HOLT

TEXAS EDITION

Decisions for Health

HOLT, RINEHART AND WINSTON
A Harcourt Education Company

Orlando • **Austin** • New York • San Diego • Toronto • London

Acknowledgments

Contributing Authors

Balu H. Athreya, M.D.
Staff Physician
Alfred I. duPont Hospital for Children
Wilmington, Delaware

Sharon Deutschlander
Department of Health and Physical Education
Indiana University of Pennsylvania
Indiana, Pennsylvania

William E. Dunscombe, Jr.
Associate Professor of Biology
Chairman, Department of Biology
Union County College
Cranford, New Jersey

Efrain Garza Fuentes, Ed.D.
Director, Patient and Family Services
Childrens Hospital Los Angeles
Los Angeles, California

Keith S. García, M.D., Ph.D.
Instructor of Psychiatry
Washington University School of Medicine
St. Louis, Missouri

Mary Gillaspy
Coordinator, Health Learning Center
Northwestern Memorial Hospital
Chicago, Illinois

Patricia J. Harned, Ph.D.
Director of Character Development and Research
Ethics Resource Center
Washington, D.C.

Craig P. Henderson, LCSW, MDIV
Therapist
Youth Services of Tulsa
Tulsa, Oklahoma
Trainer
National Resource Center for Youth Services
Norman, Oklahoma

Jack E. Henningfield, Ph.D.
Associate Professor of Behavioral Biology
The Johns Hopkins University School of Medicine
Baltimore, Maryland

Peter Katona, M.D., FACP
Associate Professor of Clinical Medicine, Infectious Disease Division, Department of Medicine
UCLA School of Medicine
Los Angeles, California

Linda Klingaman, Ph.D.
Professor
Indiana University of Pennsylvania
Indiana, Pennsylvania

Joshua Mann, M.D., M.P.H.
Clinical Assistant Professor, Department of Family and Preventive Medicine
University of South Carolina School of Medicine
Columbia, South Carolina

Tammy Mays, MLIS
Consumer Health Coordinator, National Network of Libraries of Medicine
University of Illinois at Chicago
Chicago, Illinois

Joe S. McIlhaney, Jr., M.D.
President
The Medical Institute for Sexual Health
Austin, Texas

Nancy Moreno, Ph.D.
Associate Professor, Department of Family and Community Medicine
Baylor College of Medicine
Houston, Texas

Kweethai Chin Neill, Ph.D., C.H.E.S., FASHA
Assistant Professor, Department of Kinesiology, Health Promotion, and Recreation
University of North Texas
Denton, Texas

Copyright © 2005 by Holt, Rinehart and Winston

All rights reserved. No part of this publication may be reproduced or transmitted in any form or by any means, electronic or mechanical, including photocopy, recording, or any information storage and retrieval system, without permission in writing from the publisher.

Requests for permission to make copies of any part of the work should be mailed to the following address: Permissions Department, Holt, Rinehart and Winston, 10801 N. MoPac Expressway, Building 3, Austin, Texas 78759.

CNN and **CNN Student News** are trademarks of Cable News Network LP, LLLP. An AOL Time Warner Company.

HealthLinks is a service mark owned and provided by the National Science Teachers Association. All rights reserved.

Current Health is a registered trademark of Weekly Reader Corporation.

Printed in the United States of America

ISBN 0-03-037993-8

1 2 3 4 5 6 7 048 07 06 05 04

Christine Rose, M.S.
Project Director, Innovators
  Combating Substance Abuse
Robert Wood Johnson
  Foundation
Pinney Associates
Bethesda, Maryland

Robert D. Soule, Ed.D.
Professor of Occupational
  Health
Indiana University
  of Pennsylvania
Indiana, Pennsylvania

Stephen E. Stork, Ed.D., C.H.E.S.
Assistant Professor
Department of Kinesiology,
  Health Promotion, and
  Recreation
University of North Texas
Denton, Texas

Richard Yoast, Ph.D.
Director, American Medical
  Association Office
  of Alcohol and Other
  Drug Abuse
Director, Robert Wood Johnson
  Foundation National Alcohol
  Program Offices
American Medical Association
Chicago, Illinois

Contributing Writers

Presentation Series Development

Carol Badran, M.P.H.
Health Educator
San Francisco Department
  of Public Health
San Francisco, California

Pirette McKamey
Teacher
Thurgood Marshall Academic
  High School
San Francisco, California

Inclusion Specialists

Ellen McPeek Glisan
Special Needs Consultant
San Antonio, Texas

Joan A. Solorio
Special Education Director
Austin Independent School
  District
Austin, Texas

Feature Development

Angela Berenstein
Princeton, New Jersey

Mickey Coakley
Pennington, New Jersey

Allen Cobb
La Grange, Texas

Theresa Flynn-Nason
Voorhees, New Jersey

Charlotte W. Luongo
Austin, Texas

Eileen Nehme, M.P.H.
Austin, Texas

Clementina S. Randall
Quincy, Massachusetts

Answer Checking

Hatim Belyamani
Austin, Texas

TEKS Reviewer

Thomas M. Fleming, Ph.D.
Director of Health and Physical
  Education (Retired)
Texas Education Agency
Austin, Texas

Medical Reviewers

David Ho, M.D.
Professor and Scientific Director
Aaron Diamond AIDS
  Research Center
The Rockefeller University
New York, New York

Ichiro Kawachi, Ph.D., M.D.
Associate Professor of Health
  and Social Behavior
School of Public Health
Harvard University
Boston, Massachusetts

Leland Lim, M.D., Ph.D.
Year II Resident
Department of Neurology
  and Neurological Sciences
Stanford University School
  of Medicine
Palo Alto, California

Iris F. Litt, M.D.
Professor
Department of Pediatrics
  and Adolescent Medicine
School of Biomedical
  and Biological Sciences
Stanford University
Palo Alto, California

Ronald Munson, M.D., F.A.A.S.P.
Assistant Clinical Professor,
  Family Practice
Health Sciences Center
The University of Texas
San Antonio, Texas

Alexander V. Prokhorov, M.D., Ph.D.
Associate Professor
  of Behavioral Science
M.D. Anderson Cancer Center
The University of Texas
Houston, Texas

Gregory A. Schmale, M.D.
Assistant Professor
Pediatrics and Adolescent Sports
  Medicine
University of Washington
Seattle, Washington

Hans Steiner, M.D.
Professor of Psychiatry
  and Director of Training
Division of Child Psychiatry
  and Child Development
Department of Psychiatry
  and Behavioral Sciences
Stanford University School
  of Medicine
Palo Alto, California

Professional Reviewers

Toni Alvarez, L.P.C.
Counselor
Children's Solutions
Round Rock, Texas

Professional Reviewers
(continued)

Nancy Daley, Ph.D., L.P.C., C.P.M.
Psychologist
Austin, Texas

Sharon Deutschlander
Department of Health and Physical Education
Indiana University of Pennsylvania
Indiana, Pennslyvania

Linda Gaul, Ph.D.
Epidemiologist
Texas Department of Health
Austin, Texas

Georgia Girvan
Research Specialist
Idaho Radar Network Center
Boise State University
Boise, Idaho

Linda Jones, M.S.P.H.
Manager of Systems Development Unit
Children with Special Healthcare Needs Division
Texas Department of Health
Austin, Texas

William Joy
President
The Joy Group
Wheaton, Illinois

Edie Leonard, R.D., L.D.
Nutrition Educator
Portland, Oregon

JoAnn Cope Powell, Ph.D.
Learning Specialist and Licensed Psychologist
Counseling, Learning and Career Services
University of Texas Learning Center
The University of Texas
Austin, Texas

Hal Resides
Safety Manager
Corpus Christi Naval Base
Corpus Christi, Texas

Eric Tiemann, E.M.T.
Emergency Medical Services
Hazardous Waste Division
Travis County Emergency Medical Services
Austin, Texas

Lynne E. Whitt
Director
National Center for Health Education
New York, New York

Academic Reviewers

Nigel Atkinson, Ph.D.
Associate Professor of Neurobiology
Institute For Neuroscience
Institute for Cellular and Molecular Biology
Waggoner Center for Alcohol and Addiction Research
The University of Texas
Austin, Texas

John A. Brockhaus, Ph.D.
Director, Mapping, Charting, and Geodesy Program
Department of Geography and Environmental Engineering
United States Military Academy
West Point, New York

John Caprio, Ph.D.
George C. Kent Professor
Department of Biological Sciences
Louisiana State University
Baton Rouge, Louisiana

William B. Cissell, M.S.P.H., Ph.D., C.H.E.S.
Professor of Health Studies
Department of Health Studies
Texas Woman's University
Denton, Texas

Susan B. Dickey, Ph.D., R.N.
Associate Professor, Pediatric Nursing
College of Allied Health Professionals
Temple University
Philadelphia, Pennsylvania

Stephen Dion
Associate Professor
Sport Fitness
Salem College
Salem, Massachusetts

Ronald Feldman, Ph.D.
Ruth Harris Ottman Centennial Professor for the Advancement of Social Work Education
Director, Center for the Study of Social Work Practice
Columbia University
New York, New York

Herbert Grossman, Ph.D.
Associate Professor of Botany and Biology
Department of Environmental Sciences
Pennsylvania State University
University Park, Pennsylvania

William Guggino, Ph.D.
Professor of Physiology
The Johns Hopkins University School of Medicine
Baltimore, Maryland

Kathryn Hilgenkamp, Ed.D., C.H.E.S.
Assistant Professor, Community Health and Nutrition
University of Northern Colorado
Greeley, Colorado

Cynthia Kuhn, Ph.D.
Professor of Pharmacology and Cancer Biology
Duke University Medical Center
Duke University
Durham, North Carolina

John B. Lowe, M.P.H., Dr.P.H., F.A.H.P.A.
Professor and Head
Department of Community and Behavioral Health
College of Public Health
The University of Iowa
Iowa City, Iowa

John D. Massengale, Ph.D.
Professor of Sport Sociology
Department of Kinesiology
University of Nevada
Las Vegas, Nevada

Acknowledgments continued on page 612.

Contents in Brief

Chapters

1. Health and Wellness 2
2. Making Healthy Decisions 22
3. Stress Management 50
4. Managing Mental and Emotional Health 74
5. Your Body Systems 104
6. Physical Fitness 140
7. Sports and Conditioning 168
8. Eating Responsibly 186
9. The Stages of Life 216
10. Adolescent Growth and Development 240
11. Building Responsible Relationships 260
12. Conflict Management 286
13. Preventing Abuse and Violence 316
14. Tobacco 336
15. Alcohol 368
16. Medicine and Illegal Drugs 394
17. Infectious Diseases 428
18. Noninfectious Diseases 454
19. Safety 478
20. Healthcare Consumer 506
21. Health and the Environment 528

Contents

CHAPTER 1 Health and Wellness 2

Lessons

1 **Wellness and Your Health** 4
   Cross-Discipline Activity: Language Arts 6
2 **Influences On Health and Wellness** 8
   Life Skills Activity: Using Refusal Skills 10
3 **Making Choices About Your Health** 12
   Health Journal 13
4 **Using Life Skills to Improve Health** 14
   Life Skills Activity: Practicing Wellness 16

Chapter Review 18
Life Skills in Action:
   Practicing Wellness: Molly's Physical 20

Myth & Fact

Myth: The more expensive brands are better products.

Fact: Go to page 15 to get the facts.

CHAPTER 2 Making Healthy Decisions 22

Lessons
1. **Making Decisions** 24
   - Health Journal 25
   - Cross-Discipline Activity: Social Studies 26
2. **Influences on Your Decisions** 28
   - Health Journal 29
   - Life Skills Activity: Evaluating Media Messages ... 30
3. **Examining Your Decisions** 32
   - Life Skills Activity: Making Good Decisions 32
4. **Setting Your Goals** 34
   - Health Journal 35
   - Life Skills Activity: Setting Goals 36
5. **Reaching Your Goals** 38
6. **Goals Can Change** 40
7. **Communication Skills** 42
8. **Refusal Skills** 44
   - Life Skills Activity: Using Refusal Skills 45

Chapter Review 46

Life Skills in Action:
   Making Good Decisions: Rick and the Rebels 48

CHAPTER 3 Stress Management 50

Lessons

1 Stress: A Natural Part of Your Life 52
    Cross-Discipline Activity: Language Arts 53
    Health Journal 54
    Teen Talk 55

2 How Stress Affects You 56
    Health Journal 57

3 Defense Mechanisms 60
    Health Journal 61

4 Managing Your Stress 62
    Hands-on Activity: Distress Managers 63
    Life Skills Activity: Practicing Wellness 64

5 Preventing Distress 66
    Life Skills Activity: Making Good Decisions 68

Chapter Review 70

Life Skills in Action:
    Assessing Your Health: Jared's Busy Week 72

Myth & Fact

Myth: If you swallow your gum, it will stay in your digestive system for 7 years.

Fact: Go to page 125 to get the facts.

viii | Contents

CHAPTER 4
Managing Mental and Emotional Health 74

Lessons

1 Emotions 76
2 Understanding Emotions 78
   Life Skills Activity: Assessing Your Health 79
   Hands-on Activity: Tracking Emotional States 80
3 Expressing Emotions 82
   Health Journal 84
4 Coping with Emotions 86
   Life Skills Activity: Assessing Your Health 88
5 Mental Illness 90
   Cross-Discipline Activity: Science 91
6 Depression 94
   Health Journal 95
7 Getting Help 96
   Life Skills Activity: Making Good Decisions 97
   Health Journal 98

Chapter Review 100
Life Skills in Action:
   Coping: Sabrina's Sadness 102

CHAPTER 5
Your Body Systems 104

Lessons

1 Body Organization 106
2 The Nervous System 108
   Cross-Discipline Activity: Math 109
3 The Endocrine System 112
   Health Journal 112
4 The Skeletal and Muscular Systems 116
   Hands-on Activity: Move Your Muscles 119
5 The Digestive and Urinary Systems 122
6 The Circulatory and Respiratory Systems 128
7 Caring for Your Body 134
   Life Skills Activity: Assessing Your Health 135

Chapter Review 136
Life Skills in Action:
   Practicing Wellness: Kwame's Concerns 138

Contents | ix

CHAPTER 6 Physical Fitness 140

Lessons

1 **Components of Physical Fitness** 142
   Cross-Discipline Activity: Science 144
2 **How Exercise and Diet Affect Fitness** 146
   Health Journal 147
3 **The Benefits of Exercise** 148
   Health Journal 149
4 **Testing Your Fitness** 150
   Hands-on Activity: How Often Do You Exercise? 151
   Life Skills Activity: Assessing Your Health 152
5 **Your Fitness Goals** 154
   Life Skills Activity: Practicing Wellness 155
6 **Injury and Recovery** 158
7 **Exercising Caution** 160
   Health Journal 162

Chapter Review 164

Life Skills in Action:
   Setting Goals: Mesoon's Fitness Goal 166

CHAPTER 7 Sports and Conditioning 168

Lessons

1 **Sports and Competition** 170
   Health Journal 171
   Health Journal 173
2 **Conditioning Skills** 174
3 **The Balancing Act** 178
   Life Skills Activity: Making Good Decisions 179
   Cross-Discipline Activity: Language Arts 181

Chapter Review 182

Life Skills in Action:
   Being a Wise Consumer: Shoe Shopping with Hank 184

CHAPTER 8 Eating Responsibly 186

Lessons

1. **Nutrition and Your Life** 188
   - Health Journal 189
   - Health Journal 191
2. **The Nutrients You Need** 192
3. **Making Healthy Choices** 196
   - Cross-Discipline Activity: Social Studies 197
   - Hands-on Activity: Serving Sleuths 199
4. **Body Image** 200
   - Health Journal 201
   - Life Skills Activity: Evaluating Media Messages 202
5. **Eating Disorders** 204
6. **A Healthy Body, a Healthy Weight** 208
   - Health Journal 211

Chapter Review 212

Life Skills in Action:
   - Evaluating Media Messages: Snack Facts 214

Myth & Fact

Myth: Drinking bottled water is better for you than drinking water from the faucet.

Fact: Go to page 195 to get the facts.

Contents | xi

CHAPTER 9 — The Stages of Life 216

Lessons

1. The Male Reproductive System 218
   - Health Journal 220
2. The Female Reproductive System 222
   - Life Skills Activity: Practicing Wellness 224
3. Pregnancy and Birth 226
   - Life Skills Activity: Using Refusal Skills 227
   - Cross-Discipline Activity: Science 228
4. Growing and Changing 232
   - Health Journal 234
   - Life Skills Activity: Coping 235

Chapter Review 236

Life Skills in Action:
   Assessing Your Health: Hannah's
   High School Headache 238

CHAPTER 10 — Adolescent Growth and Development 240

Lessons

1. Your Changing Body 242
   - Hands-on Activity: What Is "Normal"? 243
   - Life Skills Activity: Communicating Effectively ... 244
2. Your Changing Mind 246
   - Cross-Discipline Activity: Science 246
   - Life Skills Activity: Using Refusal Skills 247
3. Your Changing Feelings 248
   - Health Journal 249
   - Life Skills Activity: Communicating Effectively ... 250
4. Preparing for the Future 252
   - Teen Talk 254

Chapter Review 256

Life Skills in Action:
   Coping: Amira's Crush 258

CHAPTER 11 Building Responsible Relationships 260

Lessons

1 **Social Skills** 262
   Life Skills Activity: Communicating Effectively 264
2 **Sensitivity Skills** 266
   Life Skills Activity: Communicating Effectively 267
3 **Family Health** 268
   Health Journal 269
4 **Influences on Teen Relationships** 272
5 **Healthy Friendships** 274
   Health Journal 275
   Life Skills Activity: Making Good Decisions 277
6 **Teen Dating** 278
   Hands-on Activity: Diaper Budget 280
   Cross-Discipline Activity: Language Arts 281

Chapter Review 282

Life Skills in Action:
   Setting Goals: Mark and Julie's Pact 284

Myth & Fact

Myth: Family problems should be kept secret.

Fact: Go to page 270 to get the facts.

Contents | xiii

CHAPTER 12 Conflict Management 286

Lessons

1. What Is Conflict? 288
2. Communicating During Conflict 290
   - Hands-on Activity: Body Language 292
3. Resolving Conflicts 294
   - Health Journal 297
4. Conflict at School 298
   - Life Skills Activity: Making Good Decisions 299
   - Health Journal 300
5. Conflict at Home 302
   - Health Journal 303
   - Teen Talk 305
6. Conflict in the Community 306
   - Cross-Discipline Activity: Social Studies 307
7. Conflict and Violence 308
   - Health Journal 310

Chapter Review 312

Life Skills in Action:
   Communicating Effectively: Abby's Favorite Sweater ... 314

Myth: Violence only happens in bad neighborhoods or areas.

Fact: Go to page 309 to get the facts.

CHAPTER 13 Preventing Abuse and Violence ... 316

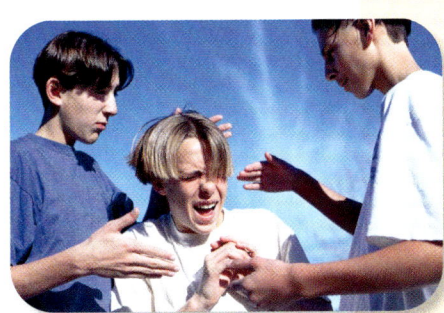

Lessons

1 **Preventing Violence** ... 318
   - Life Skills Activity: Coping ... 319
   - Health Journal ... 320
2 **Coping with Violence** ... 322
   - Hands-on Activity: Graphing Violence ... 324
3 **Abuse** ... 326
   - Cross-Discipline Activity: Social Studies ... 328
4 **Coping with Harassment** ... 330

Chapter Review ... 332

Life Skills in Action:
   Coping: Yoshi and the Bully ... 334

CHAPTER 14 Tobacco ... 336

Lessons

1 **Tobacco Products: An Overview** ... 338
2 **Tobacco's Effects** ... 340
   - Life Skills Activity: Communicating Effectively ... 342
3 **Tobacco, Disease, and Death** ... 344
   - Hands-on Activity: Blood Vessel Constriction ... 346
4 **Tobacco and Addiction** ... 348
   - Cross-Discipline Activity: Math ... 350
5 **Quitting** ... 352
   - Life Skills Activity: Making Good Decisions ... 354
6 **Why People Use Tobacco** ... 356
   - Cross-Discipline Activity: Language Arts ... 357
   - Life Skills Activity: Assessing Your Health ... 358
7 **Being Tobacco Free** ... 360
   - Health Journal ... 361
   - Life Skills Activity: Using Refusal Skills ... 362
   - Teen Talk ... 362

Chapter Review ... 364

Life Skills in Action:
   Using Refusal Skills: Josh's Tobacco Troubles ... 366

Contents | XV

CHAPTER 15 Alcohol 368

Lessons

1 **Alcohol and Your Body** 370
   Hands-on Activity: Alcohol and Your Body 373
2 **Immediate Effects of Alcohol** 374
3 **Long-Term Effects of Alcohol** 376
4 **Alcohol and Decision Making** 378
5 **Alcohol, Driving, and Injuries** 380
   Life Skills Activity: Making Good Decisions 381
6 **Pressure to Drink** 382
7 **Deciding Not to Drink** 384
   Health Journal 385
8 **Alcoholism** 386

Chapter Review 390

Life Skills in Action:
   Making Good Decisions: Aya's Tough Decision 392

CHAPTER 16 Medicine and Illegal Drugs ... 394

Lessons

1. **What Are Drugs?** ... 396
2. **Using Drugs as Medicine** ... 398
   - Life Skills Activity: Practicing Wellness ... 399
3. **Drug Abuse and Addiction** ... 402
   - Life Skills Activity: Communicating Effectively ... 403
   - Health Journal ... 404
   - Life Skills Activity: Making Good Decisions ... 405
4. **Stimulants and Depressants** ... 406
   - Hands-on Activity: Caffeine ... 407
   - Cross-Discipline Activity: Science ... 408
   - Life Skills Activity: Practicing Wellness ... 408
5. **Marijuana** ... 410
6. **Opiates** ... 412
   - Cross-Discipline Activity: Social Studies ... 412
7. **Hallucinogens and Inhalants** ... 414
8. **Designer Drugs** ... 416
   - Teen Talk ... 417
9. **Staying Drug Free** ... 418
   - Health Journal ... 418
   - Life Skills Activity: Using Refusal Skills ... 419
10. **Getting Help** ... 420

Chapter Review ... 424

Life Skills in Action:
   Using Refusal Skills: Pila's Party Predicament ... 426

Myth & Fact

Myth: As soon as a drug's effects go away, the drug is out of your system.

Fact: Go to page 422 to get the facts.

Contents | xvii

CHAPTER 17 Infectious Diseases 428

Lessons

1. **What Is an Infectious Disease?** 430
   - Cross-Discipline Activity: Social Studies 431
   - Hands-on Activity: Bacterial Reproduction 432
2. **Defenses Against Infectious Diseases** 434
   - Cross-Discipline Activity: Science 435
   - Health Journal 436
3. **Common Bacterial Infections** 438
4. **Common Viral Infections** 440
5. **Sexually Transmitted Diseases** 442
6. **HIV and AIDS** 444
   - Cross-Discipline Activity: Language Arts 447
7. **Preventing the Spread of Infectious Diseases** 448
   - Life Skills Activity: Practicing Wellness 448

Chapter Review 450

Life Skills in Action:
- Practicing Wellness: Jamal's After-School Job 452

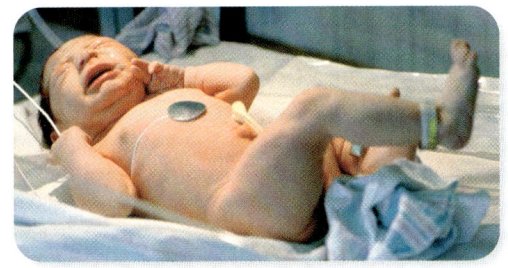

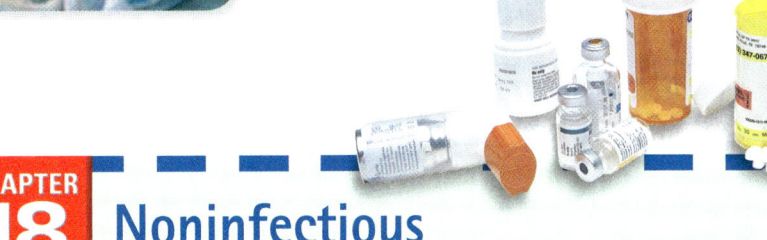

CHAPTER 18 Noninfectious Diseases 454

Lessons

1 **Disease and Disease Prevention** 456
    Life Skills Activity: Making Good Decisions 457
    Hands-on Activity: Cause and Effect 458
2 **Hereditary Diseases** 460
3 **Metabolic and Nutritional Diseases** 462
    Health Journal 463
4 **Allergies and Autoimmune Diseases** 464
5 **Cancer** 466
    Life Skills Activity: Practicing Wellness 469
6 **Chemicals and Poisons** 470
7 **Accidents and Injuries** 472

Chapter Review 474

Life Skills in Action:
    Assessing Your Health: Aaron's Asthma 476

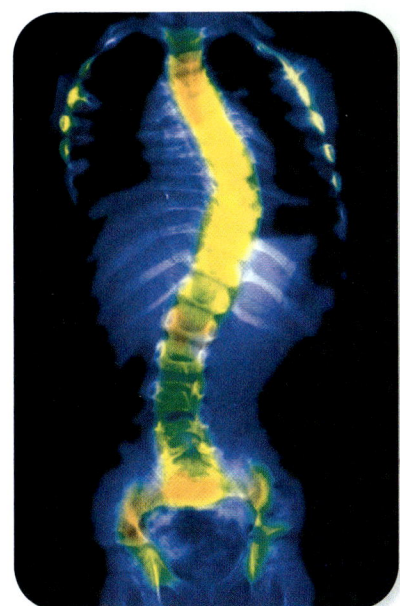

Myth & Fact

Myth: Arthritis affects only older people.

Fact: Go to page 461 to get the facts.

Contents | xix

CHAPTER 19 Safety 478

Lessons

1 **Acting Safely at Home** 480
   Life Skills Activity: Practicing Wellness 481
2 **Acting Safely at School** 484
   Health Journal 485
3 **What Is a Weapon?** 486
4 **Automobile Safety** 488
5 **Giving First Aid** 490
   Life Skills Activity: Practicing Wellness 491
   Cross-Discipline Activity: Social Studies 492
6 **Basic First Aid** 494
7 **Choking and CPR** 498

Chapter Review 502
Life Skills in Action:
   Making Good Decisions: Minhee's Dilemma 504

CHAPTER 20 Healthcare Consumer 506

Lessons

1 **Being a Wise Consumer** 508
   Hands-on Activity: The Smartest Purchase 511
2 **Healthcare Information** 512
   Cross-Discipline Activity: Social Studies 513
   Life Skills Activity: Being a Wise Consumer 514
3 **Influencing Healthcare** 516
4 **Healthcare Services** 518
   Health Journal 519
   Life Skills Activity: Communicating Effectively 521
5 **Accessing Services** 522

Chapter Review 524
Life Skills in Action:
   Being a Wise Consumer: Rafiq's Search 526

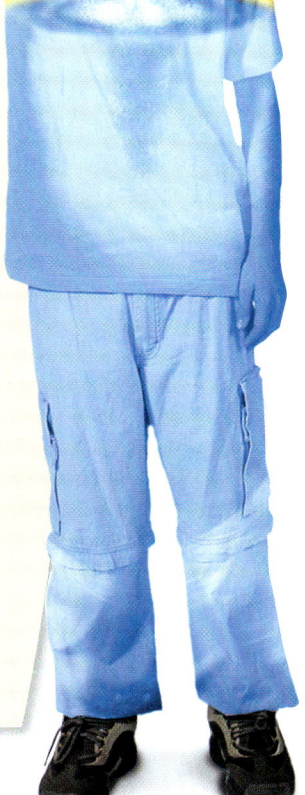

CHAPTER 21 Health and the Environment 528

Lessons

1. Healthy Environments 530
2. Meeting Our Basic Needs 532
   - Hands-on Activity: What Dissolves in Water? 532
   - Cross-Discipline Activity: Math 534
3. Environmental Pollution 536
   - Life Skills Activity: Making Good Decisions 537
4. Maintaining Healthy Environments 540
   - Health Journal 540
   - Life Skills Activity: Being a Wise Consumer 541
5. Promoting Public Health 542
   - Life Skills Activity: Practicing Wellness 543
6. A Global Community 546

Chapter Review 550

Life Skills in Action: Evaluating Media Messages:
Parking Lot or Meadow 552

Appendix

The Food Guide Pyramid 554
Alternative Food Guide Pyramids 555
Calorie and Nutrient Content of Common Foods 556
Food Safety Tips 558
BMI 559
The Physical Activity Pyramid 560
Emergency Kit 561
Natural Disasters 562
Staying Home Alone 563
Computer Posture 564
Internet Safety 565
Baby Sitter Safety 566
Careers in Health 568

Myth & Fact

Myth: Technology can solve all our environmental problems.

Fact: Go to page 531 to get the facts.

Contents | xxi

Activities

Hands-on Activity

Distress Managers 63	Blood Vessel Constriction 346
Tracking Emotional States 80	Alcohol and Your Body 373
Move Your Muscles 119	Caffeine 407
How Often Do You Exercise? 151	Bacterial Reproduction 432
Serving Sleuths 199	Cause and Effect 458
What Is "Normal"? 243	The Smartest Purchase 511
Diaper Budget 280	What Dissolves in Water? 533
Body Language 292	Glitter Handshake 548
Graphing Violence 324	

Life Skills Activity

Using Refusal Skills 10	Making Good Decisions 277
Practicing Wellness 16	Making Good Decisions 299
Evaluating Media Messages 30	Coping 319
Making Good Decisions 32	Communicating Effectively 342
Setting Goals 36	Making Good Decisions 354
Using Refusal Skills 45	Assessing Your Health 358
Practicing Wellness 64	Using Refusal Skills 362
Making Good Decisions 68	Making Good Decisions 381
Assessing Your Health 79	Practicing Wellness 399
Assessing Your Health 88	Communicating Effectively 403
Making Good Decisions 97	Making Good Decisions 405
Assessing Your Health 135	Practicing Wellness 408
Assessing Your Health 152	Using Refusal Skills 419
Practicing Wellness 155	Practicing Wellness 448
Making Good Decisions 179	Making Good Decisions 457
Evaluating Media Messages 202	Practicing Wellness 469
Practicing Wellness 224	Practicing Wellness 481
Using Refusal Skills 227	Practicing Wellness 491
Coping 235	Being a Wise Consumer 514
Communicating Effectively 244	Communicating Effectively 521
Using Refusal Skills 247	Making Good Decisions 537
Communicating Effectively 250	Being a Wise Consumer 541
Communicating Effectively 264	Practicing Wellness 543
Communicating Effectively 267	

Cross-Discipline Activity

Language Arts	6	Social Studies	328
Social Studies	26	Math	350
Language Arts	53	Language Arts	357
Science	91	Science	408
Math	109	Social Studies	412
Science	144	Social Studies	431
Language Arts	181	Science	435
Social Studies	197	Language Arts	447
Science	228	Social Studies	492
Science	246	Social Studies	513
Language Arts	281	Math	534
Social Studies	307		

Life Skills in Action

Practicing Wellness	20	Coping	334
Making Good Decisions	48	Using Refusal Skills	366
Assessing Your Health	72	Making Good Decisions	392
Coping	102	Using Refusal Skills	426
Practicing Wellness	138	Practicing Wellness	452
Setting Goals	166	Assessing Your Health	476
Being a Wise Consumer	184	Making Good Decisions	504
Evaluating Media Messages	214	Being a Wise Consumer	526
Assessing Your Health	238	Evaluating Media Messages	552
Coping	258		
Setting Goals	284		
Communicating Effectively	314		

How to Use Your Textbook

Your Roadmap for Success with *Decisions for Health*

Read the Objectives

The objectives, which are listed under the **What You'll Do** head, tell you what you'll need to know.

STUDY TIP Reread the objectives when studying for a test to be sure you know the material.

Study the Key Terms

Key Terms are listed for each lesson under the **Terms to Learn** head. Learn the definitions of these terms because you will most likely be tested on them. Use the glossary to locate definitions quickly.

STUDY TIP If you don't understand a definition, reread the page where the term is introduced. The surrounding text should help make the definition easier to understand.

Start Off Write

Start Off Write questions, which appear at the beginning of each lesson, help you to begin thinking about the topic covered in the lesson.

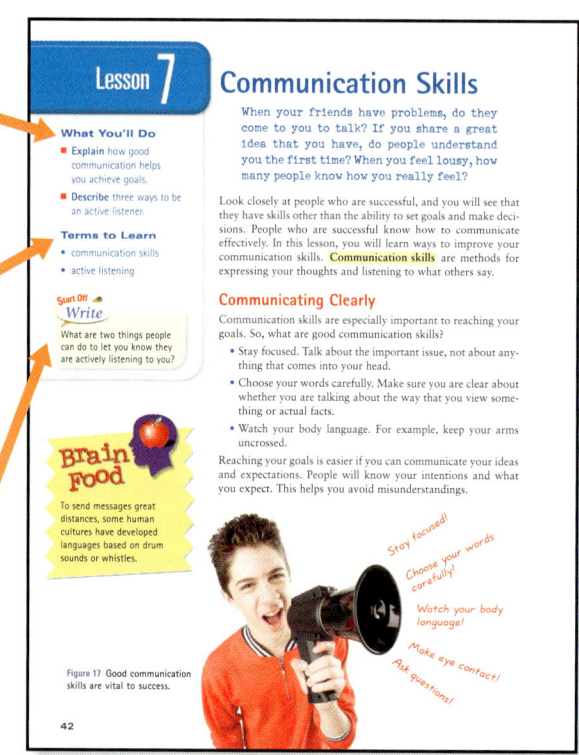

Take Notes and Get Organized

Keep a health notebook so that you are ready to take notes when your teacher reviews the material in class. Keep your assignments in this notebook so that you can review them when studying for the chapter test.

Be Resourceful, Use the Web

Internet Connect boxes in your textbook take you to resources that you can use for health projects, reports, and research papers. Go to **scilinks.org/health** and type in the HealthLinks code to get information on a topic.

Visit go.hrw.com Find worksheets, *Current Health* magazine articles online, and other materials that go with your textbook at **go.hrw.com**. Click on the textbook icon and the table of contents to see all of the resources for each chapter.

Use the Illustrations and Photos

Art shows complex ideas and processes. Learn to analyze the art so that you better understand the material you read in the text.

Tables and graphs display important information in an organized way to help you see relationships.

A picture is worth a thousand words. Look at the photographs to see relevant examples of health concepts you are reading about.

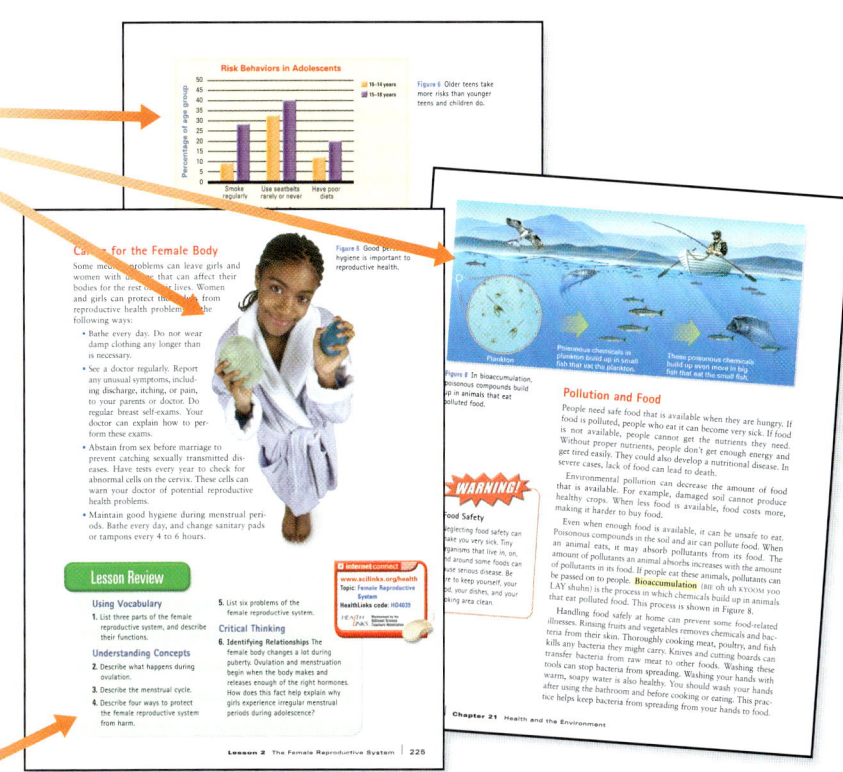

Answer the Lesson Reviews

Lesson Reviews test your knowledge over the main points of the lesson. Critical Thinking items challenge you to think about the material in greater depth and to find connections that you infer from the text.

STUDY TIP When you can't answer a question, reread the lesson. The answer is usually there.

Do Your Homework

Your teacher will assign Study Guide worksheets to help you understand and remember the material in the chapter.

STUDY TIP Answering the items in the Chapter Review will prepare you for the chapter test. Don't try to answer the questions without reading the text and reviewing your class notes. A little preparation up front will make your homework assignments a lot easier.

Visit Holt Online Learning

If your teacher gives you a special password to log onto the **Holt Online Learning** site, you'll find your complete textbook on the Web. In addition, you'll find some great learning tools and practice quizzes. You'll be able to see how well you know the material from your textbook.

Holt Online Learning
For more information go to:
www.hrw.com

Visit CNN Student News

You'll find up-to-date events in science at cnnstudentnews.com.

CHAPTER 1
Health and Wellness

Check out **Current Health**® articles related to this chapter by visiting **go.hrw.com.** Just type in the keyword **HD4CH33.**

Lessons

1. Wellness and Your Health — 4
2. Influences on Health and Wellness — 8
3. Making Choices About Your Health — 12
4. Using Life Skills to Improve Health — 14

Chapter Review — 18
Life Skills in Action — 20

> "My **grades** are good. I am able to spend time with my friends. And, I just made the **track team**. It looks like all of my **hard work** finally paid off."

Health IQ

PRE-READING

Answer the following multiple-choice questions to find out what you already know about health and wellness. When you've finished this chapter, you'll have the opportunity to change your answers based on what you've learned.

1. Which of the following defines good emotional health?
   a. getting plenty of exercise
   b. being a dependable and loyal friend
   c. accepting your strengths and weaknesses
   d. accepting new ideas and concepts

2. Mental health is the way that you
   a. recognize and cope with feelings.
   b. cope with the demands of daily life.
   c. interact with people.
   d. all of the above

3. Which of the following influences is NOT an environmental influence on your health?
   a. peer pressure
   b. pollen
   c. microscopic organisms
   d. air quality ★ 6.A

4. A set of behaviors by which you live is your
   a. attitude.
   b. heredity.
   c. life skills.
   d. lifestyle.

5. Which of the following activities is part of good hygiene?
   a. brushing your teeth
   b. getting plenty of exercise
   c. avoiding drugs and alcohol
   d. eating a healthy diet

6. Which of the following activities is an example of preventive healthcare?
   a. taking aspirin for a headache
   b. taking antibiotics to prevent infection
   c. wrapping a twisted ankle
   d. eating nutritious meals
      ★ 3.A

ANSWERS: 1. c; 2. d; 3. a; 4. d; 5. a; 6. d

Chapter 1 Health and Wellness | 3

Lesson 1

Wellness and Your Health

What You'll Do

- **Describe** the four parts of health. 1.A
- **Explain** the difference between health and wellness. 1.A

Terms to Learn

- health
- wellness
- health assessment

Start Off Write

List three things that you can do to keep your mind and body healthy.

Claudia's doctor called to tell Claudia the results of her exam. She told Claudia that all of her tests showed that she is in excellent physical health.

Good physical health is important, but there is more to health than feeling good physically. Health is a condition of your physical, emotional, mental, and social well-being. Each part of your health is equally important. To be healthy, you must balance all of these parts.

The Physical Part of Health

When you think about your health, you probably focus on your physical health. *Physical health* is the part of health that describes the condition of the body. The following suggestions are ways to take care of your body and to maintain your physical health.

- Get 8 hours of sleep every night.
- Eat nutritious food and a balanced diet.
- Get plenty of physical activity.
- Practice good hygiene. *Hygiene* is the practice of keeping clean. Cleanliness helps prevent the spread of diseases.
- Avoid drugs, alcohol, and tobacco. 1.A

Figure 1 Teens need at least 8 hours of sleep each night to stay healthy.

4 | **Chapter 1** Health and Wellness

Figure 2 Your family is an important part of your emotional health.

The Emotional Part of Health

Your emotional health affects the way you see yourself and respond to others. *Emotional health* is the way you recognize and deal with your feelings. To maintain your emotional health, you should try the following suggestions:

- Express your emotions in words rather than acting them out. Show self-control, and think before you act.
- Accept your strengths and weaknesses, and respect yourself.
- Deal with sadness appropriately and in a timely manner.

Changes that happen to you during your teen years can affect your emotional health. Added responsibility at both home and school, new feelings, and your changing body can cause you to have a wide range of emotions. Living with this range of emotions is not always a pleasant experience for teens. However, experiencing these emotions is normal. Talk to your parents or the school nurse if you are concerned about your emotional health. ★ 1.A

The Mental Part of Health

Mental health has to do with the mind. How you deal with life's demands describes your *mental health*. Being mentally healthy means that you can

- recognize and deal with stress in a positive way
- accept new ideas
- effectively solve problems

Habits that you think can affect only your physical health may also affect your mental and emotional health. For example, a poor diet and lack of sleep may leave you feeling depressed and worried as well as physically tired. ★ 1.A

Myth & Fact

Myth: Someone who is always laughing and smiling is probably emotionally healthy.

Fact: Sometimes people use smiles and laughter as a way of hiding their sadness.

Figure 3 Having friends is very important for the social health of teens.

Organizing Information Create a concept map to show how the four parts of health are necessary for total wellness.

The Social Part of Health

How well you get along with other people is a sign of your social health. *Social health* is the part of health that describes the way that you interact with people. Your family plays a large role in the support and development of your social health. You learn many of your social skills from your family. Throughout your life, your social skills continue to develop as you interact with people around you. Ways to improve your social skills include the following:

- being considerate of other people and their needs
- showing respect to others
- being dependable
- supporting people you care about when they make the right choices
- expressing your true feelings
- imagining how you would feel if you were in another person's place
- asking for help when you need it

Your relationships with others are important to healthy social development. Healthy connections with your family, friends, and groups that you have joined give you a sense of belonging and help you feel good about yourself. ★ 1.A

Assess Your Health

On a separate piece of paper, answer each item. Give yourself 4 points for each "almost always" response, 2 points for "some time" and 0 points for "almost never"

Health Habit	Almost Always	Some Time	Almost Never
I am physically active regularly.			
I eat a variety of foods, including fruits and vegetables.			
I find it easy to relax and express my feelings.			
I have close friends or relatives in whom I can confide.			
I prepare for events that I know will be stressful to me.			
I avoid risky behavior.			
I practice good hygiene.			

Scores of 23–28 means you have great health habits.
Scores of 15–22 mean your health habits are good overall, but there is room for improvement.
Scores of 7–14 indicate that many of your health habits need work.
Scores of 0–6 mean that you are taking unecessary risks with your health.

Figure 4 Check your overall health by taking this health assessment.

Wellness Is Balanced Health

When all four parts of your health are balanced, you are in a state of good health. **Wellness** is the state of good health achieved by balancing your physical, mental, emotional, and social health. If you do not maintain a balance of the four parts of health, you will not be functioning at your best.

One of the best ways to evaluate your health is to take a health assessment. A **health assessment** is a set of questions that allows you to evaluate each of the four parts of your health. Take the quiz shown in the above figure. Is anything missing in your overall health? If so, talk to your parents or a trusted adult to find out how to get this part of your health back in balance. ★ 1.A

SCIENCE ACTIVITY

Interview your doctor or nurse. Find out how they perform a yearly physical exam on patients. Ask this person about the purpose of each test that he or she runs on patients. Write a report on the information you collected.

Lesson Review

Using Vocabulary

1. Define *health*. ★ 1.A
2. Explain what *wellness* means. ★ 1.A
3. Define *health assessment*.

Understanding Concepts

4. What is good hygiene?
5. Identify the four parts of health, and briefly describe each. ★ 1.A
6. Explain the difference between health and wellness.

Critical Thinking

7. **Analyzing Ideas** Brad is an excellent student. He spends most of his time either working on homework or at the computer. Which parts of his health could be out of balance? What could he do to improve those parts of his health? ★ 1.A; 7.A

internet connect
www.scilinks.org/health
Topic: Depression
HealthLinks code: HD4026
HEALTH LINKS — Maintained by the National Science Teachers Association

Lesson 1 Wellness and Your Health

Lesson 2: Influences on Health and Wellness

What You'll Do

- **Explain** how heredity affects your health. ★ 1.A; 3.B
- **Describe** how the environment influences your health. ★ 6.A
- **Describe** how your relationships affect your health. ★ 1.A; 7.A; 10.A
- **Explain** how the media influences your health decisions. ★ 8.A

Terms to Learn

- heredity
- environment

What are inherited traits?

Ken recently moved to a new city in a different state. Ken is shy, and making new friends is hard for him. He doesn't understand why he can't be more like his sister, who is very outgoing and makes new friends easily.

Every person is unique. Even members of the same family, like Ken and his sister, can be very different. You may know that the way you look and act are influenced by many things. What you may not know is that the same things that influence the way you act also influence your health.

Heredity and Your Health

The way you look and, to some degree, the way you behave are due to heredity. **Heredity** is the passing down of traits from a parent to a child. A *trait* is a characteristic that a person has. The traits that are the easiest to identify are those that affect the way you look. For example, the color of your eyes and hair, your height, and your skin color are traits that are controlled by heredity.

However, some traits are behaviors that are influenced by heredity and that contribute to the development of your personality. For example, have you ever heard someone say, "His sense of humor is just like his dad's?"

Heredity can affect your health. Some conditions can be inherited, or passed down, from parent to child. For example, if one of your parents wears glasses due to vision problems, then you might have to wear glasses. But heredity can affect your health in much greater ways than having to wear glasses. For example, parents can pass on diseases to their children through heredity. One disease that can be inherited is cystic fibrosis (CF), which is a disease of the lungs and digestive system. ★ 1.A; 3.B; 9.A

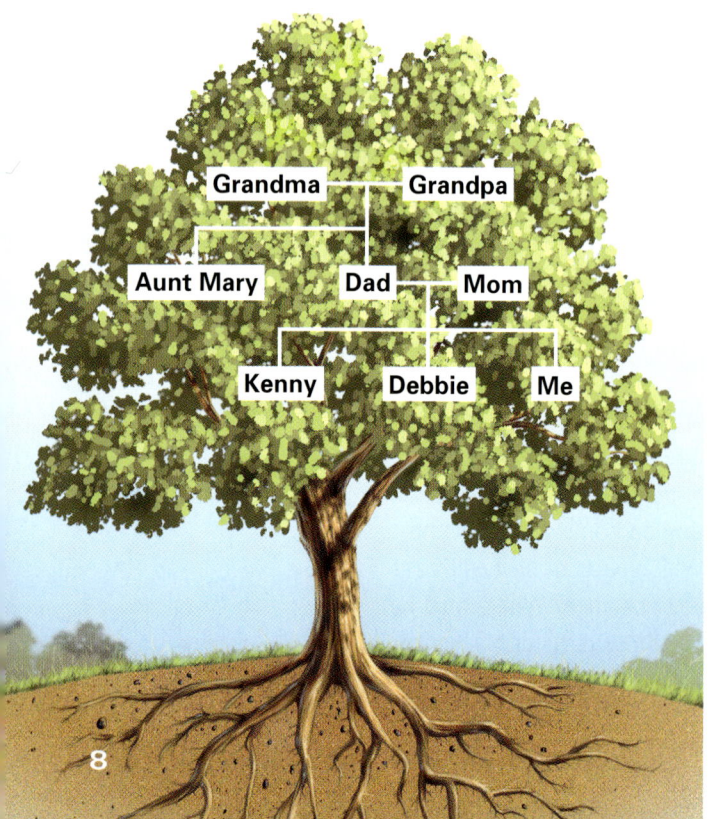

Figure 5 A family tree can help you learn about traits that have been passed down through generations of your family.

Figure 6 Asthma can be an inherited disease. Asthma attacks can be triggered by poor air quality.

Environmental Influences

If you were asked to list the things around you, you would probably name things that you can see. But there are many other things around you that you can't see, such as air, germs, smells, and noises. Whether you can see them or not, all of these things make up your environment. Your environment is everything around you, including the things you cannot see. Many factors in your environment can affect your health. For example, the air may contain particles that cause you to cough or that initiate an allergic response. Microscopic organisms can make you ill when they invade your body. Some of these irritants are things over which you have little control. For example, you may occasionally find yourself in an environment where you are forced to breathe secondhand smoke. But there are ways to make your environment a healthier place to live. The following are examples of things that you can do.

- Dispose of trash properly to prevent pollution.
- Walk, ride a bike, or use mass transit to reduce the number of cars on the road. This will reduce the amount of pollution released into the air.
- Start a recycling program for paper, plastic, and aluminum cans to save natural resources.

Remember that no matter where you live, you can help your environment. Your health and the health of your community will benefit from everyone pitching in. ★ 1.A; 6.A; 6.B

Brain Food

About 8.6 million children under the age of 18 have asthma, a chronic lung disease. Of these, 3.8 million have had an asthma attack during the previous year.

Lesson 2 Influences on Health and Wellness

Figure 7 Friends are an important influence on your life and your activities.

How Your Relationships Influence You

Your family and friends are major influences on you and your health. Your family has been responsible for teaching you about how to take care of your health. What your parents or caretakers taught you about nutrition, hygiene, and exercise has affected the way you deal with your health.

Your peers also influence your health. A *peer* is someone who is the same age or often are in the same grade as you and who has similar interests. Peers are an important part of your social health because they influence so many things that you do. Your friends may influence which classes you take and what activities you will do at school.

Friends can have either a positive or a negative effect on your health. For example, your friends can be a positive source of support when you have problems and need someone to talk to. Friends also can help each other by studying together. But peers can have a negative influence on your health if you allow them to. For example, friends who try to get you to smoke or take drugs are putting your health—and theirs—at risk. And you should remember that true friends would not ask you to do things that will harm your health or get you into trouble. Choose friends that are a positive influence on your health. And be a good influence to your friends so that they don't behave in unhealthy ways. ✪ 7.A; 7.B; 10.A; 12.E

USING REFUSAL SKILLS

Role-play with a group of four or five other students about what each of you would do if you had the opportunity to copy someone's homework. How would you tell your peers no? ✪ 12.E

Other Factors That Influence You

Have you ever come home from school, turned on the television, and saw an ad for a new snack? Maybe the people in the ad looked really cool. Then, the next time you were at the grocery store, you may have noticed that same snack and bought it. That process is what advertising is all about! When you bought the snack, did you read the ingredients? Or did you just think about the commercial you saw? If you are like many people, advertisements are a major factor in deciding which items to purchase.

The media is a major source of information about health. Some media messages give you information that will benefit you. For example, the media has taught you that bacteria can grow on sponges. You now know that you shouldn't use the same sponge over and over again. Instead, you should use a cloth that can be washed and disinfected between uses. However, not all media messages are beneficial or should be believed. Many of these messages advertise items or practices that can be harmful to your health. For example, advertisements for products that promise that you can lose a lot of weight in just a few days or weeks are deceptive, and the products may be dangerous. Be cautious about which messages you believe. You don't want to do anything that will put your health at risk. ★ 8.A; 8.B

Figure 8 Would drinking a sports drink, such as the made-up one in this figure, really make you run as fast as this athlete?

Lesson Review

Using Vocabulary
1. Define *heredity*.
2. Describe your environment.

Understanding Concepts
3. How does heredity affect your health? ★ 1.A; 3.B
4. Explain how the environment affects your health. ★ 6.A
5. How do your relationships affect the choices you make about health?
★ 1.A; 7.A; 10.A
6. How does the media influence your health decisions? ★ 8.A

Critical Thinking
7. **Analyzing Ideas** Many people argue whether heredity or the environment is a greater influence on your health. Choose one of these influences, and make a case for it being the more important factor. ★ 3.B; 7.A

internet connect
www.scilinks.org/health
Topic: Genes and Traits
HealthLinks code: HD4045
HEALTH LINKS Maintained by the National Science Teachers Association

Lesson 3

Making Choices About Your Health

What You'll Do

- **Describe** how your lifestyle can affect your health. ★ 1.A; 3.A; 12.F
- **Explain** how your attitude influences your health. ★ 1.A; 3.A
- **Identify** three ways you can take responsibility for your health. ★ 12.F

Terms to Learn

- lifestyle
- attitude
- preventive healthcare

Start Off Write

What choices can you make to improve your health?

Figure 9 Participating in a regular exercise program is one choice that you can make to have a healthy lifestyle.

Roberto and his friends were thirsty after playing a game of soccer. When they stopped at the store to get something to drink, Roberto told his friends he would rather have water than a soft drink. They laughed and told him he was too health conscious.

Sometimes you will make choices that other people may laugh at. In this lesson, you will learn the importance of making the right health choice for you.

Health Choices You Can Make

You may not have control over what color eyes you have or how tall you are, but you do have control over your lifestyle. Your **lifestyle** is a set of behaviors by which you live. Anytime that you make a choice that affects your health, you are making a choice about your lifestyle. Some of these choices will have only a short-term effect, while others can affect you for the rest of your life. For example, choosing whether or not you will exercise today may have only a short-term effect. But choosing not to smoke will certainly have a positive long-term effect.
★ 1.A; 3.A; 12.F

Taking Control of Your Health

What is your attitude about health? Your **attitude** is the way you act, think, or feel that causes you to make one choice over another. How you approach health decisions will make the difference in how well you maintain your health. Having a healthy attitude will help you to say no to situations in which you are pressured to smoke, drink alcohol, or take drugs. A healthy attitude also gives you the confidence to ignore what others may think about your choices. And a healthy attitude will give you the confidence to make choices that are right for you and that will keep you healthy. Your attitude really does make a difference! ★ 12.F

Being Responsible About Healthcare

Your parents probably took you to a healthcare provider for a physical exam before you started school. You may have gone to a dentist for a dental checkup. The purpose of these checkups is to keep you well and to find any problems before they become serious. This type of healthcare is called preventive healthcare. **Preventive healthcare** is taking the steps necessary to prevent illness or accidents. Practicing preventive healthcare requires taking actions to avoid a major health problem or injury, which may even save your life. When you buckle your seat belt, wear a helmet, or refuse to smoke or drink, you are practicing preventive healthcare. You are being proactive in your attempt to maintain your health. A *proactive* approach means that you purposefully take action to improve your personal health before a problem arises. For example, eating nutritious foods is a proactive approach. You are doing something that will improve your health.

Being responsible about your health also means knowing what to do in emergencies. Some situations can be life threatening to you or to others, and you should know how to react. Healthcare providers, such as your doctor, the school nurse, and your parents can tell you how to contact local health agencies and how these agencies can help. For example, make sure you know how to contact the poison control center and emergency services. When it comes to your health and the health of your family, you need to be prepared.

★ 3.A

Health Journal
List two people that you would trust if you needed to talk to someone about a health concern. Explain why you chose these people.

Figure 10 Having an annual exam is a proactive step in preventing health problems.

Lesson Review

Using Vocabulary
1. Define *lifestyle*.
2. What is a healthy attitude? ★ 12.F
3. Describe *preventive healthcare*. ★ 3.A

Understanding Concepts
4. Describe how your lifestyle and attitude affect your health. ★ 1.A; 3.A; 12.F
5. Explain three ways you can be responsible for your health. ★ 12.F

Critical Thinking
6. **Making Inferences** How are your lifestyle and your attitude related? Can you have a healthy lifestyle and an unhealthy attitude? Explain. ★ 1.A

Lesson 3 Making Choices About Your Health

Lesson 4

Using Life Skills to Improve Health

What You'll Do

- **Identify** the nine life skills.  1.A; 10; 11; 12
- **Explain** how using the life skills improves your health. 1.A; 10; 11; 12
- **Describe** how to assess your progress in learning the life skills. 12

Terms to Learn

- life skills
- refusal skills

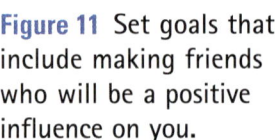

Give an example of when you would use a life skill.

> Amita told her friend for the second time that she did not want a cigarette. She also told her friend that she wanted her to think about what smoking does to her health. Her friend finally gave up pressuring her and even put out her own cigarette.

Amita made a healthy choice by saying no to her friend. Being able to say no is just one of the life skills that you can use to improve your health and wellness. **Life skills** are skills that help you deal with situations that can affect your health.

The Life Skills

Everyday you face different kinds of problems. Sometimes the problem is very simple. Other times, the problem may seem too big for you to solve. The life skills that are described below will give you the tools to deal with problems both big and small. Throughout this textbook, you will have opportunities to practice using these life skills.

Assessing Your Health Evaluate each of the four parts of your health periodically, and assess your health behaviors. One way of doing this is to take a health assessment like the one in Lesson 1. Figure out what you can do to improve your health if it is not as good as it can be.

Figure 11 Set goals that include making friends who will be a positive influence on you.

Making Good Decisions Every day, you make decisions. Making good decisions means making choices that are healthy and responsible. And you must have the courage to make difficult decisions and stick to them.

Being a Wise Consumer Read the labels on products. Compare the value and quality of the products before deciding to buy one instead of the other one.

Communicating Effectively Communication skills help you avoid misunderstandings by expressing your feelings in a healthy way. Good communication includes using good listening skills. If you really listen to what people say, they will want to listen to you as well.

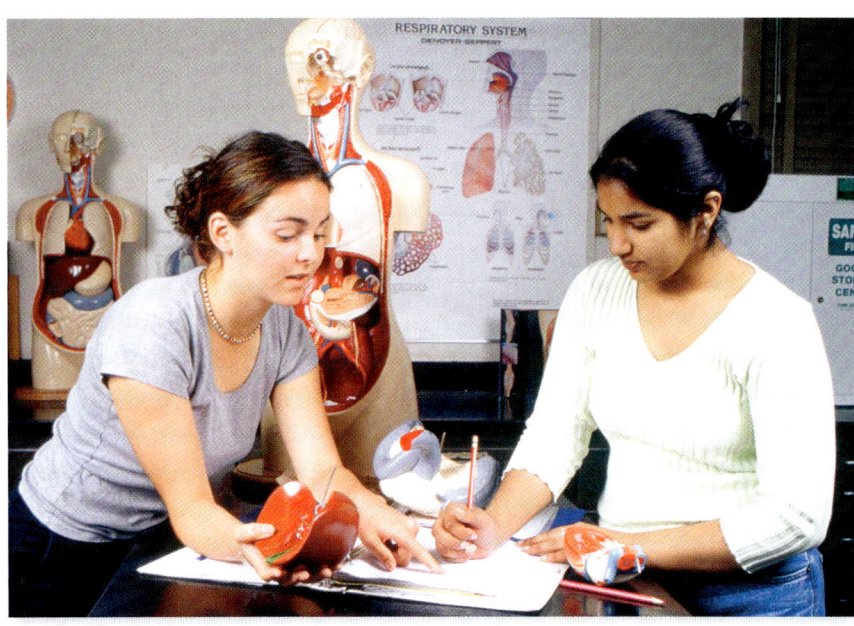

Figure 12 Good communication skills allow you to express yourself clearly and concisely.

Practicing Wellness As you are reading this textbook, you are learning about ways to be healthy. Being informed about good health habits is one way to practice wellness. Good health habits, such as eating a healthy diet, exercising, and getting plenty of sleep should be practiced daily.

Setting Goals Setting goals means aiming for something that will give you a sense of accomplishment. But make sure to set realistic goals. For example, if you decide to run 5 miles every day, give yourself some time to achieve that goal. You may have to start by running 1 mile a day. Then, you can gradually increase the distance that you run each day.

Using Refusal Skills A refusal skill is a way to say no to something that you don't want to do. This skill requires practice. But first, you must feel strongly about what things you want to avoid. If you do not know where you stand on an issue, giving in to pressure may be easy.

Coping Dealing with problems in an effective way is coping. Sometimes you may feel sad or be afraid of something, but when you learn to deal with your problem in a healthy way, then you are coping with your problem.

Evaluating Media Messages Being able to judge the worth of media messages is a challenge. Doing so takes practice because most media messages are very convincing. ★ 10; 11; 12

Myth & Fact

Myth: The more expensive brands are better products.

Fact: The less expensive store brands are often as good or better than the more expensive brand names.

Lesson 4 Using Life Skills to Improve Health | 15

Practicing Life Skills

Practice makes perfect. And by practicing the life skills, you are building lifelong habits that will help you live a healthier life. Always keep in mind that you are in charge of and responsible for your own health. Other people can help you achieve your goals, but the main responsibility is yours. You will probably feel awkward as you begin to use these skills, but do not give up. With practice, you will begin to feel more comfortable using them.

Evaluating Your Skills

As you read through the coming chapters and learn more about life skills, you may want to think about how well you are using the life skills. One way to do so is to ask yourself the following questions:

- Do I periodically evaluate the four parts of my health?
- Am I making good decisions?
- Am I setting and meeting my goals?
- Do I use refusal skills when I need to?
- Am I communicating my feelings and expectations?
- Do I compare products and services for value and quality?

If you answer no to any of these questions, you need to work harder on the skill that addresses that question. Give yourself time. Keep practicing. You will master these skills before you know it! ★ 4.B

PRACTICING WELLNESS

Your history class is having a discussion on a topic that you feel strongly about. You want to join in the discussion, but you are shy, and you don't know if you will get your point across. Which life skill would be useful now? Explain your answer.

Figure 13 Using the nine life skills helps you to be a happier and healthier person.

Figure 14 Physical activity with friends is just one way of staying healthy and well.

Staying Healthy and Well

The following statements describe ways that the nine life skills work together to improve your health and wellness.

- Using refusal skills can help you make good decisions.
- Communicating effectively can help you set and reach goals.
- Making good decisions will keep you healthy and out of trouble.
- Staying informed will alert you to areas that you need to improve on.
- Assessing all four parts of your health on a regular basis keeps your level of wellness high.
- Learning to evaluate media messages and to comparison shop makes you a wise consumer. ★ 8.A; 12.B

Lesson Review

Using Vocabulary

1. Explain what a life skill is and identify the nine life skills. ★ 1.A; 10; 11; 12
2. Define the term *refusal skill*.

Understanding Concepts

3. Explain how you would assess your progress in learning the life skills. ★ 12

4. Describe how using life skills can improve your health. ★ 1.A; 10; 11; 12

Critical Thinking

5. **Analyzing Ideas** Identify a situation for each of the life skills. How would you use each skill in these situations?

6. **Analyzing Concepts** Which of the life skills do you feel will be the most difficult one for you to use? Explain your answer.

internet connect
www.scilinks.org/health
Topic: Lifestyle Disease Research in Texas
HealthLinks code: HHTX012
HEALTH LINKS Maintained by the National Science Teachers Association

CHAPTER 1 REVIEW

Chapter Summary

■ Your health is made up of four parts: physical, emotional, social, and mental. All parts must be balanced to be healthy. ■ Wellness is a state you reach when all parts of your health are balanced. ■ Heredity, your environment, and the media influence your health. ■ Having a healthy lifestyle and attitude will improve your health. ■ Life skills help you deal with situations that can affect your health. ■ Practicing the skills and evaluating your progress in using them will help you lead a healthy life.

Using Vocabulary

For each sentence, fill in the blank with the proper word from the word bank provided below.

hygiene	heredity
environment	refusal skills
preventive healthcare	health
life skills	attitude
personal responsibility	wellness
health assessment	

1. ___ are skills that will help you deal with situations that affect your health.
2. When your physical, emotional, mental, and social health are good and in balance, you are in a state of ___.
3. The way that you act, think, or feel that affects your decisions is your ___.
4. Everything around you that affects your health is your ___.
5. Evaluating your health through a set of questions is a(n) ___.
6. The ability to say no is one of the ___.
7. The things a person does to prevent illness or accidents is ___.
8. ___ is the passing down of traits from parents to a child.

Understanding Concepts

9. What are the four parts of health? ★ 1.A
10. What are five things a person can do to promote good physical health? ★ 1.A
11. What are five things a person can do to promote good social health? ★ 1.A
12. What are two ways that heredity can affect your health? ★ 1.A; 3.B
13. What are three ways that your environment can affect your health? ★ 6.A
14. What are four influences on your health? ★ 1.A; 7.A; 8.A; 10.A
15. What are three proactive steps you can take toward preventive healthcare? ★ 3.A; 12.F
16. Explain how you can use refusal skills if your peers want you to do something that you know is wrong. ★ 11.B; 11.D; 12.B; 12.D
17. Explain what a lifestyle is. How does your lifestyle differ from your best friend's lifestyle? How are they similar? ★ 1.A; 4.A
18. How would making a decision to work out regularly affect all four parts of your health? ★ 1.A

Critical Thinking

Analyzing Ideas

19 Health is made up of four different parts—physical, emotional, mental, and social. Do you think any one part of health is more important than another part to wellness? Explain your answer. ★ 1.A

20 Describe the kind of commercial that catches your attention. Do you think the commercial will influence you the next time you are at the store? Explain your answer. ★ 8.A; 8.B

21 How do evaluating media messages and being a wise consumer contribute to each part of your wellness? ★ 1.A; 8.A

22 Do your friends and family influence your health choices in the same way? Describe a situation in which your family would have a greater influence on a health choice than your friends would. Describe another situation in which your friends would have more influence on you than your parents would. ★ 7.A; 10.E

23 A friend of yours is starting to have emotional outbursts that are affecting the way your friend is interacting with others. What suggestions could you give your friend? ★ 11.B; 11.D

Making Good Decisions

24 Your friend has been complaining about feeling bad and not being able to concentrate on school. You know that your friend has not been taking very good care of himself lately. What should you suggest to your friend to help? ★ 1.A; 4.C

25 Your friends want you to go with them on a ride in a car that belongs to their parents, and you know they don't have a driver's license. What should you do? ★ 10.D; 11.D; 12.D

Interpreting Graphics

Percentage Distribution of Asthma by Sex and Age

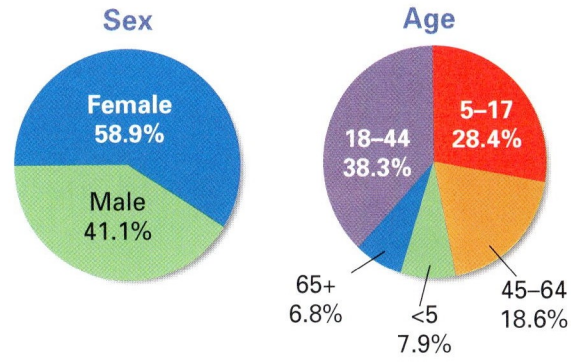

Use the figure above to answer questions 26–30. ★ M8.5.A

26 What age group do most asthma sufferers fall into?

27 What percentage of asthma sufferers are between the ages of 5 and 44?

28 If someone suffers from asthma, what sex is the person most likely to be?

29 What percentage of asthma sufferers do children from birth through age 17 make up?

30 What percentage of asthma sufferers do people over the age of 44 make up?

Reading Checkup

Take a minute to review your answers to the Health IQ questions at the beginning of this chapter. How has reading this chapter improved your Health IQ?

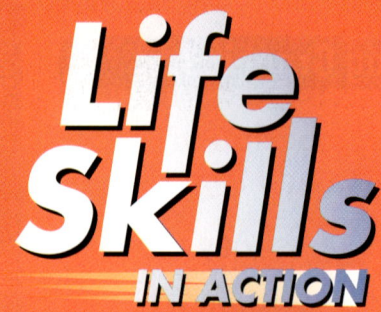

Practicing Wellness

Practicing wellness means practicing good health habits. Positive health behaviors can help prevent injury, illness, disease, and even premature death. Complete the following activity to learn how you can practice wellness.

Molly's Physical

Setting the Scene

Molly is at her doctor's office for a physical. She tells her doctor that she feels tired most of the time. Molly is worried that something may be wrong with her. After the examination, the doctor tells Molly that she is healthy and that her tired feelings may be a result of stress from her busy schedule. The doctor tells Molly to be sure that she gets enough rest and to try to reduce the stress in her life.

★ 1.A; 11.E; 11.F; 12.B

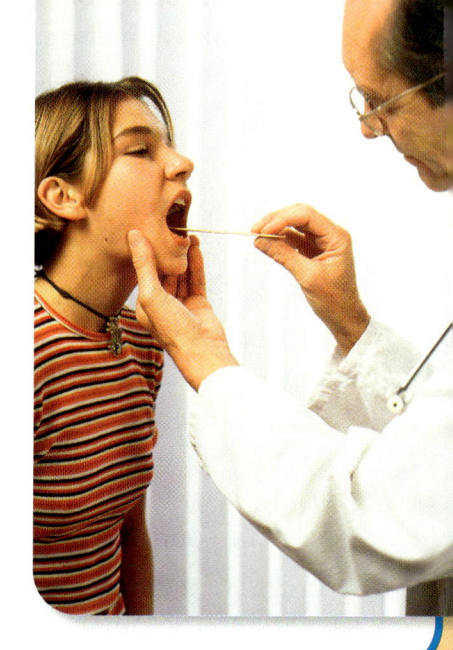

The 4 Steps of Practicing Wellness

1. Choose a health behavior you want to improve or change.
2. Gather information on how you can improve that health behavior.
3. Start using the improved health behavior.
4. Evaluate the effects of the health behavior.

Guided Practice

Practice with a Friend

Form a group of three. Have one person play the role of Molly and another person play the role of Molly's doctor. Have the third person be an observer. Walking through each of the four steps of practicing wellness, role-play the conversation between Molly and her doctor. Have Molly and her doctor discuss health behaviors that Molly could use to reduce her stress. The observer will take notes, which will include observations about what the person playing Molly did well and suggestions of ways to improve. Stop after each step to evaluate the process.

★ 12.B; 12.F

Independent Practice

Check Yourself

After you complete the guided practice, go through Act 1 again without stopping at each step. Answer the questions below to review what you did.

1. What health behaviors did Molly decide to improve?
2. Molly talked to her doctor to gather health information. What other ways could she find information about ways to improve her health behaviors? ⭐ 3.A; 4.A; 4.C
3. How can Molly evaluate the effects of the health behavior on her health? ⭐ 12.C; 12.F
4. What are some health behaviors that you would like to improve?

On Your Own

For the last month, Molly has been going to bed earlier and has cut back on her after-school activities. She does not feel tired anymore and is happy with the improvements in her health behaviors. However, while studying about cancers in her health class, she learned that she is at high risk for developing skin cancer. Make a flowchart that shows how Molly can use the four steps of practicing wellness to reduce her risk of getting skin cancer.

CHAPTER 2
Making Healthy Decisions

Lessons

1. Making Decisions — 24
2. Influences on Your Decisions — 28
3. Examining Your Decisions — 32
4. Setting Your Goals — 34
5. Reaching Your Goals — 38
6. Goals Can Change — 40
7. Communication Skills — 42
8. Refusal Skills — 44

Chapter Review — 46
Life Skills in Action — 48

Check out **Current Health** articles related to this chapter by visiting **go.hrw.com**. Just type in the keyword **HD4CH34**.

> **High school** is right around the corner, and I still have so many things to **decide**. What **courses** should I be taking? Which organizations should I join? Will I have time to play sports? Will I get to spend time with my friends from this year?

PRE-READING

Answer the following multiple-choice questions to find out what you already know about making decisions. When you've finished this chapter, you'll have the opportunity to change your answers based on what you've learned.

1. Which of the following is an important influence when you are making a decision?
   a. your values
   b. your family
   c. your friends
   d. all of the above ⭐ 7.A; 8.A; 10.A

2. Which of the following is the best example of a short-term goal?
   a. making an A in English this year
   b. making an A on your next math test
   c. going to college after high school
   d. having a successful career

3. An example of non-verbal communication is
   a. nodding your head.
   b. crossing your arms.
   c. making eye contact.
   d. all of the above ⭐ 11.D

4. Which of the following statements describes the second step for making a good decision?
   a. You identify the problem.
   b. You consider your options.
   c. You imagine the consequences.
   d. You consider your values.

5. When you accept the outcome of your decision, you accept
   a. the consequence.
   b. the outcome.
   c. personal responsibility.
   d. the rewards and benefits.

ANSWERS: 1. d; 2. b; 3. d; 4. d; 5. a

Chapter 2 Making Healthy Decisions

Lesson 1

Making Decisions

Devon is trying to decide if he has enough time to play baseball and manage his other responsibilities. He has baseball practice every day. He also has chores and homework. Devon wonders if he has time for everything.

What You'll Do

- **Explain** why a good decision is a responsible decision. ★ 12.A; 12.C
- **Describe** why personal responsibility is important in decision making. ★ 11; 12
- **Explain** how your values influence the decisions you make. ★ 12.A
- **Summarize** the six steps used in making good decisions. ★ 12.A

Terms to Learn

- good decision
- personal responsibility
- values

What are values?

Like Devon, do you ever have trouble deciding if you have enough time to do everything that you want to do? If so, you're not alone. By reading this lesson, you will learn ways to help you make decisions.

Being in Control

A lot of people tell you what to do. Your parents, teachers, coaches, and friends all want you to do one thing or another. So you might think that you have no control over your choices. However, there are many things that you do have control over. Being in control means that you can make many of your own choices. You make decisions every day. A *decision* is a choice you make and act upon. For example, you decide what clothes you wear, what lunch you eat, and who your friends are. But, your decisions should be good decisions. A **good decision** is a decision in which you have carefully considered the outcome of each choice. Along with making decisions comes personal responsibility. To take **personal responsibility** is to accept how your decision will affect yourself and other people. Therefore, a good decision is a responsible decision. ★ 12.A; 12.B

Figure 1 How is this teen taking personal responsibility for her safety?

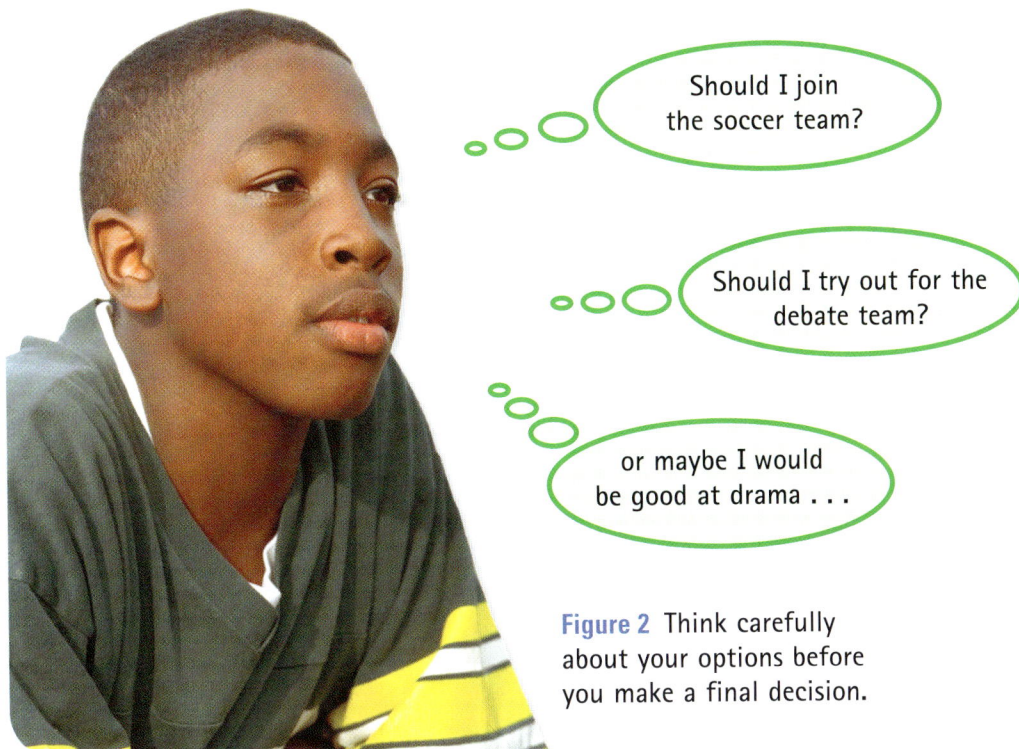

Figure 2 Think carefully about your options before you make a final decision.

Value, Character, and Decisions

Your decisions are based on your values. **Values** are beliefs that you consider to be of great importance. Many of your values come from things your parents have taught you. Other values will develop over time and will be based on experiences in your life. Although everyone does not have the same values as you, certain values are important to almost everyone. Good values include the following:

- respect for yourself and others
- responsibility
- honesty
- self-control
- trustworthiness

These values can help you live responsibly and develop good character. **Character** is the way that people think, feel, and act. If your character is based on positive values, you will develop attitudes and habits that make it easier to make good decisions. Every good decision is practice for other decisions that you will have to make. But before you can make a good decision, you must figure out exactly what the problem is. If you don't identify the problem correctly, you may make the wrong decision! So, identifying the real problem is an important first step in the decision-making process. ★ 12.A; 12.F

Health Journal

Think of one of the first decisions that you made after coming home from school. In your Health Journal, write down at least three options you had for that decision.

Lesson 1 Making Decisions

1 What's the problem?

The first step in making a good decision is to recognize the problem and clearly define it.

2 What are your values?

What is important to you? How do your personal values influence the way that you make decisions?

3 What are your options?

What are the different options you have available to you?

Figure 3 Making decisions becomes easier if you follow these six steps.

Using the six steps of decision making, explain how the founding fathers of the United States may have drawn up the Bill of Rights.

The Six Steps of Decision Making

The six steps to making a good decision are shown in Figure 3. But how you can put these steps into action? Imagine that you are working on a group project for school. You like your teammates and are glad you are grouped with them. One night after working a while, everyone decides to take a break. One student says that the group could avoid a lot of work by using his older sister's project from a few years ago. Several of the team members jump at the idea. Then, everyone looks at you. To figure out what to do, quickly run through the six steps in your mind.

1. **Identify the problem.** Is the problem about cheating, or is it about making your team mad? You decide that the real problem is cheating.
2. **Consider your values.** You value being honest.
3. **List the options.** Two options come to mind: to go along with your team or to refuse to be dishonest.
4. **Weigh the consequences.** If you refuse to cheat, your team may get mad at you. If you go along with your team, you will feel guilty about cheating.
5. **Decide and act.** You decide not to cheat, and you explain to the others why you believe cheating is wrong.
6. **Evaluate your decision.** Was it a good choice? Yes, you convinced most of your team that cheating is wrong. ★ 12.A; 12.B; 12.F

4 What are the consequences?

Did you weigh all the consequences of your decision? Did you look at all the possible outcomes?

5 Do something!

Remember that no decision is complete without action being taken.

6 How did it go?

Was your decision an effective one? If not, will you use the process to arrive at a new decision?

Putting It All Together

Deciding whether to cheat is as important as deciding what kind of career you want. For every decision, the process is the same. By following the six steps, you have a better chance of making a good decision. You may run through the six steps quickly. Other times, the six steps will take months. Either way, commit yourself to the process. Carefully work through the problem, your values, your options, and the consequences. Learn from your mistakes so that you can do even better next time!

★ 11.B; 12.A; 12.B; 12.F

Lesson Review

Using Vocabulary

1. In your own words, explain what makes a good decision. ★ 12.A; 12.F

2. What does personal responsibility mean to you? ★ 11; 12

3. Define the term *values*.

Understanding Concepts

4. List the six steps of decision making. Write a brief explanation of each step. ★ 11; 12

5. Explain why a good decision is a responsible decision. ★ 12.A; 12.C

Critical Thinking

6. **Making Inferences** Describe a scenario in which your values would help you make a good decision.

Lesson 2 Influences on Your Decisions

What You'll Do

- **Explain** the influence of your family on your decision making. ★ 7.A
- **Describe** how your peers influence your decisions. ★ 7.A; 10.A; 12.E
- **Analyze** the effect of the media on your decisions. ★ 8.A
- **Explain** why it is important to evaluate the different influences in your life. ★ 4.A; 7.B; 8.B; 10.A

Terms to Learn

- influence
- peer pressure

What is peer pressure?

Huan tells Emily that these skirts are really "in" and that Emily HAS to try one on. Emily says that she doesn't know why the skirts are so popular, because they look stupid. But she buys a skirt anyway!

You probably have clothes that you bought because they were "in." But once the clothes go "out," you won't wear them again. This lesson looks at what influences your choices and how you can evaluate these influences.

Your Family Is a Major Influence

Many things influence your decisions. An **influence** is a force that affects your choices when you have a decision to make. Members of your family have probably had the greatest influence on you so far. The members of your family set standards and have expectations that are based on their values and cultural traditions. You learn these standards, expectations, and values. And they in turn affect everything that you think and do. For example, why certain people are your friends, what you do for fun, and how you celebrate holidays are decisions that are influenced by your family. ★ 7.A

Figure 4 Your family and the cultural traditions of your family are a major influence on your decisions.

Figure 5 These teens are working together to help others. This is an example of positive peer pressure.

Your Peers Are an Important Influence

Your peers are an important influence, especially during the teen years. A peer is a person who is about your age and with whom you interact. Peers influence what you think or how you act through peer pressure. Peer pressure is the pressure that you feel to do something because your friends want you to do it. Peer pressure can be positive or negative. *Positive peer pressure* influences you to do something that benefits you. For example, if you study with a group of people who want to do well on a test, you may study harder. *Negative peer pressure* is pressure to do things that could harm you or others. For example, have you ever been mean to someone when you are around certain other people? If so, you have experienced negative peer pressure.

Peer pressure affects your life more than you may think. How many activities do you do without your friends? Who helps you choose the music you listen to or the clothes you wear? Peer pressure can even affect your health if you let it convince you to take risks with your body. Taking drugs, drinking alcohol, and getting into cars with underage or dangerous drivers are activities that you might do if you give in to negative peer pressure. There is a strong need for people to fit in, but don't let this need influence you to do harmful things. ★ 5.I; 7.A; 10.A; 12.C

Health Journal

Think of three people or things that have influenced some of your recent decisions. In two or three sentences, compare and contrast how these affected your decisions.

Figure 6 Be cautious when reading claims made by advertisers.

EVALUATING MEDIA MESSAGES

Create an advertisement for a health-related product or service. Exchange these advertisements with other students, and discuss the effect of these ads on you. How honest are the advertisements? How likely are you to buy a product if you know the claims about it are false?

Other Influences on Your Decisions

Which is better, a plain pair of sneakers or sneakers named after a famous basketball player? The truth is that the sneakers are probably about the same. But having the name of a professional basketball player on your sneakers makes you feel as if you're getting the best! That's the power of the media. You hear messages from the media every day. TV, radio, magazines, and the Internet are telling you what to buy and why to buy it. But, much of what they say is to influence you to buy their product. If commercials were accurate, you would be able to use a certain shampoo and never have hair problems. Or one bowl of cereal would give you all of the nutrients you need for the day. However, these products can't do everything that the advertisers say. Commercials are designed to make money for the company that sells the product in the advertisement. The claims are usually exaggerated.

However, the media often reports information that makes a difference. New discoveries can change what people do. For example, not long ago, people thought that aspirin was only for headaches. But studies have shown that taking an aspirin each day can prevent a heart attack in some older people. Eating habits and exercise routines often change because we learn something new. So the media can have a positive effect on your life. You just have to learn to recognize what messages are true.

★ 4.B; 8.A; 8.B

Evaluate Your Influences

If there are so many influences, how do you know whom to listen to? A good rule of thumb is to trust the people who know and care about you. Rely on them to help you evaluate what information is reliable. Family members and good friends can usually be trusted because they want what is best for you. Recall your values, and remember what is important to you. A trusted teacher or school counselor can also give you advice about good influences and bad influences. Be careful about listening to people whom you don't know very well. Evaluate their motives. Do they really have your best interests in mind? Is there evidence to support what they are saying? If not, do some research to find out the truth. Rely on the people you trust for guidance.

★ 7.A; 7.B; 10.A; 12.A; 12.B

Figure 7 These teens are having a bake sale to make money for their team. In working together, they are having a positive influence on each other.

Lesson Review

Using Vocabulary

1. Define the term *influence*. ★ 7.A

2. Explain how peer pressure works. ★ 10.A; 12.E

Understanding Concepts

3. How does your family influence your decisions? ★ 7.A

4. Identify two situations in which your peers influenced you. ★ 10.A; 12.E

5. Describe why you should evaluate the different influences on you before you make a decision. ★ 4.A; 7.B; 8.B; 10.A

Critical Thinking

6. **Making Inferences** Think of several ways that the media influences you. Separate these ways into negative influences and positive influences. ★ 8.A

internet connect
www.scilinks.org/health
Topic: Truth in Advertising
HealthLinks code: HD4103

HEALTH LINKS Maintained by the National Science Teachers Association

Lesson 2 Influences on Your Decisions 31

Lesson 3 Examining Your Decisions

What You'll Do

- **Describe** the importance of looking at the consequences of your decisions. ✪ 12.A; 12.B; 12.C
- **Explain** how using the decision-making steps becomes easier with practice. ✪ 12.B

Terms to Learn

- consequence
- precaution

Write

What are two types of consequences that a decision could have?

MAKING GOOD DECISIONS

Your friends are going to a party this weekend, and you know that someone is bringing alcohol. You don't want to make your friends angry by not going, but you also don't want to get in trouble with your parents. Using the questions in Figure 8 as a guide, determine what decision you should make. ✪ 12.A; 12.B

Neeraja made a bad decision. She told Mariah something about her friend Lee, and Lee found out. Now everyone is mad at her. Neeraja really feels sorry about what she has done!

Like Neeraja, you might have done things that you later wished you could undo. This lesson explains the importance of looking at the outcomes of our choices.

Weighing the Consequences of Decisions

Whenever you act on a decision, there is a consequence. A **consequence** is the result of an action that you take. Suppose you want to have a counselor come in and talk to your class about how to prevent teen drinking. Your action could have several consequences. Students would become more aware of the issue. Someone might even help a friend. These consequences are positive. But consequences can be negative, too. The same situation may remind someone that alcohol was responsible for a loved one's death. Decisions always have consequences, whether positive or negative. Look at the consequences and, if necessary, take precautions. A **precaution** is an action to avoid negative consequences. As a precaution, you could warn the counselor about the student's loss. ✪ 12.A; 12.B; 12.C

Figure 8 Asking yourself these questions may help you see the possible consequences of your decision.

Would my decision
- uphold my values?
- set a good example for others?
- cause emotional pain to me or others?
- help me reach my goals?
- harm me or someone else physically?
- keep me from my goal?
- help others?
- strengthen relationships with my friends?

32 Chapter 2 Making Healthy Decisions

Figure 9 Family members can be helpful when you need advice about a problem.

Practice Makes Perfect

Trying to make good decisions based on potential consequences is sometimes difficult. You may wonder how long it will take you to get good at making decisions. Just remember that the more you practice using the decision-making process, the easier it will be to use. Believe it or not, you can actually rehearse making decisions. Take a small decision, such as what you will wear tomorrow. Before you choose your clothes, think through the six decision-making steps. This idea may seem silly, but when you face a big decision, you will be glad you've walked through the steps in advance. It's also important to learn to ask your parents or other trusted adults for advice when you face problems that you don't know how to solve. Ask for their opinions on small things, and take their advice. Then, when you face big problems, you'll find that these individuals have a lot of good advice to offer!

Myth & Fact

Myth: A risk is always a bad thing.

Fact: Many times, people take risks that have positive consequences. For example, starting a business is risky, but if it succeeds, one can make a lot of money.

Lesson Review

Using Vocabulary
1. What is a consequence?
2. Define the term *precaution*.

Understanding Concepts
3. Why should you look at the consequences of your decisions? ★ 12.A; 12.B; 12.C
4. "The more you practice, the better you get" is a statement that all of us have heard before. Explain how this statement applies to the decision-making process. ★ 12.B

Critical Thinking
5. **Analyzing Ideas** You refused to participate when some other students were copying a homework assignment. What are the positive and negative consequences of your decision? ★ 12.C

Lesson 3 Examining Your Decisions | 33

Lesson 4 Setting Your Goals

Mary wants to make the basketball team. She has been going to the after-school practice everyday. And she has also been practicing on her own at home.

Mary's goal is to make the basketball team. A **goal** is something that you want and are willing to work for. This lesson will show you how to set goals.

From Decisions to Goals

When you have a goal, you are focused on accomplishing a certain task. Being focused means that you have identified something that you want to do. Being focused also helps you manage your time because there is something that you want to get done.

Goals make you feel better about yourself. Goals build self-esteem. **Self-esteem** refers to how you feel about yourself as a person and how much you value yourself. Goals help you avoid making choices that will hurt you. Let's say that Ann-Marie wants to enter a project in the science fair. One day, her friends ask her to cut science class with them. But she knows that the teacher is going to discuss the science fair that day. Her goal helped her decide not to cut class, and her self-esteem gave her the confidence to say no. ★ 12.B; 12.G

What You'll Do

- **Explain** the relationship between decisions and goals. ★ 12.B; 12.F; 12.G
- **Distinguish** between short-term goals and long-term goals. ★ 12.F
- **Explain** how your interests and values are sources of goals.
- **Identify** three sources of support for reaching a goal. ★ 7.A; 10.E

Terms to Learn

- goal
- self-esteem
- interest

Start Off Write

What is a long-term goal?

Figure 10 Accomplishing a goal is a very rewarding experience.

Figure 11 Hobbies and interests that you have now may lead to a career in the future.

Types of Goals

Did you know that you set goals every single day? When you plan to finish your homework before dinner, you set a goal. When you want to get to know someone who is new to your school, you set a goal. Some goals take a longer time to achieve than other goals do. *Short-term goals* are tasks that you can accomplish in a short period of time. For example, finishing your daily exercise routine or completing your English paper is accomplishing a short-term goal.

Long-term goals are tasks that usually take weeks, months, or even years to accomplish. Long-term goals are made up of several short-term goals. Learning how to program computers, graduating from high school, or going to college are examples of long-term goals. Being physically fit is a good example of a long-term goal. To be physically fit, you must accomplish many short-term goals. First, you must learn what it means to be physically fit. You may need to take a health course in school. Second, you must plan to eat right. To learn how to eat healthfully, you may want to read nutrition books. Third, you need to exercise regularly. So, you have to figure out what kind of exercise you like. If you like to run, you may have to add the step of buying the right running shoes for you.

You may find that one of the short-term goals is more difficult to accomplish than the other short-term goals are. But don't let one short-term goal keep you from fulfilling your final goal. Reaching goals you have set for yourself makes you feel better about who you are and more confident about your abilities. ★ 12.B; 12.F

Health Journal

Think of something that you accomplished in the last few months, and write about it in your journal. What effect did it have on your self-esteem? What do you think is the connection between fulfilling a goal and maintaining your self-esteem?

Lesson 4 Setting Your Goals | 35

Your Interests and Values

It's much easier to accomplish a goal when you really care about the goal. Goals must be based on your interests and values. An interest is something that you enjoy and want to learn more about. You might have an interest in music, sports, or even getting your dog to do tricks. Your interests often lead to goals. But your interests can and will change. For example, how many CDs do you have that you don't listen to anymore? Interests reflect tastes, and your tastes often change because something you like better comes along.

Because your goals may change when your interests change, let your values be a big influence on your goals. For example, if you value education, you will work hard in school even though your interests may change from art to history.

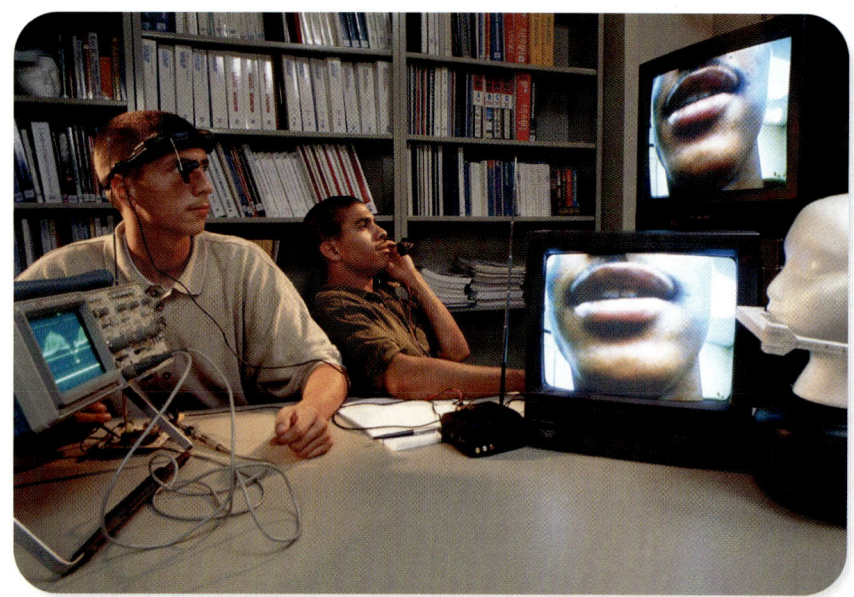

Remember that goal setting is an individual thing, so set goals that are important to you. Sometimes, you will share the same goals with others, and sometimes your goals will be different. But it will be your own interests and values that make you want to reach a goal.

★ 7.A

Figure 12 Everyone has goals. The goal of this student is to learn to read lips.

LIFE SKILLS ACTIVITY

SETTING GOALS

1. Write down at least six activities that you enjoy. Some examples of activities are music, art, writing, cooking, sports, fashion, sewing, or science.

2. Write down three of the above activities that you do well. Skip a line between each activity that you list.

3. Add more details to the items that you wrote down in step 2. For example, if you chose sports, what kinds of sports do you do best?

4. How could the items that you wrote down eventually become goals? For example, if you enjoy cooking, a goal could be to become a chef or to own your own restaurant.

Figure 13 Teamwork is important for achieving certain goals.

Your Goals and Other People

Everyone needs help to reach his or her goals. Can you think of anyone who reached a goal without having help from someone? You probably won't be able to think of many people who reached a goal without some kind of help. Even people who work alone have friends who encourage them. You probably have a goal to graduate from high school. It will be your parents, teachers, and principal who will show you the support that you may need in your efforts to reach this goal.

No matter what your goals are, you will need support. Support can be encouragement, help from your parents and teachers, or money. Your greatest source of encouragement will always be your family and friends. Remember to support your friends and family in their efforts to reach their goals, too.

★ 7.A; 10.E

Lesson Review

Using Vocabulary

1. What is a goal?

2. Define the term *self-esteem*.

Understanding Concepts

3. Explain the relationship between decisions and goals. How do your interests and values influence your goals? ★ 12.B; 12.F; 12.G

4. What are three sources of support for one of your goals? ★ 7.A; 10.E

Critical Thinking

5. **Making Inferences** Think of a career that you may like to have when you grow up. What are four short-term goals that you might have to accomplish to reach your long-term goal? ★ 12.B; 12.F

internet connect
www.scilinks.org/health
Topic: Building a Healthy Self-Esteem
HealthLinks code: HD4020
HEALTH LINKS Maintained by the National Science Teachers Association

Lesson 4 Setting Your Goals | 37

Lesson 5

Reaching Your Goals

The principal was telling the student body how proud he was to have their former student who is now the Gold Medalist Swim Champion at the assembly. He said that he had always known that students from his school would reach their goals.

What You'll Do

- **Explain** why having an action plan is important for reaching your goal. ★ 12.B; 12.G
- **Explain** the importance of learning from your mistakes.

Terms to Learn

- success
- action plan
- setback
- persistence

Start Off Write

What does being successful mean?

Having Success

If you accomplish what you set out to do, you have found success. **Success** is the achievement of your goal. You might have a goal of becoming a successful doctor or famous athlete. No matter what your goal is, you are successful when you reach that goal. So, how do you get there?

Once you've set your goal, you must have a strategy to accomplish it. An **action plan** is a map that outlines the steps for reaching your goal. An action plan

- clearly states your goal
- outlines things you need to accomplish to reach your goal
- has a timeline for reaching your goal
- lists the resources you need to reach your goal ★ 12.B; 12.G

TABLE 1 Making an Action Plan

✏️	Write down your goal.
📝	Make a list of the steps you will follow to reach your goal.
💻	Do some research to find information that you may need to reach your goal.
📅	Estimate how long it will take you to reach your goal, and write down this information.
✔️	Check your progress periodically.
🙌	Reward yourself when you have reached your goal.

38 | Chapter 2 Making Healthy Decisions

Figure 14 If you are persistent, you can reach your goal.

Setbacks

Sometimes, you can identify a goal, have an interest in your goal, and have the best action plan ever written. Yet you still do not reach your goal. Not reaching a goal happens, and it happens a lot! Many successful people had to try over and over before they reached their goals. It is easy to get discouraged when you face a setback. A <mark>setback</mark> is something that goes wrong. But setbacks are also learning opportunities. Setbacks and failures are very different. You fail only if you quit. If you have a setback, get advice and find out how to overcome this setback. What do you need to do differently? The key to reaching a goal is to be persistent. <mark>Persistence</mark> is the commitment to keep working toward your goal even when things happen that make you want to quit. If you can't achieve your goal one way, be persistent and try another way! You may succeed on your next try. ★ 12.B; 12.G

Myth & Fact

Myth: Setbacks represent failure.

Fact: Setbacks are learning tools.

Lesson Review

Using Vocabulary

1. Define *success*.
2. What is an action plan? ★ 12.B; 12.G
3. What is persistence and why is it important for reaching goals? ★ 12.G
4. What is a setback?

Understanding Concepts

5. Why is it important to have an action plan for reaching your goals? ★ 12.B; 12.G
6. Why is learning from your setbacks important?

Critical Thinking

7. **Applying Concepts** Think of a goal that you have or would like to have. Outline an action plan to achieve it. ★ 12.B; 12.G

Lesson 6

Goals Can Change

What You'll Do

- **Explain** how to keep track of your progress. ⭐ 12.B; 12.F
- **List** two reasons why goals sometimes change. ⭐ 7.A; 12.E

Terms to Learn

- assess
- coping

Start Off Write

What is one way you can track your progress in reaching a goal?

> Dominick had been doing yardwork to pay for hockey equipment. As he thought about the work he had done, he realized that he actually enjoyed working outdoors on landscaping projects.

What will happen if Dominick finds that he doesn't like hockey? Will his hard work have been for nothing? No. Dominick found that yardwork interested him, and landscaping might become his new goal. This lesson shows you how you can change your goals or start new goals.

Assessing Your Progress

When you work toward a long-term goal, seeing your progress is sometimes hard. For example, suppose you are trying to run a mile in 8 minutes. You may run every day for months in an effort to go faster. But how can you tell if you are running faster? After all, each day you come home tired and sore. Unless you have a way to track your progress, you'll probably never see it. It is important to see changes. Without seeing improvement, you may think you're getting nowhere and give up.

There's always a way to assess how you are doing. To **assess** your progress is to measure your short-term achievement towards a long-term goal. Ways to assess your short-term progress include keeping a journal or making a chart. ⭐ 12.B; 12.F

Figure 15 A savings account passbook is a good way to assess your progress on a goal to save money.

Changing Your Goals

As you track your progress, you may find that you are not progressing as much as you would like. The time might come to think about making some changes. You may do something differently to meet the same goal, or you may have to switch goals altogether. There can be many reasons to make a change. For example, your family may move away, making it hard to keep using the same resources. Maybe your interests have changed, and you don't want to reach the same goal anymore. No matter what the reason is, changing goals is not the same as quitting or failing. When you change goals, you keep working toward something. You just change directions. Even if you make a change, setbacks may occur. You may be disappointed, but you can learn to cope with it. **Coping** is dealing with problems and troubles in an effective way. One way to cope with a setback is to take a break and work on something else. When you start working on your goal again, you will feel refreshed.

★ 7.A; 10.B; 12.E

STUDY TIP for better reading

Reading Effectively After reading this lesson, rewrite the objectives at the beginning of the lesson in question form. Your questions should begin with what, why, or how. Answer each objective by writing one or two complete sentences.

Figure 16 Spend some time thinking about why you want to change goals.

Lesson Review

Using Vocabulary

1. Define the term *assess*.
2. What does *coping* mean to you? ★ 10.B

Understanding Concepts

3. Identify two reasons why goals might change. ★ 7.A; 12.E
4. What are two ways to assess your progress? ★ 12.B; 12.F

Critical Thinking

5. **Making Inferences** How could you assess your progress toward becoming a good photographer?
6. **Identifying Relationships** When have you or someone else had to change a goal?

Lesson 7 — Communication Skills

When your friends have problems, do they come to you to talk? If you share a great idea that you have, do people understand you the first time? When you feel lousy, how many people know how you really feel?

What You'll Do

- **Explain** how good communication helps you achieve goals. ★ 11.B; 11.C
- **Describe** three ways to be an active listener. ★ 10.C

Terms to Learn

- communication skills
- active listening

Start Off Write

What are two things people can do to let you know they are actively listening to you?

Look closely at people who are successful, and you will see that they have skills other than the ability to set goals and make decisions. People who are successful know how to communicate effectively. In this lesson, you will learn ways to improve your communication skills. **Communication skills** are methods for expressing your thoughts and listening to what others say.

Communicating Clearly

Communication skills are especially important to reaching your goals. So, what are good communication skills?

- Stay focused. Talk about the important issue, not about anything that comes into your head.
- Choose your words carefully. Make sure you are clear about whether you are talking about the way that you view something or actual facts.
- Watch your body language. For example, keep your arms uncrossed.

Reaching your goals is easier if you can communicate your ideas and expectations. People will know your intentions and what you expect. This helps you avoid misunderstandings. ★ 11.B; 11.C; 11.D

Brain Food

To send messages great distances, some human cultures have developed languages based on drum sounds or whistles.

Figure 17 Good communication skills are vital to success.

Figure 18 Which of these students has good listening skills?

Listen!

Good communication is more than being able to express yourself. It also depends on how well you listen to others. To be a good listener, you must use active listening skills. **Active listening** is not only hearing what someone says but also showing that you understand what the person is communicating. The following tips are examples of active listening:

- Face the person who is talking. Facing a person shows that you are interested in what that person is saying.
- Make eye contact with the other person.
- To avoid misunderstandings, restate or summarize what the person says to you.

Using good listening skills shows respect for the other person. The speaker needs to know that you heard his or her feelings, ideas, and opinions. ★ 10.C; 11.C

Lesson Review

Using Vocabulary
1. Define *communication skills*.
2. What is active listening? ★ 10.C

Understanding Concepts
3. How can good communication skills help you reach a goal?
4. What are three things you can do to be an active listener? ★ 10.C

Critical Thinking
5. **Making Predictions** Imagine your goal is to become a radio announcer. How could you convince the manager of the radio station that you have good communication skills? ★ 11.B; 11.C
6. **Making Predictions** Describe two specific things you can do to communicate better with others. ★ 11.B; 11.C; 11.D

internet connect
www.scilinks.org/health
Topic: Communication Skills
HealthLinks code: HD4022
HEALTH LINKS Maintained by the National Science Teachers Association

Lesson 8

Refusal Skills

Marina had spent a lot of time on her homework and didn't want to share it with Leah, her best friend. But she wasn't sure how to say no when Leah asked Marina to see her homework.

What You'll Do

- **Identify** four refusal skills, either verbal or nonverbal.
  ⭐ 11.B; 11.C; 11.D
- **Explain** why planning ahead is a good way to avoid risky situations. ⭐ 12.B; 12.C; 12.D; 12.G
- **Explain** why developing a support system can help you deal with peer pressure.
  ⭐ 7.A; 10.A; 12.B; 12.E; 12.F

Terms to Learn

- refusal skills
- support system

Start Off Write

What is a support system?

Refusing to do something for someone you really like is tough! How do you say no and remain friends? This lesson offers strategies to help you deal with these kinds of situations.

Say "No!"

Saying no to someone you like is very hard. Even our best friends sometimes challenge us to do things that are not good for us. But when you give in to negative peer pressure, you go against your values. For example, let's say you value your health. If you give in to your friend and start smoking, you won't stay healthy. Remember that your values are important.

When you are in a situation in which you need to say no, use refusal skills. **Refusal skills** are different ways of saying no to things that you don't want to do. Here are some examples of refusal skills that you can use.

- Say no. Be polite, but be clear. Be firm if you need to, and repeat yourself.
- Stay focused on the issue. Be true to yourself and to your beliefs.
- Stand your ground. Don't let yourself be talked into something that you know is wrong.
- Walk away. You do not have to be in a situation that you don't want to be in.
- Avoid risky situations. This can often be the easiest and safest thing to do.

Whenever you use refusal skills, use nonverbal communication, too. Stand in such a way to show that you mean no. Shake your head to also say no. These nonverbal actions will help you get your message across.

⭐ 10.B; 11.B; 11.C; 11.D; 12.D

Figure 19 The easiest refusal skill to use is to say no.

44

Plan Ahead

You can take steps to avoid dangerous situations by using refusal skills. Make a mental list of the things to which you would have to say no. Now think about how you might be tempted to do those things and how you would refuse. When you find yourself in one of these situations, you will know how to avoid them because you already ran through the situation in your mind. Role-playing risky situations with a friend may be helpful. Refusing is like any other new skill. It gets easier to use with practice! Just remember that the easiest way to prevent many of these problems is to avoid risky situations in the first place. If you have a feeling that something isn't quite right, go with your feelings. You won't regret it. ★ 5.A; 5.C; 5.J; 5.K; 11.B; 12.G

Have a Support System

The hardest part of saying no to peer pressure is feeling that you are alone and that you will lose your friends. That is not true! Real friends will support you when you stand up for what you believe. That is why you need to develop a support system. A **support system** is made up of family members and friends who will stand by you and will encourage you when times get hard. With a support system, you won't feel alone when you have to say no to someone.

It is a good idea to talk to your parents or another trusted adult when you have questions about negative peer pressure. Teachers, guidance counselors, and spiritual leaders in your community can also answer your questions. With the support of both family and friends, you will feel good about your ability to say no.

★ 7.A; 10.A; 10.E; 11.B; 11.D; 12.E; 12.F

LIFE SKILLS ACTIVITY

USING REFUSAL SKILLS

One of your friends has started smoking and, for the last few days, has offered you a cigarette. You have said no several times. With another student, role-play how you could handle the situation by using other refusal skills. ★ 5.J; 12.B

Figure 20 A support system made up of friends can be a source of encouragement.

Lesson Review

Using Vocabulary

1. Identify four refusal skills. ★ 11.B; 11.C; 11.D
2. Define the term *support system*.

Understanding Concepts

3. Why are refusal skills important? ★ 11.B; 11.C; 11.D
4. How can you avoid risky situations? ★ 5.A; 5.C; 5.J; 5.K; 12.B; 12.C; 12.D; 12.E; 12.G
5. Why is having a support system to help you deal with peer pressure important? ★ 7.A; 10.A; 12.B; 12.E; 12.F

Critical Thinking

6. **Identifying Relationships** How could you use a support system to avoid a situation in which someone wanted you to cheat? ★ 7.A; 11.B; 12.B

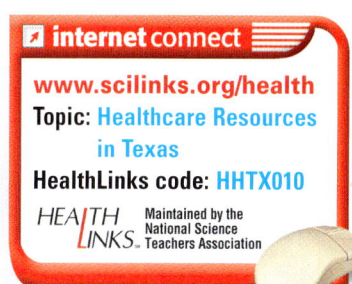

internet connect
www.scilinks.org/health
Topic: Healthcare Resources in Texas
HealthLinks code: HHTX010
HEALTH LINKS Maintained by the National Science Teachers Association

2 CHAPTER REVIEW

Chapter Summary

- A good decision is a responsible decision. ■ Values are beliefs that you consider to be of great importance. ■ There are six steps to good decision making. ■ Your family, your friends, and the media influence your decisions. ■ Peer pressure can be negative or positive. ■ There are positive and negative consequences involved in decision making. ■ Short-term goals help you achieve long-term goals. ■ Your interests and values influence your goals. ■ Success is the achievement of your goals. ■ An action plan can help you achieve goals. ■ Assess your progress toward reaching your goals. ■ Communication skills are important when speaking and listening. ■ Refusal skills are ways to say no to things that you don't want to do.

Using Vocabulary

For each sentence, fill in the blank with the proper word from the word bank provided below.

- action plan
- assess
- good decision
- persistence
- personal responsibility
- precautions
- active listening
- refusal skills
- self-esteem
- setback
- success
- values

1. If you don't progress toward a goal, you face a ___.
2. Taking ___ helps minimize negative consequences.
3. To help you reach your goal, you need to ___ your progress periodically.
4. When you accept the outcome of your decisions, you have taken ___.
5. Hearing and understanding what someone is saying are parts of ___.
6. A(n) ___ helps you reach your goal by outlining the steps you need to follow.
7. If you believe in yourself and your abilities, you have good ___.
8. When the going gets rough, you need ___ to reach your goals.

Understanding Concepts

9. How do your values influence your decisions? How do your interests influence your decisions? ★ 1.A; 7.A; 12.A
10. What are three major influences that affect your decisions? Which of these influences do you consider to be the most important? ★ 12.A
11. What are the six steps of decision making? ★ 12.A; 12.B; 12.F
12. Name two negative consequences of smoking cigarettes. Are there any benefits? ★ 5.H
13. What are three examples of short-term goals?
14. What are three examples of long-term goals? What short-term goals will you have to accomplish to reach one of your long-term goals? ★ 12.F
15. What are three sources of support for reaching your goals? ★ 7.A; 10.E
16. Write a brief action plan for making an A in one of your classes. Number and label each of the steps in your plan. ★ 12.B; 12.G

Critical Thinking

Analyzing Ideas

17 Your friend's grandmother died recently, and your friend is taking the loss very hard. She wants to talk with you about her feelings, but you're not quite sure how to help. Using your knowledge of communication skills, what could you do that may help your friend? ★ 10.C; 11.C; 11.D

18 Imagine that a friend likes working with animals. Suppose that her goal is to become a veterinarian. What sources of support could your friend use to learn more about becoming a veterinarian?

19 Having setbacks and not reaching your goals can be very disappointing and very hard to handle. Is there any value to setbacks? Explain your answer. ★ 12.F

Making Good Decisions

20 Several of your friends have started smoking cigarettes. You must decide whether you should join them. You know your parents will be very upset, and you do not want to disappoint them. You also know smoking is very unhealthy. You need to make a decision. Follow the six steps for making good decisions to decide how you will solve this problem.
★ 12.B; 12.D; 12.E

21 You are collecting tickets at a benefit dance to raise money for a charity. You see two of your friends sneak in the back door. What should you do? Should you tell the principal, should you speak directly with your friends, or should you ignore what they did? ★ 10.A; 11.D; 12.E

22 Imagine that some of your friends are planning to skip the last class of the day at school to go to a CD signing at a music store. The band is one of your favorites. Would it be OK to skip school since you would miss only one class? Explain your answer.

Interpreting Graphics

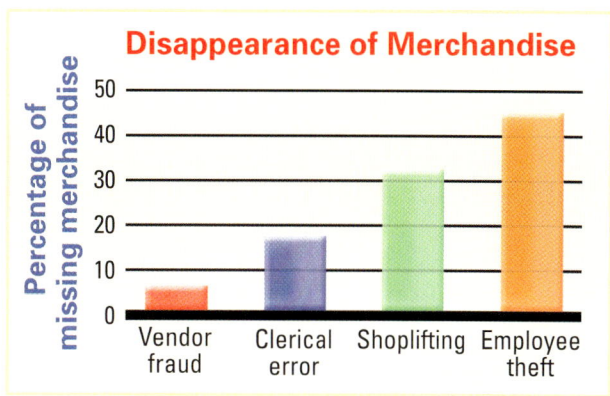

Use the figure above to answer questions 23–25. ★ M8.5.A

23 What is the most common cause of disappearance of merchandise from a store?

24 About what percentage of merchandise is lost because of shoplifting?

25 What percentage of missing merchandise is due to vendor fraud?

Reading Checkup

Take a minute to review your answers to the Health IQ questions at the beginning of this chapter. How has reading this chapter improved your Health IQ?

Life Skills IN ACTION

Making Good Decisions

You make decisions every day. But how do you know if you are making good decisions? Making good decisions is making choices that are healthy and responsible. Following the six steps of making good decisions will help you make the best possible choice whenever you make a decision. Complete the following activity to practice the six steps of making good decisions.

Rick and the Rebels

ACT 1 — Setting the Scene

Rick is riding home with his father. As they near their house, they see a group of teens vandalizing a neighbor's car. The teens start to run away. As they run past Rick and his father's car, one of the teens looks at Rick. Rick and the teen recognize each other, and Rick realizes that he knows many of the teens. Rick does not know what to do, so he goes to his sister Marcia for advice.

Guided Practice

Practice with a Friend

Form a group of three. Have one person play the role of Rick and another person play the role of Marcia. Have the third person be an observer. Walking through each of the six steps of making good decisions, role-play a conversation between Rick and Marcia as he decides what to do. Marcia can help Rick brainstorm options and help him weigh the consequences of each option. The observer will take notes, which will include observations about what the people playing Rick and Marcia did well and suggestions of ways to improve. Stop after each step to evaluate the process. ★ 7.A; 10.A; 11.B; 12.B; 12.E

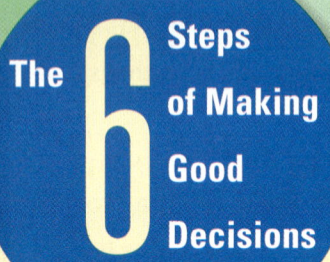

The 6 Steps of Making Good Decisions

1. Identify the problem.
2. Consider your values.
3. List the options.
4. Weigh the consequences.
5. Decide, and act.
6. Evaluate your choice.

48 | Chapter 2 Life Skills in Action

Independent Practice

Check Yourself

After you have completed the guided practice, go through Act 1 again without stopping at each step. Answer the questions below to review what you did.

1. What problem does Rick face?
2. What are some of Rick's options? What are some possible consequences of those options? ⭐ 12.C
3. Why is this decision difficult to make? ⭐ 12.E
4. How does talking with someone while following the six steps of making good decisions help? ⭐ 10.B; 11.B; 11.D
5. How would the decision-making process be different if the teen had not seen Rick?

On Your Own

At school the next day, the teen who recognized Rick stops him in the hall. The teen tells Rick, "I know what you saw. I wouldn't say anything if I were you. Your dad has a nice car—you wouldn't want anything to happen to it, would you?" Rick knows that the other teen is not making an empty threat. Write a short story about what Rick decides to do next. Be sure to write about how Rick uses the six steps of making good decisions to make his choice.

CHAPTER 3
Stress Management

Lessons
1. Stress: A Natural Part of Your Life — 52
2. How Stress Affects You — 56
3. Defense Mechanisms — 60
4. Managing Your Stress — 62
5. Preventing Distress — 66

Chapter Review — 70
Life Skills in Action — 72

Check out **Current Health** articles related to this chapter by visiting **go.hrw.com**. Just type in the keyword **HD4CH35**.

" I used to like **school** a lot, at least most of the time. But this **year** it seems like I can't **concentrate** in school, and I can't do **anything right** at home. My grades have fallen, and my parents are always mad. I hate feeling like this. I'm so stressed out that I feel tired and sick all the time. "

PRE-READING

Answer the following multiple-choice questions to find out what you already know about stress. When you've finished this chapter, you'll have the opportunity to change your answers based on what you've learned.

1. **The stress response is**
   a. a new kind of exercise.
   b. the way your body naturally responds to new situations.
   c. always harmful to your health.
   d. found only in adults. ⭐ 11.F

2. **Which of the following is part of the "fight-or-flight" response?**
   a. Your heart beats faster.
   b. Your pupils dilate.
   c. Your senses sharpen.
   d. all of the above

3. **Ways to manage stress successfully include**
   a. denying that stress exists.
   b. arguing with your parents and teachers.
   c. planning ahead for your important tasks.
   d. eating a lot of chocolate. ⭐ 12.B

4. **Your response to stress**
   a. is always bad for you.
   b. always goes away in about 24 hours.
   c. can make you grow taller.
   d. may cause you to be excited or even happy. ⭐ 11.F

5. **A defense mechanism is**
   a. medication that prevents cancer.
   b. a short-term way to handle stress.
   c. something you learn in sports.
   d. a way to completely get rid of all your stress.

ANSWERS: 1. b; 2. d; 3. c; 4. d; 5. b

Lesson 1

Stress: A Natural Part of Your Life

What You'll Do

- **Describe** the relationship between stress and stressors.
   1.A; 7.A; 11.F
- **Distinguish** between distress and positive stress.
  ★ 1.A; 11.F

Terms to Learn

- stress
- stressor
- distress
- positive stress

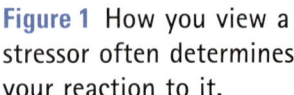

Why is some stress in your life good for you?

Jalen's parents are getting a divorce. Sometimes, Jalen hears them argue about their problems. When they do, Jalen wants to run away.

Jalen is very upset about his parents' divorce. He feels like he is always on edge. Jalen's muscles are tense, and he gets angry without warning. What is happening to Jalen?

What Is Stress?

Jalen is suffering from stress. **Stress** is the combination of a new or possibly threatening situation and your body's natural response to the situation. For example, Jalen is facing a threatening situation. He responds to the situation by feeling tense and edgy. Jalen even thinks about running away. Jalen's response is triggered by a stressor—his parents' divorce. A **stressor** is anything that causes a stress response. Stressors can be physical, such as an emergency operation to remove your appendix. Stressors can also be mental, emotional, or social. A math test may be a mental stressor. Making new friends may be a social stressor.

A stressor can be pleasant or unpleasant. Falling in love is a pleasant stressor. Falling out of love is an unpleasant stressor. Either way, stress and stressors are a normal part of life. You face stressful situations every day. But stress can be handled, so learning to recognize and cope with stress is important. ★ 1.A; 7.A; 11.F

Figure 1 How you view a stressor often determines your reaction to it.

TABLE 1 Common Stressors for Teens

arguing with a brother, sister, or friend	trying out for a sports team
moving to a new home or school	experiencing the death of a pet
getting glasses or braces	having a newborn brother or sister
arguing with a parent	being suspended from school
worrying about height, weight, or appearance	starting to use alcohol, tobacco, or other drugs
being picked as the lead in the school play	being arrested
being seriously injured or sick	experiencing the separation or divorce of a parent
worrying about family member who is seriously ill	failing classes in school
starting to date	death of brother, sister, or parent

Bad Stress and Good Stress

When a stressor triggers a stress response, your body wants to return to an unstressed condition. Sometimes, your response leaves you exhausted or sick. This response is part of negative stress, or distress. **Distress** is the negative physical, mental, or emotional strain in response to a stressor. Distress can make you sick or interfere with your life. Small things, such as forgetting your lunch money, can cause distress. Major events, such as being in a car accident, can also cause distress.

But not all stress is negative. **Positive stress**—sometimes called *eustress* (YOO stress)—is the stress response that happens when winning, succeeding, and achieving. Getting an A on a test or winning a race may create positive stress. Positive stress gives you extra energy, such as the energy boost you need to win a race. Positive stress may help you achieve more than you think you can. It can motivate, energize, and excite you. Being excited about a party is positive stress. And positive stress can leave you feeling calm, happy, and relaxed.

An event that is fun for you may distress someone else. The difference between distress and positive stress may be the way a person views and responds to the stressor. For example, some people are very shy. Meeting new people is distressful to them. Other people are more outgoing. They find it exciting to meet new people. This is positive stress for them. Whether your response to a stressor is distressing or positive often depends on your point of view. For example, writing a poem in English class causes many people distress. But for someone who loves poetry, writing a poem is positive stress. ★ 1.A; 11.A; 11.F

LANGUAGE ARTS ACTIVITY

Review the list of common stressors in Table 1. Choose a stressor, either from the list or from your own experience, and write a short story about a person dealing with the stressor.

Myth & Fact

Myth: Only unpleasant or dangerous situations are stressful.

Fact: Both pleasant and unpleasant situations can be stressful.

Lesson 1 Stress: A Natural Part of Your Life

Health Journal

List 10 items that increase distress in your life. Think about those stressors, and then rank them in order from most stressful to least stressful. Choose one stressor from your list, and describe how you cope with it.

Stressors in Your Life

Consider the following stressors:
- arguing with a brother or sister
- getting glasses or braces
- moving to a new home
- getting in trouble with a teacher
- making a speech in front of the class

These are common stressors for many teens. But not everybody feels stressed by the same event. People respond differently to the same stressor. Which of these stressors would you find the most distressing? the least distressing? Would you respond to any of these stressors positively? Would you feel motivated?

With too much stress, even positive stress, you may feel ill and exhausted. Too little stress can leave you feeling bored. The challenge is to find stressors—and a level of stress response—that leave you feeling motivated and enthusiastic. ★ 1.A; 7.A; 11.E; 11.F

Figure 2 Stress—and stressors—can be physical, mental, emotional, or social.

Stressors Never Come One at a Time

Every day, you deal with stressors you have faced many times, such as quizzes, disagreements with friends, and worrying about how you look. Most of the time, you deal with these routine stressors. But if a major life event, such as the death of a favorite grandparent, is suddenly added, your stress level may change quickly. All routine stressors may become major problems, and even small stressors may seem beyond your control. ★ 1.A; 11.E; 11.F

TABLE 2 Major Life Changes That Cause Serious Stress

- being pregnant and unmarried
- experiencing the death of a parent
- going through parents' divorce
- becoming an unmarried father
- becoming involved with drugs and alcohol
- experiencing the death of a brother or sister
- experiencing a change in your acceptance by your peers
- experiencing the death of a close friend

Teen: My parents always say that my teen years are the "best years of my life." Is this really true?

Expert: In some ways, your teen years can be wonderful. But as wonderful as these years may be, they can also be confusing and painful. This is a time of conflicting demands and mixed messages. Parents, teachers, and friends all have something to say. The good news is that the stress of your teen years won't last forever!

Lesson Review

Using Vocabulary

1. What is stress, and how is stress related to stressors? ★ 1.A; 7.A; 11.F

Understanding Concepts

2. Give an example of each kind of stress: social, physical, mental, and emotional. ★ 1.A; 11.F

3. Distinguish between distress and positive stress. ★ 1.A; 11.F

Critical Thinking

4. **Analyzing Viewpoints** Some people say, "Don't sweat the small stuff." What do you think they mean? Do you agree with them? ★ 1.A; 11.F

5. **Making Predictions** Think back to when you were in the sixth grade. Make a list of your top five stressors then. Make a list of your top five stressors today. Predict what your top five stressors may be when you are in high school. How does your list change from year to year? ★ 1.A; 11.F

Lesson 1 Stress: A Natural Part of Your Life

Lesson 2   How Stress Affects You

What You'll Do
- **Describe** the body's stress response. ⭐ 1.A; 11.F
- **Discuss** how stress may affect relationships. ⭐ 7.A; 11.E

Terms to Learn
- stress response
- epinephrine
- fatigue

Start Off Write
How might long-term responses to stress damage relationships?

On Parents Day, Terry is reading his essay to his class. He usually likes to read in class. Now, in front of all of the parents, his mouth is dry, and he feels sick.

For Terry, reading to his classmates is easy, but reading to a group of parents is very stressful. Terry's body responded naturally to the stressor by getting ready for "fight-or-flight."

Responding to Stressors

When you feel threatened, your body's immediate response is physical—your body wants to act. The **stress response**, also called the "fight-or-flight" response, is your body's reaction to a stressor. This response prepares you to fight a stressor or to run away from it (flight). Your body responds with the physical changes shown in Figure 3. These changes are an immediate and unconscious physical response to the stressor.

One of the first changes is that your body releases epinephrine. **Epinephrine** (EP uh NEPH rin) is a stress hormone that increases the level of sugar in your blood and directs the "fight-or-flight" response. A *hormone* is a chemical substance produced by glands that serves as a messenger within your body. The extra sugar released by epinephrine gives you a quick energy boost, which prepares you to fight or to run. The energy boost results from blood bringing sugar to your muscles and organs. Even if the threat is a nonphysical one, your body's first response is to prepare to fight or to run. ⭐ 1.A; 11.F

When under stress . . .
- ▶ More blood goes to brain
- ▶ Hearing and vision sharpen
- ▶ Breathing speeds up
- ▶ Heart beats faster and harder
- ▶ Epinephrine release gives energy boost
- ▶ More blood goes to legs and arms

Figure 3 Any stressor triggers a stress response. The stronger the stressor is, the stronger your body's response will be.

Lesson 3

Defense Mechanisms

What You'll Do

- **Describe** the purpose of defense mechanisms. ★ 10.B; 11.A; 11.B
- **Identify** three defense mechanisms.
- **Explain** why defense mechanisms may be harmful. ★ 1.A; 11.B; 11.E; 11.F

Terms to Learn

- defense mechanism

Start Off Write

What do defense mechanisms defend against?

Amanda had a fight with her best friend after school. When she got home, Amanda yelled at her little sister and started a fight with her. Now, Amanda is grounded.

Amanda was distressed by the fight with her best friend. Amanda loves her little sister and wasn't angry with her at all. Amanda transferred her anger from her best friend to her little sister.

Short-Term Ways to Handle Stress

Your first response to a stressor is physical. The energy boost and the other changes put a strain on your body. Your body tries to get back to normal as soon as it can. For example, to relieve physical distress, you might exercise. But relieving mental distress may not be so easy. Many people use defense mechanisms to cope with mental distress. A **defense mechanism** (di FENS MEK uh NIZ uhm) is an automatic, short-term behavior to cope with distress. Defense mechanisms include

- rationalization, making excuses instead of admitting mistakes
- displacement, shifting negative feelings about one person to another person (This is what Amanda did.)
- repression, blocking out unpleasant memories
- denial, ignoring reality or pretending that something doesn't exist
- projection, putting the blame for your problem on someone or something else ★ 10.B; 11.A; 11.B

Figure 7 Defense mechanisms may help you deal with stress in the short term.

Denial

Rationalization

Projection

Distress Affects Relationships

Your distress may affect other people. For example, your distress may hurt your ability to think clearly and to make good decisions. Your bad decisions may hurt other people even if you do not mean to. Relationships with your family may suffer. Or distress may make you angry. You may be mean to people around you. Your friends may become angry with you and avoid you. You may even lose friends because you are distressed. Distress can keep you from concentrating on schoolwork. As a result, your distress may affect your teachers.

Being friendly when you are distressed is difficult. You may not even notice how you are treating other people. So, learn what your stressors are. Know when you are stressed. Then, you can deal with your stress and will cause less damage to your relationships.
⭐ 11.E

Brain Food

In Kentucky in the mid-1990s, 13 percent of more than 5,500 middle school students reported that they had felt depressed or very sad most or all of the time. About 150 of these teens said they had thought about committing suicide.

Figure 6 Sometimes your stress makes you act in a way that hurts other people.

Lesson Review

Using Vocabulary
1. Define *stress response*. ⭐ 1.A
2. What is fatigue? ⭐ 1.A

Understanding Concepts
3. Why is the release of epinephrine important to the stress response? ⭐ 1.A; 11.F
4. Describe how stress may affect relationships. ⭐ 7.A; 11.E

Critical Thinking
5. **Making Inferences** Which do you think is more harmful to your body, being a little distressed over a long period of time or being seriously distressed for a short period of time? Explain your answer. ⭐ 1.A; 11.F

internet connect
www.scilinks.org/health
Topic: Fight or Flight
HealthLinks code: HD4040

HEALTH LINKS Maintained by the National Science Teachers Association

Figure 5 One of the long-term effects of stress is artery disease.

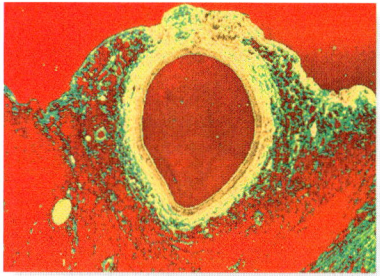

normal artery

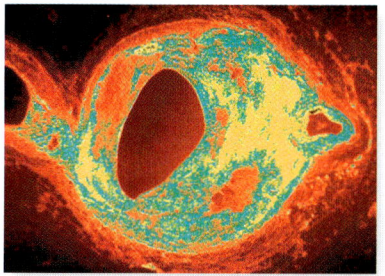

artery partly blocked by deposits related to long-term stress

TABLE 3 Long-Term Effects of Stress on the Body	
Part of body	Problem
Brain	anxiety disorder or depression; stroke (from high blood pressure)
Heart	heart disease and heart attacks
Circulatory system	high blood pressure and coronary artery disease
Immune system	increased risk of infection and disease
Digestive system	digestive problems, such as diarrhea, constipation, cramps, abdominal bloating, and a type of ulcer
Skin	including acne, hives, psoriasis, and eczema
Weight	loss of appetite and weight; cravings for "comfort foods," such as salty or sweet food, which can lead to weight gain
Other	diabetes, chronic pain (arthritis), and sleep disorders, all of which may be made worse by long-term stress

Lasting Effects of Stress

The changes caused by the stress response put your body on high alert. Your body can handle these changes for a short time. However, if the high-alert condition continues for a longer time, it can cause fatigue. **Fatigue** is a feeling of extreme tiredness. For example, your body may feel very tired after exercise. This is physical fatigue. Stress can also cause physical fatigue. In both cases, you need rest to allow your body to recover. Stress can also cause mental fatigue. Mental fatigue, like physical fatigue, causes you to feel tired all over all the time. You lose all your energy. Stress-related fatigue—physical or mental—can be relieved by removing or learning to manage the stressor.

When you are distressed continuously, you may also

- have difficulty sleeping or have frequent headaches
- have mental or emotional problems, or cry for no reason
- become depressed, bored, or frustrated
- feel tense, irritable, and overwhelmed
- have trouble concentrating on schoolwork and making decisions
- overeat without meaning to or lose your appetite

In extreme cases, distressed teens have even attempted suicide. Prolonged distress can be serious. ★ 1.A; 11.F

Figure 4 A stressor may make you feel like fighting or running away. A third way to deal with a stressor is to talk about it with a trusted adult.

Short-Term Responses to Stress

With the release of epinephrine, you get a quick surge of extra energy. As you prepare for "fight-or-flight," you may feel like Terry. Your mouth may be dry, and you may feel sick. Your muscles may tighten up. You may feel like you are extra powerful. And your vision and hearing may sharpen. These stress responses are short-term changes designed to deal quickly with the stressor.

The stress response is the same for all stressors. Both positive and negative stressors produce the same response. It is like a power surge. So, when you take action, such as running from danger or giving your speech, you burn off the extra energy. Your body begins to return to normal. You begin to relax. If you have been distressed, you may feel emotionally or mentally tired. If the stress has been positive, you may feel calm and relaxed. Either kind of stress may leave you feeling tired.

Your body can handle the power surge for only a short time. Prolonged or continuous distress is related to a variety of side effects, including heart disease and a weakened immune system. Having some stress in your life is important, but learning to use that stress to your advantage is also important. And you must let your body recover from all stress, even positive stress.

★ 1.A; 11.A; 11.F

Health Journal

Have you ever faced a "fight-or-flight" situation? What were the circumstances? What do you remember about how your body reacted to the stressor? In your Health Journal, write a paragraph about your experience.

Do Defense Mechanisms Help?

You may use defense mechanisms to cope with stressors and deal with problems. For example, it may be easy for you to deny that a stressor exists. Or you may get angry with someone and blame that person for a stressor that is really your fault. For example, you may blame your piano teacher if you cannot go the movies because you haven't practiced playing the piano. In either case, your distress is reduced and you may feel better. You think you have dealt with the stressor.

But defense mechanisms do not make the stressor go away. Defense mechanisms are temporary. They are the easy way out. Defense mechanisms delay having to deal with the stressor. In the end, the stressor is still there. Often, it becomes even worse. While defense mechanisms may help in the short term, finding other ways to manage the distress in your life is better.

★ 1.A; 10.B; 11.A; 11.B; 11.E; 11.F

Health Journal
Recall something from the past week that you felt distressed about. It can be an event at home, at school, or anywhere else. Describe the situation in detail and how you responded to the distress. Identify any defense mechanisms that you used. What other ways could you have handled the situation?

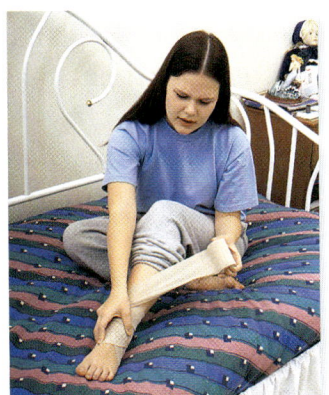

Melanie sprained her ankle at practice but told herself that her ankle was OK.

The next day at practice, Melanie convinced herself again that her ankle was not injured.

Minutes later, Melanie hurt her ankle much worse and had to leave the team.

Figure 8 Melanie refused to believe that her ankle was injured. Her denial of the injury ended up having serious consequences.

Lesson Review

Using Vocabulary
1. What is a defense mechanism?
   ★ 11.A; 11.B

Understanding Concepts
2. Identify three defense mechanisms.
   ★ 11.A; 11.B
3. Explain the purpose of defense mechanisms and why depending on them could be harmful.
   ★ 1.A; 10.B; 11.B; 11.E; 11.F

Critical Thinking
4. **Analyzing Ideas** Amanda was angry with her best friend, but she fought with her little sister. Explain why defense mechanisms may not be useful in this situation, and describe a better way that Amanda may have handled the problem. ★ 10.B; 11.E

Lesson 4 Managing Your Stress

What You'll Do

- **Identify** eight physical signs of stress. ★ 1.A
- **Identify** eight mental or emotional signs of stress. ★ 11.F
- **Discuss** three tools for managing stress. ★ 10.B; 11.A; 11.B
- **Discuss** why sharing emotions can help relieve stress. ★ 11.A; 11.B; 11.D

Terms to Learn

- stress management
- reframing
- emotions

Start Off Write

How do you know when you are stressed?

Maggie's father has a new job, so her family is moving to Florida. Maggie is angry about leaving her friends. Her twin, Mariah, is excited about living near the ocean.

Maggie and Mariah face the same stressor—moving to a new home. Maggie is distressed by the move, but Mariah sees it as exciting. How does each of the twins manage this stressor?

Recognizing Stress

Managing stress is part of mental and physical health. **Stress management** is the ability to handle stress in healthy ways. The first step to managing stress is recognizing that you are stressed. Stress—even positive stress—produces warning signs. Warning signs can be physical, mental, or emotional. Physical signs of stress include headaches, indigestion, and muscle aches. Mental and emotional signs of distress include nightmares, depression, anxiety, and mood swings. Table 4 shows some more common signs of distress. Of course, not every headache or nightmare is caused by distress. But if you have signs of distress, or if one sign lasts a long time, you probably have a stressor affecting your life.

By recognizing when you are distressed and knowing ways to reduce distress, you can protect your health. Distress that builds up may produce a variety of harmful effects. If you are distressed, find ways to get rid of the stressor. Reduce your distress to keep its effects from hurting you. ★ 1.A; 11.F

TABLE 4 Common Signs of Distress

Physical signs	Emotional and mental signs
headaches	frustration
dry mouth	depression
teeth grinding	irritability
shortness of breath	worrying
pounding heart	confusion
muscle aches	forgetfulness
fatigue	poor concentration
insomnia	loneliness

62 | Chapter 3 Stress Management

Figure 9 You can handle distress in a variety of ways, including playing a musical instrument, writing in a journal, riding your bike, or just having fun with friends.

Handling Distress

One way to manage distress is by reframing the stressor. **Reframing** is changing the way you think about a stressor, and changing your emotional response to the stressor. When you think about a problem from another point of view, you are reframing. Do you remember Maggie? She wants to be a marine biologist. She may feel better if she reframes her situation. Moving to Florida will make studying the marine animals that interest her easier. But reframing is not the only way to manage distress. Other ways to manage distress are the following:

- **Asserting Yourself** Tell other people how you feel. Speak up for yourself without hurting others.
- **Planning Ahead** Make time to do things you must do even if you don't like to do them, such as your homework.
- **Laughing** Laughter is important. Make it a habit to find something to laugh about every day. ★ 10.B; 11.B; 12.G

Hands-on ACTIVITY

DISTRESS MANAGERS

1. With your classmates, develop a survey that asks other students what causes distress for them. The survey should also ask them what they are doing, if anything, to manage distress.

2. Ask students from other classes to fill out the survey and return it to you. Tell them not to put their names on the survey.

Analysis

1. Make graphs, tables, and charts to help you interpret your survey data. Present your findings in a poster or oral report.

2. Based on your data, give recommendations for plans to manage distress.

3. Using your recommendations, produce a "Ways to Manage Distress" information sheet to give to your peers.

Lesson 4 Managing Your Stress

Figure 10 Sometimes, just talking about a problem makes the problem easier to solve.

Sharing Emotions

Sharing your emotions is a way to help manage your stress. Everybody has emotions. **Emotions** are the feelings produced as you respond to something in your life. Emotions are perfectly natural. They may be part of your response to a stressor, and they may be very powerful. For example, if you hear a noise in the middle of the night, your stress response may include feelings of fear. If you figure out what caused the noise, you may relax. Your fear will go away. But what do you do if you cannot figure out what caused the noise? Your physical response may get stronger, and your fear may grow. And as your fear increases, your physical response may become even more distressful.

Wanting to share your emotions with other people is natural. Often, just talking about your problem will help you solve it. Talk to a grownup you can trust—a parent, relative, teacher, religious leader, or guidance counselor. Choose someone who cares about you and who will take the time to listen to you. Keeping your feelings locked up inside may make your distress worse. Finding appropriate ways to share or express your feelings can make a big difference in the way you feel.
★ 10.B; 11.A; 11.B; 11.D

Distress Is Dangerous

Don't ignore signs of distress! Stressors will not just go away. Distress can lead to illness, depression, or unhealthy behavior.

LIFE SKILLS ACTIVITY

PRACTICING WELLNESS

Think of a recent incident when you were distressed and you felt unhappy or angry. Figure out what it was in the situation that left you feeling the way you did. With a friend, brainstorm ways to manage your distress. For example, could you reframe the problem? Were there ways to change your distress into positive stress? Are there ways to deal with the stressor so that its impact is reduced? How does sharing your feelings help you manage your distress? ★ 11.A; 11.B

Taking Time for Yourself

Did you know that you should have about 30 minutes every day for yourself? This personal time lets you forget all your stressors for a little while. It is time when you can relax. But how do you find that much time? You are at school all day. Your friends want to hang out. Your coach wants you to train, and your piano teacher wants you to practice. You have to clean your room. You need to walk your dog. You have homework to do. How can you find your personal time?

Step one is to list all the things you have to do. Step two is to figure out how important each item on the list is. Which tasks must be done today? Which ones can you do tomorrow? Your 30 minutes should be on today's list. Then, take your 30 minutes—go for a walk, read a book, exercise, or listen to music. Your 30 minutes is not a way to avoid your schoolwork or other responsibilities. It is a way of staying healthy and free of distress.

★ 10.B; 11.A; 11.B

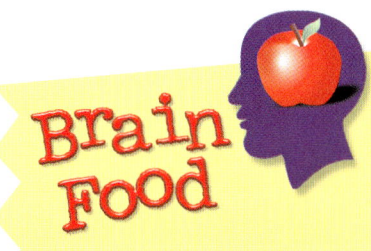

Brain Food

Just remember—If you think you can, you probably can. But if you think you can't, you probably can't. Even when you think you are swamped, you can probably find a way to make time for yourself.

Figure 11 Your mental and emotional health are important. Take time out for yourself.

Lesson Review

Using Vocabulary

1. Explain stress management in your own words, and include the term *reframing*. ★ 10.B; 11.A; 11.B

Understanding Concepts

2. Give three examples of stress management tools. ★ 10.B; 11.A; 11.B

3. Make a table, and list eight physical signs and eight mental or emotional signs of stress. ★ 1.A; 11.E; 11.F

Critical Thinking

4. **Making Predictions** Imagine that you respond to a major stressor in your life not only with the physical stress response but also with strong feelings of fear. Discuss why sharing your emotions may help relieve this distress. Predict what might happen to you if you were not able to rid that stressor from your life.
★ 11.B; 11.D; 11.E; 11.F

internet connect
www.scilinks.org/health
Topic: Stress Management
HealthLinks code: HD4095

HEALTH LINKS Maintained by the National Science Teachers Association

Lesson 4 Managing Your Stress

Lesson 5 Preventing Distress

Joshua leads a busy life. He gets up early and eats a good breakfast. He gets to school on time. After school, Joshua has soccer practice. When he gets home, he practices his clarinet and does his homework.

What You'll Do

- **Explain** why preventing distress is important. ★ 1.A; 3.A; 11.F
- **List** five ways of preventing distress. ★ 10.B; 11.A; 11.B
- **Describe** how making a plan can prevent distress. ★ 11.B; 12.G

Terms to Learn

- plan
- time management
- prioritize

Write

Describe two ways you prevent distress in your life.

Joshua gets plenty of sleep. He doesn't stay up late studying for tests. And on weekends, Joshua still has time to have fun with his friends. How does he find time to do so much?

Stopping Distress Before It Starts

Joshua wasn't always so organized. He was like a lot of busy people. Joshua finished projects at the last minute. He was late to soccer practice. His grades went down, and he wasn't able to catch up. He was tired and unhappy, but he didn't know how to stop his distress. Finally, Joshua talked with his guidance counselor and learned to prevent much of his distress.

The counselor helped Joshua make a schedule. Joshua's schedule is a plan for the next 2 weeks. A **plan** is any detailed program, created ahead of time, for doing something. On his plan, Joshua lists the things that cause him the most distress. He plans to do those things first.

You can do what Joshua did. Plan ahead. You may be able to stop much of your distress before it starts. And you will be prepared for much of the distress that you cannot stop. If you plan for stressors that are coming, you will be ready for them. With a plan, you will feel like you have control over your life. A good plan can prevent a lot of distress and will help keep you healthy.
★ 1.A; 11.B; 11.F

Figure 12 A cake recipe is a plan. By following the recipe, you can avoid disappointment and can enjoy a great cake!

Figure 13 You can prevent distress in a variety of ways.

Other Tips for Preventing Distress

Joshua has found a good way to prevent distress. Another way is to take care of your physical and mental health. A healthy, happy person handles distress better than a person who is tired or sick does. Other ways to take care of yourself include

- getting plenty of sleep (8 hours) every night
- eating lots of fresh fruit and vegetables
- setting realistic long-term and short-term goals and making plans to achieve them
- having fun and playing outside
- believing that every problem has a solution
- finding something to laugh about every day
- setting a goal to learn something new every day
- treating other people with respect, the way you want to be treated

You cannot control everything. But you can think ahead—and plan ahead—to deal with many stressors. If you have a plan and follow it, you are taking control of your life. And by taking control of your life, you can prevent distress. ★ 10.B; 11.A; 11.B

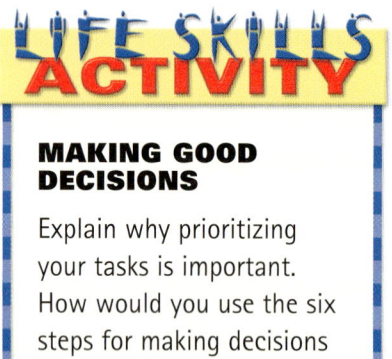

LIFE SKILLS ACTIVITY

MAKING GOOD DECISIONS

Explain why prioritizing your tasks is important. How would you use the six steps for making decisions to prioritize your school assignments and your personal time.

Compare and Contrast Review the information in Lessons 3, 4, and 5 about ways to handle stress. Compare defense mechanisms with long-term techniques, such as stress prevention and time management.

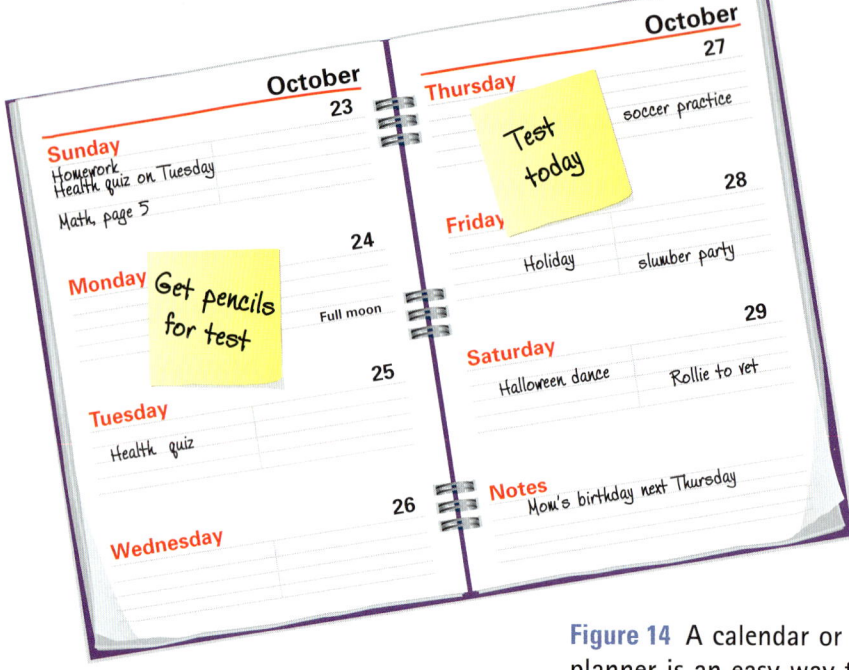

Figure 14 A calendar or planner is an easy way to keep track of important assignments and events.

Planning for School

For most teens, school and schoolwork are major sources of distress. One way to relieve some of that distress is to use time management. **Time management** is making appropriate choices about how to use your time. Start using time management by making a schedule. Use a calendar, planner, or notebook. Write down the dates when all your assignments are due. Then, write down what you need to do—and what you want to do—each day. Include time for yourself.

Look at your schedule to see if you have time for everything. Then, prioritize your tasks. To **prioritize** (prie AWR uh TIEZ) is to arrange items in the order of their importance. Decide how important a task is by imagining what will happen if you don't do it. You may have to cut the least important items from your list.

Always be sure you understand what your teacher wants you to do. If you are not sure, ask until you do understand. Arrange your assignments by due dates. Do the most urgent tasks first. Then, do the most difficult of the remaining assignments. Easier tasks are your reward for finishing harder ones. Learn to say no to things that take you away from your priorities. Time management is not always easy. But if you make—and follow—a plan for school, you'll keep a major source of distress under control.

★ 11.B; 12.G

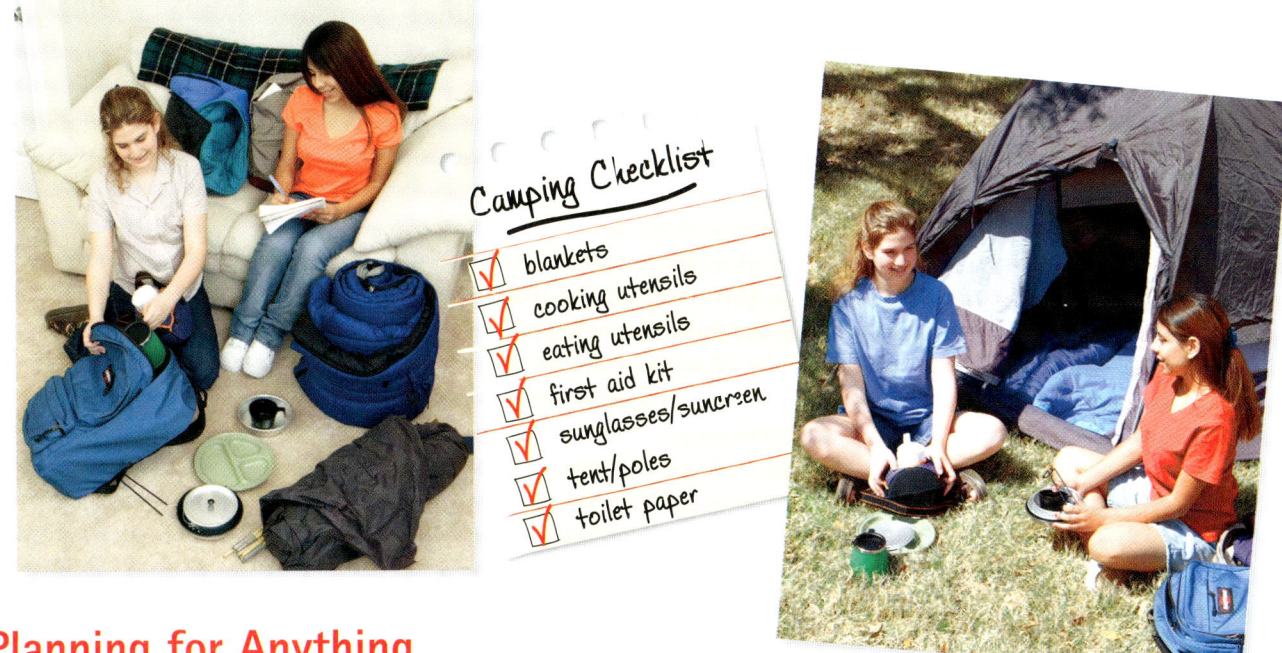

Planning for Anything

Of course, time management is just one type of plan. You can plan for any activity. And when you make a plan, it should include all the information and list all the supplies you need for a task. For example, when Joshua plans to practice his clarinet, he makes sure to bring his clarinet and his music home from school.

Planning is a way of looking ahead. When you plan, you can practice, study, or prepare for the task that faces you. Having a plan, whether for baking a cake or taking a vacation, lets you control events. You probably can't plan for everything, but a good plan will cover most problems. A plan doesn't have to be complicated. It just has to give you some control of the stressor. And by taking control, you can prevent a lot of distress.

Finally, if your plan doesn't seem to be working, ask someone for help. Find a person you trust. Ask that person to review your plan. Discuss ways to get your plan back on track. Then, follow your plan, and keep your distress under control. ★ 11.B; 12.G

Figure 15 Planning ahead is important. What would happen if you went camping and found out that you forgot the toilet paper?

Lesson Review

Using Vocabulary

1. What does it mean to plan your tasks? ★ 11.B; 12.G

Understanding Concepts

2. Explain why planning and prioritizing your activities are important ways to prevent distress? ★ 11.A; 11.B; 12.G

3. Describe five ways of preventing distress at school. ★ 10.B; 11.A; 11.B

Critical Thinking

4. **Making Inferences** Explain why preventing distress is important. ★ 1.A; 3.A; 11.A; 11.F

5. **Analyzing Ideas** Why is it important to learn something new each day and to believe that every problem has a solution? ★ 10.B; 11.B; 11.F

Lesson 5 Preventing Distress

3 CHAPTER REVIEW

Chapter Summary

- Stress is a natural part of your life. ■ Stress comes from a wide variety of sources. ■ Stress can be positive or negative. ■ Negative stress is called *distress*. ■ Something that causes a stress response is called a *stressor*. ■ When you are stressed, the hormone epinephrine is released into your bloodstream. ■ Your response to stress can be physical, mental, emotional, or social. ■ A defense mechanism, such as denial or rationalization, is a way to handle stress in the short term. ■ You can manage most of your stress. ■ Some stress can be avoided or prevented entirely. ■ An effective way to manage stress is to know what is distressful to you and to plan ahead.

Using Vocabulary

1 Use each of the following terms in a separate sentence: *positive stress*, *stress response*, *reframing*, and *prioritize*.

For each sentence, fill in the blank with the proper word from the word bank provided below.

stress	plan
stressor	defense mechanism
distress	stress management
positive stress	reframing
stress response	time management

2 Making appropriate choices about how to use your time is called ___.

3 ___ is changing the way you think about a stressor.

4 A ___ is a detailed program, created ahead of time, for doing something.

5 The combination of a new or possibly unpleasant situation and your body's natural response to it is called ___.

6 The way the body reacts to a stressor is called the ___.

7 When you learn to handle stress in healthy ways, you are doing ___.

8 A ___ is a short-term way to handle stress.

9 ___ is stress that helps you reach a goal and makes you feel good.

10 Anything that causes stress is called a ___.

Understanding Concepts

11 Describe two ways to prevent distress. ★ 10.B; 11.A; 11.B

12 Explain how major life changes may affect different people differently. ★ 1.A; 7.A; 10.E; 11.F

13 Is all stress bad? Explain your answer. ★ 1.A; 11.F

14 Describe how to use both reframing and planning to help manage your stress. ★ 10.B; 11.A; 11.B; 11.F

15 Is relieving stress important? Explain your answer. ★ 1.A; 11.F

16 Describe three social effects of stress. ★ 11.E; 11.F

17 Are defense mechanisms helpful or harmful? Explain your answer. ★ 1.A; 11.A; 11.E

18 Explain the difference between denial and rationalization.

Critical Thinking

Applying Concepts

19. Discuss how your responses to stress may affect relationships. ★ 7.A; 11.A; 11.E; 11.F

20. Imagine you have a coach who is very demanding. No matter how hard you try, the results never seem good enough for the coach. You don't want to quit. Devise a strategy to manage the stress caused by this situation. ★ 10.B; 11.A; 11.B; 11.D; 12.B

21. Dot is the captain of her chess team. Sometimes, against a tough opponent, Dot feels that she has extra energy. It seems to Dot that she can think faster than usual and that she can see several moves ahead of her opponent. Explain why Dot may be responding the way that she is. ★ 1.A; 11.F

22. Imagine that both you and your friend have been selected to take part in the school play. You are excited and motivated because you have a singing part and you love to sing. Your friend is nervous because he also has a singing part and he does not like to sing. How can you help your friend? ★ 4.C; 10.B; 11.F

Making Good Decisions

23. Marlon listed the stressors in his life. He realized that some of the stressors were things he could not control. Discuss some stress management tools that Marlon could use to handle the stressors he cannot control. ★ 3.A; 10.B; 11.A

24. Jaime is a good student. He wants to start a band and run track. Jaime's parents are worried that he won't have time to do his schoolwork and also to do these other activities. What can Jaime do to reassure his parents that his schoolwork won't suffer? ★ 7.A; 10.B; 11.B; 12.G

25. Mikela didn't do as well on a test as she thought she would. Mikela blamed the teacher for asking questions about material that Mikela hadn't studied. She also got angry with her little brother for interrupting her studying. Explain what Mikela is doing, and suggest three ways that will help her do better on her next test. ★ 10.B

26. Use what you have learned in this chapter to set a personal goal. Write your goal, and make an action plan by using the Health Behavior Contract for Stress Management. You can find the Health Behavior Contract at **go.hrw.com.** Just type in the keyword **HD4HBC10.**

Reading Checkup

Take a minute to review your answers to the Health IQ questions at the beginning of this chapter. How has reading this chapter improved your Health IQ?

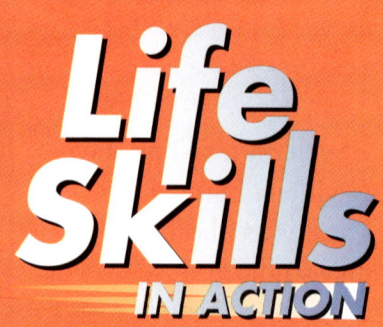

Life Skills IN ACTION

Assessing Your Health

Assessing your health means evaluating each of the four parts of your health and examining your behaviors. By assessing your health regularly, you will know what your strengths and weaknesses are and will be able to take steps to improve your health. Complete the following activity to improve your ability to assess your health.

Jared's Busy Week

Setting the Scene

Jared is very stressed out. He has a project due in his English class, and he has been putting it off for some time. He also has a big baseball game and an important math test on the same day next week. Just thinking about everything he has to do is causing him to have bad headaches and to be in a very bad mood. In fact, just last night he started yelling at his little sister for no reason.
★ 1.A; 11.E; 11.F

The 4 Steps of Assessing Your Health

1. Choose the part of your health you want to assess.
2. List your strengths and weaknesses.
3. Describe how your behaviors may contribute to your weaknesses.
4. Develop a plan to address your weaknesses.

Guided Practice

Practice with a Friend

Form a group of two. Have one person play the role of Jared, and have the second person be an observer. Walking through each of the four steps of assessing your health, role-play Jared's assessment of how his stress is affecting his health. The observer will take notes, which will include observations about what the person playing Jared did well and suggestions of ways to improve. Stop after each step to evaluate the process. ★ 1.A; 10.B; 11.E; 11.F

Independent Practice

Check Yourself

After you have completed the guided practice, go through Act 1 again without stopping at each step. Answer the questions below to review what you did.

1. Which parts of Jared's health are being affected by his stress? ⭐ 1.A; 11.F
2. How does Jared's behavior contribute to his stress? ⭐ 11.F
3. What are some things that Jared should do to reduce his stress? ⭐ 10.B; 11.B
4. Which of the four steps of assessing your health do you think is the most difficult? Explain your answer.

On Your Own

After assessing his health, Jared feels ready to solve his problems and reduce his stress. Jared notices that some of the other players on his baseball team aren't performing as well as they normally do. Jared wants to help these players assess their own health so that they can perform well again. Pretend that you are Jared, and create an educational pamphlet that lets others your age know how to assess their health.

CHAPTER 4
Managing Mental and Emotional Health

Lessons
1. Emotions — 76
2. Understanding Emotions — 78
3. Expressing Emotions — 82
4. Coping with Emotions — 86
5. Mental Illness — 90
6. Depression — 94
7. Getting Help — 96

Chapter Review — 100
Life Skills in Action — 102

Check out **Current Health** articles related to this chapter by visiting go.hrw.com. Just type in the keyword **HD4CH36**.

> "I was **nervous** about visiting my uncle when he got out of the **hospital**. He has **schizophrenia**. I was worried he would still hear voices and act strange. But now he is on new medication, and I could hardly tell that anything was wrong."

Health IQ

PRE-READING

Answer the following multiple-choice questions to find out what you already know about emotional health. When you've finished this chapter, you'll have the opportunity to change your answers based on what you've learned.

1. Which of the following statements about emotions is false?
   a. A person can't control emotions.
   b. Emotions are produced by the brain.
   c. Having a wide range of emotions is healthy.
   d. Most teens have healthy emotional lives.

2. Unpleasant emotions such as sadness
   a. are always unhealthy.
   b. are more common in teens than in adults.
   c. can be healthy because they help you learn.
   d. can never be controlled.

3. Which of the following affects teens' emotions?
   a. inherited personality traits
   b. hormones
   c. learning and life experiences
   d. all of the above

4. Mental illnesses
   a. are very rare.
   b. happen to bad people.
   c. cannot be treated.
   d. are illnesses of the brain that affect behavior.

5. Which of the following is an example of helpful nonverbal communication?
   a. screaming when you are frustrated
   b. using eye contact to show you are interested
   c. avoiding homework because you are stressed out
   d. telling your parents about how emotions are affecting you ★ 11.D

6. Which of the following is NOT an example of creative expression?
   a. making a painting
   b. participating in a play
   c. screaming
   d. writing music ★ 11.D

ANSWERS: 1. a; 2. c; 3. d; 4. d; 5. b; 6. c

Chapter 4 Managing Mental and Emotional Health | 75

Lesson 1 — Emotions

What You'll Do
- **Describe** how the brain controls emotions. ★ 1.A
- **Explain** how hormones and life changes influence emotions. ★ 1.A; 2.B

Terms to Learn
- mental health
- emotion
- emotional health
- hormone

Start Off Write

What causes emotions?

When Ricardo's mother told him that she was getting remarried, he felt strange. He was annoyed and frustrated. But he was also happy for his mother. He was confused by his feelings.

Reacting to new life experiences, such as a parent getting remarried, can be confusing. Dealing with confusing feelings in healthy ways is a large part of mental health. **Mental health** is the way people think about and respond to events in their daily lives. Emotions play a major role in a person's mental health.

An Emotional Brain

The brain produces emotions. An **emotion** is a feeling produced in response to a life event. Each emotion is related to a specific set of feelings and behaviors. For example, when something scares you, you respond with an emotion—fear. Your brain sends out messages that cause the feelings of fear. You might think about how to escape the situation. You may experience physical body changes, such as increased heart and breathing rate. You might sweat or even faint. The fear can also affect your behavior by causing you to scream or run away.

Many factors affect the emotions you feel in a situation. No two people react to situations in exactly the same way. Some people are naturally more shy or cautious in certain situations. But learning and experience can change how the brain responds to a situation. For example, a shy person can learn to be more outgoing. And experience could make a reckless person become more cautious.

Emotional health is the way a person experiences and deals with feelings. Experiencing a wide range of emotions is normal. Even unpleasant emotions can be healthy. Healthy emotions can help us appreciate relationships, success, and loss. ★ 1.A; 7.A

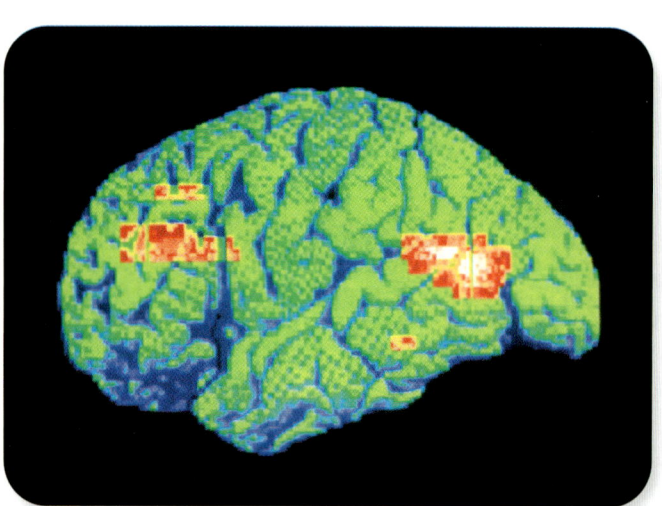

Figure 1 This scan shows activity in the brain during an emotional response.

Teens and Emotions

Both social and physical changes affect teens' emotions. Teen emotional changes are usually healthy and normal even though they can be confusing.

Changing life roles and responsibilities can affect teens' emotions. As you grow older, more will be expected from you. You could get a job to earn money. You might learn how to drive. You may be allowed to stay out late. These freedoms, responsibilities, and new experiences can lead to confusing emotions.

Hormone changes may also affect teens' emotions. **Hormones** are chemicals that help control how the body grows and functions. They are released into the blood by the brain and other organs called *glands*. Hormone changes that occur during teen development can affect emotions by causing differences in a teen's mood and energy.

Despite all these changes, teens can maintain good mental and emotional health. In fact, most teens are happy and well adjusted.
★ 1.A; 2.B

Myth & Fact

Myth: Most teens are emotionally out-of-control.

Fact: Despite the changes occurring in their lives, bodies, and brains, most teens are happy and well adjusted. ★ 1.A; 2.B

Figure 2 A person's face can show what emotion he or she is feeling.

Lesson Review

Using Vocabulary
1. Define *mental health* in your own words.
2. Define *emotion* in your own words.

Understanding Concepts
3. How does the brain influence emotions? ★ 1.A

4. How do hormones and life experiences influence emotions?
★ 1.A; 2.B; 7.A

Critical Thinking
5. **Making Inferences** You have learned that emotions are produced by the brain and that learning can change the brain's responses. How could you use this knowledge to help yourself control your emotions? ★ 4.C

internet connect
www.scilinks.org/health
Topic: Brain
HealthLinks code: HD4018
HEALTH LINKS Maintained by the National Science Teachers Association

Lesson 1 Emotions

Lesson 2 Understanding Emotions

Kate was annoyed that she could get sad so easily. Little things, such as messing up her lines in drama class, made her feel sad. Wouldn't it be better to always feel happy?

What You'll Do
- **Describe** how emotions can fit into a spectrum. ⭐ 1.A
- **Explain** how to recognize emotions. ⭐ 1.A; 11.D
- **Describe** how people have unique emotional triggers.
- **Explain** how emotions can be felt physically. ⭐ 1.A; 11.D

Terms to Learn
- emotional spectrum
- trigger

Start Off Write

How could you predict your emotional response to an event?

Feeling one emotion all the time—even happiness—would be unhealthy. Uncomfortable emotions, such as sadness, are important. They help us learn from and avoid bad experiences. Feeling a full range of emotions is a sign of emotional health.

An Emotional Spectrum

Emotions can be described as pleasant or unpleasant based on how they make you feel. An **emotional spectrum** is a set of emotions arranged by how pleasant they are. Some emotions on the spectrum are opposites, such as happiness and sadness, or love and hate. Figure 3 shows examples of opposite emotions.

Both pleasant and unpleasant emotions play an important role in learning. Situations that produce pleasant emotions make your body feel relaxed or comfortable. Situations that produce unpleasant emotions can make you feel uncomfortable. These feelings can lead you to change your behavior by seeking out some situations and avoiding other situations. ⭐ 1.A

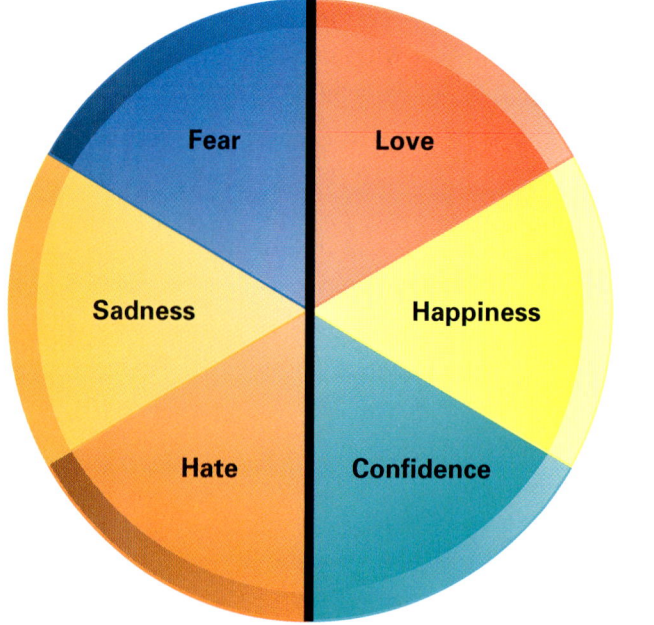

Figure 3 This emotional spectrum shows opposite emotions across from each other in the circle.

Unpleasant feelings — Pleasant feelings

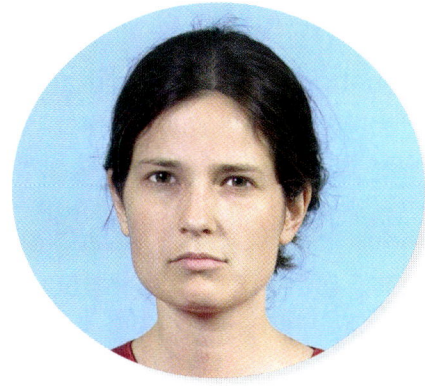
Irritation

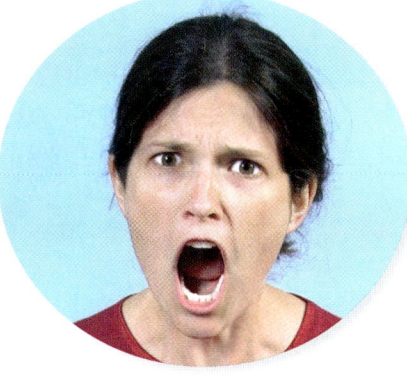
Fury

Figure 4 Each emotion can be felt at different levels of intensity.

Recognizing Emotions

Recognizing your emotions is not always easy. Sometimes, you may feel many different emotions at once. Sometimes, an emotion is hard to recognize because it is especially strong. But if you identify your emotions, you may be able to cope with problems better.

Feeling both pleasant and unpleasant emotions at once is confusing. Imagine that you are given a puppy for your birthday. But the first thing the puppy does is chew up your favorite pair of shoes. You could respond to this situation with both pleasant and unpleasant emotions. You might be happy about getting such a fun gift. You may feel love for the puppy. But you might also be angry at the puppy for ruining your shoes. Once you recognize each emotion, you can begin to cope with your anger.

Another problem with recognizing emotions is that emotions can be felt in different strengths. For example, when you feel fear, you can be a little nervous or completely terrified. You may not be able to recognize some emotions when you experience them at a different strength. You may know how to deal with feeling nervous, but you may be confused by strong anxiety. Recognizing that you feel a different strength of a familiar emotion can help you cope with the strong emotion. ★ 1.A; 11.D

LIFE SKILLS ACTIVITY

ASSESSING YOUR HEALTH

Brainstorm a list of events or situations that can produce the following emotions: love, anger, fear, happiness, and sadness. After you have made a list for each emotion, compare your list with the lists of a few classmates. Do any of the events or situations cause different emotions in different people? Do any students share emotional reactions to specific events or situations?

Know Your Triggers

If identifying emotions can be complicated, how can people understand their emotions? One way to understand your emotions is to learn what situations are likely to cause specific emotions. Situations, people, and events that cause a person to feel an emotion are called **triggers.** Each person has different emotional triggers. A trigger that angers one person may not affect another person. The same trigger could cause another person to feel sad. Knowing how certain triggers affect you is part of understanding emotions.

If you know what triggers cause specific emotions, you can often predict how a situation will affect you. Understanding your triggers can help you avoid situations that cause unpleasant emotions. It may also help you seek out situations that cause pleasant emotions.

Figure 5 If you recognize the trigger when you feel sad, you will be better able to deal with the unpleasant feelings.

Sometimes you cannot avoid triggers even when you know they will cause unpleasant emotions. In these cases, predicting your emotional response gives you a chance to prepare yourself. For example, giving a speech triggers nervousness for many people. If a person is aware of this trigger, he or she can practice giving speeches. Practicing might help the person be more comfortable. That way, the person can be less nervous in front of a real audience. You can find creative ways to deal with unpleasant emotions if you recognize your triggers ahead of time. ★ 1.A; 11.D

Hands-on ACTIVITY

TRACKING EMOTIONAL STATES

1. For 1 day, rate your emotional feelings each hour. Rate your feelings from a 1 for most unpleasant to a 10 for most pleasant. Record any triggers that you recognize.

2. For the rest of the week, rate your emotional feelings each day. Record any triggers.

Analysis

1. Compare how your emotions change through the day and through the week.

2. Did any triggers come up more than once? Do you notice any trends in what affects your emotions?

TABLE 1 Physical Responses Caused by Emotions

Emotion	Physical Response
Fear	increased heart and breathing rates, sweating, trembling, dry mouth, hot flashes or chills, dilated pupils
Anger	increased heart rate and blood pressure, pacing or agitation, red face, hot flashes, trembling or muscle tension
Sadness	poor energy or fatigue, difficulty concentrating, crying
Happiness	laughter, more energy, lower blood pressure and heart rate
Love	symptoms of fear and happiness, "butterflies" in the stomach, preoccupation with loved one

Physical Feelings

A person has emotions because of activity in the brain. This brain activity causes physical changes in the body. Emotions can change blood pressure or heart rate. Emotions can also cause muscles to tense or faces to turn red. Long-term, unpleasant emotions can even affect the immune system and make it easier to get sick.

In general, pleasant emotions, such as happiness, are associated with more comfortable physical changes. Comfortable changes can include lower blood pressure, lower heart rate, and being more energetic. Sadness and worry can be associated with fatigue and increases in heart rate, blood pressure, and muscle tension. Anger can cause hot flashes and shaking. Recognizing the physical changes caused by specific emotions can help you identify your emotions. ★ 1.A; 11.D

Lesson Review

Using Vocabulary

1. What is an *emotional spectrum*?

Understanding Concepts

2. Why might it be hard to recognize emotions? ★ 1.A; 11.D

3. Does everyone respond to emotional triggers in the same way?

4. How are emotions experienced physically? ★ 1.A

Critical Thinking

5. **Analyzing Ideas** Imagine that every Thursday, you come home from school feeling angry. You realize that your after-school band rehearsal makes you angry each week. How can you use this realization to help you deal with your anger? ★ 1.A; 11.D

Lesson 3 Expressing Emotions

What You'll Do

- **Explain** how to compare healthy and unhealthy emotions. ★ 11.D
- **Describe** communication skills that help express emotions. ★ 10.C; 11.D
- **Describe** inappropriate ways to express emotions. ★ 11.D

Terms to Learn

- body language
- active listening

Start Off Write

How can you express emotions without using any words?

Keanne felt terrible about failing her Spanish test until she talked to Janelle. Janelle listened and told Keanne she could do better next time. Keanne felt much better after talking to Janelle.

Many people feel better after expressing their emotions. Talking with a friend is just one way to express emotions. You can also communicate emotions with body language or creative projects.

Healthy Emotional Expression

All emotions—even unpleasant ones—can be a healthy part of life. Unpleasant emotions can affect our lives in good ways. For example, feeling nervous about an exam can motivate you to study harder. Feeling angry about pollution can lead you to start a recycling program for your community.

In the examples above, unpleasant emotions encouraged healthy actions. Expressing unpleasant emotions in healthy ways can help you feel better. Unpleasant emotions only become unhealthy if they are expressed in ways that are harmful to people or property. Unhealthy emotions can prevent people from solving problems. Harmful emotions can cause problems at school, at work, or in relationships. Learning to express all emotions in positive ways improves emotional health. ★ 1.A; 11.D

Figure 6 Feelings of jealousy can be used as motivation to work harder.

82 Chapter 4 Managing Mental and Emotional Health

Communication

Expressing emotions in healthy ways allows you to communicate them to other people. Communicating with other people can help you figure out why you have certain emotions. Talking about emotions can also help you feel as though you are not alone. Also, communicating with other people helps them get to know you and understand your needs.

If unpleasant emotions result from a conflict with another person, communicating with that person might resolve the conflict. That person may have misunderstood your feelings or been unaware of them. In these cases, talking can make your feelings clear. ★ 11.D

Figure 7 Communicating with other people can help you understand your emotions.

Communication Skills

There are healthy and unhealthy ways to communicate your emotions. Young children often kick and scream when they are upset. As you get older, kicking and screaming will not get you very far. Good communication skills can help you communicate emotions in healthy ways.

The first step to effective communication is to know what you want to say. If you have thought about your feelings, you can put your thoughts into words. If you do not recognize your emotions, you can talk about your confusion. Speaking calmly and clearly will allow the other person to understand you.

Emotions can also be expressed without words. **Body language** is expressing emotions with the face, hands, and posture. Being aware of your body language can help you avoid sending the wrong signals. For example, if you cross your arms and hunch your shoulders, you will look annoyed. Body language can also help you understand how others feel. If a person frowns as you speak, that person is not happy about what you are saying.

Listening to other people is a major part of communication. A good listener helps other people communicate by encouraging them to express emotions. **Active listening** is not only hearing but also showing that you understand what a person is saying. For example, eye contact lets a person know that you are paying attention. Also, asking questions can help you understand ideas that are not clear. ★ 10.C; 11.D

Did you know that some scientists study emotions in animals? Monkeys and apes use body language and facial expressions that look similar to human emotional expressions. People are studying these animals to find out more about their feelings.

Figure 8 Creating art can be a good way to express emotions and reduce emotional stress.

Creative Expression

Expressing emotions is one way of letting go of unpleasant emotions. Most people notice that they feel better after crying. And talking to someone is often a good way to let go of unpleasant feelings. But sometimes crying is not enough to get rid of uncomfortable feelings. And sometimes your feelings may be private or difficult to discuss with other people.

There are several ways to let go of uncomfortable feelings by expressing them privately. For some people, exercise is a good way to release emotions. For other people, expressing emotions in a creative way allows them to let go of discomfort. Creative ways to express emotions include drawing, painting, making sculptures, writing or playing music, dancing, acting, making films, and writing. Expressing your emotions in one of these forms can make you feel better. Using these activities to let go of emotions can be as effective as talking to another person.

Some people find it difficult to express their feelings by creating something. But even seeing how other people have expressed similar feelings creatively can be helpful. Listening to music, watching a play or movie, or reading a book can help you understand emotions in new ways. You might relate to how another person communicated an emotion through creative expression. ★ 11.D

Health Journal

Have you ever tried to express something through art? Think of something that makes you happy. In your Health Journal, draw a picture of the situation, person, or thing that makes you happy. When you are finished drawing, ask yourself if you enjoyed this activity. Do you prefer a different way to express emotions?

Unhealthy Emotional Expression

Sometimes people express emotional problems in unhealthy ways. Expressing emotions in ways that could hurt people—physically or emotionally—is unhealthy. Destroying property is another unhealthy way to express emotions. These behaviors are dangerous, and they do not help solve problems.

Most people express emotions in unhealthy ways at some point in their lives. Some common examples include raising one's voice in anger or making fun of another person. These behaviors are destructive because they encourage conflict and prevent problems from being solved. They can also hurt other people emotionally. By recognizing these behaviors, you can apologize to the person you may have hurt and avoid hurtful behaviors in the future.

Other forms of unhealthy expression are more severe. Emotional problems may lead some people to become violent. Some examples of these behaviors include setting fires or breaking windows. People who have emotional problems may also start fights, bully others, or hurt animals. Some of these people may even hurt themselves. None of these behaviors help solve a person's emotional problems. These actions only make a person's problems more difficult as he or she deals with the consequences. Frequent use of such dangerous emotional expression is a serious problem. These behaviors mean that a person needs help immediately. ★ 11.D

Figure 9 Vandalism, or destroying property, is one kind of unhealthy emotional expression.

Lesson Review

Using Vocabulary
1. What is *active listening*? ★ 10.C
2. What is *body language*? ★ 11.D

Understanding Concepts
3. How can a person distinguish between healthy and unhealthy emotions? ★ 11.D
4. List three skills that help people communicate emotions. ★ 10.C; 11.D
5. Why is it unhealthy to express emotions by damaging property? ★ 11.D

Critical Thinking
6. **Applying Concepts** How could a person who was very sad about the death of a grandparent use emotional expression to feel better? Mention at least three different kinds of expression that could help. ★ 11.D

Lesson 3 Expressing Emotions | 85

Lesson 4: Coping with Emotions

What You'll Do

- **Explain** why self-esteem is important. ★ 1.A; 11.F
- **Describe** the value of thinking through your emotions. ★ 11.D
- **Describe** how defense mechanisms and good physical and social health help us cope. ★ 1.A; 10.B; 11.B

Terms to Learn

- self-esteem
- positive self-talk
- defense mechanism

Start Off Write

How can laughter make people feel better in tense situations?

Raquel was very confused. She was furious at her mom in the morning, but after ski practice Raquel could hardly remember why she was angry at her mom. Could exercise have affected Raquel's emotions?

Exercise is one of many ways to cope with your emotions. Coping with your emotions means dealing with them in ways that show respect for others and make you feel better.

Self-Esteem

Experiencing unpleasant emotions is normal. But having these emotions does not feel good. An effective way to cope with these emotions is to improve your overall emotional health. Having good emotional health makes solving problems easier.

One thing that affects your emotional health is self-esteem. **Self-esteem** is a measure of how much you value, respect, and feel confident about yourself. Being confident and happy with one's self is a sign of high self-esteem. People who have high self-esteem have a positive view of life. People who have low self-esteem feel helpless and full of self-doubt. They also lack confidence and are easily overwhelmed by problems.

Self-esteem can influence how seriously a person is affected by unpleasant emotions. People who have high self-esteem see unpleasant emotions as temporary problems in a good life. For this reason, people who have high self-esteem are less likely to be seriously affected by unpleasant emotions.

People can improve low self-esteem by finding activities in which they can be successful. Succeeding allows people to feel good about themselves. Activities such as exercise, hobbies, volunteer work, or school groups can encourage success. ★ 11.B; 11.D

Figure 10 Volunteering to help young children can improve your self-esteem.

Figure 11 Spending time alone to think about your emotions can help you cope.

Time to Think

When you experience unpleasant emotions, simply thinking about the problem can be a good way to deal with it. Taking time out from the situation can help you look closely at your problems. Often, you will find that unpleasant emotions are based on negative thinking. *Negative thinking* is focusing on the bad side of a situation.

Thinking positively in a bad situation can help you cope with the unpleasant emotions it triggers. **Positive self-talk** is thinking about the good parts of a bad situation. Thinking this way takes practice. Positive thoughts about a bad situation might include the following: "This won't last forever," "I will have other chances," and "It doesn't always happen like this." Being able to focus on the good parts of a bad situation will help you cope until things improve. ★ 10.B; 11.B

Talking with Someone

Another way to cope with emotional problems is to talk with someone. Sometimes simply talking about emotional problems can make you feel better. And if the other person has experienced similar emotions, he or she may have helpful advice. That person might even be able to warn you against actions that could make things worse. Even if that person has never been in a similar situation, he or she may be able to help you see the problem differently. Often, another person can help by simply telling you that a problem will not last forever. ★ 10.B; 11.B; 11.D

Emotional Problems

If a person who has emotional problems does not talk about his or her feelings with someone, the problems could damage the person's emotional, mental, and physical health.

Lesson 4 Coping with Emotions

ASSESSING YOUR HEALTH

Make lists of how you might react to the following emotions: sadness, happiness, and anger. Then, in a group, decide if any of these actions are defense mechanisms.

Defense Mechanisms

The body reacts to unpleasant situations with a natural response called *stress*. Stress can be physically and mentally uncomfortable, and people have different ways of coping with it. Often people are not aware of how they cope. Automatic behaviors used to reduce uncomfortable stress are called **defense mechanisms**.

Defense mechanisms can be mature or immature. Mature defense mechanisms help people relieve stress honestly and directly. Using humor to reduce uncomfortable stress is a mature defense mechanism. Another mature defense mechanism is self-observation. This strategy involves thinking about why you are stressed and then communicating your emotions.

Defense mechanisms are immature if they help you postpone or ignore dealing with stress. *Projection* is an immature defense mechanism in which people blame others for a mistake. *Denial* is an immature defense mechanism in which a person ignores problems. Being aware of these ways of coping can help you avoid immature responses and seek out mature ones. ★ 10.B; 11.F

TABLE 2 Defense Mechanisms

Defense mechanism	Description	Example
Denial (immature)	Stress is dealt with by not thinking about stressful problems, thoughts, or feelings.	Sheila should be worried about her grades in math, but she is not studying for her next math test.
Projection (immature)	Uncomfortable thoughts or feelings are dealt with by transferring them to others.	Frederick has a crush on Rita, but he denies this and insists that she has a crush on him.
Devaluation (immature)	Stress is dealt with by assigning negative qualities to oneself or others.	Jeff is upset that he didn't make the team. Instead of admitting he is disappointed he complains about how many games the team lost last year.
Sublimation (mature)	Uncomfortable or dangerous feelings or impulses are channeled into more acceptable behaviors.	Rudy is angry with his younger sister, so he works off his frustration in the gym.
Humor (mature)	Stressful events or feelings are dealt with by focusing on amusing aspects of the situation.	Tracy dents her parents' car while driving in a snowstorm. She jokes, "At least it's not raining."
Self-observation (mature)	Emotional stress is dealt with by reflecting on thoughts, feelings, and behaviors and by expressing these emotions in a healthy way.	Selma is mad and hurt because her friend Judy did not invite her to a party. Selma talks to Judy about her feelings and asks for an explanation.

Influences You Can Control

Even though unpleasant emotions can be healthy when you learn from them, the stress they cause can be uncomfortable. One way to reduce the stress of these emotions is to maintain good physical, social, mental, and emotional health. When your overall health is stable, your mental and physical responses to stress are less severe. Also, developing habits that improve overall health can encourage pleasant emotions.

Exercising, getting enough sleep, and having a healthy diet can increase your energy and self-esteem. Forming supportive relationships with family and friends can ensure that you have someone to talk to about problems. Finding activities that you enjoy can help you to feel good about yourself and feel happy. Hobbies, such as art or music, can provide an outlet for expressing emotions creatively. If you encourage positive emotions and reduce your level of stress, you can have great emotional health. ★ 1.A; 7.A; 11.B

Figure 12 Exercise doesn't have to be an organized sport—even raking leaves is good exercise.

Lesson Review

Using Vocabulary

1. How is negative thinking related to positive self-talk? ★ 10.B; 11.B
2. Use the term *defense mechanism* in a sentence.

Understanding Concepts

3. Why is self-esteem important? ★ 1.A; 11.F
4. How can defense mechanisms help us cope with emotions? ★ 10.B; 11.B
5. What are the benefits of spending time alone and talking to other people when you are dealing with emotional problems? ★ 10.B; 11.B

Critical Thinking

6. **Analyzing Ideas** How can strong friendships, good family relationships, and healthy habits help a person handle stressful events? ★ 1.A; 11.B; 11.F

Lesson 5 — Mental Illness

What You'll Do
- **List** two factors that can lead to a mental illness. ★ 1.A
- **Describe** the differences between anxiety disorders, mood disorders, and schizophrenia. ★ 1.C
- **Explain** how some mental illnesses share symptoms. ★ 1.A

Terms to Learn
- mental illness
- anxiety disorder
- mood disorder
- paranoia

Start Off Write
What do you think causes mental illness?

Bonnie could not talk to her friends about what was happening to her father. He was acting really strange, and her whole family was scared. He kept hearing voices and slipping into long frozen silences.

Health problems that affect a person's behavior, thoughts, and emotions can be scary. But these problems are illnesses that can often be successfully treated, just like other health problems. Understanding these illnesses can make them less mysterious.

Understanding Mental Illness

The brain controls thoughts, feelings, memories, and actions. When the brain is working properly, it responds to life events with normal emotions. But the brain's responses can be changed by illnesses that affect the balance of chemicals in the brain. A **mental illness** is a disorder that affects a person's thoughts, emotions, and behaviors. One out of every six people has a mental illness.

The cause of mental illness is not completely understood. Many of these illnesses are more common in some families than in others. So, inherited traits may influence mental illness. Sometimes stressful events can trigger a mental illness, so the environment may also influence mental illness.

Mental illnesses can be grouped by the kinds of emotional and behavioral changes they cause. Anxiety disorders, mood disorders, and schizophrenia are mental illnesses. Treating these illnesses involves counseling as well as medicines that balance brain chemistry. When people who have a mental illness find and continue proper treatment, they can often live normal lives. ★ 1.A; 1.C

Figure 13 People who have a mental illness can often live normal lives with proper treatment.

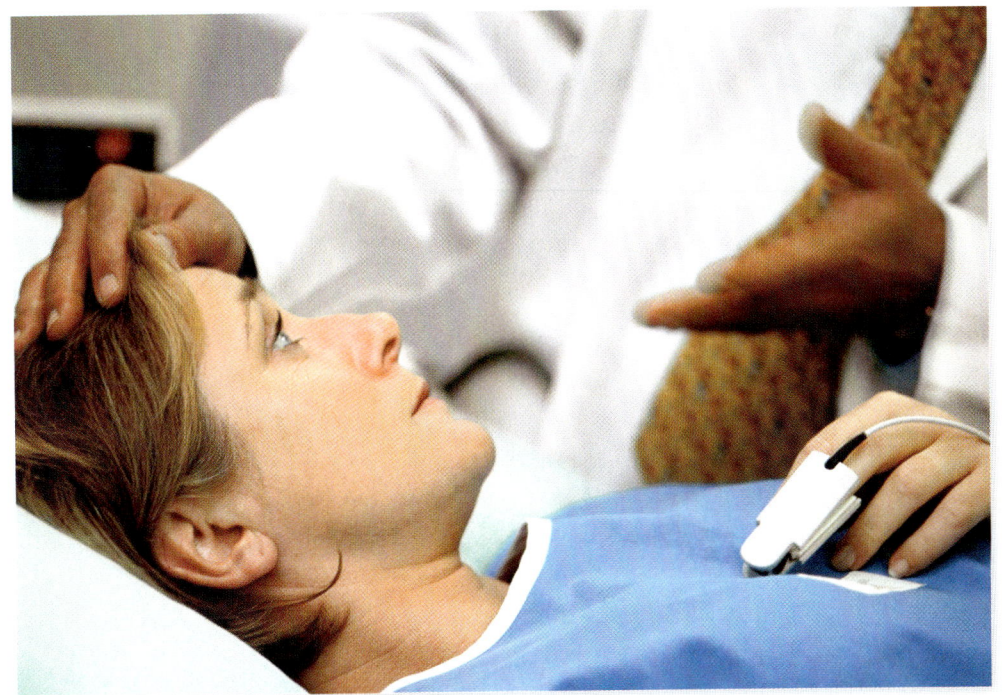

Figure 14 People who have panic attacks may feel as though they are having a heart attack.

Anxiety Disorders

Anxiety (ang ZIE uh tee) is a feeling of extreme nervousness and worry. All people have anxiety from time to time, but some people suffer from severe anxiety. An **anxiety disorder** is an illness that causes unusually strong nervousness, worry, or panic. Anxiety disorders vary in how long the nervous feelings last and in what causes those feelings to occur. Anxiety can be constant over a long time, or it may occur in short bursts.

Panic disorder is an anxiety disorder that causes a person to have brief periods of extreme anxiety called *panic attacks*. During panic attacks, people become extremely scared and may think they are having a heart attack. They may experience a fast heart rate, difficulty breathing, shaking, and lightheadedness.

Panic attacks that are triggered by specific things are called *phobias*. Common phobias include fear of animals, such as spiders, or situations, such as flying. Social phobia is a disorder that causes people to fear social situations, such as giving a speech or meeting new people.

Sometimes anxiety is triggered by repetitive thoughts called *obsessions*. Some people develop rituals, or *compulsions*, such as excessive counting or washing, to try to overcome this anxiety. This combination of anxiety and ritual activity is an anxiety disorder called *obsessive-compulsive disorder* (OCD). Medicines and counseling can usually treat people with OCD successfully.

★ 1.A; 1.C

SCIENCE ACTIVITY

Many scientists believe that using illegal drugs, such as hallucinogens, can trigger mental illness in some people. When the chemicals in these drugs reach the brain, they may cause the brain chemistry to become unbalanced. This unbalanced chemistry may lead to mental illness. Work in groups to create posters telling students that maintaining your mental health is another great reason to refuse drugs.

Bipolar Mood Disorder

A **mood disorder** is an illness in which people have uncontrollable mood changes. *Bipolar mood disorder* (BMD) is one kind of mood disorder. BMD causes a person to experience two extreme moods: depression and mania (MAY nee uh). For this reason, BMD is sometimes called *manic depression*.

Different behaviors and emotions occur during each extreme of BMD. *Depression* is a disorder that causes a mood of extreme sadness or hopelessness. Depressed people may sleep and eat more or less than they normally do. Mania is a mood that causes excessive energy and irritation. Manic people are very active and need little sleep. Their thoughts may race and become disorganized. They may talk fast and may be difficult to interrupt. The two extremes of BMD are usually separated by periods of normal moods. However, periods of depression or mania can last from weeks to months.

People who have BMD may also experience and believe things that are not real. A *hallucination* is sensing something that is not real. For example, a person may hear voices when no one is talking. A *delusion* is a false belief. Manic people may have delusions that they are famous. Or, they may think that they have a special relationship with a famous person they have never met.

Some symptoms of BMD occur in several mental illnesses. This can make BMD hard to recognize and treat. However, once people who have BMD find and continue proper treatment, they can often lead ordinary lives. ★ 1.A; 1.C

Brain Food

People who have a mental illness can lead normal or even extremely successful lives. Many famous people in history had mental illnesses that they learned to control. People who had bipolar mood disorder include composer Ludwig von Beethoven and British Prime Minister Winston Churchill.

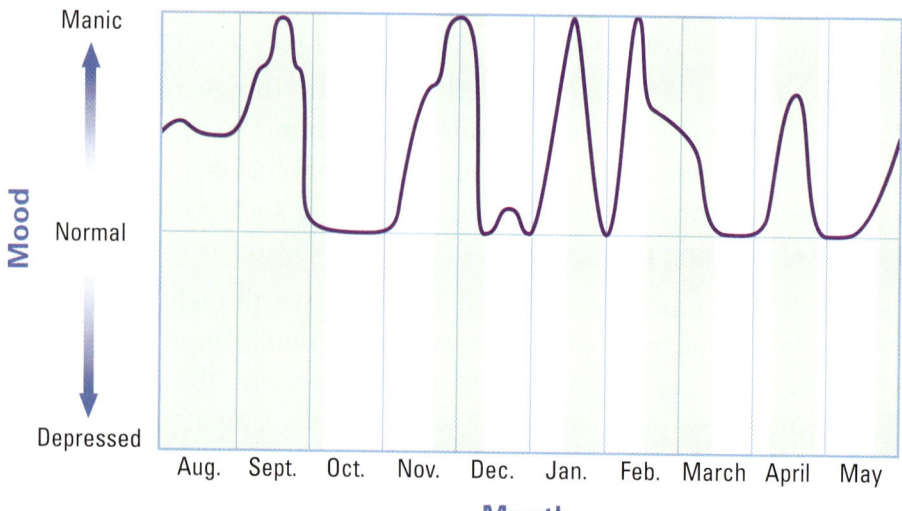

Figure 15 Green shading represents time during which a manic patient took medicine. Medicine can be used with therapy to help control mental illness.

Figure 16 Families often need help understanding and coping with a loved one's mental illness.

Schizophrenia

Schizophrenia (SKIT se FREE nee uh) is a disorder in which a person breaks from reality in several ways. People who have schizophrenia do not always have the same symptoms. Most people who have this disorder express little emotion. They usually have hallucinations and delusions, and often they feel paranoia (PAR uh NOY uh). **Paranoia** is the belief that other people want to harm someone. Many people who have schizophrenia suffer from unorganized thinking, which can lead to nonsense speech. Some people who have this disorder go through periods of time during which their bodies are frozen in one position.

Schizophrenia, like other mental illnesses, affects a person's thoughts and actions. People who have mental illness usually require life-long treatment to regain control of their lives. However, once treatment is established for people who have schizophrenia or another mental illness, they can often lead happy lives. ★ 1.A; 1.C

STUDY TIP *for better reading*

Word Origins
Consider the disease bipolar mood disorder. You know that this illness involves mood swings from depression to mania. What do you think the word *bipolar* means?

Lesson Review

Using Vocabulary

1. What is a *mental illness*? ★ 1.A; 1.C
2. What is the difference between a *mood disorder* and an *anxiety disorder*? ★ 1.A; 1.C

Understanding Concepts

3. What are two factors that play a role in causing mental illness? ★ 1.C
4. Is it possible to treat a mental illness? Explain. ★ 1.C

Critical Thinking

5. **Making Inferences** Suppose you know a person who is having hallucinations and delusions. Why might it be difficult to know exactly which mental illness this person suffers from? ★ 1.A; 1.C

internet connect
www.scilinks.org/health
Topic: Anxiety Disorders
HealthLinks code: HD4010
Topic: Bipolar Disorder
HealthLinks code: HD4014

HEALTH LINKS Maintained by the National Science Teachers Association

Lesson 6 Depression

What You'll Do

- **Describe** how depression is different from feeling sad. ⭐ 1.C
- **List** eight warning signs that someone is severely depressed. ⭐ 1.C
- **Explain** where to seek help when a person is in danger of suicide. ⭐ 1.C

Terms to Learn

- depression
- suicidal thinking

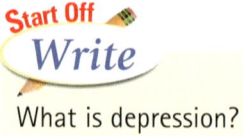

Start Off Write

What is depression?

Tim was worried about his friend Lou. Lou was not eating, he slept all the time, and he never wanted to do anything. Tim thought Lou might be depressed.

Depression is not just feeling sad. Depression is a mental illness, and it can be extremely dangerous. Knowing how to recognize depression in yourself and other people can save lives.

More Than Feeling Blue

Depression is a mood disorder in which a person feels extremely sad and hopeless for at least two weeks. Depression is different from healthy sadness. It is a mental illness, technically known as *major depressive disorder* (MDD). People who have depression may have some mixture of the following list of symptoms: extreme sadness for no reason, inability to cheer up with good news, changes in sleeping and eating patterns, tiredness or lack of energy, slowed or increased movements, difficulty concentrating or making decisions, feelings of guilt or hopelessness, and thoughts about death or suicide.

Depression can take over a person's life. It can prevent a person from caring about responsibilities and loved ones. Some people who have depression may hallucinate or have delusions. Depressed people may become detached from life by not paying attention to people or events. Without treatment, depression can continue for years. ⭐ 1.C

Figure 17 Treatment for Depression

Have depression

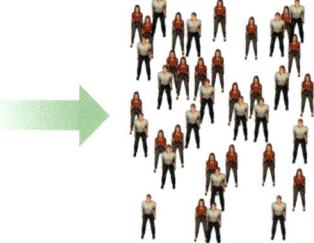

Diagnosed with depression

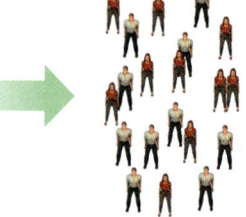

Receive proper treatment

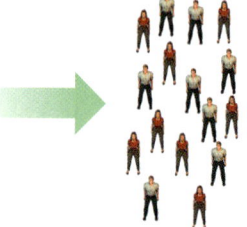

Respond successfully

Of all people in the United States who have depression, 40 percent are identified and diagnosed. Half of these people receive proper treatment. Eighty percent of those treated properly respond successfully.

Chapter 4 Managing Mental and Emotional Health

Depression Is Dangerous

The most dangerous symptom of depression is suicidal thinking. **Suicidal thinking** is the desire to take one's own life. People who have depression can be in so much emotional pain that they would rather be dead than continue to suffer. Fifteen percent of depressed people successfully commit suicide. Suicide is one of the leading causes of death among teens.

Fortunately, most patients who have depression can be treated successfully. Treatments can completely resolve symptoms in 80 percent of cases. Many suicidal patients change their minds about wanting to die once they are treated. For this reason, people should learn to recognize depression and seek treatment for it. If you or other people you know show signs of depression or suicidal thinking, you should tell an adult immediately. Suicidal thinking is an emergency condition. Someone who is thinking about suicide should be taken to a hospital emergency room.

★ 1.A; 1.C

Health Journal

Sadness is an unpleasant emotion. Unlike depression, you may be able to control sadness on your own. Think about a time that you were sad about something. In your Health Journal, make a list of things you did to try to make yourself feel better. What actions helped you the most?

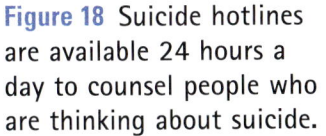

Figure 18 Suicide hotlines are available 24 hours a day to counsel people who are thinking about suicide.

Lesson Review

Using Vocabulary
1. What is *depression*? ★ 1.C

Understanding Concepts
2. How is depression different from feeling sad? ★ 1.C
3. What are eight warning signs that someone is severely depressed? ★ 1.C
4. Where can you seek help if you or someone else is in danger of suicide? ★ 1.C

Critical Thinking
5. **Making Good Decisions** If you know someone who is depressed but refuses to get help, what should you do? ★ 1.C; 4.C

internet connect
www.scilinks.org/health
Topic: Depression
HealthLinks code: HD4026

HEALTH LINKS — Maintained by the National Science Teachers Association

Lesson 6 Depression | 95

Lesson 7

Getting Help

What You'll Do

- **Explain** why one should get help for emotional problems and disorders immediately. ★ 1.A; 1.C
- **Describe** three sources of help for people with emotional problems or disorders. ★ 1.C; 3.A; 4.A
- **List** four types of mental health professionals. ★ 3.A; 4.A

Terms to Learn

- teen hotline
- counselor
- psychologist
- psychiatrist

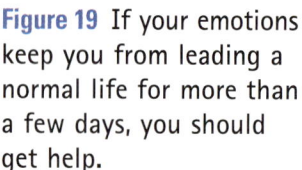

Where could you find help for an emotional problem?

Henrik was scared that something was wrong with him. He was always tired, and he couldn't get interested in anything at school. He felt really down, but should he ask for help?

It is a good idea to find help for emotional concerns even if your problems seem small. Other people can help you figure out how to cope with emotions and solve problems safely.

How Serious Is It?

Unpleasant emotions are uncomfortable, but they are not always dangerous or unhealthy. So how can you know when your feelings become unhealthy? The easiest way may be to talk to someone you trust about what you are feeling. Also, you can pay attention to your emotions over time to see if you notice sudden or major changes in how you feel.

You can ask other people for help whenever you need to. Talking to someone you trust might help you solve problems. An outside view can let you know if your problem is out of the ordinary. You should not feel ashamed or embarrassed about asking for help.

Noticing how long your unpleasant emotions last and how often they occur can help you know when they are unhealthy. Emotional triggers and the intensity of an emotion provide other clues about whether you need help. For example, extreme sadness that occurs for no reason and does not go away probably means you need help. Also, noticing how much your emotions affect your life can alert you to problems. You might need help if emotions interfere with your relationships or responsibilities at school or at home. Emotions that cause you to want to hurt yourself or others require immediate professional help. ★ 1.A; 1.C

Figure 19 If your emotions keep you from leading a normal life for more than a few days, you should get help.

Figure 20 Getting Help for Others

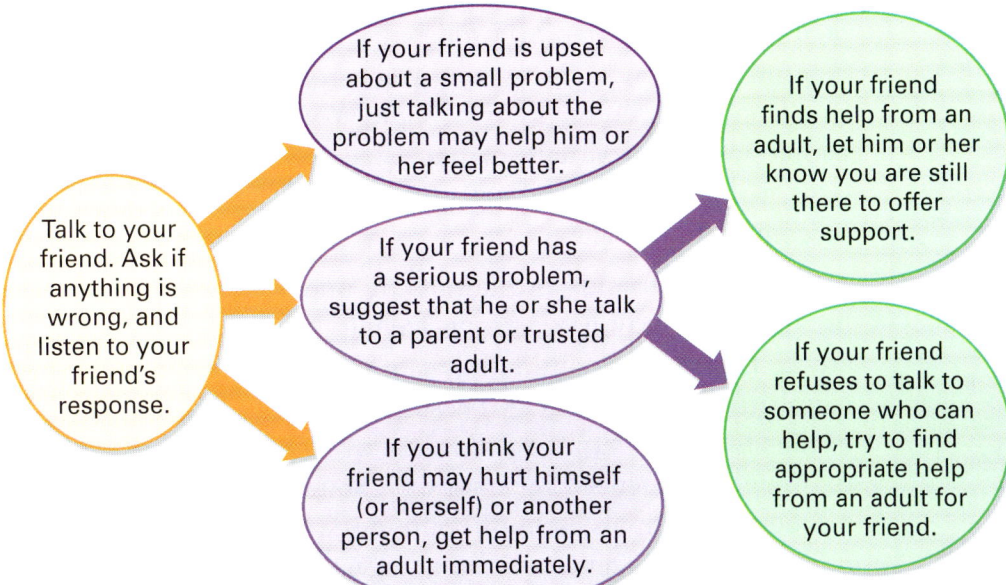

Finding Help for Other People

There are many reasons why people do not seek help for emotional problems. Sometimes they are embarrassed or ashamed. Some people think that they can handle problems alone or that problems will go away. People may be unaware that they have emotional problems or a mental illness—even when it is obvious to everyone around them. But letting a serious emotional problem or mental illness go untreated is very dangerous. People who have these problems can suffer greatly and may even hurt themselves or others. If someone you know has an emotional problem and will not ask for help, you should find help for them.
★ 1.C; 3.A; 4.A

Preventing Further Problems

If you think a friend has an emotional problem, you can let that person know that you are concerned. Your friend may want to talk to you about a problem. Some emotional problems might be solved by having a conversation.

If someone has a problem that is out of the ordinary, you could ask if he or she has spoken to an adult about the problem. You should be especially concerned if a person is depressed, has hallucinations or delusions, or is behaving dangerously. If the person will not ask for help, you can let an adult know what is going on. An adult can help the person get proper treatment. Treating mental illnesses or serious emotional problems early can prevent suicide and other violence. ★ 1.C; 3.A; 4.A; 4.C

LIFE SKILLS ACTIVITY

MAKING GOOD DECISIONS

As a class, generate a list of ideas about what you can do to help a friend who is depressed. Break up into small groups. Each group should develop a skit that acts out one of the solutions. Be sure to mention how the depressed friend responds to your actions.

Lesson 7 Getting Help | 97

Help for Emotional Problems

When people have emotional problems, they often ask other people for help. Friends, family, and trusted adults can be very helpful. People who know you well can help you see your problem from a different point of view. You may learn that other people in similar situations have had the same feelings as you have. Knowing that you are not alone in the way you feel can be comforting.

Sometimes, friends and family are unable to give calm advice because they may have strong feelings about your situation. If advice from friends and family is not enough, other community members can provide help. These people are not directly involved in the emotional situation. Because of this, they can give advice that is not influenced by emotions. Sources of help can include teachers, principals, school counselors, social workers, school nurses, clergy, peer counseling groups, and teen hotlines. A **teen hotline** is a phone number that teens can call to talk privately and anonymously about their problems.

Dealing with emotional problems can be difficult. Most people have a doctor who treats them for physical health problems. It is just as important to have people treat you for emotional health problems. ✪ 1.C; 3.A; 4.A; 4.C; 7.A

Health Journal

In your Health Journal, make a list of people you could talk to if you were having an emotional problem. Think of people who you know well, and consider where you could go if you wanted to talk to someone anonymously.

Figure 21 Some teens are trained to give peer counseling to other teens who face difficult situations.

Professional Help

If problems are keeping someone from leading a normal life for more than a few days, he or she may need professional help. Mental health professionals are trained to help people deal with emotional problems and mental illnesses.

There are many kinds of mental health professionals. *Social workers* address mental health problems by dealing with individuals and their friends and family members. A **counselor** is a professional who helps people work through difficult problems by talking. A **psychologist** (sie KAHL uh jist) is a person who tries to change thoughts, feelings, and actions by finding the reasons behind them or by suggesting new ways to manage emotions. A **psychiatrist** (sie KIE uh trist) is a medical doctor who specializes in illnesses of the brain and body that affect emotions and behavior. Psychiatrists may treat people who have a mental illness by using medicines and counseling. Individuals who have mental and emotional health concerns may try several kinds of professionals before finding which treatment works best. ★ 1.C; 3.A; 4.C; 11.B

Figure 22 Professionals can help people who have a mental illness lead happy and successful lives.

Lesson Review

Using Vocabulary

1. What is the difference between a *psychiatrist* and a *psychologist*?

Understanding Concepts

2. When should people seek professional help for their problems? ★ 1.A; 1.C; 4.C
3. Why should people get help for emotional problems and mental illnesses immediately? ★ 1.A; 3.A; 4.C
4. What are three sources of help for people with emotional problems and mental illness? ★ 1.C; 3.A; 4.A; 4.C
5. What are four kinds of mental health professionals? ★ 3.A; 4.A; 4.C

Critical Thinking

6. **Analyzing Ideas** Why would it be important to find help for a friend who heard strange voices but would not get help?

CHAPTER 4 REVIEW

Chapter Summary

- Emotions are feelings that are produced in response to life events. ■ Unpleasant emotions are healthy when we learn from them. ■ How we experience emotions is affected by inherited and environmental factors. ■ Hormones and changing life roles and responsibilities affect teen emotions. ■ Emotions may vary in intensity. ■ Knowing your triggers can help you deal with emotions. ■ Emotions are unhealthy if they interfere with relationships. ■ Good communication skills can help you solve problems. ■ Mental illnesses are disorders that affect thoughts, emotions, and behavior. ■ Suicidal thinking is an emergency condition. ■ Counselors, psychologists, or psychiatrists can help with difficult emotional problems.

Using Vocabulary

For each sentence, fill in the blank with the proper word from the word bank provided below.

- emotions
- hormones
- triggers
- mental illnesses
- body language
- self-esteem
- defense mechanisms
- delusion
- hallucination

1. Feelings that are produced in response to a life event are called ___.
2. ___ are chemicals that help control how the body grows and functions.
3. Situations that cause a person to feel an emotion are called ___.
4. ___ refers to how a person views himself or herself.
5. Automatic behaviors that are used to reduce stress are called ___.
6. Brain diseases that affect thoughts, behaviors, or emotions are called ___.
7. A(n) ___ is when a person sees or hears something that is not real.

Understanding Concepts

8. What factors in a teen's life affect emotions? ★ 1.A; 6.A; 7.A; 8.A; 12.E
9. Describe the emotional spectrum from love to hate. ★ 11.D
10. Discuss how your body feels when you are angry. ★ 1.A; 11.D
11. What are three examples of unhealthy emotional expression? ★ 11.D
12. What is the value of thinking through your emotions? ★ 10.B; 11.B; 11.D
13. How might stressful events relate to mental illness? ★ 1.A; 4.C; 11.F
14. How can you know if a person suffers from depression? ★ 1.C; 4.C
15. What symptoms might make it difficult to distinguish schizophrenia from a mood disorder? ★ 1.C; 4.C
16. What are four sources of help for people with emotional problems or a mental illness? ★ 1.C; 3.A; 4.C
17. How can mental illness be treated? ★ 1.C; 3.A; 4.C

Critical Thinking

Applying Concepts

18 You and your best friend are acting in the same play. The director always tells the actors their lines without giving them a chance to think for a few seconds to remember them. This behavior drives you crazy, and you get angry at the director. However, your best friend hardly notices, and does not feel angry at all. Why might you and your friend have such different responses to this trigger? ★ 10.B; 11.B

19 Stan was sad that his brother was leaving for college. One night, Stan feels irritable. He throws a rock at a street light and breaks it. Why might Stan have decided to damage property? What are some better ways to deal with unpleasant emotions? ★ 11.B; 11.D

20 Becky and Rachel both get bad grades on the same test, and they are both disappointed. The day after the test, Becky is still down about it and seems tired and bored. But Rachel is full of energy, in a good mood, and she studies for that class during lunch. What are some possible reasons that they are handling their disappointment in such different ways? ★ 10.B; 11.A; 11.B; 11.F

Making Good Decisions

21 Suppose that a friend says that she thinks mental illness is probably a result of being unintelligent. What can you tell her about the cause of mental illness to help her see that she is wrong? ★ 1.A; 4.C

22 A friend has been really tired lately. He mentioned that he feels sad, and he doesn't eat much. He tells you that he has thought about suicide, but not seriously. What would you do in this situation? ★ 4.C; 5.A; 11.B; 12.B

Interpreting Graphics

How Common Are Anxiety Disorders in Americans aged 18–54?

Anxiety Disorder	Percentage of Population	Number of People
Panic disorder	1.7%	2.4 million
Obsessive-compulsive disorder	2.3%	3.3 million
Social phobia	3.7%	5.3 million
Specific phobias	4.4%	6.3 million
Generalized anxiety disorder	2.8%	4.0 million

Use the figure above to answer questions 23–26. ★ M8.5.A

23 Which of the anxiety disorders is the most common in 18- to 54-year-olds?

24 How many more people (of those included in the table) have OCD than panic disorder?

25 Which of the anxiety disorders listed above is the least common in 18- to 54-year-olds?

26 What percentage of the population has a phobia?

Reading Checkup

Take a minute to review your answers to the Health IQ questions at the beginning of this chapter. How has reading this chapter improved your Health IQ?

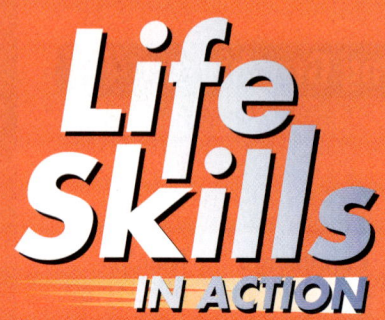

Life Skills IN ACTION

Coping

At times, everyone faces setbacks, disappointments, or other troubles. To deal with these problems, you have to learn how to cope. Coping is dealing with problems and emotions in an effective way. Complete the following activity to develop your coping skills.

Sabrina's Sadness

Setting the Scene

Sabrina's grandmother died a few months ago. Since then, Sabrina has been feeling very depressed. Sabrina's mood has affected many parts of her life. For example, her grades have been dropping because she does not always do her homework. Also, her friends are starting to avoid her because they do not think that she is much fun to be around. Sabrina's father is worried about her emotional health and asks if she wants to talk about anything. ★ 1.A; 3.A

The 5 Steps of Coping

1. Identify the problem.
2. Identify your emotions.
3. Use positive self-talk.
4. Find ways to resolve the problem.
5. Talk to others to receive support.

Guided Practice

Practice with a Friend

Form a group of three. Have one person play the role of Sabrina and another person play the role of Sabrina's father. Have the third person be an observer. Walking through each of the five steps of coping, role-play Sabrina coping with her feelings of depression. Have Sabrina ask her father for support. The observer will take notes, which will include observations about what the person playing Sabrina did well and suggestions of ways to improve. Stop after each step to evaluate the process.
★ 1.A; 10.B; 11.B; 11.D

102 | Chapter 4 Life Skills in Action

Independent Practice

Check Yourself

After you complete the guided practice, go through Act 1 again without stopping at each step. Answer the questions below to review what you did.

1. What are some positive things Sabrina can say to herself to help her cope with her problem? ★ 10.B; 11.B
2. What are some possible ways that Sabrina can resolve her problem? ★ 4.C; 11.B
3. Other than her father, who might Sabrina turn to for support?
4. Describe a time in which you could have used the five steps of coping to deal with a problem.

On Your Own

After several weeks, Sabrina is finally able to manage her feelings of depression in a healthy way. She feels happy and confident again. Unfortunately, Sabrina learns that she is doing poorly in Language Arts because she neglected her schoolwork. She is disappointed in herself and wants to improve her grade. Make a poster showing how Sabrina could use the five steps of coping to deal with her poor grade in Language Arts.

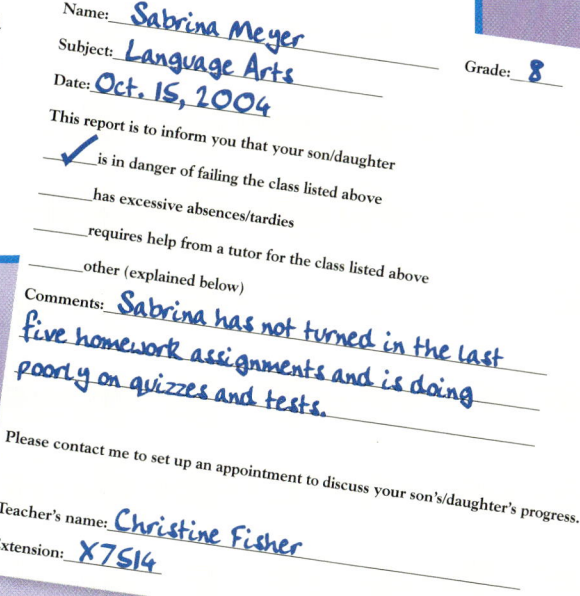

Chapter 4 Coping | 103

CHAPTER 5
Your Body Systems

Lessons

1. Body Organization — 106
2. The Nervous System — 108
3. The Endocrine System — 112
4. The Skeletal and Muscular Systems — 116
5. The Digestive and Urinary Systems — 122
6. The Circulatory and Respiratory Systems — 128
7. Caring for Your Body — 134

Chapter Review — 136
Life Skills in Action — 138

Check out **Current Health** articles related to this chapter by visiting **go.hrw.com**. Just type in the keyword **HD4CH37**.

> "I love **rollercoasters**. I always get **excited** and **scared** at the same time **when I ride** them. My heart starts racing and my palms get sweaty as the coaster climbs the first hill. And swooping through the air so fast is such a rush!"

Health IQ

PRE-READING

Answer the following true/false questions to find out what you already know about body systems. When you've finished this chapter, you'll have the opportunity to change your answers based on what you've learned.

1. Your body is made of a group of organ systems that work together in an organized way. ★ 1.A

2. If one body system is not working properly, all of the others will keep working normally. ★ 1.A

3. Everything your body does requires you to think. ★ 1.A

4. Bones are living organs. ★ 1.A

5. The muscles that help you move are the only muscles in your body. ★ 1.A

6. Food is broken down and absorbed only in your stomach. ★ 1.A

7. Your body has a system whose main function is to remove waste. ★ 1.A

8. Blood is a tissue. ★ 1.A

9. Blood is made mostly of red blood cells. ★ 1.A

10. Your lungs are hollow sacs. ★ 1.A

11. You breathe in when the diaphragm and the muscles between your ribs contract. ★ 1.A

12. As long as you feel healthy, you don't have to see a doctor regularly. ★ 1.A

13. Your body is made of trillions of cells. ★ 1.A

14. Your kidneys remove only wastes from your blood. ★ 1.A

15. Your posture has no effect on your health. ★ 1.A

ANSWERS: 1. true; 2. false; 3. false; 4. true; 5. false; 6. false; 7. true; 8. true; 9. false; 10. false; 11. true; 12. false; 13. true; 14. false; 15. false

Chapter 5 Your Body Systems

Lesson 1

Body Organization

What You'll Do

- **Describe** how cells, tissues, and organs work together in the human body. ⭐ 1.A
- **Summarize** how body systems work together. ⭐ 1.A

Terms to Learn

- cell
- tissue
- organ
- body system

Write

Name as many body systems as you can.

A computer is made of hundreds of parts that work together. When the parts of the computer work properly you can write a homework assignment, surf the Internet, or play computer games.

The human body is also a complex machine made of many parts that work together. When these parts work together, they allow you to do amazing things, such as kick a soccer ball, remember your friend's phone number, or play a musical instrument. Each part has a role to play, and each part contributes to the functions of the other parts of the body.

From Cells to Systems

Your body is made of trillions of cells. **Cells** are the simplest and most basic units of all living organisms. A group of cells that are similar and work together to perform a specific function is called a **tissue.** Two or more tissues that work together to perform a specific function are called an **organ.** Your heart, stomach, and brain are all organs. A group of organs that work together for one purpose is called a **body system.** For example, your digestive system is made of many organs that work together to provide nutrients for your body. All of your body systems work together to make your body function properly. Figure 1 shows the relationships between cells, tissues, organs, and body systems. ⭐ 1.A

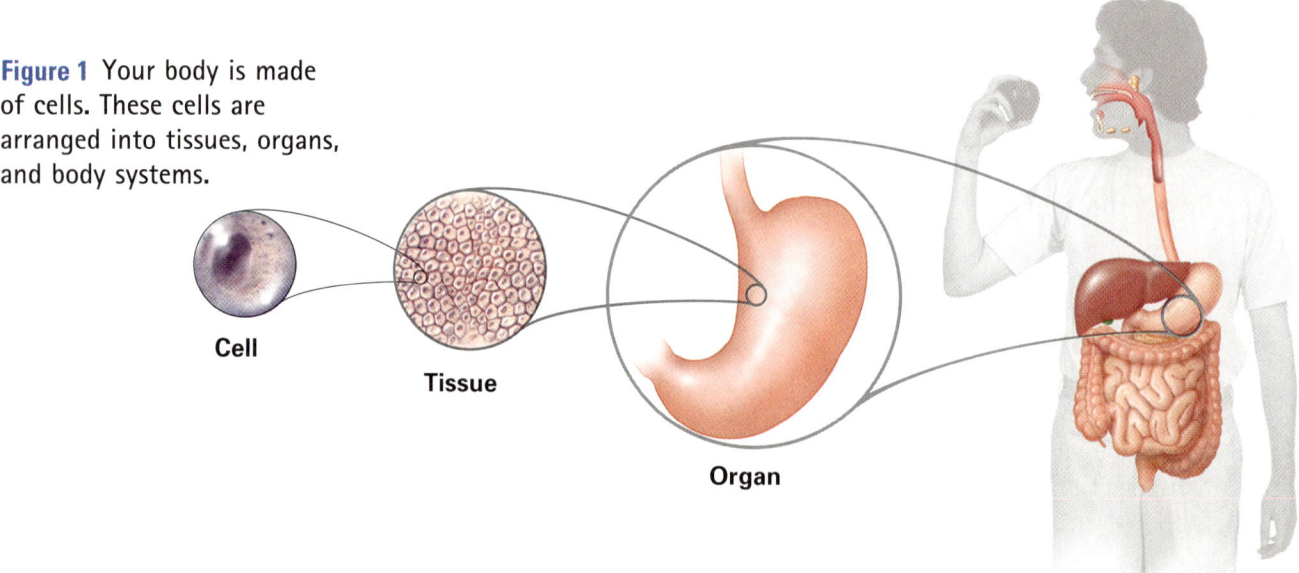

Figure 1 Your body is made of cells. These cells are arranged into tissues, organs, and body systems.

Cell

Tissue

Organ

System

TABLE 1 Your Body Systems

Body system	Function
Nervous system	controls and coordinates the activities of the body systems
Endocrine system	helps nervous system control and coordinate activities of the body; helps regulate growth
Skeletal system	provides a framework to support and protect the body
Muscular system	works with skeletal system to cause movement
Digestive system	breaks down foods into simpler substances; transfers nutrients into the blood; eliminates solid waste products from the body; stores nutrients
Urinary system	filters liquid waste products from the blood and eliminates them from the body
Circulatory system	transports and distributes gases, nutrients, and hormones throughout the body; collects and transports waste products so they can be eliminated from the body; protects the body from disease
Respiratory system	exchanges oxygen from the environment and carbon dioxide from the body

Body Systems Work Together

Each one of your body systems is made of organs that work together to perform specific functions for your body. Although each body system has a different function, the systems work together and help one another. For example, the main function of the circulatory system is to pump blood through the body. As the blood travels through the body, the blood carries materials such as oxygen, nutrients, and chemical messages to and from other body systems. Body systems depend on each other to perform their functions properly. When the body systems work together properly, they keep the body alive and healthy. ★ 1.A

Lesson Review

Using Vocabulary

1. Explain the difference between a tissue and an organ. Describe how tissues and organs work together in the human body. ★ 1.A

Understanding Concepts

2. Give an example of how two body systems work together. ★ 1.A

Critical Thinking

3. **Identifying Relationships** If you wanted to create a tissue, why would you have to create cells first?

4. **Making Inferences** How do you think the circulatory system works with the digestive system to provide nutrients to the body? ★ 1.A

internet connect
www.scilinks.org/health
Topic: Tissues and Organs
HealthLinks code: HD4100

HEALTH LINKS Maintained by the National Science Teachers Association

Lesson 2

The Nervous System

Lissa has been practicing hard for her next gymnastics meet. Sometimes she is amazed by what her body can do, such as balance on one leg on the balance beam.

What You'll Do

- **Describe** the different parts of the nervous system. ★ 1.A
- **Describe** seven common problems of the nervous system.

Terms to Learn

- nervous system
- brain
- spinal cord
- nerve

Start Off Write

What does the nervous system do?

Like Lissa's body, your body performs many amazing functions. The **nervous system** is the body system that gathers and interprets information about the body's internal and external environments and responds to that information.

Mission Control

All flights into space are controlled from Earth by Mission Control at NASA. Mission Control monitors all of the functions of the spacecraft at the same time. The nervous system acts as your body's control center. Your nervous system regulates all of your body's functions and activities at the same time.

Your nervous system is composed of your brain, spinal cord, nerves, and sensory organs, such as your eyes, ears, and the taste buds on your tongue. This system controls voluntary activities, such as walking and talking, and involuntary activities, such as the beating of your heart. It also allows you to see, hear, smell, taste, and detect pain and pressure.

The nervous system controls your body by conducting electrical messages to and from the various parts of your body. These electrical messages are called *nerve impulses*. These messages carry information that helps the organs and body systems carry out their functions correctly. ★ 1.A

Figure 2 Your nervous system allows you to perform many tasks at once without having to think too much about any one of them.

108 | Chapter 5 Your Body Systems

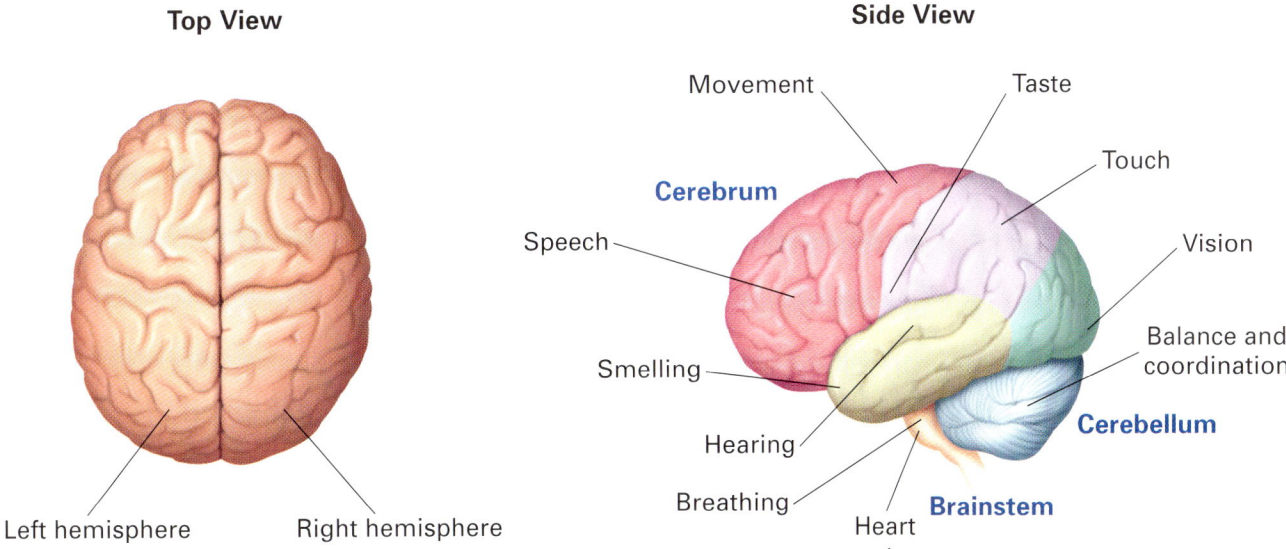

Your Brain

Thousands of different activities that happen inside your body are controlled by one organ. This organ is your brain. Your **brain** is the mass of nervous tissue that is located inside your skull. Your brain tells your body what to do by sending impulses to different parts of your body. In fact, your brain constantly receives impulses from different parts of your body. These impulses contain information about your body and about the world around you. Your brain uses this information to tell your body how to react to the environment by sending impulses to different parts of your body.

The brain consists of three parts—the cerebrum, the cerebellum, and the brainstem. Although each part has specific functions, the three parts of the brain work together to make the body systems function correctly.

- The *cerebrum* is the largest part of the brain. It is also the most complex. The cerebrum coordinates many of the activities of the body systems. The cerebrum controls your senses, including taste, smell, sight, touch, and hearing. The cerebrum also controls emotions, voluntary muscle movements, consciousness, learning, and memory.

- The *cerebellum* is the second largest part of your brain. The cerebellum controls muscle coordination, balance, and posture.

- The *brainstem* is the part of your brain that connects to the spinal cord. The brain stem controls heart rate, blood pressure, and breathing. ★ 1.A

Figure 3 Different parts of your brain control different body functions. The pink, purple, teal, and green areas are all parts of the cerebrum.

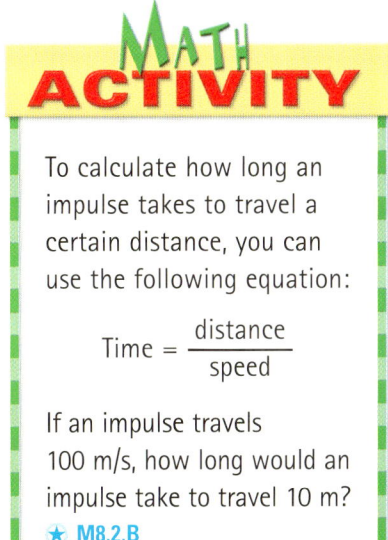

MATH ACTIVITY

To calculate how long an impulse takes to travel a certain distance, you can use the following equation:

$$\text{Time} = \frac{\text{distance}}{\text{speed}}$$

If an impulse travels 100 m/s, how long would an impulse take to travel 10 m?
★ M8.2.B

Lesson 2 The Nervous System | 109

Brain Food

Some actions in the body do not involve the brain. Many reflexive actions, such as pulling your hand away from a hot stove, are controlled by the spinal cord.

The Central Nervous System

The central nervous system, or CNS, includes your brain and spinal cord. The **spinal cord** is a bundle of nervous tissue that is about a foot and a half long and is surrounded by your backbone. The major function of the spinal cord is to relay impulses between the brain and different parts of the body. When parts of the body send impulses to the spinal cord, the spinal cord usually relays the impulses to the brain. The brain then interprets the impulses it receives and selects a response. The brain sends a response by an impulse that travels through the spinal cord back to the body part. These impulses control most of the voluntary activities of the body. ★ 1.A

The Peripheral Nervous System

The peripheral nervous system, or PNS, is composed of nerves that connect all parts of your body to the central nervous system. The central nervous system uses nerves to control the actions of different parts of the body. A **nerve** is a bundle of cells that conducts electrical signals through the body. A nerve is like an electrical cable that is made of many small wires that are bundled together. Nerves are found only in the peripheral nervous system.

Nerves serve as a means of communication between the central nervous system and the rest of the body. For example, some nerves connect the central nervous system with your skeletal muscles. These nerves tell your limbs when and how to move. Nerves that run through your skin send messages to your brain about heat, pressure, pain, and other sensations from the environment. These messages help your body respond to the world around you. ★ 1.A

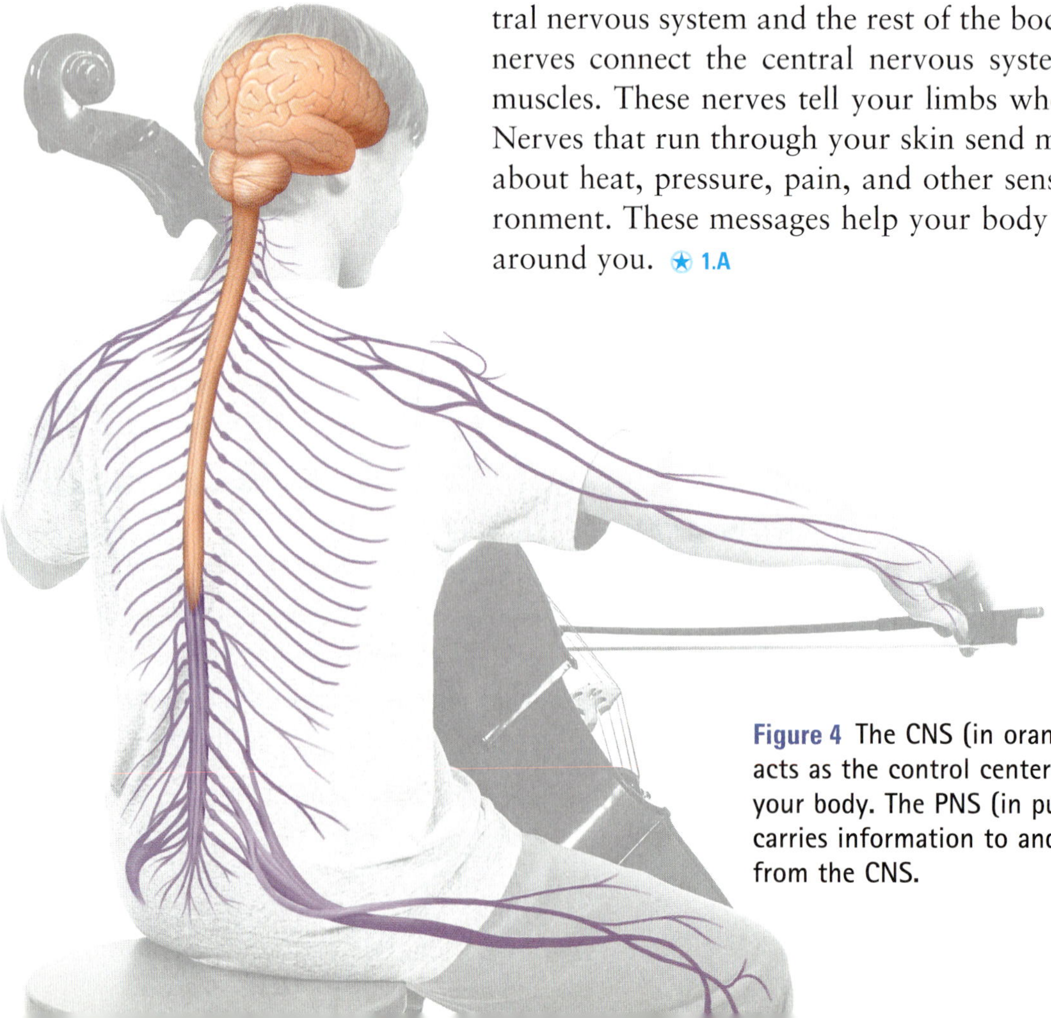

Figure 4 The CNS (in orange) acts as the control center for your body. The PNS (in purple) carries information to and from the CNS.

Common Problems of the Nervous System

If Mission Control loses contact with a spacecraft, the people on board are in danger. If any part of the nervous system does not function properly, the body may experience serious problems. Table 2 lists some of these problems.

TABLE 2 Nervous System Problems

Problem	Description	Treatment or prevention
Meningitis (MEN in JIET is)	an infection or inflammation of the protective coverings of the brain and spinal cord caused by bacteria or a virus	baterial forms treated with antibiotics; vaccine available to protect against some bacterial forms; no vaccine to treat or prevent viral forms
Rabies	a viral infection of the brain that causes irritation of the brain and spinal cord; passed by the saliva or bite of an infected animal	can be prevented by avoiding wild or unfamiliar animals; requires medical attention
Concussion	an injury to the brain caused by a blow to the head; may cause a brief loss of memory or consciousness	usually no hospitalization is required; may be prevented by wearing protective headgear
Stroke	the death of brain tissue due to a lack of blood to the brain	requires immediate medical attention and hospitalization
Paralysis	partial or total loss of the ability to use muscles; generally caused by damage to the brain or spinal cord	may be permanent; may be prevented by wearing safety gear and avoiding physical risks
Epilepsy	a disorder of the nerves and brain that is characterized by uncontrollable muscle activity	treated with medication
Cerebral palsy (SER uh bruhl PAWL zee)	a condition in which a person has very poor muscle control; caused by damage to the brain	no cure or prevention; may be helped by physical therapy

★ 3.A

Lesson Review

Using Vocabulary
1. What is a nerve?

Understanding Concepts
2. Describe the different parts of the nervous system. ★ 1.A
3. List and describe three common problems of the nervous system. ★ 1.A

Critical Thinking
4. **Making Inferences** Explain why wearing safety gear, such as bicycle helmets and seatbelts, is important to the health of your nervous system. ★ 1.A

internet connect
www.scilinks.org/health
Topic: Nervous System
HealthLinks code: HD4068

HEALTH LINKS — Maintained by the National Science Teachers Association

Lesson 2 The Nervous System 111

Lesson 3: The Endocrine System

What You'll Do

- **Identify** the different glands of the endocrine system. ★ 1.A; 2.B
- **Explain** how hormones affect growth and development. ★ 2.B
- **Describe** four common problems of the endocrine system.

Terms to Learn

- endocrine system
- hormone
- gland

Start Off Write

List some factors that could affect your growth.

Health Journal

Have you ever been frightened? How did your body respond to being frightened? What did your skin and hair do? What happened to your heartbeat and breathing? Describe a time when you were frightened and how your body responded.

Dolores was trying out for the school's cheerleading squad. When she began her try out, her heart began to race and her muscles became tense. She was really excited and nervous at the same time.

Dolores's body was responding to excitement and fear because of her endocrine system. Your **endocrine system** is a network of tissues and organs that release chemicals that control certain body functions.

Grow, Fight, or Flee

The endocrine system is composed of tissues and organs throughout the body that make and release hormones. **Hormones** are chemicals that travel in the blood and cause changes in different parts of the body. The endocrine system uses hormones to send messages to different parts of the body. For example, some of these chemical messages tell your body how to grow and develop. Other hormones help your body act during times of stress, such as when you are frightened. In a stressful situation, your endocrine system releases hormones that prepare your body to respond to the stress by defending itself or performing at its best. This response to stress is called the *fight or flight response*. It is also called an *epinephrine rush*.
★ 1.A

Figure 5 One function of the endocrine system is to prepare the body to respond to stress and fear.

Your Glands

A tissue or group of tissues that makes and releases chemicals is called a **gland**. Endocrine glands make hormones. Specific endocrine glands make and release into the blood hormones that control certain body functions. The glands of your endocrine system are located at various places in your body, but the hormones each gland releases can reach the entire body.

Your body has several endocrine glands. Each gland releases hormones that may affect many organs at one time. For example, your pituitary gland stimulates skeletal growth, helps the thyroid gland function properly, regulates the amount of water in your blood, and stimulates the birth process in pregnant women. The names and some of the functions of your endocrine glands are shown in Figure 6.

Figure 6 The Endocrine Glands ★ 1.A

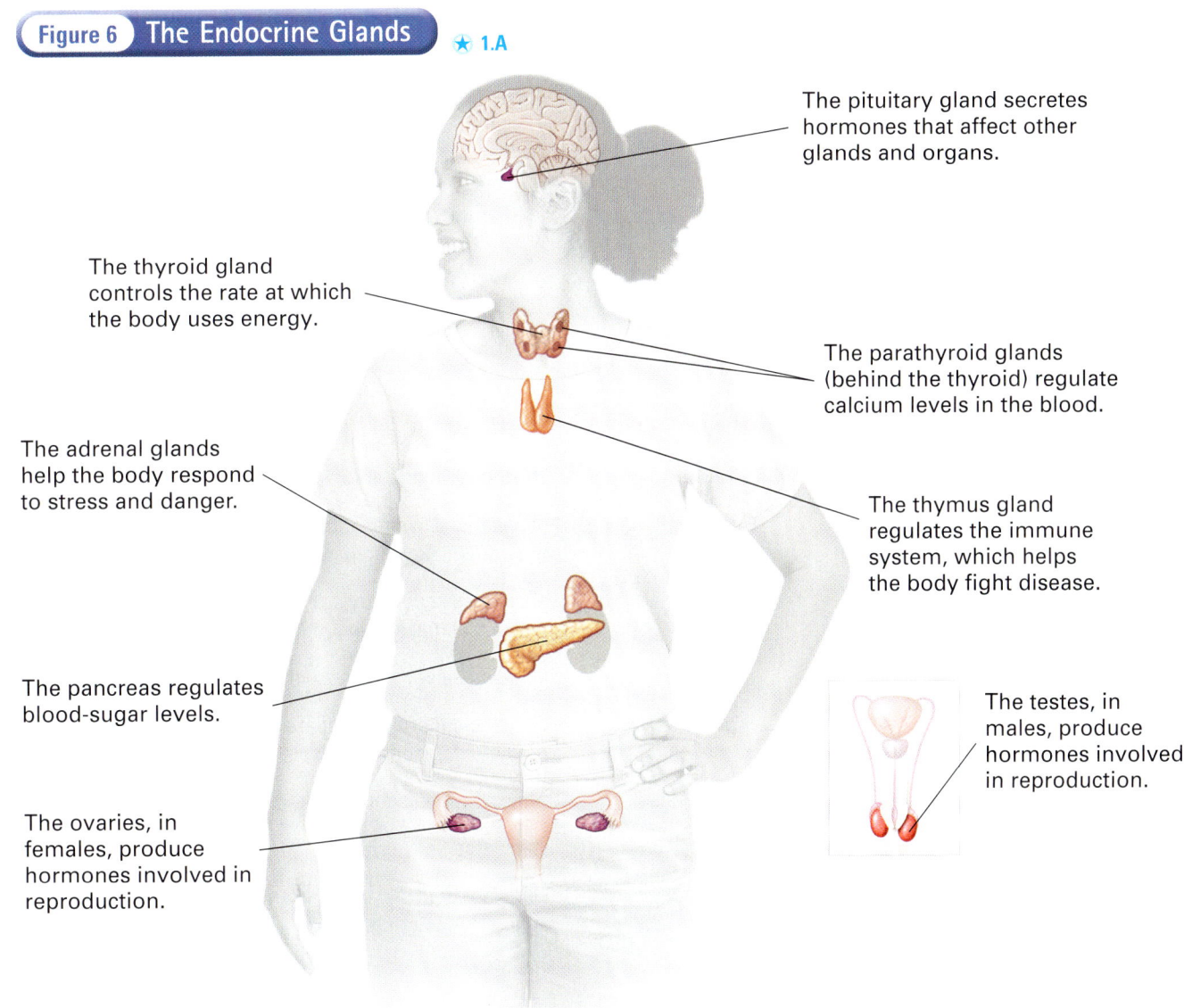

The pituitary gland secretes hormones that affect other glands and organs.

The thyroid gland controls the rate at which the body uses energy.

The parathyroid glands (behind the thyroid) regulate calcium levels in the blood.

The adrenal glands help the body respond to stress and danger.

The thymus gland regulates the immune system, which helps the body fight disease.

The pancreas regulates blood-sugar levels.

The testes, in males, produce hormones involved in reproduction.

The ovaries, in females, produce hormones involved in reproduction.

Lesson 3 The Endocrine System

Your Hormones

Your hormones control many functions of your body. Your body makes and releases different amounts of hormones at different times of the day, at different times of the month, and at different times in your life. For example, when you reach puberty, you begin to grow rapidly because your body releases more human growth hormone and more sex hormones, such as estrogen (ES truh juhn) and testosterone (tes TAHS tuhr OHN). The increased amounts of these hormones also cause other changes in your body. For example, changes in hormone levels during adolescence can cause acne. Table 3 describes the functions of some important hormones. ★ 1.A; 2.B

Figure 7 Some acne is caused by hormones, so almost everyone has it occasionally.

TABLE 3 Functions of Some Important Hormones

Hormone	Gland	Hormone function
Thyroxine (thie RAHKS een)	thyroid	stimulates body metabolism; helps regulate body growth and development
Testosterone	testis	stimulates secondary sex characteristics in males and stimulates sperm production
Estrogen	ovary	stimulates secondary sex characteristics in females
Progesterone (pro JES tuhr ohn)	ovary	allows the uterus to prepare for pregnancy and helps regulate the menstrual cycle
Insulin	pancreas	regulates the amount of sugar in the blood
Human growth hormone	pituitary	stimulates body growth
Epinephrine (ep uh NEF rin) **and norepinephrine** (NAWR ep uh NEF rin)	adrenal	stimulate the body systems and metabolism in emergencies and during stress

★ 1.A; 2.B

Common Problems of the Endocrine System

Hormones must be made and released at the right time and in the correct amounts. If your body has too much or too little of a hormone, your body systems will not work correctly. Problems with the amount of hormones can interfere with the normal structure and function of the body. Table 4 describes some of these problems.

TABLE 4 Endocrine Problems

Problem	Description	Treatment or prevention
Type II diabetes (DIE uh BEET EEZ)	a disease that is characterized by high levels of sugar in the blood; usually caused by the pancreas producing too little insulin or the body's cells not responding to insulin	may be controlled by diet and exercise; may require regular insulin injections or pills
Gigantism (jie GAN TIZ uhm)	a disorder in which an individual has a very large body size; caused by excess production of human growth hormone by the pituitary gland	may be treated with medications that reduce the production of human growth hormone
Hyperthyroidism (HIE puhr THIE royd IZ uhm)	a condition in which the thyroid gland produces too much of the thyroid hormones and many body systems become too active because of the extra thyroid hormones; can lead to rapid and unhealthy weight loss and other problems	may be treated with medications, radiation, or surgery
Hypothyroidism (HIE poh THIE royd IZ uhm)	a condition in which the thyroid gland produces too little of the thyroid hormones and many of the body systems slow down; can lead to rapid and unhealthy weight gain and other problems	treated with medications that replace the missing thyroid hormones ★ 3.A

Lesson Review

Using Vocabulary

1. What is a hormone? Where are hormones produced? ★ 1.A

Understanding Concepts

2. List six endocrine glands and one hormone that each gland produces. ★ 1.A
3. How do hormones affect growth and development? What other functions do hormones have? ★ 2.B

Critical Thinking

4. **Analyzing Ideas** Why will your body have problems if too much or too little of a hormone is produced? ★ 1.A; 2.B
5. **Identifying Relationships** If your body produced too much thyroxine, what do you think would happen to your metabolism? Would you gain weight or lose weight? ★ 1.A; 2.B

Lesson 4 — The Skeletal and Muscular Systems

What You'll Do

- **Identify** the different bones and joints in the skeleton. ★ 1.A
- **Describe** eight common problems of the skeletal system.
- **Identify** the three types of muscle. ★ 1.A
- **Explain** how muscles move the body. ★ 1.A
- **Describe** six common problems of the muscular system.

Terms to Learn

- bone
- skeletal system
- joint
- muscle
- muscular system

What do muscles do?

Lin's grandmother is 80 years old and has osteoporosis. The doctor said that Lin's grandmother's bones are very weak because they lack certain minerals.

Your body requires certain minerals and vitamins to stay strong and healthy. Many of these minerals are stored in your bones. **Bone** is a living organ made of bone cells, connective tissues, and minerals. Bone, cartilage, and the special structures that connect them make up your **skeletal system.**

Your Skeleton: Your Body's Framework

Your skeleton is the framework for your body. The bones that make up your skeletal system support your body. They also protect your organs, store minerals, and work with your muscles to help you move.

Your bones are made of two types of bone tissue. Compact bone is dense bone tissue found on the outside of all bones. Spongy bone is bone tissue that has many air spaces. It is lighter and less dense than compact bone and is found inside most bones.

The ends of many bones are covered by soft, flexible tissue called *cartilage*. Inside your bones is a soft tissue called *marrow*. Your body has two types of marrow. Red marrow makes both red and white blood cells. Yellow marrow stores fat. ★ 1.A

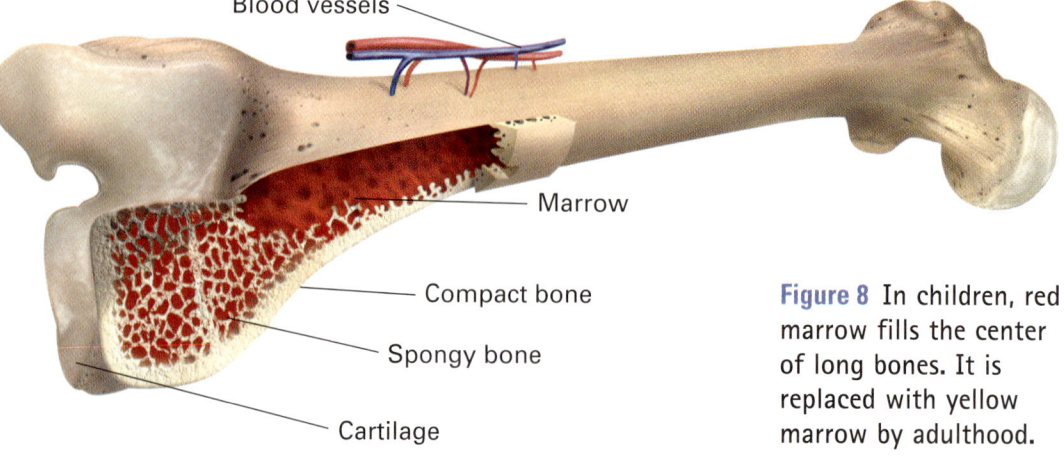

Figure 8 In children, red marrow fills the center of long bones. It is replaced with yellow marrow by adulthood.

Figure 9 The Skeletal System

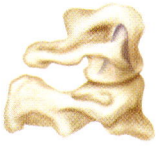

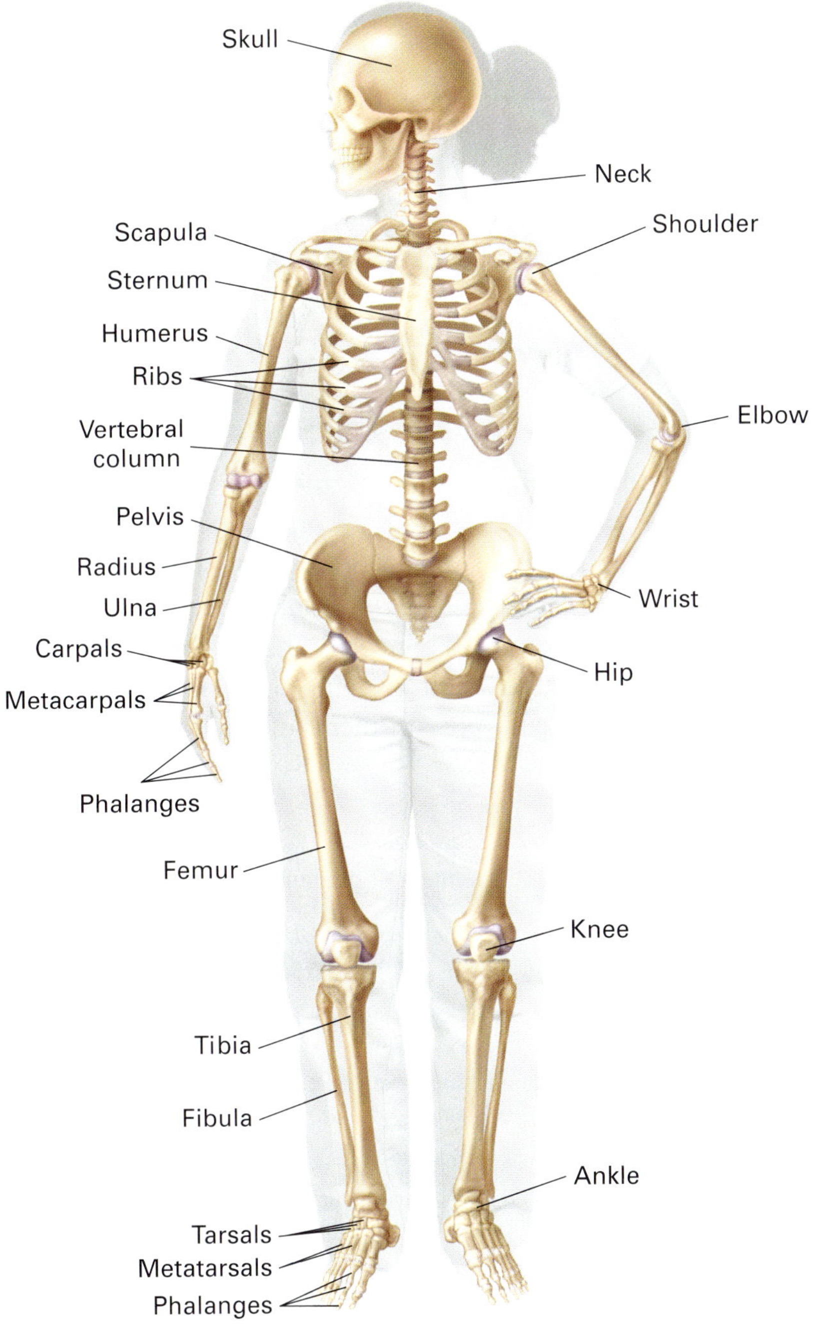

Pivot (neck)

One bone in a pivot joint rotates around the axis of the other bone in the joint. You use a pivot joint when you shake your head no.

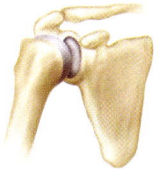
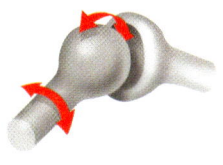

Ball and socket (hip and shoulder)

The end of one bone is shaped like a ball and fits into a cup-shaped space of the other bone. This joint allows the limbs to rotate in all directions.

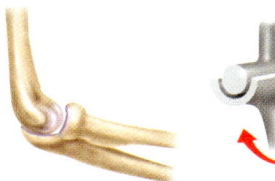

Hinge (knee and elbow)

The bones in a hinge joint are connected like the hinge of a door. This joint allows movement back and forth in one direction.

Joints

A place in the body where two or more bones connect is a **joint.** Joints allow movement when the muscles attached to the bones contract. Joints can be classified by how the bones move. Some joints allow a wide range of movement, such as those shown in Figure 9. Other joints allow little or no movement. These joints, such as those in your skull, are called *fixed joints*. The bones in most joints are held together by flexible bands of connective tissue called *ligaments*. ★ 1.A

Lesson 4 The Skeletal and Muscular Systems | 117

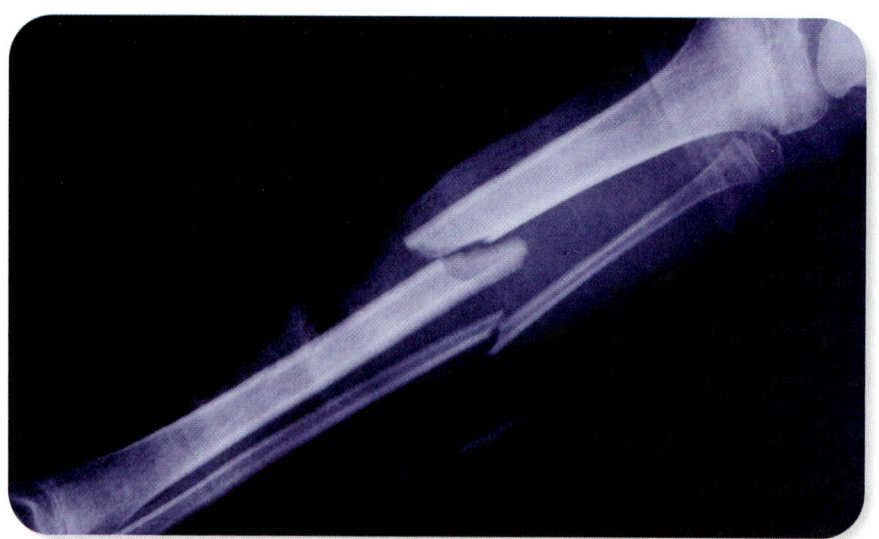

Figure 10 This X-ray image shows what broken bones look like.

Common Skeletal and Joint Problems

Injuries can cause many problems for bones and joints. Bones can break. Joints can be *dislocated*, if the bones are moved out of place. Ligaments can be stretched or torn. The skeletal system can also develop problems as a result of aging or poor diet. Table 5 lists and describes some common problems of the skeletal system.
✪ 1.A

TABLE 5 Skeletal System Problems

Problem	Description	Treatment or prevention
Osteoporosis (AHS tee OH puh ROH sis)	a disease in which the density of the bones decreases, which causes the bones to become weak and more likely to break	treated by exercise and by an increase in the amount of calcium and vitamin D in the diet
Fracture	a break in a bone; usually caused by accident or injury	most require a cast; some require surgery; may be prevented by wearing protective equipment
Osteomyelitis (AHS tee OH MIE uh LIET is)	a bacterial infection of a bone and its bone marrow	treated with antibiotics and in some cases surgery; may be prevented by cleaning all wounds, especially very deep cuts
Arthritis (ahr THRIET is)	a term used to refer to the many different types of joint inflammations	treated by physical therapy for the joint and medications that reduce the inflammation
Osteoarthritis (AHS tee OH ahr THRIET is)	the type of arthritis caused by aging; the joints are stiff and painful	treated with anti-inflammatory drugs, physical therapy, and surgery to replace the joint
Rickets	a condition in children that causes the body to have difficulty absorbing calcium and causes the bones to soften; caused by a lack of vitamin D	treated with medications that raise the levels of vitamin D in the blood
Scoliosis (SKOH lee OH sis)	curvature of the spine usually caused by uneven growth of the body	treated with exercise or a brace; may require surgery in extreme cases
Sprain	injury to the ligaments at a joint; frequently happens when the ankle rolls outward	treated with rest and ice; may require a cast; may be prevented by wearing proper shoes

Types of Muscle

Any tissue that is made of cells or fibers that contract and expand to cause movement is called **muscle.** Your body has three types of muscle. *Smooth muscle* makes up many of your internal organs, including your stomach and intestines. Smooth muscle contractions move materials such as food through internal organs. *Cardiac muscle* is the muscle found in the heart. When cardiac muscle contracts, blood is pushed through the body. The muscle that is attached to the bones is called *skeletal muscle*. Skeletal muscle is attached to the bones by connective tissues called *tendons*. When skeletal muscles contract, they pull on the bones they are attached to. This pulling causes your body to move. When skeletal muscles contract, they release energy, which helps maintain body temperature. The muscles that move your body make up your **muscular system.** ★ 1.A

MOVE YOUR MUSCLES

1. Write down the following movements: raise your arm, bend your arm, point your toe, stand up, and raise your knee.
2. Perform each movement, and use the figure to name the muscles that cause each movement.

Analysis

1. Did any movements require the use of more than one muscle? Why do you think those movements require the use of more than one muscle?

Figure 11 Your Muscles

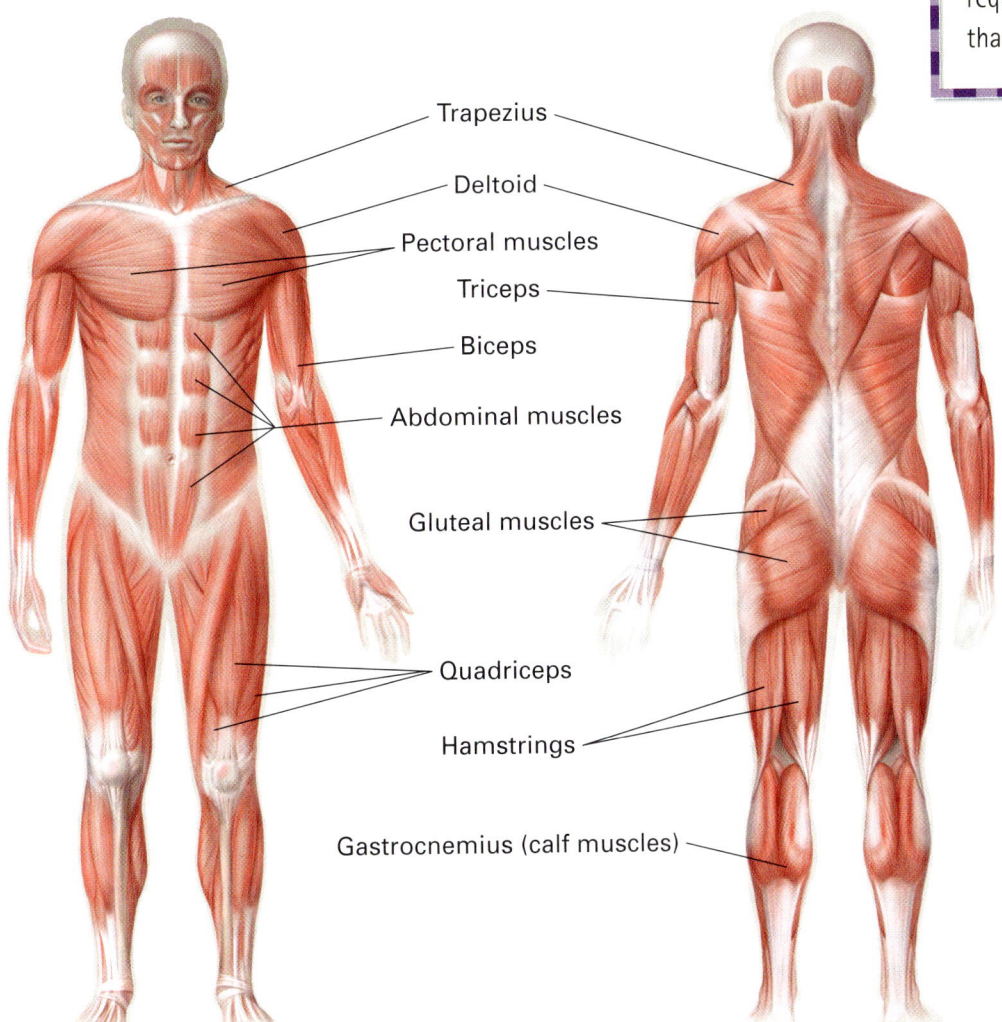

- Trapezius
- Deltoid
- Pectoral muscles
- Triceps
- Biceps
- Abdominal muscles
- Gluteal muscles
- Quadriceps
- Hamstrings
- Gastrocnemius (calf muscles)

Lesson 4 The Skeletal and Muscular Systems | 119

How Muscles Make You Move

Many different skeletal muscles must work together to make your body move. Movement of a body part is the result of muscles pulling on the bones that form a joint. When a muscle contracts, the muscle gets shorter. As the muscle contracts, the ends of the muscle are pulled toward the center of the muscle. Each end of the muscle is attached to a different bone. Therefore, as the muscle gets shorter, it pulls the two bones closer together.

When muscles contract, they can only pull the bones, not push them. To bend, or *flex,* the arm at the elbow, the biceps muscle contracts. When the biceps contracts, it pulls the bones of the forearm toward the shoulder.

The biceps can only bend the arm, it cannot straighten the arm. To straighten, or *extend,* the arm, the triceps muscle has to contract. The triceps is on the back of your arm. When the triceps contracts, it pulls the bones of the forearm away from the biceps. This movement straightens the arm. Figure 12 shows how the biceps and triceps work together to move the arm. ★ 1.A

Figure 12 Your biceps and triceps work together to move your arm. When your biceps contracts, your arm bends. When your triceps contracts, your arm straightens.

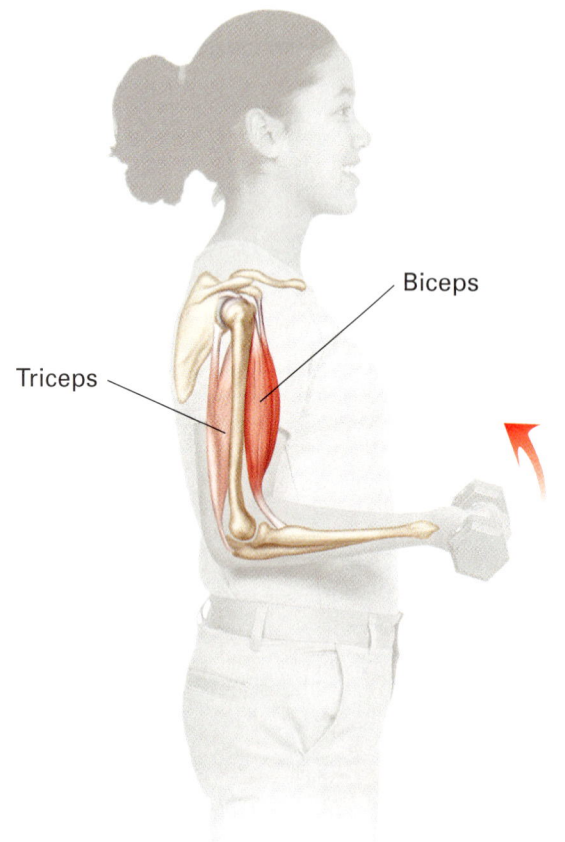

When the biceps contracts, the triceps relaxes. The forearm is pulled up, closer to the biceps, which causes the arm to bend.

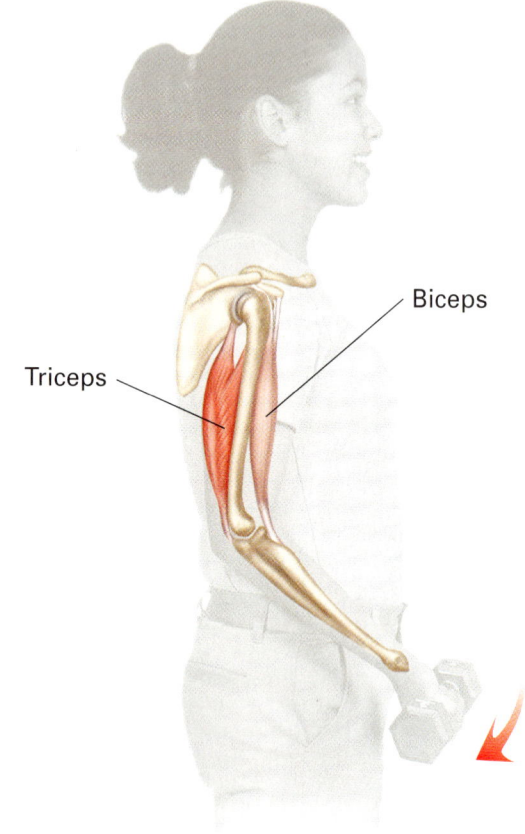

When the triceps contracts, the biceps relaxes. The forearm is pulled back, closer to the triceps, which causes the arm to straighten.

Common Muscular Problems

Muscles do most of the work of the body. Because they are used so much, muscles can become tired and sore. They can also be strained and torn. To prevent muscle injuries, you should warm up, cool down, and stretch when exercising. Table 6 describes some common problems of the muscular system.

TABLE 6 Problems of the Muscular System

Problem	Description	Treatment or prevention
Muscular dystrophy	a group of genetic diseases that lead to muscle weakness and in some cases destruction of skeletal muscle tissue	cannot be cured; may be treated with physical therapy and in some cases, surgery
Inguinal hernia (ING gwi nuhl HUHR nee uh)	a condition in which the intestine bulges through the abdominal muscles; often caused by improper lifting of heavy objects	may require surgery; may be prevented by using care when lifting heavy objects
Muscle cramp	a sudden and usually painful contraction of a muscle; often happens at night or after exercise	usually requires no treatment; may be prevented by stretching before and after exercise
Strain	overstretching and possible tearing of a muscle due to overuse or misuse	treated with rest, ice, and wrapping the injury; may be prevented by stretching before exercise
Tendinitis	inflammation of a tendon caused by aging or excessive exercise	treated with rest, hot or cold compresses, and anti-inflammatory medications; may be prevented by stretching and avoiding overuse
Shin splints	pain in the shin caused by damage or irritation to the muscles in the front of the lower leg	treated with rest, ice, and pain medication; may be prevented by not running on hard surfaces

⭐ 3.A

Lesson Review

Using Vocabulary

1. What is the difference between a bone and a joint?

Understanding Concepts

2. Explain how muscles and bones work together to cause movement of the body. What role do nerves play in causing movement? ⭐ 1.A

3. What are the three types of muscle? Give an example of each type.

4. Explain how a ball-and-socket joint works. ⭐ 1.A

Critical Thinking

5. **Identifying Relationships** Why is the brain located in the skull, and why do the ribs surround the heart? ⭐ 1.A

6. **Analyzing Ideas** Why does your body have different types of joints?

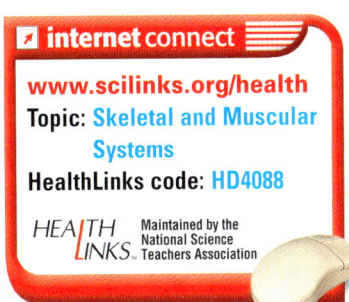

internet connect
www.scilinks.org/health
Topic: Skeletal and Muscular Systems
HealthLinks code: HD4088

HEALTH LINKS Maintained by the National Science Teachers Association

Lesson 4 The Skeletal and Muscular Systems

Lesson 5: The Digestive and Urinary Systems

What You'll Do

- **Describe** how the human body digests food and absorbs nutrients. 1.A
- **Describe** eight common problems of the digestive system.
- **Explain** how the human body excretes waste. 1.A
- **Describe** four common problems of the excretory system.

Terms to Learn

- digestion
- digestive system
- nutrient
- urinary system
- urine

Start Off Write

What is the importance of chewing your food?

To avoid being late to class, Dawn barely chewed her food as she gulped down her lunch. Then, she raced to her class and sat in her seat. Suddenly, her stomach began to hurt because she had eaten her food too fast.

Chewing your food is the first step in digestion. **Digestion** is the process by which your body breaks down the food you eat. If you don't chew your food properly, your body has a harder time breaking down the food.

Digestion: From Food to Energy

The group of organs and glands that work together to physically and chemically break down, or digest, food is the **digestive system**. Digestion takes place in the mouth, stomach, and small intestine. After digestion, the food products are absorbed into the blood. The blood carries these products to the cells of the body. The cells need these digested food products because food contains nutrients. **Nutrients** are the substances in foods that your body needs to function properly. Cells use nutrients to produce energy for all of your bodily activities, including growth, maintenance, and repair. 1.A

Figure 13 Your digestive system breaks down food into the nutrients your body needs to stay healthy.

The Journey of Food

Digestion begins in the mouth when you chew your food. Chewing makes the food particles smaller in size, which makes digestion easier. As you chew, the food is mixed with a liquid called *saliva*, which is produced by the salivary glands. Saliva moistens the food and makes it easier to swallow. Saliva also starts to break down some of the simple nutrients in the food. When food is swallowed, it is pushed by your tongue into your throat, or pharynx. From there, the food passes through your esophagus to your stomach. While in the stomach, the food particles are mixed with acidic stomach juices. The stomach churns the food and mixes the food with these juices.

After a few hours, food leaves your stomach and enters your small intestine. Most chemical digestion and absorption happen in the small intestine. Foods move through the small intestine by the contractions of the smooth muscle of the small intestine. These contractions squeeze and push the food through the organ. The liver, the gall bladder, and the pancreas all release chemicals into the small intestine. These chemicals aid digestion in the small intestine. Finally, food leaves the small intestine and enters the large intestine. No digestion happens in the large intestine. Materials that enter the large intestine are mostly waste products. These waste products are pushed out through the anus. The entire process of digestion takes about 24 hours. ★ 1.A

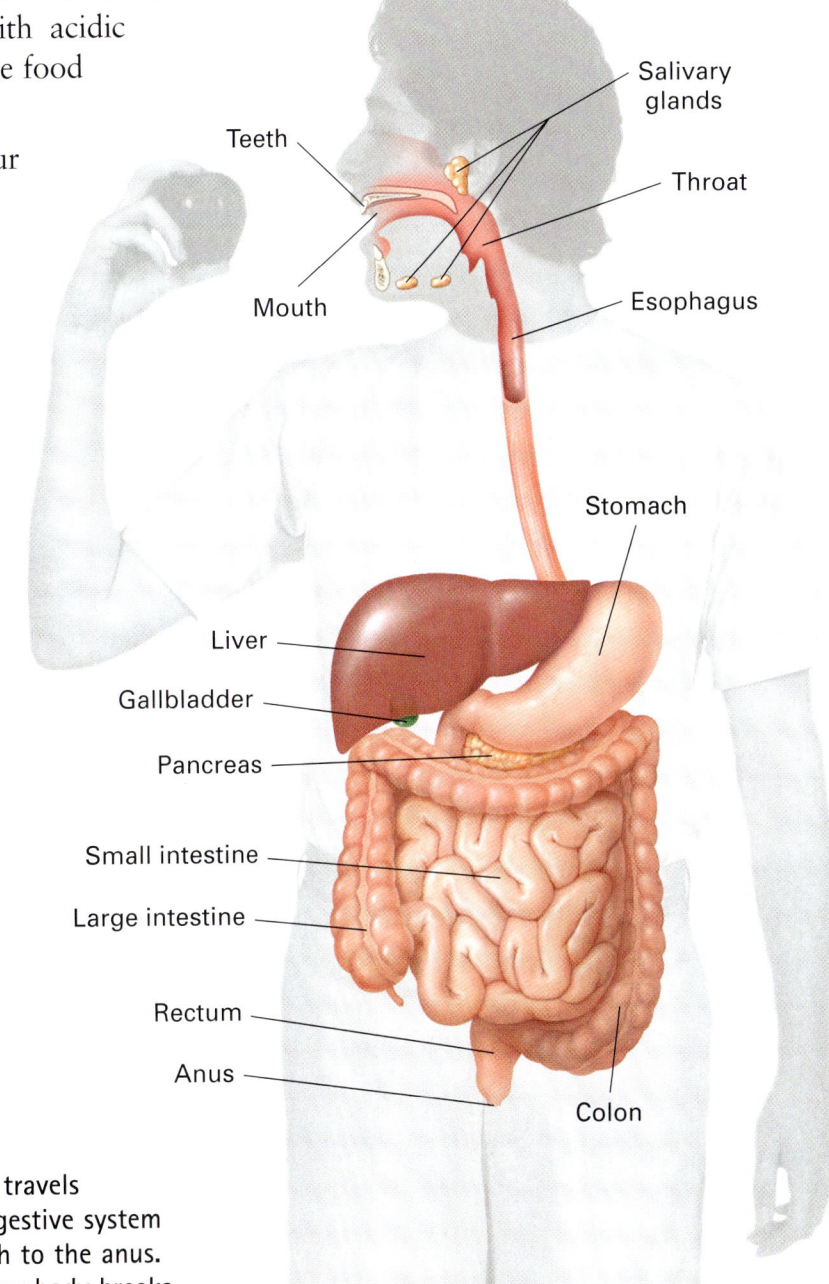

Figure 14 Food travels through the digestive system from the mouth to the anus. On the way, your body breaks down the food into nutrients it can use to stay healthy.

Lesson 5 The Digestive and Urinary Systems | 123

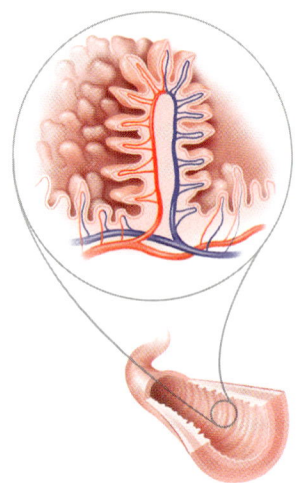

Figure 15 The villi in the small intestine are lined with tiny blood vessels. Nutrients pass from the intestine to these blood vessels.

How the Body Absorbs Nutrients

After foods are broken down, the nutrients are absorbed into the bloodstream. In the stomach, alcohol, simple sugars, and simple salts are absorbed. However, most nutrient absorption happens in the small intestine. Digested carbohydrates, proteins, and fats are absorbed in the small intestine. The inner wall of the small intestine is covered by fingerlike projections called *villi*. The villi, shown in Figure 15, increase the surface area of the intestinal wall. The greater surface area of the intestinal wall allows nutrients to pass easily from the small intestine to the blood. The nutrients are then carried in the blood to the rest of the body. The only substances absorbed in the large intestine are water and some simple salts. ★ 1.A

Common Digestive Problems

Improper chewing of foods, gulping food when you eat, or too much acid in the stomach can all lead to problems with digestion and with the digestive organs. Table 7 describes some common problems of the digestive system.

TABLE 7 Problems of the Digestive System

Problem	Description	Treatment or prevention
Indigestion (IN di JES chuhn)	pain or discomfort in the area of the stomach	treated with antacids or medication; may be prevented by eating slowly and avoiding spicy foods
Heartburn	a burning feeling in the esophagus caused by a backflow of acidic stomach contents	treated with antacids or medications that reduce the amount of stomach acid
Diarrhea (DIE uh REE uh)	an increase in the amount and number of times a person passes solid waste	treated with medication
Constipation	a condition in which passing solid waste is difficult and infrequent	treated with medication and fluids; may be prevented by eating a healthy diet and drinking lots of water
Ulcers	a round, open sore in the lining of the stomach or small intestine caused by bacteria	treated by avoiding certain foods and taking antacids and antibiotics; may be prevented by avoiding foods that irritate the stomach
Appendicitis (uh PEN duh SIET is)	inflammation of the appendix of the large intestine, which may release harmful bacteria into the abdomen	treated by surgical removal of the appendix
Hemorrhoids (HEM uhr oyDZ)	swollen tissues of the rectum and anus that contain blood vessels that may bleed	usually does not require treatment but may require surgery; may be prevented by eating more fiber
Stomach and colon cancer ★ 3.A	a tumor in the stomach, colon, or rectum of the large intestine; commonly related to age and diet	treatment involves surgical removal of the affected organ, as well as chemotherapy and radiation therapy; may be prevented by eating a healthy diet

Excretion: Removing Liquid Wastes

When nutrients reach the cells of the body, the cells use the nutrients for energy. When cells use this energy, they produce wastes. These wastes must be removed from the body. The removal of liquid wastes from the body is called *excretion*. Three of your body systems are involved in excretion: your skin releases waste products and water when you sweat, your lungs get rid of carbon dioxide and water when you exhale, and the urinary system removes waste products from your blood.

The **urinary system** is a group of organs that work together to remove liquid wastes from the blood. Your blood carries wastes from your cells to the kidneys. As blood passes through the kidneys, the kidneys clean the blood of liquid waste. The cleaned blood then leaves the kidneys and continues to move through the body. The wastes pass from the kidneys to the bladder by way of tubelike structures called *ureters*. The *bladder* is a muscular, baglike organ that stores this liquid waste until it can be released from the body. When the bladder is full, the waste leaves the body through a single tubelike structure called the *urethra*. The release of this waste from the body is called *urination*. ★ 1.A

Myth: If you swallow your gum, it will stay in your digestive system for 7 years.

Fact: Gum will pass through the digestive system at the same rate that other food particles do, which generally takes about 12 to 24 hours.

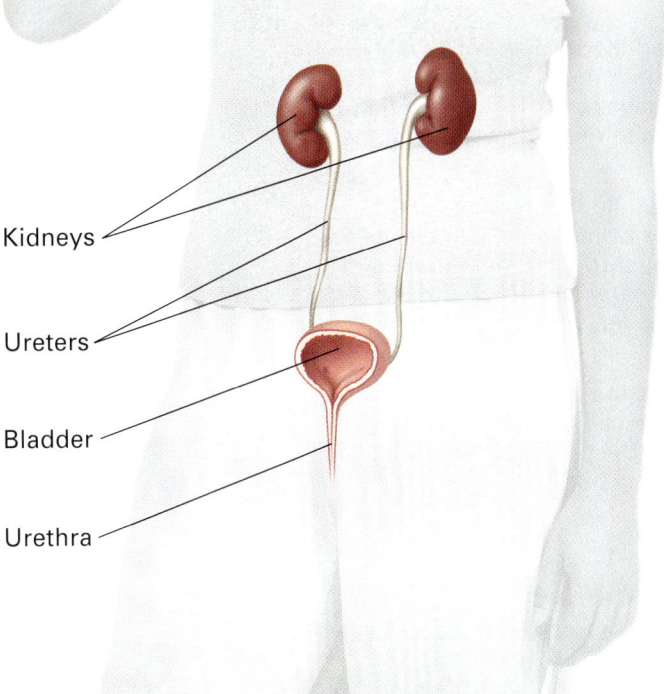

Figure 16 The urinary system removes many of the liquid waste products made by the body.

Kidneys

Ureters

Bladder

Urethra

Filtering Blood

Your kidneys clean your blood. They also help regulate the amount of water in your body. When blood enters a kidney, the blood contains nutrients, gases, water, and waste products. The kidney must remove wastes and excess water from the blood while leaving other substances in the blood. Inside your kidneys are microscopic filters called *nephrons* that remove harmful products from your blood. The nephrons remove the wastes from the blood through a process called *filtration*. Filtration is described in Figure 17. The waste products are then mixed with excess water to form a liquid waste called ==urine.== The urinary system then removes the urine and excess water from your body.

★ 1.A

Figure 17 How the Kidneys Filter Blood

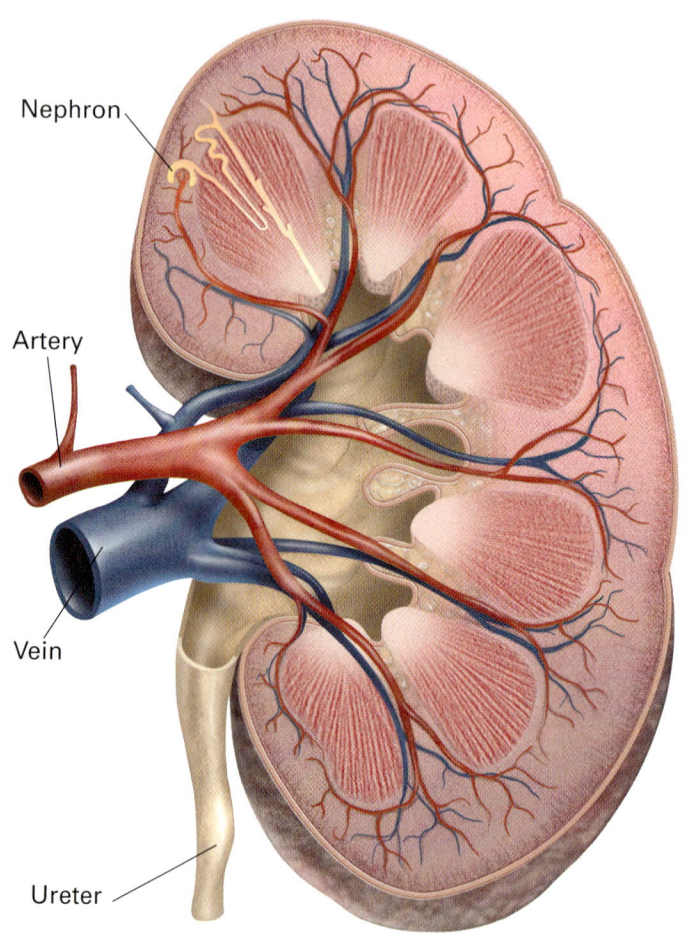

1. A large artery brings blood into each kidney.

2. Tiny blood vessels branch off of the main artery and pass through part of each nephron.

3. Water and other small substances, such as glucose, salts, amino acids, and urea, are forced out of the blood vessels and into the nephrons.

4. As these substances flow through the nephrons, most of the water and some nutrients are moved back into blood vessels that wrap around the nephrons. A concentrated mixture of waste materials is left behind in the nephrons.

5. The cleaned blood, now with slightly less water and much less waste material, leaves each kidney through a large vein to recirculate in the body.

6. The yellow fluid that remains in the nephrons is called *urine*. Urine leaves each kidney through a slender tube called the *ureter* and flows into the urinary bladder, where it is stored.

7. Urine leaves the body through another tube called the *urethra*. Urination is the process of expelling urine from the body.

Common Problems of the Urinary System

If the urinary system cannot perform its functions, waste products can build up in the blood. This buildup can lead to life-threatening conditions. The urinary system can also experience problems that are not quite as serious, but that are uncomfortable or painful. Table 8 describes some of these problems.

TABLE 8 Urinary System Problems

Problem	Description	Treatment or prevention
Urinary tract infection (UTI)	an infection of one or more of the organs of the urinary tract caused by bacteria, viruses, fungi, or parasites; more common in women than men	treated with antibiotics or antiviral drugs; may be prevented by drinking plenty of water, urinating frequently, avoiding tight clothing, and not using harsh detergents to wash clothing
Stones	crystallized mineral chunks that frequently form in the kidneys and the bladder; small, stones will leave the body with the urine; larger stones may become trapped and cause pain	treated with medications that dissolve the stones, with ultrasound waves to crush the stones, or with surgery to remove the stones; may be prevented by drinking plenty of water every day and eating a healthy diet
Urinary incontinence (in KAHN tuh nuhns)	uncontrollable loss of urine from the bladder or the inability to control urination; frequently caused by aging	treated with medication and sometimes surgery
Overactive or neurogenic (NOOR uh JEN ik) **bladder**	inability to control urination; caused by damage (by injury or a birth defect) to the nerves that go to the urinary bladder	treated with medications, surgery, or inserting a catheter

★ 3.A

Lesson Review

Using Vocabulary
1. Define *nutrient*.

Understanding Concepts
2. Describe how the body digests food and absorbs nutrients. ★ 1.A
3. List and describe two problems of the digestive system and two problems of the urinary system.
4. How does the urinary system remove wastes from the body? ★ 1.A

Critical Thinking
5. **Making Inferences** Why must the kidney filter blood to remove only waste products? What might happen if the kidney removed other materials from the blood? ★ 1.A
6. **Identifying Relationships** How does blood help the digestive system perform its function?

Lesson 5 The Digestive and Urinary Systems

Lesson 6: The Circulatory and Respiratory Systems

What You'll Do

- **Describe** how the circulatory system transports and distributes nutrients. ★ 1.A
- **Describe** seven common problems of the circulatory system.
- **Describe** the process of breathing. ★ 1.A
- **Describe** six common problems of the respiratory system.

Terms to Learn

- circulatory system
- blood
- artery
- vein
- respiratory system
- lung

What does the heart do?

Jabari's mother has high blood pressure. The doctor told Jabari's mom to change her diet and to get more exercise. Now, she has to watch the amount of salt and fat in her diet.

Jabari's mom has a problem with her circulatory system. Your **circulatory system** is a system made up of three parts—your heart, your blood vessels, and your blood.

Circulation: All Aboard!

The circulatory system is like a train that picks up objects in one town and takes them to another. The major function of the circulatory system is to transport nutrients and gases to different parts of the body where they can be used by the cells. Another function is to take waste materials from the cells to the kidneys, lungs, and skin, where the wastes can be removed. The blood does the actual carrying of these materials, but the heart is the pump that pushes the blood through the body. The heart, shown in Figure 18, is made of cardiac muscle. Every beat of your heart pushes blood through your body and back to the heart. Your blood vessels are like pipes through which the blood flows. Blood vessels are made mainly of smooth muscle and elastic tissue. ★ 1.A

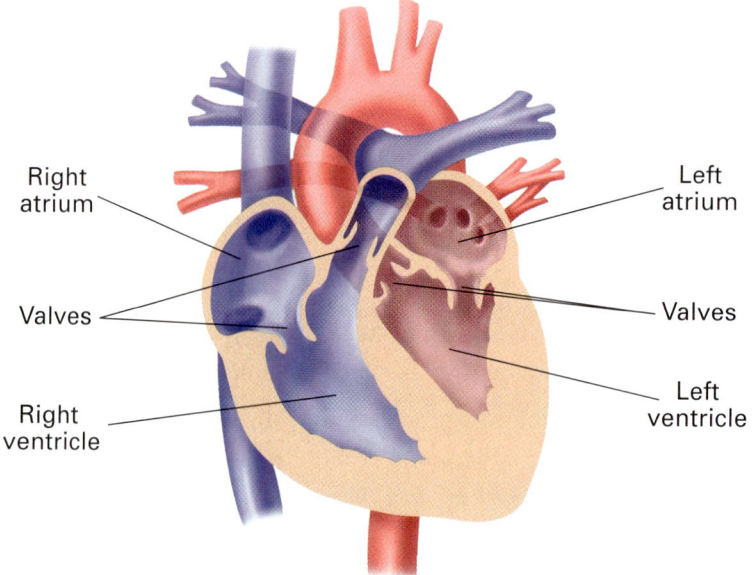

Figure 18 Your heart is a four-chambered organ that pumps blood through the body.

128 | Chapter 5 Your Body Systems

Figure 19 The Components of Blood

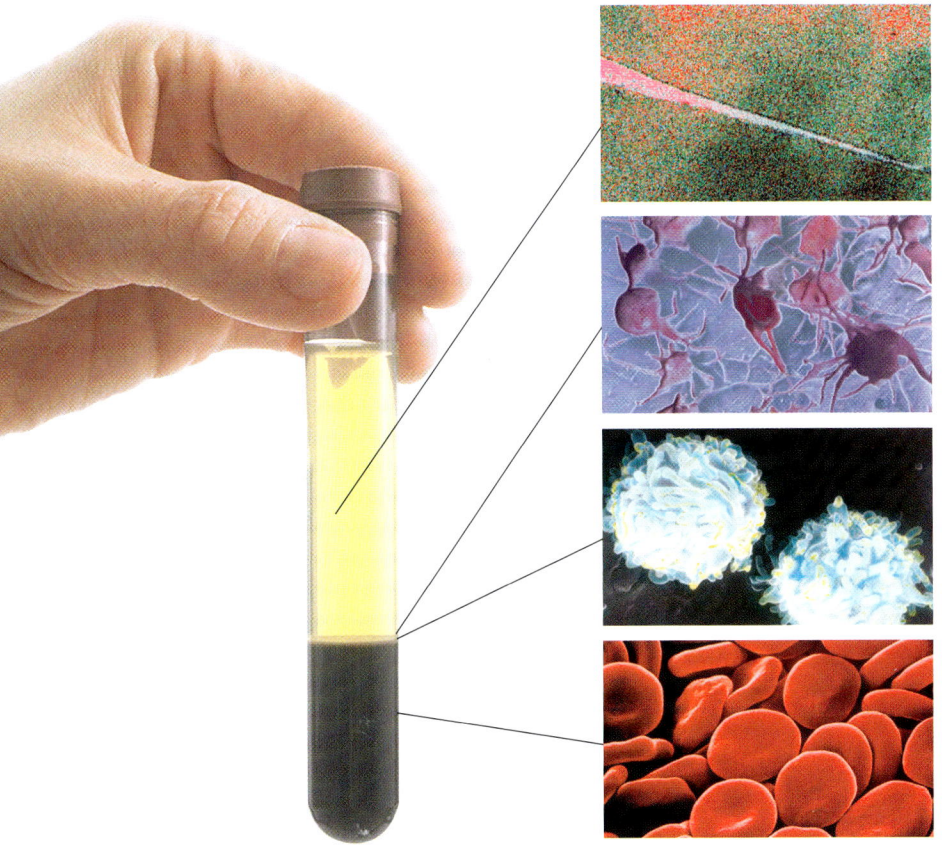

Plasma is the fluid part of blood. It is a mixture of water, minerals, nutrients, sugars, proteins, and other substances. Red blood cells, white blood cells, and platelets are carried by the plasma.

Platelets are small parts of bone marrow cells. Platelets clump together in damaged areas of your body. This clumping forms blood clots and stops you from bleeding.

White blood cells (WBCs) help you stay healthy by destroying bacteria, viruses, and other foreign particles that enter your body.

Red blood cells (RBCs) are the most abundant cells in blood. RBCs contain a protein called *hemoglobin,* which allows the RBCs to carry oxygen to the cells of your body.

What Is Blood?

Your body has about 5 liters of blood. Blood is a tissue that is made of liquid, cell parts, and two types of cells. Blood contains both liquids and solids. Approximately 55 percent of blood is a liquid called *plasma*. Ninety percent of plasma is water. Plasma carries nutrients, hormones, and waste products from one part of the body to another. Plasma also contains proteins that are important for blood clotting and fighting disease.

The other 45 percent of blood consists of solids that include blood cells and cell parts called *platelets*. The blood cells and platelets are carried by the plasma. *Platelets* are cell fragments that help repair blood vessels and form blood clots. There are two major kinds of blood cells. Red blood cells, or RBCs, are the most numerous blood cells. Red blood cells transport oxygen and carbon dioxide through the body. Red blood cells contain a protein known as *hemoglobin*. Oxygen and carbon dioxide attach to the hemoglobin. The hemoglobin carries the gases through the body. White blood cells, or WBCs, are large cells that help you stay healthy by fighting infection and protecting the body from foreign particles. Red blood cells, many white blood cells, and platelets are all made in the bone marrow.

★ 1.A

Brain Food

Your blood cells don't live as long as you do. Each type of cell has a different life span. RBCs live about 120 to 130 days. Some WBCs live a little longer than a year, and platelets live about 10 days.

Lesson 6 The Circulatory and Respiratory Systems

Figure 20 The Flow of Blood Through the Body

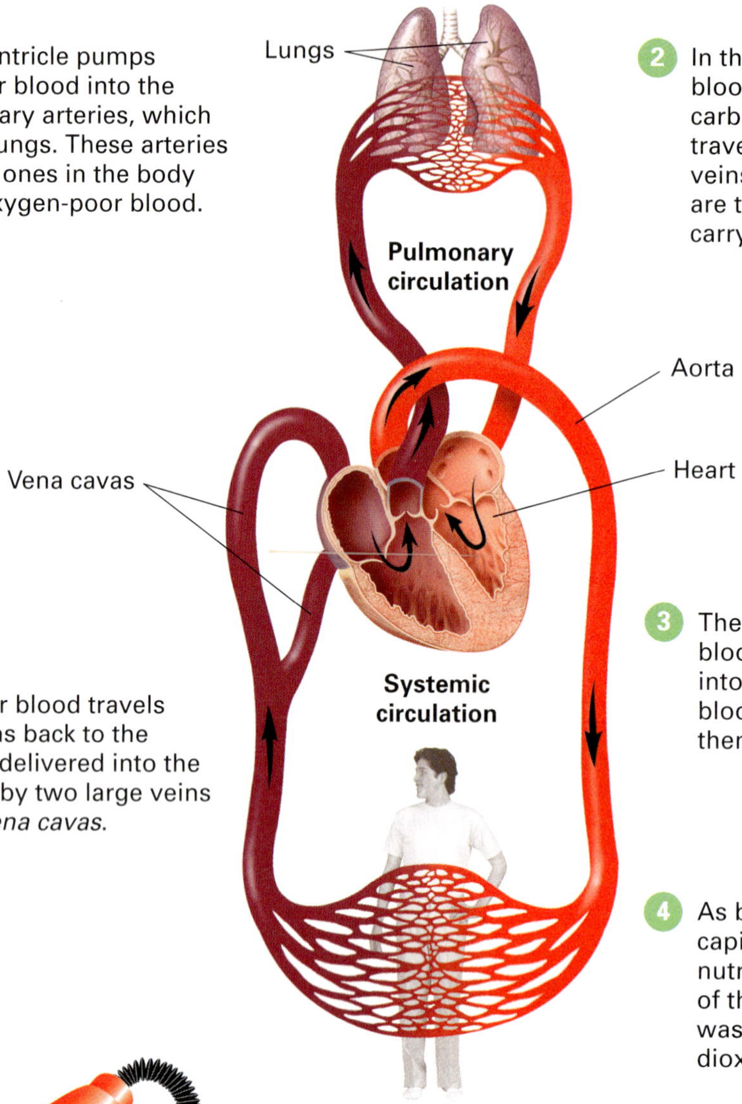

1 The right ventricle pumps oxygen-poor blood into the two pulmonary arteries, which lead to the lungs. These arteries are the only ones in the body that carry oxygen-poor blood.

2 In the capillaries of the lungs, blood receives oxygen and releases carbon dioxide. Oxygen-rich blood travels through the four pulmonary veins to the left atrium. These veins are the only ones in the body that carry oxygen-rich blood.

3 The heart pumps oxygen-rich blood from the left ventricle into the aorta. From the aorta, blood flows into the arteries and then into the capillaries.

4 As blood travels through the capillaries, it transports oxygen, nutrients, and water to the cells of the body. At the same time, waste materials and carbon dioxide are carried away.

5 Oxygen-poor blood travels through veins back to the heart and is delivered into the right atrium by two large veins called the *vena cavas*.

STUDY TIP *for better reading*

Word Origins Your circulatory system is also called the cardiovascular system. The word *cardio* means "heart" and the word *vascular* means "vessels." How does this information help you remember the parts of the circulatory system?

Supply Lines

When the heart contracts, it pumps blood into arteries. **Arteries** are blood vessels that carry blood away from the heart. The vessels that return blood to the heart are called **veins.** The microscopic blood vessels of the body that link the arteries and veins are called *capillaries*. Capillaries are where materials such as oxygen, carbon dioxide, nutrients, and waste products enter and leave the bloodstream. Figure 20 describes the flow of blood through the body. ★ 1.A

Common Circulatory Problems

The circulatory system is vital to the health of the body's cells. If cells do not get the oxygen and nutrients they need, they will die. If wastes are not removed from the cells, the cells will die. Table 9 describes some common problems of the circulatory system.
★ 1.A

TABLE 9 Problems of the Circulatory System

Problem	Description	Treatment or prevention
Hypertension (HIE puhr TEN shuhn)	abnormally high blood pressure in the arteries of the body; may increase the chance of stroke and heart attack	may be treated and prevented by losing weight; by eating a healthy diet; by not smoking; and by taking medications
Heart attack	a situation in which the blood supply to the heart is reduced or stopped, which injures the heart muscle	a medical emergency; must be treated by a medical professional
Anemia (uh NEE mee uh)	a condition in which the number of red blood cells or the amount of hemoglobin is below normal	treated with vitamin B-12, iron supplements, and medications that increase the number of RBCs
Sickle cell anemia	a genetic condition in which the red blood cells are sickle-shaped and contain an abnormal type of hemoglobin	cannot be cured and may require hospitalization at times
Leukemia (loo KEE mee uh)	a cancer of the tissues of the body that produce white blood cells	treated with chemotherapy
Hemophilia (HEE moh FIL ee uh)	a genetic disease in which the blood does not clot or clots very slowly	treated by blood transfusions and by avoiding situations that might cause bleeding

★ 3.A

The Respiratory System: Why You Breathe

Your cells use oxygen to perform their functions and produce carbon dioxide as a waste product. The **respiratory system** is the body system that brings oxygen into the body and removes carbon dioxide from the body. These gases are forced into and out of your body through breathing.

When you breathe, air enters the body through the nose and mouth. Then, air passes into the throat, or *pharynx*. After the pharynx, air passes into the voice box, or the larynx. From the larynx, air enters the windpipe, or trachea. The trachea divides into two tubes called *bronchi*, which allow the air to enter into the lungs. The **lungs** are large, spongelike organs in which oxygen and carbon dioxide are passed between the blood and the environment. ★ 1.A

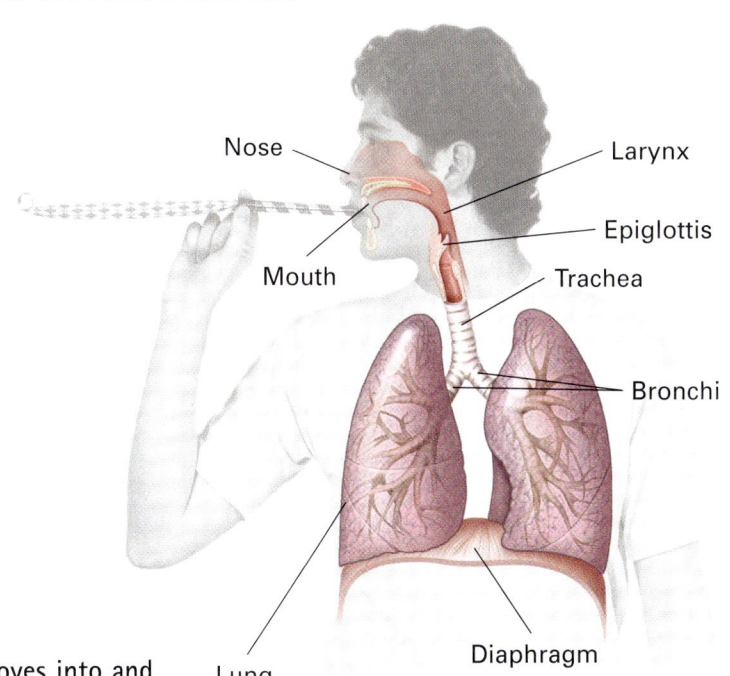

Figure 21 Air moves into and out of the body through the respiratory system.

Lesson 6 The Circulatory and Respiratory Systems | 131

How You Breathe

The movement of air into and out of the lungs is caused by movement of the diaphragm. The *diaphragm* is a dome-shaped muscle beneath the lungs. When the diaphragm and the muscles between the ribs contract, air enters the lungs. Air leaves the lungs when the same muscles relax. In the lungs, gases move between the blood and tiny air sacs called *alveoli*. Figure 22 explains what happens when you breathe. ★ 1.A

Figure 22 Breathing

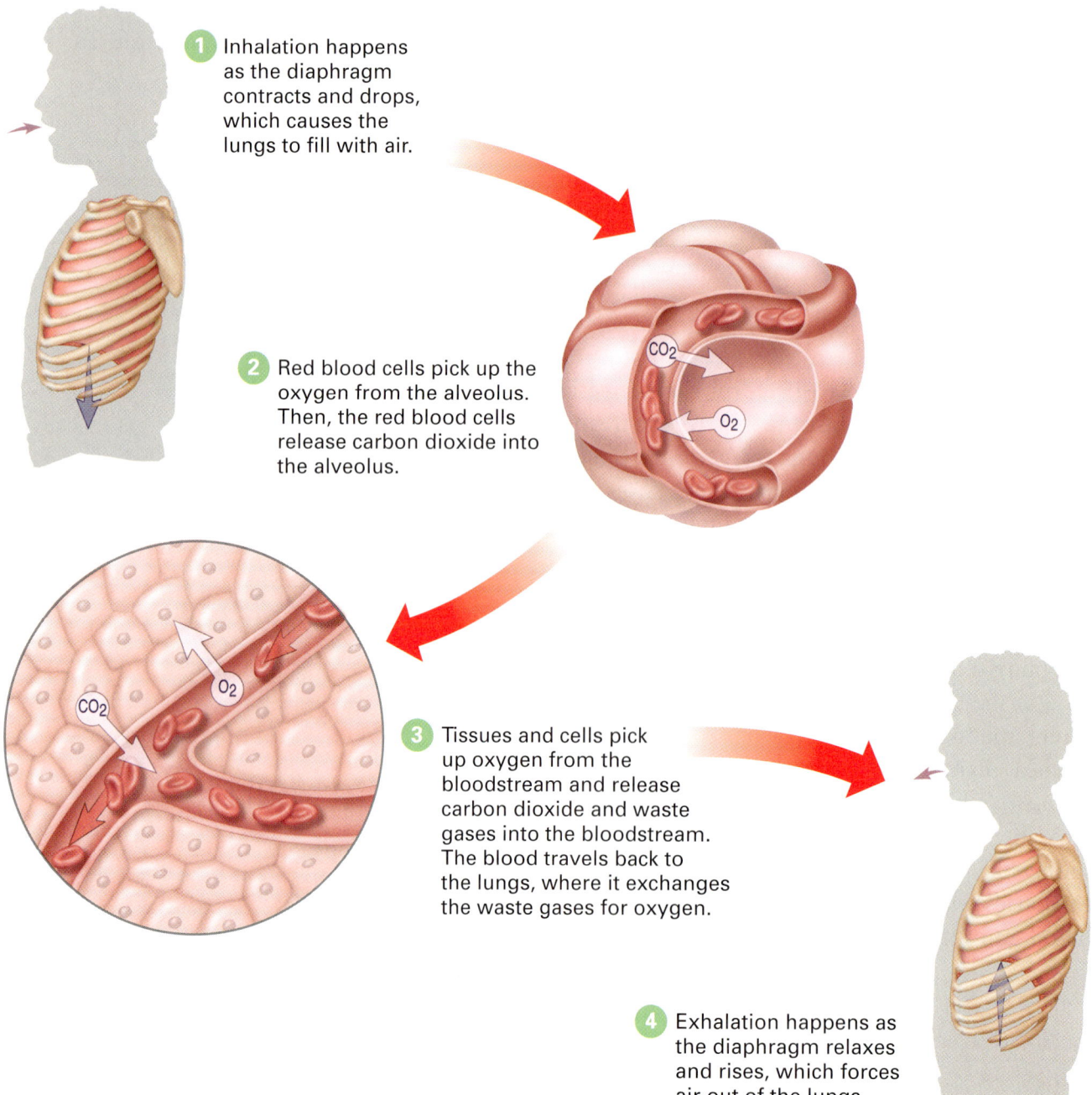

1. Inhalation happens as the diaphragm contracts and drops, which causes the lungs to fill with air.

2. Red blood cells pick up the oxygen from the alveolus. Then, the red blood cells release carbon dioxide into the alveolus.

3. Tissues and cells pick up oxygen from the bloodstream and release carbon dioxide and waste gases into the bloodstream. The blood travels back to the lungs, where it exchanges the waste gases for oxygen.

4. Exhalation happens as the diaphragm relaxes and rises, which forces air out of the lungs.

132 | **Chapter 5** Your Body Systems

Common Respiratory Problems

The air that you breathe may contain harmful materials that can affect your health. Your respiratory system helps protect you from these materials. One way to help protect your respiratory system is to avoid smoking tobacco and using drugs. Table 10 describes some common problems of the respiratory system.

TABLE 10 Problems of the Respiratory System

Problem	Description	Treatment or prevention
Tuberculosis (too BUHR kyoo LOH sis)	a contagious infection that affects the lungs and causes chest pain and difficulty breathing; caused by bacteria in the air	treated with antibiotics
Pneumonia (noo MOHN yuh)	an inflammation of the lungs in which the alveoli become filled with a thick fluid	treated with rest, fluids, and antibiotics; may be prevented by avoiding contact with infected people
Bronchitis (brahng KIET is)	an inflammation of the bronchi that often includes a cough that brings mucus into the mouth	treated with rest, aspirin, cough medicine, and antibiotics; may be prevented by avoiding individuals with bronchitis and by not smoking
Asthma (AZ muh)	an allergic response in which the airways contract and fill with large amount of mucus; caused by "triggers," such as pollen, dust, smoke, cold air, stress, or strenuous exercise	treated with drugs that widen the airway and reduce mucus production; may be prevented by avoiding triggers
Emphysema (EM fuh SEE muh)	a condition in which the alveoli in the lungs break; leads to difficulty breathing	can't be cured; can be treated with medication; may be prevented by avoiding cigarette smoke
Lung cancer	a cancer that destroys lung tissue; the most common type of cancer in women and men	treated with surgery and chemotherapy or radiation therapy; may be prevented by not smoking

★ 3.A

Lesson Review

Using Vocabulary

1. Define *blood*, and describe its parts.

Understanding Concepts

2. How does the circulatory system transport and distribute nutrients and gases? ★ 1.A

3. List and describe two problems of the circulatory system.

4. List and describe two problems of the respiratory system.

5. Describe the process of breathing. ★ 1.A

Critical Thinking

6. **Analyzing Viewpoints** Some doctors say that air pollution is causing a rise in the number of people with asthma. Why might air pollution be harmful to the respiratory system? ★ 1.A; 6.A

internet connect
www.scilinks.org/health
Topic: Respiration
HealthLinks code: HD4082

HEALTH LINKS Maintained by the National Science Teachers Association

Lesson 7　Caring for Your Body

What You'll Do

- **Explain** how the health of body systems affects total physical health. ⭐ 1.A
- **Describe** six ways to protect the body systems from harm. ⭐ 1.A; 3.A

Start Off Write

List some healthy habits that help protect your body systems.

Helen's brother Mike came home from college because he was sick. The doctor said that Mike got sick because he didn't sleep enough and ate only junk food. Mike was not taking care of his body properly.

If a car is not given the right fuel, or if any one part stops working, the car cannot be driven. If your body is not given the right fuel, or if any system does not function properly, your entire body is at risk for disease.

Body Systems and Total Health

Like the parts of a car, each system in your body depends on the other systems to maintain your overall health. If one system fails, the functioning of the other body systems is affected. One malfunction can lead to many different health problems. For example, if the kidneys are damaged or diseased, they will not be able to remove waste products from the body. As waste products build up in the blood, other organs of the body may stop working. Kidney failure can lead to weakened bones, stomach ulcers, high blood pressure, and damage to the central nervous system. Many people who experience kidney failure develop anemia because their bone marrow does not make enough red blood cells. Their blood is not able to carry enough oxygen to the cells of their body, and the cells stop functioning correctly. The resulting health problems could lead to comas, heart failure, and even death. This example shows how a simple malfunction in one body system can lead to a life-threatening disease.

Protecting your body systems is important to maintaining your health. By learning to make good health decisions now, you can protect your health for years to come. ⭐ 1.A

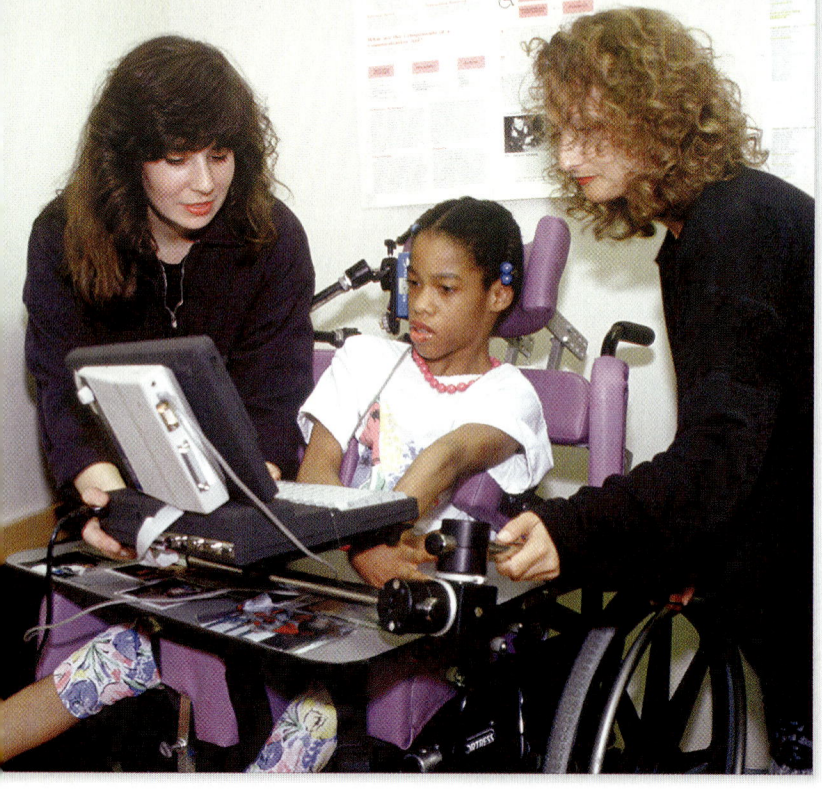

Figure 23 Cerebral palsy affects not only the nervous system but also the muscular system.

134　Chapter 5　Your Body Systems

Staying Healthy

To keep your car running properly you must take care of it and avoid accidents. You must also take care of your body to keep it functioning properly and keep it healthy. The list below contains some tips for staying healthy.

- Eat a healthy, well balanced diet. Healthy foods provide the proper amounts of nutrients that your body needs for energy. These foods also help prevent some diseases.
- Drink lots of water every day. Water helps flush waste products out of your body. Water is an important part of your blood and other body fluids.
- Get enough exercise. Exercise builds strong muscles and bones, helps maintain a healthy weight, and increases the number of blood cells and blood vessels. Building strong muscles also helps you maintain good posture, which helps your body systems function properly.
- Avoid injuries and accidents that may cause damage to body organs by wearing proper safety equipment when playing sports, riding a bicycle, or working with tools.
- Avoid using alcohol, illegal drugs, and tobacco.
- Visit a doctor for a checkup every year and any time you don't feel well. Make sure your immunizations are current; immunizations protect you from getting certain diseases. ★ 1.A; 3.A

ASSESSING YOUR HEALTH

Describe your posture. Do you slouch? When you are sitting in class, are your shoulders rounded or is your back straight? How are your feet positioned on the floor? What types of changes can you make to improve your posture?

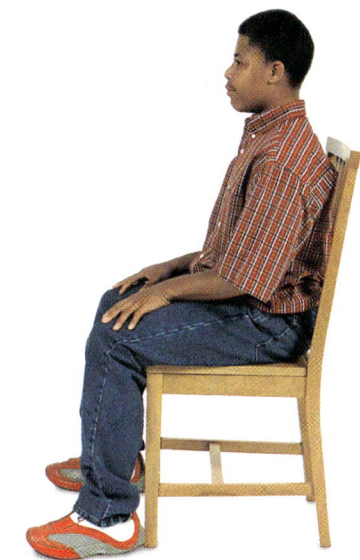

Figure 24 When you slouch, you squeeze the organs in your abdomen. If you sit up straight, your organs can rest in their proper places.

Lesson Review

Understanding Concepts

1. List six ways to care for your body systems. ★ 1.A; 3.A
2. How does the health of each body system affect the overall health of an individual? ★ 1.A

Critical Thinking

3. **Identifying Relationships** What systems of the body are affected by alcohol and tobacco smoke? Explain your answer. ★ 1.A; 6.A

Lesson 7 Caring for Your Body

5 CHAPTER REVIEW

Chapter Summary

- The body is composed of cells, tissues, organs and body systems that work together to keep the body functioning properly.
- The nervous system and the endocrine systems are the primary controlling and communicating systems of the body.
- The skeletal system forms the framework of the body and works with the muscular system to cause movement.
- The digestive system provides nutrients for the cells of the body.
- The urinary system helps the body get rid of liquid waste products.
- The circulatory system transports materials through the body.
- The respiratory system brings oxygen into the body and removes carbon dioxide from the body.

Using Vocabulary

For each pair of terms, describe how the meanings of the terms differ.

1. bone/joint
2. tissue/organ
3. artery/vein
4. gland/hormone

For each sentence, fill in the blank with the proper term from the word bank provided below.

body system(s)   hormone(s)
diaphragm   nerve(s)
urine

5. A chemical messenger that helps regulate body functions is called a(n) ___.
6. The nervous system uses ___, or bundles of cells that conduct electrical signals, to relay messages to the body.
7. A group of organs that work together for one purpose is called a(n) ___.
8. The ___ is the muscle that contracts to allow air to enter the lungs.
9. The liquid waste product expelled by the urinary system is ___.

Understanding Concepts

10. Why are the lungs and the small intestine lined by a very large number of capillaries? ★ 1.A
11. Describe how the kidneys filter blood.
12. Describe how cells, tissues, and organs work together in the human body. ★ 1.A
13. List and describe one problem of each body system.
14. Give two examples of how the health of a single organ system can affect the overall health of a person. ★ 1.A
15. How does the nervous system control the other body systems? ★ 1.A
16. How do hormones affect growth and development? What other functions does the endocrine system have? ★ 1.A; 3.B
17. Explain how muscle's ability to contract allows it to move the body.
18. List three types of joints, and explain the motion of each type.
19. Explain how your body gets energy from the food you eat. ★ 1.A
20. Describe the process of breathing. ★ 1.A

Critical Thinking

Identifying Relationships

21. How can wearing a seatbelt when riding in a car help protect the health of your body systems? ★ 3.A; 4.C; 5.A

22. Cancer patients are sometimes treated with drugs that can kill bone marrow cells. Bone marrow makes red blood cells. Based on what you know about red blood cells, why might people taking these drugs sometimes be tired and have no energy?

23. Why are some body movements not possible when a bone is broken?

Making Good Decisions

24. Use what you have learned in this chapter to set a personal goal. Write your goal, and make an action plan by using the Health Behavior Contract for improving the health of your body systems. You can find the Health Behavior Contract at **go.hrw.com.** Just type in the keyword **HD4HBC11.**

Interpreting Graphics

Daily Body Temperature Changes

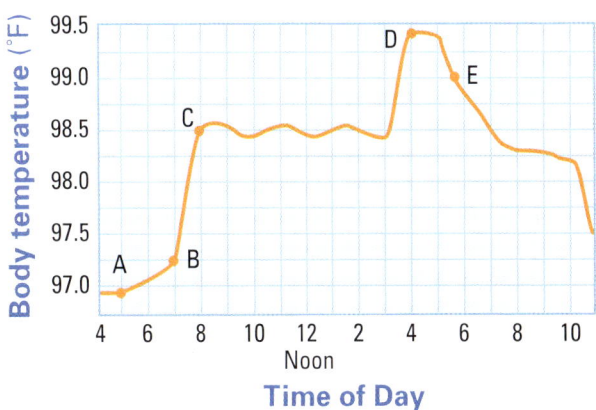

Time of Day

Use the figure above to answer questions 25–28. ★ M8.5.A

25. The graph above is a record of Tamiko's body temperature from 4 A.M. to 11 P.M. on Tuesday. Tamiko is feeling fine, and her normal body temperature is 98.6°F. School starts at 8 A.M., and Tamiko has soccer practice at 3 P.M. Why do you think Tamiko's temperature is below 98.6°F at point A on the graph?

26. Why do you think Tamiko's temperature rose at point B?

27. Why do you think Tamiko's temperature became steady at point C?

28. Why do you think Tamiko's temperature decreased at point E?

Reading Checkup

Take a minute to review your answers to the Health IQ questions at the beginning of this chapter. How has reading this chapter improved your Health IQ?

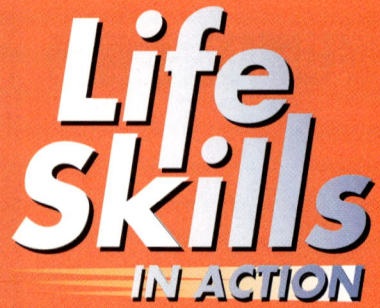

Life Skills IN ACTION

Practicing Wellness

Practicing wellness means practicing good health habits. Positive health behaviors can help prevent injury, illness, disease, and even premature death. Complete the following activity to learn how you can practice wellness.

Kwame's Concerns

ACT 1

Setting the Scene

Kwame's father has just been diagnosed with heart disease. He explained the symptoms and possible causes of the disease to Kwame. Kwame's father also told him that the disease is genetic and that several members of their family have the disease. Kwame is concerned that he might get heart disease when he is older. Therefore, he wants to change his health behaviors now to reduce his chances for getting the disease in the future. ★ 1.A; 3.B

The 4 Steps of Practicing Wellness

1. Choose a health behavior that you want to improve or change.
2. Gather information on how you can improve that behavior.
3. Start using the improved health behavior.
4. Evaluate the effects of the health behavior.

Guided Practice

Practice with a Friend

Form a group of three. Have one person play the role of Kwame and another person play the role of Kwame's father. Have the third person be an observer. Walking through each of the four steps of practicing wellness, role-play Kwame trying to reduce his chances of getting heart disease. Have Kwame talk to his father about ways to maintain a healthy heart and circulatory system. The observer will take notes, which will include observations about what the person playing Kwame did well and suggestions of ways to improve. Stop after each step to evaluate the process. ★ 1.A; 3.B

Independent Practice

Check Yourself

After you complete the guided practice, go through Act 1 again without stopping at each step. Answer the questions below to review what you did.

1. Why is it important for Kwame to adopt good health behaviors when he is young? ⭐ 1.A; 3.A
2. Describe the health behaviors that Kwame decided to improve. How do these health behaviors help maintain the health of his heart? ⭐ 1.A; 3.A
3. How can Kwame evaluate the effects of his improved health behaviors on his health? ⭐ 4.B
4. Why is it sometimes difficult to change a health behavior?

On Your Own

To reduce his risk of heart disease, Kwame has started eating a heart healthy diet and is now exercising regularly. However, he finds that his muscles become very tired and sore when he exercises. Kwame decides that he needs to work on his muscle strength. Write a short story about how Kwame can use the four steps of practicing wellness to build muscle strength.

CHAPTER 6
Physical Fitness

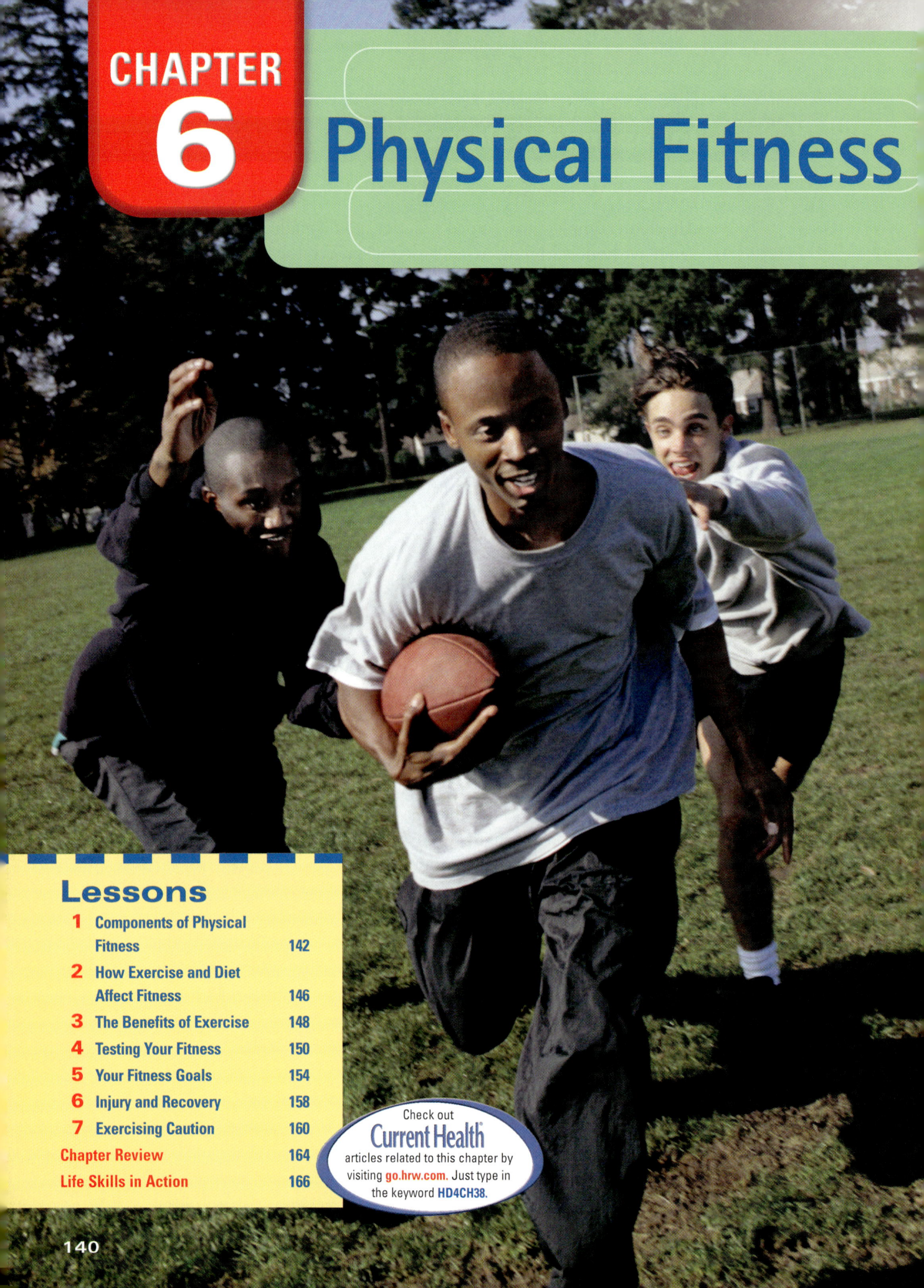

Lessons

1. Components of Physical Fitness — 142
2. How Exercise and Diet Affect Fitness — 146
3. The Benefits of Exercise — 148
4. Testing Your Fitness — 150
5. Your Fitness Goals — 154
6. Injury and Recovery — 158
7. Exercising Caution — 160

Chapter Review — 164
Life Skills in Action — 166

Check out **Current Health** articles related to this chapter by visiting **go.hrw.com**. Just type in the keyword **HD4CH38**.

" **I never** thought anything about **exercising by myself.** Then I got hurt, and **no one was around** to help me. I was lucky. A neighbor found me and took me to the hospital. Now I always exercise with my friends. "

Health IQ

PRE-READING

Answer the following multiple-choice questions to find out what you already know about physical fitness. When you've finished this chapter, you'll have the opportunity to change your answers based on what you've learned.

1. Exercise
   a. prevents disease.
   b. improves fitness.
   c. gives you a chance to make new friends.
   d. All of the above ⭐ 1.A

2. Which of the following tests flexibility?
   a. sit and reach
   b. pull-ups
   c. 1-mile run
   d. curl-ups

3. Which of the following is NOT a warning sign of injury?
   a. swelling
   b. tenderness
   c. muscle soreness
   d. numbness and tingling

4. Which of the following is a chronic injury?
   a. fracture
   b. stress fracture
   c. sprain
   d. strain

5. Which of the following activities helps prevent injury when exercising?
   a. warming up and cooling down
   b. stretching
   c. using good form
   d. all of the above ⭐ 1.A

6. Which of the following foods provides protein for strong muscles?
   a. lean meat and beans
   b. fruits and vegetables
   c. breads and pastas
   d. none of the above ⭐ 1.A

ANSWERS: 1. d; 2. a; 3. c; 4. b; 5. d; 6. a

Chapter 6 Physical Fitness

Lesson 1

Components of Physical Fitness

What You'll Do

- **Describe** the five components of physical fitness. ★ 1.A

Terms to Learn

- physical fitness
- muscular strength
- muscular endurance
- cardiorespiratory endurance
- flexibility
- body composition

What is physical fitness?

Felix and his mom were cleaning the house. She asked him to help her move some furniture. Felix hadn't noticed before, but lifting things has been easier since he started his martial arts class.

Activities such as martial arts help improve physical fitness. **Physical fitness** is the ability to do everyday tasks without becoming short of breath, sore, or tired. There are five components of physical fitness—muscular strength, muscular endurance, cardiorespiratory endurance, flexibility, and body composition.

Muscular Strength

The amount of force muscles apply when they are used is called **muscular strength** (MUHS kyoo luhr STRENGKTH). This force can be measured as the amount of weight you can lift. Strong muscles support bones and joints. Muscular strength can keep you from getting hurt. It helps you deal with falls and other accidents that can cause injury. Felix used muscular strength when he helped move the furniture.

If you can move a large amount of weight, you probably have good muscular strength. But muscular strength is only one part of physical fitness. To be fit, you need to work on all five components. ★ 1.A

The U.S. Postal Service requires many of its package handlers to be able to lift as much as 70 pounds.

Figure 1 Many everyday tasks require muscular strength.

Muscular Endurance

Felix and his mom probably had to move the furniture several times. To do all that work, they used muscular endurance (en DOOR uhns). **Muscular endurance** is the ability to use a group of muscles over and over without getting tired easily. Muscular strength and muscular endurance are related. Muscular strength lets you lift something heavy. Muscular endurance lets you lift it over and over again. ★ 1.A

Cardiorespiratory Endurance

Have you ever noticed that your heart beats faster when you're working hard? Your breathing probably gets faster too. If you have good cardiorespiratory (KAHR dee oh RES puhr uh TAWR'ee) endurance, you can probably exercise for several minutes before you notice your faster breathing. **Cardiorespiratory endurance** is the ability of your heart and lungs to work efficiently during physical activity.

Aerobic activity improves cardiorespiratory endurance. During aerobic activity, your body uses oxygen to get energy. Examples of aerobic activity are running, walking, cross-country skiing, and cycling.

The number of times your heart beats per minute is called *heart rate*. When you are resting, your heart rate is called *resting heart rate* (RHR). *Recovery time* is how long it takes your heart rate to return to RHR after activity. You can use RHR and recovery time to measure your cardiorespiratory endurance. If you are fit, your RHR will probably be lower than the RHR of someone who isn't fit. You will also have a shorter recovery time if you are fit. ★ 1.A

Myth & Fact

Myth: Jogging is a better physical activity than walking is.

Fact: Any physical activity that gets your heart going is good for you. Jogging isn't better for you than walking is. You just have to spend more time walking to get the same benefit as jogging.

Figure 2 There are many physical activities that improve cardiorespiratory endurance.

SCIENCE ACTIVITY

Some people are so flexible that they can bend their bodies in ways that seem impossible. These people are called *contortionists* (kuhn TAWR shuhn ists). Use your school library or the Internet to find out why these people are so flexible. Make a poster describing how it's possible to be a "human pretzel."

Flexibility

When you bend, twist, or reach, you're using the fourth component of fitness: flexibility (FLEK suh BIL uh tee). **Flexibility** is the ability to use joints easily.

How flexible a joint is depends on the bones of the joint. It also depends on three types of soft tissue: muscles, tendons, and ligaments. Muscle is the most elastic, or stretchy, tissue of the three. Therefore, muscle has the greatest affect on flexibility. It can be stretched more than other tissues. Tendons connect muscles to bone. Touch the back of your ankle, just above your heel. The cord that you feel is a tendon called the *Achilles'* (uh KIL EEZ) *tendon*. It attaches your calf muscle to your heel. Tendons are less elastic than muscle is. Ligaments are bands of tissue that connect the bones in a joint. Ligaments don't stretch as much as muscles and tendons do.

Flexible joints are less likely to get injured. To stay flexible, you need to lengthen the tissues around a joint, especially the muscles. Regular physical activity is usually enough to stay flexible. You can also stretch. Stretching lengthens and relaxes muscles around a joint. During a growth spurt, your bones grow faster than the muscles around them do. You may become less flexible. Regular stretching can help you stay flexible. ★ 1.A

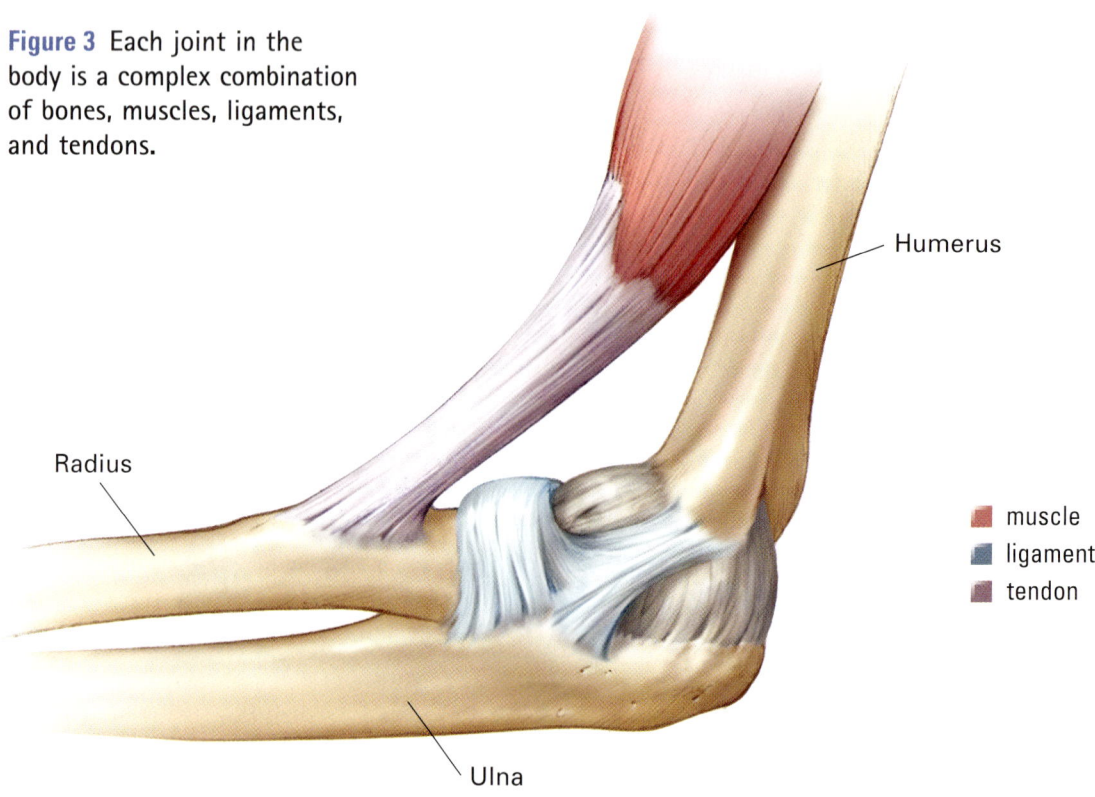

Figure 3 Each joint in the body is a complex combination of bones, muscles, ligaments, and tendons.

Figure 4 The best way to improve your body composition is through fun physical activities.

Body Composition

Has your teacher or doctor ever tested your body composition? The fifth component of fitness, **body composition,** compares the weight of fat in your body to the weight of your bones, muscles, and organs. Your body composition changes throughout your life. Women usually have a higher percentage of body fat than men do. This doesn't mean women are less healthy or less fit than men are. Women simply need more body fat than men to carry out certain body functions.

Fat plays an important role in the way your body works. However, too much fat can lead to diseases such as heart disease, diabetes, and obesity. Poor body composition can make moving some joints difficult. It also makes the heart and lungs work harder during physical activity. Activity and good nutrition are the keys to good body composition. If you get regular physical activity, you can have good body composition. Physical activity reduces fat and increases lean tissues such as muscle.

★ 1.A

Myth & Fact

Myth: You can exercise specific areas of the body to get rid of fat on them.

Fact: When you exercise, you use fat from all over your body, not just from a single area.

Lesson Review

Using Vocabulary

1. Describe the five components of physical fitness. ★ 1.A

Understanding Concepts

2. How can you use resting heart rate and recovery time to measure cardiorespiratory endurance?

Critical Thinking

3. **Identifying Relationships** How are muscular strength and muscular endurance related? Can you have muscular strength and not muscular endurance? Can you have muscular endurance and not have muscular strength? Explain your answer. ★ 1.A

internet connect
www.scilinks.org/health
Topic: Physical Fitness
HealthLinks code: HD4076

HEALTH LINKS Maintained by the National Science Teachers Association

Lesson 2
How Exercise and Diet Affect Fitness

What You'll Do

- **Describe** the relationship between exercise and physical fitness. ★ 1.A
- **Explain** how diet affects fitness. ★ 1.A

Terms to Learn

- exercise

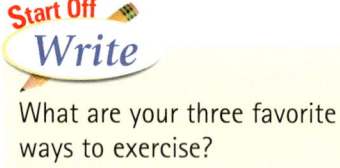

What are your three favorite ways to exercise?

Josef has been playing basketball for a few years. Practices are hard. But Josef always has a good time playing. He knows that basketball is helping him stay fit.

Today, many people don't get enough physical activity to stay fit. Therefore, we need to exercise. **Exercise** is any activity that maintains or improves your physical fitness. For Josef, basketball is a fun way to exercise.

Exercise to Be Fit

To improve your fitness, you need to exercise your body more than you normally do. This increased amount of exercise is called *overload*. Overload tires your muscles. Your body also uses fuels so your muscles can work during an overload. Your body heals itself and replaces these fuels while you rest. Muscles are made stronger during rest. Overload followed by rest gets your body ready for more hard exercise. If you slowly increase overload, your fitness keeps improving. Be careful, though. Too much exercise can cause injury.

Different activities improve different components of fitness. For example, stretching does not improve your muscular strength as much as lifting weights does. So, lifting weights is the better exercise for improving muscular strength. Stretching is better for improving your flexibility. ★ 1.A

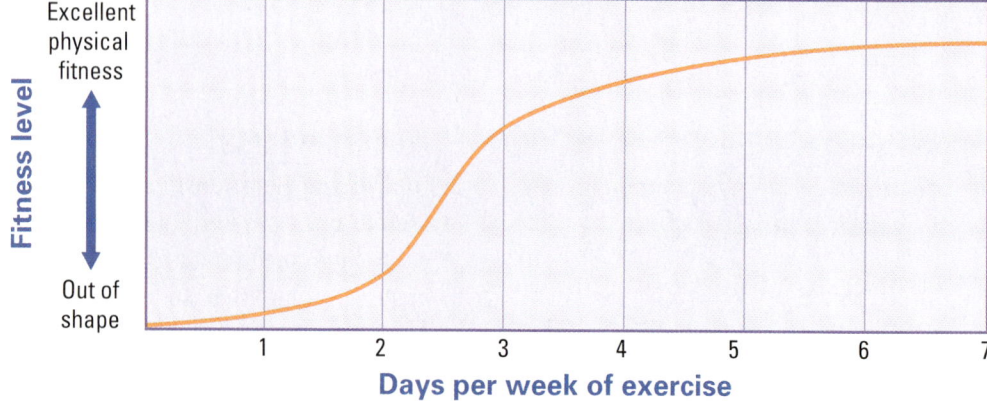

Figure 5 You should exercise 3 to 5 days per week to be fit. If you exercise 6 or 7 days a week, your risk of injury increases without further benefit to your fitness level.

Source: Gardner, James B. and J. Gerry Purdy, *Computerized Running Training Programs*.

Chapter 6 Physical Fitness

Figure 6 A balanced diet combined with exercise benefits physical fitness.

Eating Well to Exercise Well

You need to eat well to get the most from exercise. Food is fuel for physical activity. Food also provides building blocks for strong muscles and bones. Fruits and vegetables give quick energy. They also provide vitamins and minerals, which help your body repair itself after exercise. Breads and pastas give you the energy you need for exercise. Lean meats and beans give you the protein your body uses to build strong muscles. Dairy products and green, leafy vegetables provide calcium. You need calcium for strong bones and muscles.

You need good fuel to do your best during exercise. Junk food and foods high in fat don't provide good fuel. Not eating enough food also hurts how well you exercise. If you don't eat enough food, you won't have enough energy to keep going.
★ 1.A

Health Journal
List what you ate before the last time you exercised. Describe how you felt during your exercise.

Lesson Review

Using Vocabulary
1. How does exercise affect physical fitness? ★ 1.A

Understanding Concepts
2. How does what you eat affect your ability to exercise? ★ 1.A

Critical Thinking
3. **Using Refusal Skills** Alejandro runs on the track team. Alejandro knows that he races better when he eats a good meal. Some of his teammates want to go to a fast-food restaurant before their next race. They've asked him to go. What should Alejandro say to his teammates? Explain your answer.

Lesson 3 The Benefits of Exercise

What You'll Do

- **Describe** the physical benefits of exercise. ★ 1.A
- **Explain** how exercise benefits mental and emotional health. ★ 1.A
- **Describe** the social benefits of exercise. ★ 1.A

Start Off Write

What are the social benefits of exercise?

`Shelby's doctor wants Shelby to exercise more. Shelby explained that she isn't an athlete. The doctor said that physical activity isn't just sports. The doctor also said that exercise can prevent some diseases.`

Preventing disease is only one benefit of exercise. In this lesson, you will learn about how exercise is good for you.

Physical Benefits

Regular exercise helps you have good physical fitness. When you exercise regularly, you become stronger. Your heart and lungs work better. You're also more flexible. Exercise improves body composition by burning fat and increasing muscle weight. Exercise can also improve coordination, or the ability to make complicated movements.

In the short term, exercise can help prevent muscle weakness and shortness of breath. In the long term, exercise can help prevent obesity and disease such as diabetes and heart disease. Exercise burns fat and reduces your chances of obesity. Obesity is linked to both diabetes and heart disease. By reducing your chances of obesity, you reduce your chances of diabetes and heart disease. So, exercise may help you live longer. ★ 1.A

Figure 7 Exercise is good for everyone, regardless of age.

Mental and Emotional Benefits

Did you know that exercise affects your mental and emotional health? When you exercise for a long period of time, your brain makes chemicals called *endorphins* (en DAWR fins). Endorphins make you feel calm. Exercise also improves blood flow to the brain. Improved blood flow makes you feel more awake. You can also think more clearly.

Exercise is also a good way to deal with stress and improve your self-esteem. When you exercise regularly, you relieve the tension caused by stress. As you improve your fitness, you also feel better about yourself. So, exercise improves self-esteem. Exercise can improve your confidence in your abilities, too. ★ 1.A; 11.B

Social Benefits

Exercise gives you a chance to meet new people and make friends. The people you meet will have some of the same interests you have. Many of the people you meet will be on your team. But you can also make friends from other teams at games, matches, and other sporting events.

When you participate in physical activity, you are probably around people who are good influences on your fitness. You work out with people who like to exercise. So, these people are likely to encourage you to keep exercising. One way you can support each other is to cheer for one another. When someone cheers for you, it makes you feel better about yourself. And you have more fun exercising. ★ 1.A

Figure 8 Playing sports is a good way to make new friends.

Health Journal
Write about how physical activities have helped you meet new people.

Lesson Review

Understanding Concepts

1. What are the physical benefits of exercise? ★ 1.A
2. How does exercise benefit your mental and emotional health? ★ 1.A

Critical Thinking

3. **Making Inferences** Some sports don't have teams. Do you think people who participate in these sports still have the social benefits of exercise? Explain your answer. ★ 1.A

internet connect
www.scilinks.org/health
Topic: Health Benefits of Sports
HealthLinks code: HD4050

HEALTH LINKS Maintained by the National Science Teachers Association

Lesson 3 The Benefits of Exercise

Lesson 4

What You'll Do

- **Explain** why you should test your fitness.
- **Explain** why you should monitor your heart rate.
- **Describe** the tests for each of the components of fitness.  1.A; 3.A; 4.C

Terms to Learn

- target heart rate zone
- maximum heart rate

Start Off Write

How can you test your muscular strength?

Testing Your Fitness

Torey's coach wants Torey to check his heart rate during practice. Torey doesn't understand why he has to check it. But his coach says that monitoring his heart rate will help him know if his fitness is improving.

Checking heart rate is just one way to test your fitness. In this lesson, you will learn how to test the five components of fitness.

Why Test Your Fitness?

Knowing your fitness strengths can help you choose new activities to try. Knowing your weaknesses helps you plan to improve your physical fitness. Regular fitness testing also helps you check for changes in your fitness. Your physical education teacher can probably help you test your fitness. A doctor may be able to help you test some components of fitness, such as body composition.

When you decide to play a sport, you should get a sports physical. A *sports physical* is a medical checkup before playing a sport. The doctor checks your height, weight, heart rate, blood pressure, and reflexes. Your health history is an important part of a sports physical. The doctor will ask you and your parents about your past injuries. The doctor will also ask about shots, medicines, and illnesses you've had. The doctor wants to make sure it's safe for you to play a sport. ★ 1.A; 3.A

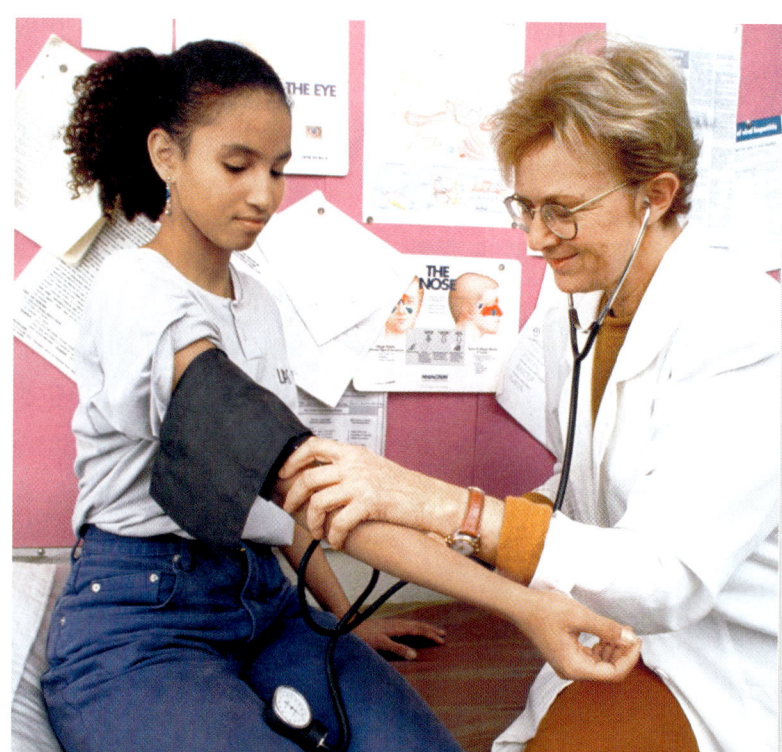

Figure 9 Everyone should visit the doctor before playing sports.

150

Hands-on ACTIVITY

HOW OFTEN DO YOU EXERCISE?

1. In small groups, discuss how often you exercise during the week.

2. Record how many boys and how many girls in your group exercise less than three times per week. How many exercise three or more times per week?

3. Combine the class results. What percentage of the class exercises less than three times per week? three or more times per week?

Analysis

1. Use the Internet or your school library to find national statistics on how often people your age exercise per week. How do your class percentages compare with the national statistics you found?

2. Is there a difference between how often boys exercise and how often girls exercise? Why do you think this is so?

Monitoring Heart Rate

Try checking your heart rate before, during, and after exercise. This can help you find out how exercise is affecting your fitness. It also helps you know if you're exercising hard enough. To improve your fitness, you need to exercise within your target heart rate zone. Your **target heart rate zone** is 60 to 85 percent of your maximum heart rate. Your **maximum heart rate (MHR)** is the largest number of times your heart can beat while exercising. You can estimate your target heart rate zone by using the following equations:

$$MHR = 220 - age$$
$$60\% \text{ of } MHR = MHR \times 0.6$$
$$85\% \text{ of } MHR = MHR \times 0.85$$

What would the target heart rate zone be for a 14-year-old? Use the equations to find out:

$$MHR = 220 - 14 = 206$$
$$60\% \text{ of } MHR = 206 \times 0.6 = 124$$
$$85\% \text{ of } MHR = 206 \times 0.85 = 175$$

So, a 14-year-old's target heart rate zone is between 124 and 175 beats per minute.

MHR isn't affected by fitness, but it decreases as you get older. Resting heart rate (RHR) is usually lower for fit people. Recovery time is also shorter. So, the lower your RHR and the shorter your recovery time, the better your cardiorespiratory endurance. ★ 3.A; 4.C

Figure 10 Heart-rate monitoring should be a regular part of exercise.

Lesson 4 Testing Your Fitness

ASSESSING YOUR HEALTH

Ask your teacher to help you measure your cardio-respiratory endurance, muscular strength, muscular endurance, and flexibility. How do your results compare to the fitness zones chart? Are there any areas in which you need to improve?

Strength, Endurance, and Flexibility

Monitoring your heart rate is just one way to check your fitness. There are also tests for each component of fitness. Some of the most common ways to test physical fitness are:

- **Muscular strength and muscular endurance** are tested with pull-ups and curl-ups. You try to do as many as you can without stopping. The more you do without stopping, the better your muscular strength and muscular endurance are.
- **Cardiorespiratory endurance** is tested by running or walking 1 mile. The faster you finish, the better your cardiorespiratory endurance is.
- **Flexibility** is tested using the sit-and-reach test. A special box measures how far you can reach when you try to reach past your toes. The better your flexibility, the farther you can reach.

Table 1 shows the fitness zones for 13- to 15-year-old boys and girls. These standards are for healthy physical fitness. You don't need to be an athlete to meet these standards. If you are fit, you will be able to meet the lowest standard for each zone. Someone who plays sports will probably meet or exceed the highest standard in each zone. If you don't meet a standard, talk to your parents and teacher. Together, you can think of ways to improve your fitness. ★ 1.A

TABLE 1 Healthy Fitness Zones for Ages 13 to 15

Activity		13	14	15
Pull-ups	Boys	1–4	2–5	3–7
	Girls	1–2	1–2	1–2
Curl-ups	Boys	21–40	24–45	24–47
	Girls	18–32	18–32	18–35
1-mile run (minutes and seconds)	Boys	10:00–7:30	9:30–7:00	9:00–7:00
	Girls	11:30–9:00	11:00–8:30	10:30–8:00
Sit and reach (inches)	Boys	8	8	8
	Girls	10	10	12

Source: FITNESSGRAM.

Estimating Body Composition

Body composition compares fat weight to lean weight in your body. Body composition cannot be directly measured, but it can be estimated. The *body mass index* (BMI) is a formula that uses height and weight to estimate body composition. A high BMI indicates that the ratio of fat weight to lean weight is high.

BMI is commonly used because height and weight are easy to measure. But it is not the only way to test body composition. Another test is the skinfold test. Someone trained to give the test pinches folds of skin at specific points on your body. A tool called a *skinfold caliper* measures the thickness of each fold of skin. The measurements are used to calculate what portion of your body is fat. Other ways to test body composition involve weighing someone under water or passing a harmless electrical current through the body. Unlike BMI, these three tests require training and special equipment. But they usually give you a better measurement of your body composition than BMI does.

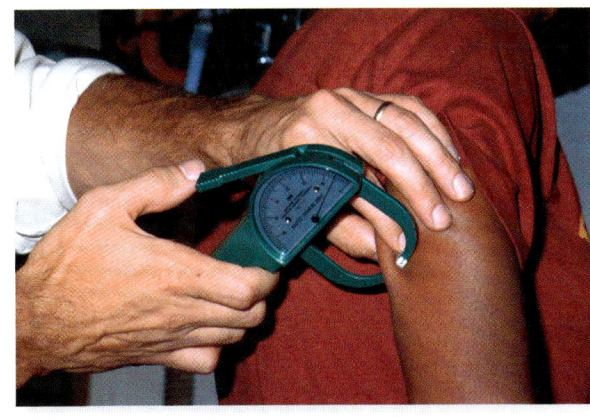

Figure 11 Though sometimes called a *pinch test*, the skinfold test does not hurt.

TABLE 2 Healthy BMI Ranges for Ages 13 to 15

Age	Girls	Boys
13	17.5–24.5	16.6–23.0
14	17.5–25.0	17.5–24.5
15	17.5–25.0	18.1–25.0

Source: FITNESSGRAM.

Lesson Review

Using Vocabulary

1. Define *target heart rate zone*.

Understanding Concepts

2. Why should you test your fitness? ★ 1.A; 3.A
3. Explain why you should monitor your heart rate. ★ 3.A; 4.C
4. List ways you can test the components of fitness.

Critical Thinking

5. **Making Inferences** Muscular endurance is the ability to use muscular strength over and over. One way to test muscular endurance is to see how many curl-ups you can do without stopping. What is another exercise you can do to test muscular endurance? Explain your answer. ★ 1.A

Lesson 5 · Your Fitness Goals

Dinah wants to play a sport, but she isn't sure what to try. Dinah knows that any sport will help her improve her fitness. But there are so many different sports!

What You'll Do

- **Explain** why you should try activities you like. ★ 1.A
- **List** five influences on physical fitness goals. ★ 7.A; 8.A; 12.E; 12.F
- **Explain** why short-term fitness goals are important. ★ 3.A
- **Describe** how intensity, frequency, and time affect physical fitness.
- **List** seven things that you could write in a fitness log.

Start Off Write
What are three things that influence your fitness?

It can be exciting to try a new activity or set new fitness goals. It can also be confusing. Your best bet is to set goals that you know you can reach. In this lesson, you'll learn about setting and meeting your fitness goals.

What Do You Want to Do?

What are your fitness strengths? What are your weaknesses? Are you trying to overcome your weaknesses? Or are you just hoping to have some fun? These are questions you might ask yourself before you choose physical activities. Most people choose activities they think are fun. If you are having fun, you are less likely to quit. If you try a lot of different activities, you are likely to find a few that you really like. Participating in many activities adds variety. It makes getting fit more fun. Even professional athletes play other sports during the off-season.

You don't have to join a team to get fit. You don't even need to play a sport. You just need to find a physical activity that you like and stick to it. There are lots of activities to try. Take a brisk walk. Hike through the woods. Shoot baskets at the park.

If you are trying to improve your fitness, try setting fitness goals. For example, you may want to improve muscular strength. If so, set a goal to be able to lift a certain amount of weight. With your goals in mind, you can choose activities that will help you improve your fitness. ★ 1.A; 12.F

Figure 12 If you enjoy your activity, you'll probably do it more often, even when you get older.

LIFE SKILLS ACTIVITY

PRACTICING WELLNESS

Write down your physical-fitness goals. List 5 things in your life that would make it difficult to meet your physical-fitness goals. Using a scale of one to five, rate how much control you have over these influences. For example, you have complete control over how much TV you watch, so you would rate it five. But you have no control over the time you spend in school. So, you would rate school one. Compare your results with your classmates' results. How would you keep these influences from preventing you from meeting your goals?

What Affects Your Goals?

You should find physical activities you enjoy. But enjoyment isn't the only thing that will affect your goals. How important do you and the people around you think physical fitness is? Pay attention to how your parents and your friends affect your goals. Parents and friends can be very supportive of your fitness goals. When they are, they help you meet them. However, friends can sometimes pressure you into trying an activity that can get you hurt.

The media can give you the wrong ideas about physical fitness. Many magazines, TV programs, and Internet sites feature people who are extremely fit. You don't need to be this fit. All you need is to be healthy. You should be able to do daily activities without becoming short of breath, sore, or tired.

Participation in any physical activity involves the risk of injury. As you set goals, you need to balance the risks against the benefits of physical activity. You shouldn't take chances, but you also need to exercise enough to stay fit.

Have you ever set a goal you had a hard time meeting? Or were the results of your goals not the results you wanted? Don't be afraid to change your goals if they are unrealistic! ★ 7.A; 8.A; 12.E; 12.F

Figure 13 Your parents and your friends influence your fitness goals.

How Will You Achieve Your Goals?

You need to make a plan to meet your fitness goals. Set fitness goals that are reasonable. If you set your goals too high at the beginning of your fitness program, you are more likely to get frustrated and quit. A good fitness plan improves physical fitness over a long period of time. Set a series of short-term goals that lead to a long-term goal. You will get a sense of accomplishment when you meet your short-term goals. ★ 12.F

Are You FIT?

If you do the same exercise program for several weeks, your fitness will stop improving. By changing parts of your program, you can see more improvement. To see improvement, you need to increase the frequency, intensity, and time of your workouts. Frequency is how often you exercise. Intensity is how hard you exercise. Time is how long you exercise. Notice that if you put the first letters of these words together, they spell *FIT*. Remembering FIT can help you remember frequency, intensity, and time.

Increasing any part of FIT can improve your physical fitness. However, improvement is gradual. When you increase one part of FIT, you should slightly decrease the other two parts. Slowly increase those two parts again so that your body can adapt to the new activity. Do not increase all three parts of FIT at the same time. Also, don't increase any one part too much. You can hurt yourself if you increase one part too much or all three at once.
★ 1.A; 3.A

> **Brain Food**
>
> Some experts include a second *T* in *FIT*. The second *T* stands for type. *Type* implies that specific physical activities improve particular components of fitness. This is called *specificity of exercise*.

Figure 14 A physical education teacher or coach can help you meet your goals.

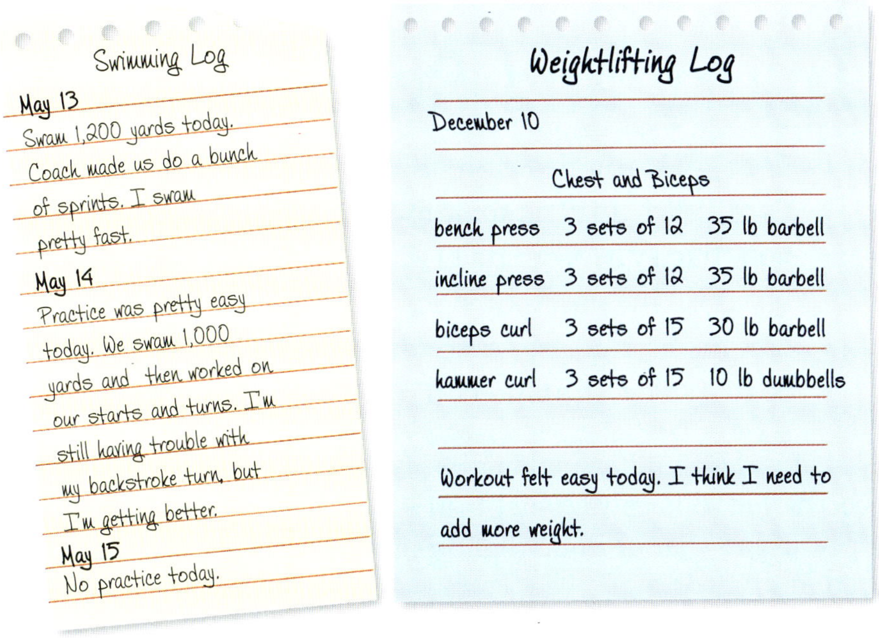

Swimming Log

May 13
Swam 1,200 yards today. Coach made us do a bunch of sprints. I swam pretty fast.

May 14
Practice was pretty easy today. We swam 1,000 yards and then worked on our starts and turns. I'm still having trouble with my backstroke turn, but I'm getting better.

May 15
No practice today.

Weightlifting Log

December 10

Chest and Biceps

bench press	3 sets of 12	35 lb barbell
incline press	3 sets of 12	35 lb barbell
biceps curl	3 sets of 15	30 lb barbell
hammer curl	3 sets of 15	10 lb dumbbells

Workout felt easy today. I think I need to add more weight.

Figure 15 Information in your fitness log should be specific to what you do.

How Can You Monitor Your Progress?

Once you've set fitness goals and started working toward them, you should monitor your progress. Are you improving as quickly as you want? To check your progress, you should test yourself often. Record your results in a fitness log. A fitness log is like a diary or a journal. You can buy a fitness log at some bookstores. Or you can use a notebook. Use a fitness log to keep track of how often and how hard you work out. You should also record how long your workouts last. You can include information about your heart rate, how you felt during your workout, and the weather conditions if you were outside. A fitness log can help you check the progress you've been making. It can help you decide if you need to change any parts of FIT to reach your goals.
★ 3.A; 12.F

Lesson Review

Understanding Concepts

1. Explain why physical activity should be fun. ★ 1.A
2. What are five things that can influence your fitness goals?
   ★ 7.A; 8.A; 12.E; 12.F
3. Why are short-term goals important? ★ 3.A; 12.F
4. How do frequency, intensity, and time affect fitness?
5. What kind of information should you write in a fitness log?

Critical Thinking

6. **Applying Concepts** Theo's parents think fitness is very important. But many of his friends would prefer to watch TV or play video games. How might Theo's parents and friends affect his fitness goals? ★ 7.A; 12.E

Lesson 6

Injury and Recovery

What You'll Do
- **Identify** six warning signs of injury. 4.C; 5.A
- **Explain** why you should let an injury heal completely. 5.A

Terms to Learn
- acute injury
- chronic injury
- rehabilitation

Write
How do you know if you are hurt?

Terry didn't realize that he was injured. His foot hurt during practice. But it didn't hurt too badly. Eventually, he couldn't run as hard as he wanted. When he finally told his coach, he had to go to the doctor. The doctor told Terry that he couldn't run for 6 weeks!

If Terry had said something to his coach earlier, he might have been able to keep running. Instead, he ignored the pain. Pain is a warning sign of injury. Ignoring the warning signs can make an injury worse.

Warning Signs of Injury

There is always a chance that you'll get hurt during physical activity. Your chances of injury increase as you exercise more often. There are two basic kinds of exercise-related injury. An **acute injury** is an injury that happens suddenly. You usually realize you have an acute injury right away. A **chronic injury** is an injury that develops over a period of time. It is sometimes hard to recognize a chronic injury.

You should not feel pain when exercising. However, don't confuse muscle soreness with injury. *Muscle soreness* is discomfort that happens a day or two after hard exercise. It is a normal result of exercise. It usually happens when you first start exercising or when you change FIT. Muscle soreness usually goes away after you exercise again. However, muscle soreness that doesn't go away may mean that you're hurt.

Six warning signs of injury are joint pain, tenderness in a single area, swelling, reduced range of motion around a joint, muscle weakness, and numbness or tingling. If you experience any of these warning signs, you should tell your parents and your coach or teacher. You may need to see a doctor.
4.C; 5.A

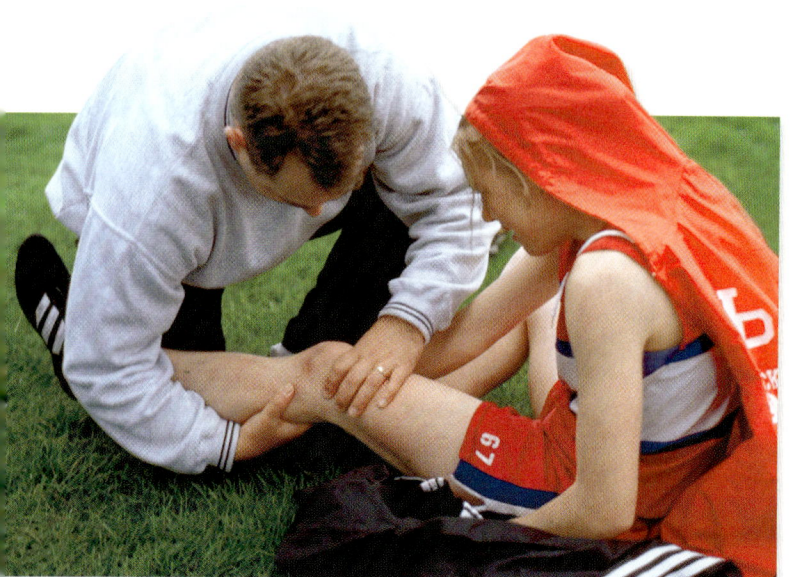

Figure 16 Coaches and trainers look for the warning signs of injury.

158   Chapter 6   **Physical Fitness**

Recovery from Injury

RICE is the treatment for most injuries. It is also useful while you heal. *RICE* stands for **r**est, **i**ce, **c**ompression, and **e**levation. Rest prevents further injury. Using ice and compressing the injured limb in bandages or tape reduces swelling. Elevating the injury also reduces swelling.

Muscles lose strength, endurance, and flexibility when they are not used. **Rehabilitation** is the process of regaining strength, endurance, and flexibility while you recover from an injury. If you return to activity before the injury is healed, you are likely to get hurt again. When you start exercising again, slowly build up to the amount of exercise you were doing before the injury.

★ 5.A

TABLE 3 Common Injuries

Injury	Type	Description
Strain	acute injury	A strain is a muscle or tendon that has been overstretched or torn. Strains are often treated using RICE. Mild strains can take as little as a week to heal.
Sprain	acute injury	A sprain occurs when a joint is twisted suddenly and out of its normal range of motion. The ligaments in the joint are stretched or torn. Sprains are treated with RICE and are sometimes placed in a splint or brace. Sprains usually take 4 to 6 weeks to heal. Bad sprains may take several months to heal.
Fracture	acute injury	A fracture is a cracked or broken bone. Most fractures are put in a cast or brace to keep the broken bone from moving while it heals. Fractures take 4 to 12 weeks to heal, depending on the location and severity of the fracture.
Stress fracture	chronic injury	A stress fracture is a tiny fracture that occurs because of too much exercise or bad form. Stress fractures are treated with RICE. They are sometimes put in a brace. Stress fractures may need 8 to 12 weeks to heal.
Tendinitis	chronic injury	Tendinitis is an irritation of a tendon caused by too much exercise or bad form. It is treated with RICE. Tendinitis can take 4 to 6 weeks to heal.

Lesson Review

Using Vocabulary
1. Describe acute and chronic injuries.

Understanding Concepts
2. Identify six warning signs of injury. ★ 4.C; 5.A

Critical Thinking
3. **Making Good Decisions** Imagine that you play soccer. Your doctor told you that you have tendinitis and that you should rest for 6 weeks. It has been 5 weeks, and your knee feels much better. Should you start playing soccer again? Explain your answer. ★ 3.A; 5.A

internet connect
www.scilinks.org/health
Topic: Sports Injury
HealthLinks code: HD4093

HEALTH LINKS — Maintained by the National Science Teachers Association

Lesson 7

Exercising Caution

What You'll Do

- **Describe** eight ways to protect yourself from injury while exercising.
  ★ 3.A; 5.A

Terms to Learn

- active rest

Write

How does stretching keep you from getting hurt?

Stella's teacher always makes the class warm up and stretch before PE. Stella didn't believe that stretching was very useful until one of her friends strained a muscle. Her friend may not have hurt himself if he had warmed up and stretched.

Warming up and stretching are just two ways you can avoid injury while exercising.

Warm Up and Cool Down

A warm-up gets you ready for exercise. It increases blood flow and loosens muscles and tendons. A warm-up also slightly raises body temperature. A fast walk and slow jog are common warm-ups. Exercising without warming up can lead to muscle and joint injuries.

A cool-down helps your body return to normal after exercise. It helps the heart return to its resting rate. Cooling down helps keep muscles from tightening up and becoming sore. A cool-down is often an easy jog or walk. ★ 5.A

Stretch

Stretching prevents injury by relaxing muscles and increasing joint flexibility. Stretching not only reduces the risk of injury. It can also help you play better. To avoid injury, stretch after a warm-up or cool-down. Stretch slowly, without bouncing. Stretches should be held about 10 to 30 seconds. If you want to improve your flexibility, you may want to hold your stretches as long as 60 seconds. ★ 5.A

Figure 17 Stretching is a good way to avoid injury.

Don't Go Too Fast

To improve fitness, you need to increase the frequency, intensity, and time of exercise. However, increasing parts of FIT too soon, too much, or all at once can cause injury. Increasing parts of FIT before the body has adjusted to exercise puts stress on the body. Exercising too frequently doesn't give the body enough time to repair itself between workouts. Over time this can lead to chronic injuries. Increasing intensity too quickly can cause you to work too hard and use poor form. Working too hard often leads to acute injuries, such as strains and sprains. Long workouts are also risky. The body gets too tired. You can lose concentration and get hurt. ★ 5.A

Improve Your Form

Doing an exercise incorrectly can hurt you. Poor form may put a lot of pressure on your muscles, joints, and bones. Using poor form over a long period of time can cause chronic injuries, such as tendinitis.

You should talk to your teacher or coach before trying a new exercise. He or she can show you the correct form and help you learn it. Your teacher or coach may decide to videotape you while you are doing an exercise. Together, you can see what you are doing right or wrong. Then, the teacher or coach can tell you ways to improve your form.

Besides videotaping, there are several other ways to check your form. Training partners can watch each other work through an exercise. They can see problems and help each other fix their form. Weight lifters and dancers also use mirrors. They can watch their own form in the mirror.

You must practice a lot to learn the correct form. But all that effort is worthwhile. Good form can keep you from getting hurt. It may also help you get better at your activity! ★ 5.A

Figure 18 Using good form can keep you from getting hurt.

Take a Break

Rest and recovery are important parts of a fitness program. Rest gives the body time to repair itself. Rest should be planned along with exercise in your fitness program. You don't have to stop physical activity completely to rest. You can reduce how hard you exercise. This reduced level of exercise is called **active rest.** Active rest lets your body repair itself while you maintain your fitness.

Taking a break can also mean that you stop doing an activity for a while. If you are injured, a long break can help your body heal. ★ 5.A

Wear the Right Clothes

Shoes are probably the most important piece of fitness clothing. Make sure your shoes fit correctly and are the right shoes for your activity. The wrong shoes are uncomfortable and may cause injury. A sports-shoe retailer can help fit you in the right shoes.

Many sports have special clothing needs. For example, football and hockey jerseys need to be large enough to go over safety equipment. However, while many sports require special clothing, you may only need shorts and a T-shirt. Fitness clothing should let you move easily. Tight clothing may cause injury. It can cut off blood flow or rub skin.

Always consider the weather when you are dressing for physical activity. Dress in layers if the weather may change. Add layers when the weather is cold. Remove layers when it's hot. Wear a hat, sunglasses, and sunscreen to prevent sunburn, even on cloudy days. ★ 3.A; 5.A

Health Journal

Describe a time when you took a break from a physical activity you enjoyed. Why did you decide to stop for a while?

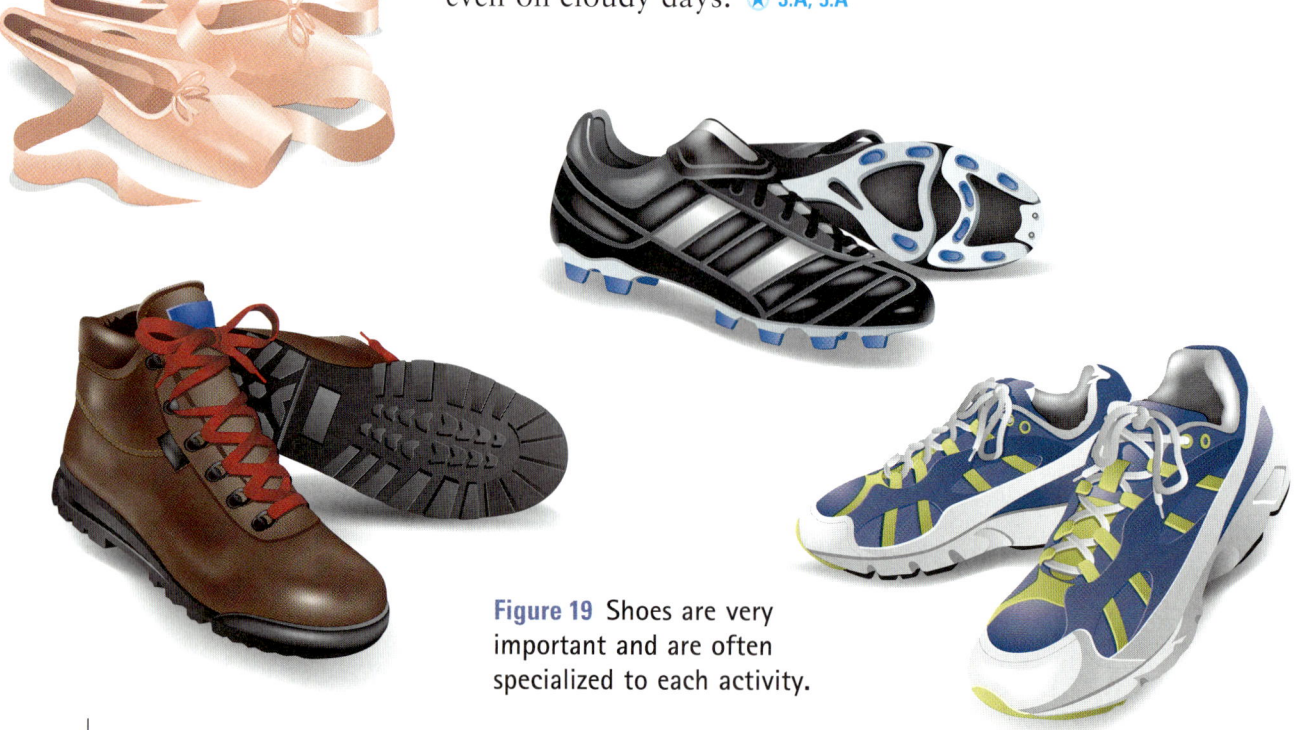

Figure 19 Shoes are very important and are often specialized to each activity.

Use Your Safety Equipment

Safety equipment serves two purposes. First, it lets you try activities that would otherwise be unsafe. For example, mountain climbing would be very dangerous without safety equipment. Climbers need ropes, harnesses, and helmets to protect them if they fall. Second, safety equipment protects you in activities that are generally safe but in which accidents could happen. Safety equipment helps you enjoy a sport by lowering your chances of getting hurt.

Collisions are a normal part of sports such as football and hockey. You're likely to fall when you in-line skate or skateboard. Safety equipment, such as helmets and pads, keeps you from getting hurt. In sports like cycling, accidents are less common. But a helmet can protect you from a head injury if an accident does happen. ★ 3.A; 5.A

Figure 20 In some sports, safety equipment has become an integral part of the activity.

Don't Exercise Alone

If you get hurt while exercising alone, there probably won't be anybody around who can help you. If you have friends around, they can help you or go get help. Exercise partners can also serve as spotters and help you work on your form. Friends also provide motivation. Exercising with someone not only is safer but also is more fun! ★ 5.A

Lesson Review

Using Vocabulary
1. What is active rest?

Understanding Concepts
2. What are eight ways to avoid getting hurt while playing sports? ★ 3.A; 5.A
3. List two reasons you should use safety equipment. ★ 3.A; 5.A

Critical Thinking
4. **Making Inferences** Josefina has been swimming with the swim team. She has been following her coach's instructions and not working too hard or too much. But she still developed tendinitis in her shoulder. Why do you think this happened?

6 CHAPTER REVIEW

Chapter Summary

- Physical fitness is the ability to do everyday activities without becoming short of breath, sore, or tired.
- The components of fitness are muscular strength, muscular endurance, cardiorespiratory endurance, flexibility, and body composition.
- Exercise improves physical fitness.
- Maximum heart rate is the largest number of times the heart can beat per minute during exercise.
- Target heart rate zone is 60 to 85 percent of maximum heart rate.
- Fitness goals are affected by enjoyment of the activity, parents and friends, the media, the risk involved, and the results of your goals.
- Increasing frequency, intensity, and time of exercise can improve fitness.
- The two types of exercise-related injury are acute injuries and chronic injuries.

Using Vocabulary

For each pair of terms, describe how the meanings of the terms differ.

1. muscular strength/muscular endurance
2. muscular endurance/cardiorespiratory endurance
3. acute injury/chronic injury

For each sentence, fill in the blank with the proper word from the word bank provided below.

physical fitness　　flexibility
body composition　exercise
maximum heart rate　rehabilitation
target heart rate zone

4. ___ is estimated by subtracting age from 220.
5. ___ helps you regain strength while you recover from an injury.
6. ___ compares fat weight to lean weight in the body.
7. To improve cardiorespiratory endurance, you should exercise in your ___.
8. ___ keeps you from losing your breath during daily activities.
9. ___ is the ability to move joints easily.
10. To stay fit, you need to ___.

Understanding Concepts

11. List the five components of fitness. ★ 1.A
12. How does not eating enough food affect fitness? ★ 1.A
13. What are eight things you can do to avoid injury during exercise? ★ 3.A; 5.A
14. What are the roles of overload and rest in exercise? ★ 1.A; 3.A
15. List six common warning signs of injury. ★ 4.C
16. How does muscle soreness differ from injury?
17. How does exercise help you live longer? ★ 1.A
18. What are the mental and emotional benefits of exercise? ★ 1.A
19. What are the social benefits of exercise? ★ 1.A
20. What part of fitness does pull-ups test? the 1-mile run?

Critical Thinking

Applying Concepts

21. Tennille had a fitness test a couple of months ago. She didn't do very well. But her PE teacher helped her make a fitness plan. She has been exercising five times a week. Should Tennille test her fitness again? Why or why not? ★ 3.A; 12.F

22. A friend of yours wants to start training for an upcoming 10-kilometer run. You are interested in training for the 100-meter dash. Based on the goals of your training, should you train with your friend? Explain your answer. ★ 4.C

23. Imagine that you play soccer. A friend of yours on the team has been frustrated lately. He doesn't have enough energy at practice. You've noticed that he eats a lot of junk food. What could you tell your friend about his diet that might help him? ★ 1.A; 3.A; 4.A; 4.C

Making Good Decisions

24. Imagine that you want to run a mile in less than 8 minutes. What kind of short-term goals could you set that would help you meet your long-term goal? ★ 12.F

25. You have been exercising by riding a bike for 10 miles three times a week. After a few weeks, you notice that your exercise isn't making you tired anymore. What could you do to make your bike riding challenging again? ★ 4.C; 12.F

26. Juanita didn't do as well as she wanted to do on her fitness assessment during PE. So, she started a new fitness program yesterday. Today, her muscles feel achy and uncomfortable. Should Juanita keep exercising? Explain your answer. ★ 1.A; 4.C

Interpreting Graphics

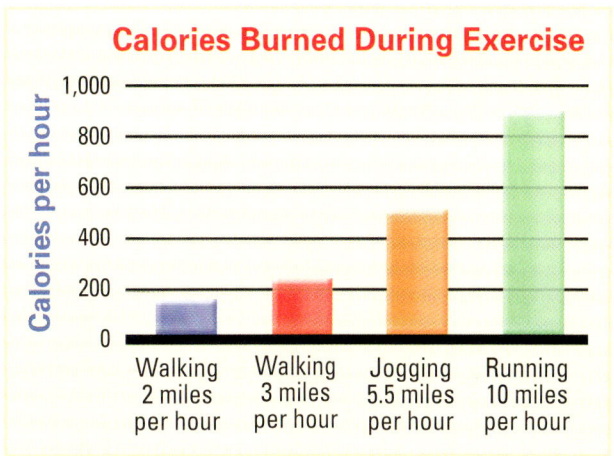

Use the figure above to answer questions 27–29. ★ M8.5.A

27. How many more Calories are burned when walking 3 miles per hour instead of 2 miles per hour?

28. Which would burn more calories, walking 3 miles per hour for 2 hours or jogging 5.5 miles per hour for 1 hour?

29. Exercising enough to burn off one pound requires using about 3,500 Calories. About how many hours of each of the following activities would be needed to lose about 1 pound?
    a. walking at 3 miles per hour
    b. running at 10 miles per hour
    c. jogging at 5.5 miles per hour

Reading Checkup

Take a minute to review your answers to the Health IQ questions at the beginning of this chapter. How has reading this chapter improved your Health IQ?

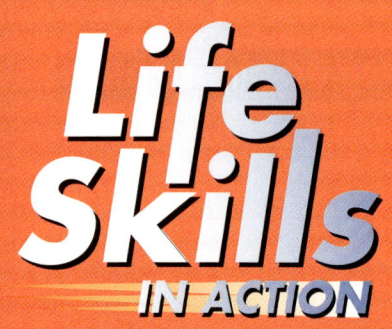

Life Skills IN ACTION

Setting Goals

A goal is something that you work toward and hope to achieve. Setting goals is important because goals give you a sense of purpose and achieving goals improves your self-esteem. Complete the following activity to learn how to set and achieve goals.

Mesoon's Fitness Goal

Setting the Scene

Mesoon is babysitting her neighbor's two young children. The children ask Mesoon to play with them. After several minutes of running around, Mesoon is surprised to find herself tired and breathing heavily. She concludes that she must be out of shape. The next day at school, Mesoon goes to her physical education teacher for advice.

The 5 Steps of Setting Goals

1. Consider your interests and values.
2. Choose goals that include your interests and values.
3. If necessary, break down long-term goals into several short-term goals.
4. Measure your progress.
5. Reward your success.

Guided Practice

Practice with a Friend

Form a group of three. Have one person play the role of Mesoon and another person play the role of her physical education teacher. Have the third person be an observer. Walking through each of the five steps of setting goals, role-play the conversation between Mesoon and her physical education teacher. Mesoon should follow the steps of setting goals as she sets a goal that will help her become physically fit. The observer will take notes, which will include observations about what the person playing Mesoon did well and suggestions of ways to improve. Stop after each step to evaluate the process. ★ 12.F

Independent Practice

Check Yourself

After you have completed the guided practice, go through Act 1 again without stopping at each step. Answer the questions below to review what you did.

1. How do Mesoon's interests influence the goal she sets? ★ 1.A
2. What long-term goal did Mesoon decide on? What are some short-term goals Mesoon needs to meet to reach her long-term goal? ★ 12.F
3. How can Mesoon measure her progress?
4. What are some goals that you can set for yourself? Remember to consider your interests and values.
5. Which of the steps of setting goals is the most difficult for you? Explain your answer.

On Your Own

A few months later, Mesoon is exercising five times a week and is happy to know that she is physically fit. However, she is worried that she might become bored with her exercise routine. Mesoon talks to her physical education teacher again to discuss her concerns. Mesoon's teacher suggests that she set a new long-term goal such as running in a 10K race or learning to lift weights to build muscle tone. Make a poster illustrating how Mesoon could use the five steps to setting goals to develop a plan for reaching her next goal.

CHAPTER 7
Sports and Conditioning

Lessons
1. Sports and Competition — 170
2. Conditioning Skills — 174
3. The Balancing Act — 178

Chapter Review — 182
Life Skills in Action — 184

Check out **Current Health** articles related to this chapter by visiting **go.hrw.com**. Just type in the keyword **HD4CH39**.

> **"I** joined the **track team** because **I like to run**. I didn't think I would like any field events, but the high jump is **awesome**! Also, I've made friends at our track meets, and the meets definitely **motivate me** to be a better athlete!**"**

Health IQ

PRE-READING

Answer the following multiple-choice questions to find out what you already know about sports and conditioning. When you've finished this chapter, you'll have the opportunity to change your answers based on what you've learned.

1. An example of an individual sport is
   a. hockey.
   b. soccer.
   c. golf.
   d. None of the above

2. The ability to make good decisions that affect everyone on a team is called
   a. teamwork.
   b. leadership.
   c. endurance.
   d. None of the above

3. Which of the following is an example of good sportsmanship?
   a. following the rules
   b. accepting defeat gracefully
   c. being modest when you win
   d. all of the above

4. Stress fractures and tendinitis are examples of
   a. overload.
   b. overuse injuries.
   c. overcommitment.
   d. None of the above

5. Which of the following is a sport skill?
   a. agility
   b. power
   c. reaction time
   d. all of the above

6. Which of the following is a sign of overtraining?
   a. decreased resting heart rate
   b. improved balance
   c. decreased performance
   d. muscle soreness

7. Overcommitment is
   a. exercising too much.
   b. taking on a new activity.
   c. spending too much time on an activity.
   d. None of the above

ANSWERS: 1. c; 2. b; 3. d; 4. b; 5. d; 6. c; 7. c

Chapter 7 Sports and Conditioning | 169

Lesson 1

Sports and Competition

Nikita joined the soccer team to get in shape. She is getting fit and making new friends. Nikita also likes playing against other teams. Playing other teams gives her a chance to work on her skills and meet new people.

What You'll Do

- **Describe** individual and team sports.
- **List** three benefits of competition.  1.A
- **List** five characteristics of a good sport. ★ 1.A
- **Explain** how friends can influence your view of sports. ★ 7.A; 10.A; 12.E

Terms to Learn

- competition
- sportsmanship
- cheating

Start Off Write

Contrast sportsmanship with cheating.

Besides improving fitness, sports can improve self-esteem. Doing well in a game or learning a new skill can help you feel good about yourself. Like Nikita, many people also find that sports help them make new friends.

Playing Sports

There are two types of sports. In *team sports*, two or more people work together against another team. People who play *individual sports* participate on their own. The two types of sports often overlap. For example, a slam-dunk competition is an individual sport that comes from basketball, which is a team sport. Also, many individual sports, such as track and field or swimming, have teams.

Sports can help you develop teamwork and leadership skills. *Teamwork* is working with other people during a game or match. *Leadership* is the ability to guide other people in an organized and responsible way. Leadership helps you make good decisions that affect everyone on your team. These skills help you work with other people both in sports and in everyday activities. ★ 1.A

Figure 1 With so many different kinds of sports, you'll be able to find something you like to do.

170

Figure 2 Competition gives you a chance to make new friends.

Competition

Why do so many people like to play sports? Some people play sports to stay fit. Other people play sports because they like competition. **Competition** is a contest between two or more people or teams. There are many different kinds of competition. You might compete for fun when you play games with your friends. Formal competition includes coaches, officials, and rules. In head-to-head competition, players are trying to see who is the most skilled. You can also compete against yourself. For example, some people are always trying to do better than they did last time.

One benefit of competition is that it can help you improve your skills and fitness. Many people who want to compete at a higher level will exercise more. Improving skills can be just as important to someone playing for fun as it is to an athlete. The only difference between these two people is the level of their goals. Whether you want to run a faster mile or to win a basketball game, competition can motivate you to improve.

Competition can help you improve your leadership and teamwork skills. It also gives you a chance to meet new people. You will probably make friends on your team. You may make friends who are on other teams. The people you compete against share an interest with you—your sport. Sharing a common interest is a natural way to make new friends. ★ 1.A

Health Journal

Write about a time when you participated in a competition. Describe the competition and how you felt afterward.

Sportsmanship

If you treat other players fairly during competition, then you are a good sport. A *good sport* practices sportsmanship. Sportsmanship is the ability to treat all players, officials, and fans fairly during competition. Losing teams may feel upset or disappointed. Winning teams may show pride and excitement. But there is no reason for a winning team to be rude to the losing side. And the losing team should not dislike the winning team.

Both fans and players should try to be good sports. A good sport does the following:

- plays his or her best at all times
- follows the rules even when there is no referee or judge
- considers the health and safety of other players
- congratulates athletes on both sides for good plays
- is gracious in defeat and modest in success

Have you ever seen a game where players yelled, cursed, or fought? These situations are examples of poor sportsmanship. It makes competition less fun for everyone. Many sports now have rules against players, coaches, and fans who are poor sports.

In many sports, the chances to lose outnumber the chances to win. For example, only one person or team out of many can win a tournament. Some people cheat to win. Cheating is trying to win by breaking the rules. Cheating is another example of poor sportsmanship. So cheating makes sports less enjoyable. ★ 7.A; 10.A

Brain Food

Professional basketball players, teams, coaches, and officials are fined millions of dollars each year for poor sportsmanship. In fact, one coach was fined $500,000 for criticizing game officials!

Figure 3 Good sportsmanship makes sports more enjoyable for everyone.

Figure 4 Support from friends and fellow players can make sports more fun.

Sports and Your Friends

Friends can have a positive and a negative influence on the things you do. If your friends get regular exercise, you are more likely to exercise. Likewise, if you are around people who'd rather watch TV, you may not want to be active. Sports can give you a chance to make friends who like physical activity. So, you are more likely to stay fit.

Friends can help you meet fitness goals. But be aware of challenges from your friends that may be dangerous. For example, don't let your friends pressure you into trying a trick or skill you know you can't do. You could get hurt. Good friends keep each other safe. ★ 7.A; 10.A; 12.E; 12.F

Health Journal

Draw a line down the middle of a page in your Health Journal. On the left, list your sports skills or accomplishments. On the right, list how your friends supported you.

Lesson Review

Using Vocabulary
1. What is competition?

Understanding Concepts
2. Compare and contrast individual and team sports.
3. What are five characteristics of a good sport? ★ 1.A
4. What are three benefits of competition? ★ 1.A

Critical Thinking
5. **Identifying Relationships** Marion has a lot of friends who spend most of their free time playing video games or watching movies. She's been thinking about joining the basketball team. What kind of influence do you think her friends might have on her goals? How might she influence her friends' goals?
★ 7.A; 10.A; 12.E; 12.F

Lesson 1 Sports and Competition

Lesson 2

Conditioning Skills

Susan's basketball coach made the team run long distances during practice. At first, Susan didn't understand how the running helped her skills. But later she realized that the running improved her endurance.

What You'll Do

- **Describe** how conditioning works. ★ 1.A
- **Describe** three principles of conditioning. ★ 1.A
- **Compare** aerobic and anaerobic exercise. ★ 1.A
- **List** six sports skills.
- **Describe** a way to avoid injury. ★ 5.A

Terms to Learn

- conditioning
- crosstraining
- aerobic exercise
- anaerobic exercise

Start Off Write

What are some ways a runner could crosstrain?

Playing sports usually means more than showing up for games. If you want to play your best, you need to prepare. Susan's basketball coach used running as a way to help her players become more fit.

How Conditioning Works

Exercise that improves fitness for sports is called **conditioning**. Conditioning works because your body is able to adjust to exercise by becoming more fit. Over time, your body adjusts to regular exercise. So, your muscles become stronger. Your endurance also gets better. And your heart and lungs become more efficient.

When you don't exercise, you lose strength. You also lose endurance. You may become short of breath more easily. If you stop exercising, your body becomes less fit. For example, while recovering from an injury, muscles in an injured limb can become weak. You will have to do additional exercise to restore strength in the limb. After an injury, someone who has been fit can regain fitness faster than someone who has never exercised. ★ 1.A

Figure 5 Swimming is an example of a conditioning exercise.

Conditioning for Competition

When you are conditioning, you need to work hard. Otherwise, your fitness may not improve. There are three principles to keep in mind when conditioning:

- *Overload* is exercising your body more than usual to improve fitness. Exercising harder, longer, or more often helps you improve your fitness.
- *Progression* (proh GRESH uhn) is the slow increase of overload over time. Progression keeps you from doing too much too soon. You can build up your fitness gradually.
- *Specificity* (SPE suh FI suh tee) is the idea that what you do affects how your fitness improves. If you want to improve a specific part of fitness or a particular skill, you need to do the right exercise. For example, distance running improves endurance.

When you condition, focus on exercises that improve your sports skills. For example, if you want to run a 10 kilometer race, you should do a lot of distance running. If you want to sprint, you should work on your muscular strength and muscular endurance. But don't be afraid to do other kinds of exercise. **Crosstraining** is doing different kinds of exercise during conditioning. Crosstraining often helps you do better at your sport. For example, many runners also lift weights. Lifting weights makes runners stronger. So, they can run faster.

Crosstraining also prevents injury. For example, runners who lift weights strengthen muscles that aren't normally used for running. These muscles often support joints. So, runners are less likely to experience a joint injury. Finally, crosstraining also keeps you from getting bored. If you do a variety of activities, you're more likely to keep exercising. ★ 1.A; 3.A

Myth & Fact

Myth: If you stop exercising, your muscles will turn into fat.

Fact: Muscle and fat are two different kinds of tissue. If you stop exercising, your muscles may become smaller. You may also gain some fat, but muscles don't turn into fat.

Figure 6 Weight lifting is just one way to do crosstraining.

Aerobic and Anaerobic Exercise

During conditioning, you need to do two types of exercise. **Aerobic exercise** (er OH bik EK suhr SIEZ) is exercise that lasts a long time and uses oxygen to get energy. Distance running and swimming are kinds of aerobic exercise. **Anaerobic exercise** (AN uhr OH bik EK suhr SIEZ) is exercise that doesn't use oxygen to get energy. It lasts a very short time. Weight lifting is an anaerobic exercise.

When conditioning, it's best to use a combination of both types of exercise. How much of each type depends on the activity. For example, most of the exercise a distance runner will do is aerobic exercise. But he or she will lift weights a couple of times a week to improve strength. ★ 1.A

> **Brain Food**
>
> You are born with a certain ratio of fast-twitch muscles to slow-twitch muscles. Fast-twitch muscles help you do anaerobic exercise, while slow-twitch muscles are used during aerobic exercise. Your muscle ratio often makes you better at some activities than others.

Sports Skills

Have you ever walked on a balance beam? Or have you ever hit a home run? What kind of skills do you think you need so that you can do these activities? The six basic sports skills are described below.

- **Agility** (uh JIL uh tee) is being able to move your body quickly and accurately. You need agility for all sports.
- **Balance** (BAL uhns) helps you stay steady. You use balance when walking on a balance beam.
- **Coordination** (ko AWR duh NAY shuhn) is using your senses and body to do tasks accurately. You need coordination for all sports.
- **Speed** is how quickly you can do something. For example, sprinters and cyclists need speed for racing.
- **Power** is a combination of strength and speed. For example, power helps you hit a home run.
- **Reaction time** is how quickly you react to something. A good reaction time helps you play sports like tennis. ★ 1.A

Figure 7 This football player is developing his agility, coordination, and speed during practice.

Listening to Your Body

During a workout, your muscles can get very tired. You may also be sore for a few days after a workout. This soreness usually goes away the next time you exercise. Soreness that doesn't go away or becomes worse may mean you are hurt. Many injuries get worse if they are not treated. If you think you're injured, tell your parents or coach right away. You may need to see a doctor. The doctor can tell you how bad the injury is and what you can do to take care of it.

You can avoid injury by getting plenty of rest between workouts. When you exercise, you tire your muscles. You also use fuel for energy during exercise. Rest gives your muscles a chance to recover from exercise and replenish fuel. Also, many injuries occur because people don't get enough rest between workouts. Be sure to schedule rest days when you are conditioning. And don't forget to warm up and cool down every time you exercise. Warming up prepares your body for exercise. Cooling down relaxes muscles. It also helps prevent muscle soreness. ★ 1.A; 5.A

Figure 8 There is a thin line between soreness and injury. Listen to your body carefully, and know the difference between them.

Lesson Review

Using Vocabulary
1. What is conditioning? ★ 1.A
2. Compare aerobic and anaerobic exercise. ★ 1.A

Understanding Concepts
3. What are three principles of conditioning? ★ 1.A; 5.A
4. What can you do to avoid injury? ★ 5.A

Critical Thinking
5. **Applying Concepts** Lorraine plays basketball. Which sports skills does she need for basketball? Explain your answer.
6. **Making Good Decisions** Imagine you play soccer. Soccer requires you to run a lot. You also need to have muscular strength. How can you use aerobic and anaerobic exercise to condition for soccer? ★ 1.A

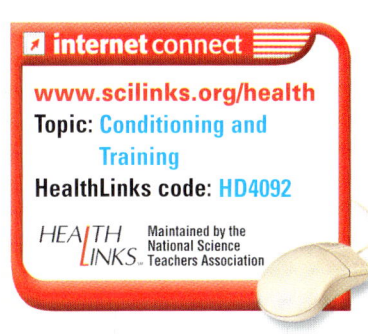

internet connect
www.scilinks.org/health
Topic: Conditioning and Training
HealthLinks code: HD4092
HEALTH LINKS Maintained by the National Science Teachers Association

Lesson 2 Conditioning Skills 177

Lesson 3: The Balancing Act

What You'll Do

- **List** five signs of overcommitment. ★ 1.A
- **Explain** how a calendar can help you manage your commitments. ★ 12.G
- **List** five warning signs of overtraining. ★ 3.A; 4.C
- **List** three causes of overuse injuries.
- **List** three reasons you might consider walking away from a sport. ★ 3.A; 4.C

Terms to Learn

- overcommitment
- overtraining
- overuse injury

How can you avoid overcommitment?

Alexis had to quit the track team. She didn't want to. But she had a hard time keeping up with practice. She was involved in too many school activities.

Alexis just couldn't keep up with everything she was doing. She had to make some tough decisions. For her, the best decision was to stop running with the track team.

Overcommitment

When you play sports, you make a commitment to yourself, your coach, and your teammates. You also make commitments when you try to improve your grades or relationships. Some people spend too much time on their commitments. **Overcommitment** is committing too much time to one or more activities. The following are signs of overcommitment.

- You begin to borrow time from one activity to do another.
- You feel like you have no free time left.
- You cannot commit to new goals. You are too busy trying to keep up with what you are already doing.
- Emergencies or unexpected changes cause you to panic. You have a hard time handling your activities.
- You miss due dates.

Overcommitment to sports can hurt your health and can lead to injury. You may be exercising too much. When you exercise too much, your body doesn't have time to recover between workouts. Also, if you have too much to do, you may not sleep enough. When you're tired, you may make mistakes that lead to injury. ★ 1.A; 3.A; 4.C

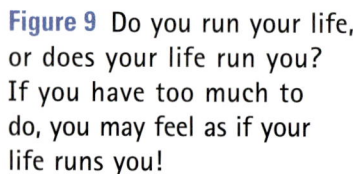

Figure 9 Do you run your life, or does your life run you? If you have too much to do, you may feel as if your life runs you!

178

Figure 10 Keeping a calendar can help you manage time commitments.

Having It All

You can prevent overcommitment by getting organized. Try using a calendar to manage your commitments. Your calendar should include activities such as team practices and club meetings. It should also include school commitments, due dates, special events, and family activities.

A schedule makes it easier to avoid overcommitment. You should check your calendar before deciding to do new activities. Don't add activities unless you have time. You may want to do something that you don't have time for. But part of growing up is learning how to evaluate your goals and values. Use your goals and values to choose between the things you need to do and the things you want to do. ★ 12.G

STUDY TIP *for better reading*

Organizing Information
You can use a calendar to prepare for your upcoming due dates, tests, and sports events. For example, if you have a health test in 4 weeks, use your calendar to make a study schedule. That way, you'll know if you're on track!

LIFE SKILLS ACTIVITY

MAKING GOOD DECISIONS

In groups, create a set of 20 note cards. On each card name an activity and the period of time it takes. For example, you may write that school is from 8 A.M. to 3 P.M. on one card. Include sports, school, family, and personal activities. Trade your set of cards with another group.

Organize a weekly schedule around the activities on the cards. Arrange the activities based on those you must do and those you want to do.

What activities were left out? Did you include physical fitness activities? Why or why not? Compare your schedule to other groups' schedules.

Lesson 3 The Balancing Act

Figure 11 Overtraining and overuse injuries can take the fun out of sports.

Overtraining

You need time between workouts to let your body recover. If you often exercise before your body has recovered, you may be overtraining. **Overtraining** is a condition caused by too much exercise. Some signs of overtraining are the following:

- You aren't doing as well during games and practice even though you're not hurt.
- You're tired all the time.
- You're less interested in the activity. You start making excuses to avoid working hard at practice and at games.
- Your resting heart rate increases.
- You get hurt more often.

To avoid overtraining, you need to make rest a part of your fitness program. Schedule days when you won't exercise or days when you'll do an easy workout. Avoid the temptation to work out hard on days when you're supposed to rest.

★ 1.A; 5.A

Overuse Injuries

Sometimes overtraining leads to overuse injuries. An **overuse injury** is an injury that happens because of too much exercise, poor form, or the wrong equipment. Stress fractures and tendinitis are common overuse injuries. People exercise too much when they are overtraining. So, they may develop an overuse injury. If you think you have an overuse injury, you should see a doctor.

Rest is the best way to heal from an overuse injury. Some people need to wear a cast, use a brace, or do special exercises while they recover. Many overuse injuries take several weeks to heal. But overuse injuries don't always mean that you have to stop exercising. For example, runners who have stress fractures may swim while their injuries heal. Also, an overuse injury doesn't mean you aren't part of a team anymore. While an injury heals, you can improve your knowledge of your sport. And you can cheer for your teammates at competitions. ★ 5.A

Brain Food

A stress fracture is not always a cracked or broken bone. In some stress fractures, the bone has grown weak. The injury is painful, but it may not appear on an X ray until it starts to heal. An X ray then shows a calcium deposit where the bone is healing.

Walking Away

Have you ever felt as if you were getting hurt all the time? Is your sport no longer fun? Does your sport take too much time? If so, think about taking a break from your sport. A break can improve your performance. A break lets you recover from injury and gives you time to evaluate your goals.

You should not continue to do an activity you don't like. Change can be hard. But leaving one sport can lead to joining another. When changing activities, don't forget your commitments to your coaches and teammates. Before you change sports, think about finishing the season of your current sport. ★ 5.A

LANGUAGE ARTS ACTIVITY

Imagine that you run for your school's track team. You have decided that you don't want to run anymore. You would like to play soccer instead. Write a letter explaining to your track coach why you are leaving the track team. Then, write a letter explaining to the soccer coach why you want to play soccer.

Figure 12 If you're thinking about changing sports, talk to your parents and coaches. They can help you make the change to another sport.

Lesson Review

Using Vocabulary

1. What is overcommitment? ★ 1.A; 12.G
2. What is overtraining? ★ 1.A

Understanding Concepts

3. List five signs of overcommitment and a way to avoid it. ★ 12.G
4. What are five signs of overtraining? ★ 3.A; 4.C
5. List three causes of overuse injuries. ★ 1.A; 5.A

Critical Thinking

6. **Making Good Decisions** Imagine that you are the captain of your school's basketball team. You used to enjoy playing basketball. But now you feel that it's not fun and it's too time consuming. You want to try participating in track instead. The city basketball championship is next week. What should you do? ★ 4.C; 12.A; 12.B

internet connect
www.scilinks.org/health
Topic: Overuse Injuries
HealthLinks code: HD4075

HEALTH LINKS. Maintained by the National Science Teachers Association

Lesson 3 The Balancing Act

7 CHAPTER REVIEW

Chapter Summary

■ Competition is a contest between two or more people or teams. ■ Conditioning is exercise that improves fitness for sports. ■ The three principles of conditioning are overload, progression, and specificity. ■ Crosstraining is doing different kinds of exercise during conditioning. ■ The two types of exercise are aerobic exercise and anaerobic exercise. ■ Six sports skills are agility, balance, coordination, speed, power, and reaction time. ■ Overcommitment is committing too much time to one or more activities. ■ Overtraining is exercising so much that performance suffers. ■ Overuse injuries are caused by too much exercise, poor form, or the wrong equipment.

Using Vocabulary

For each pair of terms, describe how the meanings of the terms differ.

1. sportsmanship/cheating
2. aerobic exercise/anaerobic exercise
3. overcommitment/overtraining

For each sentence, fill in the blank with the proper word from the word bank provided below.

crosstraining	overtraining
competition	overuse injury
conditioning	overcommitment

4. Exercise that improves fitness for sports is called ___.
5. A(n) ___ is caused by too much exercise.
6. ___ is a condition caused by too much exercise.
7. A contest between two or more teams is called ___.
8. ___ is doing different kinds of exercise during conditioning.

Understanding Concepts

9. What are five characteristics of a good sport? ★ 1.A
10. How does conditioning work? Describe three principles of conditioning. ★ 1.A
11. How does the body react when a person stops exercising regularly? ★ 1.A
12. What are six sports skills? Describe each skill.
13. Why should you make rest a part of your conditioning program? ★ 1.A; 5.A
14. What are five signs of overcommitment? How can you reduce your chances of overcommitment? ★ 1.A; 12.G
15. List five signs of overtraining. ★ 3.A; 4.C
16. Why does overtraining often lead to overuse injuries? List two examples of overuse injuries. ★ 5.A
17. What are three reasons you might consider walking away from a sport? ★ 3.A; 4.C
18. What are two kinds of sports?
19. What kind of influence can your friends have on your physical fitness? ★ 7.A; 12.E

Critical Thinking

Making Inferences

20 Josh just moved to a new town. He's excited about making new friends and thinks sports might be a good way to meet people. Do you think he should try team sports or individual sports? Explain your answer. ★ 1.A

21 Latrel has a hard time making decisions and working with other people. How do you think joining a sports team will help him develop these skills? ★ 1.A; 10.E

22 Danielle joined the track team a few weeks ago. She sometimes feels like her coach asks the team to do a lot of work during practice. Every week, the coach tells them to run a little farther or a little harder. Why do you think Danielle's coach wants the team to do a little more exercise each week? ★ 1.A

23 Last week, Sabrina ran 3 miles, went swimming, lifted weights, walked to school, and ran sprints. Identify which of these activities are aerobic exercises and which are anaerobic exercises.

Making Good Decisions

24 Imagine that you have a friend who plays rough during games. Your friend teases players on other teams. Sometimes your friend brags when your team wins. How can you help your friend understand that his or her behavior makes sports less fun? ★ 1.A; 7.A; 12.E

25 Imagine you're a basketball player. Basketball requires a lot of running and endurance. You also need strength for shooting baskets and jumping for the ball. What activities can you do for crosstraining? ★ 1.A

Interpreting Graphics

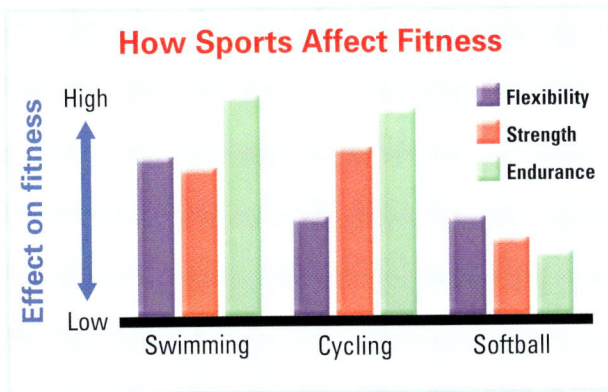

Use the figure above to answer questions 26–30. ★ M8.5.A

26 Which exercise shown in the chart improves flexibility the most?

27 If you wanted to improve your strength, which sport should you try?

28 Which sport has the greatest effect on fitness? the smallest effect?

29 Hannah plays soccer. She wants to improve her flexibility and endurance. Which of these sports would work well for crosstraining?

30 Why do you think swimming improves endurance more than softball does?

Reading Checkup

Take a minute to review your answers to the Health IQ questions at the beginning of this chapter. How has reading this chapter improved your Health IQ?

Life Skills IN ACTION

Being a Wise Consumer

Going shopping for products and services can be fun, but it can be confusing, too. Sometimes, there are so many options to choose from that finding the right one for you can be difficult. Being a wise consumer means evaluating different products and services for value and quality. Complete the following activity to learn how to be a wise consumer.

Shoe Shopping with Hank

ACT 1

Setting the Scene

Hank made the school's basketball team for the first time. He wants to buy a good pair of basketball shoes because his old ones are too worn. Hank goes to a sporting goods store and starts looking at all of the shoes. A salesperson approaches Hank and asks to help.

The 5 Steps of Being a Wise Consumer

1. List what you need and want from a product or a service.
2. Find several products or services that may fit your needs.
3. Research and compare information about the products or services.
4. Use the product or the service of your choice.
5. Evaluate your choice.

Guided Practice

Practice with a Friend

Form a group of three. Have one person play the role of Hank and another person play the role of the salesperson. Have the third person be an observer. Walking through each of the five steps of being a wise consumer, role-play the conversation between Hank and the salesperson as Hank decides which pair of shoes to buy. The observer will take notes, which will include observations about what the person playing Hank did well and suggestions of ways to improve. Stop after each step to evaluate the process.

★ 7.A; 8.A; 12.B

Independent Practice

Check Yourself

After you have completed the guided practice, go through Act 1 again without stopping at each step. Answer the questions below to review what you did.

1. What might have happened if Hank had not listed his needs before going to the store? Explain your answer.
2. Why is it important to compare several products before deciding to buy one of them? ★ 12.B ★ 4.A; 4.C
3. What are some ways that Hank can research information about products that he is considering buying?
4. Explain why it is important to evaluate your choice after using a product or service. ★ 4.C; 7.A; 8.A; 12.B

On Your Own

One day, during basketball practice, Hank sprains his ankle. Hank's doctor examines the ankle and tells Hank that he will be fine but that he should wear an ankle brace while he exercises. The doctor also gives Hank the address of a medical supply store where he can buy a good ankle brace. When Hank goes to the store, he is surprised to find many ankle braces from which he can choose. Make an outline that shows how Hank can use the five steps of being a wise consumer to select an appropriate ankle brace.

Chapter 7 Being a Wise Consumer | 185

CHAPTER 8
Eating Responsibly

Lessons

1. Nutrition and Your Life — 188
2. The Nutrients You Need — 192
3. Making Healthy Choices — 196
4. Body Image — 200
5. Eating Disorders — 204
6. A Healthy Body, a Healthy Weight — 210

Chapter Review — 212
Life Skills in Action — 214

Check out **Current Health** articles related to this chapter by visiting **go.hrw.com**. Just type in the keyword **HD4CH40**.

> **"I** don't eat **breakfast** in the mornings. Instead I just **grab** something from the **vending machine**. I usually buy lunch from the cafeteria. Many of my friends talk about trying to eat healthy, but I figure that as long as I get something to eat, I should be okay.**"**

PRE-READING

Answer the following multiple-choice questions to find out what you already know about nutrition and eating disorders. When you've finished this chapter, you'll have the opportunity to change your answers based on what you've learned.

1. How your friends eat, what your personal tastes are, and where you live influence your
   a. metabolism.
   b. energy level.
   c. digestion.
   d. diet. ★ 6.A; 7.A

2. The amount of energy your body gets from food is measured in units called
   a. grams.
   b. carbohydrates.
   c. Calories.
   d. Both (a) and (c).

3. Which of the following nutrients does your body require only in small amounts to maintain a healthy diet?
   a. water and carbohydrates
   b. vitamins and minerals
   c. carbohydrates and protein
   d. none of the above ★ 4.C

4. The Food Guide Pyramid is divided into different groups of foods. From which group does your body require the least amount of food?
   a. meats, poultry, fish, dry beans, and nuts group
   b. bread, rice, cereal, and pasta group
   c. fats, oils, and sweets group
   d. milk, cheese, and egg group
   ★ 4.C

5. If you think that one of your friends has an eating disorder, you can help him or her by
   a. telling an adult.
   b. taking care of it yourself.
   c. ignoring the problem.
   d. None of the above

ANSWERS: 1. d; 2. c; 3. b; 4. c; 5. a

Lesson 1

Nutrition and Your Life

What You'll Do

- **Explain** how the food you eat affects your health. ★ 1.A
- **Describe** the process of digestion. ★ 1.A
- **Describe** the importance of eating foods high in nutrients. ★ 1.A; 3.A; 4.C
- **Identify** seven factors that affect your food choices. ★ 6.A; 7.A; 8.A; 12.E

Terms to Learn

- nutrient
- digestion
- diet

Start Off Write

Why is practicing good nutrition important?

```
Tracy was so busy today that she did not
have time to eat lunch. Before soccer
practice, she bought a candy bar from the
vending machine. Halfway through practice,
Tracy felt tired and drained.
```

You are what you eat! How you feel and how much energy you have to be active have a lot to do with what you eat. Tracy was feeling tired during practice because she hadn't eaten enough.

Nutrition and Your Health

Your body is like a car. Without fuel, the car cannot work. If you put the wrong kind of fuel in a car, the fuel will cause problems with the engine. Your body works in a similar way. The kinds of food you eat affect your overall health. Your body needs energy for physical activity, for bone and muscle growth, and for fighting germs that cause sickness. You get this energy from the substances in the food that you eat.

Nutrition is the study of how our bodies use the food we eat to maintain our health. Practicing good nutrition will help keep your body healthy. Good nutrition means eating the right amount of healthful foods and not skipping meals. On the other hand, if the food you eat does not give your body the substances that it needs, your body will not function properly. One reason Tracy did not feel well at soccer practice was that she skipped lunch and ate an unhealthy snack. ★ 1.A; 3.A

Nutrients and Food

The substances in food that your body needs to function properly are called **nutrients.** Your body uses some nutrients to keep your body healthy. Your body uses other nutrients for energy. Your body can make some of the nutrients it needs, but most of the nutrients come from the foods you eat. For example, your body needs certain nutrients to grow strong bones. You get these nutrients for strong bones from foods such as milk or cheese. Because nutrients are so important to your health, you must eat healthful foods that are rich in nutrients. ★ 1.A

Health Journal
Summarize the journey of an apple through the human body during the process of digestion.

Using Food for Energy

The food you eat cannot be used directly as an energy source. Instead, the food goes through the process of digestion. **Digestion** is the process of breaking down food into a form your body can use.

The first step in digestion is to chew your food. The food is chopped into smaller and smaller pieces as you chew it. Once you swallow your food, it passes into your stomach. In your stomach, the food is broken down even further by strong acids and other chemicals.

The broken down food is a thick fluid that passes into your small intestine. By this time, the food you have eaten has been broken down into nutrients. The nutrients are absorbed into the blood through the blood vessels in the small intestine. The blood then carries the nutrients to your cells and tissues, where some of the nutrients are used for energy. ★ 1.A

Figure 1 The food you eat greatly affects your overall health, including your ability to stay active, study, and hang out with your friends.

Lesson 1 Nutrition and Your Life | 189

What Is a Diet?

What do you think when you hear the word diet? You may think that diet means "eating less to lose weight." A <mark>diet</mark> is a pattern of eating that includes what a person eats, how much a person eats, and how often a person eats. A person's diet is important because it describes how he or she eats every day. ★ 4.C

Influences on Your Food Choices

You may not have thought about the many things that affect your food choices. Your personal taste has a great effect on what you choose to eat. If you don't like a certain food, you are less likely to eat it, right? The overall cost of food may affect what types of food your family buys regularly. In turn, this also affects what foods you actually eat. Your family traditions may be another reason for eating some foods but not eating other foods. Also, the foods that are common in your local area may be a large part of your diet. However, these foods may be only a small part of the diet of a person who lives in a different area. The convenience of some foods may make them more appealing to you, so you may eat them more often. Finally, how and what your friends eat may influence the kinds of foods that you choose to eat. Figure 2 illustrates seven factors that influence your food choices. ★ 6.A; 7.A; 8.A; 12.E

Figure 2 Several factors may affect your food choices.

Food and Feelings

You may not realize that your feelings also affect your food choices. When you are hungry, you eat and your body's nutrients are replenished. However, many people eat even if they are not hungry. They may eat because their feelings or their surroundings make them want to eat, even if their body does not need the nutrients.

Some people eat when they feel upset or nervous. On the other hand, others don't feel like eating when they are upset or nervous. Some people feel as if they can't eat when they are very excited or happy. Then again, other people celebrate being happy by eating. Often, people feel like eating when they are at social gatherings, such as parties. Think of a time when your feelings determined what or how you ate. Knowing what types of feelings affect your diet can be helpful to you. When you eat because of your feelings instead of because of hunger, you may develop unhealthy eating habits. If you know which feelings affect you, you can stop yourself from eating when you are not hungry. Understanding what affects your eating habits will help you maintain a healthy diet. ★ 1.A

Health Journal

Keep an "eating" diary for 2 days by writing down everything you eat and drink for each meal. Next to each entry, describe the reason you ate. For example, your reasons could be excitement, stress, or hunger. Do you eat only when you are hungry? How can you change your emotional eating patterns?

Figure 3 If you understand which feelings affect your eating habits, you can make healthier decisions about food.

Lesson Review

Using Vocabulary

1. What is a *nutrient*?
2. Define *diet*.

Understanding Concepts

3. Explain how food is processed to be used as a source of energy inside your body. ★ 1.A
4. Why should you understand how your feelings affect your food choices? ★ 1.A; 4.C; 12.F

Critical Thinking

5. **Applying Concepts** Explain how the food you eat affects your overall health. ★ 1.A; 3.A
6. **Analyzing Ideas** Name three factors that affect your food choices, and give examples of how these factors affect your life. ★ 6.A; 7.A; 8.A; 12.E

internet connect
www.scilinks.org/health
Topic: Nutrition
HealthLinks code: HD4072
Topic: Foods as Fuel
HealthLinks code: HD4044

HEALTH LINKS — Maintained by the National Science Teachers Association

Lesson 1 Nutrition and Your Life

Lesson 2 The Nutrients You Need

What You'll Do

- **Identify** the six classes of essential nutrients. ★ 4.C
- **Explain** how the body uses the six classes of essential nutrients. ★ 1.A; 4.C

Terms to Learn

- Calorie
- metabolism
- carbohydrate
- fat
- protein
- vitamin
- mineral

Start Off Write

How much fat is needed in a healthy diet?

Adriana bought a bean burrito for lunch, while Rose bought a hamburger. Although these girls have very different lunches, they are receiving similar nutrients.

How can these girls be receiving similar nutrients? Many foods contain more than one nutrient. Also, different foods contain the same nutrients. This lesson will introduce you to the different types of nutrients and the foods in which these nutrients are found.

How Your Body Uses Nutrients

Your body uses some nutrients for energy. The energy is used for your body's growth, maintenance, and repair. Your body uses other nutrients to maintain certain body functions. Your body can make some nutrients. Most of the nutrients, however, must come from the food you eat. These nutrients are called the essential nutrients.

The six classes of essential nutrients are carbohydrates (KAHR bo HIE drayts), fats, proteins (PROH TEENZ), vitamins, minerals, and water. Carbohydrates, fats, and proteins provide your body with energy. Vitamins and minerals help your body use and regulate the energy from the other nutrients. Water helps transport nutrients, lubricates your joints, and regulates your body temperature.

The amount of energy your body gets from a food is measured in units called **Calories**. The process of converting the energy in food into energy your body can use is called **metabolism** (muh TAB uh LIZ uhm).

Because each nutrient plays a different role in helping your body function properly, you must have all the nutrients to stay healthy. So, you need to eat a variety of foods that provide you with the nutrients your body needs. ★ 4.C

Figure 4 Your body needs a variety of nutrients to stay healthy. Eating only one food, even if it is healthy, will not give you all the nutrients you need.

Carbohydrates

Carbohydrates are your body's main source of energy. A carbohydrate is a chemical composed of one or more simple sugars. One gram of carbohydrate has 4 Calories.

The two basic types of carbohydrates are simple carbohydrates and complex carbohydrates. *Simple carbohydrates* are sugars, such as table sugar, honey, and the sugar found in fresh fruit. Simple carbohydrates are easy for your body to digest and give your body quick energy. *Complex carbohydrates*, or starches, are made of many sugar molecules linked together. Complex carbohydrates are broken down into the simpler sugar molecules before they are used by the body. Complex carbohydrates include breads, pastas, rice, and potatoes. Fiber is a complex carbohydrate that is a healthy part of a balanced diet. Foods high in fiber include brown rice, oatmeal, and whole wheat bread. ★ 4.C

Fats

Most people think that fats are not healthful. But, a small amount of fat is essential for good health. Fats are energy-storage nutrients that help the body store some vitamins. Fats are very important, but they are needed only in small amounts. Diets that have too much fat have been linked to weight gain and heart disease. Sources of fats include butter, vegetable oil, margarine, and other dairy products. One gram of fat has 9 Calories. ★ 4.C

Proteins

You can think of proteins as building blocks for your body. Proteins are nutrients that build and repair tissues and cells. Meat, poultry, fish, eggs, milk, and cheese are animal sources of protein. Beans, nuts, and tofu are vegetable sources of protein. One gram of protein has 4 Calories. ★ 4.C

Brain Food

Sugars and starches are different kinds of carbohydrates. Breaking down whole-grain breads, whole-wheat pastas, and brown rice during digestion takes longer than breaking down foods high in sugar. This keeps us feeling full longer than if we ate only foods high in simple sugars, such as candy bars.

Figure 5 These two snacks have the same number of Calories. High-fat snacks, like the chips, will be smaller than low-fat snacks that have the same number of Calories.

Lesson 2 The Nutrients You Need 193

Vitamins

Vitamins do not provide energy, but they help keep your body healthy. **Vitamins** are organic compounds that control several body functions. Your body needs only a small amount of vitamins each day to stay healthy.

Many vitamins are found in fresh vegetables, fruits, nuts, and dairy products. Without vitamins, your body will not function properly. For example, a lack of vitamin C can cause scurvy, which is a disease that may cause tooth loss. Or without vitamin A, you may develop night blindness.

You may know people who take vitamins in the form of a pill. Taking vitamin pills is one way to get all of your vitamins. But the best way to get your vitamins is to eat a variety of fruits and vegetables. By eating fruits and vegetables, you also get the benefit of the other nutrients in these foods. ★ 1.A

Minerals

Minerals play very important roles in keeping your body healthy. **Minerals** are elements that are essential for good health. Calcium and phosphorus (FAHS fuh ruhs) keep your bones and muscles strong. Iron is necessary for your blood to deliver oxygen to your cells. Sodium and potassium help regulate your blood pressure. If your body lacks zinc you may develop coarse, brittle hair. A lack of iodine can affect your growth and may cause your thyroid gland to swell. Although minerals are very important, your body needs them only in very small amounts. Table 1 lists good sources of vitamins and minerals. ★ 1.A

TABLE 1 Good Sources of Some Important Vitamins and Minerals

Name	What It Does For Your Body	Where You Get It
Vitamin A	necessary for healthy hair and skin	carrots, sweet potatoes, and squash
Vitamin C	helps your body fight germs that cause illness	orange juice, broccoli, and papaya
Vitamin B-12	aids in concentration, memory, and balance	fish, milk and milk products, eggs, meat, and poultry
Calcium	necessary for healthy, strong bones and teeth	milk, cheese, yogurt, and sardines
Iron	necessary for healthy blood; prevents tiredness	tofu, spinach, blackeyed peas, and red meat

Figure 6 Try to drink 8 to 10 glasses of water each day. Every bit counts, even a quick drink from a water fountain.

Water

A human cannot survive for more than a few days without water. That is how important water is to your body. Your body is almost 70 percent water.

You use water to carry nutrients and waste products throughout your body. Water helps your body keep a constant temperature. The cells in your body are made mostly of water, and water is used to fill the spaces between your cells. Water surrounds your joints and keeps them moving smoothly.

If you do not get enough water every day, your body will not function properly. In fact, if you do not drink enough water, your body may dry out. The drying out of the body is called *dehydration* (DEE hie DRAY shuhn). Dehydration can lead to fainting or, in very extreme cases, death. You should drink at least 8 to 10 glasses of water a day. You should drink even more water if you exercise or play sports. Drinking water is the best way to prevent your body from drying out. However, other foods, including milk, fruits, vegetables, soups, stews, salads, and juices, are good sources of water. ★ 1.A; 4.C

Myth & Fact

Myth: Drinking bottled water is better for you than drinking water from the faucet.

Fact: Most of the time, the quality of water from a faucet is not much different from the quality of bottled water.

Lesson Review

Using Vocabulary

1. What is a carbohydrate, and how does your body use this nutrient? ★ 1.A
2. What is a Calorie?

Understanding Concepts

3. Explain why a person should eat a variety of foods each day. ★ 1.A; 4.C
4. Explain why you must drink enough water every day. ★ 1.A

Critical Thinking

5. **Making Inferences** Explain why you do not need to take vitamin pills if you have a healthy diet. ★ 1.A; 4.C

internet connect
www.scilinks.org/health
Topic: Nutrients
HealthLinks code: HD4071

HEALTH LINKS Maintained by the National Science Teachers Association

Lesson 2 The Nutrients You Need

Lesson 3 — Making Healthy Choices

What You'll Do

- **Describe** the Dietary Guidelines for Americans. ★ 4.C
- **Describe** the food groups represented by the Food Guide Pyramid. ★ 4.C
- **Explain** how to read a Nutrition Facts label. ★ 4.C
- **Describe** the difference between a serving size and a portion size. ★ 4.C

Terms to Learn

- Dietary Guidelines for Americans
- Food Guide Pyramid
- Nutrition Facts label

Start Off Write

How can the Nutrition Facts label help you make healthy choices?

When Jack gets home from school, he usually snacks on potato chips or cookies, eats dinner, and then does his homework. For the rest of the evening, he watches TV.

The way Jack spends his evening may seem normal to most teens. What Jack may not realize is that he is developing some unhealthy habits.

The Dietary Guidelines

While there may be no such thing as a good food or a bad food, there are certainly healthy and unhealthy eating habits. The **Dietary Guidelines for Americans** are a set of suggestions that will help you develop healthy eating habits.

The guidelines were created by the U.S. Department of Agriculture and the U.S. Department of Health and Human Services. The guidelines ask Americans to remember the ABCs for health: **A**im for fitness, **B**uild a healthy base, and **C**hoose sensibly. You can aim for fitness by being physically active every day. You can build a healthy base by making healthy food choices and by keeping foods safe to eat. Make sure your food is safe to eat by cooking it thoroughly. Remember to store foods properly by keeping cold foods cold and by refrigerating hot foods soon after you have used them. Finally, you can make sensible choices by choosing to eat foods that are low in fat, salt, and sugar. Following these guidelines will help you build a healthy diet and healthy eating habits. ★ 4.A; 4.C

TABLE 2 The Dietary Guidelines for Americans	
Aim for fitness	Aim to stay at a healthy weight by being physically active every day.
Build a healthy base	Choose healthy foods by using the Food Guide Pyramid. Eat plenty of fresh fruits and vegetables. Keep foods safe to eat by cooking your food fully. Store foods properly by keeping cold foods cold and by refrigerating hot foods soon after you are finished with them.
Choose sensibly	Choose foods that are low in salt, sugar, and fat.

196   Chapter 8   Eating Responsibly

Figure 7 The Food Guide Pyramid

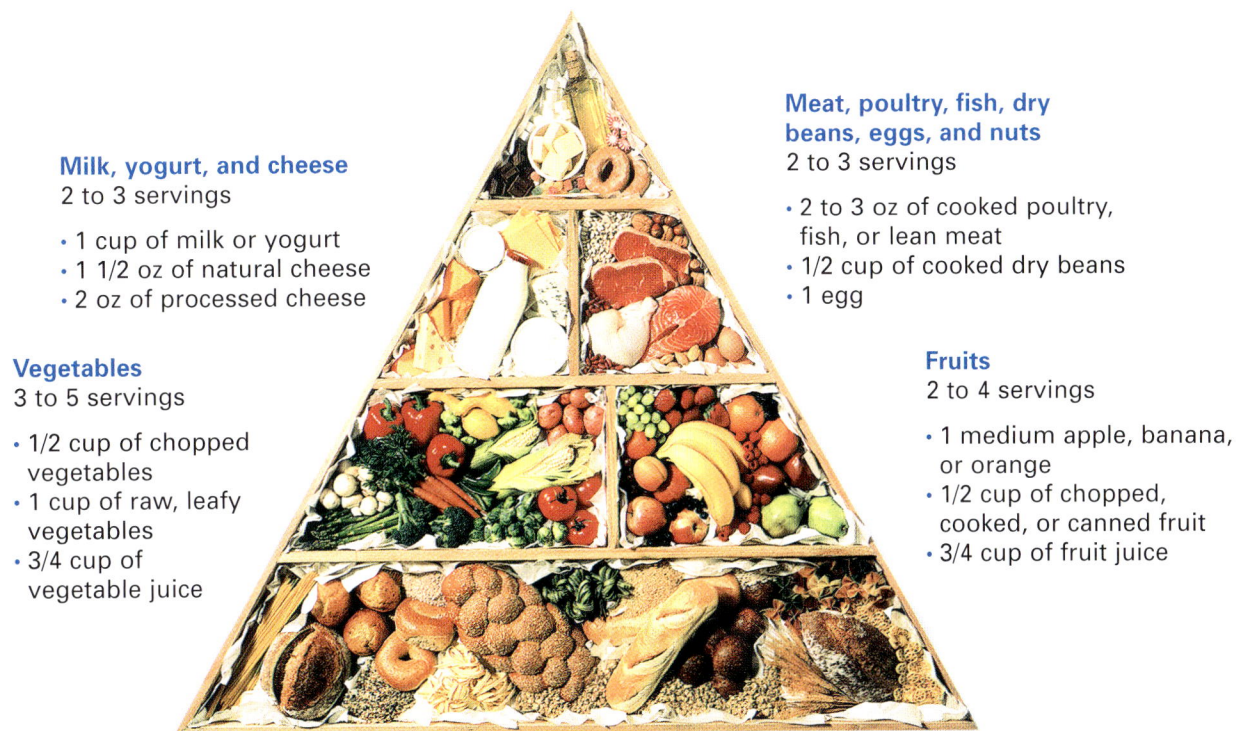

Fats, oils, and sweets
Use sparingly

Milk, yogurt, and cheese
2 to 3 servings
- 1 cup of milk or yogurt
- 1 1/2 oz of natural cheese
- 2 oz of processed cheese

Meat, poultry, fish, dry beans, eggs, and nuts
2 to 3 servings
- 2 to 3 oz of cooked poultry, fish, or lean meat
- 1/2 cup of cooked dry beans
- 1 egg

Vegetables
3 to 5 servings
- 1/2 cup of chopped vegetables
- 1 cup of raw, leafy vegetables
- 3/4 cup of vegetable juice

Fruits
2 to 4 servings
- 1 medium apple, banana, or orange
- 1/2 cup of chopped, cooked, or canned fruit
- 3/4 cup of fruit juice

Bread, cereal, rice, and pasta
6 to 11 servings
- 1 slice of bread
- 1 oz of ready-to-eat cereal
- 1/2 cup of rice or pasta
- 1/2 cup of cooked cereal

The Food Guide Pyramid

How do you know which foods are the right ones to eat? And how do you know how much of which foods to eat? The **Food Guide Pyramid** is a tool that shows you what kinds of foods to eat and how much of each food you should eat every day. In the Food Guide Pyramid, foods are separated into food groups. Each food group includes foods that contain similar nutrients. Each food group also has its own block on the pyramid. As you can see, each block is a different size. A bigger block means you should eat more of that food group. For example, the bread group is the largest block, which means you need more servings of foods from this group than the others. The *serving size* for each group is the amount of that food group that is considered healthy. The Food Guide Pyramid above shows you the recommended number of daily servings for each group. It also shows the serving sizes for each food group. ★ 4.A; 4.C

SOCIAL STUDIES ACTIVITY

In small groups, research foods from different cultures for each group of the Food Guide Pyramid. Find at least three different foods for each group. Together, create your own multicultural Food Guide Pyramid.

Lesson 3 Making Healthy Choices

Health Journal

Choose two or three of your favorite snacks and compare their Nutrition Facts labels. What nutrients are you getting from your snacks? Which snack is the healthiest, and why do you think so?

The Nutrition Facts Label

Packaged foods are required by law to have nutrition information labels. The **Nutrition Facts label** is a label found on the outside packages of food that states how many servings are in the container, how many Calories are in each serving, and the amount of nutrients in each serving. You can use the Nutrition Facts label to make your food choices.

The first part of the Nutrition Facts label shows you the serving size of the food, and how many serving sizes of the food are in the package. The second part of the label shows you how many Calories you get from eating one serving of the food. Next you will find the Percentage Daily Values section, which lists some of the nutrients found in the food. This section shows you how the amounts of the nutrients in the food campares to the amounts that are necessary for a healthy diet. These values are based on a 2,000 Calorie diet. Remember that every person has a different daily Calorie requirement. If you are unsure about how many Calories you need daily, check with your doctor or a registered dietitian. ★ 4.A; 4.C

Figure 8 Macaroni and Cheese

Serving information
Number of Calories per serving
Percentage of daily value of nutrients per serving

Nutrition Facts

Serving Size 1 cup (59 g)
Servings per Container 2

Amount per Serving	Prepared
Calories	290
Calories from Fat	90
	% Daily Value
Total Fat 10 g	14%
Saturated Fat 3.5 g	16%
Cholesterol 10 mg	39%
Sodium 30 mg	39%
Total Carbohydrate 41 g	14%
Dietary Fiber less than 1 g	3%
Sugars 4 g	
Protein 10 g	12%
Vitamin A	8%
Vitamin C	0%
Calcium	15%
Iron	8%

*Percent Daily Values are based on a 2,000 Calorie diet. Your daily values may be higher or lower depending on your Calorie needs:

	Calories	2,000	2,500
Total Fat	Less than	65g	80g
Sat Fat	Less than	20g	25g
Cholesterol	Less than	300mg	300mg
Sodium	Less than	2,400mg	2,400mg
Total Carbohydrate		300g	375g
Dietary Fiber		25g	30g
Protien		50g	60g

Hands-on ACTIVITY

SERVING SLEUTHS

1. Working in groups, choose a snack that you enjoy eating. Check the Nutrition Facts label and determine the serving size of the snack. Then, decide how much food would be in a portion.

2. Use a scale to measure the amount of vegetable shortening that is equal to the amount of fat in a serving.

3. Then, measure the amount of vegetable shortening that is equal to the amount of fat in a portion.

Analysis

1. How does the amount of fat in a serving compare with the amount of fat in a portion?

2. How will your results affect your future food choices?

What Is a Serving Size?

The Food Guide Pyramid and the Nutrition Facts label use the term *serving size*. A serving size is a standard amount of food that allows different foods to be compared with one another. The Food Guide Pyramid states how many servings of each food group you need every day and how much food is in one serving. The Nutrition Facts label shows you how much food is in one serving in a package of food. Be careful not to confuse a serving size with a *portion* of food. A portion of food is the amount of food a person wants to eat. What you need and what you want can be very different things. For example, one serving of meat is about 3 ounces (about the size of a deck of cards). You may want more than 3 ounces. You may choose a large hamburger made with 6 ounces of meat. The amount of meat in the hamburger is your portion. But, your portion counts as two servings. ★ 4.C

Figure 9 The smaller bowl is one serving of macaroni and cheese. The larger bowl is the the whole box. Which amount are you more likely to eat?

Lesson Review

Using Vocabulary

1. What are the Dietary Guidelines for Americans? ★ 4.C

2. What is the Food Guide Pyramid? ★ 4.C

Understanding Concepts

3. What is the difference between a serving and a portion? ★ 4.C

4. Explain how you use the Food Guide Pyramid to plan your daily food intake. ★ 4.A; 4.C

Critical Thinking

5. **Applying Concepts** Imagine that you plan to cut the amount of fat in your diet and you are shopping for food. What part of the Nutrition Facts label will you need to read, and how will you make your choices? ★ 4.A; 4.C

internet connect
www.scilinks.org/health
Topic: Food Pyramids
HealthLinks code: HD4043
HEALTH LINKS Maintained by the National Science Teachers Association

Lesson 3 Making Healthy Choices

Lesson 4   Body Image

What You'll Do

- **Explain** why a healthy body image is important. ★ 1.A
- **Describe** the relationship between body image and self-esteem ★ 1.A
- **List** three influences on your body image. ★ 6.A; 7.A; 8.A; 12.E
- **Identify** two strategies for building a healthy body image. ★ 12.B; 12.F

Terms to Learn

- body image
- self-esteem

Start Off Write

Who can influence your body image?

Farida and Ryan are watching TV. They see some very thin women and some very tall, muscular men. They compare themselves with the people they see on TV. Both of them think they need to lose weight.

Do you ever compare yourself with people you see on TV or in magazines, as Farida and Ryan did? If so, you are probably thinking about your body image. Your **body image** is how you feel about and see your body.

Seeing the Real You

Your body is likely to change a lot over the next few years. If you have a healthy body image, you will be able to deal with physical changes in a positive way. Keeping a healthy body image isn't always easy. A teen's weight and height may change very quickly. Sometimes, you may not feel very comfortable about all the changes. But if you can focus on what you like about your body every day, you will feel a lot better. This positive attitude will help you feel good about yourself.

If you find yourself looking at another person and wishing you were as tall as that person or thinking that you need to lose some weight, try to stop yourself. Comparing yourself with other people is natural, but doing so is not always healthy. People are often more critical of themselves than they are of other people. Remember that your body image is how you choose to see your body. Remember to accept yourself for who you are! ★ 1.A; 12.E

Figure 10 As you can see, teens come in all sizes and shapes.

200   Chapter 8   Eating Responsibly

Figure 11 **Healthy and Unhealthy Body Image**

Healthy
- I like myself.
- I like my body.
- I can do many things.
- I am a nice person.
- I like to go out and try new things.

Unhealthy
- I think I am too fat.
- I don't like my body.
- I don't think many people like me.
- I think I should go on a diet.
- I don't like to go out and try new things.

Body Image and Self-Esteem

Your body image has an impact on how you feel about yourself as a person. In other words, your body image can affect your self-esteem. **Self-esteem** is how much you value, respect, and feel confident about yourself.

A person who has a negative body image often also sees little worth in himself or herself. So, that person tends to have a low self-esteem. People who have low self-esteem tend to be less successful at school and in activities. They also tend to feel uncomfortable among their family and friends.

A person who has a positive body image tends to have high self-esteem. People who have a positive body image and high self-esteem usually are willing to try new things, and they are less likely to give up if they do not succeed at something the first time.

Your body image and your self-esteem are closely related to each other. However, they are not the same thing. Your body image is how you see and imagine your body. Your self-esteem is how much you like yourself as a person. If you see your body in a healthy way, are comfortable with your physical appearance, and value yourself as a person, you will have both a positive body image and high self-esteem. ★ 1.A; 4.C

Health Journal

Make a list of three things you like about your body. Write a paragraph about how you feel about what you have listed, and include two ways you will remind yourself of your list whenever you are feeling unsure about your body.

Influences on Body Image

Your body image has been developing since you were a baby. It will continue to develop as you get older. This development continues because throughout your life, your body image will be influenced by several factors. These factors include the following:

- your family and friends
- your teachers or coaches
- the media

Each of these factors may have a positive or a negative effect on your body image. You may have very positive experiences in which a family member or a friend says something about your physical appearance that makes you feel good. These experiences can help you have a positive body image. Then again, a friend or someone at school may say something about your appearance that makes you feel unsure about your body. This unsure feeling could lead you to develop a negative body image if you let it.

Figure 12 Sometimes, outside influences on your body image may cause you to "see" things that aren't really there.

Other people, such as teachers or coaches, may have an effect on your body image, too. Like your friends and family, teachers and coaches can help or hurt your body image. Keep in mind that most people do not mean to hurt your feelings or be critical of you.

Often the media, such as TV, magazines, movies, and music videos, changes how you feel about your body. The media often focuses on teen girls who are too thin or boys who are unusually muscular. These images may make you feel unsure about how you look. Even though your body image can be influenced by several factors, remember that how you feel about your body is your choice.

★ 6.A; 7.A; 8.A; 12.E

LIFE SKILLS ACTIVITY

EVALUATING MEDIA MESSAGES

In small groups, talk about what real people look like. Collect pictures of friends and family of different ages, and make a collage with the images. Cut out pictures of people from magazines, and make a separate collage. Compare the two collages, and discuss what you see. What can you do to change the way you feel about how a real teen should look? ★ 8.A

Building a Healthy Body Image

There are two ways to build a healthy body image. You can use "I" statements to express your feelings. Or, you can use positive self-talk to encourage yourself.

"I" statements can help you when you are dealing with people who make unkind remarks about your appearance. An "I" statement tells other people directly what bothers you about their behavior. An "I" statement can explain how you feel about the situation. The key to this strategy is to use the word *I* instead of *you*.

If you find yourself feeling uncomfortable about your body, positive self-talk can help you feel better. Positive self-talk is a way of encouraging yourself by saying positive statements to yourself. For example, instead of saying "I wish my curly hair were straight," say to yourself, "I may not always like my curly hair, but when I style it properly, it looks great." The table below gives more examples of positive self-talk and "I" statements.

★ 11.D; 12.F

TABLE 3 Strategies for Building a Healthy Body Image

Situation	Strategy	Example
Your friend tells you that you need to fix your hair, but you already spent half an hour trying to make your hair look nice.	"I" statements	I appreciate your opinion, but I think that my hair looks fine.
You recently found out that you need glasses. You are not happy about having to wear them because you are worried about what other people may think about your appearance.	Positive self-talk	I shouldn't worry about what other people think. I need glasses, so I will have to wear them. I can pick out glasses that look good on me.

Lesson Review

Using Vocabulary
1. What is self-esteem?

Understanding Concepts
2. Explain how body image and self-esteem are related. ★ 1.A
3. Identify two strategies for building a healthy body image. ★ 12.B; 12.F
4. List three influences on your body image. ★ 6.A; 7.A; 8.A; 12.E

Critical Thinking
5. **Applying Concepts** Your best friend is crying because someone told her she was overweight. What suggestions would you give your friend? ★ 4.C; 11.D

internet connect
www.scilinks.org/health
Topic: Body Image
HealthLinks code: HD4019
HEALTH LINKS Maintained by the National Science Teachers Association

Lesson 5 — Eating Disorders

Cristina's best friend Tamera has become very concerned about food and weight loss. Cristina has noticed that Tamera doesn't eat lunch very often.

What You'll Do

- **Identify** three examples of unhealthy eating behaviors. ★ 1.B
- **Explain** how overexercising is related to eating disorders. ★ 1.B
- **Identify** three eating disorders. ★ 1.B
- **Describe** how you would give or get help for an eating disorder. ★ 1.B; 4.C

Terms to Learn

- eating disorder
- anorexia nervosa
- bulimia nervosa
- binge eating disorder

Start Off Write

How can exercising too much be bad for you?

Tamera has developed an unhealthy eating behavior. This behavior may be dangerous because it can turn into an illness called an *eating disorder*.

Unhealthy Eating Behavior

The media tells us continuously that the ideal female is very thin and the ideal male is slim and muscular. As a result, many people become overly concerned about their weight. Some teen boys may try to become more muscular. Some teen girls may eat less to stay thin. Many of these attempts to have the perfect body result in unhealthy eating behaviors.

Unhealthy eating behaviors include limiting yourself to eating only certain foods, skipping meals, or eating large amounts of food at one time. For instance, when someone cuts all fat out of his or her diet, this person has an unhealthy eating behavior. Wrestlers who fast for 2 days to be at a certain weight for a match have an unhealthy eating behavior.

Unhealthy eating behaviors can affect a person's ability to learn, can disrupt his or her growth and development, and can have damaging effects on his or her overall health. The most important thing to know about unhealthy eating behaviors is that they may develop into an eating disorder. So, what makes teens develop unhealthy eating behaviors? Table 4 lists some of the reasons. ★ 1.B

TABLE 4 Why Teens Develop Unhealthy Eating Behaviors
Low self-esteem
Fear of becoming overweight
Poor skills for coping with stress
Unhealthy body image
Pressure from friends or family to be thin
Feelings of helplessness

Overexercising

The fear of becoming overweight and the stress of wanting to have perfect bodies cause many teens to exercise too much, or overexercise. While you should be physically active every day, overexercising can be harmful to your health.

People who overexercise tend to be overly concerned about their bodies and their weight. They also usually suffer from an unhealthy body image and low self-esteem. Overexercising occurs when a person exercises more intensely and for a longer period of time than is necessary for good health. There are many reasons teens overexercise. Some teens feel that their athletic abilities are what make them worthy as people. Some teens have such a poor body image that they feel they should diet to change how their body looks. When these teens eat a meal they feel ashamed or weak because they didn't follow their diet. These teens overexercise in order to burn off the Calories from the food so that they don't gain any weight.

Overexercising can be dangerous. People who overexercise may get injured easily. In addition, they may suffer from extreme tiredness and feelings of sadness or hopelessness. Teens who overexercise may have problems concentrating on school work. They also tend to be irritable and moody, and as a result, their relationships with others may be hurt. ★ 1.A; 1.B

Figure 13 Overexercising can be dangerous to your health.

What Are Eating Disorders?

An **eating disorder** is a disease that involves an unhealthy concern with one's body weight and shape. Eating disorders are caused by many emotional factors and gradually develop from unhealthy eating behaviors. People suffering from an eating disorder may try to control their weight by starving themselves. They may also overeat and then get rid of the extra food by throwing it up or using pills that make them go to the bathroom.

Eating disorders often affect teens who have low self-esteem, who suffer from depression, or who have experienced physical or sexual abuse. They also affect teens who have a negative body image. Eating disorders can affect both boys and girls. People from all cultures, races, and income levels can develop eating disorders.

Some common symptoms of people who have eating disorders include constantly talking about their weight, their bodies, or food. Also, teens suffering from an eating disorder may lose a lot of weight over a short time. ★ 1.B

Ten percent of people with eating disorders were 10 years old or younger when the disease developed, and 33 percent were between the ages of 11 and 15.

Lesson 5 Eating Disorders

Anorexia Nervosa

About 1 in every 100 teen girls develops anorexia nervosa. **Anorexia nervosa** (AN uh REKS ee uh nuhr VOH suh) is an eating disorder that involves self-starvation, an unhealthy body image, and extreme weight loss. People who have anorexia nervosa have a very intense fear of being fat and gaining weight. They also feel fat or overweight even though they are very thin. People who suffer from anorexia nervosa are often known as perfectionists who appear to be in control. But in reality, they have low self-esteem and an unhealthy body image.

People who have anorexia nervosa may eat only foods low in Calories and fat. They may spend more time playing with food than eating it. They may also wear many layers of clothing to hide their weight loss. People who have anorexia nervosa suffer from physical symptoms as well, which you can see in the figure below.

Teens who have anorexia nervosa must receive medical help. If left untreated, these people may develop long-term problems with their stomach, bowels, kidneys, and heart. In some cases, a person suffering from anorexia nervosa dies from the lack of nutrients in the body, which is caused by his or her self-starvation. ★ 1.B

Brain Food

Did you know that 39.7 percent of high school students try to lose weight? In fact, 59.7 percent of teen girls try to lose weight, while 23.1 percent of teen boys try to lose weight.

Figure 14 Some Symptoms of Anorexia Nervosa

Characteristics of a Healthy Person
- Shiny, healthy hair
- Healthy skin
- Strong nails
- Ability to maintain a healthy weight
- Energetic

Symptoms of Anorexia Nervosa
- Dry, dull hair and hair loss
- Dry skin
- Brittle nails
- Large weight loss over a short period of time
- Abdominal pain
- Growth of fine body hair
- Feels cold all the time
- Feels faint, or light headed

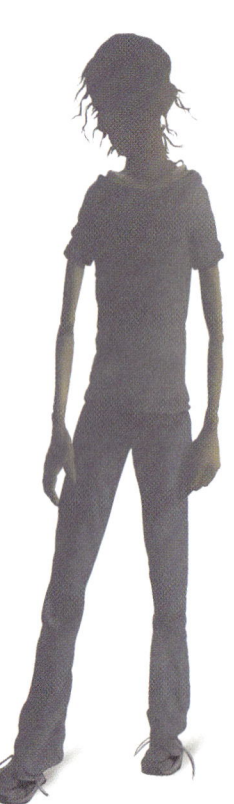

Bulimia Nervosa

Many teens suffer from bulimia nervosa. **Bulimia nervosa** (boo LEE mee uh nuhr VOH suh) is an eating disorder in which a person eats a large amount of food and then tries to remove the food from his or her body. People with bulimia nervosa cannot control how much they eat. They can eat a large amount of food in a short period of time, which is called *bingeing*. They may binge several times a day or only a couple of times a week. This type of behavior is often triggered by feelings of depression, anger, or boredom.

People with bulimia nervosa feel ashamed that they ate so much food. So, they get rid of the food by making themselves vomit, or by taking a laxative (LAKS uh tiv) (a drug that helps you have a bowel movement) or a diuretic (DIE yoo RET ik) (a drug that makes you urinate). They may also overexercise to burn off the Calories. These attempts to get rid of the food are called *purging*.

This cycle of bingeing and purging can hurt a person's natural body functions. The acid that comes up from the stomach when a person vomits eats away at the gums, teeth, and the lining of the throat. The person's cheeks and jaws may swell. Also, the person's teeth may be stained or discolored.

Many people who have bulimia nervosa don't binge and purge all of the time. Also, many people who have this disorder are not overweight. So, they often appear to be healthy. Bulimia nervosa may not be as easy to see as other eating disorders. Knowing some of the warning signs is important. A person who has bulimia nervosa may do one or more of the following:

- spend a lot of time thinking about food
- steal food
- take trips to the bathroom immediately after eating
- make themselves throw up after eating
- hide food in strange places
- exercise excessively

Bulimia nervosa puts a lot of stress on the body. As a result, a person may die. Bulimia nervosa can be treated by a doctor. ★ 1.B

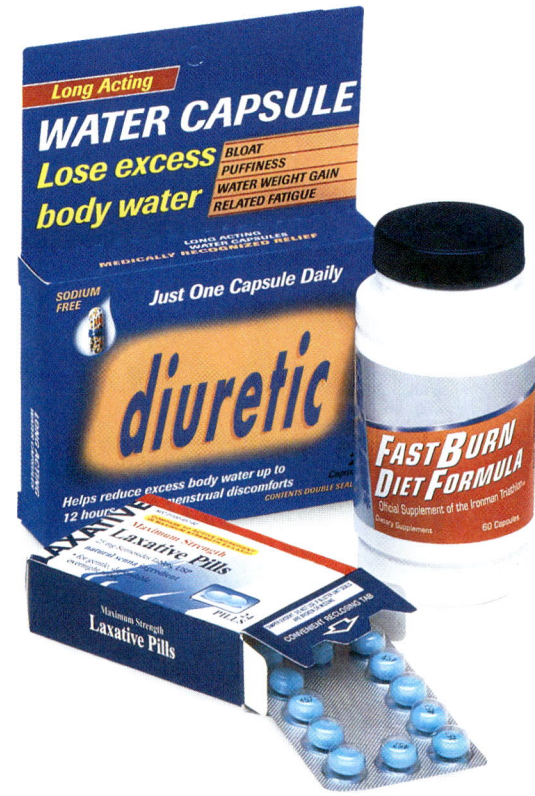

Figure 15 Some people who have bulimia use pills to help them purge. These pills can be extremely dangerous to their health.

Myth & Fact

Myth: Only women will resort to drastic measures, such as bingeing and purging, to lose weight.

Fact: About 20 percent of American men binge and purge to lose weight.

STUDY TIP *for better reading*

The word *obesity* comes from the Latin word *obesus*, which means "to devour."

Binge Eating Disorder

Binge eating disorder is an eating disorder that is often caused by emotional problems. **Binge eating disorder** is a disease in which a person cannot control how much he or she eats. People who suffer from binge eating disorder do not try to purge after they eat. Binge eaters eat a large amount of food very quickly and usually do not enjoy the food. They eat a lot of junk food, and they eat alone. In fact, they are very secretive about their eating habits. When they binge, they feel completely out of control, and when they finish, they usually feel ashamed and are disgusted with themselves. People who are binge eaters have problems controlling their weight. Eventually, binge eaters become obese. *Obesity* is a condition characterized by a large percentage of body fat.

Unfortunately, binge eaters are at risk for the health problems associated with obesity. They are at risk for high cholesterol, high blood pressure, diabetes, gall bladder and heart disease, strokes, and some forms of cancer. ★ 1.B

Giving Help

What can you do if you think a friend has an eating disorder? You must not keep your suspicions to yourself. Talk to your friend privately. In a calm and caring way, tell him or her about your concerns. Listen to what your friend has to say without interrupting. Remember that your friend may feel ashamed, embarrassed, or scared. Encourage your friend to get professional help. Your friend may refuse to get help. If so, ask for help from an adult, such as a parent, teacher, counselor, or a school nurse. Your friend may be upset with you at first, but it is very important to get help for your friend. In the long run, you may be saving your friend's life. ★ 10.C; 11.B; 11.C; 11.D; 12.B; 12.E

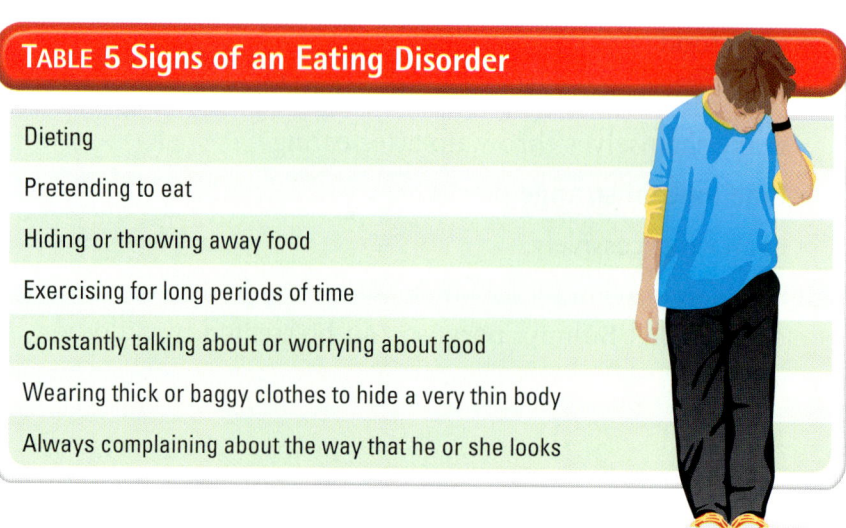

TABLE 5 Signs of an Eating Disorder
Dieting
Pretending to eat
Hiding or throwing away food
Exercising for long periods of time
Constantly talking about or worrying about food
Wearing thick or baggy clothes to hide a very thin body
Always complaining about the way that he or she looks

Getting Help

Whether you are getting help for a friend or for yourself, you may find that talking about an eating disorder is difficult. However, you must get the help you need. Most people are unable to recover from an eating disorder without professional help. Here are some steps to follow if you or someone you know needs help:

- First, find an adult you trust. This may be a parent or another adult you know.
- Find a time when you can speak to the person privately.
- Sit down, and tell the person your concerns clearly. Table 5 shows you some ways to start the conversation.

You may find that the conversation gets easier once you get started. The adult you choose to tell will likely want to help you. Sometimes, just letting someone else know helps a lot. Once someone else knows, he or she can help you with the next steps.

★ 4.C; 12.B

TABLE 6 Giving and Getting Help for an Eating Disorder

"I need your help. I am afraid that I have an eating disorder. Once I start eating, I can't stop. I'm not even always hungry when I eat."

"I need your help. I am afraid that my friend _____ has an eating disorder. I know that he/she has been throwing up after lunch almost every day."

Brain Food

Without professional help,
- 20% of people who have eating disorders die

With professional help,
- 60% of people who have eating disorders recover
- 20% of people who have eating disorders make partial recoveries
- 20% of people who have eating disorders do not improve

Lesson Review

Using Vocabulary

1. What is an eating disorder? Give three examples. ★ 1.B
2. Describe binge eating disorder. ★ 1.B
3. What is anorexia nervosa? ★ 1.B

Understanding Concepts

4. What are three examples of unhealthy eating behavior? ★ 1.B
5. How is overexercising related to eating disorders? ★ 1.A; 1.B
6. Describe the signs of bulimia nervosa. ★ 1.B

Critical Thinking

7. **Making Inferences** Why might a person find it difficult to talk about his or her eating disorder? How would this person's feelings affect his or her decision to get help? ★ 1.B; 1.D
8. **Analyzing Ideas** How would you give or get help for an eating disorder? ★ 1.B; 4.C

internet connect
www.scilinks.org/health
Topic: Eating Disorders
HealthLinks code: HD4034
HEALTH LINKS Maintained by the National Science Teachers Association

Lesson 6 A Healthy Body, a Healthy Weight

What You'll Do

- **Describe** what affects your healthy weight range. ★ 1.A; 2.A
- **Describe** the balance between energy input and energy output. ★ 1.A
- **Identify** and describe fad diets. ★ 12.A

Terms to Learn

- healthy weight range
- body mass index
- fad diet

Start Off Write

How do you find your healthy weight range?

Tracy orders a hamburger and fries while Mary orders a salad. Mary is watching what she eats because she wants to lose weight. Mary wonders how Tracy can eat all the foods that she can't and still stay slim and healthy.

What Mary may not realize is that Tracy does not eat a hamburger and fries for every meal. She may not know that Tracy is active in sports, or that Tracy walks her dog every day. Mary watches what she eats but does not exercise.

Finding Your Healthy Weight Range

Your body will go through a lot of changes in the next few years. You gain weight as you grow taller and as your body matures. You should not restrict your diet during this time because your body needs essential nutrients to fuel this period of rapid growth.

You can maintain a healthy weight by eating well and staying physically active. So, how do you know what weight is right for you? Your weight should fall into your healthy weight range. Your **healthy weight range** is an estimate of how much you should weigh depending on your height and body frame. Your healthy weight range depends on other factors, too. Your ethnicity, gender, and family traits influence your healthy weight range.

Every teen has a unique body shape and size, so it is not possible to tell exactly how much a teen should weigh. Your BMI, or **body mass index,** is a calculation that can help you determine your healthy weight range. The body mass index table, which is found in the appendix of this book, will help you find your healthy weight range. ★ 1.A; 2.A

Figure 16 Regular physical activity will help you maintain a healthy weight.

Keeping a Healthy Energy Balance

One way to stay within your healthy weight range is to maintain a healthy energy balance. Your energy balance is the balance between the Calories you get from food and the Calories you use for normal body processes and for physical activity.

If you eat more food than your body can use for your daily activities, you will gain weight. You will gain weight because your body will store the extra energy as fat. If you eat the same amount of food that your body needs daily, you will maintain your weight. Similarly, if your body needs more energy than the food you eat supplies, you will lose weight. You will lose weight because your body will draw energy from the fat stored in your body and from your muscles.

Whether you are trying to gain, lose, or maintain your weight, balancing the food you eat with physical activity will help you maintain a healthy energy balance. Therefore, you will be able to stay within your healthy weight range. ★ 1.A

Health Journal
Suppose that your weight was below your healthy weight range. Using what you have learned in this lesson, plan how you would alter your diet and your level of physical activity to reach a weight within your healthy weight range.

Fad Diets

Many people follow fad diets to lose weight quickly. **Fad diets** are diets that promise you quick weight loss with little effort. Most fad diets require you to buy special products, such as pills or shakes. Fad diets often require you to avoid many foods that contain essential nutrients. Remember that weight gain and weight loss take time. If you lose or gain weight quickly, you may harm your health. It is healthier for a person to adjust his or her energy balance instead of following a fad diet. ★ 8.A; 12.A

Figure 17 When a diet seems too good to be true, it probably is!

Lesson Review

Using Vocabulary
1. What is a fad diet? ★ 12.A
2. Define *healthy weight range*.

Understanding Concepts
3. Explain how the body gains, loses, and maintains weight. ★ 1.A; 2.A

Critical Thinking
4. **Refusal Skills** Your friend brings a bottle of diet pills to school. She wants to share the pills with you. She tells you that you can lose weight easily with these pills. What will you tell her?
★ 4.C; 8.A; 12.A

Lesson 6 A Healthy Body, a Healthy Weight

8 CHAPTER REVIEW

Chapter Summary

■ The nutrients in food provide your body with energy and the necessary substances for growth, maintenance, and repair. ■ The six classes of essential nutrients are carbohydrates, proteins, fats, vitamins, minerals, and water. ■ The Dietary Guidelines for Americans, the Food Guide Pyramid, and the Nutrition Facts label can help you make healthy food choices. ■ An unhealthy body image may lead to unhealthy eating behaviors or eating disorders. ■ Eating disorders are diseases that involve an unhealthy concern with one's body weight and shape. You can maintain your weight through proper diet and by staying physically active every day.

Using Vocabulary

For each sentence, fill in the blank with the proper word from the word bank provided below.

Food Guide Pyramid
vitamins
fats
Dietary Guidelines for Americans
fad diets
digestion
body image
eating disorders
diet
metabolism
bulimia nervosa
healthy weight range
anorexia nervosa

1. ___ is the process in which food is broken down into substances your body can use.

2. The process of converting energy from the food you eat into usable energy is your ___.

3. A set of suggestions that can help you develop healthy eating habits are known as the ___.

4. A tool that shows you what foods and how much food to eat is the ___.

5. ___ is how you see and imagine your body.

6. Anorexia nervosa and binge eating disorder are two examples of ___.

7. If you notice a friend vomiting after eating, he or she may have the eating disorder called ___.

8. Although ___ are popular, they are unhealthy because they can cause you to lose or gain weight too rapidly.

Understanding Concepts

9. Explain the process of digestion. ★ 1.A

10. What are the two ways in which your body gets the nutrients it needs in order to grow? ★ 1.A

11. What are the six classes of essential nutrients, and why are they important?

12. Explain the difference between *simple* and *complex* carbohydrates. ★ 4.C

13. Why is having a healthy body image important? ★ 1.A

14. What effects can unhealthy eating behaviors have on your body? ★ 1.A; 1.B

15. Explain how you can help a friend who may have an eating disorder. ★ 1.B; 4.C

Critical Thinking

Identifying Relationships

16. Every person's body is different. Explain how the media and TV can create a standard that affects your personal body image. ★ 8.A

17. Your friend tells you that he eats extra sugary food for lunch in order to have more energy at soccer practice. Explain why this eating behavior is a good or bad thing to do. ★ 1.A; 4.A; 4.C

18. Explain how you can use the Nutrition Facts label to choose a food that is high in vitamin C. ★ 4.A; 4.C

19. Many people in the United States are vegetarians. In other words, they choose not to eat meat, chicken, or fish. However, these foods are considered to be very good sources of protein. What other foods could a person eat in order to get protein? ★ 4.A; 4.C

Making Good Decisions

20. You are trying to decide what to eat for breakfast, and you can't decide between frosted cereal or fruit and toast. Which of these two choices will help you perform better in gym class? ★ 4.C

21. One day in class, you overhear Sarah telling another girl to take some energy pills rather than worrying about her weight. What should you do? ★ 4.C; 12.B

22. You think that your friend Michelle has an eating disorder. You decide to talk to her about it. When you do talk, she admits that there is something wrong. You suggest that she talk to an adult, but she refuses. She asks you not to say anything to anyone. What will you do? ★ 1.B; 12.B; 12.E

Interpreting Graphics

Composition of Mai's Daily Diet

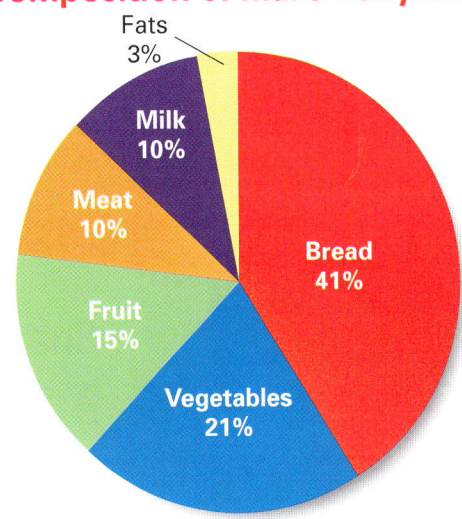

Use the figure above to answer questions 23–27. ★ M8.5.A

23. What percentage of Mai's diet consists of fatty foods?

24. What percentage of Mai's diet is NOT composed of fruits or breads?

25. How much of Mai's total daily diet is composed of meats, breads, and vegetables?

26. What percentage of Mai's diet is composed of fruits and vegetables?

27. According to the graph, Mai gets which type of nutrient the most from the foods she eats?

Reading Checkup

Take a minute to review your answers to the Health IQ questions at the beginning of this chapter. How has reading this chapter improved your Health IQ?

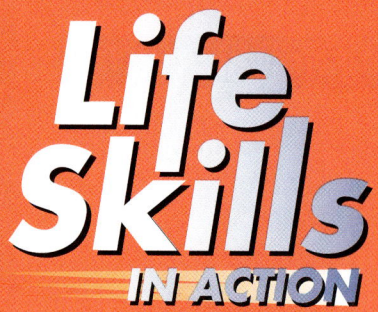

Evaluating Media Messages

You receive media messages every day. These messages are on TV, the Internet, the radio, and in newspapers and magazines. With so many messages, it is important to know how to evaluate them. Evaluating media messages means being able to judge the accuracy of a message. Complete the following activity to improve your skills in evaluating media messages.

Snack Facts

Setting the Scene

Joanna and her friend Nasreen just saw a commercial on TV for a new snack chip. The commercial said that the chip is a healthy snack because it contains only half as much fat as other snack chips do. Joanna and her friend want to know whether this snack is really healthy. ★ 4.A; 4.B; 8.A

Regular Chips

Nutrition Facts
Serving Size 1oz (28 g/12 chips)
Servings per Container 12

Amount per Serving	
Calories 160	
	% Daily Value
Total Fat 10 g	16%
Cholesterol 0 mg	0%
Carbohydrates 14 g	14%
Sugars 0g	

Reduced Fat Chips

Nutrition Facts
Serving Size 1oz (28 g/13 chips)
Servings per Container 12

Amount per Serving	
Calories 160	
	% Daily Value
Total Fat 6 g	10%
Cholesterol 0 mg	0%
Carbohydrates 19 g	16%
Sugars 0g	

ACT 1

The 5 Steps of Evaluating Media Messages

1. Examine the appeal of the message.
2. Identify the values projected by the message.
3. Consider what the source has to gain by getting you to believe the message.
4. Try to determine the reliability of the source.
5. Based on the information you gather, evaluate the message.

Guided Practice

Practice with a Friend

Form a group of three. Have one person play the role of Joanna and another person play the role of Nasreen. Have the third person be an observer. Walking through each of the five steps of evaluating media messages, role-play Joanna and Nasreen evaluating the TV commerical. Look at the Nutrition Facts labels above. Using the Nutrition Facts labels, complete the rest of the steps. The observer will take notes, which will include observations about what the people playing Joanna and Nasreen did well and suggestions of ways to improve. Stop after each step to evaluate the process. ★ 4.A; 4.B; 8.A

Independent Practice

Check Yourself

After you have completed the guided practice, go through Act 1 again without stopping at each step. Answer the questions below to review what you did.

1. What could the snack chip company gain by convincing you that their chips are healthy? ★ 4.B; 8.B
2. Is the TV commercial credible? Explain your answer. ★ 8.A; 8.B
3. What information about the healthfulness of the low-fat chips did you learn from the nutritional information? ★ 4.A
4. Are the low-fat snack chips really a healthy snack? Explain your answer. ★ 4.A; 4.C

On Your Own

The next week, Nasreen is talking to another friend at school. The friend asks Nasreen if she has tried the new shampoo made by Hair So Soft. The shampoo is expensive, but it promises to make your hair grow faster and look great. Using the commercial of the shampoo as an example, design and write an educational pamphlet that describes how to evaluate media messages.

Chapter 8 Evaluating Media Messages

CHAPTER 9
The Stages of Life

Lessons

1. The Male Reproductive System — 218
2. The Female Reproductive System — 222
3. Pregnancy and Birth — 226
4. Growing and Changing — 232

Chapter Review — 236
Life Skills in Action — 238

Check out **Current Health** articles related to this chapter by visiting **go.hrw.com**. Just type in the keyword **HD4CH41**.

> **My grandfather** and **I** have so much in common. We both **enjoy being outdoors**. We have the same favorite food. And we both like to have fun. He has lived through so many things, and I love listening to all of his stories.

Health IQ

PRE-READING
Answer the following true/false questions to find out what you already know about the human life cycle. When you've finished this chapter, you'll have the opportunity to change your answers based on what you've learned.

1. Women make new ova every month. ★ 1.D; 2.B; 2.C; 2.E

2. Removing damp clothes as soon as possible can help prevent infections of the reproductive system.

3. Many health problems suffered by adults can be avoided by making healthy decisions earlier in life. ★ 4.C; 12.F

4. Adolescents change physically, mentally, and emotionally. ★ 1.D; 2.A; 2.E

5. Grief is a process that should be avoided. ★ 1.D; 11.D

6. Everyone goes through puberty at the same age. ★ 2.A

7. Childhood is the longest stage of development. ★ 1.D

8. Sperm take several weeks to mature.

9. Children of all ages have the same mental and physical abilities. ★ 2.A; 2.C; 2.E

10. Choices made by pregnant women have little effect on the fetuses they carry. ★ 2.D

11. The blood of the mother passes through the fetus and carries nutrients and gases to the fetus.

12. Pregnancy is a simple process that has few possible complications. ★ 2.D

13. As humans age, they are more likely to develop negative health conditions, such as arthritis. ★ 1.D

ANSWERS: 1. false; 2. true; 3. true; 4. true; 5. false; 6. false; 7. false; 8. false; 9. false; 10. false; 11. false; 12. false; 13. true

Lesson 1

The Male Reproductive System

What You'll Do

- **Identify** the parts of the male reproductive system. ★ 2.C
- **Summarize** the path of sperm through the male reproductive system. ★ 2.C
- **Describe** seven problems of the male reproductive system. ★ 3.B
- **Describe** four ways to prevent common reproductive problems. ★ 3.A; 3.B; 5.D; 5.F

Terms to Learn

- sperm
- testes

What are some problems of the male reproductive system?

Raul heard his parents talking about his grandfather. His grandfather was diagnosed with prostate cancer. Raul wondered what a prostate is and what it does.

The *prostate* is a gland in the male reproductive system that makes fluid that helps carry male sex cells to the female's body. Male sex cells are called **sperm.**

The Male Body

The male reproductive system, shown in Figure 1, makes sperm and delivers them to a female's body. The **testes,** also called the *testicles,* are the organs that make sperm and the primary male sex hormone, testosterone (tes TAHS tuhr OHN). The testes are held by a sac of skin called the scrotum that hangs from the male body. The scrotum regulates the temperature of the testes so that sperm can form correctly. After leaving the testes, sperm mature in the epididymis (EP uh DID i mis). Then, the sperm are mixed with fluids made by other glands. These fluids carry the sperm out of the man's body through the penis. ★ 2.C

Figure 1 Male Reproductive Organs

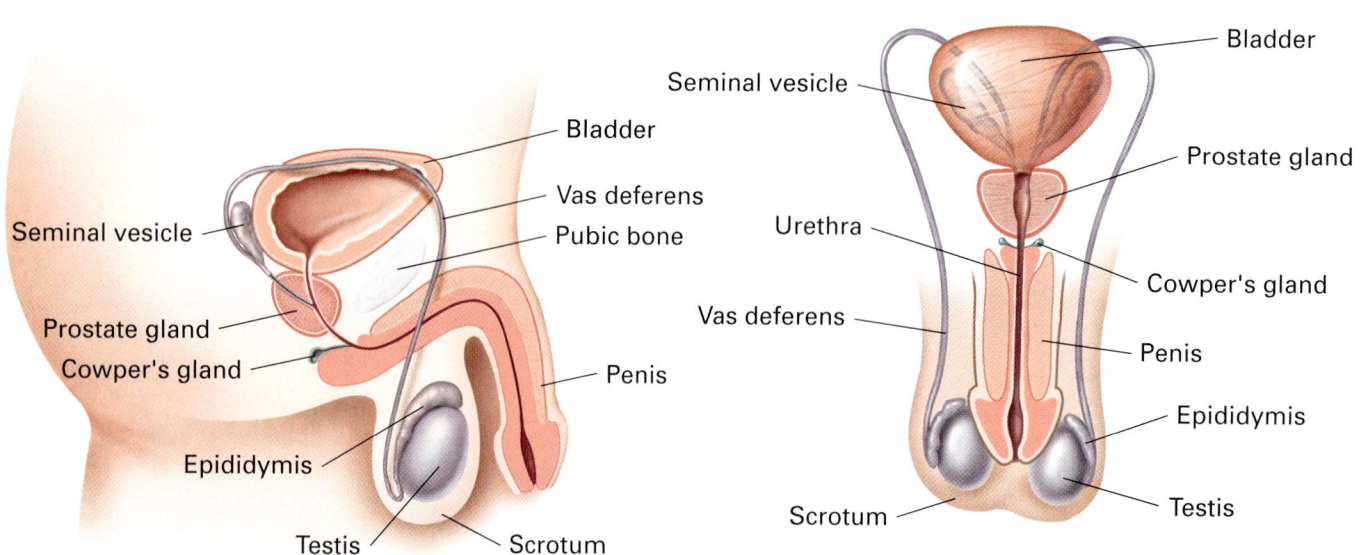

218 | Chapter 9 The Stages of Life

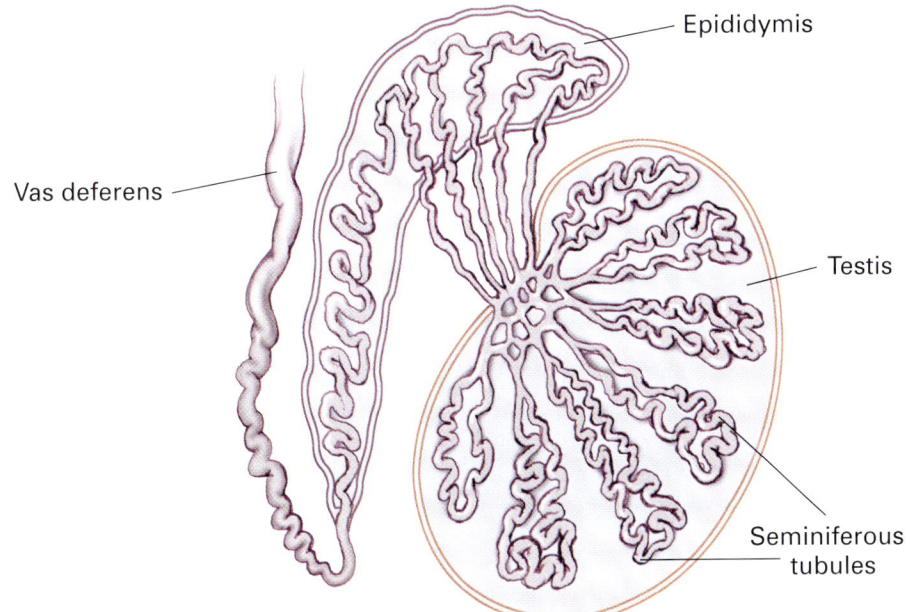

Figure 2 Sperm spend 70 days forming in the seminiferous tubules. They then spend several weeks maturing in the epididymis.

The Path Traveled by Sperm

Sperm are made inside the testes in structures called *seminiferous tubules* (SEM uh NIF uhr uhs TOO BYOOLZ). Figure 2 shows these tubules. The cells in these tubules divide so that each new sperm cell contains half of the man's genes. *Genes* are instructions for how a person's body looks and functions. While the sperm are in the testis, they form the tails that allow them to swim. The ability to swim allows sperm to reach the sex cells of a woman. The immature sperm cells then move into the epididymis, where they mature.

When the sperm are fully mature, they move into tubes called the *vas deferens* (vas DEF uh RENZ). The vas deferens run from each epididymis, out of the scrotum. They widen to form a storage area that is located just above the prostate gland. The two seminal vesicles are attached to the storage area of the vas deferens. The *seminal vesicles* (SEM uh nuhl VES i kuhlz) are glands that produce most of the fluid that carries the sperm down the urethra and out of the penis. This fluid is called *semen*.

Below the seminal vesicles, the sperm pass through the *prostate gland* on their way to the urethra. As sperm pass through the prostate gland, the prostate gland and the Cowper's glands add more fluids to the semen. The *urethra* (yoo REE thruh) is the tube that carries urine and sperm out of the body through the penis. After about 2 weeks in the man's body, the sperm break down and are reabsorbed. ★ 2.C

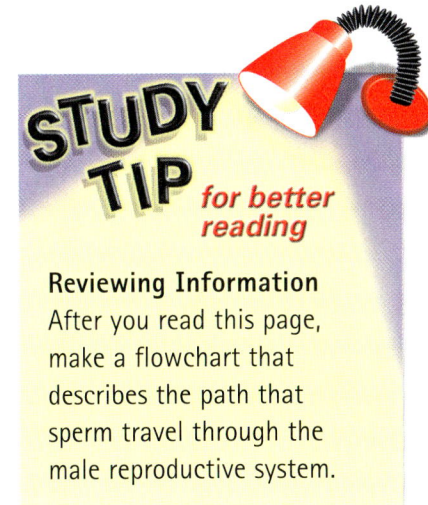

Reviewing Information After you read this page, make a flowchart that describes the path that sperm travel through the male reproductive system.

Male Reproductive Problems

Many boys and men do not recognize the importance of getting regular medical checkups. But medical checkups can help boys and men protect themselves from problems of the male reproductive system. Many of these problems can be treated easily, but some require medical care. Noticeable symptoms, such as an uncomfortable rash, a sore or lump, or painful urination, should be reported to a doctor immediately. Some problems do not have any symptoms at all, but these problems are just as dangerous as those you can see. Many problems can be found by a doctor during a regular exam. Seeking medical care is very important in preventing lasting damage to your reproductive system. Table 1 describes some problems associated with the male reproductive system. ★ 3.A; 3.B

Health Journal

Talk to your doctor about performing self-examinations. In your Health Journal, describe the process that your doctor described to you.

TABLE 1 Problems of the Male Reproductive System

Problem	Description	Treatment or prevention
Jock itch	infection of the skin by a fungus; not a sexually transmitted disease; often occurs when scrotum and groin skin stays hot and moist; symptoms are red, itchy, irritated skin	prevented by keeping the area clean and dry and by not wearing damp clothing longer than necessary; treated with over-the-counter medicated creams or ointments
Sexually transmitted diseases (STDs)	diseases passed from one person to another by sexual contact involving the sex organs, the mouth, or the rectum; may cause sores or discharge or may not cause any symptoms	prevented by abstaining from sexual activity; medical treatment is required for all STDs
Inguinal (ING gwi nuhl) hernia	a weakness in the lower abdominal wall that allows a small loop of intestine to bulge through	medical treatment and surgery required
Undescended testicle	a developmental defect in which a testicle has not descended into the scrotum; can cause damage to the testicle that prevents it from producing sperm	medical attention required; may require surgery to correct
Urinary tract infection (UTI)	infection in the urinary tract that causes frequent and burning urination; may cause urine to be bloody; can result from STD infection or other causes	medical treatment required for any symptoms; may be treated with antibiotics
Testicular cancer	uncontrolled growth of the cells of the testes; usually does not cause pain and is usually found as an enlargement of the testicle or as a pea-sized lump on the testicle	medical care required; surgery and chemotherapy usually required; identified early during testicular exams
Testicular torsion	twisting of the testicle on the nerves and blood vessels attached to it; produces swelling and pain; usually happens during athletic activity	immediate medical care required
Prostate enlargement	enlargement of the prostate gland; happens with age; causes frequent and slow urination	medical care required; may be treated with medications or surgery

★ 3.A; 3.B; 5.D; 5.F

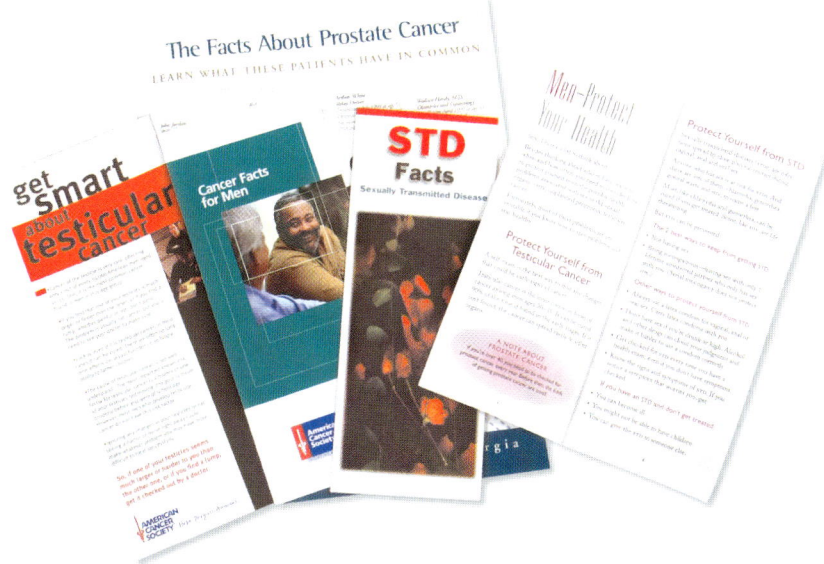

Figure 3 Doctors can provide men with information about how to care for their reproductive system.

Caring for the Male Body

Men and boys can protect themselves from reproductive health problems in the following ways:

- Bathe every day and keep skin clean and dry. Do not wear damp clothing any longer than is necessary.
- Always wear protective gear when playing sports that could cause testicular injury.
- See a doctor regularly, and report any unusual pain, swelling, tenderness, or lumps. Do regular testicular exams. Ask your doctor how to perform these exams.
- Abstain from sex before marriage to prevent catching sexually transmitted diseases. ★ 3.A; 5.D; 5.F

Lesson Review

Using Vocabulary

1. What is the difference between the testes and the scrotum? ★ 2.C

Understanding Concepts

2. List seven problems of the male reproductive system. ★ 3.B

3. Describe four ways to prevent problems of the male reproductive system. ★ 3.A; 3.B; 5.D; 5.F

4. Describe the path of sperm through the male reproductive system.

Critical Thinking

5. **Making Inferences** If someone has had sexual contact with someone else but does not have any physical signs of disease, should he or she be tested for STDs? Explain your answer. ★ 4.C

6. **Analyzing Ideas** How does wearing damp clothing increase the risk of getting jock itch? ★ 3.A

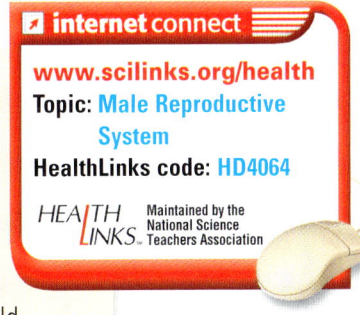

internet connect
www.scilinks.org/health
Topic: Male Reproductive System
HealthLinks code: HD4064
HEALTHLINKS Maintained by the National Science Teachers Association

Lesson 2: The Female Reproductive System

What You'll Do

- **Identify** the structures of the female reproductive system. ★ 2.C
- **Summarize** the typical menstrual cycle. ★ 2.B; 2.C
- **Describe** six problems of the female reproductive system. ★ 3.B
- **Describe** four ways to prevent common female reproductive problems. ★ 3.A; 3.B; 5.D; 5.F

Terms to Learn

- ovum
- uterus
- menstruation

What is menstruation?

Sharise's older sister Tanda got married last year. Tanda and her husband decided to have a baby. Sharise's little brother asked Sharise where the baby was inside Tanda's body.

Carrying a baby inside her body is one of the functions of a woman's reproductive system. A developing baby is carried in a pregnant woman's uterus. The **uterus** is a muscular organ of the female reproductive system that holds a fetus during pregnancy.

The Female Body

The woman's sex cell is called an **ovum** (plural, *ova*). The ova, or eggs, are stored in organs called ovaries. The ovaries also make most of the primary female sex hormone, estrogen (ES truh juhn). An ovum travels from an ovary to the uterus through a fallopian (fuh LOH pee uhn) tube. The fallopian tube is not actually attached to the ovary. The ovum is drawn into the fallopian tube and carried toward the uterus by movements of the fallopian tubes. The lower part of the uterus, where the uterus meets the vagina, is the cervix. The vagina connects the outside of the body with the uterus. A woman's breasts are also a part of her reproductive system. ★ 2.C

Figure 4 Female Reproductive Organs

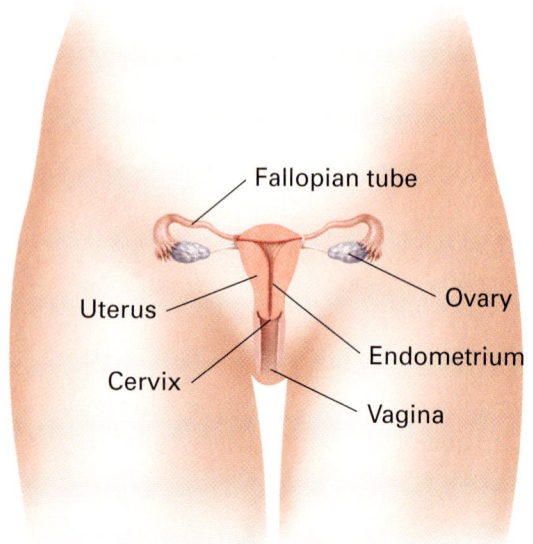
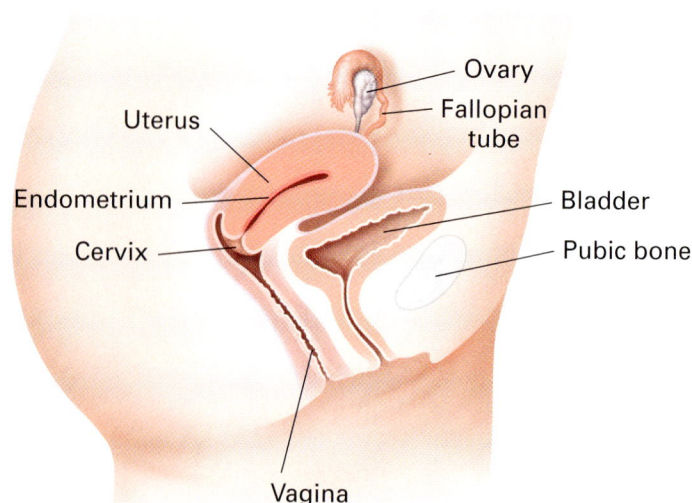

222 | Chapter 9 The Stages of Life

Ovulation

Women are born with all of the ova they will ever have. Ova contain one half of the woman's genes. Beginning at puberty, one of the ovaries releases a mature ovum every month in a process called *ovulation* (AHV yoo LAY shuhn). An ovary contains ova at various stages of development. When a hormone called *FSH* is released each month, some of the developing ova are at the right stage to finish maturing. One of these ova will dominate, and the others will be reabsorbed by the body. Then, the woman's body releases a second hormone that makes the ovary release the mature ovum. When the ovum is released, the fallopian tube draws the ovum into the tube. The sweeping movement of the tube's lining causes a current of fluid in the fallopian tube that carries the ovum toward the uterus. ★ 2.B; 2.C; 2.E

Menstruation

To prepare the uterus for pregnancy, the lining of the uterus thickens every month. The lining of the uterus is called the *endometrium* (EN doh MEE tree uhm). If the ovum is fertilized by a sperm cell in the fallopian tube, the fertilized ovum will attach to the wall of the uterus and a pregnancy will begin. If the ovum is not fertilized, the lining of the uterus will be shed. When the lining is shed, blood and tissue leave the body through the vagina. This monthly breakdown and shedding of the endometrium is called **menstruation** (MEN STRAY shuhn). This bleeding is also called a *period*.

Ovulation and menstruation happen in a cycle that lasts about 28 days. This cycle is called the *menstrual cycle*. The typical menstrual cycle is described in Figure 5. The length of the menstrual cycle varies from woman to woman. It can be as short as 21 days and as long as 35 days. The length of the menstrual period and the heaviness of the bleeding can be affected by age, stress, diet, exercise, and illness. Girls usually have their first menstrual period between the ages of 9 and 16.
★ 2.B; 2.C; 2.E

Figure 5 The Menstrual Cycle

▼ **Days 1–5:** The lining of the uterus is shed. Blood and tissue leave the body through the vagina.

Days 1–13: An ovum matures in the ovary.

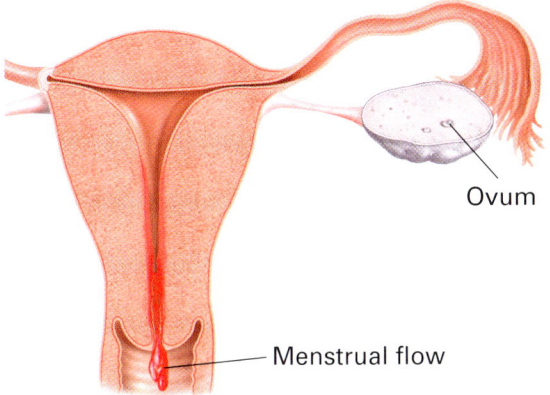

▼ **Day 14:** Ovulation—an ovum is released from the ovary.

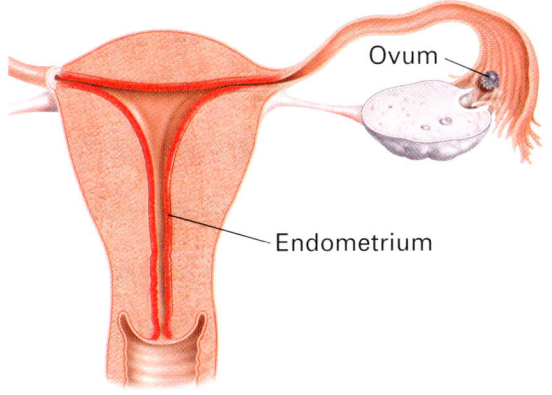

▼ **Days 15–28:** The ovum travels down the fallopian tube to the uterus. If the ovum is not fertilized, the cycle will begin again at Day 1.

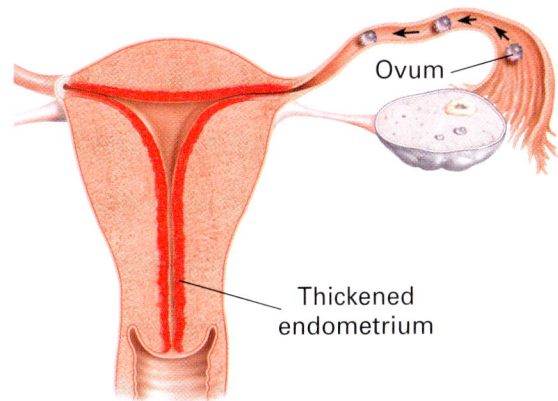

Lesson 2 The Female Reproductive System

PRACTICING WELLNESS

Research the importance of performing monthly self-examinations and getting annual examinations. Create a strategy to remember to perform self-examinations and to see a doctor every year.

Common Reproductive Problems

Most healthy young women do not have any significant problems with their reproductive system. But the changes in the female reproductive system at puberty can cause young women a great deal of stress. Many of the concerns that young women have are related to the menstrual cycle and menstruation. Girls normally have irregular periods for the first few years after starting menstruation. Irregular periods vary in length and heaviness of bleeding. Periods can come as often as every 3 weeks or as infrequently as every few months. Bleeding can last from only 1 day to 8 days. Both light and heavy bleeding are normal. Cramps, even though they may be painful, are also normal.

Some female reproductive health problems are listed in Table 2. All of these problems require medical care. Many of these problems can be avoided by maintaining good hygiene, removing damp clothes as soon as possible, and avoiding sexual activity.

TABLE 2 Problems of the Female Reproductive System

Problem	Description	Treatment or prevention
Urinary tract infection (UTI)	infection in the urinary tract that causes frequent and burning urination; may result from infection by STDs or other causes	medical treatment required for any symptoms; may be treated with antibiotics
Vaginitis	an infection of the vagina by bacteria, fungi, or protozoa that cause itching, odor, and/or discharge from the vagina; sometimes called a yeast infection	medical treatment required, may be treated with antibiotics or over-the-counter creams; may be prevented by avoiding sexual activity and by removing damp clothing as soon as possible
Endometriosis (EN do ME tree OH sis)	growth of a tissue like the endometrium outside the uterus and in the wrong place in a woman's body; during the menstrual period, this tissue bleeds and causes pain; may lead to infertility	medical attention required for severe cramps during menstrual periods; may be treated with hormones and/or surgery
Sexually transmitted diseases (STDs)	diseases passed from one person to another by sexual contact involving the sex organs, the mouth, or the rectum; may cause sores or discharge or may not cause any symptoms	medical treatment required for all STDs; prevented by abstaining from sexual activity
Toxic shock syndrome	a bacterial infection that causes fever, chills, weakness, a rash on the palms of the hands, and other symptoms; may be caused by leaving tampons in the vagina too long during menstruation	immediate medical care required; treated with antibiotics and fluids; may be prevented by changing tampons every 4 to 6 hours or not using tampons
Cervical, uterine, and ovarian cancer	uncontrolled growth of cells on the cervix, uterus, or ovary; the sexually transmitted disease HPV increases the chance of getting cervical cancer	medical care required; treated with surgery and chemotherapy; may be detected early through annual medical tests

★ 3.A; 3.B; 5.D; 5.F

Caring for the Female Body

Some medical problems can leave girls and women with damage that can affect their bodies for the rest of their lives. Women and girls can protect themselves from reproductive health problems in the following ways:

- Bathe every day. Do not wear damp clothing any longer than is necessary.
- See a doctor regularly. Report any unusual symptoms, including discharge, itching, or pain, to your parents or doctor. Do regular breast self-exams. Your doctor can explain how to perform these exams.
- Abstain from sex before marriage to prevent catching sexually transmitted diseases. Have tests every year to check for abnormal cells on the cervix. These cells can warn your doctor of potential reproductive health problems.
- Maintain good hygiene during menstrual periods. Bathe every day, and change sanitary pads or tampons every 4 to 6 hours. ★ 3.A; 5.D; 5.F

Figure 6 Good personal hygiene is important to reproductive health.

Lesson Review

Using Vocabulary

1. List three parts of the female reproductive system, and describe their functions. ★ 2.C

Understanding Concepts

2. Describe what happens during ovulation. ★ 2.B; 2.C
3. Describe the menstrual cycle. ★ 2.B; 2.C
4. Describe four ways to protect the female reproductive system from harm. ★ 3.A; 3.B; 5.D; 5.F
5. List six problems of the female reproductive system. ★ 3.B

Critical Thinking

6. **Identifying Relationships** The female body changes a lot during puberty. Ovulation and menstruation begin when the body makes and releases enough of the right hormones. How does this fact help explain why girls experience irregular menstrual periods during adolescence?

internet connect
www.scilinks.org/health
Topic: Female Reproductive System
HealthLinks code: HD4039
HEALTH LINKS Maintained by the National Science Teachers Association

Lesson 2 The Female Reproductive System

Lesson 3: Pregnancy and Birth

Humans reproduce through sexual reproduction. In sexual reproduction, the sex cells of the man and woman join together to make a new human cell. But do you know how that single cell grows into a baby?

What You'll Do

- **Describe** changes in the mother's body during pregnancy. ★ 2.D
- **Describe** three factors that affect the health of both the mother and the fetus. ★ 5.I
- **Summarize** human development before birth. ★ 1.D

Terms to Learn

- pregnancy
- embryo
- fetus
- placenta
- birth

Start Off Write
How can a pregnant woman's health habits affect the developing baby?

When the sperm from a man and the ovum from a woman join together, the genes of the mother and the father combine. This process, called *fertilization*, forms a new cell. One-half of the genes in the new cell are from the mother, and the other half of the genes are from the father.

A New Beginning

During fertilization, a single sperm penetrates the membrane that surrounds the ovum. The genes carried by the ovum and sperm combine to form a complete set of human genes. These genes will guide the development of the new human. The new cell then divides and forms more cells. This ball of cells enters the uterus and attaches to the uterine wall. The attachment of the developing cells to the uterus is called *implantation*.

Pregnancy is the time when the new cell formed during fertilization grows and develops into a baby in the woman's uterus. From the time that the ovum and the sperm unite until the end of the eighth week, the developing human is called an **embryo.** From the eighth week until birth, the developing human is called a **fetus.** A normal pregnancy generally lasts about 9 months.

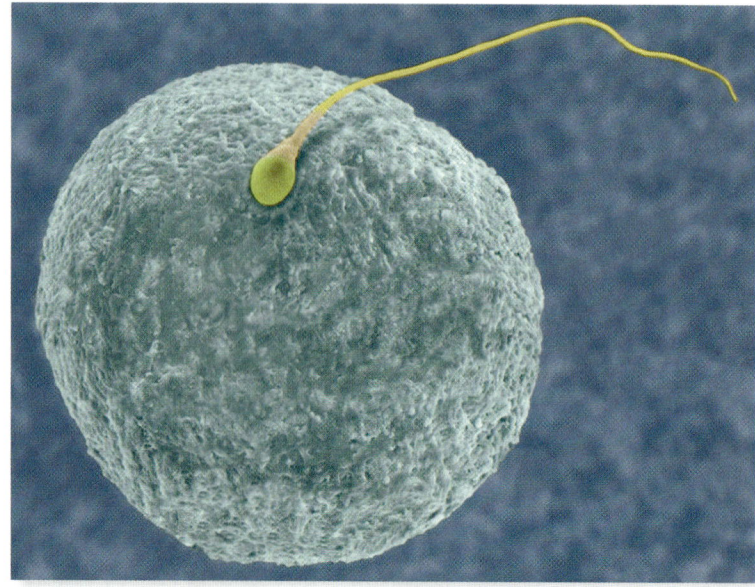
Figure 7 During fertilization, a sperm enters an ovum and the genes of the mother and father combine.

Changes in the Mother's Body

A woman's body undergoes many changes during pregnancy. As soon as implantation happens, the cells of the mother's uterus release a special hormone. Because this hormone is only released by the body during pregnancy, doctors test for this hormone to determine whether a woman is pregnant. Some of the hormones produced by a pregnant woman's body may make her nauseated. This response is called "morning sickness" and usually lasts for about 3 months. The same hormones make the woman's breasts enlarge and prepare to produce milk.

Over the 9-month period, the woman's uterus stretches to hold a full-sized newborn baby. This stretching makes her abdomen get larger. A pregnant woman may also experience swelling of her legs and difficulty sleeping as the fetus gets larger. Many women feel clumsy or uncomfortable because of the changes in their bodies. Some women may also experience emotional changes as a result of their changing hormones. ★ 2.D

USING REFUSAL SKILLS

Imagine that a pregnant woman is offered an alcoholic drink. Give three examples of what she can say or do to refuse the drink.

Nourishing the Fetus

Almost everything that goes into the mother's body enters her bloodstream and goes to the placenta. The **placenta** is an organ that grows in the woman's uterus during pregnancy and allows nutrients, gases, and wastes to be exchanged between the mother and the fetus. The mother's blood circulates on one side of the placenta. The fetus's blood circulates on the other side. Nutrients, fluid, and oxygen flow through the membrane from the mother to the fetus. Waste products and carbon dioxide flow across the placenta from the fetus to the mother.

During pregnancy, the fetus gets its only nutrition from the food its mother eats. To ensure the health of the fetus, the mother needs to eat healthy foods and take special vitamins. A mother can hurt her fetus's health by taking drugs, drinking alcohol, or smoking. She should get regular medical checkups to help protect her health and the health of the growing fetus.
★ 2.D; 5.I

Figure 8 This baby was born with fetal alcohol syndrome. The child is handicapped because her mother drank alcohol frequently while pregnant.

Lesson 3 Pregnancy and Birth

The First Trimester

A human pregnancy normally lasts 40 weeks, or about 9 months. Doctors often divide that nine months into three 3-month periods called *trimesters*. If the baby is not born until the end of the 9 months, the pregnancy is said to be "full term."

The first trimester is the first 3 months, or 12 weeks, of a pregnancy. At the beginning of this trimester, the fertilized ovum is only one cell and stays in the mother's fallopian tube for 3 days. By the end of that 3 days, that one cell has grown to about 12 cells. The embryo then enters the uterus. By the time the embryo implants, it is a rapidly growing ball of cells. The genes from the parents tell every cell of the embryo's body how to grow.

By the end of the fourth week, the heart has formed and has begun to beat. The embryo has the beginnings of a brain, and its spinal cord, arms, and legs begin to grow. At this time, the embryo is 10,000 times larger than the original fertilized ovum. By the sixth week, the embryo's head is very large in comparison with the rest of its body. At about this time, brain waves can be detected. By the eighth week, all of the major organs of the embryo's body are formed. At the beginning of the ninth week, the embryo is called a fetus. ★ 1.D

SCIENCE ACTIVITY

When two babies are born from the same pregnancy, they are called *twins*. Some twins look alike, and some do not. Use the library or the Internet to find out the difference between fraternal twins and identical twins.

Figure 9 Development Before Birth

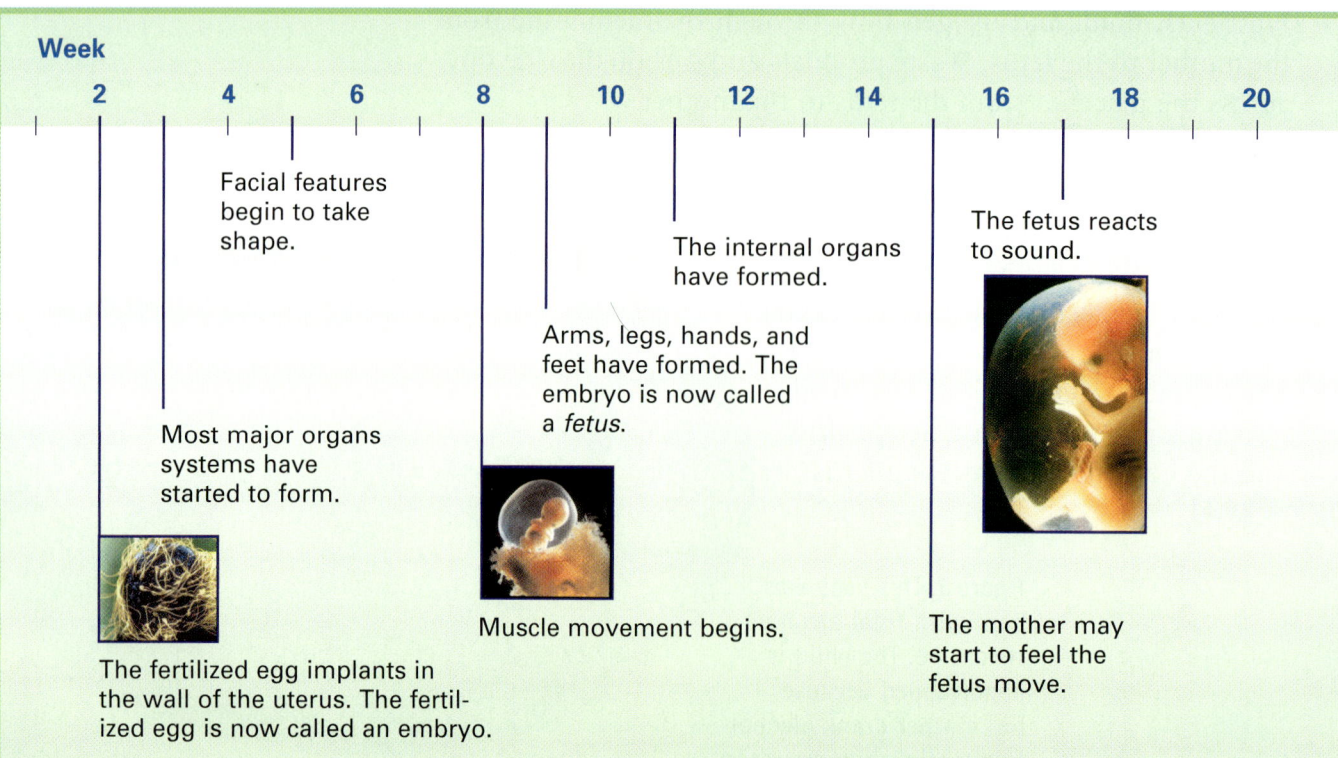

Week 2 – Most major organs systems have started to form. The fertilized egg implants in the wall of the uterus. The fertilized egg is now called an embryo.

Week 4 – Facial features begin to take shape.

Week 8 – Arms, legs, hands, and feet have formed. The embryo is now called a *fetus*. Muscle movement begins.

Week 12 – The internal organs have formed.

Week 16 – The fetus reacts to sound. The mother may start to feel the fetus move.

The Second Trimester

The second trimester is the fourth through the sixth month, or the 13th through the 27th week, of pregnancy. At the start of the second trimester, the fetus is almost 3 inches long. By the end of this trimester, the fetus will be three times that length. During the second trimester, the mother begins to feel the movement of the fetus. Between 14 and 18 weeks, a doctor can tell whether the fetus is a boy or a girl. During these 3 months, the fingers and toes grow nails. Calcium is deposited in the bones. A downy, soft hair covers the fetus's body. Eyelashes and eyebrows are developing by the end of the sixth month. ★ 1.D

The Third Trimester

The third trimester is the last 3 months, or 12 weeks, of pregnancy. At the start of this trimester, the fetus is about 10 inches long and weighs about 2 pounds. During this trimester, the fetus develops more muscle and moves more. Fat is deposited under the fetus's skin. During the first part of this trimester, the fetus's eyes open and its chest begins to "practice" breathing motions. The fetus can hear voices, and it may even recognize them. The fetus grows rapidly in both length and weight. By the end of this trimester, the fetus's organs have formed and are completely functioning. At the end of the ninth month, the baby is prepared to live outside the mother's uterus. ★ 1.D

STUDY TIP for better reading

Organizing Information
Create a timeline of the development of a fetus in the womb.

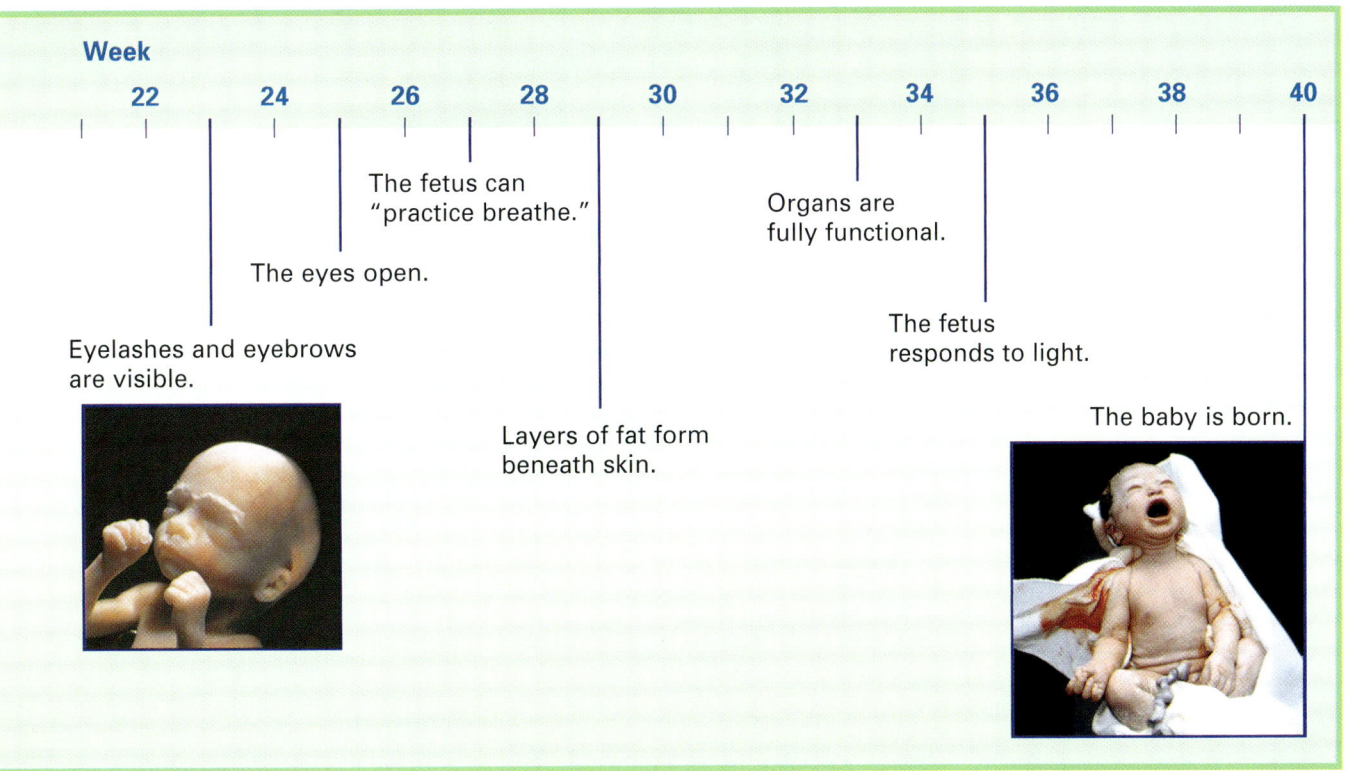

Myth & Fact

Myth: Giving birth is a natural process, so women do not need help delivering the baby.

Fact: Giving birth can be safe and easy, but during some deliveries, unexpected and life-threatening problems may arise. Delivering in the hospital with qualified doctors is the safest way to give birth.

Birth

The passage of a baby from its mother's uterus to outside her body is called **birth**. During birth, the uterus contracts many times and pushes the baby through the vagina and outside the mother's body.

Labor is the process that lasts from the time contractions start until the delivery of the child and the placenta. Labor lasts a different amount of time for every woman and every pregnancy. There are three distinct stages of labor. The first stage begins with the first contraction and lasts until the cervix has opened enough to allow the baby's head to pass through. Contractions happen every few minutes and last about a minute. The second stage starts when the cervix is completely open and lasts until the baby is delivered. During this stage, contractions happen every 2 or 3 minutes. Sometimes, doctors have to deliver a baby by a Caesarean (si ZAYR ee uhn) section, or a C-section. In this procedure, the doctor surgically removes the baby and the placenta from the mother's uterus.

After the baby is born, the doctor cuts the umbilical cord. Healthy babies breathe and cry almost immediately. The third and final stage of labor is when the placenta is delivered. In this stage, the mother's uterine contractions push the placenta, or "afterbirth," out of her body. At this time, the birth is complete.

★ 1.D

Figure 10 After a baby is born, the baby bonds with his or her parents. The parents begin to take care of the new baby.

Complications of Pregnancy and Birth

For some women, pregnancy, labor and delivery involve problems that range from very mild to life threatening. Table 3 describes some possible complications of pregnancy and birth.

TABLE 3 Possible Complications of Pregnancy and Birth

Complication	Description
Miscarriage	the loss of a pregnancy before the 20th week; can happen because a mother's body has an abnormality or because the embryo was abnormal
Ectopic pregnancy	a pregnancy in which the embryo implants outside the uterus (commonly in a fallopian tube) instead of in the uterus; after a few weeks, the fallopian tube ruptures; requires immediate medical care
Toxemia	a medical problem in which hormones cause high blood pressure, swelling of the body, and injury to the kidneys; if severe, doctors will induce labor
Gestational diabetes	abnormally high blood-sugar levels in the mother; if uncontrolled, may lead to abnormalities or death of the fetus or to medical problems in the mother
Rh incompatability	a condition in which the blood types of the mother and the fetus do not match and the mother's body forms antibodies against the fetus's blood; can cause death of the fetus
Premature birth	the birth of a baby before the 37th week of pregnancy; not harmful to the mother, but babies born too early can have medical problems or die
Breech birth	a birth in which the baby is born upside down with the bottom coming out first; may cause the baby's head to get caught by the cervix; most breech babies are delivered by C-section
Oxygen deprivation	lack of oxygen to a baby's brain during birth; may cause brain damage to the baby; may be caused by the umbilical cord being wrapped around the baby's neck during delivery
Stillbirth	the delivery of an infant that is dead after 20 weeks or more of pregnancy; good medical care can help prevent this problem; often, no cause can be found

★ 2.D

Lesson Review

Using Vocabulary

1. What is the difference between an embryo and a fetus? ★ 1.D

Understanding Concepts

2. Summarize the development of a fetus before birth. ★ 1.D

3. List three changes in the mother's body during pregnancy. ★ 2.D

4. List three factors that affect the health of both the mother and the fetus. ★ 2.D; 5.I

Critical Thinking

5. **Making Inferences** The mother's body expands to accommodate the growing fetus. What effect does this growth have on the woman's internal organs? ★ 2.D

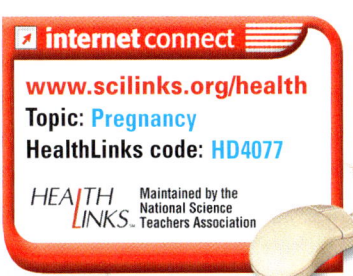

internet connect
www.scilinks.org/health
Topic: Pregnancy
HealthLinks code: HD4077
HEALTH LINKS Maintained by the National Science Teachers Association

Lesson 4

Growing and Changing

At age 1, the average human baby will weigh about three times more than at birth. By the time the child is 6 years old, he or she will weigh approximately six times more than at birth.

What You'll Do

- **Describe** development during childhood. ★ 1.D
- **Explain** development during adolescence. ★ 1.D; 2.B; 2.C; 2.E
- **Describe** what happens to the body during aging. ★ 1.D
- **Identify** the stages of grief. ★ 1.D

Terms to Learn

- infancy
- childhood
- adolescence
- puberty
- adulthood
- grief

Start Off Write

After people reach adulthood, how do their bodies continue to change?

After birth, humans go through several stages of development. These stages are infancy, childhood, adolescence, and adulthood. As we go through these stages, we grow and change.

Childhood Development

The stage of development between birth and age 1 is called **infancy**. During infancy, the baby grows quickly and learns to do a number of new things, such as sit up, crawl, and pull up to a standing position. By the end of the first year, many babies can walk and say a few words.

Childhood is the stage of development between infancy and adolescence. Childhood is divided into three stages. The first stage, early childhood, begins at age 1 and lasts until age 3. In this stage, children learn to say several words. They improve almost all of their physical skills. A child at this age can learn to pedal a small tricycle, run, and kick a ball.

After age 3, children enter middle childhood. This stage lasts until about age 6. Children in this stage begin to ask many questions. During these years, most children learn to read, make friends, and play with other children.

Late childhood lasts from age 6 until about age 11. During these years, children become more coordinated. Late childhood is a stage for exploring skills and interests. It also is a time for continued mental development. At the end of late childhood, children have many of the skills they will need during adolescence. ★ 1.D

Figure 11 Children grow rapidly and experience many mental and physical changes.

Adolescence

The time in a person's life when they mature from a child to an adult is called **adolescence.** This transition from childhood to maturity involves mental, emotional, physical, and social growth. These changes prepare you for adulthood. Adolescence begins with puberty and lasts until the person is physically mature. **Puberty** is the stage of development when the reproductive organs mature and the person becomes able to reproduce. Puberty begins at different times for different people. In general, puberty starts earlier for girls than it does for boys.

The physical changes of adolescence are caused by increased amounts of hormones in the body. Female hormones cause girls to develop breasts and begin menstruating. Male hormones cause boys to start making sperm. The voices of both boys and girls get deeper. Both boys and girls have growth spurts and begin to grow body hair. ★ 1.D; 2.B; 2.C; 2.E

Adulthood

An adult is a person who is fully grown physically and mentally. **Adulthood** is the stage of life that follows adolescence and lasts until the end of life. During adulthood, many people fulfill personal and professional goals. Adulthood is the time in life when people begin to establish careers. Many adults get married and have children. Some adults find fulfillment by participating in community activities and continuing to learn.

Adults must be responsible for their own health and safety. They must pay their bills and provide food, shelter, and clothing for themselves and, if they have a family, for their spouse and children. These responsibilities can be stressful for adults. Emotional and mental development during adolescence helps adults maintain stable home and work lives. This stability allows adults to work well with others and to provide for the needs of their families. ★ 1.D; 2.E

Figure 12 Adolescents can prepare for adulthood in many ways, including taking part in vocational programs.

Aging

Growing older, or *aging,* is a natural part of adulthood. Even during adulthood, people's bodies continue to change. Over time, their bodies begin to wear down and work less efficiently. As people age, they may encounter health problems, such as the following:

- **Arthritis** Arthritis is swelling of the joints that can cause a person to have difficulty and pain when moving. Some forms of arthritis can be treated with medication and regular exercise.

- **Alzheimer's Disease** Alzheimer's disease is a degenerative disease of the brain in which the person begins to have trouble remembering things.

- **Heart Disease** Heart disease is the number one cause of death in older adults. It can lead to heart attacks or death.

- **Cancer** Cancer is an uncontrolled growth of cells that starts in a single part of the body and can spread throughout the body. Cancer can be treated with chemotherapy, radiation, and surgery.

Figure 13 Many older adults stay healthy and active until the ends of their lives.

Some of these conditions can be improved by maintaining good health habits for an entire lifetime. Healthy habits include eating nutritious foods and exercising regularly. Many future health problems can be prevented by avoiding many risk behaviors, such as using tobacco, alcohol, and other drugs.

As they age, many adults find new ways to be fulfilled. Many older adults retire and begin to spend more time with their families and friends. Often, older adults travel and find new hobbies. Most adults stay healthy and active for most of their lives.

★ 1.D; 5.I

Health Journal

Spend some time with elderly people. Ask them about the choices they made and experiences they had when they were younger. How do their opinions and experiences differ from yours? Which of their experiences would you like to know more about? Why?

Death

Life expectancy for both men and women in the United States is the highest that it has ever been. *Life expectancy* is how long people are expected to live. People are living longer because medical advances are keeping people healthy longer.

Everyone eventually dies. *Death* is the end of life. At death, all of the body functions that are necessary for life stop. Death has many causes. Sometimes, people die because they are sick. Some people die because their bodies were injured in an accident. Other people die simply because their bodies stop working. ★ 1.D

Figure 14   Ways to Help a Grieving Person

▶ **Do** express your sympathy and show support.

▶ **Do** listen to the grieving person. Let the person share his or her grief with you.

▶ **Do** express friendship and offer to help. Reassure the person that guilt, sadness, and similar feelings are normal.

▶ **Don't** ask for details unless you are a close friend.

▶ **Don't** expect the grieving person to heal quickly. Grief is a long process.

Grief

Dealing with death is always difficult. When someone you love dies, you will probably feel grief. **Grief** is a deep sadness about a loss. Many people go through the following five stages when dealing with the death of someone they love:

1. **Denial**—The person refuses to accept that the loved one is dead.
2. **Anger**—The person is angry that his or her loved one has been taken away.
3. **Bargaining**—The person wishes that he or she could find a way to get the loved one back.
4. **Despair**—The person is sad that the loved one is gone.
5. **Acceptance**—The person accepts that the loved one is gone and begins to move on with his or her life.

Going through these stages helps people accept their loss and prepare to live their lives without the person who has died. Figure 14 lists ways to help others deal with grief. ★ 1.D; 10.B; 11.B; 11.D

LIFE SKILLS ACTIVITY

COPING

Role-play a situation in which one person is helping another person deal with the loss of a loved one.

Lesson Review

Using Vocabulary

1. Define the following terms: *infancy, childhood, adolescence,* and *adulthood.* How do these four stages of life differ? ★ 1.D; 2.B; 2.C; 2.E

Understanding Concepts

2. Explain what happens to the body during aging. What can you do to stay healthy while aging? ★ 1.D

3. What are the stages of grief? ★ 1.D

4. How does adolescence prepare you for adult roles? ★ 2.E

Critical Thinking

5. **Making Inferences** How does going through the stages of grief help you come to terms with a loss? ★ 11.D

6. **Analyzing Ideas** How can the health choices you make as an adolescent affect how you age? ★ 1.D; 5.I

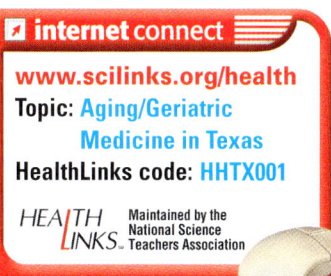

internet connect
www.scilinks.org/health
Topic: Aging/Geriatric Medicine in Texas
HealthLinks code: HHTX001
HEALTH LINKS Maintained by the National Science Teachers Association

Lesson 4 Growing and Changing

9 CHAPTER REVIEW

Chapter Summary

- The male reproductive system makes sex cells called *sperm*.
- The female reproductive system releases the sex cell called the *ovum*.
- When ovum and sperm join, the newly-formed cell develops into a baby.
- Pregnancy is divided into three trimesters and lasts about 40 weeks.
- Infancy is the stage of life between birth and age 1.
- Childhood can be divided into three stages—early childhood, middle childhood, and late childhood.
- Adolescence is the stage of development from the start of puberty to adulthood.
- During puberty, people become sexually mature.
- Aging is a natural part of life.
- Death is the end of life.

Using Vocabulary

For each sentence, fill in the blank with the proper term from the word bank provided below.

adolescence	adulthood
puberty	uterus
fetus	menstruation
ovulation	pregnancy
testes	

1. The stage of life when people become sexually mature is ___.
2. Sperm are made in the ___.
3. During pregnancy, the fetus is held inside the ___.
4. The monthly release of a mature ovum from the ovary is called ___.
5. The endometrium is discarded each month during ___.
6. After 8 weeks of pregnancy, the developing human is called a(n) ___.
7. The stage of life called ___ begins with puberty and lasts until a person is physically mature.
8. ___ is the stage of life between adolescence and death.

Understanding Concepts

9. Arrange the following steps of human development in the correct order.
   a. sperm and ovum join to form a new cell
   b. the end of all necessary life functions
   c. stage that begins at birth
   d. development inside the uterus
   e. the reproductive system matures
   f. physical and mental maturity ★ 1.D
10. List three problems of the male reproductive system.
11. List three ways to protect your reproductive system. ★ 3.A; 3.B; 5.D; 5.F
12. List three problems of the female reproductive system.
13. Describe the typical menstrual cycle. ★ 2.B; 2.C
14. Describe three changes that happen to a mother's body during pregnancy. ★ 2.D
15. List three factors that affect the health of both a pregnant woman and her fetus. ★ 5.I
16. What are the five stages of grief? ★ 1.D; 11.D
17. List four conditions associated with aging.
18. Summarize human development before birth. ★ 1.D

Critical Thinking

Analyzing Ideas

19. Why are breasts considered part of the female reproductive system? ★ 1.D; 2.C; 2.D

20. The placenta keeps the mother's circulatory system separate from the fetus's circulatory system. How can nutrients, gases, fluids, and wastes be passed between the mother and fetus if they don't share the same blood?

21. Adolescents rarely have abnormal lumps in their testes or breasts. Why is it important to start performing self-examinations early in life? ★ 3.A; 5.I

22. Why is it common for adolescent girls to have irregular menstrual cycles? ★ 1.D; 2.B; 2.C

23. Many bacteria, fungi, and protists like to live in a warm, moist environment. How can changing your clothes after you exercise help prevent some reproductive health problems? ★ 4.C

Making Good Decisions

24. Imagine that your friend recently lost his mother in an accident. He is angry because she left him. He is also angry with himself for being angry at his mother. What could you do to help your friend? ★ 11.C; 11.D

25. Imagine that your grandmother was diagnosed with cancer. Your mother tells you that many people in your family have had different kinds of cancers, including colon cancer and lung cancer. What health decisions can you make now to help you reduce the risk of getting cancer as you age? ★ 3.A; 5.I

Interpreting Graphics

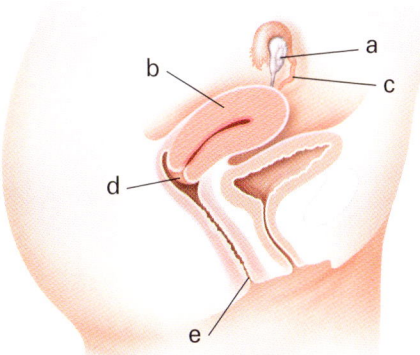

Use the figure above to answer questions 26–31.

26. The figure above shows the female reproductive system. Using the letters on the figure, identify the following structures: ovary, uterus, vagina, and fallopian tube.

27. What is the function of structure **b**?

28. Name the structure labeled **d**. What is the function of this structure?

29. Which structure releases a mature ovum every month?

30. What is the lining of structure **b** called?

31. What happens to structure **d** during the first stage of labor?

Reading Checkup

Take a minute to review your answers to the Health IQ questions at the beginning of this chapter. How has reading this chapter improved your Health IQ?

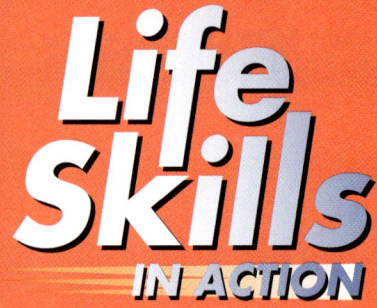

Life Skills IN ACTION

Assessing Your Health

Assessing your health means evaluating each of the four parts of your health and examining your behaviors. By assessing your health regularly, you will know what your strengths and weaknesses are and will be able to take steps to improve your health. Complete the following activity to improve your ability to assess your health.

Hannah's High School Headache

Setting the Scene

It's the end of summer, and Hannah is just weeks away from starting high school. She spent most of the summer worrying about going to a new, larger school. Hannah was very happy in middle school—she was a good student and was popular. However, most of Hannah's friends will be going to a different high school than she will and she is concerned about the difficulty of high school classes. Hannah's mother notices that Hannah is nervous and asks her if she wants to talk about it.

★ 1.D; 7.A; 10.E; 11.B; 11.D

The 4 Steps of Assessing Your Health

1. Choose the part of your health you want to assess.
2. List your strengths and weaknesses.
3. Describe how your behaviors may contribute to your weaknesses.
4. Develop a plan to address your weaknesses.

Guided Practice

Practice with a Friend

Form a group of three. Have one person play the role of Hannah and another person play the role of Hannah's mother. Have the third person be an observer. Walking through each of the four steps of assessing your health, role-play the conversation between Hannah and her mother. In the conversation, Hannah should assess how her transition from middle school to high school is affecting her health. The observer will take notes, which will include observations about what the person playing Hannah did well and suggestions of ways to improve. Stop after each step to evaluate the process. ★ 11.D

Independent Practice

Check Yourself

After you have completed the guided practice, go through Act 1 again without stopping at each step. Answer the questions below to review what you did.

1. Which parts of Hannah's health are most affected by her move from middle school to high school? Explain your answer.

2. What can Hannah do to improve her social health?

3. What plan did Hannah develop to address her weaknesses?

4. What are some concerns you have about going to high school? How can you prevent your worries from negatively affecting your health?

On Your Own

After a month at her new high school, Hannah is involved in several extracurricular activities and has made many new friends. Schoolwork, activities, and her social life keep Hannah very busy. She is enjoying herself, but she feels tired much of the time. Make a flowchart that shows how Hannah can use the four steps of assessing your health to help her decide what to do.

Chapter 9 Assessing Your Health | 239

CHAPTER 10
Adolescent Growth and Development

Check out **Current Health** articles related to this chapter by visiting **go.hrw.com.** Just type in the keyword **HD4CH42.**

Lessons

1. Your Changing Body — 242
2. Your Changing Mind — 246
3. Your Changing Feelings — 248
4. Preparing for the Future — 252

Chapter Review — 256
Life Skills in Action — 258

> **"I** never thought that **growing up** would be so hard. My **body** is changing in so many ways. Sometimes, I don't know how to **feel** or act. Sometimes, I do things that I don't really want to do, just to fit in with my friends. But I'm still working hard at school, and I'm looking forward to my future. **"**

PRE-READING

Answer the following multiple-choice questions to find out what you already know about adolescent growth and development. When you've finished this chapter, you'll have the opportunity to change your answers based on what you've learned.

1. Puberty is the stage of development
   a. between childhood and adulthood.
   b. when your reproductive system becomes mature.
   c. after adolescence.
   d. when your endocrine system stops working. ★ 1.D

2. Infatuation is
   a. a desire to get to know someone better.
   b. admiration for someone while not seeing that person's flaws.
   c. accepting the consequences of your actions.
   d. a desire to belong.

3. Which of the following activities will help you get organized?
   a. redoing things you've already done
   b. making a weekly to-do list
   c. waiting until the evening to do everything you need to do
   d. relying on your memory to keep track of everything you need to do

4. A clique is a small group of people who accept
   a. certain types of people and exclude others.
   b. everybody.
   c. only people that are susceptible to peer pressure.
   d. only people that have many responsibilities. ★ 10.E

5. Which of the following statements is false?
   a. Boys and girls grow and change at the same age.
   b. Many adolescents experience mood swings.
   c. Adolescents take more risks than children or adults do.
   d. Romantic relationships during adolescence help prepare teens for adult relationships. ★ 2.A

ANSWERS: 1. b; 2. b; 3. b; 4. a; 5. a

Chapter 10 Adolescent Growth and Development | 241

Lesson 1: Your Changing Body

How did your friend suddenly get taller than you? Why did your older brother, sister, or friend grow so much over the last year? He or she probably began puberty.

What You'll Do

- **Summarize** the role of the endocrine system in growth and development. ★ 2.B
- **Compare** the changes that happen in males with the changes that happen in females during puberty. ★ 2.C

Terms to Learn

- puberty
- hormone

Start Off Write

What are some factors that affect your development?

Adolescence is the stage of development between childhood and adulthood. **Puberty** (PYOO buhr tee) is the part of adolescence when the reproductive system becomes mature.

What Makes You Grow?

The changes that happen during puberty are caused by hormones. A **hormone** is a chemical made in one part of the body that is carried through the bloodstream and causes a change in another part of the body. Hormones are made and released by the endocrine (EN doh KRIN) system, which is illustrated in Figure 1. The hormones that cause sexual maturation are called the *sex hormones*. *Testosterone* (tes TAHS tuhr OHN) is the male sex hormone. *Progesterone* (pro JES tuhr OHN) and *estrogen* (ES truh juhn) are the sex hormones of females. Estrogen and testosterone are found in both males and females. Males have more testosterone than females do. Females have more estrogen than males do. ★ 2.B

Figure 1 The Endocrine System

The thyroid gland secretes thyroxine, which helps regulate body growth and development.

The pituitary gland secretes human growth hormone and follicle-stimulating hormone. These hormones stimulate physical growth and the development of the reproductive organs.

The adrenal gland secretes cortical sex hormones, which help regulate the development of sex characteristics that signal the physical differences between males and females.

The testes secrete testosterone. Testosterone affects sperm production and the development of male sex characteristics.

The ovaries secrete estrogen and progesterone. Estrogen affects the development of female sex characteristics. Progesterone allows the uterus to prepare for pregnancy.

Individual Differences in Development

Many different factors affect your development. These factors include heredity, nutrition, your weight and fitness level, and your general health. In addition, boys and girls mature at different times and at different rates. And not every boy or girl changes in the same way or at the same time as his or her classmates. Some people develop earlier or later than others do. Nothing is wrong with developing differently than others do. Your body will develop at the time that is right for your body. However, if you are concerned that you may have a problem, see your doctor. Your doctor can tell you whether you are growing normally. ★ 2.A; 2.B; 2.C; 2.E

Figure 2 These girls are the same age, but one of them has grown faster than the other.

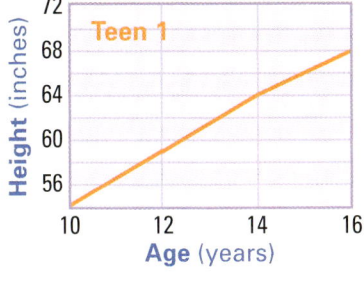 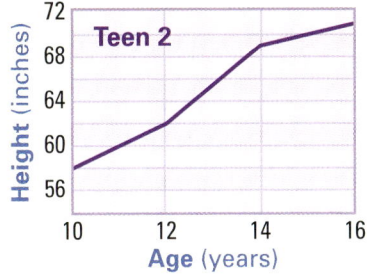

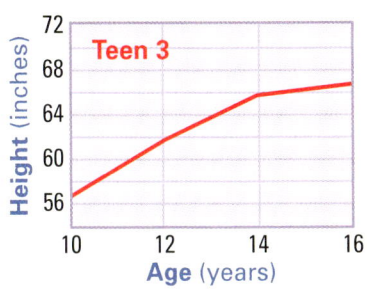 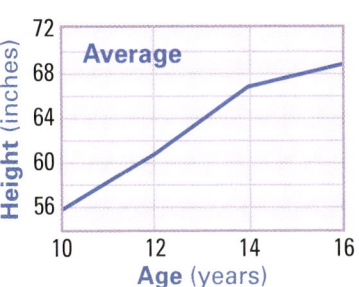

WHAT IS "NORMAL"?

1. Analyze the graphs for Teens 1, 2, and 3.
2. Find the average of the data in the three graphs by adding the three heights for each age and then dividing by three. Plot the new data on a new graph.

Analysis

1. Compare your new graph with the graph labeled "Average." How are these graphs similar?
2. How are the graphs of three teens alike? How are the graphs different?
3. What does the term *average height* mean?

★ 2.A; M8.5.A

The human body has between 50 and 100 different hormones.

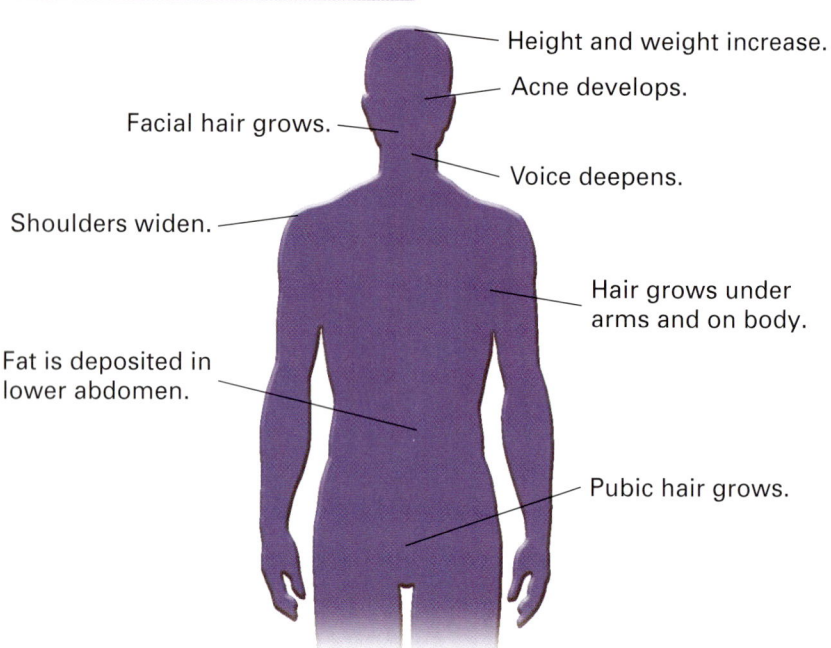

Figure 3 How Males Change

Physical Changes in Boys

Everyone goes through puberty at different times, but for boys, puberty generally begins between age 10 and age 14. Testosterone is responsible for many of the physical changes that happen to boys during puberty. One major change is rapid growth in both height and weight. This rapid growth can cause adolescent boys to feel awkward or clumsy. At about the same time, coarse hair begins to grow on the body and face. The voice gets deeper. Bones become denser, and muscles grow bigger and stronger. Fat is deposited on the back of the neck and the lower abdomen. Many boys also get acne (AK nee), or pimples. About one-third of boys develop fatty tissue in the breast area during puberty. In most cases, these breast changes go away in a few months. ★ 2.C

LIFE SKILLS ACTIVITY

COMMUNICATING EFFECTIVELY

The changes that happen during puberty can cause a lot of stress. Stress is your body's natural response to new and possibly unpleasant situations. Stress often results in mental or physical tension. List five aspects of puberty that you think are particularly frightening or stressful. Discuss your concerns with a parent or doctor. Write down some of their suggestions for coping with these changes.

★ 2.A; 2.B; 2.E

Figure 4 How Females Change

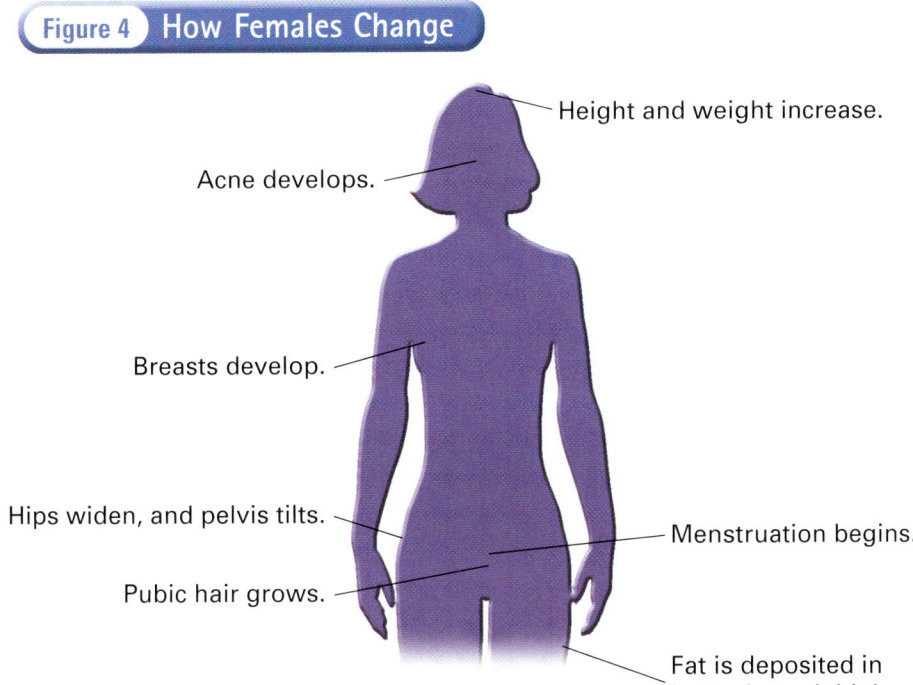

Physical Changes in Girls

Girls generally begin puberty earlier than boys do. In girls, puberty usually begins between age 8 and age 13. Estrogen is responsible for most of the physical changes that happen to girls during puberty. Generally, breast development is the first change to be noticed. Body hair begins to grow shortly after the beginning of puberty. The hips widen, and bones become more dense. Like boys, girls may also develop acne. Menstruation (MEN STRAY shuhn) usually begins between age 10 and age 16. Menstruation is the monthly discharge of blood and tissue from the body through the vagina. Menstruation is the signal that a girl's body is mature enough to become pregnant. ★ 2.C

Lesson Review

Understanding Concepts

1. What role does the endocrine system play in growth and development? ★ 2.B
2. List three changes that happen to both girls and boys during puberty. ★ 2.B; 2.C
3. How do boys develop differently from girls during puberty? ★ 2.A; 2.C

Critical Thinking

4. **Making Inferences** Girls generally begin puberty before boys do. How does this fact explain why girls often weigh more than boys do at age 11? ★ 2.A; 2.E
5. **Analyzing Ideas** If everyone develops differently, why do people discuss average growth and development? ★ 2.A

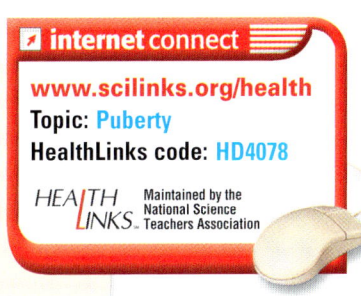

internet connect
www.scilinks.org/health
Topic: **Puberty**
HealthLinks code: **HD4078**
HEALTH LINKS Maintained by the National Science Teachers Association

Lesson 2: Your Changing Mind

What You'll Do

- **Explain** how your mental abilities change during adolescence. ★ 2.E
- **List** the six major categories of adolescent risk behavior.
- **Describe** how changes during puberty can affect risk-taking behavior in adolescents. ★ 2.A; 2.E

Terms to Learn

- abstract thought

Start Off Write

Why do teens act differently than children do?

Science Activity

As people grow from infants to adults, they learn many mental skills. Scientists have done studies to find out when and how children learn these skills. Use the library or the Internet to research the timeline of mental development in children. Write a short summary of the mental skills children have before they reach adolescence.

As a child, Keesha read mystery novels, but she could never figure out who "did it" until the end. As she got older, she began to be able to solve the mysteries by herself. Her ability to analyze the clues had changed.

In addition to the physical changes that happen during adolescence, mental changes also happen. During adolescence, your way of thinking starts to change from that of a child to that of an adult.

Development of Mental Abilities

The stages of human development involve both physical changes and mental changes. Adolescence is a time when people mature both physically and mentally.

Children have many of the same mental abilities as adults do. However, as children get older, their ability to think critically, or analyze ideas, improves. During adolescence, you begin to rely more on critical thinking, particularly your ability for abstract thought. **Abstract thought** is thought about ideas that are beyond what you see or experience. You learn to form and evaluate hypotheses. You begin to think critically about topics that are not part of your current surroundings or that don't directly affect you. You may begin to consider complex moral and ethical ideas. These new abilities are why adolescents usually become more concerned with justice, love, self-discovery, politics, and philosophy.
★ 2.A; 2.E

Figure 5 As you get older, you become better able to perform complex mental tasks, such as building models.

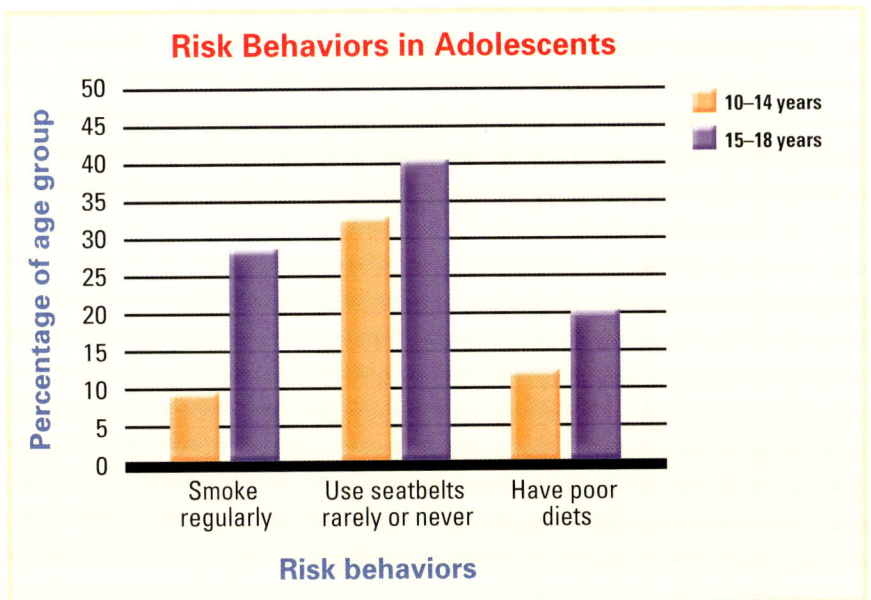

Figure 6 Older teens take more risks than younger teens and children do.

Development of Behavior

Adjusting to all the changes of adolescence can be difficult. As a way to deal with the mental, physical, emotional, and social changes they are going through, adolescents may participate in behaviors that place them at risk of illness or injury. These risky behaviors fall into six main categories—sexual activity, tobacco use, alcohol and drug use, unnecessary physical risks, poor nutrition, and lack of exercise. By taking some of these risks, adolescents may feel more in control of their lives. Sometimes, adolescents wrongly think that taking risks will make others like them better.

One of the most important tasks of adolescence is learning to make good decisions about your health. The ability to think abstractly helps you understand both the short-term and the long-term consequences of your actions. This knowledge can help you choose not to behave in risky or harmful ways. ★ 2.A; 2.E; 12.F

USING REFUSAL SKILLS

Role-play the following situation: Heather is at a party and her friend Brian is drinking alcohol. He offers her a beer and calls her a wimp when she says no. Create three responses that will help Heather avoid drinking alcohol. What can Heather do to avoid this situation in the future?

Lesson Review

Understanding Concepts

1. Explain how the mental abilities of an adolescent and a child differ. ★ 2.E

2. List the six main categories of adolescent risk behavior.

3. Why do adolescents take more risks than children or adults do? ★ 2.A; 2.E

Critical Thinking

4. **Making Inferences** How do changes in mental abilities affect adolescent behavior? ★ 2.A; 2.E

Lesson 3

Your Changing Feelings

What You'll Do

- **Identify** six emotional and social changes that happen during adolescence. ★ 2.E
- **Explain** how additional responsibility prepares teens for adulthood.
- **Describe** how peer pressure can affect your opinions and attitudes. ★ 7.A; 10.A; 12.E

Terms to Learn

- independence
- responsibility
- peer
- clique

Start Off Write

How do you think changes during adolescence prepare teens for adulthood?

Andrew sometimes worries that he's not normal. Sometimes, he feels happy and laughs a lot. Sometimes, he feels sad and lonely. Other times, he feels angry, and he doesn't know why.

Have you ever felt like Andrew? Adolescents often experience emotional and social changes. The changes that Andrew is going through affect how he feels. Learning to deal with these changes is another important task of adolescence.

Mood Swings

All the changes of puberty may lead to mood swings. You may feel happy one day and sad, angry, or anxious the next. You may feel that no one understands or cares what you are going through. Mood swings are a common part of adolescence, and almost everyone has them. However, mood swings should not keep you from functioning normally or make you feel like hurting yourself or someone else.

If you feel hopeless or helpless for longer than a few days or the feeling is particularly severe, you should talk with your parents or another trusted adult. These people can help you find ways of dealing with your emotions.

If you ever feel as though you may hurt yourself or someone else, seek help immediately! Talking to a parent or another trusted adult is very important. If you cannot reach any of these people, most communities have places where you can go to get help.
★ 2.A; 2.E

Figure 7 Adolescents often experience a wide range of emotions in a single day.

Attraction to Others

Another part of adolescence is the beginning of romantic attraction to others. *Attraction* is admiration for someone that may include the desire to get to know that person better. Early in adolescence, attraction usually takes the form of infatuation, or a "crush." *Infatuation* is admiration for someone while not recognizing that person's flaws. Crushes usually last for only a short time—a few weeks or maybe a few months. These feelings are completely normal and are a part of becoming a young adult.

Later in adolescence, or in early adulthood, most people begin to form romantic relationships based on love. *Love* is deep affection for someone and is based on a true desire for the other person's best interests. In a healthy relationship, the other person should respond with the same kind of love. Learning to develop, nurture, and even deal with the loss of these relationships are important ways to prepare for adult relationships.

★ 2.E; 7.A

Belonging

During adolescence, your friendships may change, too. Many adolescents begin to care more and more about being accepted. *Acceptance* means being approved of by others, or being welcomed into a group of friends. Making friends is part of getting ready for adulthood. Friends who accept you can help you deal with the stresses of growing up. Choosing your friends wisely can help you protect your health. Your emotional health can benefit from the support of friends. And good friends can encourage you to do the right things.

> **Health Journal**
> Think of a time when you were dealing with a problem of belonging and acceptance. Write about how you felt and what you did to solve the problem. Did you choose a good solution? Explain your answer.

Unfortunately, adolescents can become too focused on being accepted. They sometimes pretend to be someone they're not. Sometimes, they participate in risky behaviors because they think that these behaviors will make others like them. People who pressure you to do something unhealthy or unwise are not very good friends.

★ 2.E; 7.A; 10.A

Figure 8 Feeling that others accept you can boost your self-esteem.

Independence

Independence is very important to adolescents. **Independence** is being free of the control of others and relying on your own judgment and abilities. Independence usually increases throughout adolescence. By the end of adolescence, most people are responsible for taking care of themselves.

Your new-found independence may include later curfews, the right to make some of your own decisions, and permission to go out with your friends. At times, you may feel frustrated when you are not given the independence you want. Your parents or guardians are only looking out for your best interest. To get more independence, you will need to show them that you can handle more independence. ★ 2.E; 11.C

Responsibility

The best way to gain more independence is to show your parents or guardians that you are responsible and that you can be trusted. **Responsibility** is the act of accepting the consequences of your decisions and actions. You may have to show that you are responsible by doing more chores, getting a part-time job, or baby-sitting. When you can show others that you are dependable and that you understand the consequences of your actions, they will treat you more like an adult.

By learning to be responsible, adolescents prepare for adult roles. Adults must be responsible and dependable when they have jobs and families, because others will rely on them. Responsibility also helps you to be a good role model for others. Younger children are likely to imitate what they see. Seeing you act responsibly will help them learn to be responsible. ★ 2.E; 11.C

LIFE SKILLS ACTIVITY

COMMUNICATING EFFECTIVELY

Name one area of your life in which you would like to gain more independence. Write a letter to your parents that explains why you feel you need more independence and what responsibilities you can accept to show that you are ready for the additional freedom.

Figure 9 Many teens take on more responsibilities. In return, they get more independence.

Peer Groups and Cliques

Your **peers** are those people of about the same age or grade as you with whom you interact every day. These are your classmates, your friends, and your brothers and sisters. Your peers influence your opinions and actions. How you interact with your peers influences your behavior in certain ways. This influence is called *peer pressure*. Peer pressure can be positive or negative. Negative peer pressure encourages you to do unhealthy or unsafe things. Positive peer pressure encourages you to do healthy and safe things. Choosing good friends will help you avoid negative peer pressure to do things you may not want to do.

A **clique** (KLIK) is a group of people who accept only certain types of people and exclude others. Cliques can keep you from developing friendships with people who look or think differently than you. Acting in a cliquish, snobbish way shows a lack of respect and kindness toward others. ★ 7.A; 10.A; 10.E; 12.E

Myth: Belonging to one social group means you can't be friends with people outside that social group.

Fact: Being friends with one group of people should not prevent you from being friends with other people. Having different friends helps you learn to respect people's differences.

Figure 10 Many adolescents form groups of friends, but those groups should be accepting of others.

Lesson Review

Using Vocabulary

1. What is the difference between a peer and a clique?

Understanding Concepts

2. List six emotional and social changes that happen during adolescence. ★ 2.E

3. Explain why responsibility is important for adolescents. ★ 2.E; 7.A

Critical Thinking

4. **Using Refusal Skills** List three ways that your peers may affect your opinions and actions. How can you be more aware of peer pressure? ★ 7.A; 10.A; 12.E

5. **Analyzing Ideas** Describe how mood swings and a desire for acceptance can affect your social and physical health. ★ 2.A; 2.E

Lesson 4

What You'll Do

- **List** two ways to identify and explore your interests. ★ 6.A; 7.A
- **Describe** how organization and study skills affect your success in school. ★ 11.B; 12.G
- **Explain** how exploring career opportunities can help you plan for your future. ★ 12.F; 12.G

Terms to Learn

- extracurricular activity
- elective class

Start Off
Write

How can exploring your interests help prepare you for a future career?

Preparing for the Future

When Ana was little, she wanted to be a princess. Then, she wanted to be an astronaut. She also wanted to be a firefighter, a doctor, a teacher, an artist, a spy, and a game-show host. Now, she is interested in police work.

Like Ana, you have probably changed your mind about what you want to do. Your interests will continue to change as you get older. Being involved in different activities can help you decide what you enjoy and what you do well. These activities may also help you explore careers that you may enjoy as an adult.

Discovering Your Interests

Doing well in school is an important part of preparing for the future. Activities other than studying can be just as important. **Extracurricular activities** are activities that you do that aren't part of your schoolwork. Clubs, sports, and volunteering are all extracurricular activities. These activities are a great way to make friends and to identify and explore your interests and talents. **Elective classes** are classes that you can choose to take for a grade but are not required. Some electives may include band, choir, shop, and keyboarding. Elective courses enrich your education and help you learn new skills.

Activities should be a source of enjoyment, not of stress. You must be careful not to do too much. Activities should not keep you from doing your schoolwork, spending time with your family, or getting enough rest. ★ 6.A; 7.A

Figure 11 You can explore your interests by participating in extracurricular activities.

Getting Organized

Juggling school, friends, family, and other activities requires a lot of organization. Being disorganized forces you to spend a lot of time redoing things you've already done. By being more organized, you can reduce stress and be more productive.

To be organized, you need both skills and supplies. Most importantly, you need discipline. You must be willing to spend a little time planning in advance, to save a lot of time later. Sometimes, taking the time to be organized seems like too much trouble, but in the end you'll be glad you did. Here are some tips for becoming more organized:

- At the beginning of each week, spend at least 20 minutes planning what needs to be done that week. Every evening, spend about 5 minutes planning what needs to be done the next day.
- Use a filing cabinet, a bookshelf, or your locker to organize the different projects that you are working on. Keep your locker neat and free of clutter.
- Discuss other ways to be better organized with friends or adults who you think are well organized.

If you take these steps, you should find that you will get more work done in less time. Being organized leaves more time for relaxation and other activities. ★ 11.B; 12.G

Figure 12 An organized locker and backpack can save you time and space. A day planner can help you keep track of assignments and their due dates.

Lesson 4 Preparing for the Future | 253

Figure 13 When reading a textbook, you should take notes about important topics by using a notebook.

Your Schoolwork

In middle school and high school, you must learn study skills to succeed in your education. You need to learn how to take notes in class, read a textbook, and study for tests. Here are some tips for taking notes and reading textbooks:

- On the left side of the paper, write down important topics. Write details or explanations under these main topics.
- Compare notes with a friend. Make sure both of you wrote down all of the important points. Read these notes daily.
- Before class, read the lesson in the textbook that relates to the class. Take notes in a notebook while you read.
- Look for key words. Some textbooks highlight key words or list them at the beginning or end of the chapter.

Here are some tips for studying for tests:

- Begin studying 2 or 3 days before the test. Avoid "cramming" the night before.
- Study with a friend, and ask each other questions.
- Get plenty of rest the night before the test.

These skills can help you succeed in any class. But if you think you need additional help in any subject, ask a friend, your parents, or your teacher for help. ★ 12.G

Teen: Sometimes, I wait until the last minute to do homework or other projects. How can I stop doing this?

Expert: The best way to avoid waiting until the last minute, or procrastinating, is to spend a little time studying or working on an assignment each day. Reviewing your notes within a day or two of the class helps reinforce in your mind the information you heard in class. If you review your notes often, this practice will become second nature, and you will be less likely to procrastinate.

Planning for Your Future

You will soon have to make decisions about what you will do with your adult life. What kind of career do you want to have? If you continue your education, what will you study? To answer these questions, ask yourself, "What do I enjoy doing? What topics in school interest me, and in which areas do I do well?" You also need to think about the lifestyle you want to have. How much time do you want to spend with your family? How much are you willing to work? You will need to decide what makes you happy. For example, if you enjoy helping people, you may be interested in teaching or social work.

You can explore careers in many ways. You could go to work with an adult. You could volunteer at a hospital or charity. You could get a part-time or summer job. If you are interested in a certain career, look for ways to gather information about that field. Keep in mind that most people change their mind about their career at least once after finishing high school. But thinking about your future now will help you make good decisions later.
★ 12.F; 12.G

Myth: You should know what you want to do as an adult before you finish high school.

Fact: Most people don't decide what their final career will be until they attend college or technical school, or even much later in life.

Figure 14 One way to explore future careers is to volunteer.

Lesson Review

Understanding Concepts

1. How can extracurricular activities and elective courses help you identify your interests? ★ 6.A; 7.A

2. How do organizational skills and study skills affect your success in school? ★ 11.B; 11.F; 12.B; 12.G

3. How does exploring career opportunities help you prepare for the future? ★ 12.F; 12.G

Critical Thinking

4. **Analyzing Ideas** How can being organized affect your health? ★ 11.B; 11.F; 12.B; 12.G

10 CHAPTER REVIEW

Chapter Summary

- Boys and girls undergo significant physical changes during puberty. This growth and development is affected by chemicals called *hormones*.
- Mental, emotional, and social changes are also an important part of adolescence.
- During adolescence, people begin to rely more on their ability to think abstractly.
- Adolescents usually become more independent and responsible.
- During adolescence, teens feel a strong desire for acceptance. This desire may cause adolescents to participate in risky behaviors.
- Developing healthy relationships is an important part of adolescence.
- Adolescents also start thinking about future careers and prepare for the future by doing well in school and participating in extracurricular activities.

Using Vocabulary

1. Use each of the following terms in a separate sentence: *puberty*, *clique*, and *extracurricular activity*.

For each pair of terms, describe how the meanings of the terms differ.

2. clique/peer
3. extracurricular activity/elective class
4. puberty/hormone
5. independence/responsibility

For each sentence, fill in the blank with the proper word from the word bank provided below.

| abstract thought | hormones |
| independence | responsibility |

6. Your ___ cause(s) changes in different parts of your body.
7. Forming and evaluating hypotheses is a form of ___.
8. You have ___ when you are free from the control of others.
9. When you accept the consequences of your actions, you are showing ___.

Understanding Concepts

10. How is puberty the same for everybody? How is it different? ★ 2.B; 2.C; 2.E
11. What is the role of the endocrine system in growth and development? ★ 2.B
12. How does responsibility prepare adolescents for adulthood? ★ 2.E
13. What emotional and social changes happen during adolescence? ★ 2.A; 2.E
14. How do mental abilities change during adolescence? ★ 2.E
15. Give an example of negative peer pressure. Give an example of positive peer pressure. ★ 10.A
16. How can understanding your interests help you prepare for the future? ★ 12.F
17. What six types of risk behaviors increase during adolescence?
18. How could all of the changes of adolescence lead to risk-taking behaviors? ★ 2.A; 7.A; 12.E
19. What is the difference between puberty and adolescence? ★ 1.D; 2.B; 2.E
20. How does being organized affect your success in school? ★ 1.D; 2.B; 2.E

Critical Thinking

Analyzing Ideas

21. During puberty, higher levels of estrogen cause women's bones to become denser. At menopause, the body releases less estrogen. How may this affect women's bone density? What result would this have on women's overall health? ★ 1.D; 2.E

22. A perfume manufacturer guarantees that its product will make you more attractive to the opposite sex because it contains hormones. Do you think this claim is valid? Why or why not? ★ 4.A; 4.C; 8.A

23. What are some possible long-term consequences of not accepting responsibility for your actions? ★ 11.B; 12.B; 12.D

Making Good Decisions

24. Imagine that you started dating someone at your school. Everything was going fine until your date offered you an illegal drug. He or she refuses to date you unless you try the drug. You are uncomfortable with this pressure. What should you do in this situation? ★ 7.A; 11.D; 12.E

25. A group of your friends are having a party on Saturday night. You invite a new student to come with you to the party. At the party, one of your friends pulls you aside and tells you not to ask the new student to other parties. When you ask why, she says that the new student is "not like us." What should you do? ★ 10.A; 11.A; 11.C; 11.D; 12.E

26. At the beginning of the semester, your science teacher gives you a list of all the assignments that will be due during the semester. Some of these assignments will take you a long time to complete. How can you make sure your assignments will be completed on time this semester? ★ 12.G

Interpreting Graphics

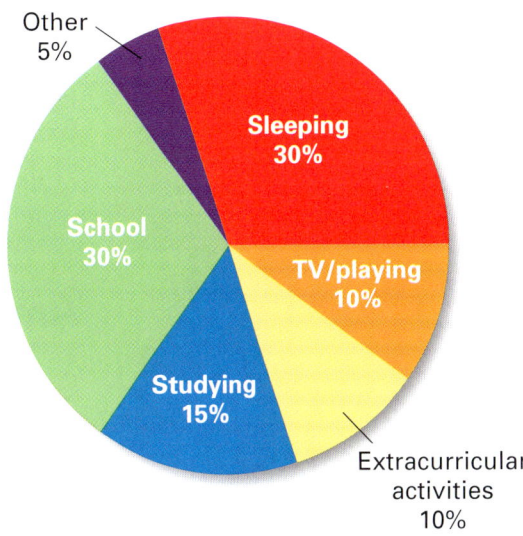

Tara's Time Management

Use the figure above to answer questions 27–30. ★ *M8.5.A

27. The graph above shows the percentage of time Tara spends on different tasks during a typical day. How much time, in hours, does Tara spend playing or watching TV?

28. How much time, in hours, does Tara spend sleeping each day?

29. How much total time, in hours, does Tara spend on scholastic activities? How much more time, in hours, does Tara spend on non-scholastic activities?

30. What advice would you give to Tara about her lifestyle?

Reading Checkup

Take a minute to review your answers to the Health IQ questions at the beginning of this chapter. How has reading this chapter improved your Health IQ?

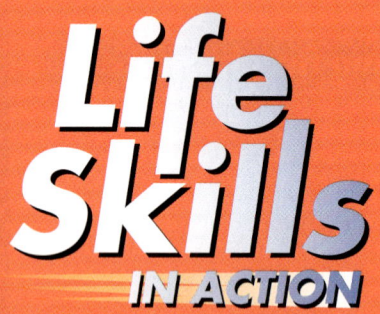

Life Skills IN ACTION

Coping

At times, everyone has to face setbacks, disappointments, or other troubles. In order to deal with these problems, you have to learn how to cope. Coping is dealing with problems and emotions in an effective way. Complete the following activity to develop your coping skills.

Amira's Crush

Setting the Scene

Amira has had a crush on Jason for several years. Last week, she finally had the courage to invite him to a school dance, but he turned her down. Since then, Amira has been very depressed. Amira's friend Tracy has been trying to cheer her up, but Amira keeps thinking about Jason's rejection.
★ 2.E; 10.B; 11.B

The 5 Steps of Coping

1. Identify the problem.
2. Identify your emotions.
3. Use positive self-talk.
4. Find ways to resolve the problem.
5. Talk to others to receive support.

Guided Practice

Practice with a Friend

Form a group of three. Have one person play the role of Amira and another person play the role of Tracy. Have the third person be an observer. Walking through each of the five steps of coping, role-play Amira coping with Jason's rejection. Have Tracy support Amira. The observer will take notes, which will include observations about what the person playing Amira did well and suggestions of ways to improve. Stop after each step to evaluate the process. ★ 11.B

Independent Practice

Check Yourself

After you complete the guided practice, go through Act 1 again without stopping at each step. Answer the questions below to review what you did.

1. Aside from depression, what other emotions could Amira feel? Explain.

2. What are some positive things Amira could tell herself to help her cope with this situation? ⭐ 4.C; 11.B

3. Explain why talking with others could help Amira cope. ⭐ 11.B; 11.D

4. Describe a time when you had to cope with a problem similar to Amira's. What did you do to cope?

On Your Own

Tracy tells Amira that she should still go to the dance. Tracy says that she can set Amira up with her cousin and that they can all go to the dance together. Amira reluctantly agrees because she doesn't want to miss out on the dance. However, Amira is very nervous because she has never been on a blind date before. Draw a comic strip showing how Amira could use the five steps of coping to deal with the blind date.

CHAPTER 11
Building Responsible Relationships

Lessons

1. Social Skills — 262
2. Sensitivity Skills — 266
3. Family Health — 268
4. Influences on Teen Relationships — 272
5. Healthy Friendships — 274
6. Teen Dating — 278

Chapter Review — 282
Life Skills in Action — 284

Check out **Current Health** articles related to this chapter by visiting **go.hrw.com**. Just type in the keyword **HD4CH43**.

" I stutter, and that makes it hard to talk. Some kids used to **make fun** of me. They'd get **right in my face** and pretend to stutter. I go to classes that help me speak more clearly, but when people tease me, I get nervous and I stutter again. Juanita and Katie were the first people to tell kids to cut out the teasing. It was a relief to have friends who cared and stood up for me. **"**

Health IQ

PRE-READING

Answer the following multiple-choice questions to find out what you already know about relationships. When you've finished this chapter, you'll have the opportunity to change your answers based on what you've learned.

1. Which of the following help you communicate?
   a. your words
   b. your behavior
   c. the way you stand
   d. all of the above ★ 11.D

2. Tolerance is
   a. rude.
   b. a way to show respect.
   c. always appropriate.
   d. All of the above ★ 11.C

3. Aggressiveness is
   a. pushy and disrespectful behavior.
   b. a healthy way of sharing feelings.
   c. a healthy way to cope with hard times.
   d. None of the above ★ 10.B

4. Healthy self-esteem helps you become
   a. more selfish.
   b. aggressive.
   c. a better friend.
   d. None of the above

5. The best way to cope with change in the family is to
   a. talk to a trusted adult.
   b. pretend it isn't happening.
   c. wait until someone asks about it.
   d. keep it a secret. ★ 10.B

6. Unhealthy relationships
   a. are always with people you don't like.
   b. will take care of themselves.
   c. should be resolved quickly.
   d. None of the above

ANSWERS: 1. d; 2. b; 3. a; 4. c; 5. a; 6. c

Lesson 1

Social Skills

You probably spend most of your day interacting with other people. Your family, friends, teachers, and teammates all affect you and depend on you. Having good social health allows you to get along with the people you meet every day.

Having good social health means having clear, healthy relationships. A **relationship** is an emotional or social connection you have with another person or group. One of the ways you keep your relationships healthy is to use good social skills.

Expressing Yourself

The ability to communicate well is an important social skill. One requirement of communication is to express yourself. You have to be able to express yourself clearly so that people around you know what you are thinking and feeling. Think about what you are going to say. Stick to your point. Speak clearly, and ask questions to make sure your listener understands you.

Sometimes, expressing feelings can be hard. Using a form of art can help. You can express your feelings through writing or poetry. Painting, dancing, sculpting, and playing a musical instrument are all healthy ways of expressing your feelings without using words. ★ 11.D

What You'll Do

- **Explain** why clearly expressing yourself is important. ★ 11.D
- **List** four characteristics of active listening. ★ 10.C
- **Describe** the ways of expressing body language. ★ 11.D
- **Contrast** assertive behavior with passive behavior and with aggressive behavior. ★ 10.D; 11.C; 11.D
- **Describe** the three aspects of personal responsibility. ★ 12.B
- **Explain** how refusal skills help maintain healthy relationships. ★ 12.B; 12.E

Terms to Learn

- relationship
- active listening
- body language
- behavior

What is active listening?

Figure 1 Sometimes art is a great way to express your feelings.

Understanding Others

Expressing yourself is only half of the process of communication. The other half is understanding others. Understanding the thoughts and feelings of other people takes practice. Being a good listener helps you understand others. Good listening is more than just hearing. It's using active listening skills. **Active listening** is hearing and thoughtfully responding as a person is speaking. Active listening includes the following behaviors:

- paying attention to the person speaking
- making eye contact
- nodding when you understand
- asking questions when you don't understand

Active listening is participating in a conversation in which the other person does most of the talking. ★ 10.C

Understanding Body Language

Becoming a good listener helps you understand what people are saying. But people also express themselves by using body language. **Body language** is a way of communicating by using facial expressions, hand gestures, and body posture. You see and use body language every day. A smile usually means someone is happy. A person who has a tilted head and scrunched eyebrows is probably confused. A person who is holding his or her head high and standing tall is probably confident.

But body language is not always easy to read. For example, a person who is sitting with his or her arms and legs crossed and who is not smiling may be afraid or angry. A person who is slightly frowning may be sad. But he or she may be deep in thought. When you don't understand a message, ask about it. Likewise, if your friend says she is happy but her body language seems sad, tell her that you are confused. Ask her to tell you how she is really feeling. Sending the same message with your words and your body language will help people understand you.
★ 11.D

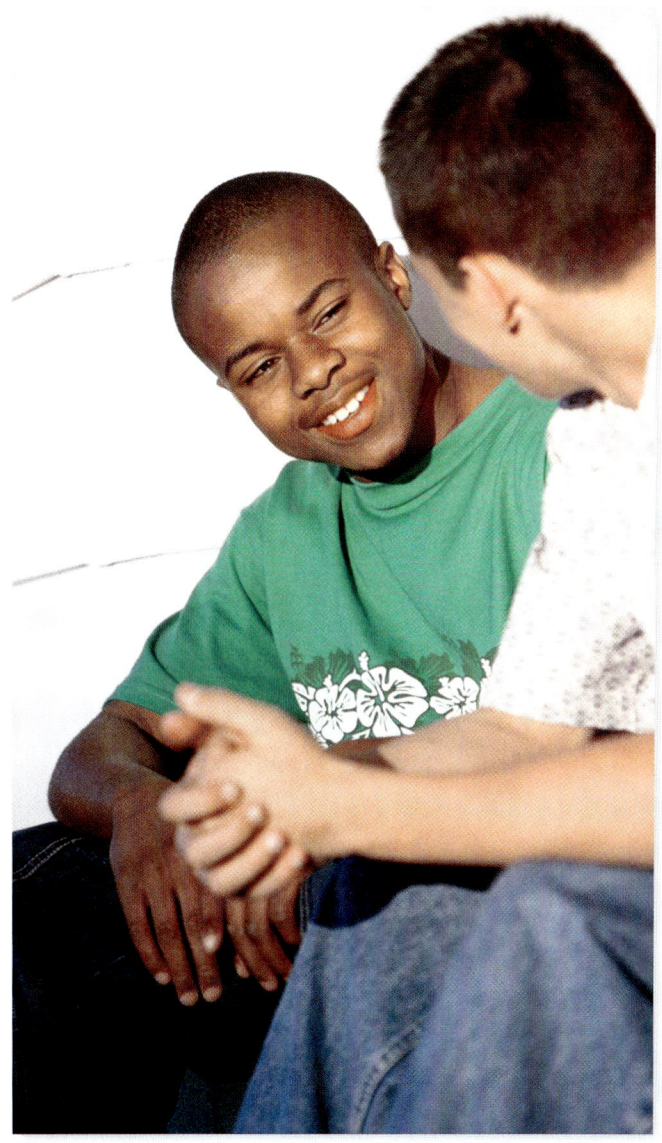

Figure 2 Active listening skills help you understand what people are saying.

Figure 3 Debaters use assertive behavior. Everyone takes turns respectfully stating his or her position.

Communicating Through Behavior

You send messages through your words and your body language. You also send messages through your behavior. Your **behavior** is how you choose to respond or act. In every situation, you can choose from many ways to respond. For example, if someone cuts in front of you in line, what would you do? A *passive* response would be to say and do nothing. An *aggressive* response would be to be pushy and disrespectful, by shouting or threatening, for example. Respectfully asking the person who cut in front of you to go to the end of the line would be an assertive response. *Assertive* behavior is expressing your thoughts and feelings in a respectful way. Assertive behavior is helpful in relationships. It shows that you care about yourself. But it also shows that you care about the thoughts and feelings of others. When you care about yourself and others and put your caring into action, you are demonstrating good character.

★ 10.D; 11.C; 11.D

LIFE SKILLS ACTIVITY

COMMUNICATING EFFECTIVELY

In small groups, build a single, free-standing tower by using index cards and masking tape. Use no words to communicate while you are building your tower. Use behavior and body language to communicate your ideas to each other. After all the groups have built a tower, discuss how you managed to build the towers without talking. What was the most difficult part of completing this task? What types of communication did you and the members of your group use? What other tasks have you done in which words were not used to communicate?

Character and Personal Responsibility

Your behavior, thoughts, and feelings are all part of your character. Relationships are affected by the character of the people in them. Developing good character, which is based on positive values, will help you have healthy relationships. One value that helps relationships is responsibility. Taking *personal responsibility* means doing your part, keeping promises, and accepting the consequences of your actions. When people take responsibility for their actions, they are on the right track to having healthy relationships. ★ 12.B

Refusal Skills

One way to take personal responsibility is to use refusal skills whenever you need them. Plan ahead to avoid risky situations in the first place. But if you find yourself in a risky situation, remember that you can choose a healthy response. Refusing risky behavior helps keep you and those around you safe and healthy. If you are confronted with an unhealthy choice, say, "No." Stand your ground. Remember your values. If people keep pressuring you, walk away.

Figure 4 Using refusal skills can keep you from smoking.

Using refusal skills shows that you care about your relationships. It shows that you take responsibility for the consequences of your decisions. For example, refusing a cigarette when offered one shows that you respect your health, your family, and the law. ★ 12.B; 12.E

Lesson Review

Using Vocabulary
1. Define *body language*.

Understanding Concepts
2. Explain why clearly expressing yourself is important. ★ 11.D
3. List four characteristics of active listening. ★ 10.C
4. Describe three ways of expressing body language. ★ 11.D
5. Explain how refusal skills help you maintain healthy relationships. ★ 12.B; 12.E

Critical Thinking
6. **Applying Concepts** While playing catch, Salvador threw the ball over Tomas's head. The ball went through a neighbor's window. How can Salvador show personal responsibility? Describe an aggressive response, a passive response, and an assertive response to the problem.
★ 10.D; 11.C; 11.D

Lesson 1 Social Skills

Lesson 2

Sensitivity Skills

What You'll Do

- **Explain** four ways to develop empathy. ★ 11.D
- **Explain** why tolerance is important to relationships. ★ 11.B; 11.C; 11.D

Terms to Learn

- empathy
- tolerance

Why is tolerance important to relationships?

Derek's little brother, Toby, always wants to hang around with Derek and Terrel. He wants to do everything they do and go where they go. Derek thinks his brother is a pest. He wants Toby to find his own friends and to stop trying to tag along.

When Derek talked to Toby, he learned that Toby felt hurt and left out. Toby said that Derek used to play with him a lot but now he doesn't even want to spend time with him. Derek understood how Toby was feeling and promised to spend more time with him. Sharing and understanding another person's feelings is called **empathy** (EM puh thee).

Developing Empathy

Healthy communication in relationships is more than just getting your point across. It includes understanding the feelings of the people around you. You can start developing empathy by being a good listener and by being a good reader of body language. When you are talking with people, try to identify their feelings. Be specific. For example, you could say,

- "You seem upset at what your sister did."
- "You seem excited about moving to a new city."
- "You seem disappointed with the part you got in the play."

Figure 5 People with wheelchairs have to overcome physical obstacles every day. Being aware of the barriers people face helps you understand their lives.

If you are wrong, the person you are talking to can help you identify the feelings correctly. Developing empathy takes practice. But showing empathy for your family and friends is a great way to show that you respect them and care about their feelings.

Another way to develop empathy is to become aware of the kinds of problems people face every day. For example, have you ever used a wheelchair? If not, imagine how a person in a wheelchair visits a friend whose apartment building has stairs at the front door. He or she may feel angry or hurt. Imagining someone else's point of view helps you better understand the person. ★ 11.D

Showing Tolerance

Empathy helps people understand each other's feelings. Tolerance (TAHL uhr uhns) helps people get along. Tolerance is the ability to overlook differences and accept people for who they are. People like different foods and different music. People have different traditions and values. Even friends disagree about some ideas. By showing tolerance, you show people that you respect them for who they are, not because they are just like you.

Showing tolerance can help you build relationships with people who are different from you. But not all differences should be overlooked. What if a person wants to hurt people, steal, or show disrespect for other people's property? Should you show tolerance for that behavior? No. Tolerance supports responsible behavior, not unhealthy or dangerous behavior. Talk to a trusted adult about anybody who is behaving dangerously.

Tolerance is not just something to use to get along with strangers. Family members need to use tolerance with each other, too. Respect all the generations of your family, and learn from them. Being polite, listening, and treating each other with respect helps you show your family members that you care about them. ★ 11.B; 11.C; 11.D

LIFE SKILLS ACTIVITY

COMMUNICATING EFFECTIVELY

Learning about other cultures helps you practice tolerance. Conduct library research about a holiday or event in history that is important to a culture you would like to learn about. Interview some people of that culture to find out how they celebrate that holiday or why that historical event is important to them. Prepare a brief report explaining what you learned, and share it with the class.

Figure 6 By overlooking a few differences, these brothers can get along and have fun together.

Lesson Review

Using Vocabulary
1. Define *empathy*. Use the word *empathy* in a sentence.
2. What is tolerance? ★ 11.C

Understanding Concepts
3. Explain four ways to develop empathy. ★ 11.D
4. Explain why tolerance is important to relationships.
★ 11.B; 11.C; 11.D

Critical Thinking
5. **Making Good Decisions** Brad and Troy are friends. They each root for rival baseball teams. How can tolerance help their relationship? ★ 11.C
6. **Making Good Decisions** Kyla and Emma are 13. When Kyla's mother was away, Kyla took the car and drove to the store. Should Emma show tolerance for Kyla's behavior? Explain your answer.
★ 11.C; 11.D

Lesson 2 Sensitivity Skills

Lesson 3: Family Health

What You'll Do

- **Explain** how a family's structure can change over time. ★ 7.A; 9.A
- **Explain** how both adults and teens can provide nurturing in a family. ★ 9.B
- **Explain** why family roles and responsibilities change. ★ 7.A; 9.A
- **Identify** three disruptive changes that families face. ★ 9.B
- **Explain** two ways to cope with family problems. ★ 9.B; 11.B; 11.D

Terms to Learn

- nurturing

Start Off Write

What are two healthy ways to cope with family problems?

After school, Felipe helps his family by looking after his brother and his cousin. He helps them with their homework and keeps them out of trouble. Felipe's sister, Rita, helps by starting dinner.

Felipe and Rita have important jobs in their family. They are students, and they help care for their family after school. You probably have roles to play in your family, too. Fulfilling your roles in your family helps your family stay healthy. Living in healthy families gives people the love and care they need to grow. Providing the care and other basic things that people need to grow is called **nurturing** (NUHR chuhr ing).

Family Structure

The job of every family is to nurture its members. But that does not mean that every family looks the same or has the same structure. The figure below shows some common family structures. Families don't always keep the same structure. For example, the two spouses in a couple are a family before they have children. They become a nuclear (NOO klee urh) family after they have children. If they adopt children, they can become an adoptive (uh DAHP tiv) family, too. If a grandparent moves in, they will live as an extended family. ★ 7.A; 9.A

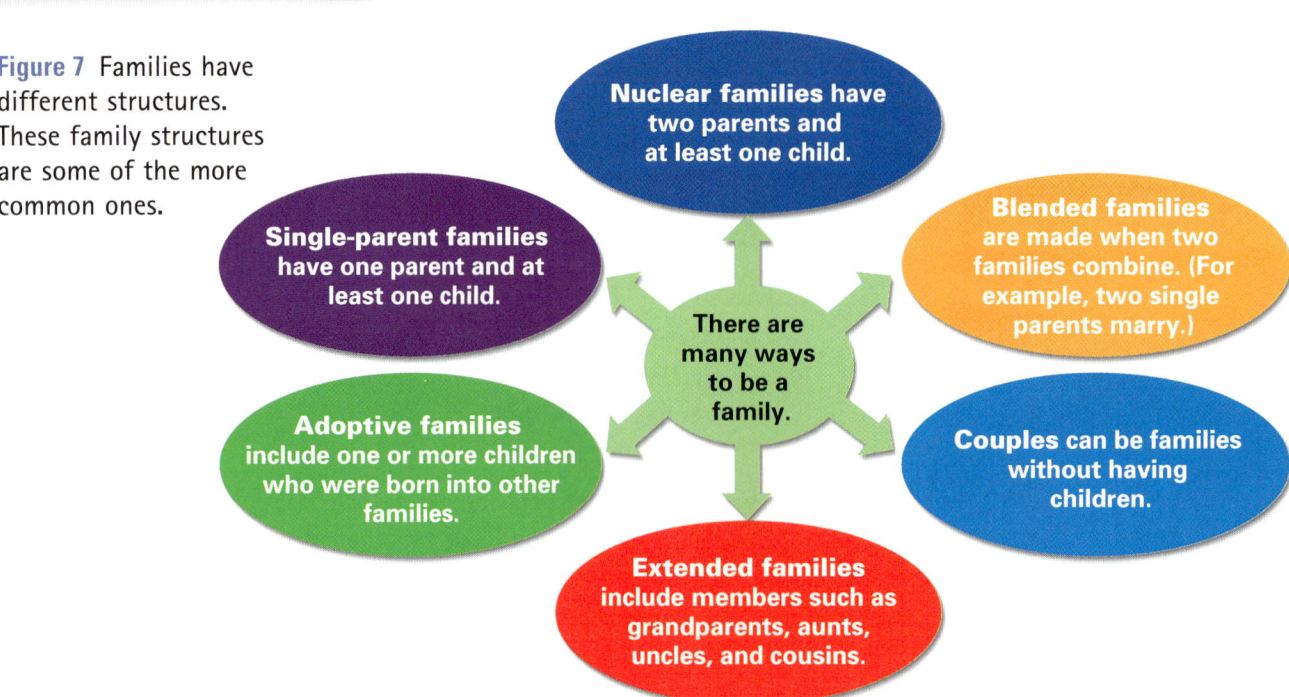

Figure 7 Families have different structures. These family structures are some of the more common ones.

Figure 8 There are roles for everyone in a family. You may help by doing some of the shopping.

Family Roles

Healthy families may have different structures, but all healthy families provide nurturing. Parents or other adults in the family are responsible for most of the nurturing in a family. Adult responsibilities include providing food, clothing, shelter, basic care, and love. Adults protect the health and safety of everyone in the family. Adults also teach children basic skills and values.

When you care for the members of your family in any way, you are also nurturing them. You help care for your family by showing respect and cooperation. The other roles you have depend on what your family needs. For example, if you have younger brothers and sisters, you may be responsible for looking after them. You may also help with the cooking, housecleaning, shopping, or laundry. Your friends may have different roles in their families if their families have different needs. ★ 7.A; 9.A; 9.B

Changing Roles

Roles within a family can change. Your roles change as you gain responsibility and learn to do more things. When a family's needs change, many family roles change, too. For example, if a baby is born, caring for the baby will require a new set of responsibilities. If your older sister leaves for college, someone will have to take on the household responsibilities she had. Maybe your mother used to stay home. If she now has a job outside the home, she has taken on an additional role. Her role change can lead to other role changes. For example, you may have to begin getting dinner ready before she gets home. ★ 7.A; 9.A; 9.B

Health Journal

You are a role model for your younger brothers and sisters because they look up to you. Record the time you spend with a younger brother or sister for one week. What did you do together? What was good about spending time as a positive role model? Describe one way you can be a better role model for younger brothers and sisters.

Lesson 3 Family Health | 269

Family Changes

A certain amount of change is normal. But sometimes change is difficult. Over time, some problems can become very disruptive, often causing families to change the way they live. Common problems include the following:

- **Health problems** It can be hard for a family to cope with the long illness of a close family member. The care of a sick person is important and takes a lot of time. If the person who is sick has held a job and now can no longer work, the loss of income can affect the family, too.

- **Money problems** Money problems can happen for many reasons. For example, a parent could lose a job, or a car may need to be replaced suddenly. Money problems sometimes lead to other problems between family members.

- **Relationship problems** When family members don't get along, the whole family is affected. When parents separate or divorce, the structure of the family changes. Adjusting to the new arrangement can be hard.

Most major problems should be handled by adults. But the problems can affect everybody. Members of the family may feel worried, angry, or feel other effects of negative stress. Sometimes talking about these problems with parents or other family members helps. Counseling offices often have many resources that can help, too. ★ 7.A; 9.A; 9.B

Myth: Family problems should be kept secret.

Fact: One of the best ways to cope with family problems is to talk with a trusted adult about them.

Figure 9 If family changes cause problems for you, try talking with a trusted adult.

Figure 10 Sometimes, talking to grandparents can help you solve problems.

Coping with Problems

One of the best ways to cope with problems is to talk about them. Adult family members, such as parents or grandparents, can help. Teachers, coaches, and school counselors can also help. Talking about your feelings to people who can help you often keeps problems from creating other problems. If you or a friend have problems that are affecting your relationships, health, or schoolwork, find someone you can talk with about the problem.

Another good way to cope with family problems is to hold regular family meetings. In family meetings, families set aside time to talk. Everyone in the family gets a chance to speak about his or her feelings and concerns. Everyone should listen carefully to the person speaking and act respectfully. As problems arise, family members can work together to solve them. Writing down what you talk about at a family meeting can help you keep track of problems and make sure the problems are being resolved.
★ 9.B; 11.B; 11.D

STUDY TIP *for better reading*

Organizing Information Create a flow chart that illustrates the organizational steps leading to a family meeting. Make another flow chart that illustrates how to follow up on a problem.

Lesson Review

Using Vocabulary
1. What is nurturing? ★ 9.B

Understanding Concepts
2. Explain how a family's structure can change over time. ★ 7.A; 9.A
3. Explain why family roles and responsibilities change. ★ 7.A; 9.A; 9.B
4. Explain how both adults and teens can provide nurturing in a family.
★ 9.B

5. Identify three disruptive changes a family might face. Explain two healthy ways of coping with family problems.
★ 7.A; 9.A; 9.B

Critical Thinking
6. **Applying Concepts** Josh is very close to his grandmother. She recently moved into a nursing home. Josh is worried about her. What is a healthy way for Josh to cope with his feelings?
★ 10.B; 11.B; 11.D

Lesson 3 Family Health

Lesson 4: Influences on Teen Relationships

What You'll Do

- **Describe** how you can tell if a message in the media is a good influence on relationships. ★ 4.A; 8.A
- **Describe** three types of relationships that may influence your actions. ★ 7.A; 8.A; 12.E

Terms to Learn

- media

Start Off Write

How can you tell if a message in the media is a good influence on your relationships?

Mia is annoyed at the way women are shown in some magazines, ads, TV shows, and movies. She is bothered that women are often included just to look pretty. And she gets really annoyed when the female characters are helpless!

TV shows, movies, music, magazines, and all other public forms of communication are the **media.** The media can influence what you think about yourself and how you get along with others. You are responsible for choosing how you will get along with people. But how do you choose? You can start by examining what influences you, the way Mia does.

Media Influences

You are surrounded by messages that influence how you get along with others. Listen closely to the words in your favorite song. Are they disrespectful or violent? Do the characters in the TV shows and movies you watch do things that are against your values? If so, these things may be bad influences on you. They may encourage you to act like the characters in the songs, TV shows, and movies. Messages that encourage healthier, safer, and stronger relationships are good influences. Surrounding yourself with good influences helps you make healthy choices. ★ 4.A; 8.A

Figure 11 The media can influence how you treat people.

Real People as Influences

Another influence on your behavior is your experience with people. Examples of such influences are discussed below.

- **Your family** The first group you belonged to was your family. Your family taught you values, traditions, and ways to get along with others. In your family, you have probably learned how to cooperate, solve problems, and show healthy affection.

- **Your role models** Trusted adults, such as parents, teachers, and coaches, may have influenced how you treat people. For example, if they have helped and supported you, you have learned how to give help and support.

- **Your peers** You spend a lot of time with your peers. They have a big influence on your relationships and your health. Your teammates, classmates, and friends have all taught you how to interact with people your own age. When they pressure you to do things you should not do, they are using *negative peer pressure*. Peers who pressure you to do your best are using *positive peer pressure*. Positive peer pressure is a way that you and your friends can help each other reach healthy goals.

All of your relationships affect the other relationships you have. You learn something from everybody. Use the good lessons from each relationship in all of your other relationships. ★ 7.A; 12.E

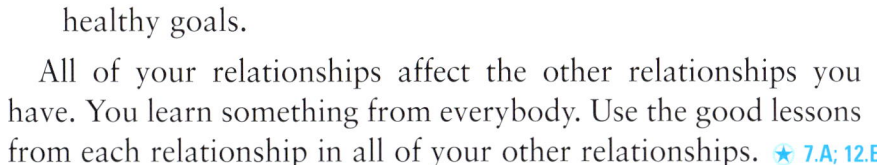

Figure 12 When friends encourage each other to do well in school, they are using positive peer pressure.

Lesson Review

Using Vocabulary
1. Define *media*.

Understanding Concepts
2. Describe three kinds of relationships that influence you. ★ 7.A; 8.A; 12.E

3. How can you tell if a media message is a good influence? ★ 4.A; 8.A

Critical Thinking
4. **Applying Concepts** Why are violent movies rated to keep young people from seeing them? ★ 4.A; 8.A

Lesson 5

What You'll Do

- **Describe** four ways you can build your self-esteem. ★ 7.A; 7.B; 12.B
- **List** five qualities of good character. ★ 11.C; 12.B
- **List** three ways to make new friends. ★ 7.A; 10.A; 11.C
- **Explain** why keeping friendships healthy is important. ★ 7.A; 7.B
- **Explain** three ways to resolve unhealthy relationships. ★ 7.B; 11.D; 12.B

Terms to Learn

- unhealthy relationship

Start Off Write

What are qualities of a good friend?

Healthy Friendships

All of Brenda's friends tell Brenda their problems. She is a good listener and always seems to understand what is wrong. Sometimes she can offer a solution, but usually she just listens and tries to be a good friend.

Besides your family, good friends are some of the most important people in your life. When you were younger, you and your friends only played together. As you grow up, your friends can become more like a second family. Friends help you work on projects and reach goals. Friends help you do well in school and stay physically fit. The number of friends you have doesn't matter. What matters is that you and your friends keep each other safe and healthy.

Building Self-Esteem

Before you can be a good friend to others you have to be good to yourself. Your *self-esteem* is the way you feel about yourself as a person, or how you value yourself. You can build healthy self-esteem. Practice treating yourself the way a good friend would treat you. Respect yourself. Encourage yourself to make healthy decisions. Be assertive about reaching goals. Building healthy self-esteem is not the same as being selfish. Being selfish is caring only about how your decisions affect you. People who have healthy self-esteem also respect the well-being of others. In fact, building healthy self-esteem also helps you develop the skills you need to treat your friends in the same way you want them to treat you. ★ 7.A; 7.B; 12.B

Figure 13 Healthy self-esteem can help you build good relationships.

Figure 14 Good friends care about each other and look out for each other.

Friendship and Character

The skills you use to be good to yourself should also help you treat your friends well. Good friends promote good character in each other. You can promote good character by demonstrating the following traits:

- **Caring** Good friends care about each other and look out for each other's well-being. They try to be aware of how each other is feeling.
- **Respect** Good friends respect each other, their families, and their values.
- **Dependability** Good friends keep their promises. They are around when they are needed, especially during hard times. Good friends are also careful when they borrow your things.
- **Loyalty** Good friends are loyal. They stick by you when other people may turn against you. They don't stop being friends with you to be friends with others.
- **Honesty** Good friends are honest. Good friends are even honest when the truth is difficult to say or hear. ★ 7.A; 10.A; 11.C; 12.B

Health Journal

Why do friends stop being friends? In your Health Journal, write down some of the difficulties of staying friends with someone.

Making New Friends

Knowing these qualities can help you be a good friend to others. It can also help you identify people who may make good friends. Making new friends is fun. You can make new friends by joining a club or group, volunteering to help with a community project, or simply talking with someone after class. No matter how you meet new friends, being good to each other over time will help you keep each other healthy. ★ 7.A; 7.B; 12.B

Lesson 5 Healthy Friendships | 275

Preventing Trouble

If a friend tells you that he or she is going to hurt himself or herself or others, tell a trusted adult as soon as possible.

Friendship and Health

Friends are important people, so choosing friends wisely is important, too. Friendships affect you and your health. For example, talking to a friend about minor problems is one way to help cope with them. Likewise, a friendship that causes negative stress can have a negative effect on your health, your schoolwork, and your family life.

One way to keep friendships healthy is for the friends to support each other. You can support each other by cheering for each other in activities or by helping out during difficult times. If a friend gets hurt, you may help him or her get from class to class. If a friend seems troubled, ask about what the problem may be. When a friend has a problem, help the best you can. If a friend trusts you with personal information, don't tell other people about that information. On the other hand, if a friend is involved in something that puts him or her or anyone else at risk, you can be a good friend by telling a parent or another trusted adult as soon as possible.

Good friends create positive peer pressure for each other. Making a healthy choice by yourself can be hard. But you may have more confidence if a friend supports your decision. When friends support each other, they make the relationship stronger.

★ 7.A; 7.B; 10.A; 11.B; 11.C; 11.D; 12.B

Figure 15 Good friends support you and help you when you need it.

Resolving Unhealthy Relationships

Not all relationships are healthy. An <mark>unhealthy relationship</mark> is a relationship with a person who hurts you or who encourages you to do things that go against your values. Try to resolve unhealthy relationships right away. Talk to your parents about resolving an unhealthy relationship. If you cannot talk to your parents, talk to another trusted adult, such as a grandparent, teacher, or coach. And use your refusal skills. Say "No" whenever you need to. Stick to your values. If all else fails, never be afraid to walk away.

Not all unhealthy relationships are with people you don't like. It's very hard when friendships become unhealthy. But sometimes friends begin to make irresponsible or dangerous choices. One way to deal with these friends is to be as honest as you can. You are not responsible for your friends' behavior. But you can encourage your friends to make healthy choices. Remind these friends that you care. And remind them that they can choose to change their behavior before they hurt themselves or someone else.

MAKING GOOD DECISIONS

In a group with two or three of your classmates, brainstorm examples of unhealthy friendships. Choose one example. What could the friends do to resolve this unhealthy relationship?

Figure 16 If a friend is choosing harmful behavior, talk to that friend and encourage him or her to make better choices.

Lesson Review

Using Vocabulary

1. What is an unhealthy relationship? ⭐ 7.A; 10.A

Understanding Concepts

2. Describe four ways you can build your self-esteem. ⭐ 7.A; 7.B; 12.B

3. Explain why keeping friendships healthy is important. ⭐ 7.A; 7.B

4. Explain three ways to resolve an unhealthy relationship. ⭐ 7.B; 11.D; 12.B

5. List five qualities of good character and three ways to make new friends. ⭐ 11.C; 12.B

Critical Thinking

6. **Applying Concepts** Jennifer's friend is upset because her dad and mom are talking about separating. How can Jennifer help her friend? ⭐ 10.C; 11.B; 11.C; 11.D; 12.B

Lesson 6

Teen Dating

What You'll Do

- **Describe** four benefits of group dating. ★ 2.E; 10.E
- **List** eight healthy ways to show affection. ★ 7.A; 11.D
- **Describe** five ways to be clear about showing affection. ★ 11.B; 11.D
- **Explain** four benefits of sexual abstinence. ★ 5.D; 5.E; 5.F
- **Explain** how refusal skills can be used to promote sexual abstinence. ★ 5.D; 5.E; 5.F; 11.D; 12.B

Terms to Learn

- dating
- sexual abstinence

Write

What are some healthy ways you can show affection?

> Every time Sally sees Martin, her heart beats faster and her palms get sweaty. She is embarrassed, but she shouldn't be. Sally has a crush.

Sally is not alone. Having a crush is very common. During your early teenage years, you may begin to have closer friendships with members of the opposite sex. You may start feeling physically attracted to them. You may even have a crush on someone, the way Sally does. You may find yourself attracted to someone you have never met. Or you may look at an old friend in a new way. This can be a very exciting and confusing time. You may find yourself wanting to do things that you are not ready for or that scare you. These new feelings, challenges, and responsibilities are complicated. So, it's a good idea to have a plan before you are faced with them in real life.

Dating

One of the ways people get together is by dating. **Dating** is going out with people you find attractive and interesting. One of the best ways to begin dating is by group dating. The group can have the same number of boys and girls or different numbers of boys and girls. Groups can date by going together to places, such as the movies, parties, or dances. Group dating can help boys and girls learn how to have healthy relationships with each other and how to talk to each other socially. Group dating gives you a lot of people to talk to. Best of all, group dating is fun! ★ 2.E; 10.E

Figure 17 Group dating gives people in a group a chance to go out together.

Showing Affection

Whether or not you are dating, there are many healthy ways for teens to show affection for each other. Here are some examples:

- giving a smile or a kind laugh to someone
- telling someone how much he or she means to you
- remembering a birthday
- writing a card, a note, or a letter
- giving a small gift, such as a flower
- cheering for someone at a game or performance
- spending time together
- holding hands

Showing affection is an important part of being close friends. When friends show each other that they care, they help remind each other that they matter. Sometimes, telling people that you care for them helps them remember to make healthy decisions. And knowing that you are liked and loved feels good. ★ 7.A; 11.D

Being Clear

Sometimes, letting someone know how you feel is difficult. You may feel shy or awkward. But as long as you are clear and respectful, you're doing OK. Remember that simple expressions are usually the clearest. And not everyone appreciates the same form of affection. A smile usually says a lot. Expressing affection aloud can be more difficult. Planning out what you're going to say may help. You don't want to read a script, but planning may help you say what you mean. Pay attention to the other person's response. If the other person seems uncomfortable, you should back off and give him or her time to respond. If the person's response is not clear, ask about it.

All affection is based on respect. For example, when people ask not to be touched, don't touch them. Respecting their wishes shows that you like them. If you feel uncomfortable about the way someone is showing you affection, say so. Tell the person to stop. If the person does not stop, talk with a parent about the problem. ★ 11.B; 11.D

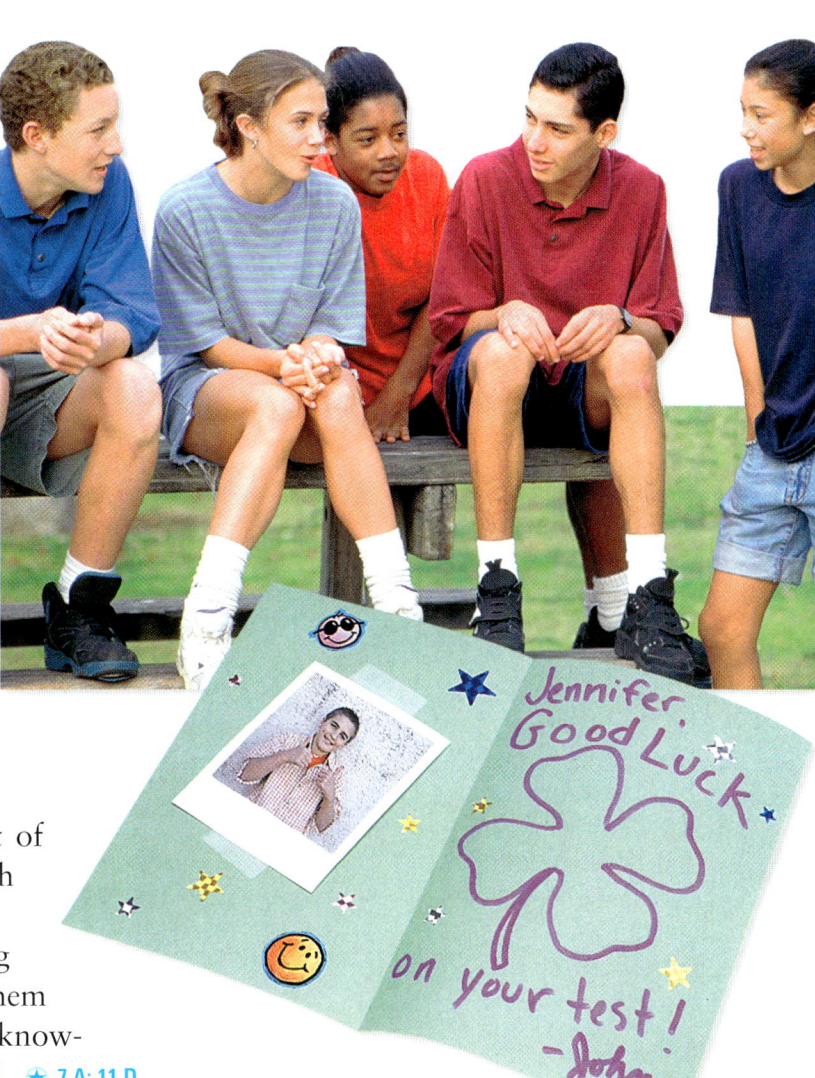

Figure 18 You can show affection for your friends by spending time with them or by sending one of them a card.

Lesson 6 Teen Dating

Figure 19 Some teachers ask teens to try to carry a sack of flour with them everywhere, just to see what caring for a baby all day might be like. Carrying a sack of flour is tough. And caring for a baby is much tougher!

Sexual Abstinence

Sexual feelings are normal and healthy. You may experience increased sexual feelings and desires as a teen. These desires can make sexual activity tempting. But sexual activity requires maturity and the *commitment* (or promise) found in marriages. The best way to show that you care about yourself, your family, and your friends is to practice sexual abstinence (SEK shoo uhl AB stuh nuhns) before you are married. **Sexual abstinence** is the refusal to take part in sexual activity. Planning can make sexual abstinence easier. Setting limits before you are in a situation in which you feel sexual desire helps you maintain abstinence. If you want to talk about your feelings and ways to deal with them, talk to your parents or another trusted adult.

The benefits of choosing abstinence include the following:

- being sure you will not cause an unwanted pregnancy
- being absolutely sure you will not get diseases that are spread by sexual activity
- being absolutely sure you will not be hurt emotionally from sexual involvement
- demonstrating care for yourself, your family, and your future

Abstinence is the healthiest choice for teens to make. It can help protect you physically and emotionally. It can help you keep from changing your life in dangerous and harmful ways.

★ 5.D; 5.E; 5.F

Hands-on ACTIVITY

DIAPER BUDGET

1. Hypothesize the cost of buying diapers for a baby for 1 year.

2. Ask a clinic, a hospital, or a new mom how many times a baby needs changing during the first year. The number of diapers needed may change throughout the year. Get estimates for the first 32 weeks and the last 20 weeks.

3. Go to the store and find out how many packages of disposable diapers would be needed during 1 year.

4. Find out how much each package of diapers costs.

5. Calculate the cost of buying disposable diapers for a baby for a whole year.

Analysis

1. Was your estimate accurate, low, or high?

2. What would have improved your estimate?

3. If you earned $8.00 per hour, how many hours would you have to work to buy all the diapers a baby would use in a year?

4. What do you think is a major problem that teenage parents face?

TABLE 1 Responding to Pressure

Pressure	Response
"You're the only person in the class who hasn't had sex."	"That's not true. But that doesn't even matter. Abstinence is my choice."
"If you really loved me, you would."	"If you really loved me, you'd respect my decision."
"It would mean so much to me."	"It would mean much more to our relationship if we wait until we are married."
"Is there something wrong with you?"	"There is nothing wrong with me. But if you think so, maybe we should stop seeing each other."

★ 5.D; 11.D; 12.B

LANGUAGE ARTS ACTIVITY

Abstinence requires good decision making and clear communication. Read a novel or short story about teens. Note where in the story decisions and communication are important. How do the characters show good decision-making and communication skills? How could they improve?

Maintaining Abstinence

Refusal skills can help you maintain abstinence. Use them. If anyone pressures you, say no with your words, actions, and body language. Table 1 shows some helpful responses to pressure. Stick to your values. Walk away, or call for a ride home. Try to avoid putting yourself in risky situations. And, of course, never pressure other people to do anything they don't want to do.

You have a lot to do right now: you have responsibilities at school, at home, and with your friends. All of those responsibilities are important. You need the time and emotional energy to take care of them and to grow. Sexual activity does not prove you are grown up or independent. In fact, you can show you are gaining healthy independence by choosing abstinence to protect your health and your future. ★ 5.D; 5.E; 5.F; 11.D; 12.B

Lesson Review

Using Vocabulary

1. Define *sexual abstinence*.

Understanding Concepts

2. Describe four benefits of sexual abstinence. ★ 5.D; 5.E; 5.F

3. List eight ways to show healthy affection. ★ 7.A; 11.D

4. Describe five ways to be clear about showing affection. ★ 11.B; 11.D

5. Describe four benefits of group dating. ★ 2.E; 10.E

Critical Thinking

6. **Using Refusal Skills** Kathy and Brian are close friends. At a party, Brian asks Kathy if she wants to go upstairs to be alone. Kathy does not want to go. How can refusal skills help Kathy? ★ 5.F; 11.D; 12.B

internet connect
www.scilinks.org/health
Topic: Abstinence
HealthLinks code: HD4002
HEALTH LINKS. Maintained by the National Science Teachers Association

Lesson 6 Teen Dating

11 CHAPTER REVIEW

Chapter Summary

- Good social skills, such as communication skills and assertive behavior help keep your relationships healthy. ■ Empathy helps you understand how other people feel. ■ Tolerance helps you respect and accept people. ■ Being a family is a lot of work. ■ Teens can help by cooperating and fulfilling their roles. ■ All families have problems sometimes. ■ One good way to cope with the stress of problems is to talk with a trusted adult. ■ Teen relationships are influenced by the media, family, role models, and peers. ■ Unhealthy relationships should be resolved as soon as possible. ■ Group dating is a healthy choice for teens. ■ Sexual abstinence is the only sure way to avoid pregnancy, some diseases, and the emotional scars of early sexual involvement.

Using Vocabulary

1 Use each of the following terms in a separate sentence: *media*, *tolerance*, and *empathy*.

For each sentence, fill in the blank with the proper word from the word bank provided below.

sexual abstinence	relationship
body language	nurturing
active listening	dating
empathy	tolerance
unhealthy relationship	media
behavior	influence

2 The way you choose to act is called your ___.

3 ___ means not taking part in sexual activity.

4 ___ is a way of sending a message by using facial expressions, hand gestures, and body posture.

5 TV shows, radio, movies, and newspapers are all examples of the ___.

6 A social connection between a person and another person or group is called a ___.

7 ___ is going out with people you like.

Understanding Concepts

8 Explain what to do if someone shows you affection in a way you don't like. ★ 11.D

9 Contrast assertive behavior with passive behavior and aggressive behavior. ★ 10.D; 11D

10 Describe the three aspects of personal responsibility. ★ 11.D; 12.B

11 Explain how refusal skills can be used to promote sexual abstinence. ★ 5.D; 5.E; 5.F; 11.D; 12.B

12 If you could not use words, how could you express how you are feeling? ★ 11.D

13 How can your relationships influence each other? ★ 7.A; 10.A; 10.E; 12.E

14 How can empathy and tolerance help relationships? ★ 7.A; 11.C; 11.D

15 Explain active listening. ★ 10.C

16 Give two reasons why your role in your family may change. ★ 7.A; 9.A; 9.B

17 Describe six different family structures. ★ 7.A

18 List three ways to show tolerance to family members. ★ 10.D; 11.B; 11.C; 11.D; 12.B

Critical Thinking

Identifying Relationships

19 While Miguel was in line for lunch, Gwen stepped in front of him to be with her friends. Describe three responses from Miguel: one passive, one assertive, and one aggressive. How might Gwen respond assertively to each of Miguel's behaviors? ★ 11.B; 11.C; 11.D

20 How is maintaining abstinence an example of assertive behavior? Why would it be dangerous to be passive when faced with pressure to be sexually active?
★ 5.D; 11.D; 12.B

21 How might building your own self-esteem help you to show tolerance?
★ 11.B; 11.C; 11.D; 12.B

Making Good Decisions

22 When Kevin's dad lost his job, Kevin's family had to make a lot of changes. Kevin was upset because he didn't know what would happen next. Kevin had trouble sleeping and focusing on school. What could Kevin do to help himself handle this big change? How might Kevin's older brother help him? ★ 9.A; 9.B; 10.B

23 Deepak never cuts class. But Deepak saw a movie and the most interesting character left school one day to go on an adventure. Deepak thought this idea sounded like fun. He wants to try it. If you were his friend, what would you say to Deepak? How could you help him decide what to do?
★ 11.D; 12.B; 12.E

24 Paul takes money from his mother's purse without asking. When his mother asks him about taking the money, he denies it. Paul wants his friend Johan to steal money from his parents so that they can both go to the movies. What should Johan do to resolve this unhealthy relationship? ★ 10.A; 10.B; 11.B; 11.D; 12.B

25 Fred's sister, Tess, just got married and moved out of the house. Tess used to do the laundry and some cooking. How will her leaving affect other roles in the household? What can Fred do to help make this change smooth? ★ 9.A; 9.B

Interpreting Graphics

Changes in the Structure of a Family

	1994	1999	2004
Adults living at home	mother, father	mother	mother, grandmother, grandfather
Children born into family	boy, girl	boy, girl	boy, girl
Adopted children	none	boy	boy

Use the table above to answer questions 26–28.

The table above shows how one family's structure changed over time.

26 What family structure is shown in 1994?

27 What two family structures help describe the family in 1999?

28 What three family structures help describe the family in 2004?

Reading Checkup

Take a minute to review your answers to the Health IQ questions at the beginning of this chapter. How has reading this chapter improved your Health IQ?

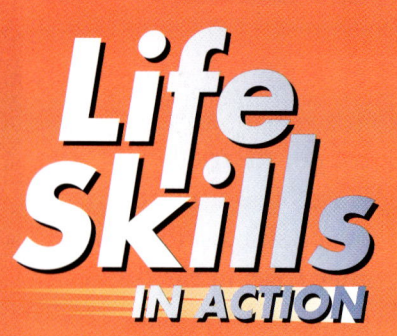

Life Skills IN ACTION

Setting Goals

A goal is something that you work toward and hope to achieve. Setting goals is important because goals give you a sense of purpose and achieving goals improves your self-esteem. Complete the following activity to learn how to set and achieve goals.

Mark and Julie's Pact

Setting the Scene

Mark and his friend Julie just received their grades from their first math quiz. Neither of them did very well, and both of them are disappointed. After class, Mark asks Julie if she wants to study with him for the next quiz. Julie agrees and tells Mark that she wants to earn a good grade in the class.

The 5 Steps of Setting Goals

1. Consider your interests and values.
2. Choose goals that include your interests and values.
3. If necessary, break down long-term goals into several short-term goals.
4. Measure your progress.
5. Reward your success.

Guided Practice

Practice with a Friend

Form a group of three. Have one person play the role of Mark and another person play the role of Julie. Have the third person be an observer. Walking through each of the five steps of setting goals, role-play Mark and Julie working together to set a goal of earning good grades in their math class. Have Mark and Julie support each other as they work toward their common goal. The observer will take notes, which will include observations about what the people playing Mark and Julie did well and suggestions of ways to improve. Stop after each step to evaluate the process. ★ 7.A; 11.B; 11.D; 12.B; 12.E; 12.F

Independent Practice

Check Yourself

After you complete the guided practice, go through Act 1 again without stopping at each step. Answer the questions below to review what you did.

1. What values did Mark and Julie consider before setting their goal?
2. What are some ways that Mark and Julie could measure their progress toward their goal? ★ 12.B; 12.F
3. How could Mark and Julie's common goal help strengthen their friendship? ★ 7.A
4. Describe a goal that you and a friend can work on together.

On Your Own

At the end of the semester, Mark and Julie are happy to learn that they both earned an A in their math class. Mark knows that setting the goal was useful because it helped him stay focused on his problem. He decides to set a goal to make the track team this year. Write a short story about how Mark could use the five steps of setting goals to prepare for the track team tryouts.

Chapter 11 Setting Goals

CHAPTER 12
Conflict Management

Lessons

1. What Is Conflict? — 288
2. Communicating During Conflict — 290
3. Resolving Conflicts — 294
4. Conflict at School — 298
5. Conflict at Home — 302
6. Conflict in the Community — 306
7. Conflict and Violence — 308

Chapter Review — 312
Life Skills in Action — 314

Check out **Current Health** articles related to this chapter by visiting **go.hrw.com**. Just type in the keyword **HD4CH44**.

> "Last year, my **best friend** and I got into an **argument** about some **money** that she owed me. It wasn't much money, but it turned into a huge fight, and we haven't spoken since. I can't help but think that if we had handled the argument better, we might still be friends."

Health IQ

PRE-READING

Answer the following true/false questions to find out what you already know about managing conflict. When you've finished this chapter, you'll have the opportunity to change your answers based on what you've learned.

1. Most conflicts lead to violence.
2. Most conflicts can be avoided.
3. Respecting other people's opinions can help you avoid conflicts. ✪ 11.C
4. The words we use in a conflict can determine the outcome of the conflict. ✪ 11.D
5. Body language is not a real form of communication. ✪ 11.D
6. Bullies usually pick on others because of their own insecurities. ✪ 7.A
7. Conflict can occur often between neighbors because of how close they live to each other.
8. Compromise means giving up and letting the other person have what he or she wants. ✪ 10.D
9. Peer mediation is effective because the mediators are closer to the age of the people in conflict. ✪ 10.E; 12.E
10. Most people are affected by violence at some point in their lives even if it isn't directed specifically at them.
11. Aggression is the same as violence.
12. The way you manage conflict now will affect how you manage conflict in the future. ✪ 12.F

ANSWERS: 1. false; 2. false; 3. true; 4. true; 5. false; 6. true; 7. true; 8. false; 9. true; 10. true; 11. false; 12. true

Lesson 1

What Is Conflict?

Jean borrowed some books from Susan. Jean borrowed them weeks ago, and Susan wants them back but hasn't said anything to Jean. Susan is trying to forget about it but gets more upset every day.

What You'll Do

- **Describe** the three major sources of conflict. ⭐ 6.A; 7.A
- **Describe** three signs that conflict is happening or is about to happen.
- **Describe** three ways to avoid conflict. ⭐ 10.D; 11.A; 11.C; 11.D

Terms to Learn

- conflict

Start Off Write

What was the cause of the last conflict you were in?

Conflict can happen anywhere, with anyone, and can be about anything. **Conflict** is any clash of ideas or interests. The way we deal with conflict will determine whether the conflict will end in a healthy way. If you don't learn how to deal with conflict, you will face a lot of serious problems.

Major Sources of Conflict

You can probably think of a conflict you have been in or seen at school even within the past few weeks. Conflicts happen all the time when people are in contact with one another. Conflicts are usually about one of the following three things:

- **Resources** Many conflicts happen when two or more people want the same thing but only one can have it.

- **Values and Expectations** Many conflicts happen because of different ideas about what is important or how things should be done.

- **Emotions** Many conflicts happen because of hurt feelings or anger. These feelings are usually a reaction to rudeness or insensitivity. ⭐ 6.A; 7.A

Figure 1 Conflicts can happen anywhere and can be about almost anything. What do you think caused these conflicts?

Recognizing the Signs of Conflict

There are usually a lot of warning signs that conflict is about to occur. Identifying these signs can allow you to identify conflict and avoid it or begin working to solve it. Some of these signs are listed below.

- **Disagreement** The first and surest sign that conflict is happening is disagreement with another person over an issue.
- **Emotions** When conflict begins, you may feel emotions such as frustration, resentment, or anger.
- **Others' Behavior** If you notice another person becoming angry or frustrated about a disagreement, then a conflict is happening.

Avoiding Conflict

There are several ways to stop conflict before it happens or before it gets too serious. A few of the ways are listed below.

- **Pick your battles.** Many conflicts aren't worth having. Decide which conflicts are important to you, and avoid getting into the conflicts that aren't important.
- **Respect different opinions.** Everyone has a right to his or her own opinion. You shouldn't feel the need to always change other people's opinions.
- **Take a break.** Often, putting off a conflict for a short time can give you time to think about the conflict. You may decide that the conflict is unnecessary. ★ 10.D; 11.A; 11.C; 11.D

Figure 2 By recognizing conflict, these two friends were able to take steps to solve the conflict.

Lesson Review

Using Vocabulary
1. What is conflict?

Understanding Concepts
2. What are the three major causes of conflict? ★ 6.A; 7.A
3. What are three signs that a conflict is happening or is about to happen?
4. What are three ways to avoid conflict? ★ 10.D; 11.A; 11.C; 11.D

Critical Thinking
5. **Applying Concepts** Describe a conflict that might happen over resources. Describe another conflict that might occur because of emotions.

Lesson 1 What Is Conflict?

Lesson 2

Communicating During Conflict

What You'll Do

- **Explain** the importance of communication in a conflict.  5.K; 11.D
- **Describe** appropriate ways to express yourself in a conflict. ★ 10.D; 11.D
- **Describe** body language and its importance during a conflict. ★ 11.D
- **Describe** the importance of listening in a conflict. ★ 10.C; 10.D; 11.D

Terms to Learn

- body language

Start Off Write

How would you describe body language?

Jennifer borrowed $10 from her friend Lisa and promised to pay Lisa back in 2 days. It's been 2 weeks, and Jennifer has yet to pay Lisa back. Lisa calmly reminds Jennifer of this, and Jennifer repays her.

If Lisa had not approached Jennifer calmly, Lisa might not have gotten her money back. The way in which you choose to communicate can determine if and how the conflict is resolved.

The Conflict Cycle

The way in which you deal with conflict often depends on how you have handled conflict in the past and on how you have seen others handle conflict. Figure 3 shows how the way in which we manage conflict is part of a cycle. Different people manage conflict differently. For example, you may manage conflict by avoiding the conflict, solving the problem, or becoming very angry. When a conflict happens in your life, you respond to the conflict in the way that is most familiar to you. There are then consequences for your response. These consequences can be positive or negative. The consequences of how we manage a conflict then affect the way we deal with the next conflict that arises. ★ 11.D

Figure 3 The way that you handle conflicts now affects the way that you will handle conflicts in the future. This is called the *conflict cycle*.

290 | Chapter 12 Conflict Management

Express Yourself

Staying calm usually becomes difficult when you are faced with conflict. Both sides are usually emotional and sensitive to the issue. One or both sides feel frustration and anger. However, this is the most important time to stay calm. Staying calm allows you to express yourself without frustration and anger. In a conflict, the other side needs to understand your position and your feelings about the conflict. Expressing yourself in a calm and clear manner will allow the other side to hear what you have to say. If you speak in an angry or threatening manner, the other side will probably stop listening to you. If you feel like you are losing your temper, stop! Take a few deep breaths, and remind yourself to stay calm. You can even ask the other person to give you a moment to think. ★ 5.K; 11.A; 11.C; 11.D

Choose Your Words

Choosing the right words when expressing yourself during a conflict is also very important. Several tips on choosing the right words in a conflict are listed below.

- Speak openly and honestly.
- Be sure only to use words that explain how you feel.
- Do not use abusive or threatening language.
- Do not make demands or threats.
- Avoid words that threaten the other person, such as insults.
- Avoid using the word *you*. In a conflict, this word usually comes before an insult or an accusation. Instead, use the word *I* or *me* to describe your feelings. ★ 5.K; 11.C; 11.D

Figure 4 By expressing themselves clearly and calmly, these teens increase the chances that their conflict will end well.

Figure 5 The way you use your body can communicate many things about how you feel. Can you tell in which of these pictures the girl is unhappy?

Brain Food

Gestures and body language can mean different things in different cultures. For example, in Japan, if you want someone to come to you, you turn your palm down and move your fingers up and down. In the United States, this gesture means "goodbye."

Body Language

When you think of communication, you probably think of speaking and using words. However, there is another way that you communicate your feelings to another person. The way that you use your body while you speak can communicate a lot about your feelings to other people. **Body language** is communication that is done by the body rather than by words. Body language can include how you are standing, whether or not you make eye contact, or the expression on your face. Your body language can be as important as verbal communication when you are in conflict. Like the words you use, your body language can determine if a conflict ends well or ends poorly. If your body language is relaxed it sends the message that you are open to talking and listening to others. This gives you a better chance of solving conflicts. ★ 11.D

Hands-on ACTIVITY

BODY LANGUAGE

1. Find a partner in your class. Make sure that you each have a piece of paper and a pen or pencil.

2. You and your partner should take turns describing the things you did the previous weekend. As your partner describes his or her weekend, record every time your partner uses his or her body to communicate. How is your partner sitting? How does your partner use his or her hands while talking. How does your partner's head move while he or she is talking? What are your partner's facial expressions?

Analysis

1. When you are done, compare your observations with your partner's observations. What types of body language, if any, did you both use? Which one of you used more body language? How did your body language fit with what you were talking about? ★ 11.D

Listening

When communicating in a conflict, you must also focus on your listening skills. Sharing your own feelings and thoughts in a conflict is very important. You must also give the other person time to share his or her feelings and thoughts. If you do not listen to the other person, the conflict cannot be solved.

One of the ways you can hear what the other person has to say is through active listening. *Active listening* is listening to what the other person is saying, thinking about it, and either asking questions or restating what the person said. This type of listening allows you to understand people better and lets people know that you are listening to them.

Another important way that you can be an active and effective listener is through your body language. Your body language can communicate whether you are listening to others and whether you care about what they are saying. For example, pay attention to your posture. You should face the other person and keep your arms unfolded. Always make eye contact and have an interested look on your face. These are just a few of the ways that you can communicate nonverbally to others that you are listening. ★ 10.C; 10.D; 11.D

TABLE 1 Tips for Listening

Make eye contact.

Use open body language.

Focus on what the speaker is saying rather than on what you plan to say next.

Don't fold arms or use closed body language.

Don't interrupt. Wait until the other person is done speaking before you speak.

Don't let your eyes wander. Pay attention to the person who is speaking.

Lesson Review

Using Vocabulary

1. What is body language?

Understanding Concepts

2. Why is the way that you communicate in a conflict important? ★ 5.K; 11.D

3. Why should you listen to the other person in a conflict? ★ 10.C; 10.D; 11.D

4. What is active listening? ★ 10.C

Critical Thinking

5. **Making Inferences** Why is listening to the other person necessary when solving a conflict? What may happen if you don't listen? ★ 5.K; 10.C

internet connect
www.scilinks.org/health
Topic: Communication Skills
HealthLinks code: HD4022

HEALTH LINKS Maintained by the National Science Teachers Association

Lesson 2 Communicating During Conflict

Lesson 3

Resolving Conflicts

Sarah and her brother were fighting about whose turn it was to do the dishes. Finally, they agreed that Sarah would wash the dishes and that her brother would dry them.

What You'll Do

- **Describe** negotiation as a tool to resolve conflict. ★ 10.D
- **Compare** compromise and collaboration as tools for resolving conflict. ★ 10.D
- **Explain** how mediation is used to resolve conflicts. ★ 10.D
- **List** the advantages of peer mediation. ★ 10.D; 12.E

Terms to Learn

- negotiation
- compromise
- collaboration
- mediation
- peer mediation

Start Off Write

How is compromise useful in resolving conflicts?

Although they may not have realized it, Sarah and her brother used negotiation and compromise to settle their conflict. Negotiation and compromise are just two of the tools that can be used to resolve conflicts.

Negotiation

Resolving a conflict means finding a solution with which everyone is pleased. The first step to resolving a conflict is negotiation. **Negotiation** (ni GOH shee AY shuhn) is the act of discussing the issues of a conflict to reach an agreement. Negotiation requires both parties in a conflict to describe their feelings and their needs. It also requires each party to understand and respect the other person's position. Being good at negotiation takes time and practice. When used properly, negotiation allows you to solve conflicts easily and calmly. It usually also insures that both parties get at least some of what they want out of a conflict.

★ 10.D

Figure 6 Negotiation is used in many situations. This man is negotiating for the release of hostages.

294 Chapter 12 Conflict Management

Figure 7 By negotiating and compromising, these teens were able to solve their argument in a way that pleased them both.

Compromise and Collaboration

When you are trying to solve a conflict in a way that pleases both sides, you may have to agree to give something up in order to get something that you want. **Compromise** (KAHM pruh MIEZ) is a solution to a conflict in which each side gives up something to reach an agreement. Compromise is something we all must learn to do, because it is a skill that we will need throughout our lives.

Collaboration is another skill for solving conflicts. **Collaboration** (kuh LAB uh RAY shuhn) is a solution to a conflict in which both sides work together to get what they want. When it is possible, collaboration is better than compromise because it does not require anyone to give anything up. Collaboration allows both parties to walk away from a conflict feeling like they both got what they wanted. Imagine that you and a friend are arguing about which movie to rent. A compromise would be letting your friend pick the movie and your friend promising that you can have the good seat to watch the movie. Collaboration would be if you picked a movie that you both like and then watched it together. ★ 10.D

STUDY TIP for better reading

Word Origins The word *mediate* comes from the Latin *mediatus* meaning "divided in the middle." Knowing this makes it easier to remember that a mediator is someone who splits up a conflict by getting in the middle.

Mediation

Sometimes, collaboration is not a possible solution to a conflict. Even compromise can fail when both sides are unwilling to give up anything. Conflicts can reach a point at which neither person is willing to collaborate or compromise. In this case, a good strategy is the use of mediation. **Mediation** (MEE dee AY shuhn) is a process in which another person, called a *mediator*, listens to both sides of the conflict and then offers solutions to the conflict. Having a third party involved in resolving a conflict can make the resolution of that conflict much faster and easier. A mediator can keep the conflict from getting out of control.

Not just anyone can be a mediator. A mediator must have certain skills to be effective. A good mediator has the following characteristics:

- **Special Training** Special training is required to know how to effectively resolve a conflict between two other people.
- **Objectivity** This means that the mediator does not take the side of either person or group in the conflict.
- **Understanding** To resolve the conflict, a mediator must understand what each person or group wants and why they want it.
- **Ability to Control the Situation** A good mediator focuses on resolving the conflict and keeps it from becoming angry or violent. If the conflict begins to turn angry, a good mediator quickly gets the discussion back on track. ★ 10.D

Figure 8 This conflict has reached a point where no progress is being made. If this happens, mediation may be needed.

Peer Mediation

Many schools now have peer mediation programs. **Peer mediation** is mediation in which the mediator is of similar age to the people in the conflict. One advantage of peer mediation is that it is usually easier to access, because peer mediation programs are available at many schools. Younger people also often feel that a peer can better understand their needs. Peer mediation must not be taken lightly. Becoming a peer mediator requires much work. Mediators must have training and practice. Going into a conflict without this training and practice might make the conflict worse. An untrained mediator might also end up involved in a conflict that he or she wasn't part of to begin with. If you are considering starting a peer mediation program, you should begin by talking to a few other schools that have successful programs for direction. ★ 10.D; 12.E

Health Journal

Describe a conflict that you have had in which mediation would have been helpful. Why would the presence of a mediator have made this conflict easier to resolve?

Figure 9 This trained peer mediator is helping two classmates solve a conflict.

Lesson Review

Using Vocabulary

1. What is negotiation? ★ 10.D
2. What is the difference between collaboration and compromise? ★ 10.D
3. What is mediation? ★ 10.D

Understanding Concepts

4. What advantages does peer mediation have over mediation by someone who is not a peer? ★ 10.D; 12.E

Critical Thinking

5. **Applying Concepts** Imagine that you and a friend are arguing about what to do. You say that it is a beautiful day and suggest going to a park. Your friend says that she is hungry and would rather go and eat lunch. How could this situation be solved through compromise? How could it be solved through collaboration? ★ 10.D

Lesson 3 Resolving Conflicts

Lesson 4

Conflict at School

Every day when Kisha went to school, a girl named Angela made fun of her clothes. The more upset Kisha got, the more Angela teased her. Why was Angela so mean to Kisha?

Angela teased Kisha because Angela didn't feel very good about herself. Being teased is just one of the ways that conflict can arise at school.

Teasing

We have all probably teased someone or have been teased in our lives. You may think that teasing is harmless, but every time you tease someone, you hurt that person emotionally, even if you don't mean to. If you are being teased, there are several ways that you can deal with the teasing.

- **Ignore it.** People usually tease other people to make them upset or to get attention. If you ignore them, they will quickly lose interest.
- **Make a joke.** By making a joke, you show the person that teasing doesn't bother you. This will usually make the person lose interest in teasing you.
- **Confront the teaser.** If you tell the teaser how his or her words make you feel, he or she may understand and stop the teasing. ★ 6.A; 7.A; 11.B; 11.D

What You'll Do

- **Describe** four possible sources of conflict at school. ★ 6.A; 7.A
- **Discuss** a strategy for preventing school conflicts from interfering with education. ★ 11.B; 11.D

Terms to Learn

- bully
- intimidation

How do bullies scare other people?

Figure 10 Often, being teased can be as painful emotionally as being beaten up is painful physically.

298

Bullying

Some people feel the need to scare or abuse others. These people are called *bullies*. A bully is a person who constantly picks on or beats up smaller or weaker people. Bullies are usually people who struggle with their own self-esteem. Picking on others, especially those smaller and weaker than themselves, makes bullies feel stronger and more important.

Bullying is not always physical. Sometimes, people bully other people without physically touching them. This is called *intimidation*. Intimidation is the act of frightening others through the use of threatening words and body language.

Most people who are victims of a bully feel helpless. However, you can do several things if someone is bullying you.

- **Ignore the bully.** If a bully sees that his or her threats are not bothering you, he or she may leave you alone.
- **Talk to the bully.** Tell the bully how his or her behavior makes you feel. Ask the bully why he or she feels the need to pick on you.
- **Stand up to the bully.** Tell the bully that you will not put up with his or her behavior any longer. Tell the bully that if the bullying continues, you will report it to an adult.
- **Report the bully.** If the bullying continues or if any violence occurs, report the bully to an authority figure, such as a parent, teacher, or school principal. ★ 6.A; 7.A; 11.B; 11.D

Figure 11 The teen on the right is using intimidation to scare the other teen.

LIFE SKILLS ACTIVITY

MAKING GOOD DECISIONS

Imagine that you have a classmate who has been causing problems for you. He has been demanding that you do his homework and that you give him a dollar every day. He says that if you don't do this, he will beat you up. Make a list of the ways that you could deal with this situation. List the pros and cons for each option. Which option is the best one?

Health Journal

Have you ever had a conflict at school? If so, write about this conflict in your Health Journal. What was the conflict about? How was the conflict resolved?

Conflict with Teachers

Another type of conflict you may face at school is conflict with a teacher. Conflict with a teacher might arise for many reasons. Maybe you think a teacher is too strict or unfair. A teacher may think that you aren't trying hard enough in class or that you are being disrespectful. Conflict with a teacher can usually be solved by talking to the teacher. When you talk to a teacher about a conflict, you should remember a few things.

- **Pick the right time and place.** Do not discuss a conflict with a teacher during class. Find the teacher after class. Tell him or her that you would like to talk. Ask what would be a good time.
- **Stay calm.** Never become aggressive or overly angry when talking to a teacher or anyone else.
- **Focus on solving the problem.** Do not waste time trying to decide whose fault the conflict is. Instead, work to solve the problem.

If talking to the teacher doesn't work, talk to your parents, another teacher, or a principal to get help. ★ 6.A; 7.A; 10.D; 11.D

Cultural Conflict

Your school is made up of people of different races, religions, and backgrounds. These types of differences between people can sometimes cause anxiety, fear, and anger. These feelings usually arise because people misunderstand the values of people who are different from them. The key to avoiding or dealing with this kind of conflict is communication. You can often learn a lot by talking to somebody who is different from you. You might even learn that you aren't so different after all. ★ 6.A; 7.A; 11.D

Figure 12 School classes often contain members of many different cultures. Sometimes conflicts can arise because of these differences.

Making the Grade

You should not allow conflicts at school to interfere with your education. Remember that you are at school to learn. Your grades and education come first. At some time, you may find yourself in a conflict that begins to affect your grades or causes you to fall behind in your education. If this kind of conflict happens, you must find a way to resolve the conflict or to keep it from interfering with your learning. Remember that communicating your needs to other people is your best tool for dealing with conflict. The more you keep your feelings inside, the longer the conflict will last and the more your education will suffer. Most schools have counselors who can help you with problems that interfere with your education. ★ 10.D; 11.D

Figure 13 By talking calmly with his teacher, this teen is resolving a conflict before it begins to interfere with his education.

Lesson Review

Using Vocabulary
1. What is a bully?
2. What is intimidation?

Understanding Concepts
3. What are four possible sources of conflict at school? ★ 6.A; 7.A
4. Why should you resolve school conflicts quickly? ★ 11.B; 11.D

Critical Thinking
5. **Making Inferences** Often, people who are bullied become bullies themselves, and pick on weaker people. What do you think the reason for this is?

Lesson 4 Conflict at School

Lesson 5

What You'll Do

- **Identify** four possible sources of conflict at home.
  ⭐ 7.A

Terms to Learn

- sibling rivalry

Start Off Write

Why do teens have conflicts with their parents?

Conflict at Home

If you have a brother or sister, you've probably had at least a few conflicts with him or her. Even if you are an only child, you've probably had arguments with your parents or caregivers.

Many conflicts can arise between people who live together. When a conflict arises in the home, the conflict usually affects everybody in the home. For this reason, knowing how conflicts can arise at home and how to resolve these conflicts is very important.

All in the Family

You spend a lot of time with your family or caregivers. There are often many differences between members of a family or household. There can be differences in age, tastes, and personality. Because you spend so much time around the people in your home, there are plenty of opportunities for these differences to cause conflict. Like other conflicts, conflicts in the home should not go on for too long. Resolving conflicts is even more important when conflicts are in the home. In the home, you are less able to walk away if the conflict gets out of control. Usually, you can rely on your parents or caregivers to help resolve conflicts in the home. However, you need to develop your own skills for resolving conflicts as well. Developing these skills will allow you to make quicker and better solutions to conflicts in the home.
⭐ 7.A; 9.B

Figure 14 Every family is different. However, every family has the potential for conflict.

Conflict with Parents

Conflict can arise between you and your parents or caregivers for many reasons. A few of the most common reasons that conflicts arise between teens and parents are listed below.

- **Rules** You may think that your parents' rules are unfair. You may also feel that you deserve more freedom than your parents allow you. Your parents may think that you are being disrespectful by not following the rules.
- **Responsibilities** As you get older, your parents may expect you to take on more responsibility.
- **Expectations** You may think that your parents expect too much of you. They may think that you are not doing the things that are expected of you.
- **Difference of Opinion** Your parents might disagree with your choices, such as the friends or activities you choose. You may feel that your parents make decisions for you with which you disagree.

Health Journal

Think about the last time you had a conflict with a parent or caregiver. How did you feel when you were arguing with your parent or caregiver? What are some ways that you could have better handled the situation?

Remember that your parents or caregivers have your best interests in mind. You need them for direction and advice. Parents or caregivers have experienced more than you have. They know things that you have not yet learned. Listening to and obeying their advice and rules is usually wise. Do not allow anger at a parent or caregiver to get out of control. You must use good communication skills with your parents or caregivers. If you don't share your feelings, you cannot expect any conflict to end well. 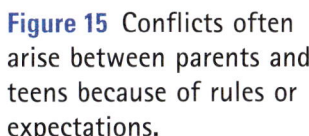 7.A; 11.D

Figure 15 Conflicts often arise between parents and teens because of rules or expectations.

Lesson 5 Conflict at Home

Conflict with Siblings

Many people have *siblings,* or brothers and sisters. If you have siblings, you have probably had conflicts with them. As you get older and develop your own sets of friends, conflict sometimes increases. There are several common reasons for conflict between siblings.

- **Sharing Possessions and Space** Often, siblings must share their possessions and their space. This can create many opportunities for conflict.
- **Jealousy** Many times, one sibling thinks that the other sibling gets to do more or gets more attention from parents.
- **Age Differences** Age differences between siblings can mean that the siblings have different interests or responsibilities. These differences can create conflict. ★ 7.A

Sibling Rivalry

Sometimes, you and your siblings can develop what is called *sibling rivalry.* **Sibling rivalry** is competition between siblings. It is natural to compare yourself and your accomplishments to your siblings and their accomplishments. Some sibling rivalry can be healthy. However, you may sometimes feel that you are not as good as your sibling. This can make you angry or depressed, or it can cause conflict between you and your sibling. If this happens, you should talk about the rivalry. You may find that your sibling feels that he or she isn't as good as you, either. By talking about the problem, you can solve it and develop a better relationship with your sibling. ★ 7.A; 11.D

Figure 16 Because siblings usually live together and often have to share space and belongings, they have many opportunities for conflict.

Conflict Between Parents

One of the toughest conflicts to deal with in a family is conflict between your parents or caregivers. When your parents fight, you often feel like you have no control. You may even think that the conflict is your fault. Remember that conflict is natural and happens even between people who love each other very much.

Although conflict between parents is not your fault, it can still affect you very much. When family members are not getting along, their conflict affects everyone in the family. If you are feeling uncomfortable or becoming worried about conflict between your parents, communicate your feelings. Let your parents know that their conflict is affecting you. Communication and honesty are the keys to dealing with conflict, even when the conflict isn't directly related to you. ★ 7.A; 11.D

Figure 17 Even if they love each other very much, parents can still get into conflicts. Conflicts between parents can affect everyone else in the home.

teen talk

Teen: My parents argue a lot about things such as bills or dinner. When they argue, I worry that they don't love each other. Should I worry?

Expert: Even people who love each other will be in conflict from time to time. In fact, a reasonable amount of conflict is healthy and can benefit a relationship.

Lesson Review

Using Vocabulary
1. Define *sibling rivalry* in your own words.

Understanding Concepts
2. What are four possible sources of conflict at home? ★ 7.A
3. What are four reasons that conflict might arise between a parent and child? ★ 7.A
4. What are three reasons that conflict might arise between siblings? ★ 7.A

Critical Thinking
5. **Making Inferences** If two siblings are very close in age, do you think it increases or decreases the chances for sibling rivalry? Explain your answer.

Lesson 6

Conflict in the Community

What You'll Do

- **Identify** two possible sources of conflict in the communities. 6.A; 7.A

Start Off Write

What are some differences between people in your community?

Joaquín's dad is mad at a neighbor because the neighbor's dogs bark all night. Joaquín's dad has complained many times to the neighbor and is now considering calling the police.

Neighbors often have different opinions about how things should be done. Because neighbors and other members of a community live near one another, differences can often cause conflict. For a community to be a safe and happy place to live, these conflicts must be resolved.

Conflict with Neighbors

As seen in the situation above, conflict can sometimes arise between neighbors. Avoiding or getting away from conflict with neighbors may be difficult because this conflict happens where you're living. So, you should solve these conflicts when they arise. Some tips for dealing with conflicts you have with neighbors are listed below.

- **Be tolerant.** Remember that your neighbors have as much right to their opinions as you do.
- **Communicate.** If your neighbor is upsetting you, be sure that he or she knows you are upset. Then you can work to solve the problem.
- **Compromise.** Be flexible and willing to make sacrifices in conflicts with neighbors.
  6.A; 6.B; 7.A; 11.D

Figure 18 Neighbors, such as the ones shown here, usually live very close to one another, which can increase the chances for conflict.

Figure 19 Most communities contain members of many different races, cultures, and backgrounds. These differences sometimes lead to conflict.

Cultural Conflict

Communities in the United States are becoming filled with more and more people from different cultural backgrounds. This new diversity provides a wonderful opportunity for you to grow and learn from others who are different from you. Unfortunately, diversity can also cause increased conflict because of the fear and anxiety many people have in reaction to those who are different from them. The way to solve these problems is to communicate, listen, and observe. By talking to people who come from different backgrounds, you can learn about and address your differences. You can also learn about the many things that you may have in common. Remember also to be tolerant of other cultures. Being tolerant means realizing that other people have as much right to their beliefs as you do. It also means treating others with the respect they deserve.
★ 6.A; 7.A; 11.D

SOCIAL STUDIES ACTIVITY

To which culture do your ancestors belong? Research your family history, and write a short paper on the culture to which your family belongs. How does this culture influence your family life today?

Lesson Review

Understanding Concepts

1. What are two possible sources of conflict in the community? ★ 6.A; 7.A
2. Why do neighbors sometimes have more opportunities for conflict? ★ 7.A
3. What is a benefit of increased cultural diversity in a community?

Critical Thinking

4. **Making Inferences** By realizing the things that you have in common with somebody from a different culture, you can better understand him or her and avoid conflict. Can you think of two examples of beliefs or practices that are probably the same in most cultures? ★ 7.A; 9.A

Lesson 7 Conflict and Violence

What You'll Do

- **Describe** the relationship between aggression and violence. ★ 5.K
- **Identify** four signs that violence is about to happen. ★ 5.K
- **Describe** five ways to control anger. ★ 5.K; 10.B; 11.D
- **Discuss** the importance of avoiding and preventing violent situations. ★ 5.K

Terms to Learn

- violence
- aggression

Start Off Write

How do you control your anger?

`Gene cut in the lunch line in front of Eric. Eric got very angry and threatened Gene. Gene pushed Eric, and they got into a fist fight. Both of them were sent to the principal's office.`

Gene and Eric allowed their conflict to get out of control, and the result was violence. **Violence** is physical force used to cause damage or injury. A conflict can become violent for many reasons, such as lack of communication or uncontrolled anger. Most of the time, there are clues that violence is about to happen. By knowing what signs to watch for, you can avoid violence.

Aggression

Any action or behavior that is hostile or threatening to another person is called **aggression.** Aggression does not always lead to violence, but it is usually the first step. While violence is more dangerous physically, aggression can be just as damaging emotionally. Aggression is used to intimidate or frighten others. Bullies are often aggressive without ever physically harming a person. This doesn't make them any less frightening. Many people that have been bullied report that the threat of violence is as scary and damaging as violence itself. Many times, a conflict that starts with aggressive behavior ends in violence.
★ 5.K

Figure 20 If it is handled poorly, a conflict that could have been resolved calmly can become violent.

308 Chapter 12 Conflict Management

Conflict Can Lead to Violence

If a conflict gets out of control, it can result in violence. When people in a conflict stop communicating, anger grows and violence can result. Knowing when conflicts are beginning to get out of control allows you to avoid violent situations. Watch for the following signs when you are in a conflict:

- **Lack of Communication** When people in a conflict stop communicating with one another, anger usually increases, which can lead to violence. Remember that communication means sharing your feelings openly and honestly. People can talk for hours and still not communicate.

- **Aggression** One clear sign that violence might happen is aggressive speech or body language. Be careful if a person is using name-calling, insults, and threats, or if he or she is entering your personal space. These are signs that he or she may be close to becoming violent.

- **Anger** When a person becomes overly angry, there is a chance that he or she might become violent. Watch for signs that a person is very angry, such as screaming or crying.

- **Group Pressure** Sometimes, people like to see others fight. These people will sometimes encourage their friends to become violent in a conflict. This type of peer pressure is very powerful. Often, the person will become violent because he or she doesn't want to look weak in front of friends.

★ 5.K; 10.A; 12.E

Myth & Fact

Myth: Violence only happens in bad neighborhoods or areas.

Fact: Violence can occur anywhere.

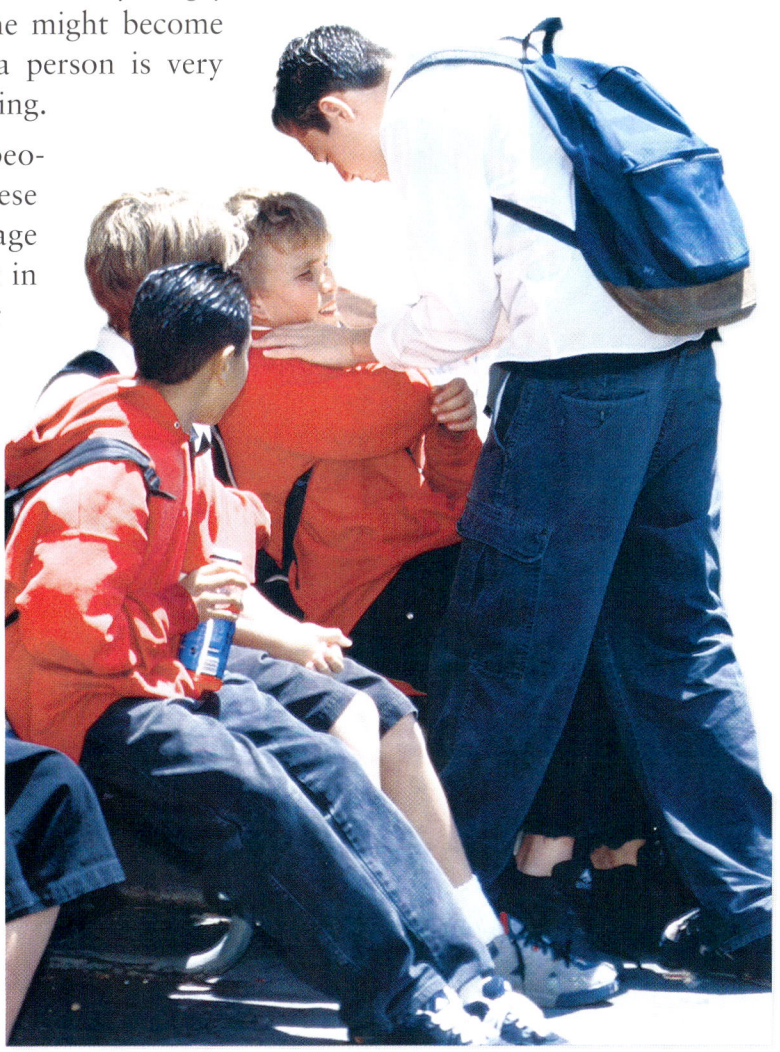

Figure 21 Uncontrolled anger can quickly lead to violent outbursts like the one shown here.

Controlling Anger

In a conflict, you cannot control the other person's behavior. However, you can control yourself and your emotions. If you can manage your anger, you can think clearly and resolve a conflict without violence. There are several ways to manage your anger.

Health Journal
When you feel really angry, what are some of the things that you do to calm down? What works best?

- **Take a break.** If you are in a conflict and you are becoming too angry, take a break from the conflict and calm down. If you stay in the conflict, you will only become more angry. Taking a break allows you to to calm down and think about the conflict. Then you can return to the conflict and work to resolve it peacefully.

- **Exercise.** Exercising can release much of the energy that is created by your anger. Many people find that they are more calm after exercising. You could go jogging or take a walk to the park. Whatever you choose to do, exercise will take your mind off your anger and allow you to calm down.

- **Talk to someone.** When you are very angry, talking to someone about your anger can help you feel better. Choose someone who is not involved in the conflict that is causing your anger. Talk about what caused you to become angry and why it caused you to become angry. Then talk about different ways to resolve the conflict.

- **Stop and think.** When you are very angry, stop and think about what might happen if you do not control your anger. If you become violent, there will be consequences. These consequences could include injury, punishment by authorities, or the end of a friendship. When you consider these consequences, you will realize that controlling your anger is worth the effort.

- **Get help.** If you have an ongoing problem with controlling anger, you should seek the advice of a trained counselor.

★ 5.K; 10.B; 11.D

Figure 22 If you get too angry, it is sometimes best to remove yourself from the situation and take a break by yourself to calm down.

Avoiding and Preventing Violence

If you are able to recognize situations that may become violent, many times you can avoid violence. If you believe that a situation or conflict is about to become violent, it is usually best to walk away. If the conflict is important, it can always be addressed later when both parties have had a chance to calm down and think about the conflict.

If you are threatened with violence, or if you hear somebody threaten violence against another person, you should always be safe and tell someone. Report any threats of violence to an adult or authority figure immediately. If you do not report threats of violence, you are only increasing the risk of violence happening in the future. You have probably heard stories about shootings at schools and in other places throughout the country. Many of the individuals who committed these crimes threatened others with violence before they actually committed violent acts. Many of these threats were not reported to the appropriate authority figures. You have an obligation as a responsible youth and citizen to make other people aware of any threat against them or someone else. ★ 5.K; 11.D

Myth & Fact

Myth: It's always bad to tell on others.

Fact: You should always report threats of violence. If you don't, the consequences could be very serious.

Figure 23 If you hear someone threatening violence against anyone else, you should immediately report the threat to an authority, such as a school counselor.

Lesson Review

Using Vocabulary
1. Describe the relationship between aggression and violence in your own words. ★ 5.K

Understanding Concepts
2. What are four signs that violence is about to happen? ★ 5.K
3. What are five ways to control anger? ★ 5.K; 10.B; 11.D

Critical Thinking
4. **Making Good Decisions** Imagine that a friend of yours has told you that he is going to attack a classmate who has been bullying him. Should you report the threat? What might happen if you don't report the threat? ★ 5.K; 10.B; 11.D

12 CHAPTER REVIEW

Chapter Summary

■ Conflict is any clash of ideas or interests. ■ The way you communicate during a conflict can often determine whether the conflict ends positively or negatively. ■ Body language is as important as words are in a conflict. ■ There are many tools for resolving conflicts, including negotiation, compromise, collaboration, and mediation. ■ Conflicts can occur at school with peers or with teachers. ■ Conflicts at school should be resolved before they interfere with education. ■ All families have conflict within them. ■ Conflicts between two family members usually affect the whole family. ■ If aggression is left uncontrolled, it can lead to violence. ■ Controlling anger and avoiding violent situations are two ways to prevent violence.

Using Vocabulary

For each pair of terms, describe how the meanings of the terms differ.

1. negotiation/mediation
2. compromise/collaboration
3. aggression/violence

For each sentence, fill in the blank with the proper word from the word bank provided below.

peer mediation   body language
sibling rivalry   intimidation
bully

4. Frightening others with threatening words and body language is called ___.
5. A person who likes to pick on smaller and weaker people is a(n) ___.
6. An important part of communication is ___, or how we use our bodies to communicate.
7. A useful tool in some conflicts is ___, in which somebody of similar age to the people in the conflict helps them to reach a solution.
8. When brothers and sisters compete with each other, the competition is called ___.

Understanding Concepts

9. For what reason do people usually tease other people? ★ 7.A
10. What are three possible sources of conflict in the home? ★ 7.A; 9.B
11. Why are there more opportunities for conflict to occur between two people who are neighbors than between two people who aren't neighbors? ★ 7.A
12. What is required for negotiation to take place? ★ 10.D
13. Why is collaboration better than compromise when it is possible? ★ 10.D
14. When is mediation a good strategy for solving a conflict? ★ 10.D
15. Why should a peer mediator be trained in mediation? ★ 10.D; 12.E
16. What are the four signs that violent behavior might be about to happen? ★ 5.K
17. Briefly describe how bad communication can negatively affect a conflict. ★ 5.K; 11.D

Critical Thinking

Making Inferences

18. Many times, when a person teases another person, he or she does it only when a group of people is watching. What might be the reason that a person who teases others likes to do so in front of an audience? ★ 7.A; 10.A

19. Mediation is an important tool for solving conflicts between individuals. It is also sometimes used in the court system to prevent long and costly trials. Can you think of another type of situation in which mediation would be a useful tool? Describe the situation, and explain how mediation could be helpful. ★ 10.D

20. Imagine that two friends of yours are arguing. The first friend is ignoring the second friend and rolling his eyes. The second friend gets mad and calls the first friend a name. The first friend begins yelling and poking the second friend in the chest. The second friend then hits the first friend and starts a physical fight. In this situation, name all of the things that should have happened differently to keep violence from occurring. ★ 5.K; 11.D

Making Good Decisions

21. Imagine that another student at school has been calling you names and making fun of your clothes. The statements are bothering you. Describe a plan for handling the situation, and explain why this plan is the best plan. ★ 6.A; 7.A; 10.D; 11.D

22. Imagine that you have heard a student making threats of violence against another student. You think he might be joking, but you can't be sure. Should you tell somebody? Explain your answer.
★ 5.K; 11.D

Interpreting Graphics

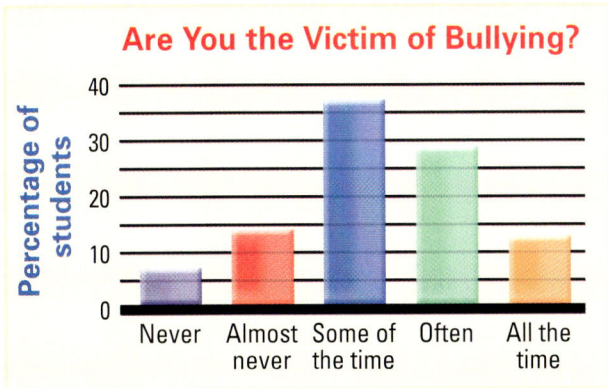

Use the figure above to answer questions 23–28. ★ M8.5.A

23. The graph above shows the results of a survey of students at a local school. About what percentage of the people in the survey are being bullied?

24. Which category had the fewest responses? Which category had the most responses?

25. About how many people were included in the survey?

26. About what percentage of the people report being bullied often or all the time?

27. About what percentage of the people report being bullied never or almost never?

28. About what percentage of the people report being bullied some of the time?

Reading Checkup

Take a minute to review your answers to the Health IQ questions at the beginning of this chapter. How has reading this chapter improved your Health IQ?

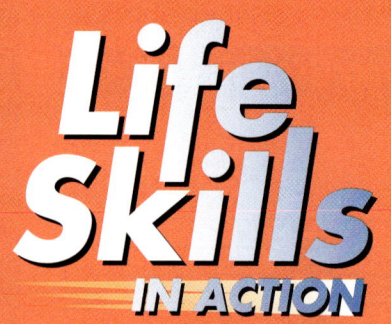

Communicating Effectively

Have you ever been in a bad situation that was made worse because of poor communication? Or maybe you have difficulty understanding others or being understood. You can avoid misunderstandings by expressing your feelings in a healthy way, or communicating effectively. Complete the following activity to develop effective communication skills.

Abby's Favorite Sweater

Setting the Scene

Abby's best friend, Ella, borrowed Abby's favorite sweater over a month ago. At first, Abby did not want to let her borrow it because Ella does not always take good care of her own clothes. But Ella promised to be careful with the sweater and to return it within a week. Now Abby is very angry and wants the sweater back.

The 4 Steps of Communicating Effectively

1. Express yourself calmly and clearly.
2. Choose your words carefully.
3. Use open body language.
4. Use active listening.

Guided Practice

Practice with a Friend

Form a group of three. Have one person play the role of Abby and another person play the role of Ella. Have the third person be an observer. Walking through each of the four steps of communicating effectively, role-play a conversation in which Abby confronts Ella about the sweater. Have Abby communicate her feelings to Ella without using unhealthy expressions of anger. The observer will take notes, which will include observations about what the person playing Abby did well and suggestions of ways to improve. Stop after each step to evaluate the process.

★ 5.K; 10.D; 11.D

Independent Practice

Check Yourself

After you complete the guided practice, go through Act 1 again without stopping at each step. Answer the questions below to review what you did.

1. How can Abby show calm behavior when asking Ella for her sweater? ★ 11.D

2. What words or phrases should Abby avoid using when asking for her sweater? ★ 5.K; 10.D; 11.D

3. Describe some examples of open body language that Abby might use in this situation. ★ 11.D

4. Why is it important to use healthy communication skills when expressing anger? ★ 5.K; 11.D

On Your Own

After their conversation, Ella finally returned the sweater to Abby. Abby found a stain on the sweater but was happy to finally have it back. A week later, Ella asks to borrow a pair of Abby's jeans. When Abby says no, Ella becomes very upset. Draw a comic strip of the conversation between Abby and Ella. In the comic strip, Abby should use the four steps of communicating effectively to explain her position without making Ella angry.

CHAPTER 13
Preventing Abuse and Violence

Lessons
1. **Preventing Violence** — 318
2. **Coping with Violence** — 322
3. **Abuse** — 326
4. **Coping with Harassment** — 330

Chapter Review — 332
Life Skills in Action — 334

Check out **Current Health** articles related to this chapter by visiting **go.hrw.com.** Just type in the keyword **HD4CH45**.

"Talking about the **attack** was hard, but I'm glad **I did it**. After I got out of the **emergency room**, I tried to forget it. But I couldn't sleep, and I was really scared. I finally asked my grandmother if she had a minute to talk. We talked, and I started to cry really hard. She gave me a hug, and we kept talking. It is a big help to know that she is there for me.**"**

PRE-READING

Answer the following multiple-choice questions to find out what you know about preventing violence and abuse. When you've finished this chapter, you'll have the opportunity to change your answers based on what you've learned.

1. You can help avoid violence by
    a. avoiding violent people.
    b. planning ahead.
    c. scaling down conflicts.
    d. All of the above ⭐ 5.C; 5.K

2. Threats of violence
    a. are usually jokes.
    b. should always be taken seriously.
    c. are seldom important.
    d. are ways of scaling down conflicts. ⭐ 5.K

3. In a violent situation, your first priority is to
    a. protect yourself and seek safety.
    b. protect your money and other valuables.
    c. plan how you are going to get back at the person hurting you.
    d. make sure everyone around you is safe. ⭐ 5.K

4. Abuse happens to people in
    a. cities.
    b. rural areas.
    c. suburbs.
    d. All of the above ⭐ 5.C

5. Harassment can be an unwanted
    a. touch.
    b. comment.
    c. joke.
    d. All of the above ⭐ 5.C

6. One of the best ways to cope with abuse, violence, and harassment is to
    a. tell a trusted adult as soon as possible.
    b. work through the problem on your own.
    c. toughen up.
    d. ignore it. ⭐ 5.C; 5.K

ANSWERS: 1. d; 2. b; 3. a; 4. d; 5. d; 6. a

Preventing Abuse and Violence | 317

Lesson 1

Preventing Violence

What You'll Do

- **Identify** seven signs that a conflict may become dangerous. ⭐ 5.K
- **Describe** three general rules that can help you avoid violence. ⭐ 5.K
- **Describe** five ways to scale down conflicts. ⭐ 5.K
- **Explain** how to respond to a threat of violence. ⭐ 5.K
- **Explain** how respecting yourself and others helps you avoid violence. ⭐ 5.K; 11.C

Terms to Learn

- threat

Start Off Write

What are three signs that a conflict might become dangerous?

Sheila noticed the crowd in the hall. She could see the boys at the center of the crowd yelling at each other. She wished that they could talk things out, but the crowd wasn't helping. The crowd was cheering for the boys to start fighting.

What would happen to Sheila if she raced into the middle of the crowd and got between the two boys? Quite likely, she would get hurt. Thinking ahead and imagining the consequences of your choices can help you stay safe from violence. You cannot always prevent or avoid violence. Sometimes, violence happens in spite of the best planning. But thinking ahead can help.

Spotting Dangerous Situations

Some situations are more likely than others to lead to violence. Watch out for conflicts that look like they are getting out of hand. Signs of trouble include the use of shouting, profanity, and aggressive physical contact. Avoid any conflict involving gangs, weapons, or drugs. These conflicts may also lead to violence. Just as Sheila thought, crowds may encourage an argument to turn into a fight. Unfortunately, sometimes people choose violence just to avoid backing down in front of a crowd. ⭐ 5.K

Figure 1 Aggressive physical contact during an argument is a sign that a situation could become dangerous.

318 | Chapter 13 **Preventing Abuse and Violence**

Planning Ahead

Preventing and avoiding violence is not a science. You cannot always know when you are walking into a dangerous area or situation. But sometimes violence is avoidable. Plan ahead. Imagine how some choices could lead to trouble. For example, imagine you are going to a friend's house before dark. You know it will be dark when you go back home. Walking in the dark can be dangerous. So, before you leave home, make plans to get home safely. If you forget to make plans ahead of time, you can make a plan later, but then you may have fewer safe options. Some examples of plans are shown in the figure below. In addition, here are some general rules that can help you avoid violence.

- Avoid dangerous places. Never walk in areas you know to be dangerous.
- Avoid people who use violence to solve problems. People who are violent with others will probably be violent with you.
- Make sure your parents or guardians know where you are going, who is with you, and when you'll be home. ★ 5.K

COPING

Role-play healthy responses to the following situations:

- You hear a peer threaten to harm others.
- You witness a peer verbally attacking another student.
- Your friends are plotting to get back at a student who pushed one of them into a locker.

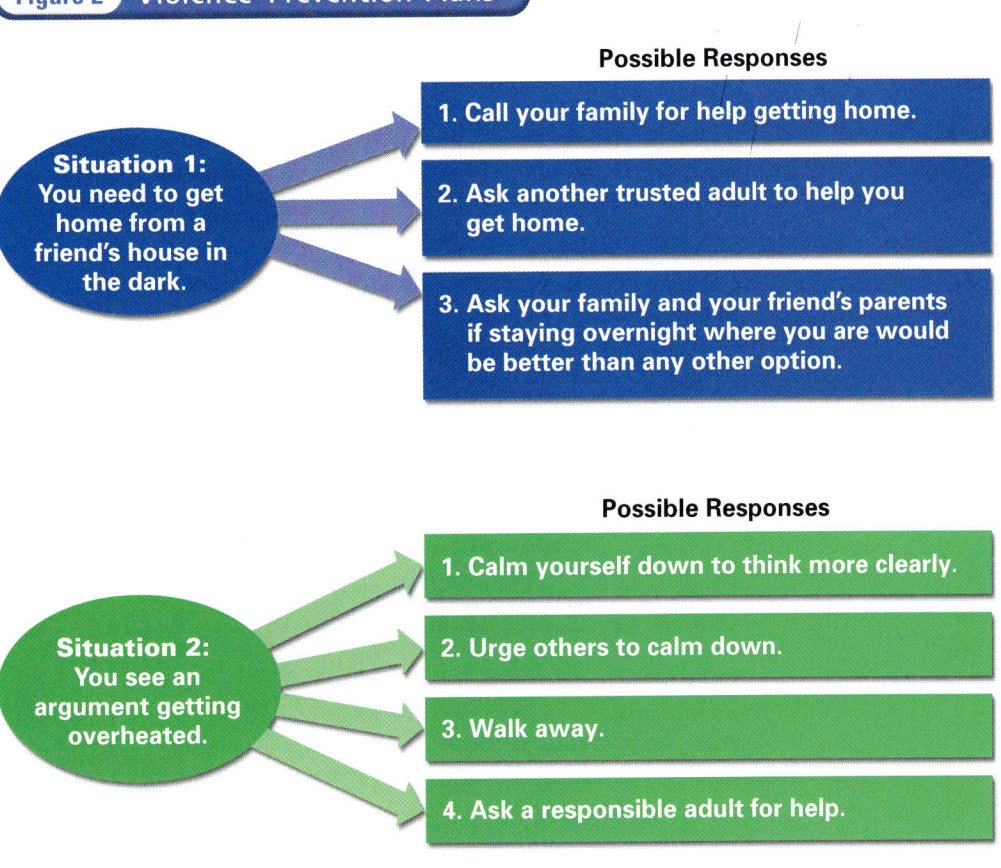

Figure 2 Violence-Prevention Plans

Possible Responses

Situation 1: You need to get home from a friend's house in the dark.

1. Call your family for help getting home.
2. Ask another trusted adult to help you get home.
3. Ask your family and your friend's parents if staying overnight where you are would be better than any other option.

Possible Responses

Situation 2: You see an argument getting overheated.

1. Calm yourself down to think more clearly.
2. Urge others to calm down.
3. Walk away.
4. Ask a responsible adult for help.

Lesson 1 Preventing Violence

TABLE 1 Tools for Scaling Down Conflicts	
Tool	How it works
Empathy	Empathy is sharing the feelings of others. When you know what another person feels, you can better understand why he or she is upset.
Reason	Reason is thinking carefully. When you think carefully, you can consider what is best for everybody in the conflict.
Tolerance	Tolerance is respecting and accepting people in spite of differences. At the end of a conflict, you still may not agree with each other. But respecting each other helps avoid problems in the future.

Figure 3 Taking a break from a conflict can help prevent violence.

Scaling Down Conflicts

Part of planning ahead is knowing how to handle conflicts. When a conflict becomes dangerous, walk away. Try to keep minor conflicts from becoming dangerous. When you are part of a minor conflict that begins to get loud or physical, scaling it down can make it less risky. The following guidelines can help you scale down a minor conflict.

- Allow yourself time to calm down before you speak.
- Let the other person know you are not interested in getting into a violent conflict.
- Change the focus of the conversation with a direct statement such as, "I think we both need time to cool off."
- Try changing the subject by making an inoffensive joke.
- You can always take a break or walk away.

Some tools to help you are listed in the table above. ★ 5.K

Taking Threats Seriously

Sometimes, people give clear signs that they intend to become violent. A **threat** is any serious warning that a person intends to cause harm. Anyone who threatens violence should be taken very seriously. Tell a parent or another trusted adult about any threat as soon as possible. Make sure the adult understands that you take the threat very seriously. If the adult ignores you, tells you to be brave, or says the threat was probably a joke, tell someone else. Keep telling people until the threat of violence has been addressed. ★ 5.K

Health Journal

Write down a list of people who could help you if you were threatened by violence. Write down how you would report threats to these people.

Respecting Yourself and Others

Respect helps prevent violence. If you respect yourself, you'll make decisions that help you take care of yourself. You'll avoid dangerous situations and conflicts and will work to scale down conflicts. Respecting others also helps prevent violence. For example, if someone mistakenly bumps into you, be understanding. Mistakes happen. If you mistakenly bump into someone else, apologize and move on.

Sometimes, anger and the heat of the moment can influence people to be disrespectful of others, especially during a conflict. Being respectful is especially hard if someone is being disrespectful to you. But responding in a disrespectful way can make matters worse. Show respect once you have resolved a conflict. Shake hands. Show the person that you respect him or her even though you had a disagreement. This can help prevent future conflicts.

Respecting parents, teachers, and other authority figures can also help prevent violence. Adults can help you resolve conflicts, and they can bring some dangerous situations back under control. Challenging adults with disrespectful actions or language is unacceptable and can lead to problems. ★ 5.K; 11.C

Figure 4 Treating the people around you with respect helps prevent violence.

Lesson Review

Using Vocabulary
1. Define *threat*.

Understanding Concepts
2. Identify seven signs of trouble in a conflict. ★ 5.K
3. List three ways to avoid potentially violent situations. ★ 5.K; 11.C
4. Describe five ways to scale down conflicts. ★ 5.K; 11.C
5. Explain how to respond to a threat of violence. ★ 5.K

6. Explain how respecting yourself and others helps prevent violence. ★ 5.K; 11.C

Critical Thinking
7. **Making Good Decisions** Two older students threaten Grace at a basketball game. They tell her that they will be waiting outside for her. What should Grace do? ★ 5.K
8. **Applying Concepts** Keith is in an argument and gets pushed. What should he do? ★ 5.K

Lesson 1 Preventing Violence

Lesson 2 Coping with Violence

What You'll Do

- **Describe** six healthy ways to protect yourself from violence. ★ 5.K
- **Explain** why victims must report violence. ★ 10.B; 11.B
- **List** four community resources available to victims of violence. ★ 6.A; 11.B
- **Explain** the roles of the police, family, friends, and counselors in recovery. ★ 7.A; 11.B

Start Off Write

What are three healthy ways that you can protect yourself from violence?

Raul was standing alone on the subway platform. Three guys came up to him and told him to hand over his wallet and his watch. Raul did. The guys pushed him to the ground and ran. Raul was too scared to move. For weeks afterward, Raul had trouble sleeping. And he didn't want to take the subway anymore.

Teens, such as Raul, are twice as likely as other age groups to be victims of violence. Homicide (or murder) is the second-leading cause of death for teens. Not all violence ends in robbing or killing. But all violence hurts people. A violent person can be young or old and can be male or female. And anyone can become a victim of violence. Try to prevent and avoid violence when you can. But you may find yourself in a violent situation anyway. You can learn to cope with that, too. Coping with violence begins with understanding the different kinds of violence you may face.

Spotting Violence

Keeping an eye out for violence as it is happening can help you avoid it. For example, if you recognize violence you may call for help. And recognizing violence can stop you from being violent, too.

You already know what many kinds of violence look like. Pictures and sounds of violence are often in the news. Music lyrics, TV shows, movies, and video games often have violent images or messages. But spotting violence in real life can be harder. For example, you would recognize someone hitting another person as violence. But unwanted touching and bullying are violence, too. Holding someone too tightly is a violent act. Anytime one person intentionally hurts another, he or she is being violent. ★ 5.K

Figure 5 Holding someone too tightly is a form of violence.

Figure 6 When you find yourself in a violent situation, seek safety first. Call for help as soon as possible.

Seeking Safety

When you are confronted with risky or violent situations, your first priority is your safety. You can reduce the risk of becoming a victim of violence by learning to protect yourself. The following tips can help you stay safe:

- When you are home alone, keep your doors and windows locked. Do not open the door for anyone you do not know. These strangers include repairmen and even uniformed officers. If the people at your door say they are police officers, call the police department. Ask why police officers are visiting your home. Call a trusted adult, and ask him or her to come to your home immediately.

- Do not walk alone at night. If you are walking with someone at night, walk in lighted areas.

- If you think someone is following you, go to a public place where others can see you. Tell people to help you. If you are close to home, go inside and lock the door. Call the police.

- If someone bothers you in public, use direct eye contact while telling him or her to leave you alone, or loudly yell "Help!" Yell and do anything that might attract attention.

- If someone threatens you for your money or jewelry, throw it toward him or her and run in the opposite direction.

- If you are attacked, get away any way you can. Try screaming, hitting, or kicking your attacker. 5.K; 11.B

STUDY TIP *for better reading*

Organizing Information
Create a table with two columns: "Dangerous problem" and "Response." For each of the situations listed on this page, write a response. Your responses should be specific to your neighborhood.

Lesson 2 Coping with Violence | **323**

Letting People Know

Figure 7 You can report violence to any adult you trust. Try to record the details of the violence as accurately as you can.

Talking about violence can be scary. Sometimes, victims of violence are ashamed or afraid. They think that the violence was too personal or embarrassing to talk about. But there is nothing shameful about being a victim. It can happen to anyone.

Reporting the violence can help victims get the help they need. If the victim needs medical help, he or she should get it right away. A parent or trusted adult should report the violence to the police. The police can take steps to stop the dangerous person from hurting people again.

When you report violence, speak directly and honestly. Tell the adult exactly what happened. Describe what happened as clearly as you can. Describe the violent person or people. Report any words you remember from the attack. Reporting violence soon after it happens may help you better remember important details. But if you are the victim of violence that happened a while ago, and you never told anyone, you should still tell someone. Report it just the way you would if it happened earlier today.

★ 5.K; 11.B; 11.D

Hands-on ACTIVITY

GRAPHING VIOLENCE

1. Watch the evening news for two evenings. Remember to bring a pencil and paper.

2. Keep track of all the violent stories on the news shows. Write a short description of each violent story. Save your descriptions.

3. Organize the violent acts into categories. Place each story into one of your categories.

Analysis

1. What categories did you choose? Why did you choose those categories?

2. Make a bar graph to show the number of acts in each category. Which category had the greatest number of violent acts?

3. Compare your graph with the graphs of your classmates. Can you compare data from graphs that use different categories?

4. As a class, choose a set of categories that everyone can use.

5. On your own, organize the violent acts using these new categories and make a new graph.

6. Compare the new graphs. Is it easier or harder to compare data than it was in question 3? Explain your answer.

Helping Your Friends

If your friends are victims of violence, they need help, too. You cannot help them alone. Try to convince them to talk to a parent or another trusted adult about the problem. If your friends cannot go to an adult relative or another adult they know, perhaps they can use community resources, such as the following:

- police departments
- hospitals or clinics
- victim support groups
- crisis hotlines ★ 5.K; 6.A; 7.A; 11.B

Recovering from Violence

Just telling someone what happened helps some victims begin to recover, or get back to normal. Talking can help victims regain some security. Talking to the police and other authorities can stop the violent person from hurting people again. Talking with family can help a victim begin to feel safer, too.

Friends and family may not know quite what to do for the victim. But the best thing to do is to be there to listen. Friends and family may help the victim feel safe if they are calm and caring. Knowing that the people around the victim are caring and supportive is comforting.

Some victims need to get help from counselors. When talking to counselors, victims need to talk openly and honestly about their feelings. These conversations are confidential (KAHN fuh DEN shul). What the counselor and victim talk about is private. In most cases, no one else will know the details of the conversation, unless the victim chooses to tell someone else. ★ 5.K; 10.B; 11.B

Figure 8 Violence is bad and can change your life. However, many victims recover to live normal, happy lives.

Lesson Review

Understanding Concepts

1. List three reasons why identifying violence is important. ★ 5.K; 7.A; 10.B
2. List four community resources available to victims of violence. ★ 6.A; 11.B
3. Explain the roles of police, family, friends, and counselors in recovery. ★ 7.A; 11.B
4. Why must victims report violence? ★ 5.K

Critical Thinking

5. **Applying Concepts** While your parents are out, a man comes to the door. He is dressed like a workman. He tells you that your parents asked him to measure for new carpeting. What can you do to be safe? ★ 5.K

Lesson 2 Coping with Violence | 325

Lesson 3: Abuse

What You'll Do

- **Describe** why abuse is often complicated and hard to resolve. ✦ 5.C
- **Describe** five effects of abuse. ✦ 5.C
- **Describe** the best first step a victim of abuse can take. ✦ 5.C
- **Explain** why reporting abuse is very important. ✦ 5.C

Terms to Learn

- abuse

Start Off Write

Why is reporting abuse important?

Reporting violence is hard. Many victims of violence are afraid and embarrassed. Victims of abuse often have an even tougher time. Victims of abuse are often hurt by the people they trusted the most.

Abuse and Its Victims

One of the most serious problems a person can deal with is abuse. **Abuse** is harmful or offensive treatment. Abuse can be physical, sexual, verbal, or emotional. Some forms of abuse are described in the table on the next page. Abuse can happen between strangers. But most of the time, abuse happens between people who know each other, such as family members and friends. Furthermore, abusers are often much more powerful than their victims. Anyone can be a victim of abuse, but victims of abuse are often children or the elderly. It is hard to understand how people can hurt people they say they care about, but such abuse does happen. Close relationships between abusers and victims make many cases of abuse complicated and hard to resolve.

Abuse happens in every city and town. You usually cannot tell by looking who has been abused. All forms of abuse are wrong and harmful. The abuser sometimes makes the victim feel responsible for the abuse. Abusers use this trick to make the abuse seem OK. Abuse is never OK. Victims should place the blame back on the abuser and seek help right away. ✦ 5.C

Figure 9 Who has been abused? You cannot usually tell by looking.

326 Chapter 13 Preventing Abuse and Violence

TABLE 2 Definitions and Examples of Abuse

Problem	Definition	Examples
Physical abuse	any physical act meant to cause bodily harm to another person	physical contact that results in bruises, burns, broken bones, or head injuries; wounds or cuts; twisted arms or legs
Sexual abuse	any sexual contact with a child; any unwanted sexual act or touch between individuals of any age that continues after a person has been told to stop	touching another person's body in an unwanted sexual way such as kissing or fondling; forcing a person to perform a sexual act against his or her will
Verbal abuse	the use of hurtful words to intimidate, manipulate, hurt, or dominate another person	shouting profanity, ridiculing, teasing; using put-downs; making fun of another person
Emotional abuse	the repeated use of actions or words that imply a person is worthless or powerless	continually degrading someone; using threatening words or actions; repeatedly being insensitive to another's feelings
Neglect	the failure of parents or caregivers to meet the physical, emotional, social, and educational needs of a child or other dependant	not providing a child with food and clothing; teaching harmful behaviors; withholding love and affection; keeping a child from receiving a proper education

The Effects of Abuse

All abuse is harmful. Some victims suffer physical harm. Some may feel fear, shame, or anger. Sometimes, victims try to avoid these feelings by pretending the abuse did not happen. Some victims use alcohol or other drugs to "numb" their pain. But that does not work. Unfortunately, victims of abuse sometimes wind up abusing others in an attempt to deal with their own pain. And hurting other people only causes more problems.

The effects of abuse are not limited to the immediate pain of being physically or emotionally hurt. The effects of abuse can build up over time. The longer the abuse happens, the more the victim's overall health can be affected. Victims of abuse often cannot stop the abuse by themselves. Victims should seek help immediately from trusted adults who can help stop the abuse. If the first adult told about the abuse does not help, the victim should keep telling people until the abuse stops. ★ 5.C

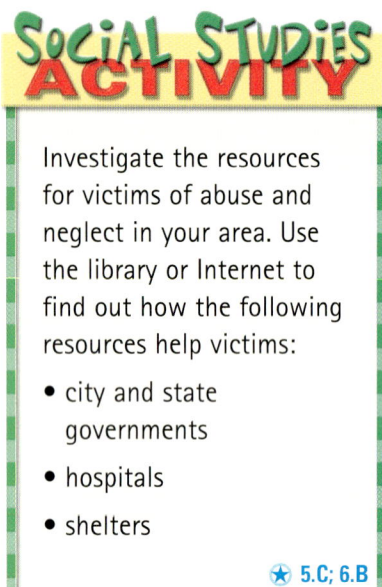

Social Studies Activity

Investigate the resources for victims of abuse and neglect in your area. Use the library or Internet to find out how the following resources help victims:

- city and state governments
- hospitals
- shelters

★ 5.C; 6.B

Help

No one deserves to be abused. And people who have been abused are not responsible for the abuse. Protect yourself from abusive situations by following the tips below.

- Stay away from people who you see being abusive to others.
- Stay away from people who act violently.
- Tell an adult about any abuse you know about.
- Trust your instincts. Don't do anything that seems wrong to you, even if someone else says it's OK.

Abuse that takes place in families or in close relationships is more difficult to prevent and escape. But you can take steps to protect yourself or anyone you know from being abused at home. Use the resources in your school or community to report what is happening. Talk to an adult. If an adult close to you is the abuser, you can ask another adult for help. Some people who can help you are suggested in the figure below. ★ 5.C

Figure 10 People Who Can Help

Family Members
parents
grandparents
aunts and uncles
older brothers and sisters

School Staff
teachers
principals
guidance counselors
group activity leaders
coaches
school nurses

Local People
neighbors
friends' parents
music teachers
spiritual and religious leaders
youth-group leaders

Health Professionals
family doctors
local hospital workers
nurses
social workers

Community Professionals
police officers
firefighters
abuse agency workers
crisis hotline workers

Breaking the Silence

Health professionals and counselors agree that abuse is never the fault of the victim. They also agree that the best way to make abuse stop is to tell someone. Abused people often do not seek help because the abuser has promised never to do it again. Abusers will often do special things for the victim to keep the victim from telling. The victim may enjoy the special attention and forgive the abuser. But abusive people may never stop abusing unless they get help. If nothing is done, the abuse can happen again.

Reporting abuse is often very difficult. Sometimes, victims do not tell because they are afraid of what will happen. They may worry that the family will break up or someone will be sent to jail. Others worry that no one will believe them. Victims are often ashamed and think they are responsible for what has happened. These problems can prevent victims from seeking help. But reporting abuse is very important. Help for victims and abusers is available only when people who can help know about the problem. The first step is to identify a trusted adult. The next step is to begin telling that person about the abuse. A simple statement such as "I need to talk to someone" can be a good opener. Most adults will be able to pick up the conversation from there and guide the discussion. Once people know, they can help. ★ 5.C; 11.D

Figure 11 Posters like this encourage victims of abuse to get help.

Lesson Review

Using Vocabulary

1. What is abuse? ★ 5.C

Understanding Concepts

2. Describe why abuse is often complicated and hard to resolve. ★ 5.C
3. Explain why reporting abuse is very important. ★ 5.C
4. Describe the best first step a victim of abuse can take. ★ 5.C
5. Describe five effects of abuse. ★ 5.C

Critical Thinking

6. **Understanding Relationships** Why might children and the elderly be common victims of abuse? ★ 5.C

internet connect
www.scilinks.org/health
Topic: Abuse and Violence
HealthLinks code: HD4003
HEALTH LINKS. Maintained by the National Science Teachers Association

Lesson 4 Coping with Harassment

Esteban's ears stick out. They always have. At his old school, nobody seemed to notice. But at his new school, one kid at the lunch table told Esteban that he looked like a bowtie. Everyone laughed, and he laughed too. Now, everybody says it all the time. Esteban is embarrassed. He wants the teasing to stop.

What You'll Do

- **Contrast** joking with harassment.  5.C; 5.K
- **Summarize** a way to stop harassment. 5.C; 5.K

Terms to Learn

- harassment

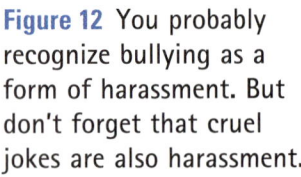

How can you stop harassment?

Joking around is part of being friends. Laughing is part of having a good time. But sometimes, joking is mean. Sometimes, mean jokes are aimed at a group or a single person, such as Esteban. This kind of teasing can hurt.

Just a Joke?

Healthy joking is fun for everybody. But when people who joke are trying to hurt or control someone else, that is not healthy. It's mean. Even if you don't intend to hurt anyone's feelings, you may. If someone tells you that he or she is uncomfortable with your jokes or any other attention from you, you need to stop. If you don't stop, your behavior becomes harassment (huh RAS muhnt). **Harassment** is any repeated, unwanted joke, comment, touch, or behavior. Unwanted jokes, behavior, or touching that relate to a person's gender or sexuality are *sexual harassment*. Anyone can be a victim of harassment. Harassment is never acceptable. 5.C; 5.K

Figure 12 You probably recognize bullying as a form of harassment. But don't forget that cruel jokes are also harassment.

Figure 13 Being assertive can help you stop harassment.

Stopping Harassment

If someone is harassing you, act assertively. You are not responsible for the harassment. But you can take responsibility for stopping it. State very clearly with words and body language that the attention is not welcome. Use clear statements such as

- "Please stop talking to me that way."
- "Don't touch me."
- "That's not funny. Please don't tell jokes like that around me."

If that doesn't work, use your refusal skills to show that you will not let the harassment continue. Make it clear that you will report the harassment to an adult if it happens again. If the harassment continues, report it immediately to a parent, a teacher, or another trusted adult. 5.C; 5.K; 11.D

Myth & Fact

Myth: Only girls and women experience sexual harassment.

Fact: One recent study indicated that 79 percent of boys reported that they were victims of sexual harassment.

Lesson Review

Using Vocabulary
1. Define *harassment*.
2. What is sexual harassment? 5.C; 5.K

Understanding Concepts
3. Summarize a way to stop harassment. 5.C; 5.K
4. Contrast healthy joking with harassment. 5.C; 5.K

Critical Thinking
5. **Applying Concepts** Your friends and you go to a local swimming pool on a hot summer day. One of your friends starts to tease a girl in your group about how skinny she looks in a bathing suit. The teasing continues until the girl starts to cry. What would you do? 5.C; 5.K

Lesson 4 Coping with Harassment

13 CHAPTER REVIEW

Chapter Summary

- Good ways to prevent violence include avoiding dangerous conflicts, planning ahead, scaling down conflicts, taking threats seriously, and respecting yourself and others.
- Your first responsibility in a violent situation is to seek safety.
- Reporting violence helps victims get the help they need.
- Recovery from violence may take time and the help of family, friends, and counselors.
- Abuse is harmful or offensive treatment, often from someone the victim trusts.
- The best way to handle abuse is to talk with a parent or trusted adult as soon as possible.
- Harassment can be any unwanted touch, joke, comment, or behavior.
- Assertive behavior and refusal skills can help stop harassment.

Using Vocabulary

For each sentence, fill in the blank with the proper word from the word bank provided below.

threat
harassment
physical abuse
sexual abuse
neglect
verbal abuse
emotional abuse

1. A person telling you that he plans to hurt another person is making a ___.
2. The failure to provide food or clothes to a dependent child is one form of ___.
3. Any sexual contact with a child is ___.
4. Repeatedly giving someone unwanted attention is a form of ___.
5. ___ can result in bruises, burns, and broken bones.

Understanding Concepts

6. Describe how planning ahead can help you avoid violence.
7. Describe six healthy ways to protect yourself from violence.
8. If someone threatens you with violence, what should you do? ★ 5.K
9. How does respecting authorities help prevent violence? ★ 5.K
10. Explain why violence and abuse must be reported. ★ 5.C; 5.K
11. Explain the difference between harassment and joking. ★ 5.C; 5.K
12. Are all kinds of violence easy to spot? Explain your answer. ★ 5.K
13. Explain how a person who has been abused might begin talking to a trusted adult about his or her problem. ★ 5.C
14. Describe a confidential relationship. ★ 5.C; 5.K
15. How do empathy, tolerance, and reason help scale down minor conflicts? ★ 5.K
16. How does respecting yourself help keep you safe? ★ 5.K
17. Why should someone being abused seek help right away? ★ 5.C
18. Explain how to help your friends when they are victims of violence. ★ 5.K; 11.B

Critical Thinking

Identifying Relationships

19. Drinking alcohol makes it harder for people to think clearly. Why may conflicts involving alcohol be more likely to become violent than conflicts between people who have not been drinking? ★ 5.H; 5.K

20. Abusers are often more powerful than their victims. How may this relationship influence the way victims respond to the abuse? How does telling a trusted adult about the abuse help victims have more power than they would have on their own? ★ 5.C

21. You know that you should walk away if you are faced with violence. What could happen if somebody responded to violence with more violence? ★ 5.K

Making Good Decisions

22. Imagine that someone is harassing you about your name. How can you use assertiveness and refusal skills to help stop the harassment? ★ 5.C; 5.K; 11.B; 11.D

23. Aaron spends all afternoon at school rehearsing for a school play. When rehearsal is over, he sits under a tree to study and wait for the bus. But he falls asleep. He misses the last bus home. When he wakes up, it's dark. No one is around. The school is locked. He has no phone or money. Aaron lives 3 miles from school. Near the school is a mall, a fire station, and a bank. What should Aaron do? ★ 5.K; 11.B

24. On the way to school, a student you do not know tells you he is mad at his math teacher, Mr. Roberts. He tells you that he is going to make Mr. Roberts sorry for telling his parents about his bad behavior at school. You can tell the boy is very angry. What should you do? ★ 5.K; 11.B

25. Use what you have learned in this chapter to set a personal goal. Write your goal, and make an action plan by using the Health Behavior Contract for preventing abuse and violence. You can find the Health Behavior Contract at **go.hrw.com**. Just type in the keyword **HD4HBC12**.

Reading Checkup

Take a minute to review your answers to the Health IQ questions at the beginning of this chapter. How has reading this chapter improved your Health IQ?

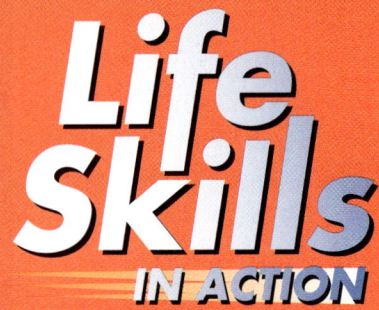

Life Skills IN ACTION

Coping

At times, everyone has to face setbacks, disappointments, or other troubles. To deal with these problems, you have to learn how to cope. Coping is dealing with problems and emotions in an effective way. Complete the following activity to develop your coping skills.

Yoshi and the Bully

Setting the Scene

Last week, Yoshi had a run-in with a bully at school. After a brief argument, the bully began threatening Yoshi and pushing him around. Since then, Yoshi has been pretending to be sick so that he can stay home. Yoshi's father realizes that he is not ill and tells him that he has to go back to school. However, Yoshi is afraid to go back to school. He tells his father that he is worried that the bully will come after him again. ★ 5.C; 5.K; 11.B

The 5 Steps of Coping

1. Identify the problem.
2. Identify your emotions.
3. Use positive self-talk.
4. Find ways to resolve the problem.
5. Talk to others to receive support.

Guided Practice

Practice with a Friend

Form a group of three. Have one person play the role of Yoshi and another person play the role of his father. Have the third person be an observer. Walking through each of the five steps of coping, role-play Yoshi coping with his fears. Yoshi's father should offer advice and encouragement when Yoshi goes to him for support. The observer will take notes, which will include observations about what the person playing Yoshi did well and suggestions of ways to improve. Stop after each step to evaluate the process. ★ 5.C; 5.K; 11.B

Independent Practice

Check Yourself

After you have completed the guided practice, go through Act 1 again without stopping at each step. Answer the questions below to review what you did.

1. What problem does Yoshi face? What emotions are caused by this problem? 11.F

2. What are some positive things you could say about yourself if you were in Yoshi's place? 10.B; 11.B

3. What are some ways Yoshi can resolve his problem? 10.B; 11.B

4. How does talking with someone help you cope? 10.B; 11.B

5. Which of the five steps of coping is the most difficult for you? Explain your answer.

On Your Own

Later that week, Yoshi returns to school. But when Yoshi goes to track practice after school, his coach tells him that he has been temporarily suspended from the team because of the fight with the bully. The news makes Yoshi very angry. He doesn't think that being pushed around is the same as being in a fight and doesn't think he should be punished for it. Write a short story about how Yoshi could use the five steps of coping to deal with the suspension.

CHAPTER 14
Tobacco

Lessons

1. **Tobacco Products: An Overview** — 338
2. **Tobacco's Effects** — 340
3. **Tobacco, Disease, and Death** — 344
4. **Tobacco and Addiction** — 348
5. **Quitting** — 352
6. **Why People Use Tobacco** — 356
7. **Being Tobacco Free** — 360

Chapter Review — 364
Life Skills in Action — 366

Check out **Current Health** articles related to this chapter by visiting **go.hrw.com**. Just type in the keyword **HD4CH46**.

> **I recently quit using chewing tobacco. I was starting to get sores in my mouth**, and I felt like I was always sneaking around to **hide my habit**. Now I never use tobacco, and the doctor said that I was smart. I quit before the sores became cancerous.

PRE-READING

Answer the following true/false questions to find out what you already know about tobacco. When you've finished this chapter, you'll have the opportunity to change your answers based on what you've learned.

1. Smoking pipes or cigars can be as deadly as smoking cigarettes.

2. Nicotine is a drug.

3. Tobacco only affects a person after years of use. ★ 5.H

4. Tobacco increases the risk of lung, mouth, throat, pancreatic, and bladder cancer. ★ 5.I

5. It is against the law to sell any tobacco product to someone under the age of 18.

6. A person can easily quit smoking when he or she really wants to quit. ★ 5.H

7. Young people do not become addicted to tobacco products as easily as adults do. ★ 5.H

8. Sometimes, medicine can help a person quit using tobacco. ★ 5.J

9. Positive peer pressure from friends can influence a teen to avoid tobacco. ★ 12.E

10. Once a person has used tobacco, quitting the habit will not help him or her recover from the health effects. ★ 5.H

11. Advertisements can encourage a false understanding of tobacco's effects. ★ 8.A

12. Tobacco smoke can increase asthma symptoms in nonsmokers. ★ 5.I

ANSWERS: 1. true; 2. true; 3. false; 4. true; 5. true; 6. false; 7. false; 8. true; 9. true; 10. false; 11. true; 12. true

Lesson 1

Tobacco Products: An Overview

What You'll Do

- **Identify** three chemicals found in cigarettes. ★ 5.H; 5.I
- **Describe** how nicotine from smokeless tobacco enters the bloodstream. ★ 5.H
- **List** four smokable tobacco products besides cigarettes. ★ 5.H

Terms to Learn

- nicotine
- carbon monoxide
- tar

Start Off Write

Why do you think smoking is a health risk?

Shawn's dad smoked a pipe every evening. It looked relaxing to Shawn. But his teacher told him that pipe tobacco can be just as dangerous as cigarettes are.

Both cigarettes and pipe tobacco contain hundreds of dangerous chemicals. Even though some forms of tobacco may look safer than others do, all tobacco products are unhealthy.

Tobacco and Cigarettes

Tobacco is a plant that has been used for centuries to make many products. Tobacco products contain nicotine (NIK uh TEEN). **Nicotine** is a highly addictive drug found in all tobacco products. Within seconds of inhaling or chewing tobacco products, nicotine enters the blood and reaches the brain. Nicotine raises the heart rate and blood pressure. This drug can make people feel dizzy, relaxed, or energetic.

The most common tobacco product is the cigarette. To make cigarettes, tobacco leaves are dried and hundreds of chemicals are added to them. These chemicals keep tobacco moist, make it taste better, and help it burn. Burning a cigarette causes the chemicals to form even more chemicals. When a person inhales cigarette smoke, thousands of chemicals enter the lungs.

Two dangerous chemicals in cigarette smoke are carbon monoxide (KAHR buhn muh NAHKS ied) and tar. **Carbon monoxide** is a gas that makes it hard for the blood to carry oxygen. **Tar** is a sticky substance that can coat the airways and can cause cancer. These chemicals are also present in the air around smokers. ★ 5.H; 5.I

Figure 1 The air around a person smoking cigarettes is filled with the dangerous chemicals found in cigarette smoke.

Smokeless Tobacco

Tobacco products are not always smoked. The two main types of smokeless tobacco are *chewing tobacco* and *snuff*. Each type consists of chopped tobacco leaves, chemicals, and flavoring. Chewing tobacco can be loose or pressed together to form a small bunch. Snuff is more powdery than chewing tobacco and is either loose or wrapped in a pouch.

Though snuff can be sniffed through the nose, most smokeless tobacco users place tobacco between the cheek and gum. They suck on the tobacco and then spit it out along with saliva. The nicotine in this tobacco is absorbed through the mouth. From there, nicotine enters the blood. ★ 5.H

Other Tobacco Products

Most tobacco products contain similar chemicals. Pipe tobacco, cigars, and clove cigarettes are smokable tobacco products. The smoke from these products contains thousands of harmful chemicals. Smokers do not always inhale smoke from these products into the lungs. But this smoke often has higher levels of nicotine than cigarette smoke does. And smoke can release nicotine into the blood through the mouth.

Bidis (BEE deez) are unfiltered cigarettes that are wrapped in brown leaves and tied with thread. They come in flavors, such as strawberry and chocolate. Bidis are appealing to teens because of the flavors. But smoke from bidis has high levels of carbon monoxide, nicotine, and tar. Bidis are just as dangerous as cigarettes are. ★ 5.H

Myth & Fact

Myth: Tobacco is not as dangerous as alcohol or other drugs are.

Fact: More deaths are caused by tobacco use every year than by the use of all other drugs combined—including people killed in alcohol-related car accidents.

Figure 2 Many different products are made from tobacco.

Lesson Review

Using Vocabulary
1. Define *nicotine*.
2. How are carbon monoxide and tar related? ★ 5.H; 5.I

Understanding Concepts
3. How does nicotine from smokeless tobacco enter the blood? ★ 5.H; 5.I
4. List four smokable tobacco products besides cigarettes. ★ 5.H

Critical Thinking
5. **Applying Concepts** How might smoke from cigarettes, pipe tobacco, cigars, bidis, and clove cigarettes be harmful to nonsmokers? Explain. ★ 5.H; 5.I

Lesson 2

Tobacco's Effects

The Food and Drug Administration (FDA) monitors the safety of foods, drinks, and medicines. It requires companies to list a product's ingredients on its package.

What You'll Do

- **Describe** immediate and chronic effects of smokable and smokeless tobacco.
  ★ 5.H; 5.I; 12.C
- **Describe** the effects of environmental tobacco smoke. ★ 5.H; 5.I; 6.A
- **Explain** how tobacco affects social and emotional health.
  ★ 5.H; 5.I; 12.C

Terms to Learn

- chronic effect
- environmental tobacco smoke (ETS)

Start Off Write

How can smoking affect a person's social health?

But the FDA does not monitor tobacco products. Ingredients for tobacco products are not listed on the package. Safety testing is not required for these products. To make wise decisions about tobacco, you need to learn about tobacco's effects.

Early Effects of Smoking

When someone inhales chemicals from a tobacco product, the body is affected immediately. Upon the first puff, clothes, hair, and skin begin to smell like smoke. The first lung-full of smoke can cause nausea and dizziness. When the body is not used to nicotine or other chemicals, they can make a person sick.

Many of the early effects of smoking become chronic (KRAHN ik) if a person keeps smoking. A **chronic effect** is a consequence that remains with a person for a long time. Chronic effects of smoking remain with smokers at least as long as they keep smoking. Bad breath is a chronic effect that begins soon after a person starts smoking. Persistent coughing, excess mucus, and discolored teeth can also appear shortly after a person begins smoking.

Another chronic effect that begins soon after starting to smoke is shortness of breath. Tar in the lungs blocks oxygen from reaching the blood. Also, carbon monoxide from tobacco smoke passes to the blood through the lungs. High levels of this gas make it harder for the blood to carry oxygen. As a result, the body works harder and breathes faster. These effects can impair physical ability—even in trained athletes. ★ 5.H; 5.I; 12.C

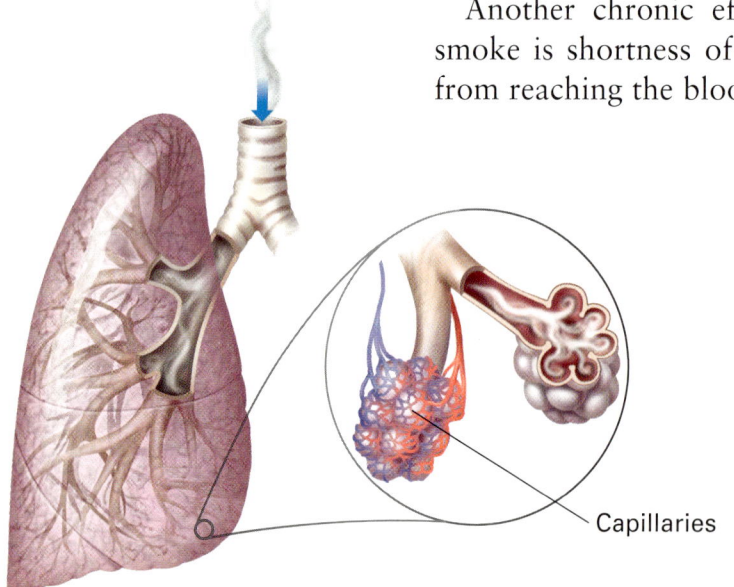

Figure 3 Normally, blood absorbs oxygen through capillaries. But if carbon monoxide from tobacco smoke fills the lungs, the blood will absorb carbon monoxide instead of oxygen.

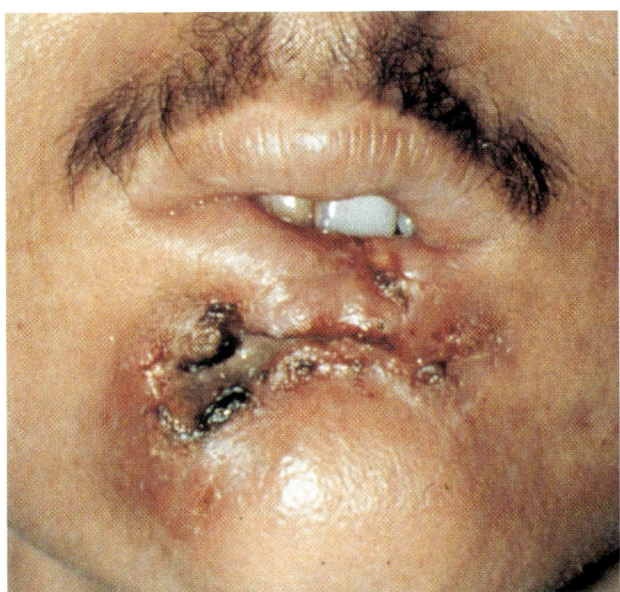

Figure 4 Chewing tobacco can cause cancer that disfigures the face.

Effects of Smokeless Tobacco

Imagine having a conversation with someone who constantly spits out a brown liquid. Using chewing tobacco and snuff is unattractive as well as dangerous. In addition to bad breath and yellow teeth, these products can cause gum disease. After a person uses smokeless tobacco for a while, white sores often appear in the mouth and on the gums. These sores are chronic problems for smokeless tobacco users. Eventually, these sores may become cancerous and require surgical removal. Cancer and the surgeries to remove it can disfigure a person's face. These problems can cause difficulty with eating or speaking. ★ 5.H; 5.I; 12.C

Environmental Tobacco Smoke

Chemicals from tobacco smoke fill the air around smokers. The mix of exhaled smoke and smoke from the end of lit cigarettes is called **environmental tobacco smoke (ETS).** ETS, or secondhand smoke, is unhealthy to everyone who breathes it. Nonsmokers who breathe ETS can experience some of the same health problems that affect smokers. These nonsmokers have a higher risk of lung cancer and heart disease than nonsmokers who avoid ETS.

ETS is especially dangerous for children because they are still growing. Children with parents who smoke can have reduced lung growth. These children are also more at risk for respiratory illnesses, such as severe asthma. So, many parents try to keep their children away from smoky environments. ★ 5.H; 5.I; 6.A

Brain Food

A typical cigarette or a pinch of snuff can contain 0.5 to 1.4 milligrams of nicotine. Soaking the tobacco from a pack of cigarettes in a few ounces of water overnight can make an effective insecticide.

Figure 5 ETS may affect people in nonsmoking areas if the smoking areas are not fully enclosed by walls and doors.

Contact Lenses

Sidestream smoke is smoke that escapes from a burning cigarette. This smoke can coat contact lenses with nicotine and tar, making the lenses irritate the eyes. Washing the nicotine and tar off the lenses is difficult because these chemicals can be absorbed into the lenses.

Reducing Tobacco's Effects

Until recently, smoking was permitted in most buildings in the United States. Once people understood the dangers of ETS, many cities made laws against smoking in public places. Even where there are no laws against smoking inside, many businesses do not allow it. Other businesses allow smoking only in certain areas of a building. However, unless these areas are completely separated from nonsmokers, ETS can still affect people in the building.

A more effective way to reduce the effects of tobacco is for people to stop using it. This would reduce the effects on both nonsmokers and people who use tobacco. As soon as people quit using tobacco products, their bodies begin to heal. If they quit early enough, tobacco's chronic effects can disappear. The longer people use tobacco, the more difficult it is for the body to recover from the damage. ★ 5.J; 6.B

LIFE SKILLS ACTIVITY

COMMUNICATING EFFECTIVELY

In a group, research facts about smokers' and nonsmokers' rights. Each group should choose a side to represent. Then prepare for a debate about whether smokers should be able to smoke in public places. Pair up with a group who has prepared to represent the other side of the issue and debate the issue. Remember that listening is an important part of communication. After the debate, ask yourself if your own opinions about smokers' rights have changed at all.

Social and Emotional Health Effects

Tobacco can affect more than physical health. Tobacco users spend a large amount of money to pay for their habit. And using tobacco can have serious legal, social, and emotional effects.

In most states, possessing tobacco products is illegal for people younger than 18 years old. Teens under the age of 18 who try to buy tobacco can face legal punishment. Any store that sells to underage teens also risks legal trouble. Also, laws against indoor smoking can cause difficulties for smokers who want to take part in social events.

Tobacco use can put friendships in danger. Some friends may be uncomfortable around people who are using tobacco. Other friends may know that ETS threatens their health.

Tobacco use can also strain relationships with parents. The effects of tobacco are not easy to hide. Teen smokers usually have to lie to their parents in order to keep their habit a secret. Lying and keeping secrets can be emotionally difficult.

Some smokers also have emotional difficulty because they know that they are risking their health. Many smokers have known someone who died from a smoking-related disease. Being unable to stop smoking can be confusing and frustrating. And knowing that smoking risks the health of others can increase the emotional burden of smoking.

★ 5.H; 5.I; 6.A; 12.C

Figure 6 Stores that sell tobacco suffer legal punishment if they are caught selling tobacco to people under the age of 18.

Lesson Review

Using Vocabulary
1. Define *chronic effect*.

Understanding Concepts
2. Describe the immediate and chronic effects of smoking. ★ 5.H; 5.I; 12.C
3. What are some early effects of using smokeless tobacco? ★ 5.H; 5.I; 12.C
4. How can ETS affect a person? ★ 5.H; 5.I; 6.A

Critical Thinking
5. **Making Inferences** If a teen smokes a cigarette at a friend's house after school, a parent who drives this teen home would probably smell smoke in the teen's hair and clothes. How could this incident strain the relationship between the parent and the teen? ★ 12.C

Lesson 3

Tobacco, Disease, and Death

What You'll Do

- **Describe** how cancer is related to tobacco use. ★ 5.H; 5.I
- **List** two respiratory diseases caused by tobacco. ★ 5.H; 5.I
- **Explain** how tobacco makes the heart work harder. ★ 5.H; 5.I

Terms to Learn

- cancer
- chronic bronchitis
- emphysema

Start Off Write

How can smoking lead to cancer?

Before Mandy's grandmother died of emphysema, she used oxygen tanks to breathe. Mandy knew that her grandmother used to smoke and this caused her emphysema.

Emphysema (EM fuh SEE muh) is a lung disease that can be caused by smoking. Tobacco use causes many kinds of diseases. Several of these diseases can lead to death. In the United States, about 400,000 deaths are caused by tobacco use each year.

Cancer

In 1964, the Surgeon General concluded that smoking can cause lung cancer. **Cancer** is a disease in which damaged cells grow out of control and destroy healthy tissue. These cells grow in lumps called *tumors*. All tobacco products contain cancer-causing chemicals. Smoking causes about 20 percent of all cancers.

Lung cancer causes more deaths than any other cancer does. Smoking and exposure to ETS are thought to cause 90 percent of all lung cancers. However, smokers and other tobacco users are also at risk for other kinds of cancer. Tobacco use can cause cancers of the mouth, throat, bladder, pancreas, and kidney.

The earlier people start using tobacco, the higher their risk of getting cancer and other tobacco-related diseases is. This risk increases with the length of time that tobacco is used and the amount used each day. However, the risk begins to drop as soon as a person quits. ★ 5.H; 5.I

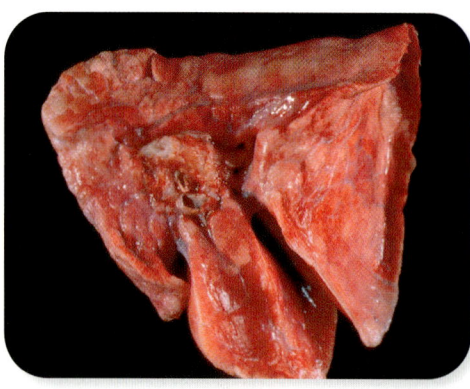
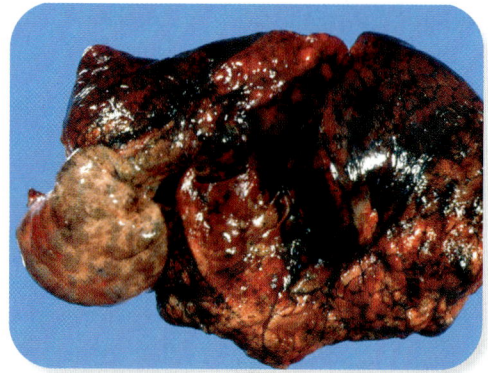

Figure 7 The lung on the left is from a nonsmoker. The lung on the right shows cancerous tissue due to smoking.

Figure 8 Tobacco companies are required to put warnings on all products.

Respiratory Disease

When people smoke tobacco, chemicals in the smoke touch the cells lining their airways and lungs. This can damage these cells and lead to respiratory diseases.

The two most common smoking-related respiratory diseases are chronic bronchitis (KRAHN ik brang KIET is) and emphysema. **Chronic bronchitis** is a disease in which the lining of the airways becomes very swollen and irritated. This irritation makes a person produce large amounts of mucus and cough a lot. Chronic bronchitis can make it hard for a person to breathe.

People with emphysema also have trouble breathing. **Emphysema** is a disease in which the tiny air sacs and walls of the lungs are destroyed. This damage is permanent—holes in the air sacs do not heal. Many people with emphysema depend on machines to help them breathe.

Cigarette smoke causes over 80 percent of all cases of chronic bronchitis and emphysema. Eventually, these diseases can lead to heart failure and death. The risk for these diseases increases with the number of cigarettes a person smokes each day and how long a person smokes. ★ 5.H; 5.I

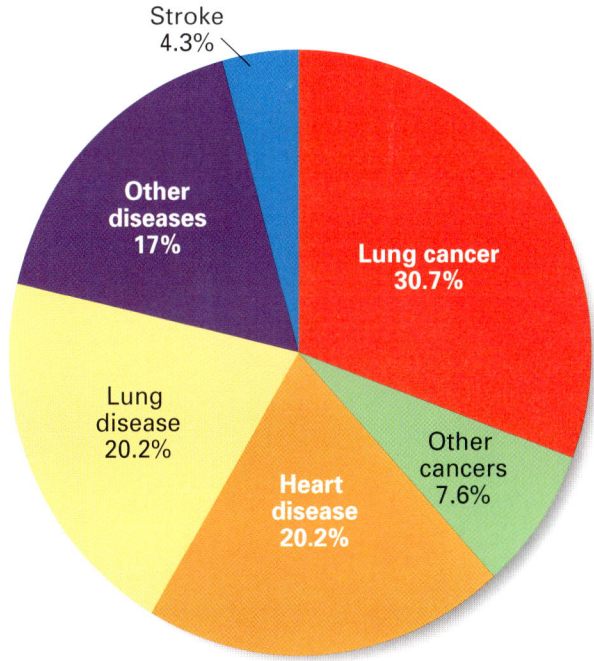

Causes of Smoking-Related Deaths

- Stroke 4.3%
- Other diseases 17%
- Lung cancer 30.7%
- Lung disease 20.2%
- Heart disease 20.2%
- Other cancers 7.6%

Source: Centers for Disease Control and Prevention.

Figure 9 About 51 percent of all smoking-related deaths are caused by lung diseases.

Lesson 3 Tobacco, Disease, and Death

Hands-on ACTIVITY

BLOOD VESSEL CONSTRICTION

1. Find two straws with diameters of different sizes.
2. Place each straw in a glass of water.
3. Blow into the first straw for 10 seconds.
4. Blow into the second straw for 10 seconds.

Analysis

1. Was one of the straws more difficult to blow into? If you think of the straws as blood vessels, which straw would represent a constricted blood vessel?
2. How does this experiment demonstrate how the heart must work harder when blood vessels are tighter?

Cardiovascular Diseases

Cardiovascular diseases are diseases of the circulatory system. These problems include heart disease, chronic high blood pressure, and stroke. Each year, smoking-related cardiovascular diseases cause about 150,000 deaths in the United States. This number includes about 30,000 nonsmokers who were exposed to ETS.

Smoking causes the heart to work harder. When chemicals from smoke enter the blood, they decrease the amount of oxygen that can enter the blood. With less oxygen in the blood, less oxygen flows through the body. To make up for this loss of oxygen, the heart must pump faster.

In addition, smoking constricts, or tightens, the blood vessels. This tightening makes it difficult for blood to flow and causes the heart to work even harder. The stress on the heart increases the risk of heart disease or heart attack.

Constricted blood vessels become even more dangerous when a person has a blood clot. A *blood clot* is a solid mass of blood particles that can form when the blood flow slows. If a clot cannot fit through a blood vessel, it will block the flow of blood. If a blood vessel that leads to the heart is blocked, a person may have a heart attack. If blood flow to the brain is blocked, a person may have a stroke. If blood flow to the arms or legs is blocked, a person may experience strong pain. In severe cases, body parts that do not get enough blood must be removed. ★ 5.H; 5.I

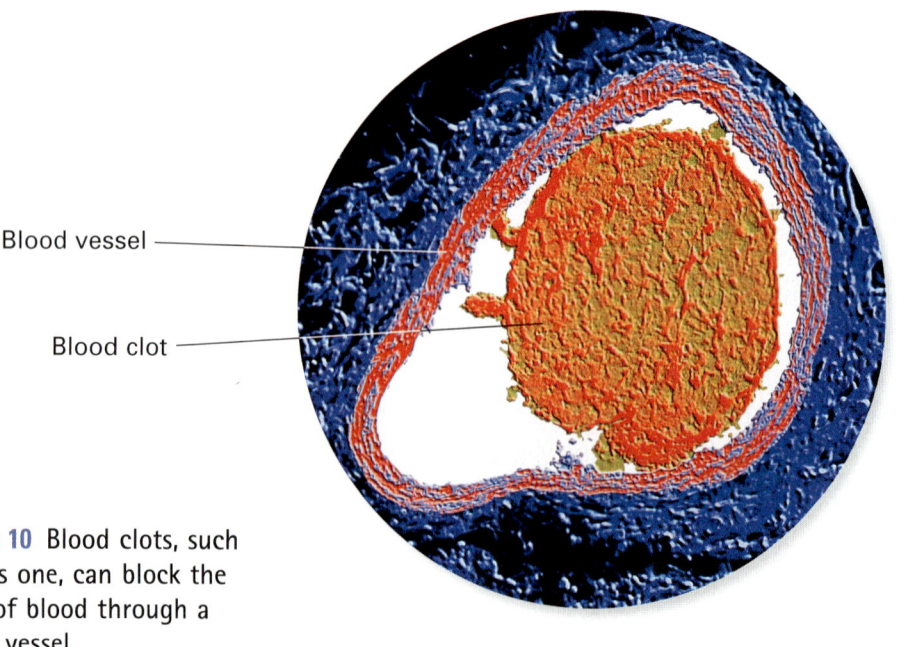

Figure 10 Blood clots, such as this one, can block the flow of blood through a blood vessel.

Other Health Problems Caused by Tobacco

Cancers and respiratory and cardiovascular diseases are not the only diseases caused by tobacco. Most tobacco products increase the risk of gum and dental diseases. Smoking during pregnancy can lead to pregnancy complications, such as premature birth. Smoking cigarettes can also cause several eye diseases. Some chemicals in tobacco products can lead to clouding of the lenses. Also, constricted blood vessels can reduce blood flow to the eyes, causing eye muscles to weaken.

Using tobacco also makes it easier for people to get sick and harder for them to recover. Smokers are more likely to get colds and the flu than nonsmokers are. And smokers with colds or the flu do not recover as quickly as nonsmokers do. This is because chemicals in tobacco products make it harder for the body to attack bacteria and viruses that enter the body. ★ 5.H; 5.I

STUDY TIP for better reading

Interpreting Graphics
Use the pie chart to determine what percentage of deaths are caused by alcohol, illegal drug use, and motor vehicles combined. Is this greater than or less than the percentage of deaths caused by tobacco?

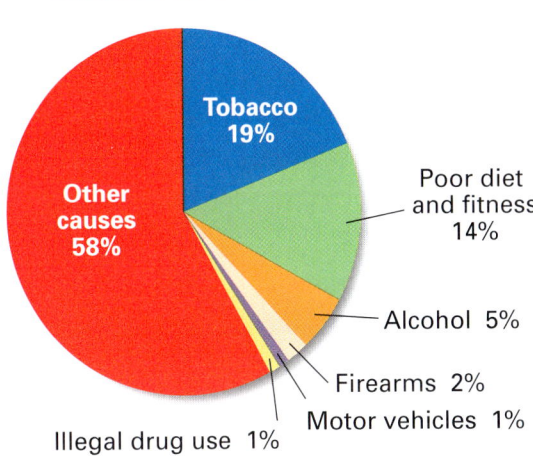

Causes of Death

Source: Journal of American Medical Association.

Figure 11 Tobacco use causes more than twice the number of deaths caused by alcohol, illegal drugs, motor vehicles, and firearms combined.

Lesson Review

Using Vocabulary
1. How are emphysema and chronic bronchitis similar? ★ 5.H; 5.I

Understanding Concepts
2. How is cancer related to tobacco use? ★ 5.H; 5.I
3. What are two respiratory diseases caused by smoking? ★ 5.H; 5.I

Critical Thinking
4. **Analyzing Ideas** Smoking can decrease the amount of oxygen in the blood. You learned that the heart tries to pump faster to make up for the lack of oxygen. Do you think a faster flow of blood would make up for the lack of oxygen? Why or why not?

internet connect
www.scilinks.org/health
Topic: Lung Cancer
HealthLinks code: HD4063
Topic: Smoking and Health
HealthLinks code: HD4090

HEALTH LINKS Maintained by the National Science Teachers Association

Lesson 4

What You'll Do

- **Explain** why nicotine is addictive. ★ 5.H
- **Explain** how someone can form a tolerance to nicotine. ★ 5.H
- **Describe** the different kinds of dependence. ★ 5.H; 5.I
- **Explain** how individual differences affect addiction. ★ 5.H; 5.I

Terms to Learn

- tolerance
- physical dependence
- drug addiction
- psychological dependence
- withdrawal

Start Off Write

How does nicotine affect people?

Tobacco and Addiction

Rob took a smoking break after every hour of doing homework. Gradually, he realized that he couldn't concentrate without taking smoking breaks. Why was it so hard to concentrate?

Rob had trouble concentrating because he was becoming addicted to cigarettes. Regular use of tobacco products leads to nicotine addiction.

Nicotine

All forms of tobacco contain the drug nicotine. Tiny molecules of nicotine enter the blood through tissues in the mouth and the lungs. These molecules reach the brain within seconds of using tobacco. Once in the brain, nicotine molecules attach to *receptors* on nerve cells. A receptor is a place on a cell where a specific molecule can attach. A molecule attaches to a receptor much like a key fits into a lock. When nicotine attaches to a receptor, the brain sends chemical messages through the body. These messages cause nicotine's effects, such as increased heart rate and increased blood pressure.

Nicotine is a very powerful drug. Only a small amount of nicotine is needed to produce an effect. Most people feel dizzy and nauseous and may even vomit when they first use tobacco. This happens because their bodies are not yet used to nicotine's effects. After the body becomes used to nicotine, the drug's effects are less obvious, but more dangerous. ★ 5.H

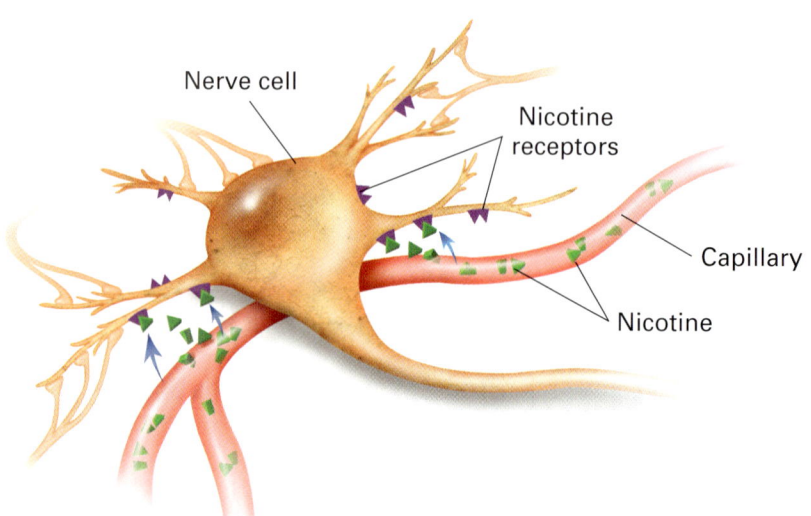

Figure 12 Nicotine in the blood attaches to nicotine receptors on nerve cells in the brain.

Figure 13 As tolerance increases, a smoker needs nicotine just to feel normal.

Tolerance and Dependence

The more a person uses a drug, the less effect the drug has. Experienced tobacco users rarely feel dizzy from tobacco because their bodies are used to nicotine. The process of the body getting used to a drug is called **tolerance.** People with tolerance to nicotine need more tobacco in order to feel its effects. This is why most smokers slowly increase how often they smoke.

Tolerance occurs as the body adapts to the effects of drugs. The brain physically changes by forming more receptors for nicotine. These extra receptors prevent the original amount of nicotine from causing effects such as increased heart rate. Only with more nicotine attaching to the new receptors can these effects occur. When people increase the amount of tobacco they use, nicotine's effects return.

Once nicotine has caused a person's brain to change, that person is dependent. **Physical dependence** is a state in which the body needs a drug to function normally. People who are physically dependent experience fewer effects from tobacco. In fact, these people have to use tobacco just to feel normal. Physical dependence develops quickly in most tobacco users. It is a sign that they are addicted to nicotine. **Drug addiction** is the inability to control one's use of a drug. ★ 5.H; 5.I

Myth & Fact

Myth: Uncomfortable symptoms occur only when a person quits using tobacco.

Fact: Uncomfortable symptoms begin to occur if a person goes longer than usual without using a tobacco product. One reason that a person continues using tobacco is to avoid the discomfort.

Psychological Dependence

Drug addiction affects the mind as well as the body. Some people use tobacco so often that they think that they need it to feel energetic or relaxed. They may get so much pleasure from tobacco that they even enjoy holding and lighting cigarettes. These people have a mental need for tobacco. **Psychological dependence** is a state in which you think that you need a drug in order to function. Psychological and physical dependence are both parts of drug addiction. 5.H; 5.I

Withdrawal

When tobacco users are dependent on nicotine, they feel uncomfortable without tobacco. At first, they may get edgy and feel a desire for tobacco. If they don't use tobacco, they will have withdrawal. **Withdrawal** is the way in which the body responds when a dependent person stops using a drug. Withdrawal from nicotine can cause people to feel anxious, irritable, and tired. It can also cause headaches and poor concentration. Once people build up a tolerance, they may use tobacco to avoid withdrawal. 5.H; 5.I

MATH ACTIVITY

Suppose that the time it takes a man to answer a math problem is increased by 0.45 seconds when he quits smoking. In 1 week, withdrawal has decreased and it takes him 1.1 seconds to answer a math problem. If he got 0.2 seconds faster during this week, how long did it take him to answer a math problem before he quit smoking? M8.5.A

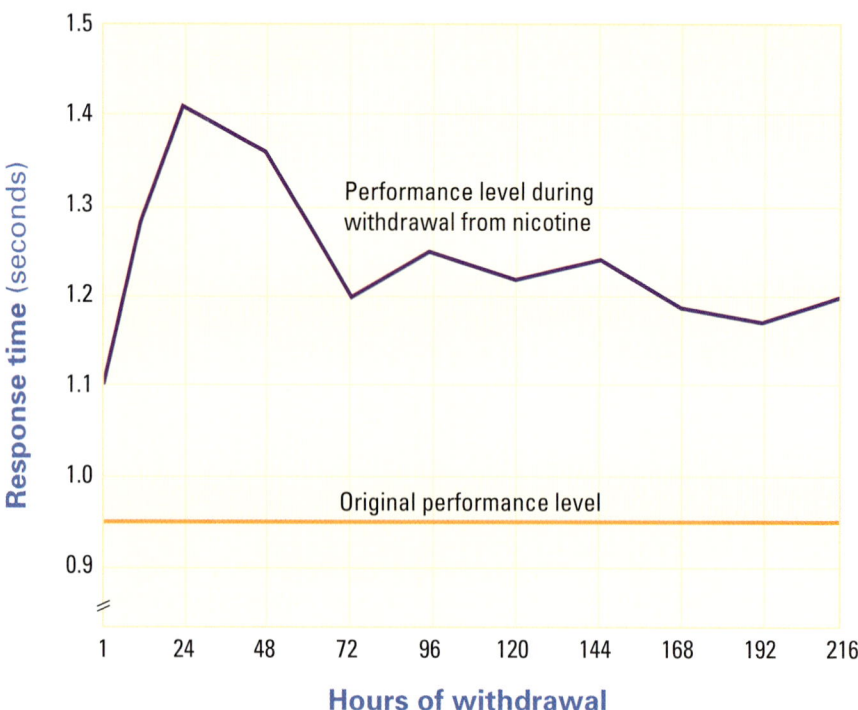

Figure 14 This graph shows withdrawal's effect on response time for solving math problems. Eventually, the reaction time returns to normal.

Source: *Handbook of Neurotoxicology.*

Figure 15 Individual differences make quitting different for every person.

Different Responses to Tobacco

No two people are exactly alike, and no two people are affected by tobacco in exactly the same way. Some people become addicted to nicotine after a short period of smoking. Others try one cigarette and never smoke again. And while some people can quit using tobacco on the first try, others can't quit even after getting emphysema.

Social factors and family history may influence the way in which different people respond to tobacco. Some people grow up in places where smoking is acceptable. Others are born with a brain chemistry that makes nicotine more enjoyable. Scientists are trying to understand the reasons behind such differences. Understanding these reasons may make treating addiction easier.
★ 5.H; 5.I

Lesson Review

Using Vocabulary

1. What is the difference between physical and psychological dependence? ★ 5.H; 5.I

2. Use the word *nicotine* in a sentence about addiction. ★ 5.H; 5.I

Understanding Concepts

3. What are the steps to forming an addiction to tobacco products?
★ 5.H; 5.K

4. Why is it easier for some people to become addicted? ★ 5.H; 5.I

Critical Thinking

5. **Making Predictions** The first time a person tries a cigarette, that person will probably feel sick. What do you think would happen to a person who regularly smokes but then tries chewing tobacco? Would the person feel sick? Why or why not?
★ 5.H; 5.I

internet connect

www.scilinks.org/health
Topic: Nicotine
HealthLinks code: HD4069
Topic: Drug Addiction
HealthLinks code: HD4028

HEALTH LINKS Maintained by the National Science Teachers Association

Lesson 4 Tobacco and Addiction

Lesson 5

Quitting

Nick's father had tried to quit smoking many times, but he always started again as soon as a problem came up at work or at home. Why was quitting so hard?

What You'll Do

- **Explain** why quitting a tobacco habit is so difficult. ★ 5.H
- **Describe** strategies for quitting a tobacco habit. ★ 5.J
- **Explain** how tobacco-free nicotine products help people quit smoking. ★ 5.J

Terms to Learn

- relapse
- cessation
- nicotine replacement therapy (NRT)

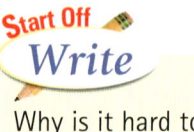

Start Off Write

Why is it hard to quit using tobacco?

Nick's father may start smoking when problems come up because he thinks smoking helps him relax. Quitting a tobacco addiction is very difficult. But there are several ways to quit, and people can keep trying until they are successful.

Quitting Isn't Easy

Each year, nearly 20 million people in the United States try to quit smoking. But only 3 percent have long-term success. Unfortunately, most people who try to quit relapse within a few months. To **relapse** is to begin using a drug again after stopping for awhile. People often relapse when trying to quit an addiction to tobacco.

Why is quitting so tough? Quitting is difficult because physical and psychological dependence and the discomfort of withdrawal make nicotine very addictive. Nicotine changes the brain to make a person want more nicotine. It is hard to quit using an addictive drug—even when people know that the drug makes them sick. Some researchers think that nicotine is one of the hardest drugs to stop using.

It is easier for a person who has used tobacco for a short time to quit than for a person who has used tobacco a long time. Over time, the body changes more and more, making it even more difficult to quit a tobacco habit.
★ 5.H; 5.I; 12.C

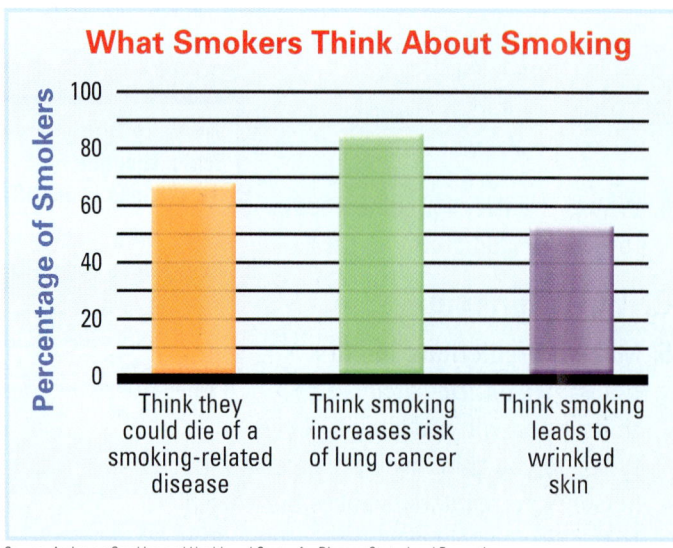

Figure 16 Quitting is hard even for smokers who realize that smoking is dangerous.

Source: Action on Smoking and Health and Center for Disease Control and Prevention.

352 | Chapter 14 Tobacco

Figure 17 Spending time with people who don't use tobacco can make quitting a tobacco addiction easier.

Planning

Making a serious attempt to quit using tobacco takes thought, commitment, and planning. There are many different ways to quit. A method that works for some people may not work for others. Just as there are individual differences in a person's response to tobacco, there are differences in a person's ability to quit.

Choosing the right method can make quitting easier. Some people can quit by deciding to suddenly and completely stop. This method is called quitting "cold turkey." However, most people need help from doctors, health professionals, or cessation (se SAY shuhn) counselors. Cessation is the act of stopping something entirely and permanently. Some tobacco users may prefer to join a support group of other people who are also trying to quit. Such groups may meet regularly with a counselor. However, an informal group of friends can also be effective.

Most people need to make changes in order to avoid situations that tempt them to use tobacco. If people are used to smoking when drinking coffee, they could drink tea or juice instead. If people are used to chewing tobacco with friends, they could ask friends not to chew tobacco near them. People who want to quit need to plan ways to avoid temptations. ★ 5.J; 12.C

LIFE SKILLS ACTIVITY

MAKING GOOD DECISIONS

Write a short story about a person who smoked cigarettes for many years. Describe how this person realizes the need to quit smoking. Then describe how difficult it is to quit. The person may try several different methods before finding a plan that works. Perhaps this person finds that quitting with friends who want to end their tobacco habit is a helpful way to quit. Or the person may find that avoiding places where people smoke is the most helpful way to quit. End your story with a brief description of the benefits that quitting brings to this person's life.

Using Medicines

Several kinds of medicine can help people quit using tobacco. Some of these medicines can be bought at a store, but others can be taken only with a doctor's prescription. Research has shown that people who use both medicine and counseling have the most success quitting.

One of the hardest parts of quitting a tobacco habit is withdrawal from nicotine. Some medicines can reduce the discomfort of withdrawal. **Nicotine replacement therapy (NRT)** is a form of medicine that contains safe amounts of nicotine. NRT replaces some of the nicotine that people used to get from tobacco products. These small amounts of nicotine reduce withdrawal discomfort so that quitting is easier. Nicotine gum and patches are the most common forms of NRT. Over several weeks, people reduce their use until they no longer need NRT. This method helps the body slowly get used to functioning without tobacco products.

All medicines used to help with cessation of tobacco use are tested for safety before they can be sold. However, they are drugs, and they can be dangerous if they are not used correctly. Also, most tests on these medicines have studied adults who want to quit using tobacco. It is important for anyone—especially children and teens—to talk to a doctor before using these medicines.

★ 5.J; 12.C

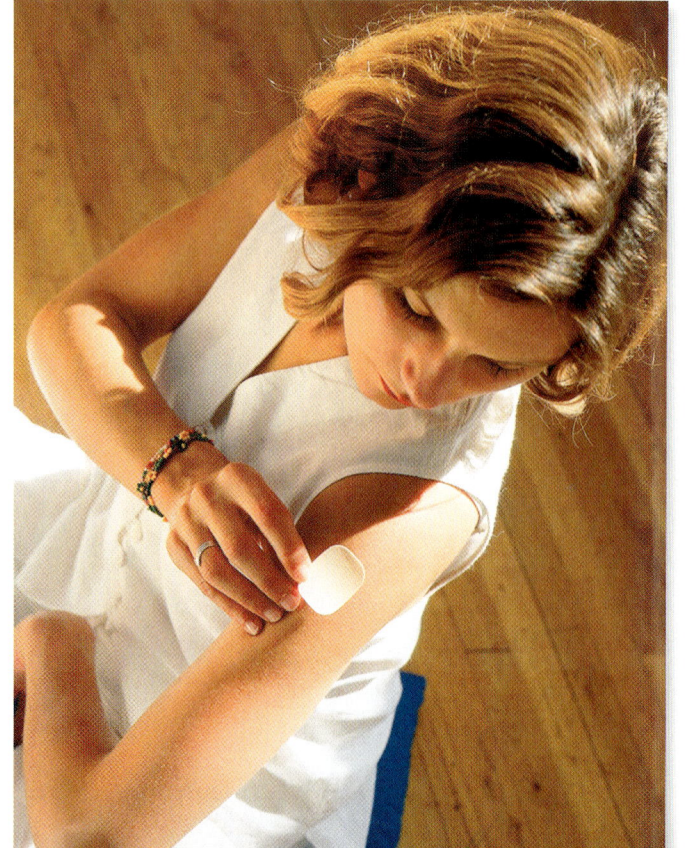

Figure 18 NRTs are drugs developed to help people quit using tobacco.

Why Quit?

It is never too early or too late to quit using tobacco. Quitting at any age reduces the risk of getting diseases caused by tobacco. Quitting once a disease has developed keeps the problem from getting worse. However, the benefits of quitting are greater the earlier that a person stops.

Positive changes in health begin immediately after a person quits using tobacco. Just one day after quitting, the level of carbon monoxide in a smoker's body can return to normal. The body's ability to recover from illness and resist infection increases immediately. After quitting, people catch fewer colds. People also recover faster when they become sick. Even mouth sores from chewing tobacco can heal if the user quits before they become cancerous.

Quitting also helps people who live with tobacco users. Getting rid of ETS reduces the risk of disease for nonsmokers. People who love and care about the tobacco user can stop worrying about that person's health. People report feeling better about life in general once they have quit using tobacco. After a while, people who quit notice the independence of being free from the addictive need for a drug. Quitting a tobacco habit is one of the most beneficial things a person can do for his or her health and life.

★ 4.C; 12.C; 12.F

Figure 19 As soon as a person quits using tobacco, his or her body begins to recover.

Lesson Review

Using Vocabulary

1. What is nicotine replacement therapy? ★ 5.J

2. Define *cessation* in your own words.

Understanding Concepts

3. Why is quitting tobacco difficult once you are addicted? ★ 5.H; 5.I

4. Describe different methods of quitting smoking. ★ 5.J

Critical Thinking

5. **Applying Concepts** If NRTs contain the drug nicotine, how can they help people quit an addiction to nicotine? ★ 5.J

6. **Making Inferences** If a smoker quits using cigarettes, what positive changes may he or she notice immediately? in a week? ★ 5.H; 5.I

Lesson 6

Why People Use Tobacco

What You'll Do

- **Describe** how peers can influence tobacco use. ★ 7.A; 12.E
- **Explain** how family and role models can influence people to use tobacco. ★ 7.A
- **Discuss** how advertising can influence tobacco use. ★ 8.A

Terms to Learn

- peer pressure
- modeling

Start Off Write

How can peer pressure help a person avoid tobacco?

Iris was pleased that her friend Zoey spoke up so strongly about not wanting to smoke a bidi. After Zoey refused the tobacco, Iris had a much easier time refusing it, too.

Even though Iris did not want to smoke, she felt pressured to try it until Zoey spoke up. Pressure to try tobacco can come from many places. Being aware of these pressures can help you avoid their influence.

Why Would Anyone Ever Start?

Why would anyone begin a habit that causes nausea and dizziness at first and can lead to serious diseases or even death? Some people enjoy the relaxed or energetic feelings caused by nicotine. But many different pressures can influence people to try tobacco. Teens often feel the most pressure from peers. Your *peers* are friends and other people who are the same age as you. **Peer pressure** is a strong influence from a friend or a classmate.

Peer pressure often influences a person's ideas about tobacco. Just seeing other teens smoking can make cigarettes seem tempting. Using tobacco may seem like an easy way to make friends or to act like an adult. Sadly, teens who try tobacco do not always understand that they are at risk for addiction and disease. ★ 7.A; 12.E

Do Smokers Have More Friends Than Nonsmokers Do?

Smokers think . . .

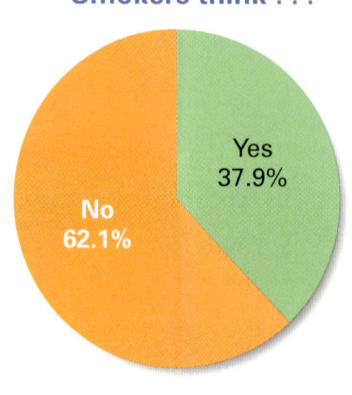

Nonsmokers think . . .

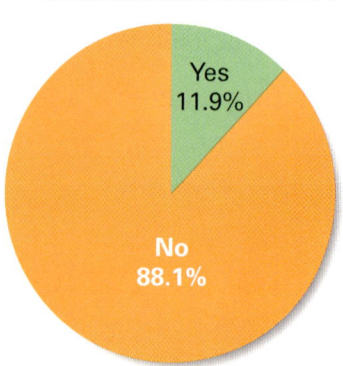

Figure 20 Though some people who smoke think that smokers have more friends than nonsmokers do, most nonsmokers disagree.

Source: Center for Disease Control and Prevention.

356 Chapter 14 Tobacco

Figure 21 Children of smokers are two times more likely to smoke than children of nonsmokers are.

Family and Role Models

Peers are not the only source of pressure to try tobacco. Watching someone who you admire use tobacco can strongly influence your beliefs about tobacco. Actors who use tobacco in movies or on TV can make tobacco seem appealing. Some tobacco companies pay for actors to use their products in movies. These companies know that some people may buy that brand of tobacco if they think a favorite actor uses it.

Family members may also influence teens to try tobacco, even if they don't intend to. Seeing parents or siblings smoke may cause a young person to think that smoking is safe. Children often base their behavior on what they see around them. Basing your behavior on how others act is called **modeling.** Research has shown that children of parents who smoke are more likely to become smokers than children of nonsmokers are.

However, pressure from family members can work in the opposite direction, too. Parents who do not use tobacco are a positive influence. Also, watching a loved one become ill or die from a tobacco-related disease is very difficult and painful. This experience can pressure a person to never try tobacco. ★ 7.A

LANGUAGE ARTS ACTIVITY

Have you ever seen a movie or a TV show in which a character smoked or used chewing tobacco? Write a paragraph about whether that character made the tobacco seem safe or appealing. Or, invent a character, and write a brief story about that person using tobacco in a way that makes it seem dangerous and unappealing.

Lesson 6 Why People Use Tobacco

Figure 22 Advertising can be used to promote tobacco products, but it can also send antismoking messages.

ASSESSING YOUR HEALTH

Do you feel tempted to try tobacco, or have you already tried it? If so, write yourself a letter weighing the pros and cons of using tobacco. If you are not tempted, write yourself a letter outlining all of the reasons you do not want to use tobacco.

Advertising and Tobacco Promotion

Even people who have never tried a cigarette can usually name the most popular brands of tobacco. Tobacco companies spend large amounts of money each year to advertise and promote their products. *Promotion* is making a product seem wonderful by hosting games or concerts, giving out free products, or setting up displays in stores. In 1999, $8.24 billion was spent promoting tobacco. In other words, these companies spent nearly $1 million an hour!

People in tobacco ads often look young, attractive, healthy, and fit. Ads often show beautiful scenes, such as beaches and mountains, where people enjoy nature. These images are not at all related to the health problems caused by tobacco products.

Some brands of tobacco are designed to attract different groups of people. Some products are aimed at men, women, or young people. Teens are more likely to use specific brands of tobacco. If teens recognize a particular brand, they will be more likely to try that brand if they decide to smoke.

Because of lawsuits against tobacco companies, there are now more restrictions against designing tobacco products for teens. Several efforts have been made to advertise the dangers of tobacco use. Since 1966, all tobacco packaging has been required to show a warning from the Surgeon General. This label warns people about specific dangers of tobacco. Recently, anti-tobacco groups have advertised the dangers of tobacco products on billboards and TV. These advertisements encourage teens to avoid tobacco. ★ 8.A; 8.B

Internal Pressures

Sometimes the strongest pressures to use tobacco come from our own thoughts. Some people like to take risks. Others are rebellious or curious. Certain people may have trouble facing peer pressure. Even boredom can tempt some people to try tobacco. Whatever the reason, trying tobacco is not worth the risks. Smoking is dangerous. Satisfying curiosity, rebellious feelings, or boredom in another way can save a person's life.

People who have emotional problems can be easily tempted to try tobacco. Tobacco may give them a false sense of control. However, addictive drugs do not help solve emotional problems. Drugs can even make some problems worse by causing health or social problems. Getting help from counselors, friends, and others is a much better way to cope with problems. ★ 5.I; 12.C

Most People Don't Use Tobacco!

Remembering that most people do not use tobacco can help you resist pressure to try tobacco. Although many people die from smoking-related diseases in the United States every day, most Americans do not smoke. Tobacco users and advertisements can make smoking seem popular. But about 75 percent of the people in the United States do not use tobacco. The number of young people who use tobacco has been declining since the late 1990s. More and more people are deciding not to use tobacco.

Figure 23 Satisfying your curiosity about smoking is not worth the health risks of using tobacco.

Lesson Review

Using Vocabulary

1. Define *peer pressure*. ★ 7.A; 12.E

Understanding Concepts

2. How can peers pressure teens to try tobacco? ★ 7.A; 12.E

3. How can family members influence teens' ideas about tobacco? ★ 7.A

4. How can advertising influence teens' ideas about tobacco? ★ 8.A

Critical Thinking

5. **Applying Concepts** Why do some tobacco companies promote products by hosting sporting events or concerts? How could these events pressure people to use tobacco? ★ 8.A; 8.B; 12.E

6. **Analyzing Ideas** Why do you think that the number of young people who use tobacco has been declining since the late 1990s?

Lesson 7 — Being Tobacco Free

What You'll Do

- **Describe** four ways to refuse tobacco products. ★ 5.J; 11.B
- **Explain** how positive peer pressure can help you resist tobacco. ★ 10.A; 12.E
- **Describe** how to have a tobacco-free social life. ★ 5.J; 7.A

Start Off Write

Why is it healthy to avoid places where tobacco is used?

Jon is angry with his friend Sonesh. Sonesh laughed at Jon for saying, "No, thanks," when the snuff was passed around.

In a case like Jon's, leaving may be the best way to get out of an uncomfortable situation. However, there are many different ways to reject tobacco and feel good about your choice.

Rejecting an Offer

Most teens will be offered tobacco at some point in their lives. Planning for that experience ahead of time can help build confidence. Planning can also make saying no to tobacco less stressful. Teens who practice refusing tobacco are less likely to start using tobacco. Being prepared makes a difference.

You never need to give a reason for not wanting to smoke or chew tobacco. Simply saying, "No" or "No, thanks," is enough to make your opinion known. If someone asks why you are refusing, you can simply reply, "Because I don't want to." You might feel more comfortable by explaining, "No, thanks. My parents would kill me." But you don't owe anyone an explanation.

Other ways to make yourself more comfortable include making a joke or changing the subject. A joke is a healthy way to get out of an uncomfortable situation. And changing the subject can prevent someone from repeating the offer.

People who pressure others are often unsure about their own decisions. You may be able to influence someone by suggesting a different activity. Responding to an offer by saying, "Cigarettes are gross—let's just go get a soda," could sound like fun to the person offering tobacco. However, if people cannot accept your refusal, you can leave. ★ 5.J; 11.B

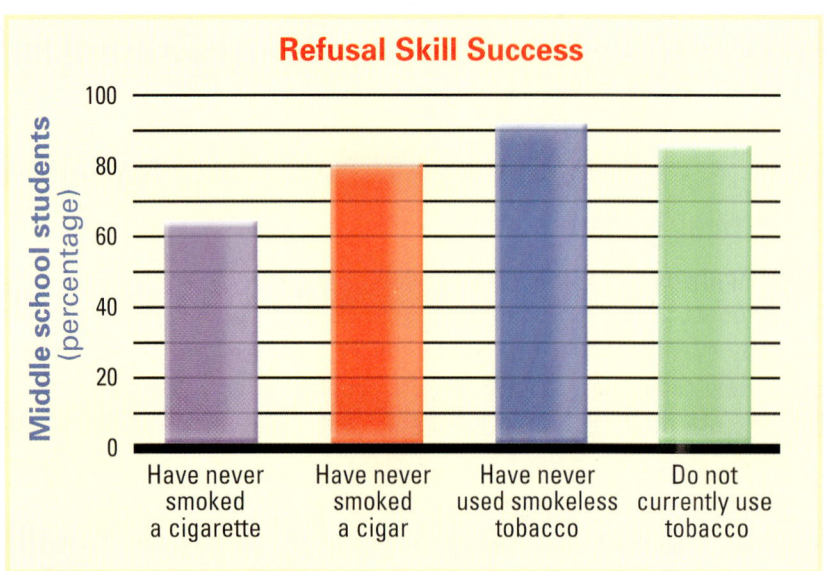

Figure 24 Most teens your age do not use tobacco in any form.

Source: Center for Disease Control and Prevention.

360 | Chapter 14 Tobacco

Figure 25 Resisting smoking is easier when you are in a smoke-free environment.

Avoiding Tobacco Environments

One of the best ways to resist trying tobacco is to avoid places where it is used. Situations that make tobacco use seem acceptable are risky. Also, you are more likely to be offered tobacco when you are with many tobacco users. People who spend less time in tobacco environments are less likely to try tobacco. Avoiding environments where tobacco is used also helps tobacco users use less tobacco.

People who have quit using tobacco can be tempted to relapse if they are surrounded by tobacco use. This temptation is especially strong if a person quit very recently. Smelling tobacco smoke and seeing people smoke tobacco can cause cravings in ex-smokers. Being around tobacco smoke can even cause withdrawal symptoms in these people. Similarly, seeing people use smokeless tobacco can tempt someone to slip back into a smokeless tobacco addiction. Avoiding environments where tobacco is used can help people escape the temptation to start using tobacco again.

Staying away from tobacco environments is important for your health even if you aren't tempted to smoke. These places contain ETS, which is harmful for everyone. Avoiding places where tobacco is used is especially important for people who have asthma, allergies, or other respiratory problems.

Often, you can predict where and when tobacco will be present. But sometimes you cannot predict this. And sometimes, avoiding tobacco environments is impossible—especially if a family member uses tobacco. In these cases, you can leave the area when a cigarette is lit. You can also ask the person to use tobacco outside. ★ 5.J; 11.B

Health Journal

Can you think of a time when you used refusal skills to let someone know that you did not want to do something? The situation could be about anything, even telling someone you didn't want to eat brussel sprouts. In your Health Journal, write a paragraph about how you communicated your refusal. Did you use the strategies mentioned in this lesson?

LIFE SKILLS ACTIVITY

USING REFUSAL SKILLS

Act as a positive role model by writing a letter to a younger friend or family member. Tell the person why using tobacco is dangerous and offer him or her some advice on how to avoid tobacco. You may want to give specific examples of tobacco-related diseases. You could also give specific examples of what he or she could say to refuse tobacco.

Teen: How can I keep my younger sister from smoking?

Expert: When you decide not to smoke, you will set a great example for your younger sister. You can also talk with her about the physical and social health problems caused by smoking.

Setting an Example

Tobacco users aren't the only people who have the power to influence others. By choosing not to chew or smoke tobacco, you can be a positive influence. You can set an example for people who are unsure about whether they want to try tobacco. Being strong enough to refuse tobacco is impressive. Friends will respect a person who is willing to set a strong example. Your actions could even influence younger brothers or sisters who look up to your decisions.

You may want to look at other people who have chosen to be tobacco free as examples for your own decisions. Their actions and support could make refusing drugs easier for you.

Friends who don't use tobacco can pressure you with a helpful kind of peer pressure. *Positive peer pressure* is an influence from friends that helps you do the right thing. You and your friends can use this pressure to help each other stay tobacco free.
★ 5.J; 12.E

Figure 26 Student groups that speak out against tobacco use can be a source of positive peer pressure.

Figure 27 Joining an after-school activity can be a fun and tobacco-free way to make friends.

Tobacco-Free Social Health

Being tobacco free leads to a healthy social life as well as strong physical health. Friendships based only on tobacco are not as strong as friendships with people who share your interests. And friends who do not smoke may find being around you easier if you do not smoke.

Relationships with family and other adults may also improve when a person does not use tobacco. Without secrets or guilt to deal with, parents and other adults can be a source of support and friendship. And when teens make healthy decisions about tobacco, their parents may trust them to make other good decisions.

Good physical and social health can lead to good emotional health. Strong relationships with friends and family are a major part of being emotionally healthy. Deciding to be tobacco free is a step toward complete health. ★ 7.A; 9.B; 12.E

Lesson Review

Understanding Concepts

1. Describe four ways to refuse tobacco products if they are offered to you. ★ 5.J; 11.B
2. How can positive peer pressure help you refuse tobacco? ★ 10.A; 12.E
3. How can being tobacco free improve your social health? ★ 5.J; 7.A; 9.B

Critical Thinking

4. **Using Refusal Skills** Imagine that your friend Beth quit smoking a few months ago. The two of you go to a party where half of the people are smoking and the room is full of smoke. Beth says that she is tempted to have a cigarette. What can you do to help her resist this temptation? ★ 5.J; 12.E

Lesson 7 Being Tobacco Free

14 CHAPTER REVIEW

Chapter Summary

■ Tobacco products contain hundreds of chemicals. ■ The effects of tobacco products begin immediately. ■ Smoking is harmful to nonsmokers who breathe environmental tobacco smoke. ■ Cancer and respiratory and cardiovascular diseases can be caused by tobacco use. These diseases can lead to death. ■ Nicotine is addictive. People can become dependent on nicotine and can experience withdrawal if they stop using tobacco. ■ Quitting a tobacco habit is difficult. There are many methods of quitting. ■ Peer pressure, family, and advertising can influence people to use tobacco. ■ Using tobacco can create social and legal problems for teens. ■ Teens can refuse tobacco and be tobacco free.

Using Vocabulary

For each pair of terms, describe how the meanings of the terms differ.

1. tolerance/withdrawal
2. physical dependence/psychological dependence

For each sentence, fill in the blank with the proper word from the word bank provided below.

carbon monoxide	modeling
chronic bronchitis	NRT
chronic effects	peer pressure
emphysema	tobacco

3. ___ and ___ are the two most common respiratory diseases caused by smoking.
4. ___ is positive when it helps teens make good, healthy decisions.
5. People can use ___ to help them quit a tobacco habit by reducing withdrawal.
6. When harmful effects of smoking do not go away, they are ___.
7. ___ is a gas found in cigarette smoke.

Understanding Concepts

8. How does nicotine from smokeless tobacco enter the bloodstream? ★ 5.H; 5.I
9. How do positive peer pressure and negative peer pressure differ? ★ 10.A
10. Name different kinds of cancer that can be caused by tobacco use. ★ 5.H; 5.I
11. Why does using tobacco make the heart work harder? ★ 5.H; 5.I
12. What makes nicotine addictive? How does tolerance to nicotine develop? ★ 5.H; 5.I
13. What is it so hard to quit using tobacco? ★ 5.H; 5.I
14. Why do people not know the exact ingredients contained in tobacco products?
15. How can family members help each other refuse tobacco products? ★ 5.J; 7.A; 9.A; 9.B
16. How could advertising teach teens about tobacco's dangers? ★ 8.A; 12.E
17. Why do people usually feel sick and dizzy when first trying tobacco products? ★ 5.H; 5.I

Critical Thinking

Applying Concepts

18. Andy wants to try smoking but plans to quit before experiencing any dangerous effects. What can you tell Andy about immediate and chronic effects of smoking that will help him make a good decision? ★ 4.C; 5.H; 5.I

19. Jane has been smoking a pack of cigarettes a day for several years until one day, she finally decides that it's time to quit. A few hours into her first smoke-free morning, she begins to feel edgy, nervous, and irritable and has a terrible headache. Why is Jane feeling this way? ★ 5.H; 5.I

20. Tom and Matt both smoke. Tom wants to quit because he notices an effect on his ability to swim on the school's team. They decide to quit together. Matt quits quickly and never smokes again. Tom takes weeks to stop and relapses twice over the next year. Why did they have such different experiences with quitting? ★ 5.H; 5.I

21. Lucy's parents were heavy smokers, but Lucy never used tobacco products. However, she recently noticed that she has a persistent cough and her asthma has gotten worse. What may have caused these problems? ★ 5.H; 5.I; 6.A

Making Good Decisions

22. Sarah's family just moved, and Sarah has been eager to make friends in her new school. The first group of girls that Sarah spoke to invited her to meet them after school so that they could smoke cigarettes and chat. Sarah doesn't want to smoke. What should Sarah do? ★ 5.J; 11.B; 11.D

23. Imagine that you are at a party in a room full of smoke. A friend asks you if you'd like a cigarette. When you say, "No, thanks," he laughs and says that you're already breathing the smoke from the air around you, so you're practically smoking. Is he right? How can you refuse to let tobacco damage your health? ★ 5.H; 5.I; 6.A; 6.B; 11.B

Interpreting Graphics

Use the figure above to answer questions 24–26.

24. Who is this ad trying to reach?
25. Why do you think a company would make an ad like this to advertise something like a cigarette?
26. Why is this ad misleading?

Reading Checkup

Take a minute to review your answers to the Health IQ questions at the beginning of this chapter. How has reading this chapter improved your Health IQ?

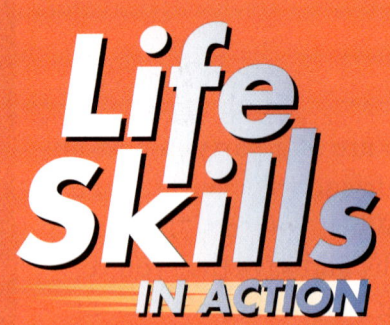

Life Skills IN ACTION

Using Refusal Skills

Using refusal skills is saying no to things you don't want to do. You can also use refusal skills to avoid dangerous situations. Complete the following activity to develop your refusal skills.

Josh's Tobacco Troubles

Setting the Scene

Josh goes to the park to meet his friend Kendal. When he arrives at the park, Kendal introduces Josh to his older cousin Brian. Brian is visiting from out of town. As the three of them are talking, Brian takes out a pack of cigarettes and offers Josh and Kendal a cigarette. Josh doesn't smoke, and he knows that Kendal doesn't either. However, Josh is surprised when Kendal takes a cigarette.

The 5 Steps of Using Refusal Skills

1. Avoid dangerous situations.
2. Say "No."
3. Stand your ground.
4. Stay focused on the issue.
5. Walk away.

Guided Practice

Practice with a Friend

Form a group of four. Have one person play the role of Josh, another person play the role of Kendal, and a third person play the role of Brian. The fourth person should be an observer. Walking through each of the five steps of using refusal skills, role-play what Josh should say to Kendal and Brian. Kendal and Brian should try to convince Josh to smoke. The observer will take notes, which will include observations about what the person playing Josh did well and suggestions of ways to improve. Stop after each step to evaluate the process. ★ 10.E; 11.A; 11.D; 12.D; 12.E

Independent Practice

Check Yourself

After you have completed the guided practice, go through Act 1 again without stopping at each step. Answer the questions below to review what you did.

1. Which refusal skill was the easiest to use? Explain.
2. Which refusal skill was the most effective in this situation? Explain.
3. Is using refusal skills with a stranger easier than it is with a friend? Explain.
4. Why is it important to know how to use more than one refusal skill?

On Your Own

A week after the meeting in the park, Josh is home alone. Kendal stops by to talk to Josh. Josh tells Kendal that he was disappointed in Kendal for smoking. Kendal tells Josh that it was not a big deal but that he thinks Josh should try smoking at least once. Kendal says that everyone experiments with cigarettes. Think about what you would say to Kendal if you were Josh. Write a skit about the conversation between Josh and Kendal that concentrates on Josh's use of refusal skills.

⭐ 11.A; 11.D; 12.E

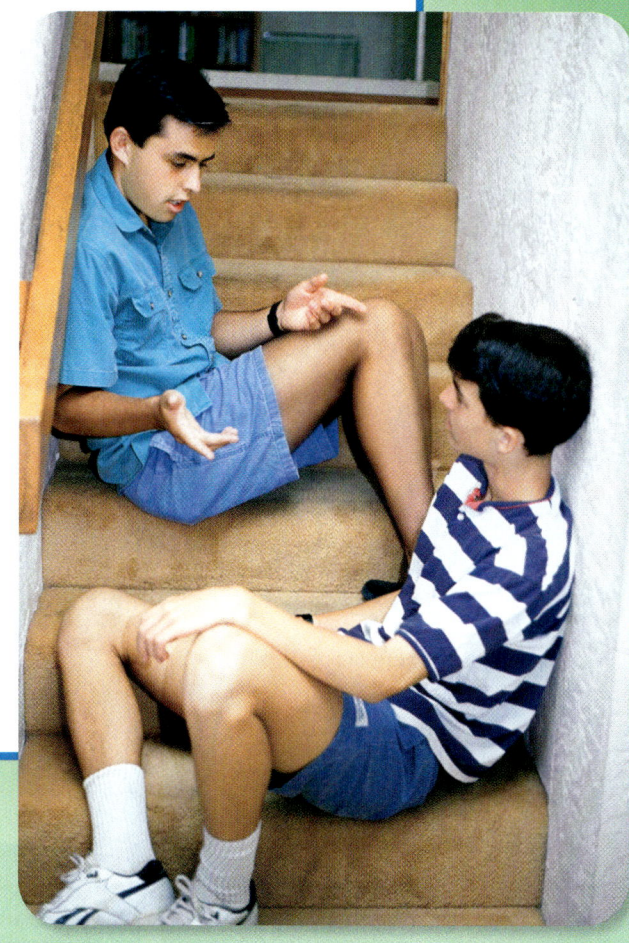

CHAPTER 15
Alcohol

Lessons

1. Alcohol and Your Body — 370
2. Immediate Effects of Alcohol — 374
3. Long-Term Effects of Alcohol — 376
4. Alcohol and Decision Making — 378
5. Alcohol, Driving, and Injuries — 380
6. Pressure to Drink — 382
7. Deciding Not to Drink — 384
8. Alcoholism — 386

Chapter Review — 390
Life Skills in Action — 392

Check out **Current Health** articles related to this chapter by visiting **go.hrw.com.** Just type in the keyword **HD4CH47**.

"I am worried about my friend Michael. Recently, he has been sneaking bottles of beer out of his parents' refrigerator. At first it seemed like a joke, but now it seems to be a habit."

PRE-READING

Answer the following multiple-choice questions to find out what you already know about alcohol. When you've finished this chapter, you'll have the opportunity to change your answers based on what you've learned.

1. Your central nervous system includes your
   a. arms and legs.
   b. stomach and urinary tract.
   c. brain and spinal cord.
   d. digestive and reproductive systems.

2. Which is NOT an effect of drinking alcohol?
   a. relaxed, clear thinking
   b. loss of coordination
   c. poor concentration
   d. blurred vision   5.H

3. The human brain is usually fully mature by
   a. birth.
   b. early childhood.
   c. puberty.
   d. adulthood.

4. How much alcohol can a teen drink and still legally drive?
   a. one beer
   b. two beers
   c. one glass of wine
   d. none   5.L

5. The degree of alcohol intoxication is accurately measured by
   a. the amount of alcohol in the beverages you've drunk.
   b. the percentage of alcohol in your blood.
   c. the number of hours you've been drinking.
   d. the number of drinks you've had in one sitting.

6. Which of the following statements about alcoholism is NOT true?
   a. It is curable.
   b. It is treatable.
   c. It is a disease.
   d. It is lifelong.   5.H

ANSWERS: 1. c; 2. a; 3. d; 4. d; 5. b; 6. a

Lesson 1

Alcohol and Your Body

Marta and her friends are writing a play about how alcohol affects a person's life. Marta knows that drinking alcohol can make you sick but isn't sure how it does.

What You'll Do

- **Describe** how the body processes alcohol. ★ 5.H; 5.I
- **Explain** blood alcohol concentration. ★ 5.I
- **Identify** three factors that affect an individual's reaction to alcohol. ★ 5.H

Terms to Learn

- central nervous system (CNS)
- depressant
- blood alcohol concentration (BAC)

Start Off Write
What happens to your body when you drink alcohol?

Marta learns that there are different kinds of alcohol, that all kinds are dangerous, and that all are drugs. Like any drug, alcohol changes a person's physical or psychological state.

Types of Alcoholic Beverages

Alcohol is one of the oldest substances made and drunk by humans. It is a colorless, bitter-tasting liquid. Most alcohol comes from plants that have been *fermented*, or processed to produce alcohol. For example, wine comes from fermented grapes and other fruits. Beer is made from fermented grains, including barley and wheat. Some spirits and liquors, such as whiskey, vodka, brandy, and gin, are made from fermented plants and then processed further to increase their alcohol content.

Beverage alcohol, also called ethanol (ETH uh NAWL), is only one type of alcohol. Other alcohols, such as wood alcohol, or methanol (METH uh NAWL), were created for other purposes. These alcohols are poisonous and can permanently damage the body. Never drink methanol or other nonbeverage alcohols. A few teaspoons of methanol can cause blindness. A few tablespoons can cause death.

Figure 1 Alcoholic beverages come in all shapes, sizes, and flavors. And all of them can be deadly.

Alcohol in Your Body

When you swallow alcohol, it goes into your stomach and small intestine. Alcohol is then absorbed into the bloodstream and is carried to every part of your body.

Alcohol has very little nutritional value. In fact, alcohol acts as a poison or a drug in your body. In excessive amounts, alcohol is a poison. Alcohol's main effect is as a drug on the central nervous system. The **central nervous system (CNS)** consists of the brain and spinal cord. The CNS controls speech, thinking, memory, judgment, and learning. It also controls emotions, breathing, senses, and movement. Alcohol is a CNS depressant. A **depressant** is a drug that slows body functioning. Alcohol depresses the ways in which your CNS controls your body. Alcohol also affects your kidneys, liver, and digestion.

At low levels, such as one drink, alcohol affects your mood. Some drinkers feel more active and less shy. The alcohol makes them feel more relaxed and friendly. This initial feeling from one or two drinks is one of alcohol's effects on the brain. The pleasant feeling is one reason some adults drink. But some drinkers want to drink more. They think that if one drink makes them feel good, several drinks will make them feel even better. The result can be deadly. ★ 5.H

Alcohol and Your Brain

Alcohol affects the parts of your brain that control behavior. As the amount of alcohol in your blood increases, your thinking, memory, and judgment are impaired. Your ability to tell the difference between what is safe and what is dangerous is reduced. With a little more alcohol, you lose control of speech, movement, and coordination. Walking and even standing become difficult. As alcohol levels increase, your CNS becomes more depressed. Sleep, coma, and even death—by alcohol poisoning—can occur. ★ 5.H; 5.I

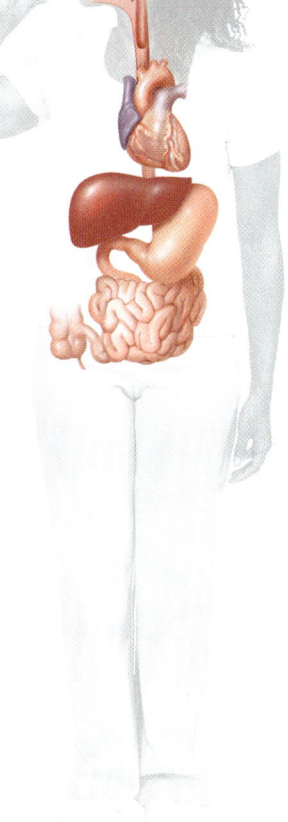

Figure 2 Alcohol's Path Through Your Body

Brain
Within 10–15 heartbeats, alcohol in the bloodstream reaches the brain.

Mouth
Alcohol enters the body.

Liver
Alcohol is converted into water, carbon dioxide, and energy.

Small intestine
Most alcohol enters the bloodstream through the small intestine.

Esophagus
Alcohol travels down the esophagus from the mouth to the stomach.

Heart
The heart pumps alcohol in the bloodstream throughout the body.

Stomach
Some of the alcohol enters the bloodstream in the stomach, but most alcohol passes into the small intestine.

TABLE 1 What Are the Effects of Alcohol?

Blood-alcohol concentration (BAC)	Physical effects	Mental effects
= 1 drink/1 hour (0.02–0.04)	mild relaxation; reaction time slowed	acting silly; telling people things you wouldn't usually tell them
= 2 drinks/1 hour (0.03–0.06)	slight to minor impairment of memory; slight impairment of balance, speech, vision, reaction time, and hearing	reduction in judgment and self-control; belief that you are functioning better than you really are
= 3 drinks/1 hour (0.05–0.14)	minor to significant impairment of coordination, balance, speech, vision, reaction time, and hearing; loss of physical control	moderate to severe impairment of judgment and perception; feeling very happy and lightheaded

Myth & Fact

Myth: Alcohol gives you extra energy.

Fact: Alcohol is a depressant. It affects your central nervous system, slows you down, and impairs the functioning of your mind and your body.

Alcohol in the Blood

Blood alcohol concentration (BAC) is the amount of alcohol in the bloodstream. It is measured in percentages. For example, a BAC of 0.08 percent means that a person has 8 parts of alcohol per 10,000 parts of blood in the body. Blood alcohol concentration is often called *blood alcohol level* (BAL). These terms mean the same thing, and both use the same scale of measurement. BAC, or BAL, is the result of how much alcohol you drink and how quickly you drink it. The amount of alcohol in your blood greatly affects how your mind and body react.

As alcohol is absorbed into the liver from the blood, the liver changes alcohol into waste products, such as water and carbon dioxide. Your body gets rid of these wastes through breathing and urination. Your liver can process only about two-thirds of an ounce of liquor or 8 ounces of beer per hour. So, if you drink more than one drink an hour, your body absorbs alcohol faster than it can be changed. The rest of the alcohol continues to circulate in your blood. And as you continue to drink, your BAC continues to increase. Having food in your stomach can slow down the absorption of alcohol into the blood, but food will not speed up the rate at which you process alcohol. In fact, there is nothing you can do to speed up this process. Only time will allow your BAC to go down. ★ 5.H; 5.I

Individual Reactions to Alcohol

Each person's body reacts to alcohol a little differently. You may see a wide variety of reactions among people. And one person's reactions may be different each time the person drinks alcohol. Why? Alcohol's effects on the body are influenced by several factors. For example, women absorb and metabolize alcohol differently than men do. Women tend to have more body fat and to reach a higher BAC faster than men who drink the same amount do. And a heavier or larger person must drink more alcohol than a smaller person does to reach the same BAC.

An individual's health, amount of sleep, and medications may also affect his or her reaction. And how people expect alcohol to make them feel and their mood may also affect their reaction to alcohol. For example, if a person expects to lose control, he or she more likely will. A person's positive or negative mood also affects his or her reaction to alcohol. ★ 5.H

Factors Affecting Individual Reactions to Alcohol

- How much and how fast a person drinks
- Body weight
- Food in the stomach
- Genetic vulnerability
- Alcohol tolerance (drinking history)
- Gender

Figure 3 Alcohol's effects on a person, or on different people, depend on several factors. The same amount of alcohol can have very different effects. Even one drink may be enough to get a person into trouble.

Hands-on ACTIVITY

ALCOHOL AND YOUR BODY

1. With a partner, create a list of alcohol's effects on body systems and a list of alcohol's effects on emotions.

2. Based on the information you have collected, design and make a poster or pamphlet warning people about alcohol consumption.

Analysis

1. Compare the two lists, and note any similarities or differences.

Lesson Review

Using Vocabulary

1. Define *blood-alcohol concentration* (BAC).
2. What is a depressant? ★ 5.I

Understanding Concepts

3. How does your body process alcohol? ★ 5.H; 5.I
4. How does an increasing BAC affect your body? ★ 5.I

Critical Thinking

5. **Making Inferences** What are three factors that influence a person's reaction to alcohol? ★ 5.H

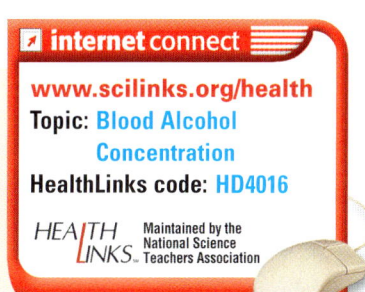

internet connect
www.scilinks.org/health
Topic: Blood Alcohol Concentration
HealthLinks code: HD4016

HEALTH LINKS — Maintained by the National Science Teachers Association

Lesson 2

Immediate Effects of Alcohol

What You'll Do

- **Describe** how alcohol affects a person's behavior. ★ 5.1
- **Identify** two risks of drinking alcohol. ★ 5.1

Terms to Learn

- intoxication
- alcohol poisoning
- hangover

Write

What are some effects of drinking alcohol?

Thomas felt terrible on Saturday morning. He drank beer at a friend's house on Friday night and was really sick. He threw up several times before he went to sleep.

Why would drinking alcohol make Thomas sick?

Losing Control

Alcohol causes intoxication (in TAHKS i KAY shuhn). **Intoxication** is the physical and mental changes produced by drinking alcohol. Mild intoxication may cause mental effects such as feeling relaxed and friendly. As intoxication increases, your feelings and behavior may become exaggerated and your judgment, sense of risk, concentration, and self-control decrease. And alcohol may produce unexpected feelings. After having some drinks, someone who is sad may unexpectedly become very angry.

At the same time, alcohol is causing physical effects. For example, if you are mildly intoxicated, you may feel lightheaded. As BAC rises, you become less responsive to the things that are going on around you. As intoxication increases, thinking clearly becomes impossible. Anything requiring mental or physical coordination, such as walking or driving, is seriously affected. Drinking too much alcohol can cause alcohol poisoning. **Alcohol poisoning** is the damage to physical health caused by drinking too much alcohol. It is a drug overdose, and it can be fatal.

Thomas was sick the next day, too. He had a hangover. A **hangover** is the uncomfortable physical effects caused by alcohol use, including headache, dizziness, stomach upset, nausea, and vomiting. These effects result when the body processes alcohol. The process upsets the body's water balance and causes the blood to become more acidic than it normally is. As a result, a person who has a hangover does not feel well. ★ 5.1

Figure 4 Drinking affects both physical and mental abilities. Don't ride with someone who has been drinking.

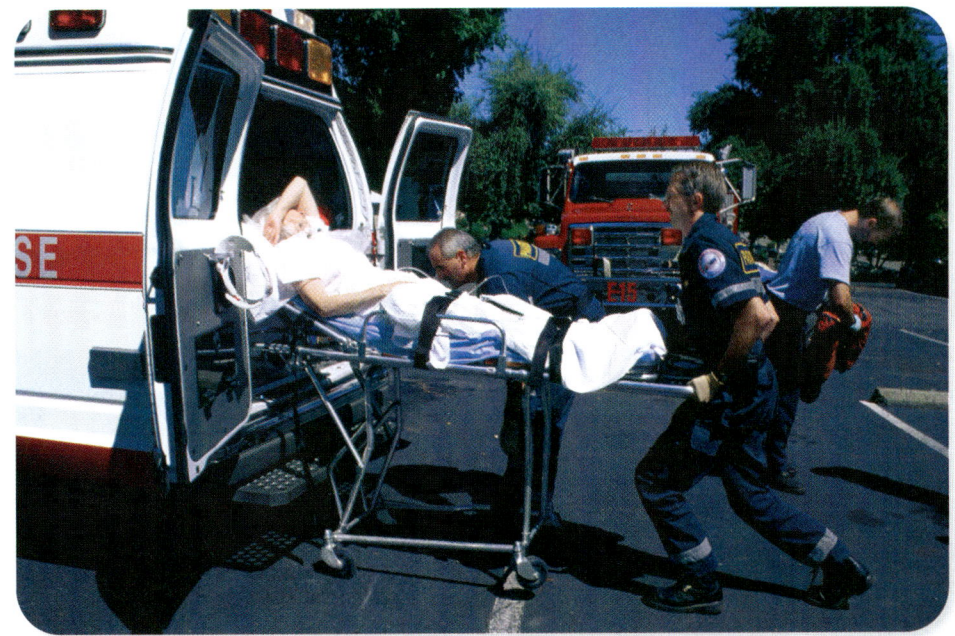

Figure 5 Heavy drinking can lead to alcohol poisoning or death. Don't risk death. Control your life and don't drink.

Injury and Harm

As BAC rises, you become less likely to see risks or predict possible harmful consequences. You become less alert and less aware of what is going on around you. These factors decrease your ability to recognize or protect yourself from possible dangers. When you combine this loss of judgment with your loss of coordination and concentration, injuries become more likely.

Drinking also makes you less aware of other people's feelings. You may have trouble understanding what other people say or do or what they intend. And alcohol can change your mood quickly. You may have been happy a minute ago, but now you are angry. These mood swings can play a major role in causing arguments, injuries, and violence. Alcohol is often involved in fights, assaults, car crashes, robberies, or abuse of others. But alcohol is not an excuse for harming others or for damaging property. You are still responsible for your actions. 5.1

Lesson Review

Using Vocabulary

1. What is alcohol poisoning? 5.1
2. Define *intoxication* in your own words. 5.1

Understanding Concepts

3. Identify two risks of drinking alcohol. 5.1

Critical Thinking

4. **Making Inferences** When some people drink, they think they can do anything. What are some of alcohol's effects that may lead to that feeling? 5.1
5. **Analyzing Ideas** Why is alcohol often related to violent incidents? 5.1

Lesson 3

Long-Term Effects of Alcohol

What You'll Do

- **Identify** two long-term effects of drinking alcohol. ★ 5.H; 5.I
- **Explain** why it is dangerous for pregnant women to drink alcohol. ★ 5.I

Terms to Learn

- cirrhosis
- tolerance
- fetal alcohol syndrome (FAS)

Write

Why is it dangerous for a pregnant woman to drink alcohol?

Benny's aunt, who has been drinking alcohol for many years, is very ill. She has liver damage and stomach problems caused by her long-term heavy drinking.

Benny's aunt has *cirrhosis* (suh RO sis), a liver disease related to long-term alcohol abuse. Because this disease affects the way in which the body processes food and gets rid of wastes, it is very serious.

Alcohol's Effects

Cirrhosis is a deadly disease that replaces healthy liver tissue with useless scar tissue. Cirrhosis is most often the result of long-term exposure to alcohol. In cirrhosis, the liver has difficulty removing poisons, such as alcohol and drugs, from the blood. These toxins build up in the blood and may affect brain function. Cirrhosis has made Benny's aunt very ill.

Alcohol also affects the brain. If you drink regularly as a teen, before your brain is fully mature, alcohol may change your brain physically. These physical changes may have negative effects on learning, memory, and verbal skills. Failure in school is more likely. Teenage drinking has also been shown to increase the risk of alcohol abuse.

Regular, heavy drinking can lead to alcohol tolerance. **Tolerance** is a condition in which a person needs more of a drug to feel the original effects of the drug. So, the more alcohol you drink, the more alcohol you need to get the same effects. Another problem with alcohol is alcohol abuse. *Alcohol abuse* is the inability to drink in moderation or at appropriate times. Alcohol abuse happens whenever drinking interferes with your health or well-being or keeps you from handling your responsibilities. ★ 5.H; 5.I

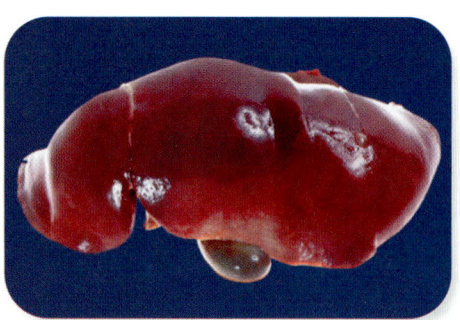

Healthy liver

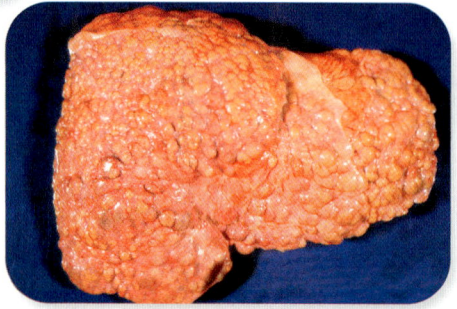

Damaged liver

Figure 6 A healthy liver is shown above. A liver damaged by alcohol abuse, shown on the right, cannot keep a body healthy.

Alcohol and Pregnancy

What is the connection between alcohol and pregnancy? Alcohol affects judgment, decision making, and emotions. Because alcohol affects the parts of the brain that process information and control behavior, drinking alcohol makes self-control and sexual abstinence less likely. You are more likely to take chances and to do things that are dangerous.

A person who has been drinking is less able to recognize danger than a sober person is. So, someone who is drinking is less able to protect himself or herself. As a result, a drinker's chances of being a victim of violence increase. For women, drinking increases the chances that they will become the victim of a sexual assault. Drinking also increases the chances that a woman may have unplanned and unwanted sex or pregnancy.

A mother who drinks during her pregnancy may harm the nervous system and organs of the developing fetus. This group of birth defects that affect an unborn baby that has been exposed to alcohol is called **fetal alcohol syndrome (FAS).** Fetal alcohol syndrome may include mental retardation, organ abnormalities, and learning and behavioral problems. Some problems, such as mental retardation, are lifelong. Any woman who is or thinks she may be pregnant should abstain from alcohol—there is no known safe level of alcohol during pregnancy. ★ 5.I

Figure 7 A fetus gets nutrients from its mother's blood. When the mother gets drunk, the fetus is bathed in alcohol and may suffer permanent damage.

Lesson Review

Using Vocabulary

1. What is FAS? ★ 5.I

2. In your own words, define *tolerance* of alcohol. ★ 5.H; 5.I

Understanding Concepts

3. What are two long-term effects of drinking alcohol? ★ 5.H; 5.I

4. What is the danger of alcohol use during pregnancy? ★ 5.I

Critical Thinking

5. **Making Inferences** Why may a young person's drinking be more harmful than an adult's? ★ 5.H; 5.I

internet connect
www.scilinks.org/health
Topic: Drug and Alcohol Abuse
HealthLinks code: HD4029
HEALTH LINKS Maintained by the National Science Teachers Association

Lesson 3 Long-Term Effects of Alcohol

Lesson 4

Alcohol and Decision Making

What You'll Do

- **Explain** how drinking alcohol affects a person's ability to make decisions. ★ 5.I
- **Describe** the relationship between alcohol and violence. ★ 5.I

Terms to Learn

- inhibition

Write

How does alcohol affect a person's ability to make decisions?

Clayton's older brother Roger is in high school. Roger has friends who drink, but Roger has decided not to drink. He told Clayton that alcohol can get you into trouble.

Clayton has seen some of his brother's friends when they have been drinking. He is glad Roger doesn't drink, and Clayton has decided he will not drink either.

Alcohol Influences Social Decisions

Many adults have a drink or two without any trouble. But the decision to drink—or not to drink—alcohol often determines the consequences of other social decisions. When alcohol is added to a situation, an unknown element is added. People who have been drinking often act differently from the way they act when they are not drinking.

Alcohol in your brain reduces your fear of certain behaviors. The alcohol relaxes your inhibitions. An **inhibition** is a mental or psychological process that restrains your actions, emotions, and thoughts. For example, a person may usually be very shy about talking to strangers at a party. But after a couple of drinks, the person's inhibitions are reduced, and the person may start a conversation with anyone who walks by, even complete strangers. Talking to people isn't necessarily dangerous. But because alcohol reduces one's inhibitions, a person may make other choices that are far more harmful than talking.

Alcohol also makes you less likely to recognize risks or dangerous situations. As a result, you might start a fight with someone. Or you may take physical risks that would seem unreasonable if you were sober, such as riding with a drunk driver. ★ 5.I

Figure 8 It is often hard to decide not to drink when others around you are drinking. But not giving in to peer pressure to drink is one of the bravest things you can do.

378

Figure 9 Alcohol often affects families and may lead to family violence and physical abuse.

Alcohol and Violence

Alcohol impairs people's judgment and reduces their inhibitions. As a result, alcohol increases the chances that a person will become involved in violence. The violence may be directed at

- the drinker (he or she may become angry or depressed and try to hurt himself or herself)
- others (the drinker may start a fight with someone)
- property (the drinker may become angry and try to destroy someone's property)

When a person loses control of his or her emotions, social situations may become tense or violent. The mixture of alcohol, reduced inhibitions, and unclear thinking is a major factor in child abuse, arguments, fights, and crimes—such as robbery, assault, and vandalism. The risk of self-injury, depression, and suicide increases as you drink more. And alcohol is a major cause of boating accidents, drowning, car crashes, and illegal drug use. ★ 5.1

Alcohol Doesn't Help

When you use alcohol to try to solve or forget problems, you only postpone solutions. In fact, your problems are likely to get worse.

Lesson Review

Using Vocabulary

1. In your own words, explain the term *inhibition*.

Understanding Concepts

2. Describe a situation in which alcohol may lower a person's inhibitions and lead to a dangerous situation for that person. ★ 5.1

3. How is alcohol related to violence? ★ 5.1

Critical Thinking

4. Making Inferences Some people drink to help them avoid bad feelings and to solve their problems. Explain how drinking affects a person's ability to handle problems. ★ 5.1

Lesson 4 Alcohol and Decision Making

Lesson 5

Alcohol, Driving, and Injuries

What You'll Do

- **Explain** how alcohol impairs a person's ability to drive. ★ 5.I
- **Describe** how people are trying to stop drunk driving. ★ 5.A; 5.J
- **Identify** three types of injuries other than driving injuries in which alcohol may be involved. ★ 5.I

Terms to Learn

- reaction time

Why is drinking and driving so dangerous?

The leading cause of death for people ages 15 to 20 is motor vehicle crashes. In fact, about 16,000 people of all ages die from alcohol-related traffic crashes every year.

Why is the mixture of alcohol and automobiles so deadly? First, a car traveling at 60 miles an hour is dangerous even under ideal conditions. Second, when the driver has been drinking and is impaired by alcohol, bad things may happen.

A Deadly Decision

When alcohol gets to the brain, it impairs judgment, reflexes, and vision. A person's ability to drive is affected even if he or she doesn't feel the alcohol's effects. Even one drink can slow a driver's reaction time. **Reaction time** is the amount of time from the instant your brain detects an external stimulus until the moment you respond. For example, a driver who comes to a stop sign may not be able to stop. A drinking driver can't respond to dangerous situations in time.

Alcohol has other deadly effects. It blurs a driver's vision and reduces a driver's coordination, memory, ability to figure distances, judgment, and concentration. Drivers who have been drinking cannot think clearly or steer or brake properly. And the more alcohol a person drinks, the less able he or she is to drive a car. The only sure way to avoid alcohol-related injuries and death is not to ride with someone who has been drinking. And never drink and drive! ★ 5.I

Figure 10 In 2000, more than 6,300 drivers ages 15 to 20 were killed in auto crashes. More than 1 in 3 of those drivers had been drinking.

Figure 11 Don't risk injury or death by riding with someone who has been drinking. Call a parent or a friend to take you home.

Stopping the Injuries

The deaths and injuries caused by drunk driving are completely preventable. Groups such as SADD (Students Against Destructive Decisions) and MADD (Mothers Against Drunk Driving) have formed to educate people about the dangers of drunk driving. Over the past few decades, a combination of stronger laws, stricter enforcement, and increased public education about these issues has reduced the numbers of crashes and fatalities.

Alcohol is also involved in many other types of injuries, disabilities, and even death. Alcohol is responsible for drownings, fires, falls, accidents while operating machinery, and injuries that happen during leisure activities, such as sports and games. The way to avoid these injuries is the same as the way to reduce injuries and death from drunk driving: do not drink in the first place. ★ 5.A; 5.J

MAKING GOOD DECISIONS

You need to get home from a party where alcohol is being served. A friend offers you a ride home. The ride sounds like a great idea until you notice that your friend smells like alcohol. What do you do? Explain how you made your decision.

Lesson Review

Using Vocabulary

1. What is reaction time?

Understanding Concepts

2. What is the connection between alcohol consumption and the ability to drive? ★ 5.I

3. What is the simplest way to prevent drunk driving? ★ 5.A; 5.J

Critical Thinking

4. **Making Inferences** Explain how alcohol's effects may be responsible for injuries that are not related to driving. ★ 5.I

5. **Analyzing Ideas** What are four things that should be included on a poster that educates students about alcohol and driving? ★ 5.I

Lesson 6 · Pressure to Drink

What You'll Do

■ **Identify** three pressures that tempt teens to drink alcohol. ★ 6.A; 7.A; 8.A; 12.E

Start Off Write

How might you feel pressured to drink?

Alex felt bad. He had offered his friend Sam a beer at a party. Sam refused, and Alex laughed at Sam. Later, Alex realized that he didn't want to drink either.

Pressures come in two kinds: pressures inside yourself, or internal pressures, and pressures from outside, or external pressures. When Alex offered Sam a beer, Alex may have felt pressure inside his own mind to drink or to push Sam to drink.

Internal Pressures

Perhaps the most common internal pressure for teens is curiosity. They want to know what it feels like to drink. They want to know what alcohol tastes like. And curiosity is often tied to a desire to be like other people you see. For example, you may see your parents or some of your friends drinking. As a result, you may be curious about their experiences and want to drink.

Most teens have an inner need to be accepted and to be part of a group. So, when some teens see others drinking, they may join in so that they don't feel left out or different. To fit in, you may feel the pressure to try alcohol even if you don't really want to drink.

Teens may drink because they think that drinking makes them look mature and adult or that drinking will impress others. Some teens have low self-esteem and think that alcohol will make them happier or more successful. Finally, some teens drink to deal with problems or unpleasant emotions. They hope that alcohol will make the feelings go away. But alcohol cannot solve any of these problems, and it might make them worse. ★ 7.A; 12.E

Figure 12 There are better ways than drinking, such as volunteering, to prove that you are growing up.

External Pressures

Internal pressure to drink may be triggered by external pressures, such as advertisements for alcohol. Alcohol advertising is everywhere—TV, radio, Web sites, magazines, and billboards. The advertising message is that drinking is attractive and normal. But the purpose behind that message is to get you to buy and drink that brand of alcohol. Ads are filled with good-looking, smart, sexy, happy, athletic, and popular people. Ads never show people who have alcoholism or who are unhappy, injured, vomiting, or hung over. And some people actually believe the ads. They drink alcohol, hoping they will be like the people on TV or in the magazines.

External pressures to drink also come from seeing people drinking in different places and situations, such as at parties, sporting events, family gatherings, and restaurants. Sometimes, people may pressure you directly by offering you a drink and encouraging you take it. When you're around people who drink a lot, you get the impression that drinking is what everybody does. But it isn't! The fact is that the majority of people drink only occasionally, drink lightly, or don't drink at all. Most of the time, people don't notice that other people are not drinking.

When you are offered something alcoholic to drink, remember how alcohol can affect you and your relationships. The choice is always yours. Make a wise decision. ★ 6.A; 7.A; 8.A

Figure 13 Alcohol advertisements may target legal drinkers, but they are seen by and influence underage drinkers.

Lesson Review

Understanding Concepts

1. What are three pressures to drink that teens may feel? ★ 6.A; 7.A; 8.A; 12.E
2. Explain why the messages contained in advertisements for alcohol may be misleading. ★ 4.A; 8.A

Critical Thinking

3. **Making Inferences** How do ads for alcohol influence some people to drink? ★ 8.A
4. **Analyzing Ideas** Identify an external pressure to drink, and explain how it may trigger or increase an internal pressure to drink. ★ 6.A; 7.A; 8.A; 12.E

Lesson 6 Pressure to Drink

Lesson 7 Deciding Not to Drink

What You'll Do

- **Identify** three steps you would take when deciding not to drink alcohol.  5.J; 5.K
- **Identify** two ways to resist internal pressures to drink.  5.J; 5.K

Start Off Write

What should you ask yourself when deciding not to drink?

> Vernon was worried about his family. His parents were getting divorced. One of his brother's friends tried to convince Vernon that drinking beer would make him feel better. Vernon was tempted to drink it.

Vernon was feeling pressured to drink. How could he resist the pressure? How could he refuse the beer he was offered?

Making the Decision Not to Drink

Sometimes, pressure from other people to do something makes it difficult to say no. But the decision to drink or not to drink is always your decision. Vernon knew that he had a problem—he was upset about his parents' divorce. His brother's friend said that beer would help him forget his problem. But drinking beer doesn't feel right to Vernon. He has a tough choice to make.

Vernon knows that making a decision about drinking alcohol involves the same steps that making any good decision does. First, Vernon must consider his *values*, or the beliefs that are of great importance to him. Second, he must also consider all his options. Right now, Vernon has two options: he can choose to drink or he can choose to refuse. Sometimes, he may have more than two options. But he should consider all of them. Third, Vernon must weigh the consequences of each option. For example, if Vernon chooses not to drink, he may still be upset, but he will avoid the negative effects of drinking alcohol, including feeling guilty about drinking.

Finally, once Vernon has made his decision, he must take action. Vernon decided not to take the beer, and he left the room where people were drinking. Looking back on his decision, Vernon knows that he made the right choice.  5.J; 5.K

Figure 14 It's easier to decide not to drink if you are with friends who share your values.

Resisting Internal Pressures

Some of the pressure to drink that Vernon felt was internal. He wanted to stop worrying and to feel better. Sometimes, internal pressures may be hard to identify. If you have trouble figuring out what is wrong, ask someone you trust for help. For example, if you're unhappy, lonely, or feeling bad about yourself, talk to someone who can help. Is there an adult whom you trust at school, in your family, at church or in your neighborhood? Sometimes, an adult can offer ideas and viewpoints you haven't considered. Once you have identified the problem, make your decision the same way you would make any other good decision.

Sometimes, you may need to take some time to think about what you really need. Ask yourself some questions: What activities and people make me happy? What makes me feel like an adult and in charge? What are the likely consequences if I drink? What pressures do I really feel, and how can I avoid or stop them? If you think about how drinking could hurt you or get you into trouble, resisting internal pressures to drink may be easier. Write down your thoughts. When you stop and think for yourself, you can make the good decision not to drink.
★ 5.J; 11.D; 12.C

Health Journal
Think of someone whom you admire for his or her maturity. What is it about that person that you admire? In your Health Journal, write about what makes a person mature and how you can work on becoming a mature person.

Figure 15 When people do things that make them feel good about themselves, such as having a summer job, alcohol becomes less important to them.

Lesson Review

Understanding Concepts
1. What are two ways that you could help a friend resist pressures to drink? ★ 5.J; 5.K
2. What are three steps you would take when deciding not to drink alcohol? ★ 5.J; 5.K; 11.D; 12.C

Critical Thinking
3. **Making Good Decisions** How could talking to a trusted adult help a person resist internal pressures to drink? ★ 5.J; 11.B

Lesson 8

Alcoholism

What You'll Do

- **Compare** physical dependence and psychological dependence. ⭐ 5.H
- **Describe** how alcoholism can affect a person's social, mental, and emotional health. ⭐ 5.H; 5.I
- **Identify** three factors that contribute to alcoholism. ⭐ 3.B
- **Describe** how a person can overcome alcoholism. ⭐ 5.J; 5.K

Terms to Learn

- alcoholism
- physical dependence
- psychological dependence
- recovery

Start Off Write

What causes alcoholism?

Silvia knew that her father felt bad about firing Lloyd, his friend and employee. Lloyd has an illness called alcoholism and has not been able to stop drinking.

Silvia's father told Sylvia that Lloyd's alcoholism was affecting the way Lloyd did his job. **Alcoholism** is a disease in which a person is physically and psychologically dependent on alcohol.

Physical Dependence

When a person's body processes high levels of alcohol for a long period of time, the body's reactions to alcohol change. The body develops a tolerance for alcohol. As a person drinks more and more, the central nervous system adjusts for the effects of alcohol. Eventually, a drinker must drink increasing amounts of alcohol to produce the same effect.

In some cases, a person's body becomes physically dependent on alcohol. **Physical dependence** is the body's chemical need for a drug. Dependence happens over time. It may develop quickly or slowly. And it may develop at different levels of drinking. Often, a drinker doesn't know that he or she is dependent until he or she tries to stop drinking and becomes ill.

A drinker who is physically dependent on alcohol has the illness of alcoholism. The symptoms of alcoholism include a strong craving to drink, tolerance to alcohol's effects, loss of control, and physical and emotional dependence on alcohol.
⭐ 5.H

Figure 16 Some people feel that they can't relax or get through the day without alcohol. These feelings may be a sign of dependence on alcohol.

Warning Signs of Teen Alcohol Abuse

- Loss of interest in school, sports, or other activities that used to be important
- Uncharacteristic withdrawal from family, friends, or interests
- Heightened secrecy about actions or possessions
- Association with a new group of friends who drink
- Smell of alcohol on breath or sudden, frequent use of breath mints
- Association with an older crowd
- Association with known alcohol users
- Getting upset easily and experiencing frequent changes in emotions
- Defiance toward parents and other adults
- Skipped classes or days of school
- Getting into trouble in school
- Change in appearance or hygiene

Figure 17 Most teens do not even drink alcohol. But you may have a friend or a relative who is drinking, so you should be aware of the warning signs.

Psychological Dependence

In addition to being physically dependent on alcohol, people who have alcoholism become psychologically dependent on alcohol. **Psychological dependence** is a person's emotional or mental need for a drug. The life of a person who has alcoholism revolves around drinking. Alcohol controls his or her personality, feelings, and daily routines. As a result, alcohol plays a major role in how he or she deals with other people, especially family members.

Someone who has alcoholism feels the need to drink to cope with responsibilities, stress, and problems. He or she drinks to feel normal—or not to feel bad—and to deaden his or her feelings. And once the physical and psychological dependence have taken control, a person who has alcoholism finds it almost impossible to stop drinking. This inability to quit makes the person feel even worse, which leads to more drinking. Psychological dependence often comes before—and may outlast—physical dependence. But both types of dependence grow over time with regular drinking. Both are part of this lifelong illness. And both types of dependence must be addressed in treating alcoholism. ★ 5.H

Myth: Alcohol is safer than illegal drugs are.

Fact: Just like other drugs, alcohol is addictive, mind altering, and health damaging. Alcohol is illegal for people under 21 to purchase in the United States.

Figure 18 Alcoholism is found in both sexes and in all populations, nationalities, and age groups. It is a disease, not a character flaw.

Factors That Contribute to Alcoholism

Alcoholism is a complex illness, and a number of factors may contribute to it. First of all, a person must be exposed to alcohol. If you never drink alcohol, you cannot become an alcoholic. A person develops alcoholism because alcohol is available and he or she drinks it regularly. Frequent, heavy use of alcohol can lead to tolerance and dependence.

Another factor that contributes to alcoholism is emotional pain. Some people drink to deal with feelings of sadness, anger, or shame. Alcohol makes these feelings seem more bearable. Other people start drinking because they lost a loved one, or because they don't like themselves, or because they feel powerless and alone. To these people, alcohol seems to reduce the strength of these feelings and seems to make the world a better place.

Once a person has started drinking, his or her genetic makeup may be a factor in his or her alcoholism. Certain genes make some people more likely to develop alcoholism when they drink. This means that children of people who have alcoholism may be at greater risk for alcoholism than other children are.

Alcoholism is a chronic illness. A *chronic illness* is a condition that lasts a year or longer, limits what a person can do, and may require constant care. Diabetes and heart disease are two other chronic illnesses. Like most other chronic diseases, alcoholism is not curable, but it is treatable. ★ 3.B; 5.H

Overcoming Alcoholism

Many people who have alcoholism want to overcome their illness. People can recover from the illness and be free from most of its symptoms. **Recovery** is learning to live without alcohol. Recovery halts alcoholism and allows the person to lead a healthier, normal life. But recovery is a lifelong effort.

A requirement of any alcoholism treatment program is abstinence from alcohol. A person who has alcoholism is always at risk of the effects of the illness returning if he or she begins to drink again. So, recovery from alcoholism requires that the person who has the disease must want to stop drinking. But the person's physical and emotional dependence on alcohol can make stopping very difficult. The person's decision to recover is critical to success.

In fact, the decision to stop drinking is the first step to recovery. The next step is treatment. Treatment may involve both medical care to improve physical health and counseling to redirect life and emotions. Counseling often includes participation in groups with other people who are trying to recover. Groups such as Alcoholics Anonymous (AA) provide support and may be the main treatment tool. These groups are important for providing ongoing support. And people close to someone who has alcoholism may also need help and support. In order to move on with their lives, they must overcome the hurt they experienced because of their loved one's drinking-related behaviors. For example, some families get counseling, too, or join support groups such as Al-Anon and Alateen.

★ 5.J; 5.K

Figure 19 Talking with others who have been close to a person who has alcoholism can give support to an alcoholic's family.

Lesson Review

Using Vocabulary

1. What is alcoholism, and how can it affect a person's health? ★ 5.H; 5.I

Understanding Concepts

2. Compare physical dependence with psychological dependence. ★ 5.H

3. What are three factors that contribute to alcoholism? ★ 3.B; 5.H

Critical Thinking

4. **Making Inferences** What is recovery, and why is recovery so difficult for a person who has alcoholism? ★ 5.J; 5.K

5. **Analyzing Ideas** Explain how psychological dependence on alcohol may be stronger than physical dependence. ★ 5.H

internet connect
www.scilinks.org/health
Topic: Alcoholism
HealthLinks code: HD4007
HEALTH LINKS Maintained by the National Science Teachers Association

15 CHAPTER REVIEW

Chapter Summary

- Alcohol comes in a variety of forms. ■ All types of alcohol can be dangerous. ■ Alcohol is a depressant that affects the central nervous system and slows body functioning. ■ Alcohol quickly affects the brain and other parts of the body. ■ Alcohol's effects on the brain may make a person more likely to be involved in violence. ■ Alcohol's long-term effects include alcohol abuse and liver disease, such as cirrhosis. ■ Alcohol can reduce inhibitions and allow people to do things that they usually would not do. ■ Alcohol's effects on the body and brain make it dangerous to drink and drive. ■ Pressure to drink may come from sources outside a person. ■ Some pressure to drink may be inside a person's mind. ■ It is possible to resist the pressure to drink by considering all your options and understanding the consequences of drinking alcohol. ■ Alcoholism is an illness in which a person is physically and emotionally dependent on alcohol.

Using Vocabulary

1 Use each of the following terms in a separate sentence: *tolerance, BAC, depressant,* and *alcoholism.*

2 In your own words, write a definition for the term *physical dependence.*

For each sentence, fill in the blank with the proper word from the word bank provided below.

inhibition	cirrhosis
reaction time	intoxication
hangover	recovery
fetal alcohol syndrome (FAS)	tolerance

3 ___ is the time from the instant your brain detects an external stimulus until the moment you respond.

4 Physical and mental changes produced by drinking alcohol are ___.

5 ___ is a liver disease caused by alcoholism.

6 A(n) ___ is a mental process that restrains your thoughts and actions.

7 The group of birth defects that can occur when pregnant mothers drink alcohol is called ___.

Understanding Concepts

8 Describe alcohol's path through your body when you take a drink. ★ 5.I

9 How does alcohol affect a person's mental, physical, emotional, and social health? ★ 5.H; 5.I

10 Why is recovery a life-long process? ★ 5.H

11 How can talking to a trusted adult reduce the pressures a teen may feel to drink alcohol? ★ 7.A; 10.B

12 What is being done to reduce the number of injuries and deaths related to drunk driving? ★ 5.J; 5.K

13 What are three pressures to drink alcohol that teens may face? ★ 6.A; 7.A; 8.A; 12.E

14 Describe two of the possible causes of alcoholism. ★ 3.B; 5.H

Critical Thinking

Identifying Relationships

15 Describe how drinking alcohol may increase the chances that a person will become the victim of violence. ★ 5.I

16 Why is it necessary for a person who has alcoholism to want to stop drinking if he or she is going to be successful? ★ 5.H; 5.I

17 Describe alcohol's effects on the CNS. ★ 5.I

18 Advertisements in magazines and on TV are carefully designed to convince certain people to buy and use the products that the ads are selling. Describe one beer commercial you have seen on TV. Whom do you think the commercial was trying to influence? Explain your answer. ★ 8.A

Making Good Decisions

19 Using the steps for making good decisions, describe how a person might decide to resist external pressures to drink alcohol. ★ 10.B; 11.D

20 Imagine that you see your friend drink a couple of beers at a party. When you ask her about it, she says she isn't worried because she couldn't feel any effects from the alcohol. What could you tell her about alcohol's effects to help her not drink again? ★ 4.C; 5.H; 5.I

21 Imagine that a person who has alcoholism has decided he wants to quit drinking. What are three steps he should take to reach his goal? ★ 5.J; 5.K

22 How might drinking alcohol make a person's existing social and emotional problems even worse? ★ 5.H; 5.I

23 Use what you have learned in this chapter to set a personal goal. Write your goal, and make an action plan by using the Health Behavior Contract for not drinking alcohol. You can find the Health Behavior Contract at **go.hrw.com.** Just type in the keyword **HD4HBC13.**

Reading Checkup

Take a minute to review your answers to the Health IQ questions at the beginning of this chapter. How has reading this chapter improved your Health IQ?

Chapter 15 Review | 391

Life Skills IN ACTION

Making Good Decisions

You make decisions every day. But how do you know if you are making good decisions? Making good decisions is making choices that are healthy and responsible. Following the six steps of making good decisions will help you make the best possible choice whenever you make a decision. Complete the following activity to practice the six steps of making good decisions.

Aya's Tough Decision

Setting the Scene

Aya's friend Katie has an older brother who is in college. Katie's brother is home for the summer and often drinks beer after dinner. One day, Katie tells Aya that she has been drinking some of her brother's beer and that she really likes it. Her brother assumes that their father is drinking the beer and hasn't said anything about the missing beer. Aya knows that Katie is doing something wrong, but she doesn't know what to do about it.

Guided Practice

Practice with a Friend

Form a group of four. Have one person play the role of Aya, another person play the role of Katie, and a third person play the role of a trusted adult. Have the fourth person be an observer. Walking through each of the six steps of making good decisions, role-play Aya deciding what to do about Katie's drinking. When she acts on her decision in step 5, Aya may talk to Katie and the trusted adult. The observer will take notes, which will include observations about what the person playing Aya did well and suggestions of ways to improve. Stop after each step to evaluate the process. ★ 4.C; 11.B; 11.C; 11.D; 12.A

The 6 Steps of Making Good Decisions

1. Identify the problem.
2. Consider your values.
3. List the options.
4. Weigh the consequences.
5. Decide, and act.
6. Evaluate your choice.

Independent Practice

Check Yourself

After you complete the guided practice, go through Act 1 again without stopping at each step. Answer the questions below to review what you did.

1. What values did Aya consider before making her decision?
2. If this decision was difficult to make, explain what made it difficult. If it was not difficult, explain what made it easy.
3. How does weighing the consequences help in making a good decision?
4. Which of the six steps of making good decisions was the most difficult for you? Explain your answer. What can you do in the future to make this step easier for you?

On Your Own

One evening, Aya goes over to Katie's house and finds her acting silly and laughing with her brother. Aya suspects that Katie is drunk and says so. Katie laughs and tells Aya that her brother found out about her drinking and is now buying extra beer. Katie's brother asks Aya not to tell anyone. He says he's keeping an eye on Katie so she doesn't get into trouble when she's drinking. Think about what you would do if you were Aya. Make an outline that shows how Aya can use the six steps of making good decisions to decide what to do in this situation. ★ 4.C; 12.B

CHAPTER 16
Medicine and Illegal Drugs

Lessons

1. What Are Drugs? — 396
2. Using Drugs as Medicine — 398
3. Drug Abuse and Addiction — 402
4. Stimulants and Depressants — 406
5. Marijuana — 410
6. Opiates — 412
7. Hallucinogens and Inhalants — 414
8. Designer Drugs — 416
9. Staying Drug Free — 418
10. Getting Help — 420

Chapter Review — 424
Life Skills in Action — 426

Check out **Current Health®** articles related to this chapter by visiting **go.hrw.com**. Just type in the keyword **HD4CH48**.

> **"Nobody** in my family **knew** that I used **cocaine** until I got **caught stealing** a portable **CD player** from a store. I wanted to sell it to get money to buy cocaine. When I got caught, I freaked out. I really didn't even care that I was in trouble for stealing because I was so upset that I couldn't get more drugs.**"**

PRE-READING

Answer the following multiple-choice questions to find out what you already know about medicine and illegal drugs. When you've finished this chapter, you'll have the opportunity to change your answers based on what you've learned.

1. Which of the following statements gives the correct relationship between drugs and medicine?
   a. A drug is a type of medicine.
   b. A medicine is not a drug.
   c. All drugs can be used as medicines.
   d. Some drugs can be used as medicines.

2. Which statement about prescription drugs is NOT true?
   a. You need a doctor's approval to use prescription drugs.
   b. Prescription drugs should never be shared with another person.
   c. People can't get addicted to prescription drugs.
   d. Prescription drugs are usually stronger than over-the-counter drugs.

3. When a person's body needs a drug in order to function properly, the person has a
   a. physical dependence.
   b. side effect.
   c. drug prescription.
   d. hallucination. ✪ 5.H

4. Heroin is a kind of
   a. stimulant.
   b. depressant.
   c. opiate.
   d. hallucinogen.

5. Which of the following is a good reason to avoid drugs?
   a. to stay healthy
   b. to stay out of trouble
   c. to save money
   d. all of the above ✪ 5.H, 5.I

6. A good person to ask for help with a drug problem is
   a. a teacher.
   b. a school counselor.
   c. a parent or caretaker.
   d. All of the above

ANSWERS: 1. d; 2. c; 3. a; 4. c; 5. d; 6. d

Lesson 1

What Are Drugs?

In today's world, you hear a lot about drugs. You hear about all kinds of drugs, from drugs that are used to treat diseases and save lives to illegal drugs that can cause many problems. But what is a drug?

What You'll Do

- **Explain** what makes a substance a drug. ★ 5.H; 5.I
- **Identify** five different ways that drugs can enter the body. ★ 5.I

Terms to Learn

- drug

Start Off Write

What happens to a drug after you swallow it?

What Is a Drug?

Many different substances are considered drugs. But what is it about these substances that makes them drugs? A **drug** is any chemical substance that causes a change in a person's physical or psychological state. What makes drugs any different from the food you eat? After all, food can make you feel better, and it improves the way your body works. The difference is that your body needs food every day to work properly. Unlike food, drugs do not give your body nourishment. You should take drugs only to treat an illness or a disorder. ★ 5.H; 5.I

How Drugs Enter Your Body

Almost all drugs that you take into your body end up in your bloodstream. However, drugs can be taken and can enter the bloodstream in several different ways. Figure 2 shows the different ways that drugs can enter the body. ★ 5.I

Figure 1 All of these products contain drugs.

Figure 2 How Drugs Enter the Body ⭐ 5.I

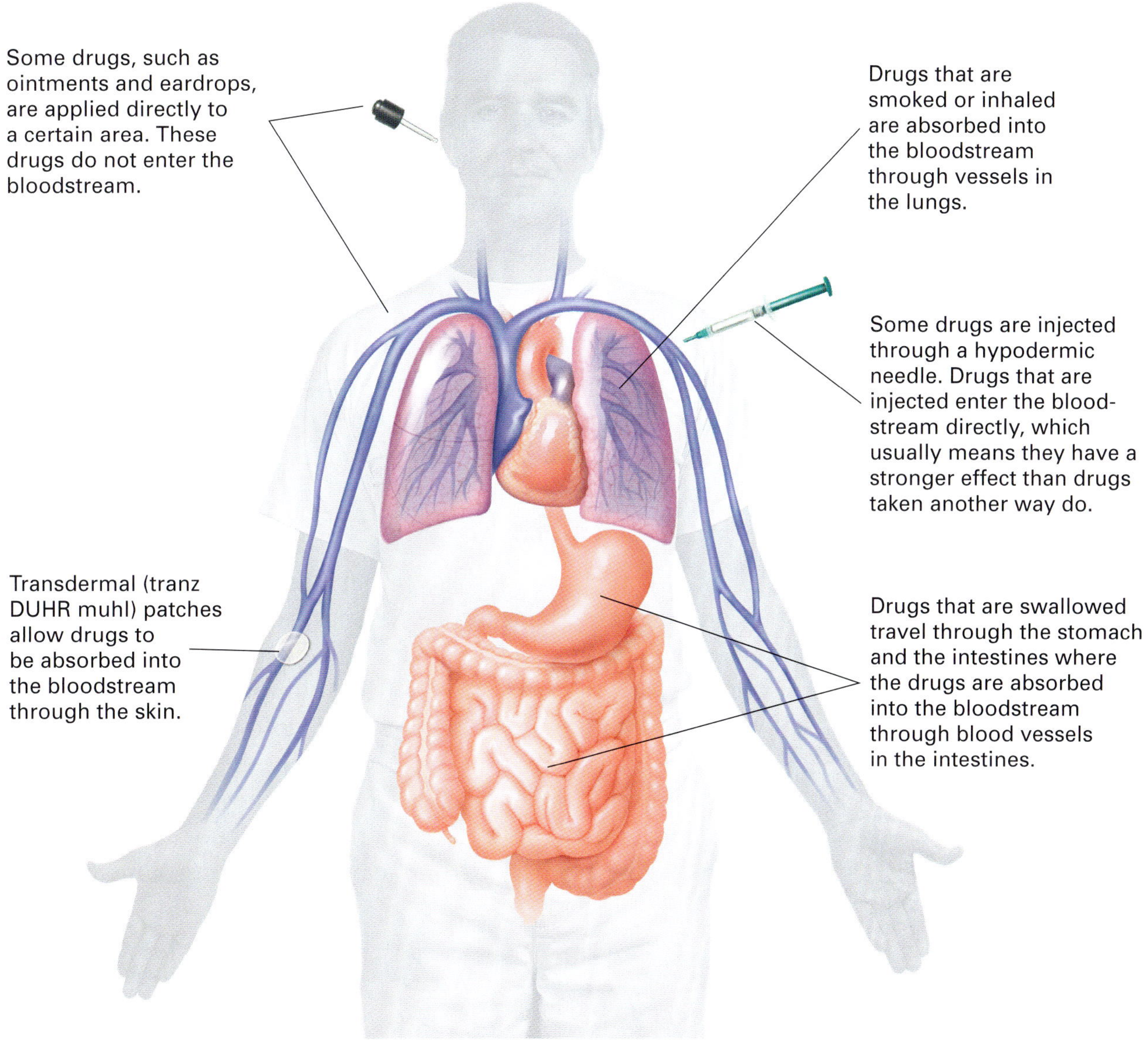

Some drugs, such as ointments and eardrops, are applied directly to a certain area. These drugs do not enter the bloodstream.

Drugs that are smoked or inhaled are absorbed into the bloodstream through vessels in the lungs.

Some drugs are injected through a hypodermic needle. Drugs that are injected enter the bloodstream directly, which usually means they have a stronger effect than drugs taken another way do.

Transdermal (tranz DUHR muhl) patches allow drugs to be absorbed into the bloodstream through the skin.

Drugs that are swallowed travel through the stomach and the intestines where the drugs are absorbed into the bloodstream through blood vessels in the intestines.

Lesson Review

Using Vocabulary

1. What makes a substance a drug?
2. How are drugs different from food? ⭐ 5.H; 5.I

Understanding Concepts

3. Compare and contrast the ways that drugs enter the bloodstream. ⭐ 5.I

Critical Thinking

4. **Applying Concepts** Imagine that a patient has been taking a certain amount of a painkiller in swallowed form. The patient's doctor later decides that the drug should be injected instead. Should the amount of drug the doctor injects be larger than the amount that the patient was swallowing? Explain your answer. ⭐ 5.H; 5.I

internet connect
www.scilinks.org/health
Topic: **Drugs**
HealthLinks code: **HD4030**

HEALTH LINKS Maintained by the National Science Teachers Association

Lesson 1 What Are Drugs?

Lesson 2 Using Drugs as Medicine

What You'll Do

- **Compare** prescription medicines and over-the-counter medicines.
  ★ 3.A; 4.B; 4.C
- **Identify** three possible dangers of using medicines.
  ★ 5.I
- **Explain** how the government approves a drug.

Terms to Learn

- medicine
- prescription medicine
- over-the-counter medicine
- side effect
- Food and Drug Administration

Start Off Write

What could happen if you took too much of a drug?

If you've ever been sick, you've probably taken drugs to feel better. Some drugs can cure disease. Some drugs just make you feel better while you're sick. If you've taken a drug for either of these purposes, then you have used medicine.

Medicine is any drug that is used to cure, prevent, or treat illness or discomfort. There are many different kinds of medicines, and there are also instructions for using each kind. Following instructions when taking medicine is very important. Not following instructions can be very dangerous to your health.

Prescription Medicine

Using any medicine is always safer under a doctor's care. Some medicines can be harmful or dangerous if they are not used properly. For this reason, certain medicines can be bought only with a prescription (pree SKRIP shuhn). A *prescription* is a written order from a doctor for a certain medicine or treatment. Prescriptions are always for a certain amount of a medicine, and they contain instructions on when and how often a medicine should be taken. Medicine that can be bought only with a written order from a doctor is called **prescription medicine**.
★ 3.A

Figure 3 Reading Prescription Medicine Labels

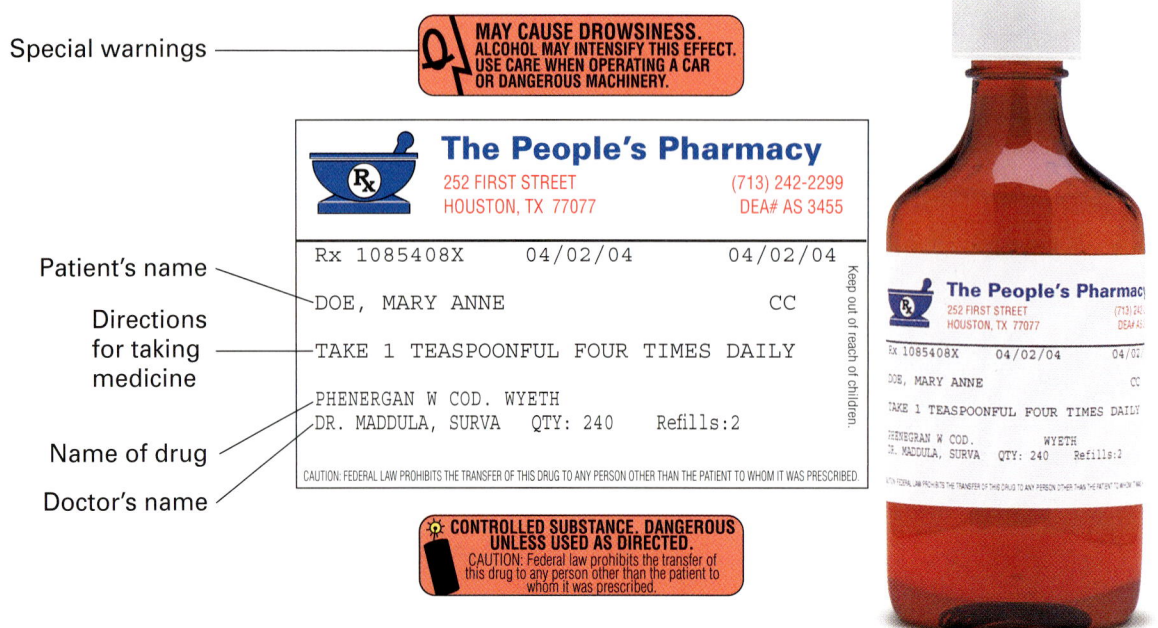

398 Chapter 16 Medicine and Illegal Drugs

Figure 4 Reading Over-the-Counter Medicine Labels

List of ingredients

Special warnings

See Carton for complete information.
Active Ingredient (in each tablet) — **Purpose**
Aspirin 325 mg ....PainReliever/Fever Reducer
Warnings: Reye's Syndrome: Children and teenagers should not use this medicine for chickenpox or flu symptoms before a doctor is consulted about Reye's Syndrome, a rare but serious illness reported to be associated with aspirin.
Alcohol Warning: If you consume 3 or more alcoholic drinks every day, ask your doctor whether you should take aspirin or other pain relievers/fever reducers. Aspirin my cause stomach bleeding. **Do not use** if you are allergic to aspirin. **Ask a doctor before use** if you have bleeding problems, asthma, ulcers, or stomach problems (such as heartburn, upset stomach, or stomach pain) that persist or recur. **Ask a doctor or a pharmacist before use** if you are taking a prescription drug for anticoagulation (thinning the blood), diabetes, gout, or arthritis. **Stop use and ask a doctor** if pain or fever persists or get worse, redness or swelling is present, new or unexpected symptoms occur, or ringing in the ears or loss of hearing occurs. These could be signs of a serious condition. **If pregnant or nursing a baby, seek the advice of a health professional before use. It is especially important not to use aspirin during the last 3 months of pregnancy unless directed to do so by a doctor. Keep out of reach of children.** In case of overdose, get medical help immediately. **Directions:** Do not take more than 10 days for pain or 3 days for fever. Adults and children 12 years and older: Take 1 or 2 tablets with water every 4 hours. Do not exceed 12 tablets in 24 hours. Children under 12 years: Consult a doctor.

Directions for taking the medicine

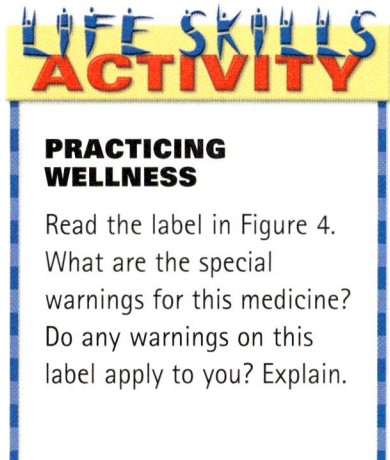

Over-the-Counter Medicine

Many medicines are safe enough that they can be used without a doctor's care as long as the instructions are followed. These medicines are called over-the-counter medicines. An <mark>over-the-counter medicine</mark> is any medicine that can be bought without a prescription. Before you take any over-the-counter medicines, read the label to learn how to use it properly. There are many kinds of over-the-counter medicines, including aspirin, cough syrup, antacids, sleeping pills, and eyedrops. Over-the-counter medicines fill the shelves at every neighborhood drugstore. ★ 4.B; 4.C

Drug Interactions

Sometimes, the effect of a drug can be different from expected if the drug is taken at the same time as another drug. This unexpected effect is called a *drug interaction*. Drug interactions can cause serious problems. You should always be very careful when taking more than one drug at a time. If you are on any medication, you should talk to a doctor or pharmacist before taking additional medication. ★ 5.I

LIFE SKILLS ACTIVITY

PRACTICING WELLNESS

Read the label in Figure 4. What are the special warnings for this medicine? Do any warnings on this label apply to you? Explain.

Lesson 2 Using Drugs as Medicine | 399

Side Effects and Drug Allergies

Most drugs have side effects. A side effect is any effect that is caused by a drug and that is different from the drug's intended effect. Side effects are usually no worse than dry mouth, drowsiness, or a headache. With some drugs, however, side effects can include nausea, hair loss, dizziness, and exhaustion. Most medicine packages describe a drug's known side effects. You can also ask your doctor or pharmacist about the possible side effects of a medicine. If you are taking a medicine and experience unexpected side effects, you should consult a doctor immediately.

Sometimes, a person can have a very bad reaction to a medicine that causes little or no side effects in most people. This kind of reaction is called a *drug allergy*. Drug allergies can cause a number of health problems. These problems can be as minor as a rash or as serious as the inability to breathe. Unfortunately, there is no way to know if you are allergic to a drug until you have taken it. If you begin to experience negative effects from taking any medicine, you should talk to a doctor right away. If you know that you are allergic to a drug, you should also wear a medical identification tag. This tag will tell doctors about your drug allergy if you ever need to be treated while you are unconscious. ★ 5.I

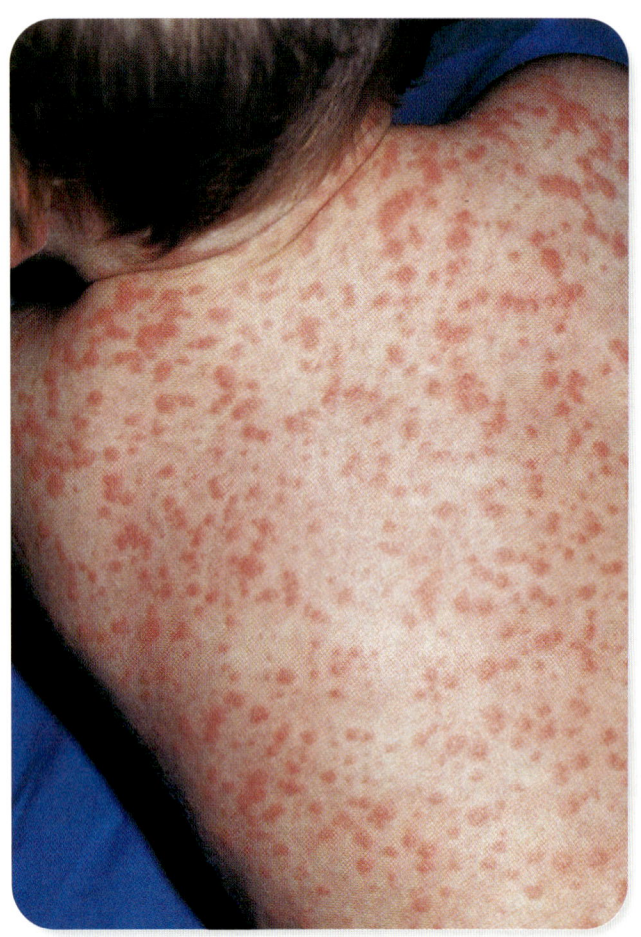

Figure 5 Drug allergies can cause a number of problems, such as a rash.

Tolerance

When you take a medicine for a long time, its effects can become weaker. If you need large amounts of the medicine to get the same effect as before, then you have developed a tolerance. *Tolerance* is the body's ability to resist the effects of a drug. Even a person who is tolerant of a drug may, under certain circumstances, take an overdose and be harmed. An *overdose* is the taking of a larger amount of a drug than a person's body can safely process. An overdose can result in a coma, brain damage, or even death. You should always talk to a doctor or pharmacist before taking more medicine than you were instructed to take. ★ 5.H; 5.I

The Food and Drug Administration

Before a drug can be sold as a medicine in the United States, it has to be approved by the Food and Drug Administration (FDA). The **Food and Drug Administration** is a government agency that controls the safety of food and drugs in the United States. Before a drug can be approved for use by the FDA, it must go through an approval process.

Herbal Supplements

Sometimes, substances that have medicinal effects are sold as herbal supplements. Although herbal supplements may seem very safe, they have not been tested and approved by the FDA. You should always talk to a doctor before you take any herbal supplement.

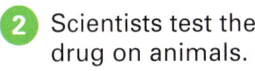

Figure 6 Drug Approval Process

1. Scientists develop or discover a new drug.
2. Scientists test the drug on animals.
3. If the animal testing shows the drug to be safe, then testing begins on healthy humans.
4. The drug's usefulness is tested on humans who have the disorder that the drug is meant to treat.
5. If tests on humans show that the drug is useful and safe, then the drug's creators can apply to the FDA for approval of the drug.
6. The FDA reviews the research and approves or rejects the drug.

Lesson Review

Using Vocabulary

1. Explain the difference between prescription medicines and over-the-counter medicines. ★ 3.A; 4.A; 4.B; 4.C
2. What is the difference between a side effect and a drug allergy? ★ 5.I

Understanding Concepts

3. Why can some drugs be bought only with a prescription? ★ 5.H; 5.I
4. Explain the steps that must occur before a drug can be approved by the FDA.

Critical Thinking

5. **Making Inferences** Both codeine and aspirin are used to treat pain. But codeine can be bought only with a prescription, while aspirin can be bought over the counter. What might be the reason for this difference? ★ 4.C; 5.I

6. **Analyzing Ideas** The FDA's drug approval process usually takes about eight years. What might be a benefit of having such a lengthy approval process for drugs? What might be a disadvantage? ★ 4.B; 4.C

internet connect
www.scilinks.org/health
Topic: Medicine Safety
HealthLinks code: HD4066

HEALTH LINKS — Maintained by the National Science Teachers Association

Lesson 3: Drug Abuse and Addiction

What You'll Do

- **Explain** what drug addiction is and how it happens. ★ 5.H
- **Compare** physical dependence and psychological dependence. ★ 5.H; 5.I
- **Identify** three types of problems related to drug abuse and drug addiction. ★ 5.H; 5.I

Terms to Learn

- drug addiction
- physical dependence
- psychological dependence

How can a drug addiction affect a person's relationships?

Jared is worried about his uncle, who has been very sick. Jared's parents told Jared that his uncle is recovering from a drug addiction. How did Jared's uncle become addicted to drugs, and why is his uncle sick if he isn't taking the drugs anymore?

Jared's uncle is sick because he stopped taking a drug that his body had come to need. This problem happens to people who suffer from drug addiction. **Drug addiction** is the uncontrollable use of a drug.

Drug Addiction

The path to addiction usually starts with drug abuse. *Drug abuse* is the misuse of a drug on purpose or the use of any illegal drug. When a drug is abused over a period of time, the result can be drug addiction. A person who is addicted to a drug cannot control their use of the drug because they have become dependent on the drug. *Dependence* on a drug means needing the drug in order to function properly. A person who is dependent on a drug will suffer negative effects when he or she stops taking the drug. There are two types of dependence: physical dependence and psychological (SIE kuh LAHJ i kuhl) dependence. Usually, a person who is addicted to a drug suffers from both types of dependence. ★ 5.H

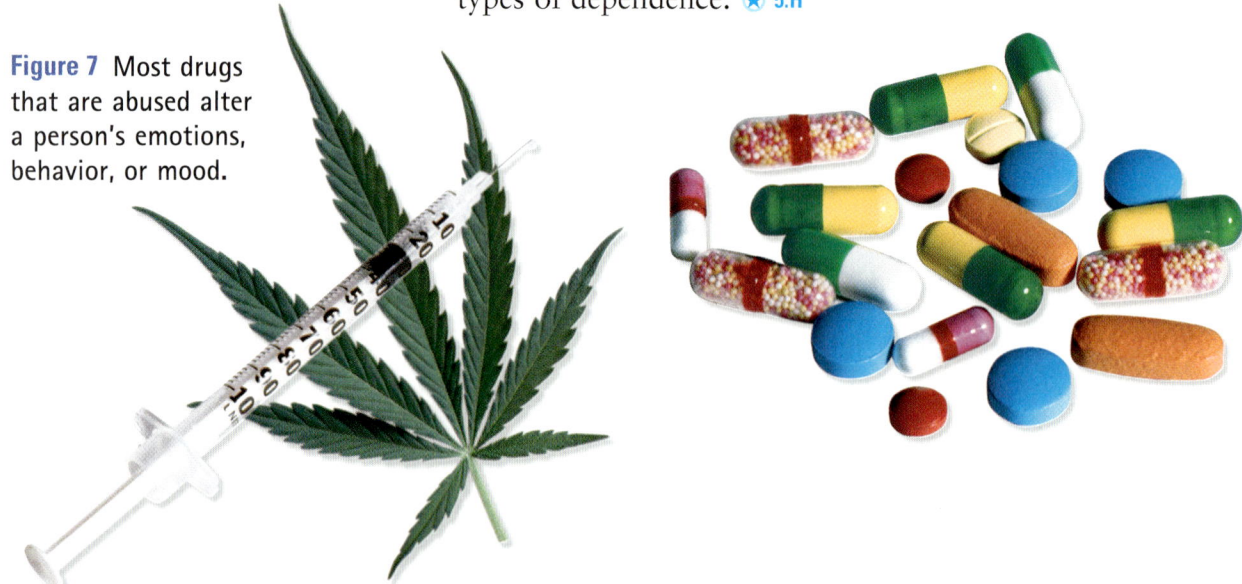

Figure 7 Most drugs that are abused alter a person's emotions, behavior, or mood.

Figure 8 How Addiction Happens

Experimentation → Using the drug every now and then → Craving and seeking out the drug → Using the drug very often → Addiction

Physical Dependence

Dependence on a drug changes the levels of certain chemicals in a person's body and makes the person's body need the drug to function properly. This type of addiction is called physical dependence. **Physical dependence** is the body's chemical need for a drug. An addicted person may experience withdrawal when he or she stops taking a drug. *Withdrawal* is the process that occurs when an addicted person stops taking a drug. Withdrawal can include many negative symptoms. These symptoms may include anxiety, fever, cramps, nausea, trembling, and seizures. Heroin, alcohol, and tobacco are just a few of the drugs that can cause physical dependence and withdrawal.
★ 5.H; 5.I

Psychological Dependence

Sometimes, a person can have a psychological need for a drug. This kind of addiction is called psychological dependence. **Psychological dependence** is a person's emotional or mental need for a drug. A person who is psychologically dependent on a drug has strong cravings for the drug. He or she also relies on the drug to control his or her emotions or to escape from problems. A person who is psychologically dependent on a drug may experience some physical withdrawal symptoms when he or she stops using the drug. These symptoms can include depression, nervousness, sleeplessness, and irritability. Drugs that can create a psychological dependence include marijuana, LSD, and Ecstasy. ★ 5.H; 5.I

LIFE SKILLS ACTIVITY

COMMUNICATING EFFECTIVELY

Create a public service announcement that warns young people of the dangers of drug abuse and addiction. Your announcement should include descriptions of physical dependence, psychological dependence, and withdrawal. Be sure that your announcement is attention-grabbing and informative. Your announcement could be a poster, a radio advertisement, or an item that has your message printed on it.

Health Journal

Imagine that a younger brother or sister has asked you about using drugs. In your Health Journal, explain to him or her how abusing drugs could affect his or her life.

Drug Addiction and Relationships

People who abuse drugs may seem to be hurting only themselves. However, an addiction can also affect others, especially the people closest to the addicted person. We spend most of our time with our families and friends. When we have a problem, they are usually the first to know. So when a person becomes addicted, that person's family and friends are usually affected by the addiction more than anyone else is. A person who is addicted to drugs often has mood swings. Talking to him or her can be very difficult. People with drug addictions can also be very irritable. This irritability can lead to many arguments. Sometimes, these arguments can even lead to violence.

A person who is addicted to drugs may lie to his or her family or friends. Often, drug addiction and the behavior that goes with it can cause a person to destroy friendships and lose the respect of his or her family. 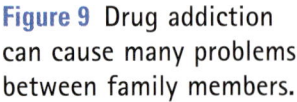 5.H; 5.I

School Problems Due to Drug Addiction

Home is not the only place in which a drug addiction can cause problems. A person who is addicted to drugs may have difficulty focusing on anything other than the drug. A drug-addicted person's performance at school almost always worsens. An addicted person begins to pay less and less attention at school, and his or her grades begin to suffer. This poor performance can have many consequences. These consequences can include failure, expulsion, or the need to repeat a grade. Problems in school can also result in difficulty getting into college or getting a job after graduation. 5.H; 5.I

Figure 9 Drug addiction can cause many problems between family members.

The Cost of Drug Addiction

A drug addiction can be an expensive problem. The cost of drugs is often very high. Some addicts must spend hundreds of dollars on drugs each day just to feel normal. Because many drug-addicted people have a hard time keeping a job, they must find other ways to support their habits. Too often, they turn to crime. Many drug-addicted people begin by stealing money or property from family and friends. As their need for the drug increases, they are often driven to commit more serious crimes—such as burglary and robbery—to buy drugs. ★ 5.I

MAKING GOOD DECISIONS

Many people who abuse drugs suffer another serious consequence: going to jail. Many states have mandatory drug sentencing laws. These laws place limits on the lowest amount of jail time that a person can receive for certain drug crimes. Research mandatory drug sentencing laws. How may the existence of mandatory sentencing laws further influence your decision to refuse drugs?

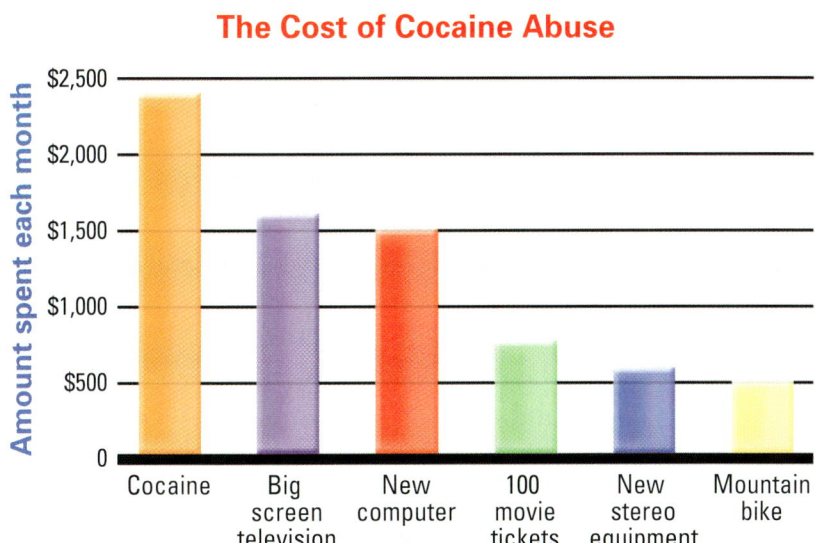

Figure 10 Some addicts spend $2,500 or more on cocaine each month.

Lesson Review

Using Vocabulary

1. Define *addiction* in your own words. ★ 5.H; 5.I

2. What is the difference between physical dependence and psychological dependence? ★ 5.H; 5.I

Understanding Concepts

3. Why does drug addiction sometimes lead a person to commit crimes? ★ 5.I

4. What are three problems that drug addiction can cause? ★ 5.H; 5.I

Critical Thinking

5. **Making Good Decisions** A doctor prescribes a prescription painkiller for you. She warns you that this particular medicine can be addictive if it is misused. What questions would you ask your doctor to learn how to avoid becoming addicted to this medicine? ★ 5.H; 5.I

internet connect
www.scilinks.org/health
Topic: Drugs & Drug Abuse
HealthLinks code: HD4031
Topic: Drug Addiction
HealthLinks code: HD4028
HEALTH LINKS Maintained by the National Science Teachers Association

Lesson 4

Stimulants and Depressants

What You'll Do

- **Explain** the difference between stimulants and depressants. ★ 4.A; 4.C
- **Describe** the effects and dangers of stimulants and depressants. ★ 5.H; 5.I

Terms to Learn

- stimulant
- depressant

Why does caffeine make you feel more awake?

Have you ever felt more awake and alert after having a soda or a cup of tea? Have you ever felt sleepy after taking a medicine for a cough or a headache? These feelings are the effects of stimulants and depressants.

Drugs are often grouped by their effects on people. Stimulants and depressants are two of the largest groups of drugs. You may take some of these drugs every day. Some of these drugs are dangerous and addictive.

Stimulants

Some of the most commonly used drugs are stimulants. A **stimulant** (STIM yoo luhnt) is any drug that increases the body's activity. Stimulants cause your heart rate and breathing to speed up. The increased beating of the heart causes blood pressure to increase. The effects of stimulants on the body make you feel more awake and alert. Some stimulants have only mild effects. One example is caffeine, which can be found in tea, coffee, some soft drinks, and chocolate. However, some stimulants are very dangerous. The stimulants cocaine, crack cocaine, and methamphetamine (METH am FET uh MEEN) are among the most addictive drugs that exist. These drugs can cause you to stay awake for days at a time and can cause a heart attack. Deaths due to misusing and abusing stimulants are common.

★ 4.A; 4.C; 5.H

Figure 11 The average person in the United States consumes 210 milligrams of caffeine each day, or about the amount of caffeine contained in six cans of cola.

Cocaine and Crack Cocaine

Cocaine and crack cocaine may be the most widely abused illegal stimulants. *Cocaine* is a powerful stimulant that is produced from the coca plant, a plant that is native to South America. Cocaine is a fine white powder. Cocaine is usually inhaled through the nose, although some users also inject it. *Crack cocaine* is cocaine that has been altered into a form that can be smoked, called a "rock." The effects of crack cocaine are more intense but shorter lasting than the effects of regular cocaine.

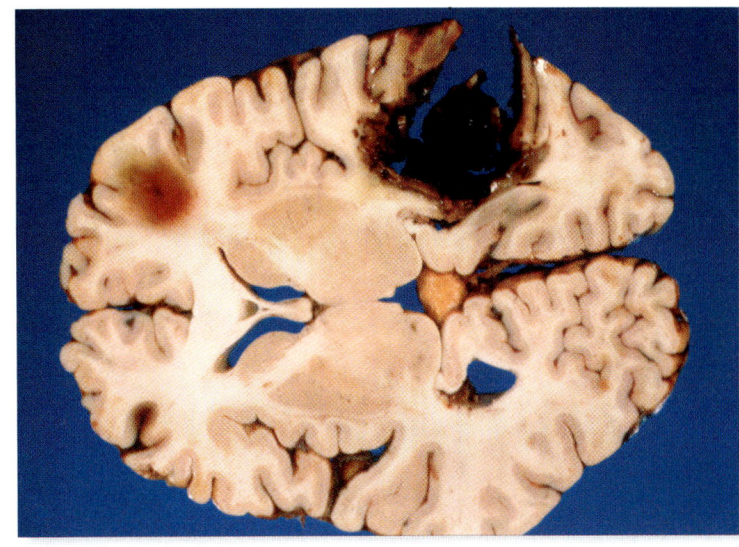

Figure 12 Long-term use of cocaine can cause brain injuries such as the one shown above.

Using cocaine or crack cocaine immediately raises the heart rate and blood pressure. Both drugs cause intense feelings of euphoria (yoo FAWR ee uh). *Euphoria* is a physical and mental sense of well-being. These feelings are very brief. They are followed by physical illness and a sense of depression. Both drugs are incredibly addictive. Because the effects of both cocaine and crack cocaine are so short-lived, people must use the drug often to make the effects last. Taking the drug so often increases the chances of addiction and overdose. Overdosing on cocaine or crack cocaine can cause a heart attack or a stroke, either of which can cause brain damage or death. ★ 4.A; 4.C; 5.H

Methamphetamine

Another very powerful stimulant is called *methamphetamine*. Methamphetamine is synthetic (sin THET ik), which means that it is produced in a laboratory. In recent years, abuse of methamphetamine, commonly called *meth*, *crystal*, or *crystal meth*, has risen sharply. Illegal methamphetamine usually appears as a yellowish "rock," which is crushed and then either smoked, injected, or inhaled through the nose. Methamphetamine has intense effects that can last for hours, and it is extremely addictive. The short-term effects of methamphetamine use include feelings of euphoria, decreased appetite, and increased body temperature. Repeated use of methamphetamine can cause severe damage to the body, including permanent kidney or liver damage. An overdose of methamphetamine can cause brain damage or death.
★ 4.A; 4.C; 5.H

Hands-on ACTIVITY

CAFFEINE

1. For the next week, record every serving of coffee, caffeinated soft drink, tea, or chocolate that you consume.
2. At the end of the week, score yourself by adding 3 points for every serving of coffee, 2 points for every serving of cola or tea, and 1 point for every serving of chocolate.

Analysis

1. How does your score compare with the scores of your classmates? Are you taking in more or less caffeine than your classmates are?

Lesson 4 Stimulants and Depressants

TABLE 1 Common Depressants

Drug	Type of depressant	What it looks like	Effects
Valium™ (diazepam)	tranquilizer		relaxes muscles; reduces anxiety; causes drowsiness
Seconal™ (secobarbital)	barbiturate		causes drowsiness and sleep; affects mood and coordination; can be very addictive
Rohypnol™ (flunitrazepam)	hypnotic		severely impairs judgment and muscle control; causes slurred speech, drowsiness, and memory loss

SCIENCE ACTIVITY

The chemical formula for Rohypnol is $C_{16}H_{12}FN_3O_3$. What does this mean? Research how to read a chemical formula. What do the letters represent? What do the numbers represent?

Depressants

Any drug that decreases activity in the body is called a **depressant.** Depressants cause your heart rate and breathing to slow down and your blood pressure to drop. Depressants, also called *sedatives* (SED uh tivz), can have a range of effects, from mild relaxation to deep sleep. Types of depressants include tranquilizers (TRAN kwil IEZ uhrz), barbiturates (bahr BICH uhr its), and hypnotics (hip NAHT iks). *Tranquilizers* are mild depressants that are used in small doses to treat anxiety. *Barbiturates* are strong depressants that are used to treat sleep disorders and seizures. *Hypnotics* are extremely powerful depressants that can cause sleep, loss of muscle control, and loss of memory. Abusing depressants can be very dangerous. Depressants can be very addictive, and an overdose can cause coma, brain damage, or death. Depressants also interact strongly with alcohol. Mixing even a small amount of depressants with alcohol can produce severe effects, including an accidental overdose. ★ 4.A; 4.C; 5.H; 5.I

LIFE SKILLS ACTIVITY

PRACTICING WELLNESS

Since they were created in the 1930s, barbiturates have been used for many medical purposes. They have also been widely abused and have caused many deaths. Research the history of barbiturates and the dangers of using them. Include information on the medical uses of barbiturates, what barbiturates do to your body and central nervous system, and the dangers of using barbiturates. When you are finished, use your research to create an informative brochure that you can pass out to the members of your class.

Rohypnol

Rohypnol (roh HIP NAHL) is an extremely powerful hypnotic depressant. Rohypnol was originally created for use during surgery and for use as a prescription drug used to treat sleep disorders. However, Rohypnol has recently become a drug of abuse for many people. Known also as "roach," "roofies," or "rope," Rohypnol tablets are small and white.

The effects of Rohypnol usually last about 8 hours. These effects include sleepiness, slurred speech, impaired judgment, difficulty walking, and loss of muscle control. These effects are increased when the drug is mixed with alcohol. Many users of Rohypnol also experience blackout. *Blackout* is the inability to remember anything that happened while under a drug's effects. Because Rohypnol causes a user to lose self-control and then forget everything, some people have used this drug to perform sexual assaults. Rohypnol is not currently approved for any medical use in the United States. However, it is approved in Mexico, in most of Latin America, and in some parts of Europe. ★ 4.C; 5.I

Figure 13 Much of the illegal Rohypnol in the United States is smuggled from other countries. This agent is searching a car that is crossing the border between the United States and Mexico.

Lesson Review

Using Vocabulary

1. What is the difference between a stimulant and a depressant? ★ 4.A; 4.C

Understanding Concepts

2. What effects do all stimulants have? What effects do all depressants have? ★ 5.H; 5.I

3. What are the dangers of abusing stimulants? What are the dangers of abusing depressants? ★ 4.A; 4.C; 5.H; 5.I

Critical Thinking

4. **Making Inferences** Which of the types of depressants listed in the text would a doctor most likely prescribe for a person who has an anxiety disorder? Explain. ★ 4.C

5. **Making Inferences** Imagine that a person takes a depressant. One hour later, the person is nearly asleep and has very little muscle control. The person's speech is also slurred. The next day, the person does not remember taking the drug. What type of depressant might this person have taken? Explain. ★ 4.C; 5.I

Lesson 4 Stimulants and Depressants

Lesson 5

Marijuana

Steven was at a friend's house when his friend's brother offered them some marijuana. When Steven said that he didn't do drugs, his friend told him, "It's just marijuana. It's totally harmless." Is that statement correct? Is marijuana really harmless?

What You'll Do

- **Describe** the most common effects of marijuana. ★ 4.C; 5.I
- **Identify** the dangers of continued marijuana use. ★ 5.H; 5.I

Terms to Learn

- marijuana
- THC

Start Off Write

Is marijuana a harmless drug? Explain.

Marijuana (MAR uh WAH nuh) is not harmless. It may not cause the physical addiction or overdoses that many other illegal drugs cause, but using marijuana can cause many other problems. These problems can seriously affect your physical and emotional health.

What Is Marijuana?

Marijuana may be the most popular drug of abuse. But what is marijuana? And what are its effects? **Marijuana** is the dried flowers and leaves of the *Cannabis* (KAN uh BIS) plant. Marijuana is known by many different names, including *grass, weed, pot, dope, Mary Jane, green, bud,* and *reefer*. Marijuana produces a wide range of effects, which can differ greatly from person to person. For example, some users experience stimulant-like effects, while others experience depressant-like effects. The most common effects of marijuana are mild euphoria, distortion of time and distance, and reduced energy and coordination. Other effects include increased sensitivity to sights and sounds, increased appetite, decreased memory, and an increase in reaction time. Most often, marijuana is smoked, but it can be mixed with food and eaten. The active substance in marijuana is a chemical called *tetrahydrocannabinol*, or **THC** for short. Different marijuana plants may contain very different levels of THC.
★ 4.C; 5.I

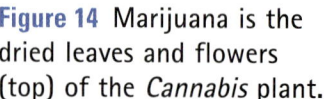

Figure 14 Marijuana is the dried leaves and flowers (top) of the *Cannabis* plant.

410　Chapter 16　Medicine and Illegal Drugs

The Long-Term Effects of Marijuana

Using marijuana over a long period of time can cause serious problems. Marijuana often decreases a person's ability to think and concentrate. Marijuana also decreases energy and the desire to perform tasks or pursue goals. These effects can cause a marijuana user to perform poorly at school or work. These effects can also make reaching goals difficult.

The long-term effects of using marijuana can also threaten a person's physical health. Because marijuana is usually smoked, using the drug over a long period of time can cause many of the same health effects as smoking cigarettes can. In fact, some studies have shown that unfiltered marijuana smoke contains more poisonous substances than tobacco smoke contains. Smoking marijuana can cause lung cancer and circulatory problems. Smoking marijuana can also cause *emphysema* (EM fuh SEE muh), which is a painful and deadly lung disease. ★ 5.H; 5.I

Brain Food

Hemp is a cousin of marijuana and is used for a number of purposes. Many products are made from hemp, including rope, clothing, and paper. Although hemp is closely related to marijuana, it contains little or no THC, so it cannot produce a "high."

Figure 15 Marijuana can make concentrating very difficult.

Lesson Review

Using Vocabulary

1. Define *THC* in your own words.

Understanding Concepts

2. What are three negative effects of using marijuana? ★ 4.C; 5.H; 5.I
3. Why does marijuana use sometimes affect a person's performance at school? ★ 4.C; 5.I

Critical Thinking

4. **Making Inferences** Some of the dangers of marijuana are related to smoking this drug. Does that mean that eating the drug is safe? Explain. ★ 4.A; 4.C; 5.I
5. **Making Inferences** Like many other drugs, marijuana reduces coordination and causes drowsiness and increased reaction time. What are some of the dangers of these effects? ★ 5.I

Lesson 6 Opiates

Opiates may be the most effective drugs ever discovered for the treatment of pain. Opiates may also be the most addictive and dangerous drugs ever discovered.

What You'll Do

- **Describe** the addictive nature of opiates. ★ 5.H; 5.I
- **Identify** uses and dangers of prescription opiates. ★ 5.I
- **Describe** heroin and its dangers. ★ 5.H; 5.I

Terms to Learn

- opiate

Why is it important to follow instructions when taking a prescription drug?

What Are Opiates?

Any drug that is produced from the milk of the opium poppy is called an **opiate** (OH pee it). The opium poppy is a flowering plant that grows in Europe and Asia. When the seed pods of opium poppies are cut, they produce a milky white liquid. This liquid, called *opium* (OH pee uhm), is used to make all opiates.

Opiates Are Addictive

Opiates are extremely addictive. They are commonly abused because of the strong "high" that they produce. Opiates can cause addiction very quickly, sometimes with just one use. Opiates can also cause users to develop a strong tolerance. This tolerance increases the danger of overdose. Opiate addiction may be one of the hardest drug addictions to break. People who are addicted to opiates experience many withdrawal symptoms. These symptoms can include cramps, vomiting, muscle pain, shaking, chills, and panic attacks. Many people who are breaking an addiction to an opiate must slowly decrease the amount of the drug used. Others must use a less dangerous drug that imitates the abused drug's effects. The reason for this is that the symptoms of opiate withdrawal are very bad. Sudden withdrawal from opiates is so painful that an addicted person will usually use the drug again to stop the pain of withdrawal. ★ 5.H; 5.I

Social Studies Activity

The use of opium and morphine has a long history in the United States and in the rest of the world. Do research and write a short paper about the history of opium and morphine.

Figure 16 All opiates come from the milk of the opium poppy.

Prescription Opiates

The most commonly used opiates can be bought with a prescription at any neighborhood pharmacy. Opiates have many medical uses and are prescribed to treat many medical conditions. All opiate drugs have painkilling properties, and some opiate drugs are also useful in treating coughs and intestinal problems. Unfortunately, even opiates that are used as medicine can be misused or abused, which can eventually lead to addiction. Addiction to prescription opiates usually happens because users fail to follow a doctor's instructions. ★ 4.A; 4.C; 5.H

Heroin

Heroin (HER oh in) may be the most powerful and addictive opiate that exists. *Heroin* is a drug that is made from morphine (MAWR FEEN). *Morphine* is one of the chemical substances in the milk of the opium poppy. Heroin can be inhaled through the nose or smoked. However, the most popular and most dangerous way to take heroin is by injection. The effects of heroin include euphoria, sleepiness, a warm feeling in the skin, shallow breathing, and nausea.

Repeatedly injecting heroin, especially with unclean needles, can cause skin infections, open wounds, and scarring. Another danger of injecting heroin, or any drug, is getting a disease from a shared needle. When a person uses a needle to inject drugs, some of his or her blood remains on the needle. This blood can spread diseases such as hepatitis or HIV to the next person that uses the needle. ★ 4.A; 4.C; 5.H; 5.I

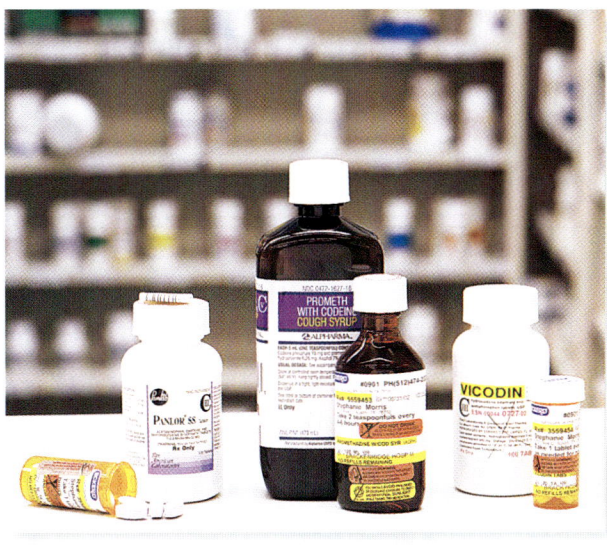

Figure 17 Some opiates are sold as prescription painkillers. Even though these drugs are sold legally, they can still cause addiction.

Lesson Review

Using Vocabulary

1. What are opiates? ★ 4.C

Understanding Concepts

2. What are three uses of prescription opiates? ★ 4.C; 5.H

3. What are three of the withdrawal symptoms that a person who is addicted to heroin may experience? ★ 5.H; 5.I

4. How does sharing needles spread diseases? ★ 4.C; 5.H; 5.I

Critical Thinking

5. **Making Inferences** Using unclean needles to inject heroin can cause a number of health risks. Does that mean that using clean needles to inject heroin is safe? Explain. ★ 4.A; 4.C; 5.I

Lesson 7: Hallucinogens and Inhalants

What You'll Do

- **Identify** the dangers of using hallucinogens and inhalants. ★ 5.I
- **Explain** how flashbacks happen. ★ 5.I

Terms to Learn

- hallucinogen
- flashback
- inhalant

Write

Why is it dangerous to sniff glue?

Hallucinogens (huh LOO si nuh juhnz) and inhalants (in HAYL uhnts) are drugs that are capable of producing very intense effects. Along with these effects are some very real dangers.

Hallucinogens

Can you imagine a drug so powerful that it can cause a person to see something that isn't actually there? Such drugs exist, and they are called hallucinogens. A **hallucinogen** is any drug that causes a person to hallucinate. To *hallucinate* is to see or hear things that are not actually present. The effects of a dose of a hallucinogen are often referred to as a "trip." The length of a trip depends on the type and amount of the drug that is taken and can last from minutes to days. Table 2 lists examples of hallucinogens and their dangers. ★ 5.I

TABLE 2 Common Hallucinogens

Common names	How it is taken	Effects	Dangers
LSD, acid, blotter	licked, swallowed	hallucinations, euphoria, inability to judge time or distance, sleeplessness, and loss of appetite; effects last 5 to 10 hours	psychological dependence, flashbacks, increased blood pressure and heart rate, loss of judgment, and psychosis (an inability to tell what is real and what is not)
Magic mushrooms, shrooms	swallowed	hallucinations, euphoria, inability to judge time or distance, sleeplessness, loss of appetite, and nausea; effects last 4 to 6 hours	psychological dependence, loss of judgment
PCP, angel dust, dust, sherm, superweed, ozone	swallowed, smoked, injected	hallucinations, euphoria, loss of coordination, sleeplessness, loss of appetite, nausea, and feelings of superhuman power; effects last 3 to 12 hours	violent behavior, memory loss, difficulty speaking or thinking, psychological dependence, brain damage, coma, and death
Peyote, buttons, cactus, mescaline	swallowed, smoked	powerful hallucinations, severe nausea, euphoria, inability to judge time or distance, sleeplessness, and loss of appetite; effects last 9 to 10 hours	psychological dependence, flashbacks, increased blood pressure and heart rate, loss of judgment, and psychosis

Chapter 16 Medicine and Illegal Drugs

Flashback

Flashbacks are one of the many dangers of using hallucinogens. A **flashback** is an event in which a hallucinogen's effects happen again long after the drug was originally taken. Flashbacks may occur days, weeks, or even years after the drug was taken. Flashbacks may last for a few seconds or for several hours. How and why flashbacks happen is not known. Flashbacks can happen at any time and can be as strong as the drug's original effects. ★ 5.1

Inhalants

Another dangerous class of drugs is known as inhalants. An **inhalant** is any drug that is inhaled and absorbed into the bloodstream through the lungs. Common inhalants include household cleaners, spray paint, and some glues. Other inhalants are gases such as *Freon* (FREE AHN), which is used in air conditioners, or *nitrous oxide* (NIE truhs AHKS IED). Nitrous oxide is also called "laughing gas" or "whip-its."

Inhalants produce very short, intense effects that may last no longer than a minute or two. Effects of inhalants include hallucination, lack of coordination, distortion of time and distance, and difficulty speaking or thinking. The use of inhalants is incredibly dangerous. Inhalants can replace the oxygen flowing to your brain with another chemical. This lack of oxygen causes brain cells to die and can cause immediate death. Use of inhalants can cause brain damage. ★ 5.1

Myth & Fact

Myth: Because doctors and dentists sometimes use nitrous oxide as a mild anesthetic, it must be safe.

Fact: When used medically, nitrous oxide is given in small amounts by a trained doctor. When it is used out of a doctor's care, nitrous oxide can cause brain damage or death.

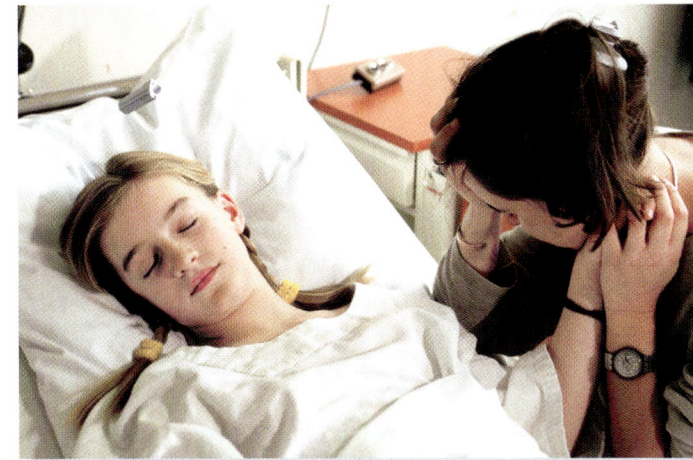

Figure 18 Inhalants can cause severe brain damage or even death, even after only one use.

Lesson Review

Using Vocabulary
1. What are hallucinogens?
2. What is an inhalant?

Understanding Concepts
3. What are flashbacks? ★ 5.1
4. What are two dangers of using inhalants? ★ 5.1

Critical Thinking
5. **Making Inferences** If substances such as glue or paint can be used as inhalants, why are these substances still sold legally?

Lesson 8

Designer Drugs

A new group of drugs is quickly rising in popularity. These drugs use clever nicknames and false promises of safety to attract users. However, these drugs, called designer drugs, have the potential to kill.

A **designer drug** is a drug that is produced by making a small chemical change to a drug that already exists. A designer drug has many of the same effects as its parent drug has. However, it can also have new and unpredictable effects all its own. Dozens of new designer drugs are now available. Many of these drugs are so new that their dangers are not yet fully known. However, a few designer drugs are widely used, and their dangers have been well-known for some time.

What You'll Do

- **Identify** three examples of designer drugs. ★ 4.C
- **Describe** the dangers of using designer drugs. ★ 4.C; 5.I

Terms to Learn

- designer drug
- Ecstasy
- GHB
- Ketamine

Why is Ecstasy dangerous?

Ecstasy

One of the most popular designer drugs is called Ecstasy. **Ecstasy** (EK stuh see) is the common name given to the chemical MDMA. MDMA is a mind-altering drug that was created from the powerful stimulant methamphetamine. Ecstasy is also known by a number of other names, including *X*, *Adam*, *XTC*, and *E*. Ecstasy is normally taken as a pill, although it can also be crushed and snorted. The effects of Ecstasy include an increased sensitivity to touch, hallucinations, tingling in the skin, and increased energy. The effects of Ecstasy usually last for 4 to 6 hours. Side effects can include dry mouth, nausea, confusion, blurred vision, muscle tension, and dehydration. In some cases, Ecstasy can cause seizures. *Seizures* (SEE zhuhrz) are short episodes in which an overload of brain activity causes violent shaking in the muscles. Other dangers of Ecstasy use are heart failure and death. Continued use of Ecstasy causes sleep disorders, memory loss, and brain damage.
★ 4.C; 5.I

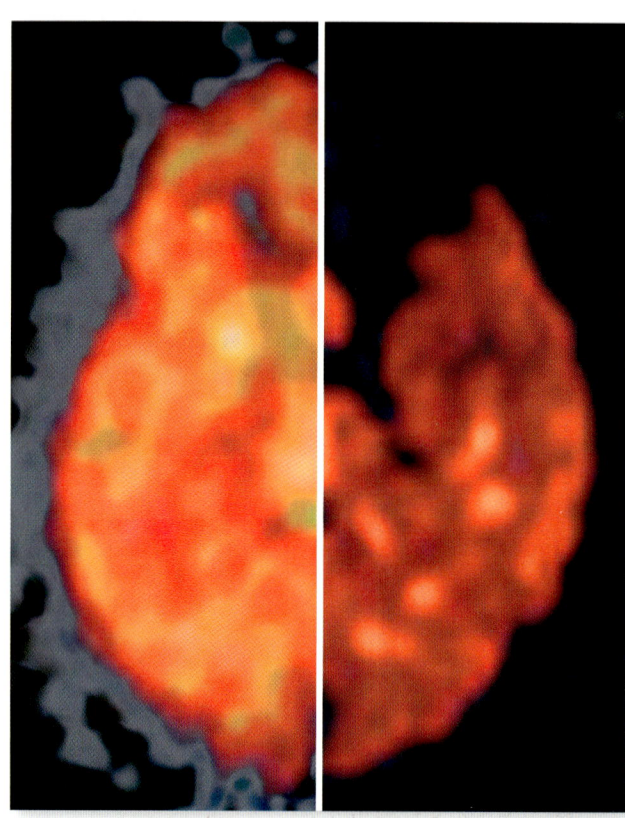

Figure 19 These two images compare the brain activity in two people. Brain activity has stopped in the darkened area of the Ecstasy user's brain.

Normal brain   Brain of an Ecstasy user

416   Chapter 16   Medicine and Illegal Drugs

GHB

Another very dangerous designer drug that is rising in popularity is called GHB. **GHB** is a drug that is made from the anesthetic *GBL*, a common ingredient in pesticides. GHB is also known as *G, Gamma-oh, Liquid X, Georgia Home Boy,* and *Fantasy*. GHB is a relatively new drug. In the late 1980s and in the 1990s, GHB was sold legally as an herbal supplement. In fact, it wasn't until the year 2000 that a federal law was passed to outlaw GHB. GHB normally appears as a clear, colorless liquid that looks almost identical to water. Sometimes, it also appears as a white powder. The effects of GHB include increased energy, euphoria, muscle relaxation, and increased sensitivity to touch. Other effects include dizziness, vomiting, loss of memory, trouble breathing, and an inability to move. In many cases, people who take GHB lose consciousness. This loss of consciousness is called "scooping out" or "carpeting out" and can last for hours. Many people who "carpet out" on GHB never wake up. The GHB causes them to stop breathing, and they die. Death is even more likely when GHB is combined with other drugs, especially alcohol. ★ 4.C; 5.I

Figure 20 GHB is a colorless liquid that resembles water.

Ketamine

Another popular designer drug is called Ketamine (KEET uh MEEN). **Ketamine** is a powerful drug that is closely related to the hallucinogen PCP (angel dust). Ketamine is used most often during surgery on people or animals. To recreational users, the drug is known as *Special K, Kit Kat,* or *Vitamin K*. Users of Ketamine experience a sense of *dissociation* (di SOH see AY shuhn), which means "separation from reality." Other effects include hallucination, numbness, an inability to move, and loss of memory. The dangers of Ketamine are not yet fully known. However, many users hurt themselves while on the drug because they are unable to feel pain. In other cases, Ketamine has been known to cause permanent memory loss and coma. ★ 4.C; 5.I

> **teen talk**
>
> **Teen:** I've heard people talk about "date-rape drugs." What does that mean?
>
> **Answer:** There have been many reports of people being sexually assaulted after taking GHB, Ketamine, or Rohypnol. Because these drugs make a user unable to move or to remember events, they leave victims powerless to defend themselves. Often, these drugs are slipped into a victim's drink when he or she is distracted.

Lesson Review

Using Vocabulary

1. What is a designer drug? ★ 4.C; 5.I

Understanding Concepts

2. What dangers are involved in using designer drugs? ★ 4.C; 5.I

3. List three designer drugs.

Critical Thinking

4. **Making Inferences** Why is it difficult to know all of a drug's effects if the drug has only existed and been used for a short time? ★ 5.H; 5.I

Lesson 9

Staying Drug Free

There are many reasons to stay drug free. One person's reasons for staying drug free might be completely different from another person's reasons. But some reasons hold true for everybody.

What You'll Do

- **Discuss** five reasons for remaining drug free. ★ 4.C; 5.H; 5.I; 5.L
- **Describe** six strategies for refusing drugs. ★ 5.J; 5.K

Start Off Write

What is one of your personal reasons to stay drug free?

Health Journal

Because everybody has different goals, everybody has his or her own reasons to stay drug free. Describe three of your goals, and explain how using drugs could keep you from reaching these goals.

Reasons to Stay Drug Free

1. **Staying Healthy** Drugs can cause many health problems. These problems can be as harmless as lack of energy. They can also be as serious as coma, brain damage, cancer, or death. Protecting your health and doing drugs do not go together.

2. **Staying in Control** Drugs seriously affect the way you behave. Often, people who take drugs act in ways that they would never act if they were not on drugs. This change in behavior is especially true of people who are addicted. Losing control of the way you act can have serious consequences. Staying drug free ensures that you are in control of your actions.

3. **Making Good Decisions** Using drugs seriously impairs judgment and can cause difficulty in thinking. The decisions that a person makes while on drugs may not be the same decisions that he or she would have made when he or she was not on drugs. Making the right decisions is important. Doing so is difficult or impossible while on drugs.

4. **Staying Out of Jail** If you are caught using illegal drugs, you could be sent to jail. Going to jail takes away your freedom and can ruin many of your plans for the future. By staying away from illegal drugs, you can keep your freedom and your future.

5. **Saving Your Money** Drug use can be very expensive. A drug addiction can waste even more money. By avoiding drugs, you can avoid a number of serious financial problems.
★ 4.C; 5.H; 5.I; 5.L

Figure 21 One reason to avoid drugs is to stay competitive in sports.

Refusing Drugs

Avoiding drugs is the right choice, but it can be hard. Pressure to do drugs can come from many places. Developing skills for refusing drugs and avoiding situations in which you may be pressured to do drugs are very important. The clearest and best way to refuse drugs is simple: You say, "No, thank you." Usually, those three words are enough. However, sometimes the pressure to do drugs is strong. The person or people that are pressuring you sometimes will not take "no" for an answer. In this case, there are certain strategies that you can use. First, make it clear that you do not want the drugs. If that doesn't work, give a reason for not using drugs. You could say something like "I have a big test tomorrow. I really need to study," or "I'm supposed to babysit my sister tonight." You should also try suggesting another activity, such as going out for food or playing a game. If all of these strategies fail, remember that the easiest way to get out of a pressure situation is to leave.

There are many ways to say no to drugs. However, the best way to avoid drugs is to avoid pressure situations altogether. Avoid the places and situations in which you know drugs will be present. In this way, you can make sure that you never feel pressured to start using drugs. ★ 5.J; 5.K; 11.D

Figure 22 Knowing how to refuse drugs is important.

LIFE SKILLS ACTIVITY

USING REFUSAL SKILLS

Imagine that somebody at a party has just asked you to do drugs. Find a partner in your class, and work together to think of 10 ways that you could refuse the drugs.

Lesson Review

Understanding Concepts

1. What are five reasons to stay drug free? ★ 4.C; 5.H; 5.I; 5.L
2. Why might using drugs lead you to make poor decisions? ★ 5.I
3. What are six ways to refuse drugs? ★ 5.J; 5.K; 11.D

Critical Thinking

4. **Making Inferences** Is there a connection between any two of the reasons to stay drug free? Explain. ★ 4.C; 5.L
5. **Applying Concepts** Describe a situation in which there might be pressure to do drugs. ★ 7.A; 12.E

Lesson 10 — Getting Help

What You'll Do

- **Explain** the importance of recognizing a drug problem.
  ✯ 12.A; 12.B
- **Discuss** three different options for treating drug abuse or addiction.
  ✯ 5.J; 5.K; 10.E

Terms to Learn

- intervention
- treatment center
- detoxification

Start Off Write

How could a support group help a person who used to abuse drugs?

Paula is very proud of her brother Eddie. One year ago, he was addicted to cocaine. Paula and her family confronted her brother and enrolled him in a drug treatment program. Now, Eddie is off of drugs and is returning to college. What did Eddie need to get better?

There are many ways to treat drug problems. The right treatment is different for every addicted person. Eddie needed to stay in a place where health professionals could help him with his problem. He was lucky that he was able to get the help he needed. However, to get the right help, a person must know when and how to ask for help.

Knowing When You Need Help

The first step in getting help for drug abuse is simply to realize that the problem exists. Because people who abuse drugs tend to make excuses and hide their abuse, recognizing a drug abuse problem can be very hard. Recognizing a problem can be even harder if you are the one who has the problem. However, it is very important because treatment for a drug abuse problem cannot start until the problem is recognized. Anytime a person repeatedly abuses drugs, that person has a drug abuse problem for which they need help. ✯ 12.A; 12.B

Figure 23 Getting help for a drug addiction is often as simple as asking for help.

Figure 24 An intervention is sometimes necessary to get an addicted person to accept help.

Helping Someone Else

You may notice that a friend is acting differently from usual. He or she may have become distant or less interested in activities that he or she used to enjoy. He or she may also be suddenly having problems at school or at home. This friend may simply be having some hard times. However, these problems may also be signs of drug abuse. If you think a friend needs help, the first step is to get him or her to admit the problem. It may be very difficult for someone to admit that he or she has a drug problem. In this case, an intervention (IN tuhr VEN shuhn) may be necessary. An **intervention** is a gathering in which the people who are close to a person who is abusing drugs try to get the person to accept help by relating stories of how his or her drug problem has affected them. If you are planning an intervention, it is usually best to seek the advice or help of a professional counselor. ★ 4.C; 5.J; 11.D

Counseling

Once a person who abuses drugs has recognized the problem, he or she is ready to get help. Sometimes, a person's problem can be helped through counseling. Through counseling, the person may discuss his or her problems with a person who is trained to offer advice and solutions for emotional problems. By addressing the emotional problems behind a drug problem, a person who abuses drugs is more likely to stay off drugs. Although counseling is a good start toward ending a drug problem, some people need a stronger approach. ★ 4.C; 5.J; 12.F

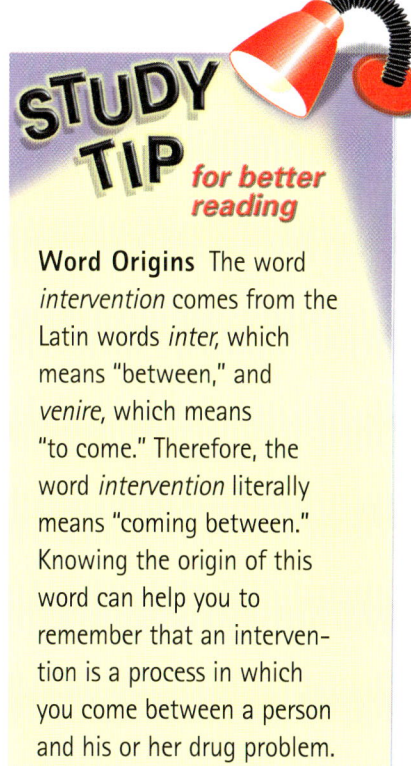

STUDY TIP *for better reading*

Word Origins The word *intervention* comes from the Latin words *inter*, which means "between," and *venire*, which means "to come." Therefore, the word *intervention* literally means "coming between." Knowing the origin of this word can help you to remember that an intervention is a process in which you come between a person and his or her drug problem.

Figure 25 Treatment centers offer counseling and support for people who are fighting an addiction.

Treatment Centers

Some people get help for their drug problems at treatment centers. A treatment center is a facility with trained doctors and counselors where people who abuse drugs can get help for their problems. While the people who abuse drugs stay at a treatment center, they participate in many therapy sessions, group discussions, and activities aimed at solving their drug problems. Spending time in a treatment center also helps people who abuse drugs stay away from things that may tempt them to use drugs again.

The first step that a person who abuses drugs takes at any treatment center is detoxification (dee TAHK suh fuh KAY shuhn). Detoxification is the process by which the body rids itself of harmful chemicals. A person who has been abusing a drug almost always has traces of that drug in his or her blood. These traces contribute to his or her addiction because the drug never fully leaves his or her body. Detoxification can be a long and extremely painful process. During this process, all traces of a drug are removed from a person's system. Detoxification includes the process of withdrawal, which can be very difficult and painful. ★ 4.C; 5.K

Myth & Fact

Myth: As soon as a drug's effects go away, the drug is out of your system.

Fact: The effects of a drug may stop after a few hours. However, the drug actually remains in your bloodstream for some time. Traces of some drugs can be found in the bloodstream for up to 2 months after the drug was taken.

Support Groups

Even after receiving treatment for drug abuse, the person may have difficulty adapting to life without drugs. An easy and effective way to deal with this problem is to become a member of a support group. A *support group* is a group of people who have undergone the same or very similar problems. In a support group, people discuss their problems and work together to find solutions or comfort. Numerous support groups exist for people who used to abuse drugs. Often, the family or friends of a person who abuses drugs may find that they also need the type of comfort or advice that a support group can offer. Therefore, many support groups have been formed for the family and friends of people who abuse or who have abused drugs.

★ 4.C; 5.K; 10.E

Recovery Is Never One Step

A person addicted to drugs can take many different paths to get well. However, there is no easy way to solve a drug abuse problem. No matter how a person chooses to work on his or her problem, the path to recovery is long and difficult. Many people who used to abuse drugs will always have to fight the urge to use drugs. These people will require ongoing treatment, usually in the form of a counselor or a support group.

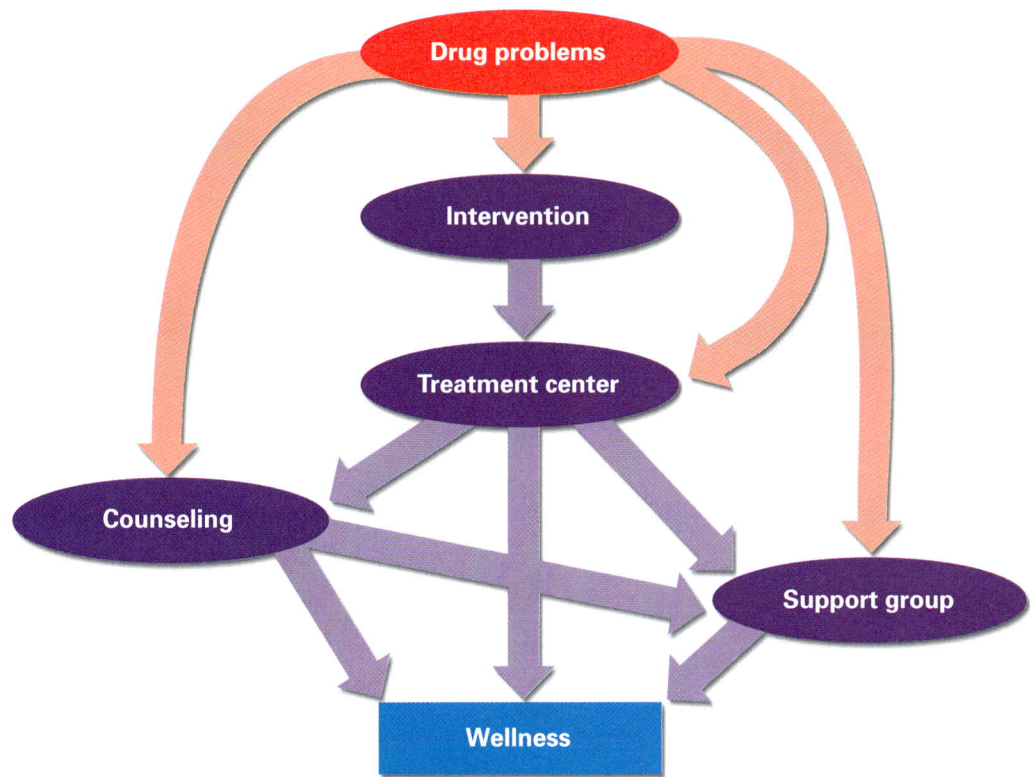

Figure 26 The Many Paths to Wellness

Lesson Review

Using Vocabulary

1. Describe an intervention. ★ 5.J; 5.K
2. What is a treatment center? ★ 5.J; 5.K

Understanding Concepts

3. Why is recognizing a drug problem so important? ★ 12.A; 12.B
4. What are three different options for treating drug abuse or addiction? ★ 5.J; 5.K; 10.E

Critical Thinking

5. **Applying Concepts** Why do you think detoxification is the first step a drug abuser takes at a treatment center? ★ 5.H; 5.I
6. **Making Inferences** What advantages might a support group have over counseling? ★ 10.E

Lesson 10 Getting Help

16 CHAPTER REVIEW

Chapter Summary

- A drug is any chemical substance that causes a change in a person's physical or psychological state. ■ Many drugs are used as medicine. When using medicine, it is important to follow safe practices, such as following the directions on the bottle. ■ If used properly, drugs can be very valuable. But misusing drugs can lead to drug abuse or even addiction. ■ Drug abuse can quickly get out of control. Drug abuse causes problems in every part of a person's life by interfering with relationships and school. ■ Recovering physically and psychologically from drug abuse is much harder than refusing drugs is. But there are several treatment options for people who abuse drugs.

Using Vocabulary

For each pair of terms, describe how the meanings of the terms differ.

1. drug/medicine
2. prescription medicine/over-the-counter medicine
3. stimulant/depressant
4. physical dependence/psychological dependence

For each sentence, fill in the blank with the proper word from the word bank provided below.

medicine	intervention
side effect	THC
depressant	treatment center
Ecstasy	detoxification

5. A(n) ___ is any effect that is caused by a drug and that is different from the drug's intended effect.
6. ___ is the active substance in marijuana.
7. A(n) ___ is any drug that is used to cure, prevent, or treat illness or discomfort.
8. ___ is the common name given to the chemical MDMA.
9. A(n) ___ is a facility with trained doctors and counselors where drug abusers can get help for their problems.

Understanding Concepts

10. How does the body absorb drugs that are swallowed?
11. How does tolerance put a drug user at high risk for an overdose? ★ 5.I
12. Why can some drugs be bought only with a prescription? ★ 4.C; 5.H; 5.I
13. What are the steps of the drug approval process?
14. What is the source of all opiates? ★ 4.C
15. How does a flashback occur? ★ 5.I
16. What are three examples of designer drugs? How are designer drugs created? ★ 5.I
17. List the five reasons to stay drug free that are listed in this chapter. Which is the best reason for you? Explain. ★ 4.C; 5.H; 5.I; 5.L
18. Why is recognizing a drug problem important? ★ 12.A; 12.B
19. What options does a person have for getting help with a drug problem? ★ 5.J; 5.K; 10.E

Critical Thinking

Applying Concepts

20. Imagine that you have just taken a drug. A few minutes later, you notice that your heart is beating much faster and that you are breathing faster. You feel very awake and very alert. What type of drug have you taken? Explain your answer. ★ 4.C; 5.I

21. Imagine that you have taken a drug. You feel restless. You have difficulty judging time, and you begin to see colors and patterns that were not there before. What type of drug have you taken? Explain your answer. ★ 4.C; 5.I

Making Good Decisions

22. You are sick and are taking a prescription cough medicine that your doctor gave to you. Suddenly, you get a headache. The school nurse offers to give you some medicine for your headache. What should you do? ★ 4.A; 4.C

23. A doctor prescribes a medicine for you. The doctor tells you that the medicine may cause stomachaches and thirst. After 3 days of taking this medicine, you do not have a stomachache and you are not thirsty, but you have a small rash on your arms. Your friend says that the rash is probably nothing and will go away. What should you do? ★ 4.A; 4.C

24. Imagine that you have a bad cough. You took the medicine that your doctor gave you, but it isn't helping. Your friend has some cough syrup that she bought at the store. She says it works great, and she offers to share it with you. Is sharing her medicine a good idea? Why or why not? ★ 4.A; 4.C; 5.I

Interpreting Graphics

The People's Pharmacy
252 FIRST STREET
HOUSTON, TX 77077
(713) 242-2299
DEA# AS 3455

Rx 1085407C   01/02/04   01/02/04
BROWN, THOMAS   CC
TAKE 1 TABLET EVERY 6 HOURS
AS NEEDED FOR PAIN
TYLENOL W COD #3   30MG   MCNEI
DR. ORLANDO, ANTHO QTY: 30   NO REFILL
CAUTION: FEDERAL LAW PROHIBITS THE TRANSFER OF THIS DRUG TO ANY PERSON OTHER THAN THE PATIENT TO WHOM IT WAS PRESCRIBED.
Keep out of reach of children.

CONTROLLED SUBSTANCE. DANGEROUS UNLESS USED AS DIRECTED. CAUTION: Federal law prohibits the transfer of this drug to any person other than the patient to whom it was prescribed.

MAY CAUSE DROWSINESS. ALCOHOL MAY INTENSIFY THIS EFFECT. USE CARE WHEN OPERATING A CAR OR DANGEROUS MACHINERY.

Use the figure above to answer questions 25–30.

25. What type of drug is contained in this bottle?

26. How much of this drug should be taken at one time?

27. How often should this drug be taken?

28. Are there any special precautions that the user of this drug should take when using this medicine? What are these precautions?

29. Who is the only person allowed to take this drug?

30. What is this medicine intended to treat?

Reading Checkup

Take a minute to review your answers to the Health IQ questions at the beginning of this chapter. How has reading this chapter improved your Health IQ?

Chapter 16 Review | 425

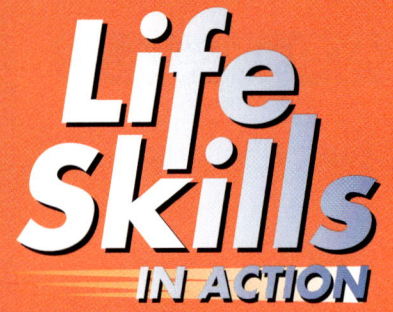

Using Refusal Skills

Using refusal skills is saying no to things you don't want to do. You can also use refusal skills to avoid dangerous situations. Complete the following activity to develop your refusal skills.

Pila's Party Predicament

Setting the Scene

Rosa has invited Pila to a party. Pila doesn't really know any of the kids who will be at the party, but she has heard there might be drugs at the party. Pila really likes Rosa, but the thought of going to the party makes Pila uncomfortable.

★ 5.K; 5.L; 11.A; 11.D

The 5 Steps of Using Refusal Skills

1. Avoid dangerous situations.
2. Say "No."
3. Stand your ground.
4. Stay focused on the issue.
5. Walk away.

Guided Practice

Practice with a Friend

Form a group of three. Have one person play the role of Rosa and another person play the role of Pila. Have the third person be an observer. Walking through each of the five steps of using refusal skills, role-play what Pila should say to Rosa. Rosa needs to be convincing. The observer will take notes, which will include observations about what the person playing Pila did well and suggestions of ways to improve. Stop after each step to evaluate the process.

Independent Practice

Check Yourself

After you have completed the guided practice, go through Act 1 again without stopping at each step. Answer the questions below to review what you did.

1. Which refusal skills did you use? How did you use them?
2. How hard was it to refuse to go to the party?
3. When was it a good time to walk away?
4. Which refusal skill do you think is your weakest? Explain. ★ 11.A; 11.D

ACT 2 — On Your Own

Later that week, Pila is bored at home. She knows Rosa is at the party. The phone rings. Rosa has called to ask Pila if she is sure she doesn't want to come to the party. Rosa says she won't take no for an answer. Think about how you would say no to Rosa if you were Pila. Write a skit about the telephone conversation between Rosa and Pila. Be sure to stress Pila's use of refusal skills.
★ 5.J; 5.K; 11.D

Chapter 16 Using Refusal Skills | 427

CHAPTER 17
Infectious Diseases

Lessons

1. **What Is an Infectious Disease?** — 430
2. **Defenses Against Infectious Diseases** — 434
3. **Common Bacterial Infections** — 438
4. **Common Viral Infections** — 440
5. **Sexually Transmitted Diseases** — 442
6. **HIV and AIDS** — 444
7. **Preventing the Spread of Infectious Diseases** — 448

Chapter Review — 450
Life Skills in Action — 452

Check out **Current Health** articles related to this chapter by visiting **go.hrw.com**. Just type in the keyword **HD4CH49**.

> **"Six** months ago, I started feeling very **tired** all of the time. I thought I was just working hard at school and not getting enough **sleep**. When I went to the doctor, he told me I had *mononucleosis*. He said that was why I was so tired.**"**

PRE-READING

Answer the following multiple-choice questions to find out what you already know about infectious diseases. When you've finished this chapter, you'll have the opportunity to change your answers based on what you've learned.

1. Which of the following diseases is NOT an infectious disease?
   a. strep throat
   b. cancer
   c. influenza (the flu)
   d. tuberculosis ★ 3.B

2. Which of the following diseases is NOT a contagious disease?
   a. tuberculosis
   b. bacterial sinusitis
   c. common cold
   d. AIDS ★ 3.B

3. Which of the following symptoms are symptoms of a common cold?
   a. rash
   b. fever
   c. runny nose
   d. vomiting

4. Antibiotics are drugs that are used to treat
   a. viral infections
   b. bacterial infections
   c. the flu
   d. HIV

5. HIV is spread through
   a. sexual contact.
   b. the sharing of needles.
   c. a blood transfusion.
   d. All of the above ★ 3.D

6. Which of the following is NOT a first-line defense against germs?
   a. skin
   b. tears
   c. saliva
   d. fever

7. Which of the following behaviors cannot spread mononucleosis?
   a. sharing food
   b. kissing
   c. holding hands
   d. drinking after an infected person ★ 3.A

ANSWERS: 1. b; 2. b; 3. c; 4. b; 5. d; 6. d; 7. c

Lesson 1: What Is an Infectious Disease?

What You'll Do

- **Identify** five types of infectious agents. ★ 3.B
- **Describe** ways in which infection can spread. ★ 3.B; 3.C
- **Describe** bacterial and viral infections. ★ 3.B
- **Explain** how antibiotics fight bacterial infections. ★ 3.A; 3.B

Terms to Learn

- infectious disease
- bacteria
- antibiotic
- virus

Start Off Write

How do infections spread?

Terrence woke up one morning feeling horrible. He had a high fever, and his whole body ached. The doctor said that Terrence had the flu. What caused this illness?

Terrence caught the flu from his friend. He had been infected with the virus that causes influenza (IN floo EN zuh).

Infectious Diseases

There are many kinds of illnesses. Examples include cancers, heart diseases, and diabetes. However, these are not infectious diseases. An **infectious disease** (in FEK shuhs di ZEES) is any disease that is caused by an agent that can pass from one living thing to another. Infectious agents are very tiny and usually cannot be seen with the naked eye. There are many different types of infectious agents, and they exist almost everywhere. Some infectious diseases, such as tuberculosis and smallpox, are contagious, while others, such as sinusitis, are not. A *contagious disease* is a disease that can be passed directly from one person to another person.

★ 3.B

TABLE 1 Disease-causing Organisms

Infectious agent	How it looks	What it is	Examples
Bacterium		a one-celled organism that is found everywhere	strep throat, tuberculosis, sinus infections
Virus		an extremely small organism that consists of only a protein coat and some genetic material	cold, influenza
Fungus		a fungus relies on other living or dead organisms to survive; yeasts, molds, and mildews are included in this group	athletes' foot, ringworm
Protozoan		a single-celled organism; much more complex than a bacterium; protozoal infections usually come from infected water or food	amebic dysentery
Parasite		an organism that lives in a host organism; draws nourishment from a host; some may be very large	tapeworm, malaria

★ 3.B

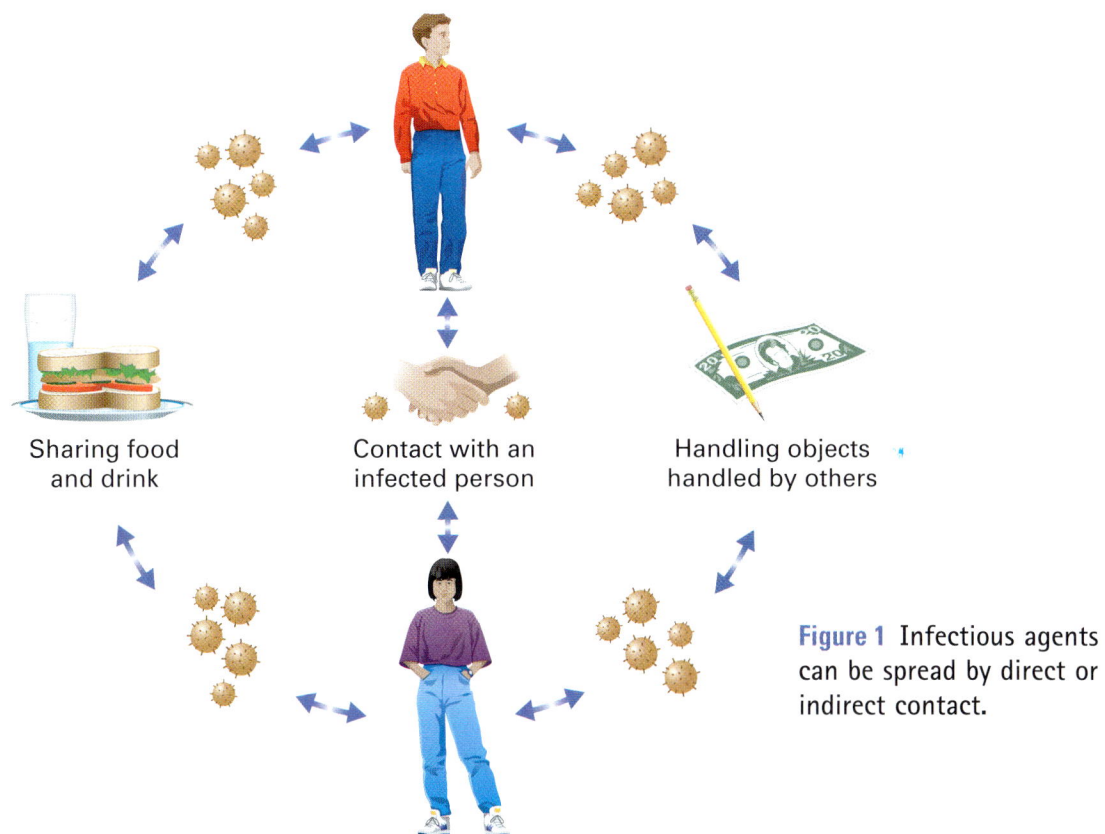

Figure 1 Infectious agents can be spread by direct or indirect contact.

How Infection Spreads

Not all infections are contagious, but those that are contagious can spread in many different ways. Infections can spread directly or indirectly from person to person, from animal to person, from insect to person, or even indirectly from food or water to a person. Sometimes, a person can be infected by handling an object that was previously touched by an infected person or that simply has an infectious agent on it. When infections pass between people, they are normally passed by touching, or by sharing food or drink. Infectious disease may be spread when one person coughs or sneezes, releasing germ-filled water droplets into the air. If another person inhales these droplets, that person may become infected.

Sometimes, infections can spread from a single source to many people, causing an epidemic. An *epidemic* is a widespread occurrence of a disease. For example, in 1832, many people in a neighborhood in London, England, were dying from a bacterial disease called *cholera (KAHL uhr uh)*. The government searched for months for the source of this infection. They finally discovered that the disease was being passed through water contaminated with human sewage. A broken pump that was used by the entire neighborhood to supply water to their homes was responsible for this disaster. ★ 3.B; 3.C

Research one of the three major outbreaks of the bubonic plague. Explain how this disease was spread from person to person.

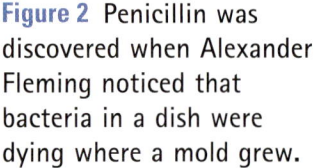

BACTERIAL REPRODUCTION

1. A certain bacterium reproduces itself every 20 minutes. Assume that there is one bacterium. In 20 minutes, there are two bacteria; in 40 minutes, there are four bacteria; and so on.
2. Make a graph that shows the growth of the bacteria in 20-minute intervals. The graph should go up to 2 hours.

Analysis

1. How many bacteria would there be at the end of 1 hour? at the end of 2 hours?
2. You may notice that the number of bacteria starts increasing more quickly as time goes on. What is the reason for this?

Bacterial Infections

Many serious infections are caused by bacteria. **Bacteria** (bak TIR ee uh) are very small, single-celled organisms that are found almost everywhere. Some examples of infections that bacteria cause are tetanus, ulcers, and tuberculosis. Although many types of bacteria can cause infection, you benefit from bacteria, too. Millions of bacteria live in your body. They help protect you from harmful bacteria and help you digest your food. ★ 3.B

Antibiotics

In 1928, Alexander Fleming, a Scottish scientist, was cleaning some trays in which he had been growing bacteria. He noticed something strange. In one dish, a mold had begun to grow. And the bacteria directly around the mold were dead. The mold had produced something toxic to the bacteria. Fleming had just discovered the first antibiotic, penicillin (PEN i SIL in).

An **antibiotic** (AN tie bie AHT ik) is a drug that kills or slows the growth of bacteria. Before the discovery of antibiotics, doctors had few if any tools to fight bacterial infections. Penicillin turned out to be an incredibly effective tool for fighting bacterial infections. And it is still the most commonly used antibiotic. Since the discovery of penicillin, scientists have discovered and created dozens of other antibiotics. Different antibiotics are used to treat different infections. Some new antibiotics are even specially designed through the use of computers. Examples of commonly used antibiotics are penicillin, ampicillin (AM puh SIL in), and erythromycin (e RITH roh MIE sin). ★ 3.A

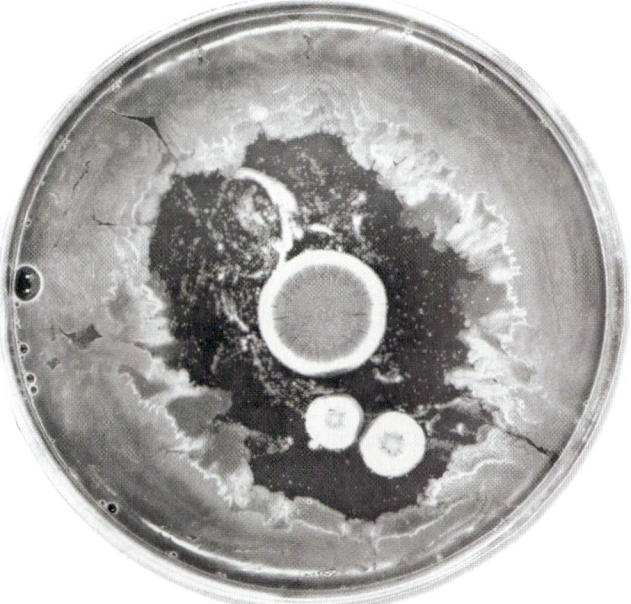

Figure 2 Penicillin was discovered when Alexander Fleming noticed that bacteria in a dish were dying where a mold grew.

Viral Infections

Many infections are caused by germs called viruses. A **virus** is an extremely small particle that consists of an outer shell and genetic material. Unlike bacteria, viruses cannot reproduce by themselves. The only thing a virus can do is attach to and enter a host cell. It then takes over that host cell's machinery to make more viruses. Most scientists agree that viruses are not living organisms because viruses cannot reproduce outside of a host.

The symptoms of a viral infection vary and may include nasal congestion and a sore throat, as in a cold, or body aches and fever, as in the flu. Medications are now available to fight certain viral infections, such as herpes and HIV/AIDS. However, many of these medications, especially those used to treat HIV, have very unpleasant side effects. Today, many people are vaccinated to prevent them from getting certain viral infections. 3.B

Myth: Antibiotics are available to treat most infections.

Fact: Antibiotics are available to treat most bacterial infections. However, antibiotics are useless against viral infections.

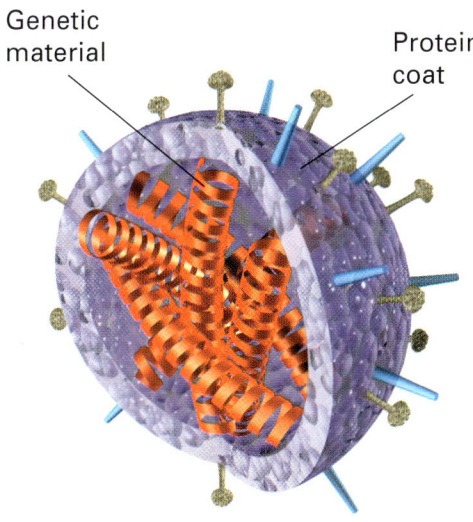

Figure 3 A virus usually is made of only a protein coat and genetic material.

Lesson Review

Using Vocabulary

1. How is an infectious disease different from a disease like cancer? 3.B

2. What is a virus? 3.B

Understanding Concepts

3. What type of infections are antibiotics used to fight? 3.A; 3.B

4. Describe how coughing or sneezing can pass an infection to another person. 3.B; 3.C

5. How are viruses different from bacteria? 3.B

Critical Thinking

6. **Making Inferences** In the 1832 cholera epidemic in London, was the infection contagious? Explain. 3.B

Lesson 2

Defenses Against Infectious Diseases

What You'll Do

- **Describe** how the body keeps germs out. ★ 1.A; 3.A
- **Explain** how the body fights diseases internally. ★ 1.A; 3.A

Terms to Learn

- immune system

How does your body defend itself against disease?

When Diana got sick last summer, she had a very high fever, which caused her to have chills and a terrible headache. What caused Diana's fever?

Infections can cause fever. Although Diana's fever made her feel awful, it was actually helping her body fight the infection that was making her sick. A fever raises your body temperature, which may kill the organisms that are causing the infection. It may also increase the rate at which your body fights the infection.

Your Body's Defense System

Everywhere you go, you encounter germs that can cause very serious illnesses. In fact, even as you read this, there are millions of germs on your body. So why don't you get sick more often? The answer is that your body has a defense system to protect you from most infections. The first part of this defense system is made up of physical barriers, such as your skin, saliva, and nasal hairs. These physical barriers keep the majority of germs from entering your body. However, some germs do manage to get past these physical barriers. And that's when your immune system takes over. The **immune system** is made up of organs and special cells that fight infection. Without your immune system, your body would be powerless against most of the agents that cause infections and disease.
★ 1.A; 3.A

Figure 4 There are dangerous germs wherever you go. Your body's immune system protects you from almost all of these germs.

Figure 5 Physical Barriers to Infection

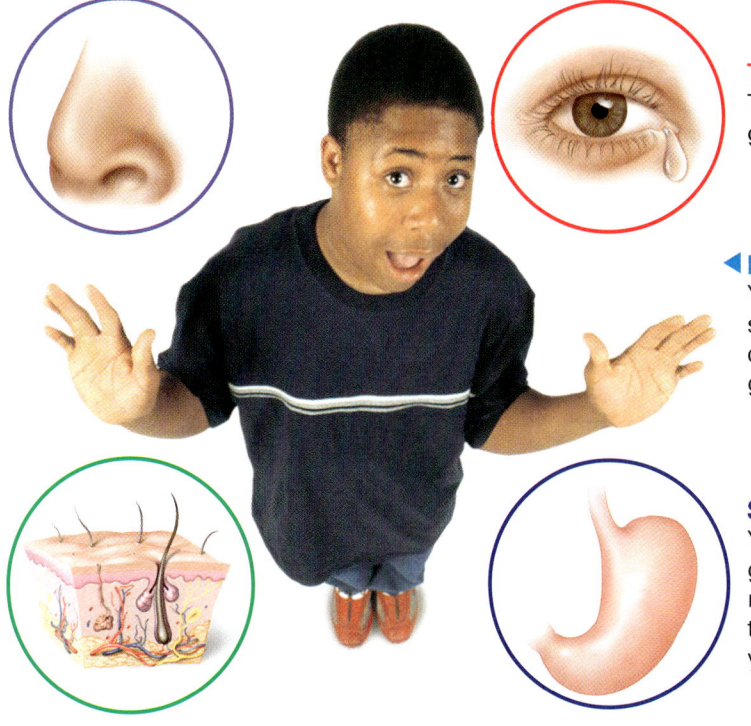

Nose Your nose contains mucus and tiny hairs, which both trap germs and keep them from entering your body.

Tears Tears wash dirt and germs from your eyes.

Mouth Your mouth contains saliva, which contains chemicals that kill germs.

Skin The outer layer of the skin is tough and keeps germs from entering your body.

Stomach Your stomach contains gastric juices that kill many of the germs that do make it into your body.

The Front Line: Keeping Germs Out

Your body's defense system has several physical barriers to keep germs from getting into your body. Some of these barriers are as follows:

- **Skin** When a germ tries to invade your body, the first thing it comes into contact with is the skin. Your skin is actually made of many layers of cells. The cells on the outside are tough and dead, which makes it difficult for a germ to get through. These cells are also constantly falling off, taking germs with them.

- **Hairs** The hair around your eyes and nose traps germs and keeps them from getting into your body. The large airways of the lungs also have tiny hairs called *cilia* that keep germs out of the lungs.

- **Tears** Your eyes produce tears that wash germs out of your eyes.

- **Mucus** The sticky substance that exists in your nose and other parts of your body is called mucus. Mucus not only traps germs but also contains chemical defenses to attack and destroy the germs.

- **Saliva and Stomach Acid** Most of the germs that enter your mouth and stomach are killed by saliva and stomach acid. ★ 1.A; 3.A

SCIENCE ACTIVITY

Joseph Lister was the physican who introduced the concept of washing your hands as a way to prevent the spread of disease. This is where the name of the mouthwash, *Listerine*, came from. Research Lister's germ theory.

Lesson 2 Defenses Against Infectious Diseases

Figure 6   The Internal Immune System

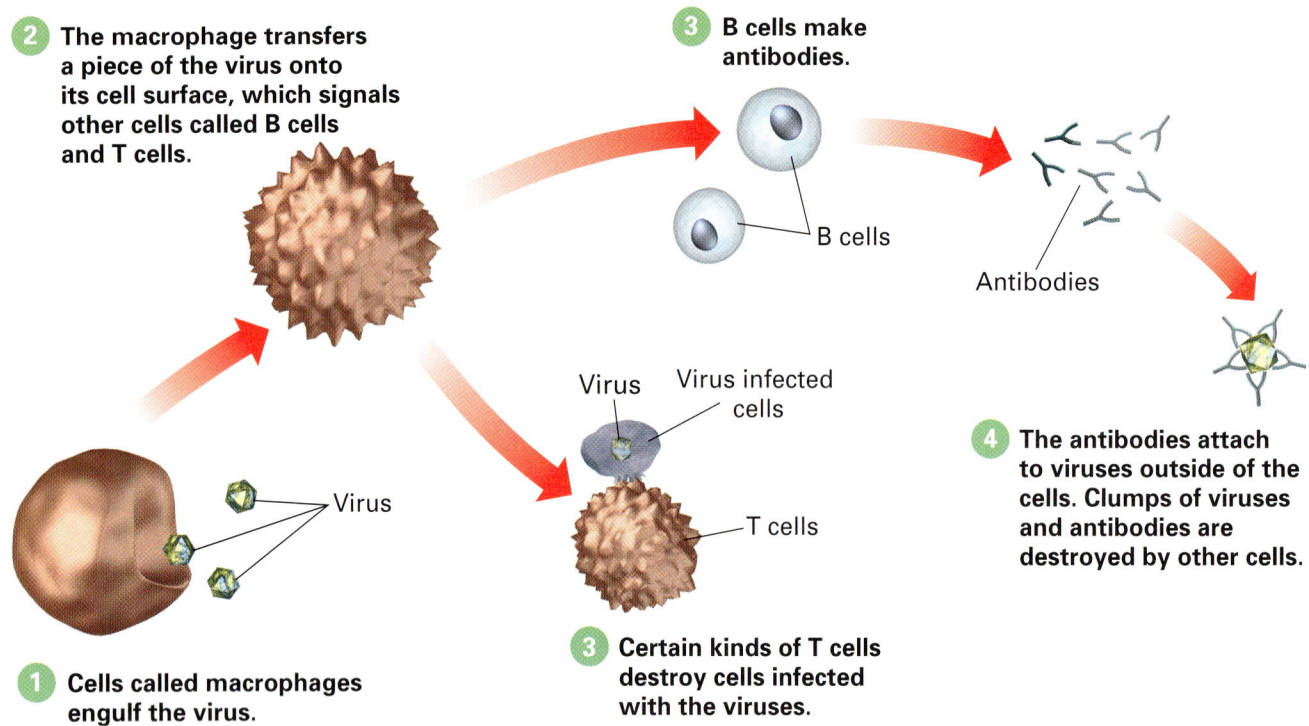

① Cells called macrophages engulf the virus.

② The macrophage transfers a piece of the virus onto its cell surface, which signals other cells called B cells and T cells.

③ B cells make antibodies.

③ Certain kinds of T cells destroy cells infected with the viruses.

④ The antibodies attach to viruses outside of the cells. Clumps of viruses and antibodies are destroyed by other cells.

Your Body's Internal Defenses

In the event that a germ gets through the physical barriers of the defense system, it still has to do battle with the inner workings of the immune system. The reaction of the body to a germ that has gotten in is called an *immune response*.

Imagine that a virus has entered your body and invaded your body's cells. This is the immune response that would follow:

1. Cells called *macrophages* (MAK roh FAYJ uhz) engulf the cells that have been infected by viruses.
2. The macrophages signal cells called *T cells* and cells called *B cells*.
3. The B cells produce antibodies, which are substances that destroy germs. The T cells help destroy the virus-infected cells.
4. Antibodies attach to other viruses outside of the cells. This signals other cells to destroy the viruses.

A particular antibody works on only one particular germ. However, your body remembers how to make the antibodies for every disease that you have ever had. If that disease attacks you again, your body remembers how to fight it. That is why once you have had certain diseases, such as chicken pox, you rarely catch them again. This is called *immunity*. ★ 1.A; 3.A

Health Journal

Write a short story (one or two pages) in which you are a bacterium or a virus. Tell what happens as you infect someone's body. Describe how you get into the body, what you do once you get in, and what happens when you encounter the immune system.

Keeping Your Immune System Strong

Keeping your immune system strong is very important. The healthier your immune system is, the less you will get sick. A healthy body and a healthy immune system go hand in hand. Think of it this way: if you take care of your body, then your body will take care of you. To strengthen your immune system, you have to eat right and exercise regularly. You should also get the vaccinations you need and go the doctor regularly to make sure that your body is healthy. If you get very ill, you can sometimes take certain medications to give your immune system a boost.

Understanding what keeps your immune system strong also means understanding what makes it weak. The immune system can be weakened by certain behaviors. For example, if you are not getting enough sleep or if you are not getting all of the vitamins that you need in your diet, your immune system may suffer. Engaging in certain activities, such as using alcohol, tobacco, or illegal drugs, can seriously weaken your immune system. ★ 1.A; 3.A

Figure 7 Regular exercise keeps your immune system strong.

Lesson Review

Using Vocabulary
1. Describe the immune system in your own words. ★ 1.A; 3.A

Understanding Concepts
2. What are five things that your body uses to keep germs out? ★ 1.A; 3.A
3. What is an immune response? ★ 3.A
4. Why can't you catch chicken pox twice? ★ 3.A
5. List four things that you can do to make sure that your immune system stays strong. ★ 3.A

Critical Thinking
6. **Making Inferences** What would happen to you if your body had no immune system? ★ 3.A; 3.B; 3.C

Lesson 2 Defenses Against Infectious Diseases

Lesson 3

Common Bacterial Infections

What You'll Do

- **Describe** the causes and symptoms of three common bacterial infections. ★ 3.B; 3.C

What are three diseases that are caused by bacteria?

Myth & Fact

Myth: Strep throat is no big deal.

Fact: If strep throat goes untreated, many complications can result—some of which can be fatal.

Last summer, Marina had a bad cough and a high fever. The doctor wanted to test her for tuberculosis. Marina didn't want to be tested, but the doctor said it was very important. Why was it so important for Marina to have this test?

Marina had to be tested for tuberculosis because this infection is not only life-threatening but also very contagious. Bacterial infections can be very dangerous if they are allowed to go untreated.

Strep Throat

Strep throat is an infection caused by a bacterium called *streptococcus*. This bacterium can be spread from person to person through sharing food and drink or touching. The main symptom of strep throat is pain when you swallow. Strep infection can also make you feel achey and feverish. If your doctor thinks you may have strep throat, he or she may perform a throat culture. A throat culture is a test in which a doctor uses a cotton swab to wipe the back of your throat. The material on the swab is then tested for strep-throat bacteria. If the test is positive, your doctor will give you an antibiotic. It's important to take the antibiotic for the full course of treatment, even if you feel better in a few days. Otherwise, the infection could return.
★ 3.A; 3.B; 3.C

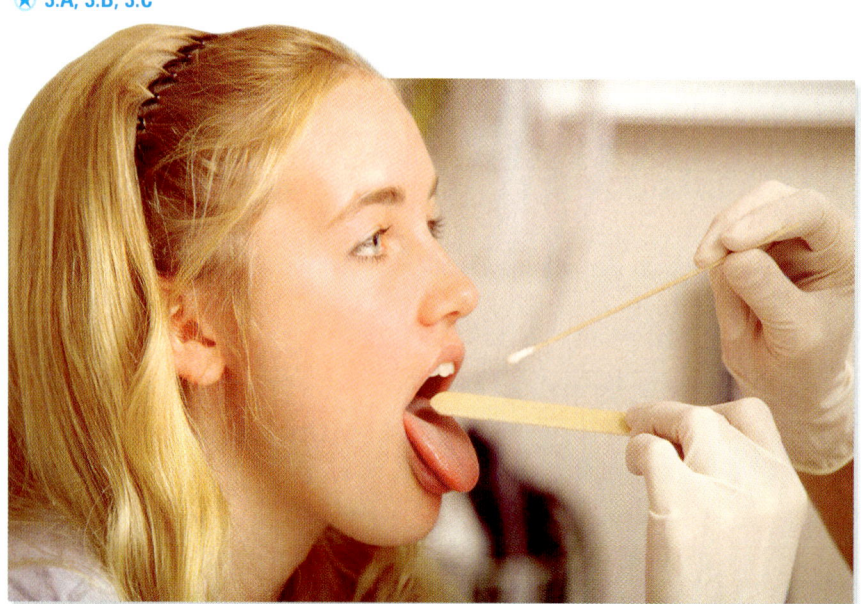

Figure 8 A throat culture is a very simple and painless test that can show whether or not you have strep throat.

Tuberculosis

Tuberculosis (too BUHR kyoo LOH sis) is a bacterial infection caused by very slow-growing organisms from a family of bacteria called *mycobacteria* (MIE koh bak TIR ee uh). Tuberculosis affects a large percentage of the world's population and kills about 3 million people a year. Tuberculosis is spread by coughing, which releases the bacteria into the air. This cough can infect an average of 80 other people.

The symptoms of tuberculosis are persistent cough, weakness, fever, and sweating. By doing a skin test, such as a PPD test, your doctor can tell if you have been exposed to tuberculosis. To treat tuberculosis, doctors use combinations of up to five antibiotics. Even with treatment, some cases of tuberculosis are deadly. All cases of tuberculosis must be reported to the health department which then must track and test all of the people that have been in contact with the infected person. ★ 3.A; 3.B

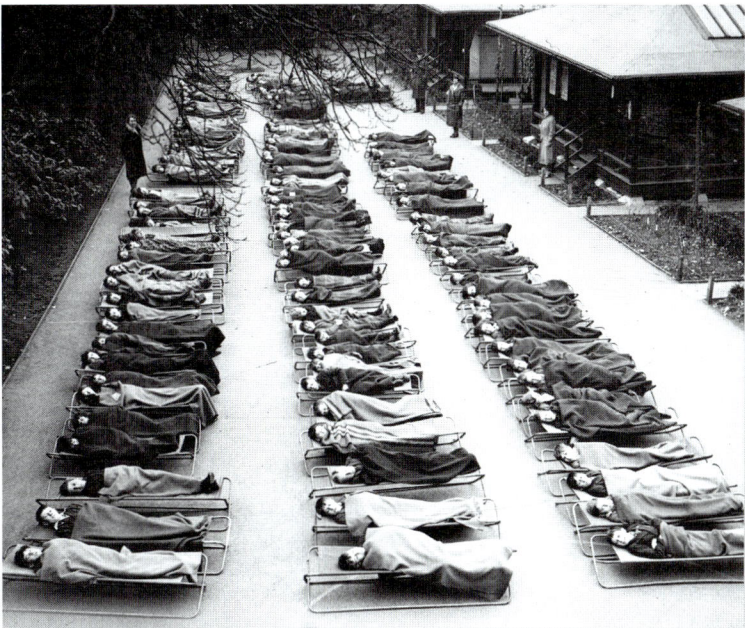

Figure 9 At the beginning of the 20th century, tuberculosis was still fatal. Tuberculosis patients, like the ones above, were kept in special hospitals so that they would not infect others.

Sinus Infections

The *sinuses* are open areas in your skull that are located behind your face and above your mouth. These areas can fill with mucus and become infected with bacteria. This condition is called *sinusitis* (SIEN uhs IET is). Symptoms include congestion, a runny nose, fever, or a headache. Sinusitis is usually not contagious. Sinus infections are often confused with colds or flu because of similar symptoms. ★ 3.B; 3.C

Lesson Review

Understanding Concepts

1. Describe three bacterial infections. Are these infections contagious? ★ 3.B; 3.C
2. What are three symptoms of tuberculosis? ★ 3.B
3. How does sinusitis occur? ★ 3.B
4. What is one danger of allowing tuberculosis to go untreated? ★ 3.B; 3.C

Critical Thinking

5. **Analyzing Ideas** Why does the health department track people who have been in contact with tuberculosis patients? ★ 3.A; 3.B; 3.C

internet connect
www.scilinks.org/health
Topic: Bacteria
HealthLinks code: HD4012
HEALTH LINKS — Maintained by the National Science Teachers Association

Lesson 3 Common Bacterial Infections

Lesson 4

Common Viral Infections

What You'll Do

- **Identify** three common viral infections. ★ 3.B
- **Explain** what a vaccine is. ★ 3.A

Terms to Learn

- vaccine

Start Off Write

What are some symptoms of the flu?

Myth: You catch a cold by being outside in cold or wet weather.

Fact: Colds are caused by viruses, not by weather.

Tomás remembers one day last year when half of the people in his math class were sick with a cold. What caused so many people in the math class to get sick at one time?

The illness that struck so many of the people in the math class was caused by a common cold virus. Colds are just one of the many infections caused by viruses. Every year, viral infections cause thousands of days of missed school and work. Severe acute respiratory syndrome (SARS), a viral infection that suddenly appeared in 2003, was even fatal to many people.

The Common Cold

The average person catches about two colds a year. The common cold is actually caused by many different viruses. Cold viruses are usually passed from person to person by touch. However, they can also be passed by sneezing or coughing. When you have a cold, stay away from other people as much as possible so that you do not spread the disease. Washing your hands frequently can also lower the risk of catching or spreading a cold.

Cold symptoms usually include sore throat, sneezing, congestion, headache, and a runny nose. Because the cold is caused by many different viruses, developing a medicine that protects you from the cold is very difficult. A medicine that works on one cold virus would probably not work against other cold viruses. ★ 3.A; 3.B

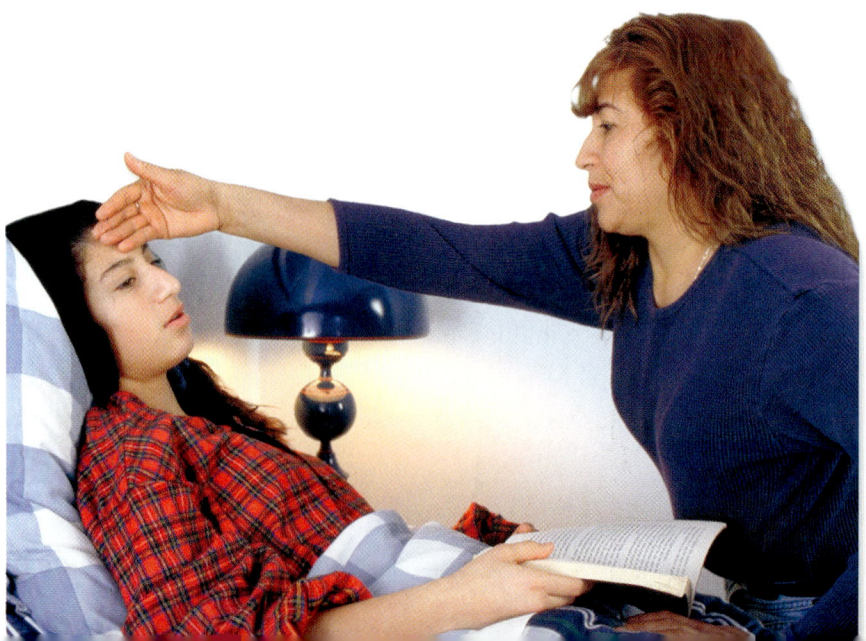

Figure 10 Although a cold is not a very serious illness, it can make you feel miserable.

Influenza

Influenza, or "the flu," is actually a virus from one of the two groups of viruses called *influenza A* and *influenza B*. Influenza can be passed by touching, coughing, or sharing food and drink. Symptoms of influenza include fever, chills, and body aches as well as all the symptoms of a cold virus. These symptoms can be very mild or very severe.

A **vaccine** is a substance that is used to keep a person from getting a disease. The flu vaccine changes every year as different types of influenza travel worldwide. Even though your body develops immunity to any virus that infects you, influenza viruses change all the time, which means that you may have the flu many times in your life. ★ 3.B; 3.C

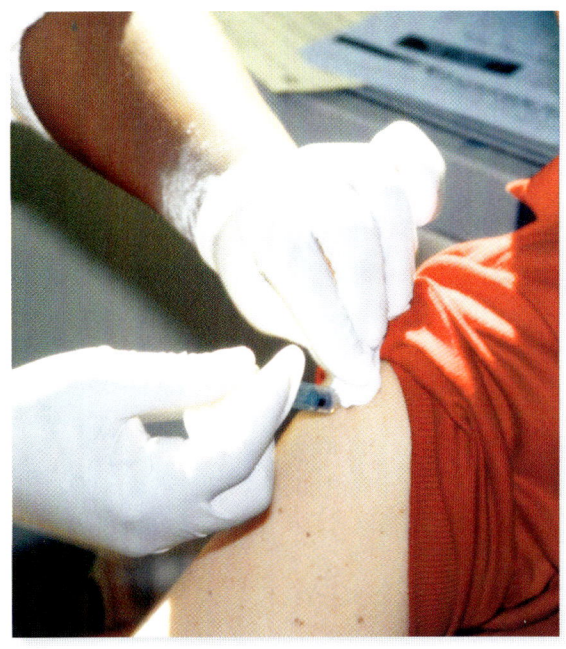

Figure 11 Getting a flu shot is a lot less painful than catching the flu.

Mononucleosis

Infectious mononucleosis (MAHN oh NOO klee OH sis) is caused by a virus called *Epstein-Barr virus*, or *EBV*. Mononucleosis is passed through infected saliva, which is why it is sometimes called "the kissing disease." But kissing isn't the only way to catch mononucleosis. It can also be passed by sharing food or drink. The symptoms of mononucleosis are swollen glands in the neck, fever, feeling tired, and sore throat. The liver and spleen can also be affected. In fact, the spleen may stay swollen for a month or longer. Care must be taken during this month to not rupture, or burst, the spleen. The disease is easily diagnosed by a blood test. About one-half of those infected have no symptoms at all, while others stay ill for many weeks. Currently, there is no cure for mononucleosis. ★ 3.B; 3.C

Brain Food

Every once in a while, a particularly deadly type of influenza develops. In the winter of 1918–1919, a deadly type of influenza killed tens of millions of people worldwide.

Lesson Review

Using Vocabulary

1. Define *vaccine*. ★ 3.A

Understanding Concepts

2. Why is creating a vaccine to fight the common cold difficult? ★ 3.A; 3.B
3. What are three common viral infections? ★ 3.B
4. What are the symptoms of the three diseases that you studied in this lesson? ★ 3.B; 3.C

Critical Thinking

5. **Analyzing Concepts** If cold weather is not responsible for catching the flu, then why do more people get the flu in the winter? ★ 3.A; 3.B

internet connect
www.scilinks.org/health
Topic: Viruses
HealthLinks code: HD4104
HEALTH LINKS Maintained by the National Science Teachers Association

Lesson 5

Sexually Transmitted Diseases

What You'll Do

- **Explain** why abstinence is the only sure way to avoid sexually transmitted diseases.  3.D; 5.D; 5.F
- **Identify** six common sexually transmitted diseases.  3.D

Terms to Learn

- sexually transmitted diseases
- sexual abstinence

Start Off Write

What are sexually transmitted diseases?

Every year, there are 15 million new cases of disease that are spread through sexual contact. And many of these diseases have no cure!

Many painful and dangerous diseases, such as herpes are passed from person to person through sexual contact. These diseases are called sexually transmitted diseases. **Sexually transmitted diseases,** or STDs, are contagious infections that are spread from person to person by sexual contact. There are over 75 kinds of sexually transmitted diseases.

What Are STDs?

STDs are transmitted through an exchange of bodily fluids during sexual contact. Many different types of infections can be transmitted sexually. These infections can be caused by bacteria, viruses, fungi, or other infectious agents. Although some STDs can be treated successfully, many STDs still have no cure.

Symptoms of an STD depend on the type of infection. Some symptoms include a discharge from the genitals, sores in the genital area, a rash, and pain while urinating. Some people can have an STD but show no symptoms at all. These people are called *carriers*. Carriers are very dangerous because they can transmit an infection without even knowing it.

STDs are very common. In fact, as many as one out of every five Americans may have an STD. With so many people infected, the only certain way to keep from catching these diseases is by abstinence. **Sexual abstinence** is the deliberate choice to refrain from all sexual activity. 3.A; 3.B; 3.D; 5.D; 5.F

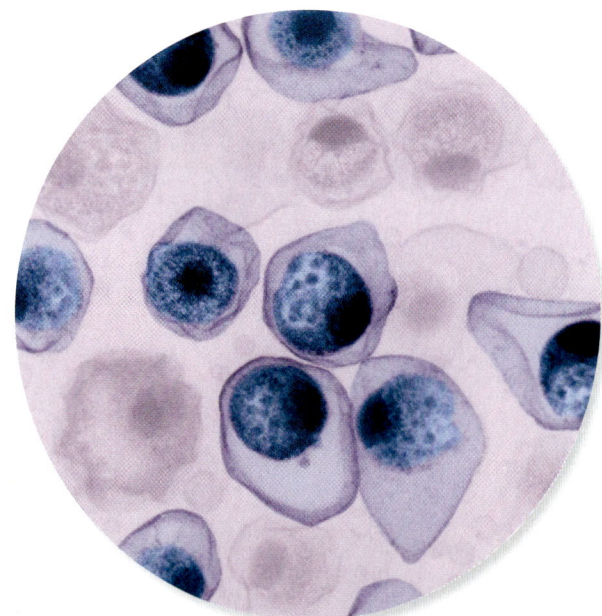

Figure 12 Chlamydia is the most common sexually transmitted bacterial disease. It is caused by a bacterium that lives within certain cells.

TABLE 2 Common STDs

Disease	Symptoms	Treatment or cure	Long-term consequences
Chlamydia (kluh MID ee uh)	Some people show no symptoms, especially women. Others have a discharge from the genitals, painful urination, and severe abdominal pain.	Chlamydia can be cured with antibiotics taken by mouth.	Sterility and liver infection can result from Chlamydial infections.
Human papillomavirus (HYOO muhn PAP i LOH muh VIE ruhs) (HPV)	Some people show no symptoms; others have warts on the genital area, and women have an abnormal Pap-smear test.	HPV can be treated, but not cured. Sometimes, warts can be removed. Pap-smear tests help to identify precancerous conditions.	If left untreated, cervical cancer can occur in women.
Genital herpes (JEN i tuhl HUHR PEEZ)	Herpes causes outbreaks of painful blisters or sores around the genital area that recur, swelling in the genital area, and burning during urination.	Herpes cannot be cured. Treatment with antiviral medication can decrease the length and frequency of outbreaks and can decrease the spread of herpes.	If left untreated, herpes may cause cervical cancer in women. Herpes can cause deformities in unborn babies.
Gonorrhea (GAHN uh REE uh)	Some people show no symptoms. Other people have a discharge from the genitals, painful urination, and severe abdominal pain.	Gonorrhea can be cured with antibiotics, although a new strain of bacteria has shown resistance to antibiotics.	Sterility, liver disease, testicular disease can result from gonorrheal infections in not treated.
Syphilis (SIF uh lis)	Symptoms, if present, are sores, fever, body rash, swollen lymph nodes.	Syphilis can be cured with antibiotics.	If left untreated, mental illness, heart and kidney damage, and death can result.
Trichomoniasis (TRIK oh moh NIE uh sis)	Symptoms include itching, discharge from the genitals, and painful urination.	Trichomoniasis can be cured with medication.	Trichomoniasis has been linked to an increased risk of infection by HIV.

★ 3.A; 3.B; 3.D

Lesson Review

Using Vocabulary

1. What is a sexually transmitted disease? ★ 3.B
2. What is abstinence, and why is abstinence the only certain way to prevent STDs? ★ 3.D; 5.D; 5.F

Understanding Concepts

3. Name the six STDs listed in this lesson and the symptoms of each. ★ 3.B

Critical Thinking

4. **Analyzing Concepts** Is an STD that doesn't show symptoms, such as Chlamydia, still contagious? Explain your answer. ★ 3.B; 3.C; 3.D

Lesson 5 Sexually Transmitted Diseases

Lesson 6

HIV and AIDS

HIV and AIDS, which were only discovered in the early 1980s, have already killed millions of people, and millions more are currently infected.

What You'll Do

- **Explain** the difference between HIV and AIDS. ★ 3.D
- **List** four ways that HIV can be spread from person to person. ★ 3.B; 3.C; 3.D
- **Describe** how HIV and AIDS have become a worldwide problem. ★ 3.B; 3.C; 3.D

Terms to Learn

- HIV
- AIDS

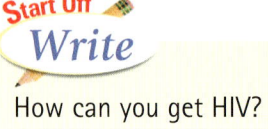

How can you get HIV?

Are HIV and AIDS the same thing? The answer is no. HIV and AIDS are different, but they are very closely linked. Learning the difference between HIV and AIDS and knowing how to protect yourself can help you understand and avoid this deadly disease.

What Are HIV and AIDS?

Acquired immune deficiency syndrome, or **AIDS**, is a serious viral disease that destroys the body's immune system. AIDS is caused by a virus called *human immunodeficiency virus* (HYOO muhn IM myoo noh dee FISH uhn see VIE ruhs), or **HIV**. Remember that HIV is a virus and that AIDS is a disease that results from infection by the HIV virus. A person can be infected with HIV and not be suffering from AIDS.

Once a person has been infected with HIV, the virus stays in a person's body for a long period of time—sometimes years—before any symptoms appear. This period of time is known as the *incubation period*. The majority of people infected with HIV develop AIDS and die. Since the first four cases of AIDS were reported in California in 1981, there are now hundreds of millions of cases all over the world. In some parts of Africa, as many as one in every four people are infected with HIV. ★ 3.B; 3.D

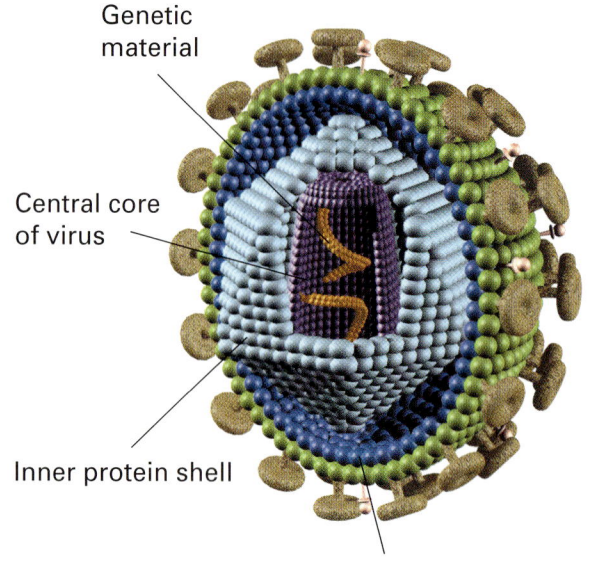

Figure 13 HIV is the virus that causes AIDS.

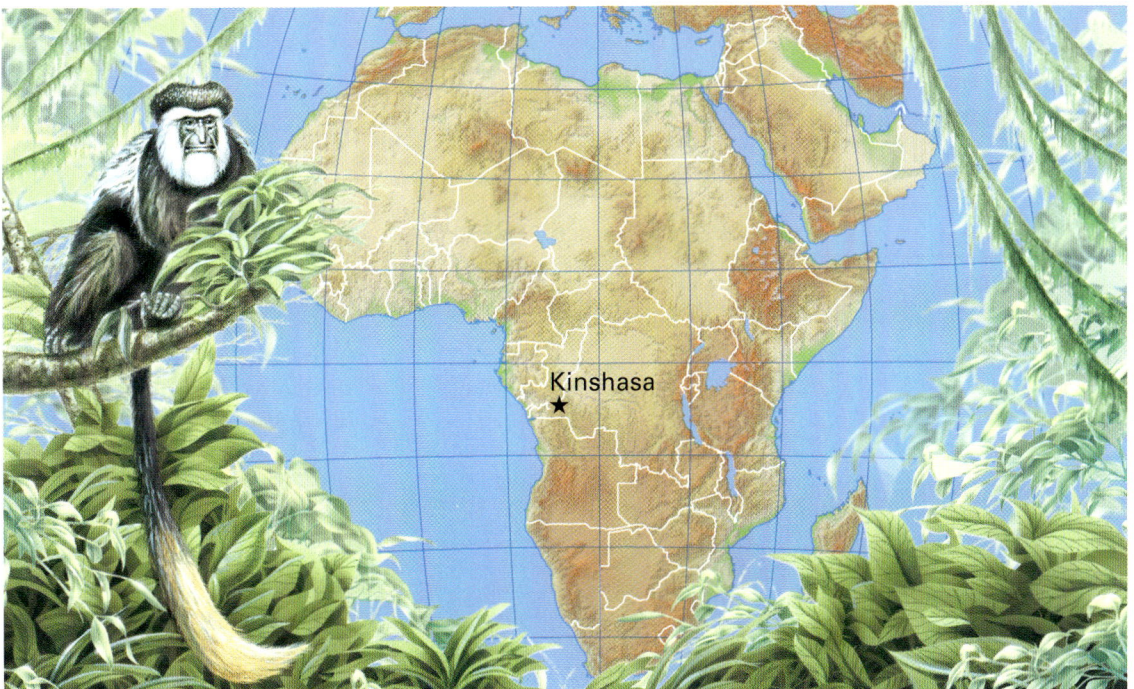

Figure 14 Scientists believe that the first cases of HIV were passed to humans from monkeys. The earliest known case of HIV happened in Kinshasa, in Africa's Congo region.

Where Did HIV Come From?

Although nobody knows for sure, most scientists think that HIV came from central Africa where the African green monkey lives. This monkey has been known to be infected with Simian immunodeficiency virus (SIM ee uhn), or SIV, which is very similar to HIV. It is thought that some SIV particles changed slightly to become HIV and somehow contaminated the blood of a hunter while he was slaughtering a monkey for food. Recent studies of a blood sample taken in Africa in 1959 have revealed the first known case of HIV. It wasn't until 1981 that the first cases of AIDS began to appear outside of Africa. HIV/AIDS is now a global problem. ★ 3.D

How HIV Is Spread

The following are methods by which HIV can be spread:

- **Sexual Contact** This is the most common way that HIV is spread from person to person.
- **Sharing Hypodermic Needles** When needles are used to inject drugs, blood can remain on the needle and be passed to the next user.
- **Blood Transfusion** This form of transmission is now rare in this country, thanks to thorough testing of the blood supply.
- **Mother to Child** HIV can be transmitted from a mother to her unborn child through their shared blood supply, or from a mother to her child through breast milk. Because of new drug treatments, these types of transmission are also rare in this country. ★ 3.B; 3.C; 3.D

Brain Food

Although the oldest known case of HIV in a human dates to 1959, it was not until the mid-1980s that this case was uncovered. The blood sample that contained the HIV had been frozen and put away since it was collected in 1959.

Lesson 6 HIV and AIDS

Figure 15 The Effects of AIDS on the Body

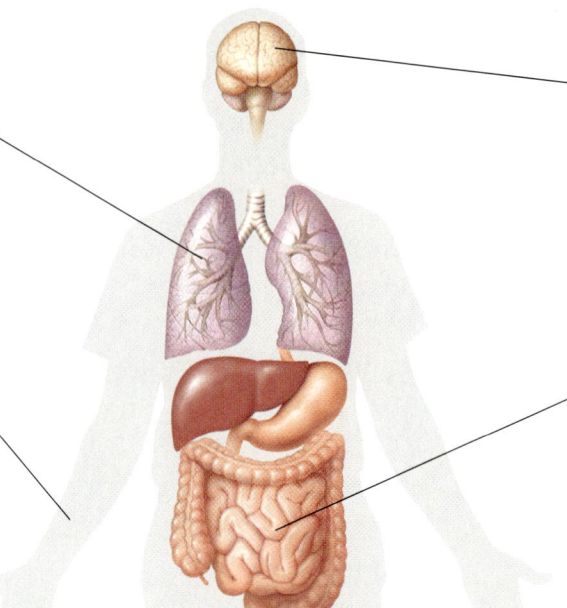

Lungs
AIDS can leave the body open to pneumonia. Pneumonia is a serious lung infection. Often, pneumonia is the reason many AIDS patients die.

Skin
AIDS sufferers often get a type of skin cancer called *sarcoma*. This cancer creates brown or blue sores on the skin. Many AIDS sufferers are covered in these sores.

Nervous system
HIV infection and AIDS can cause many problems in the nervous system. These problems include mental problems, loss of vision, and paralysis.

Digestive system
AIDS can cause many digestive problems. These problems include frequent diarrhea and intestinal infections.

The Effects of AIDS on the Body

Because HIV attacks the immune system, it destroys your body's ability to fight infections. Once patients develop full-blown AIDS, their lifespan is usually shortened. Often AIDS sufferers get an *opportunistic infection,* or an infection that happens only in people whose immune systems are not working very well. Others get some kind of cancer, such as lymphoma (cancer of the lymph nodes) or sarcoma (a cancer of the skin). ★ 3.D

How HIV and AIDS Are Treated

The time that passes from when a person is infected with a disease and when he or she actually gets sick is called the *incubation period*. In AIDS, the incubation period can be over 10 years. The only treatment available for AIDS is a combination of several drugs and is called *combination therapy*. These drugs slow the reproduction of the HIV virus and lengthens the incubation period of HIV. A second type of treatment is usually needed for AIDS patients who suffer from opportunistic infections. Different types of opportunistic infection require different kinds of treatments. Unfortunately, these treatments only delay the progress of the disease, and most patients die from AIDS. ★ 3.A; 3.D

Myth & Fact

Myth: A combination of many drugs has allowed people with HIV to live comfortably for many years.

Fact: The drugs used to treat HIV cause people infected with HIV to feel weak and physically ill. People who take these drugs must take dozens of pills every day. These drugs are also extremely expensive.

The HIV/AIDS Epidemic

Since the first cases of AIDS were reported, the disease has spread to every country in every continent. In this country, there are larger pockets of infection in places such as New York City, San Francisco, and Los Angeles. However, HIV also exists in small towns and rural areas. HIV is a huge problem in the rest of the world too. The African continent has been hardest hit by the HIV epidemic. In some parts of Africa, as many as one in four people is infected. HIV infection is rapidly spreading in parts of Asia as well. In less developed countries, poor medical care and little education about the disease make this problem worse. In fact, the problem is getting worse everywhere. As of the writing of this book, about 40 million people worldwide are infected with HIV and over 22 million have already died from it. ★ 3.B; 3.D

Research the history of HIV and AIDS from 1982 to 1986. Write a report on your research. Include how scientists gathered their data and finally discovered that a virus caused AIDS.

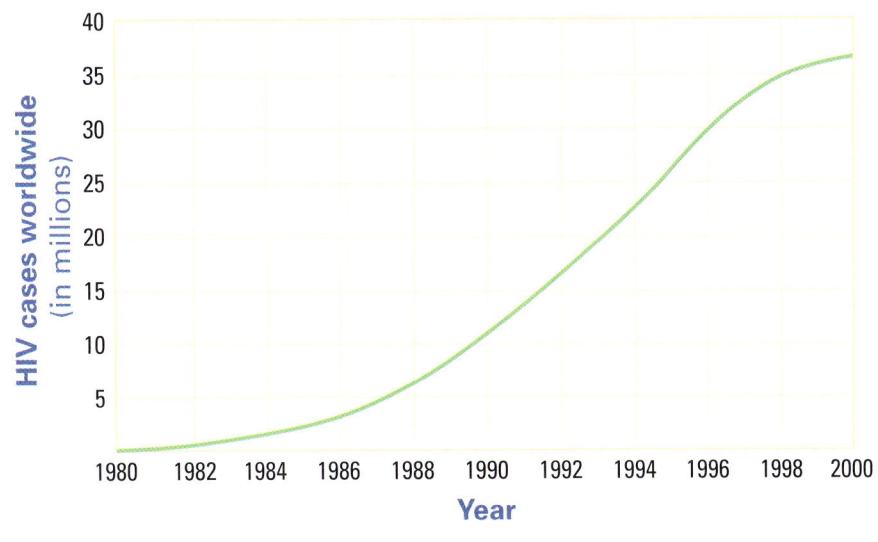

Source: Joint United Nations Program on HIV/AIDS

Figure 16 This graph shows a worldwide increase in the number of people living with HIV and AIDS.

Lesson Review

Using Vocabulary

1. In your own words, describe the difference between HIV and AIDS. ★ 3.D

Understanding Concepts

2. What are four ways that HIV can be passed from person to person? ★ 3.B; 3.C; 3.D

3. Which continents have avoided the HIV/AIDS epidemic? ★ 3.B; 3.C; 3.D

Critical Thinking

4. **Analyzing Ideas** Imagine that you are in charge of decreasing the number of new HIV infections in Africa. What are three things that you would do? ★ 3.A; 3.B

www.scilinks.org/health
Topic: AIDS Research in Texas
HealthLinks code: HHTX002
HEALTH LINKS Maintained by the National Science Teachers Association

Lesson 7

Preventing the Spread of Infectious Diseases

Last year, Roland caught the flu and was sick for almost a week. This year, Roland is doing everything he can to keep from catching the flu again.

What You'll Do

- **Identify** situations and behaviors that increase or decrease the risk of catching an infectious disease. ★ 3.B; 3.C
- **Describe** four ways to prevent infectious diseases from spreading to others. ★ 3.B; 3.C
- **Explain** the importance of getting vaccinations. ★ 3.A; 3.C

Start Off Write

What is the best way to avoid catching a cold or the flu?

No matter what you do, you are going to get sick every once in a while. However, there are things that you can do to reduce your risk of catching or spreading an infectious disease.

Protecting Yourself

There are many ways to protect yourself from getting infections. The best way to avoid infection is to try to stay away from people who have a contagious disease, such as a cold or flu. However, this is not always possible. Sometimes, you have to be around an infected person, such as a sick family member. Other times, an infected person may not know that he or she is infected and may unknowingly pass the infection to others. However, avoiding people with certain diseases is not always necessary. For example, you can't catch HIV from casual contact. Table 3 lists a few simple things that you can do to reduce your risk of catching an infection. ★ 3.A; 3.B; 3.C

PRACTICING WELLNESS

Do this activity with a partner. Make a list of eight diseases you have learned about. Next to each disease in your list, write two symptoms of the disease and what you can do to protect yourself from that particular disease.

TABLE 3 Protecting Yourself from Infections

What to do	How it helps
Wash your hands and bathe regularly with soap and warm water	Washing your hands and bathing remove germs from your body, which lowers your risk of infection.
Avoid contact with people who have a contagious infection.	Staying away from known sources of infection is the easiest way to avoid becoming infected.
Do not eat or drink after others.	Eating or drinking after other people, even if those people don't look sick, is a very easy way to catch an infection. By not sharing food or drink, you protect yourself from possible infection.
Eat a balanced diet, get enough sleep, and exercise regularly.	Eating the right foods, exercising, and getting enough sleep make your body stronger and more able to fight infections.

★ 3.A; 3.B; 3.C

448   Chapter 17   Infectious Diseases

Protecting Others

Being considerate to others by preventing the spread of any infection is very important. If you have a cold or flu, for example, you should wash your hands regularly. This will keep germs off of your hands and will prevent you from spreading infections by touch. Also, if you are coughing or sneezing, try to cough or sneeze into your elbow rather than into your hand or into the air. Last, if you know that you have a contagious infection, avoid situations in which you are in contact with people. For example, if you are sick with a contagious infection, you should stay home from school so that you don't infect your classmates. ★ 3.A; 3.B; 3.C

Getting Your Shots

Remember that a vaccine is a substance that is used to make a person immune to a certain disease. But how does a vaccine work? Vaccines are made of inactivated, or weakened, germs that trick the body into thinking that it has been infected. In turn, this trick causes your body to produce antibodies that can be used if you are exposed to the infection in the future. Therefore, you become immune to the disease without ever getting sick. There are many vaccines currently available. All of these vaccines go through testing and are considered very safe, although they occasionally can have side effects. Early childhood vaccinations include hepatitis, measles, mumps, rubella (German measles), polio, diphtheria, tetanus, pertussis (whooping cough), and chickenpox. Ask your doctor if you have had all of the vaccinations that you need. ★ 3.A; 3.B

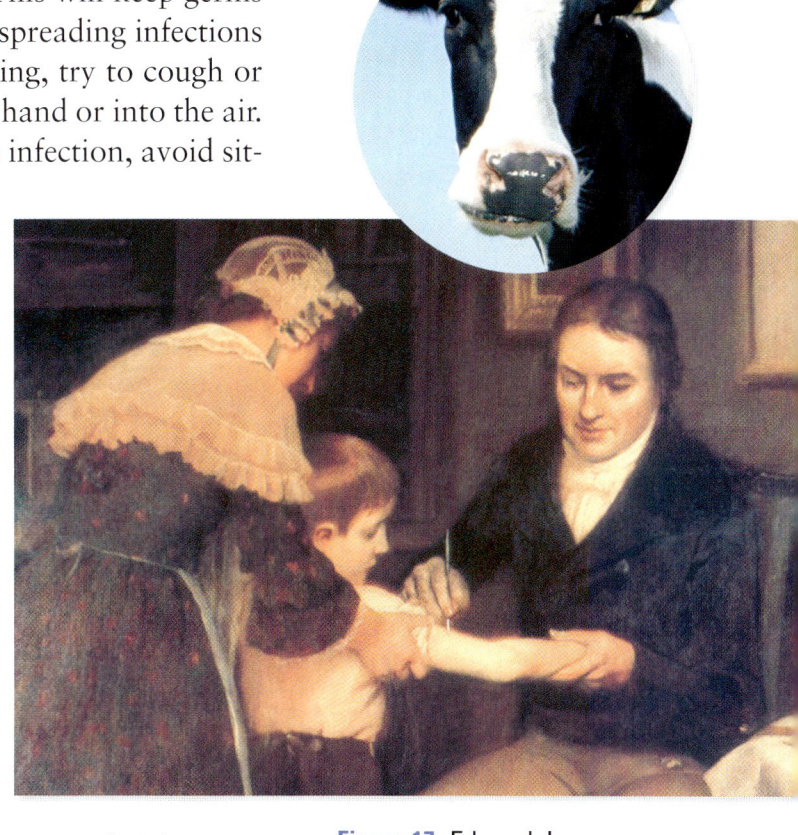

Figure 17 Edward Jenner developed the first vaccine for smallpox from a similar virus called *cowpox*, a disease that mainly infected cattle.

Lesson Review

Understanding Concepts

1. What is the best way to avoid infection? ★ 3.A; 3.B; 3.C

2. What are four other things that you can do to reduce your chances of catching an infection? ★ 3.A

3. Why should you stay home from school if you are sick? ★ 3.A; 3.B

Critical Thinking

4. **Making Inferences** If you have had all of the vaccinations that your doctor recommends, does that mean that you can stop worrying about avoiding infections? Explain. ★ 3.B; 3.C

Lesson 7 Preventing the Spread of Infectious Diseases

17 CHAPTER REVIEW

Chapter Summary

■ Infectious diseases are caused by infectious agents that invade the body. ■ Some infectious diseases are contagious, and some are not. ■ Germs can be passed from person to person in many ways. ■ The most common types of infections are bacterial infections and viral infections. ■ Antibiotics are drugs that fight bacterial infections. ■ The immune system is your body's main weapon against infection. ■ Sexually transmitted diseases are passed from person to person by sexual contact. ■ Abstinence, or avoiding all sexual contact, is the only sure way to avoid STDs. ■ HIV is a virus that causes a deadly disease called *AIDS*. ■ Knowing how to protect yourself and others from infectious diseases is very important.

Using Vocabulary

For each pair of terms, describe how the meanings of the terms differ.

1. infectious disease/contagious disease
2. AIDS/HIV
3. bacteria/virus
4. immune system/immune response

For each sentence, fill in the blank with the proper word from the word bank provided below.

abstinence   HIV
STDs   bacteria
sinuses   antibiotic
vaccine

5. A(n) ___ is a drug that kills bacteria or slows the growth of bacteria.

6. The ___ are open areas in your skull that are located behind your face and above your mouth.

7. ___ are contagious infections that are spread from person to person by sexual contact.

8. ___ is avoiding all sexual contact.

Understanding Concepts

9. List three examples of infections that are contagious, and describe how each one can be passed from person to person. ★ 3.B; 3.C

10. What virus causes mononucleosis? ★ 3.B

11. Describe how a vaccine works. ★ 3.A; 3.B

12. What are three activities or behaviors that could weaken your immune system? ★ 1.A; 3.A; 3.C

13. Arrange the following steps in the immune response in the correct order.

    a. The B cells produce antibodies, which are substances that destroy germs. The T cells help destroy the virus-infected cells.

    b. Antibodies attach to viruses and signal other cells.

    c. Cells called *macrophages* engulf the cells that have been invaded by viruses.

    d. The macrophages signal cells called *T cells* and cells called *B cells*. ★ 1.A

14. What does it mean that the incubation period of HIV was about 5 years for a certain patient? ★ 3.B; 3.C

450   Chapter 17   Review

Critical Thinking

Applying Concepts

15. Would a doctor prescribe an antibiotic for you if you had a cold? Explain. ★ 3.A; 3.B

16. Imagine that you have a fever, body aches, runny nose, sore throat, and a headache. What type of infection might you have? Explain. ★ 3.B

17. Stewart is taking an antibiotic medicine for a sinus infection. His friend Lewis has strep throat. Stewart is not worried about catching Lewis's infection because Stewart is taking antibiotics. Should Stewart be worried? Will the antibiotics protect him from catching Lewis's infection? ★ 3.A; 3.B; 3.C

18. Steven, Lourdes, and Dionne ate together at a restaurant last night. Steven and Dionne shared a soda, Dionne and Lourdes shared a sandwich, and all three shared a basket of french fries. A day later, all three of them were sick. Describe two ways that this infection could have spread to all three of them. ★ 3.B; 3.C

Making Good Decisions

19. You just got over mononucleosis, and you've been feeling well for the last week. You want to start playing football again before the season is over. However, you know that there is a chance you could damage your spleen. What should you do? ★ 3.C

20. Imagine that you are on the school basketball team. You have a big game coming up next week, but you have caught the flu. Should you go to practice anyway? What might happen if you do go to practice? ★ 3.A; 3.B; 3.C

Interpreting Graphics

Deaths Due to AIDS from 1981 to 2000

Age group	AIDS deaths
Under 15	5,086
15–24	8,726
25–34	129,781
35–44	181,633
45–54	78,788
55 or older	34,368

Use the table above to answer questions 21–25. ★ M.8.5.A

21. How many people under the age of 15 died from AIDS between 1981 and 2000?

22. Which age group had the most AIDS deaths?

23. How many more people in the age group of 15–24 died from AIDS than did people in the 25–34 age group?

24. Why do you think that most of the people who died of AIDS between 1981 and 2000 were 35 or older?

25. How many people died of AIDS between 1981 and 2000?

Reading Checkup

Take a minute to review your answers to the Health IQ questions at the beginning of this chapter. How has reading this chapter improved your Health IQ?

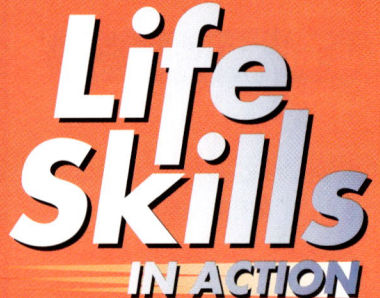

Life Skills IN ACTION

Practicing Wellness

Practicing wellness means practicing good health habits. Positive health behaviors can help prevent injury, illness, disease, and even premature death. Complete the following activity to learn how you can practice wellness.

Jamal's After-School Job

Setting the Scene

Jamal volunteers at a daycare center after school. He really enjoys his work and hopes to be a pediatrician some day. However, since he started working at the daycare, Jamal has noticed that he has been getting sick more frequently. He thinks that this is happening because several of the children in the center have colds. Jamal doesn't want to quit working at the center, but he doesn't want to be sick all the time either. ★ 3.B; 3.C

The 4 Steps of Practicing Wellness

1. Choose a health behavior you want to improve or change.
2. Gather information on how you can improve that health behavior.
3. Start using the improved health behavior.
4. Evaluate the effects of the health behavior.

Guided Practice

Practice with a Friend

Form a group of two. Have one person play the role of Jamal, and have the second person be an observer. Walking through each of the four steps of practicing wellness, role-play Jamal working to reduce his chances of catching colds from the children at the daycare center. Have Jamal identify at least one health behavior that he can improve. The observer will take notes, which will include observations about what the person playing Jamal did well and suggestions of ways to improve. Stop after each step to evaluate the process. ★ 3.A; 3.B; 3.C

452 | Chapter 17 Life Skills in Action

Independent Practice

Check Yourself

After you complete the guided practice, go through Act 1 again without stopping at each step. Answer the questions below to review what you did.

1. What are some health behaviors that Jamal may need to change or improve to avoid getting sick? ⭐ 3.A

2. What resources can Jamal use to find information about good health behaviors? ⭐ 4.A; 4.C

3. How can Jamal evaluate whether the changes in his health behaviors are effective? ⭐ 4.A; 4.B

4. What health behaviors do you practice to reduce your chances of getting sick? ⭐ 3.A

On Your Own

Jamal learned several health behaviors that reduced his chances of getting colds. He adopted several of the behaviors and did not become sick as often. Now, Jamal's younger sister has the flu. Jamal does not want to catch the flu, and he does not want to infect the children at the daycare center. Imagine that you are Jamal and make a pamphlet for the parents and children at the daycare center that describes how to avoid getting and spreading the flu. Be sure to emphasize the four steps of practicing wellness in your pamphlet.

CHAPTER 18
Noninfectious Diseases

Check out **Current Health** articles related to this chapter by visiting **go.hrw.com.** Just type in the keyword **HD4CH50.**

Lessons

1. Disease and Disease Prevention — 456
2. Hereditary Diseases — 460
3. Metabolic and Nutritional Diseases — 462
4. Allergies and Autoimmune Diseases — 464
5. Cancer — 466
6. Chemicals and Poisons — 470
7. Accidents and Injuries — 472

Chapter Review — 474
Life Skills in Action — 476

" I'm pretty lucky. The most serious **disease** I usually get is a **cold**. But my mom has **high blood pressure,** and my cousin has **sickle cell** disease. They both take medicine every day. I'm not sure how they got their diseases, but I hope that I can avoid the diseases. "

PRE-READING

Answer the following multiple-choice questions to find out what you already know about noninfectious diseases. When you've finished this chapter, you'll have the opportunity to change your answers based on what you've learned.

1. Noninfectious diseases can be caused by
   a. viruses.
   b. bacteria.
   c. toxins and poisons.
   d. None of the above ★ 3.B; 3.C

2. Which of the following diseases is caused by an allergy?
   a. stroke
   b. eczema
   c. diabetes
   d. cancer ★ 3.B; 3.C

3. Smoking cigarettes may cause
   a. lung cancer.
   b. heart disease.
   c. emphysema.
   d. All of the above ★ 3.B; 3.C

4. A head injury resulting from an automobile accident may cause
   a. brain disease.
   b. a cold.
   c. a broken leg.
   d. kidney disease. ★ 3.B

5. Some metabolic diseases can be treated by
   a. eating potato chips and candy.
   b. sleeping a lot.
   c. drinking water every day.
   d. eating a special diet. ★ 3.A

6. Obesity is related to which of the following conditions?
   a. high blood pressure
   b. type 2 diabetes
   c. heart attack
   d. all of the above ★ 3.B; 3.C

7. One way for adults to avoid cancer is to
   a. have periodic medical checkups.
   b. read articles about cancer.
   c. not eat ice cream.
   d. do breathing exercises. ★ 3.A; 3.B

ANSWERS: 1 c; 2 b; 3 d; 4 a; 5 d; 6 d; 7 a

Lesson 1

Disease and Disease Prevention

What You'll Do

- **Explain** what a noninfectious disease is. ★ 3.C
- **Explain** the relationship between risk factors and noninfectious diseases. ★ 3.B; 3.C
- **Identify** three strategies for preventing noninfectious diseases. ★ 3.A; 3.B

Terms to Learn

- disease
- noninfectious disease
- risk factor

Start Off Write

How might you get a disease that cannot be passed from person to person?

A car hit Sanjay while he was riding his bicycle. He wasn't wearing a helmet and had severe head injuries.

If Sanjay had worn his helmet, his risk for brain injury would have been reduced by 88 percent. Now, Sanjay's head injuries may cause permanent brain damage and brain disease.

Noninfectious Diseases and Injuries

A **disease** is any harmful change in the state of health of your body or mind. Diseases may be caused by infections or by a lack of certain nutrients. A disease may result if your immune system is not working normally. Or you may be born with certain diseases. Some diseases result from injuries.

Diseases are classified as infectious or noninfectious. A **noninfectious disease** is a disease that is not caused by a virus or a living organism. Noninfectious diseases include immune system disorders, diseases of organs or systems, and nutrition disorders.

Diseases produce signs and symptoms. A *sign* of a disease, such as a fever, is something another person can see or measure. A *symptom* of a disease, such as a sore throat, is a feeling of pain or discomfort you have when you are sick. Some diseases have several signs and symptoms. And different diseases may produce the same signs and symptoms. But it is possible to have a disease and not have symptoms. ★ 3.B; 3.C

Figure 1 People who have noninfectious diseases can lead active and happy lives.

TABLE 1 Common Noninfectious Diseases

Disease	Description
Allergy	an overreaction by the body to something that is harmless to most people, such as pollen or peanuts
Alzheimer's disease	a brain disorder that gets worse over time and that affects a person's memory and behavior
Asthma	an abnormal reaction of the respiratory system that causes shortness of breath, wheezing, and coughing
Cancer	a group of diseases that can attack any type of body tissue, in which cell growth is uncontrolled
Circulatory system diseases	a group of diseases that affect the heart and blood vessels, such as hardening of the arteries, high blood pressure, and heart failure
Muscular dystrophy	a group of diseases that cause muscle tissue to get weaker over time

Noninfectious Diseases and Risk Factors

Many noninfectious diseases cannot be prevented. Some of them are inherited from parents, and some are present at birth but are not inherited. A person's age, gender, and, in some cases, race also play a role in some noninfectious diseases. So does diet, or the type and amount of food you eat. All these factors—age, gender, race, and diet—are what doctors call risk factors. A **risk factor** is a characteristic or behavior that raises a person's chances of getting a noninfectious disease.

You have no control over some risk factors, such as how old you are, whether you are a boy or a girl, and the racial group to which you belong. You cannot change these characteristics.

But there are other risk factors, such as how much food you eat, that you can control. And in some cases, the risk factors you can control are the most important ones. For example, lung cancer is one of the leading causes of death in this country. Some lung cancer may be inherited, and some may be caused by poisons in the environment. But the single most common cause of lung cancer is tobacco smoke. Smoking is something you do or don't do. It is a choice you make. Smoking is a *risky behavior*, or something you choose to do that increases your chances of getting a noninfectious disease.

Even if you could live a risk-free life—and you cannot—you might still have a noninfectious disease. But by making good decisions, such as exercising, eating a healthy diet, and choosing not to smoke, you can minimize your chances of disease.

★ 3.A; 3.B; 3.C

Brain Food

Scientists have learned that a wide variety of things in the environment can trigger an asthma attack. These triggers include dust mites, cockroach particles, tobacco smoke, paint fumes, and weather changes. These triggers are risk factors that increase a person's chances of having an asthma attack. ★ 3.B; 3.C

Preventing Noninfectious Diseases

Scientists, like the one in Figure 2, study diseases to find ways to prevent or cure them. In fact, some noninfectious diseases, such as some cancers, can be prevented.

Diseases caused by injuries, especially head and spine injuries, are preventable. Wearing a helmet when you ride your bicycle and wearing a seat belt when you ride in a car will prevent most injury-related diseases.

Obesity, or weighing at least 20 percent more than your recommended weight, is related to a variety of noninfectious diseases, including type 2 diabetes, heart disease, and high blood pressure. A nutritious diet and regular exercise can help prevent these noninfectious diseases.

Most cases of mouth and throat cancer can be prevented if people don't smoke or chew tobacco. Liver diseases and other diseases can be prevented by not abusing alcohol. So, many noninfectious diseases are preventable. ★ 3.A; 3.B; 3.C

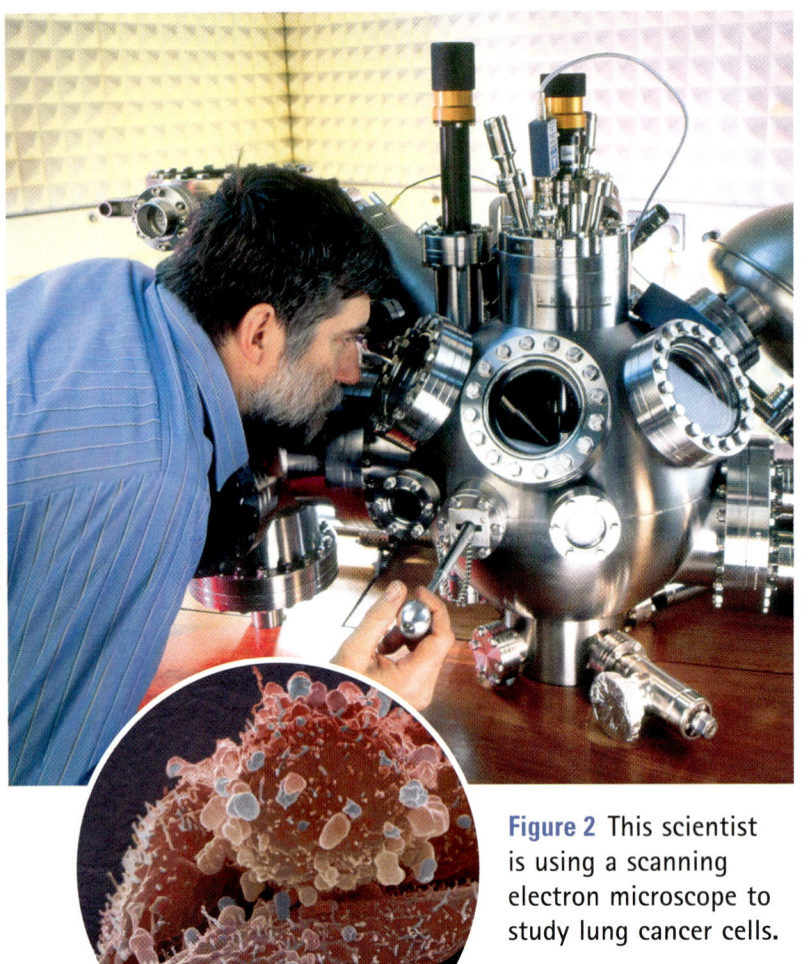

Figure 2 This scientist is using a scanning electron microscope to study lung cancer cells.

Lung Cancer Cells

Hands-on ACTIVITY

CAUSE AND EFFECT

Suppose you are a physician in a small town. Over a 2-year period, you see a number of patients who have similar symptoms and complaints. Despite all your efforts, you cannot find a disease that matches their symptoms. You know that they all live within 3 miles of an abandoned manufacturing plant, and you know that some of these patients are related to each other.

1. Write a list of questions that you would ask these patients to help you determine the cause of their problems.

2. Make a list of other people you would interview or consult for information.

Analysis

1. Do you think this disease is infectious or noninfectious? Why?

2. Do you think this disease is genetic, related to health behaviors, or caused by something in the environment? Explain your answer.

Living with Noninfectious Diseases

Most noninfectious diseases cannot be cured, but they can be treated. To *treat* a disease is to provide medical care to someone who has that disease. Treatment is usually given to control symptoms or to slow or stop the progress of a disease. For example, type 2 diabetes can be treated with medication, exercise, and a healthy diet. Allergies and asthma can usually be controlled with medication. Some heart diseases can be treated with medication, diet, and exercise.

Other noninfectious diseases, such as some types of cancer, can be treated with surgery or radiation therapy. Some heart diseases require surgery or medication. Cancer, heart disease, and other noninfectious diseases can be controlled if they are discovered and treated properly. With appropriate medical care, someone who has a noninfectious disease may live a healthy, active life. ★ 3.A

MAKING GOOD DECISIONS

Some noninfectious diseases are caused by harmful lifestyle behaviors. List four unhealthy lifestyle behaviors, and then list the alternative healthy lifestyle choices.

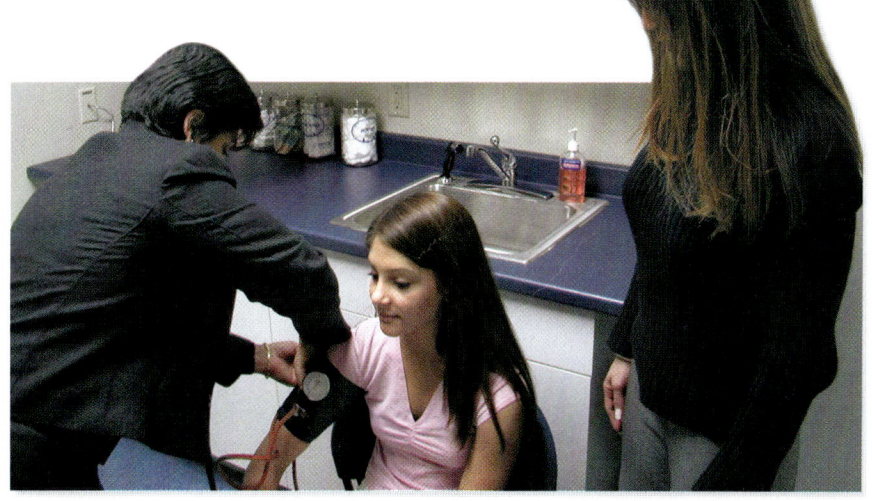

Figure 3 If you have high blood pressure, you should have your blood pressure checked frequently. Your doctor will probably take your blood pressure each time you visit.

Lesson Review

Using Vocabulary

1. What is a noninfectious disease? ★ 3.B; 3.C

Understanding Concepts

2. Explain the relationship between risk factors and noninfectious diseases. ★ 3.B; 3.C

3. Describe three strategies for preventing noninfectious diseases. ★ 3.A; 3.B

Critical Thinking

4. **Making Predictions** Poor diet and too little exercise are risk factors for heart disease. If you eat right and get plenty of exercise, will you never have a heart attack? Explain your answer. ★ 3.A; 3.B; 3.C

5. **Applying Concepts** Marcos has a cousin who was born with a damaged heart valve. Should Marcos be afraid of catching his cousin's heart problem? Explain your answer. ★ 3.A; 3.B; 3.C

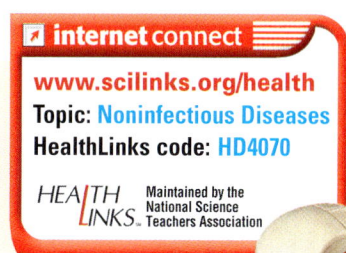

internet connect
www.scilinks.org/health
Topic: Noninfectious Diseases
HealthLinks code: HD4070

HEALTH LINKS. Maintained by the National Science Teachers Association

Lesson 2 Hereditary Diseases

What You'll Do

- **Describe** how genes are related to hereditary diseases. ★ 3.B; 3.C
- **Give** three examples of hereditary diseases.

Terms to Learn

- hereditary disease

Start Off Write

What do genes do?

Shawn's father has sickle cell disease. Shawn was tested for the disease when he was born. Fortunately, Shawn did not inherit sickle cell disease.

Sickle cell disease causes red blood cells to change shape. These changed cells do not carry oxygen through the body as well as normal red blood cells do. They are more likely to get stuck in blood vessels, which causes painful and dangerous clots.

Genes and Hereditary Diseases

Sickle cell disease is a hereditary disease. A **hereditary disease** is a disease caused by defective genes inherited by a child from one or both parents. Hereditary diseases are caused by changes in the structure of genes. *Genes* control the activities of cells and determine a person's physical characteristics. Genes are passed from parents to offspring. For example, the color of your eyes is controlled by genes that you inherited from your parents.

If a gene changes, the change may cause a hereditary disease. For example, in sickle cell disease, a change in a gene causes the change in the shape of the red blood cells. As a result, red blood cells become sickle shaped instead of disk shaped.

Some hereditary diseases, such as sickle cell disease, are caused by changes to one gene. Other hereditary diseases, such as breast cancer and colon cancer, may involve changes in more than one gene. And Down syndrome results when a person is born with part or all of an extra chromosome 21. ★ 3.B; 3.C

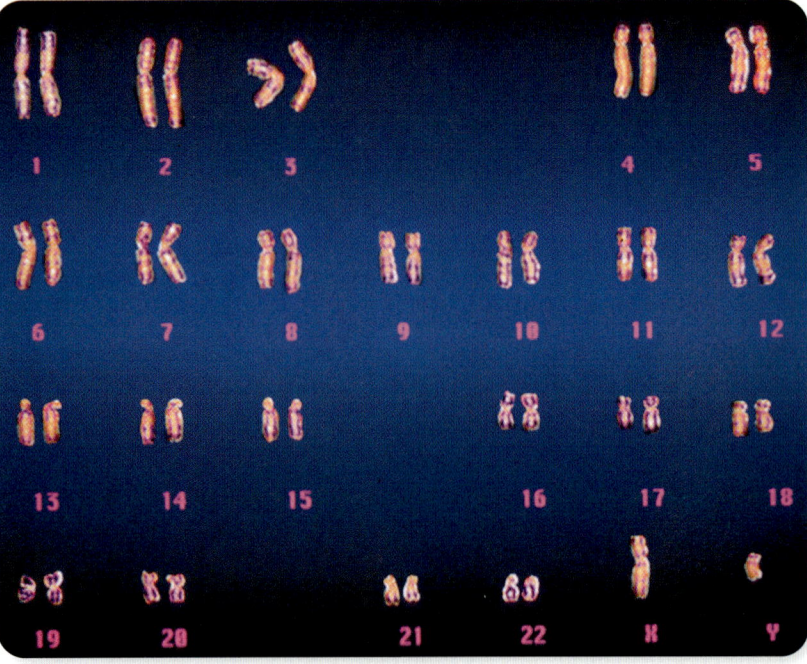

Figure 4 In cells, genes are found on structures called chromosomes. Humans have 23 pairs of chromosomes.

- Sickle cell disease
- Cystic fibrosis
- Phenylketonuria (PKU)
- Muscular dystrophy
- Hemophilia
- Tay-Sachs disease

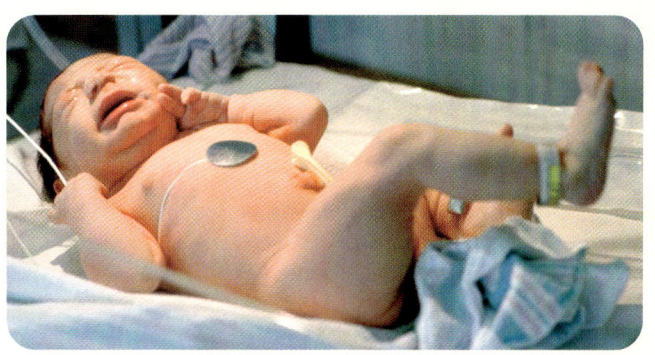

Figure 5 Newborn babies may be tested for a variety of hereditary diseases.

Living with Hereditary Diseases

Because doctors are able to test for a number of hereditary diseases, they can often reduce the problems the disease might cause. For example, newborns can be tested for a variety of diseases. One such disease is *phenylketonuria* (FEN uhl KEET oh NOOR ee uh), or PKU. If untreated, PKU can cause mental retardation. But infants who test positive for PKU are put on a special low-protein diet. The harmful effects of PKU can be prevented if the diet is started right away and is followed throughout life.

Down syndrome and cystic fibrosis (SIS tik fie BROH sis), or CF, are two other hereditary diseases. People who have these diseases have inherited genetic information that prevents parts of their bodies from functioning normally. People who have CF may have trouble breathing. Down syndrome may affect a person's ability to learn. People who have hereditary disease may experience medical problems. However, these problems can be reduced if the disease is detected early. ★ 3.A

Myth & Fact

Myth: Arthritis affects only older people.
Fact: There are several types of arthritis. One type is probably inherited and it affects children. While it is true that the frequency of arthritis increases with age, nearly three out of every five arthritis sufferers are under age 65.

Lesson Review

Using Vocabulary
1. What is a hereditary disease? ★ 3.B; 3.C

Understanding Concepts
2. How are genes related to hereditary diseases? ★ 3.B

Critical Thinking
3. **Analyzing Ideas** Explain the good points and the bad points of knowing about hereditary diseases. Which do you think are more important? Why? ★ 3.A; 3.B

internet connect
www.scilinks.org/health
Topic: **Hereditary Disease Research in Texas**
HealthLinks code: **HHTX008**

HEALTH LINKS — Maintained by the National Science Teachers Association

Lesson 3
Metabolic and Nutritional Diseases

What You'll Do

- **Describe** how metabolism and nutrition are related to disease. ★ 1.A; 3.A; 3.B
- **Identify** two examples of metabolic diseases.
- **List** two ways to prevent metabolic diseases. ★ 3.A

Terms to Learn

- metabolism

Why is a healthy diet important in preventing noninfectious diseases?

When Dale was born, the doctor discovered that he had a problem with his metabolism. Now, Dale follows a special diet and leads a normal life.

Dale was born with a disease called *PKU*. People who have PKU are unable to use a certain amino acid found in some foods.

Your Metabolism

Most of the time, you do not even think about your metabolism (muh TAB uh LIZ uhm). **Metabolism** is the process by which the body converts the energy in food into energy the body can use. This process takes place after digestion, when your body metabolizes carbohydrates, protein, fat, vitamins, and minerals. But many things can go wrong with your metabolism. A metabolic disease, such as PKU or diabetes, is one that prevents the body from using one or more nutrients.

Some metabolic problems happen before birth and some happen after. Problems may be hereditary, related to nutrition and diet, or have some other cause. In some cases, these problems may be caused by drugs and medication. For example, some hormonal medications may raise blood pressure and cause fat to build up in the blood.

Nutrition and diet are important to metabolism. *Nutrition* is the result of all the processes, including digestion and metabolism, by which your body takes in nutrients in food and uses the nutrients to maintain your health. Poor nutrition and diet may also cause problems. For example, too little vitamin D can cause rickets, a disease that may lead to deformed bones. Too little vitamin A may cause blindness, while too much vitamin A may cause liver disease and hair loss. ★ 1.A; 3.A; 3.B

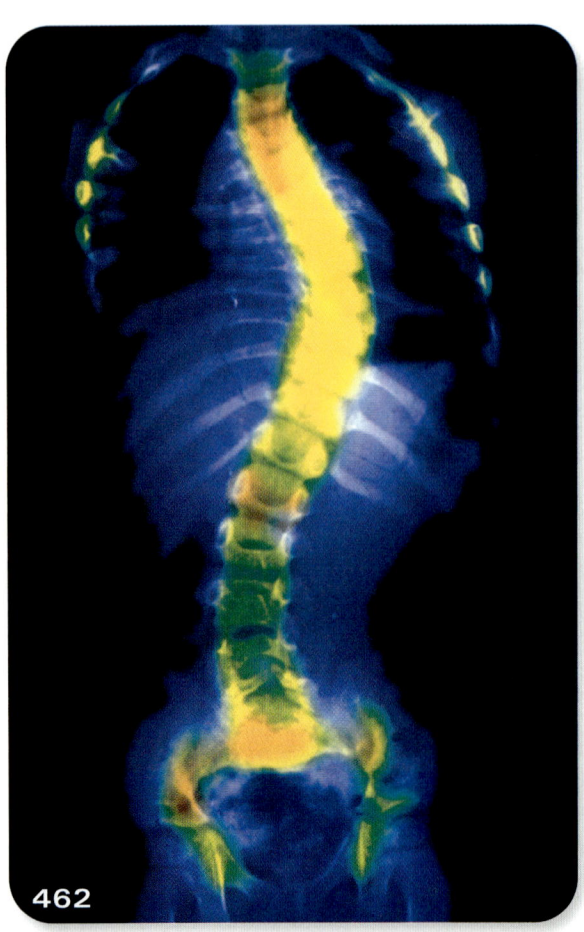

Figure 6 Rickets, a metabolic disease caused by too little vitamin D, caused this spine to curve.

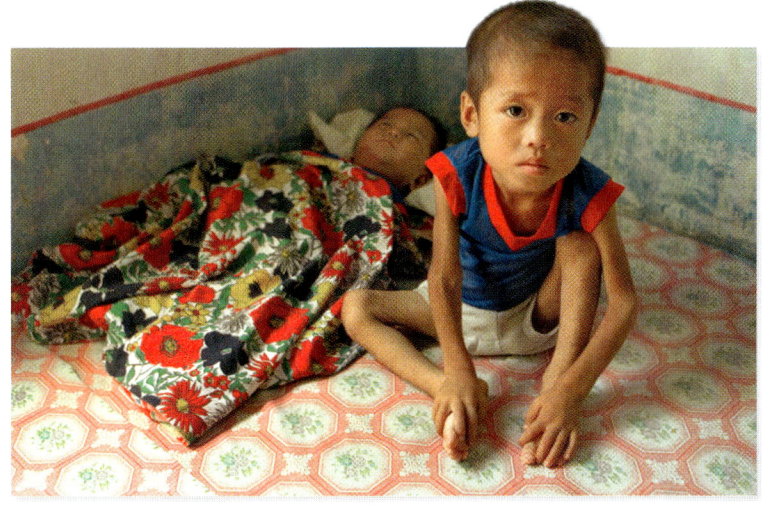

Figure 7 This child suffers from malnutrition, which can be especially harmful to children, because their bodies are growing and changing rapidly.

Preventing Nutritional Diseases

A nutritious diet is important to have a normal life. A nutritious diet has the proper balance of fat, carbohydrates, protein, vitamins, and minerals. An improper or unhealthy diet may lead to *malnutrition*, which is poor nourishment caused by a lack of nutrients. Malnutrition, such as too little Vitamin A, may cause disease. But diseases, such as PKU, may also cause malnutrition. Good nutrition and good health are very closely linked.

Eating the right amount of food is just as important as eating the right kind of food. If you take in more energy than you use, your body stores the extra energy as fat. Too much stored fat may lead to obesity. Obesity is linked to heart disease, high blood pressure, some types of cancer, type 2 diabetes, and a variety of other diseases.

What can you do to avoid nutritional problems? Eat a nutritious and balanced diet. Choose foods that are low in fat, sugar, and salt. Minimize your time in front of the TV and computer. Don't eat snacks while you are watching TV. Finally, get some exercise. Spend 20 to 30 minutes a day in vigorous activity of some kind. 3.A; 3.B

Health Journal

In your Health Journal, list the food changes you would have to make if you had PKU and could not eat milk, dairy products, meat, fish, chicken, eggs, beans, and nuts.

Lesson Review

Using Vocabulary

1. What is metabolism? 1.A

Understanding Concepts

2. How are metabolism and nutrition related to disease? 1.A; 3.A; 3.B
3. Identify two metabolic diseases.
4. What are two ways to prevent metabolic diseases? 3.A

Critical Thinking

5. **Analyzing Ideas** How is physical exercise important in maintaining your metabolism? 1.A; 3.A

Lesson 4

Allergies and Autoimmune Diseases

What You'll Do

- **Explain** what it means to have an allergy.  3.B
- **Describe** two ways to treat allergies and autoimmune diseases. ★ 3.A

Terms to Learn

- allergy
- autoimmune disease

Start Off Write

What is the purpose of your immune system?

Every fall, Shari suffers from severe allergies. Shari's doctor did some tests, and found out that Shari is allergic to tree pollen.

When Shari breathes in pollen from certain kinds of trees, her eyes get red and swollen. Her nose gets stuffy. She feels tired. Shari is not alone. Like Shari, many people have allergies.

Being Allergic

Shari's allergy is to tree pollen. But people can be allergic to a wide variety of substances, including strawberries, shellfish, peanuts, cats and dogs, or milk. An **allergy** is an overreaction of the immune system to something in the environment that is harmless to most people. Something that causes an allergy is an *allergen* (AL uhr juhn). Almost anything can be an allergen. Your immune system protects your body by responding to invading proteins or other substances. Usually, the proteins are part of harmful bacteria or other microorganisms. If your immune system responds to harmless proteins in pollen, dust, or other allergens, you have an allergy.

Normally, your own body cells do not trigger an immune response. Your immune system recognizes the difference between "self" and "not self." Sometimes, however, immune cells make a mistake. They attack the body cells that they are supposed to protect. Your body reacts as if it is allergic to itself. An **autoimmune disease** (AWT oh i MYOON di ZEEZ) is a disease in which a person's immune system attacks certain cells, tissues, or organs of the body. ★ 3.B

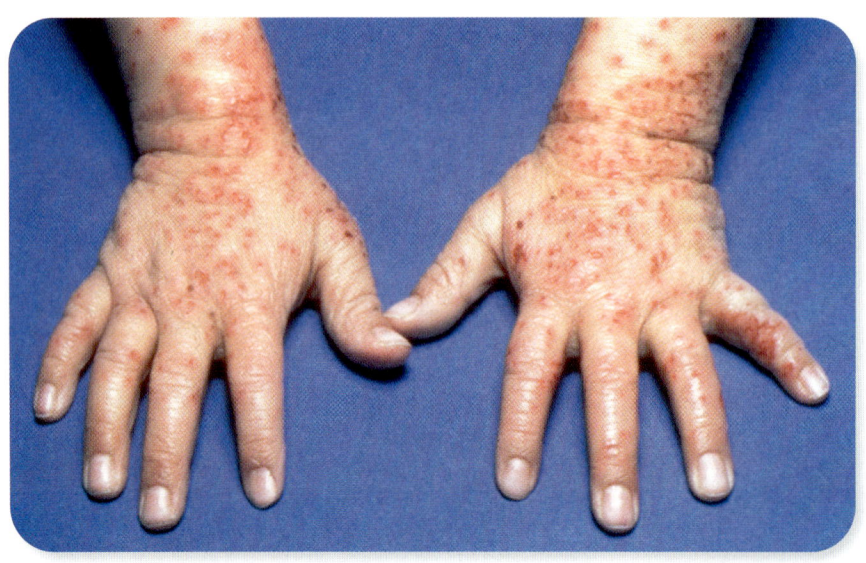

Figure 8 Eczema is a skin rash caused by a high sensitivity to allergens in the environment.

Living with Immune Reactions

Most allergies and autoimmune reactions cannot be prevented. For one thing, genetics plays a part in both allergies and autoimmune diseases. You cannot change your genetic inheritance. And it is not possible to avoid allergens such as dust and pollen. Therefore, it is not possible to prevent allergies and autoimmune diseases totally. However, treatments for many of these diseases are available. Most allergies and autoimmune diseases are treated with medication. For example, Shari cannot always stay indoors to avoid tree pollen. She will probably take medication to relieve her itchy eyes and stuffy nose.

You can take steps to reduce allergy reactions. Always follow your doctor's advice. Avoid things to which you know you are allergic. Avoid contact with allergens such as peanuts or cats and dogs. Reduce the dust in your house or your room. Treat allergy attacks early, before they get worse. ★ 3.A

Myth & Fact

Myth: Eczema is caused by an emotional disorder.

Fact: Eczema is not caused by an emotional disorder. However, emotional factors such as stress can make eczema worse. Using stress management can reduce stress, anxiety, anger, or frustration and can limit the possibility of an eczema flare-up.

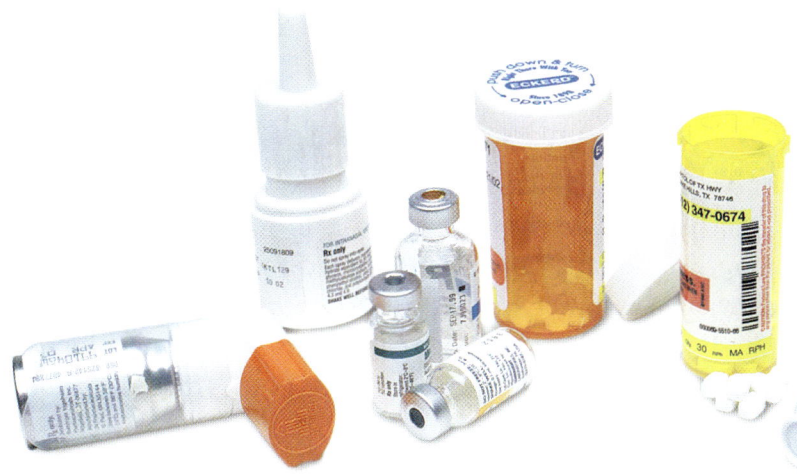

Figure 9 A wide variety of medications is available to treat the symptoms of allergies.

Lesson Review

Using Vocabulary
1. What is an allergy?

Understanding Concepts
2. What are two ways to treat allergies and autoimmune diseases?

Critical Thinking
3. **Identifying Relationships** Maria thought she was catching colds in September and October, but she realized that she has a runny nose and itchy eyes every fall. What factors should Maria explore to see if she has allergies?

internet connect

www.scilinks.org/health
Topic: Asthma
HealthLinks code: HD4011
Topic: Immune System
HealthLinks code: HD4059

HealthLinks Maintained by the National Science Teachers Association

Lesson 5

Cancer

What You'll Do

- **Explain** how the growth of cancer cells is different from the growth of normal cells. ★ 3.B
- **Identify** three ways to treat cancer. ★ 3.A

Terms to Learn

- cancer
- tumor
- malignant
- benign
- biopsy

How do doctors treat cancer?

Lyndie's mom has just been diagnosed with breast cancer, and Lyndie is worried. Lyndie and her mom talk about breast cancer and look on the Internet to learn more about it.

Lyndie discovered that breast cancer is the most common kind of cancer among women. Lyndie also learned that because her mom has breast cancer, she is also at risk for getting it.

What Is Cancer?

Cancer is a disease in which cells grow uncontrollably and invade and destroy healthy tissues. But where does cancer come from? Every day, cells in a body die and are replaced. Cell replacement is natural and continuous. This process is controlled by the instructions in DNA. Unfortunately, sometimes the DNA instructions in a cell get changed. Then the cell's shape, size, and behavior change. The cell's growth becomes abnormal. It divides and forms more abnormal cells. As these cells grow, they form tumors. A **tumor** is a mass of abnormal cells.

A tumor may be malignant (muh LIG nuhnt) or benign (bi NIEN). **Malignant** tumors are cancerous and can be life threatening. Malignant tumor cells spread to other parts of the body. They invade other organs and tissues. And they tend to get worse. **Benign** tumors are not cancerous and are usually not life threatening. Benign tumor cells do not spread to other organs or tissues. ★ 3.B

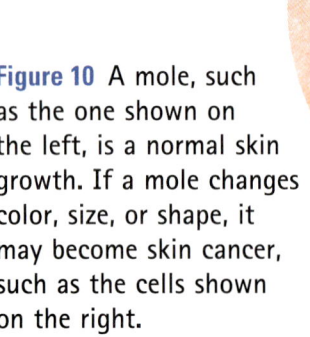

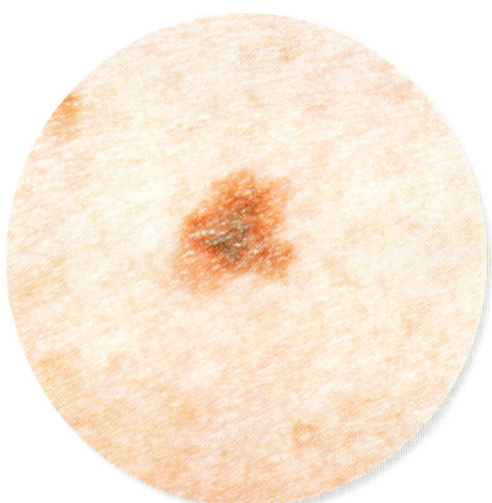

Normal cells **Cancer cells**

Figure 10 A mole, such as the one shown on the left, is a normal skin growth. If a mole changes color, size, or shape, it may become skin cancer, such as the cells shown on the right.

466 | Chapter 18 Noninfectious Diseases

Common Types of Cancer

Cancer can affect any tissue or organ of the body. Some cancers, such as small-cell lung cancer, grow and spread very quickly. Other cancers, such as some skin cancers, grow more slowly. In adult women, the most common types of cancer are breast, ovarian, and lung cancers. In adult men, the most common types of cancer are prostate, colon, and lung cancers. In children, leukemia (loo KEE mee uh) is a common cancer. Leukemia is cancer of the white blood cells, which grow in bone marrow.

Skin cancer is one of the most common types of cancer. Most skin cancer is caused by exposure to the ultraviolet (UV) rays in sunlight. UV light changes the DNA in some skin cells, and cancer results. Exposure to UV rays may cause *basal cell carcinoma* (kar suh NOH muh), the most common type of skin cancer, or *melanoma* (MEL uh NOH muh), the most serious type of skin cancer. Skin cancer can affect anyone regardless of skin tone.

⭐ 3.B

Brain Food

Basal cell carcinoma (BCC), the most common of all cancers, starts in the bottom of the outer skin layer. BCC usually grows very slowly and can usually be cured. *Melanoma* also develops in the outer layer of the skin. Melanoma is curable if it is caught early. But if it is not detected, melanoma spreads rapidly to other organs. Once melanoma spreads, it is often fatal.

Figure 11 Types of Cancer

- ▶ **Skin cancer**—the most common type of cancer—is usually caused by too much exposure to sunlight.

- ▶ **Lung cancer** in both men and women is closely linked to cigarette smoking. Lung cancer is the No. 1 cause of deaths due to cancer in the United States.

- ▶ **Colon and rectal (colorectal) cancer**—cancer that affects the lower end of the digestive tract—is the second most common cancer in the United States.

- ▶ **Leukemia** causes cancerous white blood cells to interfere with production of healthy white blood cells.

- ▶ **Lymphoma** (lim FOH muh) is cancer of the cells in the lymph system. It may spread throughout the body and weaken the immune system.

- ▶ **Breast cancer** is most often seen in women over 50, but younger women and even men can develop breast cancer.

- ▶ **Reproductive organ cancers** affect both men and women. In men, these cancers strike the testicles and the prostate gland. In women, these cancers strike the ovaries, cervix, and uterus.

No Warning Signs

Some cancers, such as some types of leukemia, do not show any of the cancer warning signs. Doctors must rely on other tests to detect and diagnose those cancers.

Diagnosing and Treating Cancer

Cancer is often found when a person describes one or more of the cancer warning signs to a doctor. The doctor usually orders a biopsy (BIE OP see) to confirm whether the patient has cancer. A **biopsy** is a sample of tissue that is removed from the patient and that is sent to a specialist to see if cancer cells are present. If cancer cells are detected, the doctor will order other tests to determine the size and location of the cancer. The doctor and the patient can then plan how to treat the cancer.

The following are three major cancer treatments:

- **Surgery** Doctors remove cancer cells from the body. This method works best on cancer that has not spread to other parts of the body.
- **Chemotherapy** (KEE moh THER uh pee) Chemicals are used to destroy cancer cells. This method is used to fight cancers that have spread.
- **Radiation** (RAY dee AY shuhn) High-energy rays from radioactive materials are used to shrink or kill cancer cells. This method is usually used in combination with surgery and chemotherapy. ✪ 3.A

Figure 12 Even though cancer does not usually strike young people, it can. Learn these cancer warning signs.

Cancer Warning Signs

- **C**hange in bowel or bladder habits
- **A** sore that does not heal
- **U**nusual bleeding or discharge
- **T**hickening or lump anywhere
- **I**ndigestion or difficulty swallowing
- **O**bvious change in a wart or mole
- **N**agging cough or hoarseness

Preventing Cancer

Some cancer cannot be prevented. It may be caused by hereditary factors, or it may be related to aging or gender. But some cancers are the result of lifestyle choices. In general, men who smoke are 22 times more likely to get lung cancer than men who don't smoke. And a leading cause of skin cancer is prolonged exposure to sunlight. Other kinds of cancer are caused by alcohol abuse or by exposure to chemicals in the environment.

There are ways to reduce your chances of getting cancer. Making healthy choices, such as eating a nutritious diet, not smoking or using alcohol, and using sunscreen, will help you avoid some types of cancer.

You cannot prevent all types of cancer, so early detection is very important. Regular visits to a doctor will help detect cancer early. Your doctor can show you self-exams that may detect cancer in its early stages. The earlier most cancers are detected, the better the chances that they can be treated successfully.

★ 3.A; 3.B; 3.C

PRACTICING WELLNESS

Research skin cancer. Create a public service announcement warning teens about skin cancer and telling them how to avoid it.

Figure 13 Skin cancer is a common kind of cancer, but the risk of getting skin cancer can be reduced by applying sunblock.

Lesson Review

Using Vocabulary

1. What is a biopsy? ★ 3.A

Understanding Concepts

2. Describe how the growth of cancer cells is different from normal cell growth. ★ 3.B

3. What are three ways to treat cancer? ★ 3.A

Critical Thinking

4. Making Inferences Some kinds of radiation can damage DNA. Why might there be a relationship between radiation and cancer? ★ 3.B

5. Analyzing Ideas Why do people who spend a lot of time in the sun have a higher risk of skin cancer than people who spend most of their time indoors?
★ 3.B; 3.C

Lesson 6 Chemicals and Poisons

Hattie's lung disease makes it hard for her to breathe. Some days, air pollution makes her disease worse, and she can't leave home.

What You'll Do

- **Identify** four possible sources of environmental poison.  5.A; 6.A
- **Describe** how environmental poisons may cause disease. ★ 3.B

Terms to Learn

- poison
- toxin

Start Off Write

What do air pollution and cigarette smoke have in common?

Air pollution may contain chemicals and tiny particles of soot and dust that irritate Hattie's lungs. Hattie listens to the weather report each morning to find out whether air pollution will be a problem that day.

Exposure to Environmental Dangers

Your *environment* is all of the living and nonliving things around you. Some parts of the environment may be harmful. For example, natural and manufactured chemicals are all around us. We use chemicals in our home, on our lawns and gardens, and in our industrial processes. Chemicals are necessary and useful. But some of the chemicals we use are poisons. A **poison** is something that causes illness or death on contact or if it is swallowed or inhaled. Some poisons, such as detergents, are clearly marked. Other poisons, such as the exhaust fumes from cars, are not. Poisons may be solids, liquids, or gases.

Some poisons are toxins. A **toxin** is a poison produced by a living organism. For example, plants such as poison ivy and some mushrooms produce toxins. Some animals, such as certain snakes, bees, and frogs, produce toxins. Bacteria and other microorganisms make toxins that may cause disease. ★ 5.A; 6.A

TABLE 2 Sources of Environmental Dangers

	Bees, wasps, and other stinging insects are usually relatively harmless, but, for a few people, an insect sting can be life threatening.
	Many common household chemicals, garden chemicals, and even medicines can cause illness, injury, or death.
	Water and air pollution, at low levels, can be irritating and relatively harmless. At higher levels, water and air pollution can threaten health and can even be deadly.
	Poison ivy and its relatives usually cause only an itchy rash that goes away after a few days. Some people, though, are very sensitive, and the rash can cause a serious reaction.

Figure 14 You are surrounded by a variety of environmental dangers. Learning what the dangers are and how to avoid them will help protect you from diseases caused by these dangers.

Diseases Caused by Environmental Poisons

Environmental poisons may cause a wide variety of diseases. For example, air pollution can trigger asthma attacks and other allergic reactions. Air pollution and cigarette smoking can cause a lung disease called emphysema (EM fuh SEE muh). Alcohol, aspirin, and cigarette smoking can cause birth defects. A chemical called *vinyl chloride,* which is used to make many plastic products, can cause liver cancer or brain tumors. And sometimes infants and children eat paint chips and other things that contain the element lead. Lead is a poison that can damage the brain, kidneys, liver, and other organs. Small amounts of lead may cause behavioral changes and learning problems. Severe lead poisoning may produce convulsions and death.

You cannot escape all of the possible poisons in your environment. Learning what the possible dangers are is the best way to avoid them. ★ 3.B

Brain Food

Allergic asthma affects about 3 million children and 7 million adults in the United States. Despite improvements in air quality in the last 15 years, asthma has increased as an illness and as a cause of death in the United States.

Lesson Review

Using Vocabulary

1. What are toxins?
2. What is the difference between a poison and a toxin? ★ 5.A; 6.A

Understanding Concepts

3. What are four possible sources of environmental poison? ★ 5.A; 6.A
4. Describe how environmental poisons may cause disease. ★ 3.B; 6.A

Critical Thinking

5. **Making Inferences** Your brother has a summer job mowing and taking care of the grass at a golf course. What are two environmental dangers he should be aware of? ★ 6.A
6. **Analyzing Ideas** "If the dose is big enough, all things are poison." Do you think this statement is true or false? Explain your answer. ★ 3.B; 5.A; 6.A

Lesson 7

Accidents and Injuries

What You'll Do

- **Explain** how accidents and injuries may cause disease. ★ 3.B; 5.A
- **Identify** strategies to prevent accidents and minimize injuries. ★ 3.A; 5.A

Terms to Learn

- accident
- traumatic injury

How can you avoid serious injuries?

> Alice was diving at the lake, but she didn't see the rocks under the surface. She hit the rocks and injured her spinal cord. She could not move her legs.

Alice was lucky. The damage to her spinal cord was not permanent. After several months, Alice regained the use of her legs and she was able to walk again.

Diseases Caused by Injuries

Accidents are the most common noninfectious medical problem among young people. An **accident** is any unexpected event that causes damage, injury, or death. Many accidents cause only minor injuries. But accidents may also cause serious injuries, such as Alice's temporary paralysis, or even death. Accidents usually cause traumatic injuries. A **traumatic injury** is an injury caused by physical force. Head injuries are a good example.

Injuries can cause disease. For example, a traumatic head injury can damage the brain. Brain damage can cause several problems, such as seizures, inability to use arms and legs, loss of memory, loss of coordination, loss of speech, and a variety of other symptoms. Most of these problems are the same as those caused by brain tumors and other brain diseases. ★ 3.B; 3.C; 5.A

Accidents

Accidents are the leading cause of death among 10- to 14-year-olds. In 1999, for instance, accidents were responsible for 39.6 percent of all deaths in this age group.

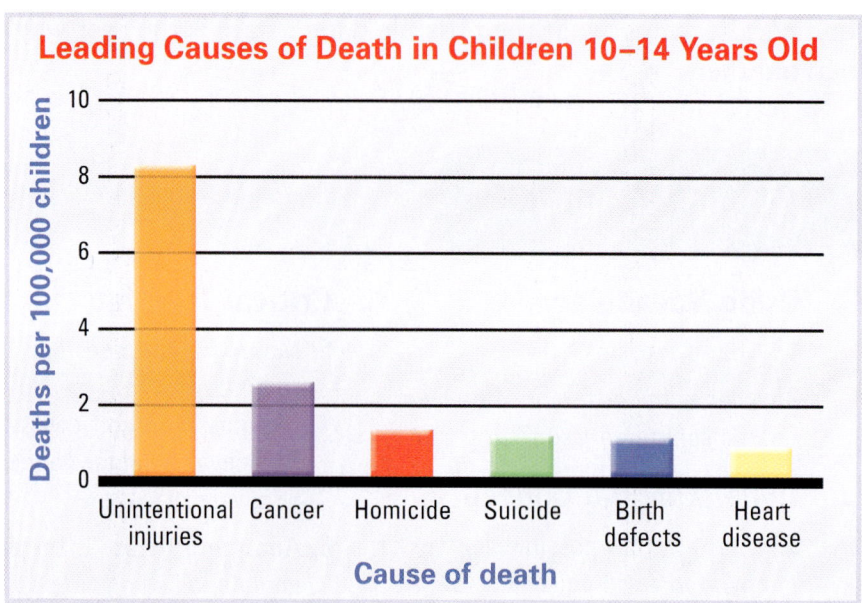

Figure 15 The leading cause of death among young people 10 to 14 years old is unintentional injuries. Many of these deaths could be prevented.

Preventing Traumatic Injuries

Most accidental injuries are minor. The difference between minor and serious injuries may be small. A few seconds can make a difference to a drowning victim. An inch may mean life or death to a gunshot victim. But many accidents are not beyond your control. In fact, most injuries that teens suffer are preventable. Prevent injury to yourself and others. Make healthy choices about safety. Follow a few simple rules and you can avoid most teen injuries.

- Do not drink alcoholic beverages. Alcohol plays a role in a large percentage of automobile and swimming accidents.
- Do not play with guns. Learn gun safety.
- Always wear a well-fitting helmet and other safety gear when you ride a bicycle or skateboard.
- Always wear appropriate and well-fitting safety gear when you play a sport.
- Learn CPR.
- Wear a seatbelt every time you ride in a car. ★ 3.A; 5.A; 6.B

Figure 16 Traumatic injuries that may change your life can be prevented or reduced by wearing all the appropriate safety equipment.

Lesson Review

Using Vocabulary

1. What is an accident? ★ 5.A

2. How does a traumatic injury differ from other types of injuries? ★ 3.B

Understanding Concepts

3. Explain how accidents and disease are related and how using proper safety equipment may prevent disease. ★ 3.A; 3.B; 5.A

Critical Thinking

4. **Making Good Decisions** You want to buy a skateboard. You can't afford to buy a helmet, too. Should you buy the skateboard anyway? Why or why not? ★ 3.A; 12.B

5. **Making Inferences** Why is it important to include diseases caused by injuries in a chapter about noninfectious diseases? ★ 3.A; 3.B; 5.A

18 CHAPTER REVIEW

Chapter Summary

■ A noninfectious disease is a disease that is not caused by a virus or living organism. ■ There are several types of noninfectious diseases, including hereditary diseases, nutritional and metabolic diseases, immune system defects, and cancers. ■ Hereditary diseases are caused by a defect in the genes that a person inherits from one or both parents. ■ Metabolic diseases prevent the body from using one or more nutrients. ■ An allergy is an unusual reaction to something in the environment. ■ Cancer can attack any organ of the body. ■ The environment is full of chemicals. Most chemicals are useful, but some are poisonous. ■ Poisons and toxins in the environment cause some noninfectious diseases. ■ Accidents and injuries can cause noninfectious diseases.

Using Vocabulary

1 Use each of the following terms in a separate sentence: *disease, noninfectious disease, hereditary disease,* and *cancer*.

For each sentence, fill in the blank with the proper word from the word bank provided below.

risk factor	malignant
allergy	benign
autoimmune disease	poison
cancer	toxin
tumor	traumatic injury

2 A(n) ___ is a poison produced by a living organism.

3 Sometimes, the physical force of an accident can cause a(n) ___.

4 A ___ is a mass of abnormal cells.

5 If your immune system overreacts to something in the environment, you probably have a(n) ___.

6 A(n) ___ tumor is cancerous and may be life threatening.

7 A(n) ___ is a characteristic or behavior that raises your chances of getting a noninfectious disease.

Understanding Concepts

8 What are three types of noninfectious diseases? Give an example of each type. ★ 3.B; 3.C

9 Explain how good nutrition can help prevent disease. ★ 1.A; 3.A

10 Identify two common causes of cancer, and explain how to minimize the risk of cancer from those causes. ★ 3.A; 3.B

11 How could a traumatic brain injury cause disease? ★ 3.B; 5.A

12 Explain how hereditary diseases are caused by genes. ★ 3.B; 3.C

13 What are three common allergens? ★ 3.B

14 Why is it important for people who have inherited risk factors for heart disease to eat a healthy diet and get plenty of exercise? ★ 1.A; 3.A; 3.B

Critical Thinking

Making Inferences

15. Why is it important to know whether a disease is infectious or noninfectious? ★ 3.A; 3.B; 3.C

16. In some magazines, you see advertisements for vitamin pills that give you hundreds or even thousands of times the daily requirement for some vitamins. Why might taking vitamins in such large doses be dangerous? ★ 3.A; 3.B; 4.A

17. Imagine that you read in the newspaper a story about a woman who had a tumor the size of a watermelon removed from her abdomen. Doctors estimate that the tumor had been growing for years. Was this tumor likely to have been malignant or benign? Explain your answer. ★ 3.B; 3.C

Making Good Decisions

18. In your favorite magazine, you read that certain foods—foods that you like—contain chemicals that increase your risk of having stomach cancer. The risk is fairly small for teens, but increases greatly as a person gets older. Explain how you would decide whether to continue to eat these foods. ★ 3.A; 3.B; 4.A; 4.C; 12.A; 12.B; 12.F

19. Imagine that someone has discovered a drug that will increase your metabolism and help you lose weight fast. Unfortunately, the drug has a side effect. Sometimes, but not always, the drug damages the liver and causes heart attacks. Would you take this new diet drug or not? Explain your answer. ★ 3.A; 3.B; 4.A; 4.C; 12.A; 12.B; 12.F

20. Arnold has a new skateboard. Maria wants to ride it, but she has no helmet. Maria tells Arnold that she will wear his helmet, which is much too big for her. Should Arnold let Maria try his skateboard anyway? Explain your answer. ★ 3.B; 5.A

21. Use what you have learned in this chapter to set a personal goal. Write your goal, and make an action plan by using the Health Behavior Contract for Noninfectious Diseases. You can find the Health Behavior Contract at **go.hrw.com**. Just type in the keyword **HD4HBC14**.

Reading Checkup

Take a minute to review your answers to the Health IQ questions at the beginning of this chapter. How has reading this chapter improved your Health IQ?

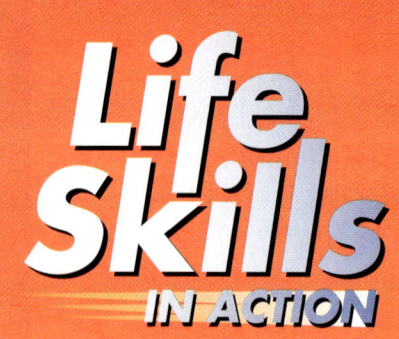

Life Skills IN ACTION

Assessing Your Health

Assessing your health means evaluating each of the four parts of your health and examining your behaviors. By assessing your health regularly, you will know what your strengths and weaknesses are and will be able to take steps to improve your health. Complete the following activity to improve your ability to assess your health.

Aaron's Asthma

Setting the Scene

Aaron has asthma. He knows that too much strenuous exercise may cause him to have asthma attacks. In spite of this, Aaron wants to join the school soccer team. Many of his friends joined the team and Aaron feels left out when they practice after school. Aaron talks to his mother about how not being a part of the team is making him depressed.

★ 3.B; 4.A; 4.C

The 4 Steps of Assessing Your Health

1. Choose the part of your health you want to assess.
2. List your strengths and weaknesses.
3. Describe how your behaviors may contribute to your weaknesses.
4. Develop a plan to address your weaknesses.

Guided Practice

Practice with a Friend

Form a group of three. Have one person play the role of Aaron and another person play the role of Aaron's mother. Have the third person be an observer. Walking through each of the four steps of assessing your health, role-play a conversation between Aaron and his mother. Have Aaron assess how his asthma affects the different parts of his health. Have Aaron's mother support Aaron as he talks about his concerns. The observer will take notes, which will include observations about what the person playing Aaron did well and suggestions of ways to improve. Stop after each step to evaluate the process.

★ 3.A; 3.B; 4.A; 12.A; 12.B; 12.C

Independent Practice

Check Yourself

After you complete the guided practice, go through Act 1 again without stopping at each step. Answer the questions below to review what you did.

1. How does Aaron's asthma affect the four parts of his health? ⭐ 1.A
2. What are some possible strengths that Aaron may have in his social health? What are some possible weaknesses? ⭐ 1.A
3. How can Aaron improve his social health if he is unable to join the soccer team? ⭐ 1.A
4. Describe a time when a weakness in your physical health affected a different part of your health. ⭐ 1.A

ACT 2 — On Your Own

After talking with Aaron, Aaron's mother tells him to make an appointment to talk to his doctor. During the appointment, Aaron and his doctor discuss the possibility of Aaron participating in soccer. Draw a comic strip that illustrates Aaron's doctor's appointment. In the comic strip, Aaron should follow the four steps of assessing your health to assess whether his asthma will interfere with him playing soccer.

Chapter 18 Assessing Your Health | 477

CHAPTER 19 Safety

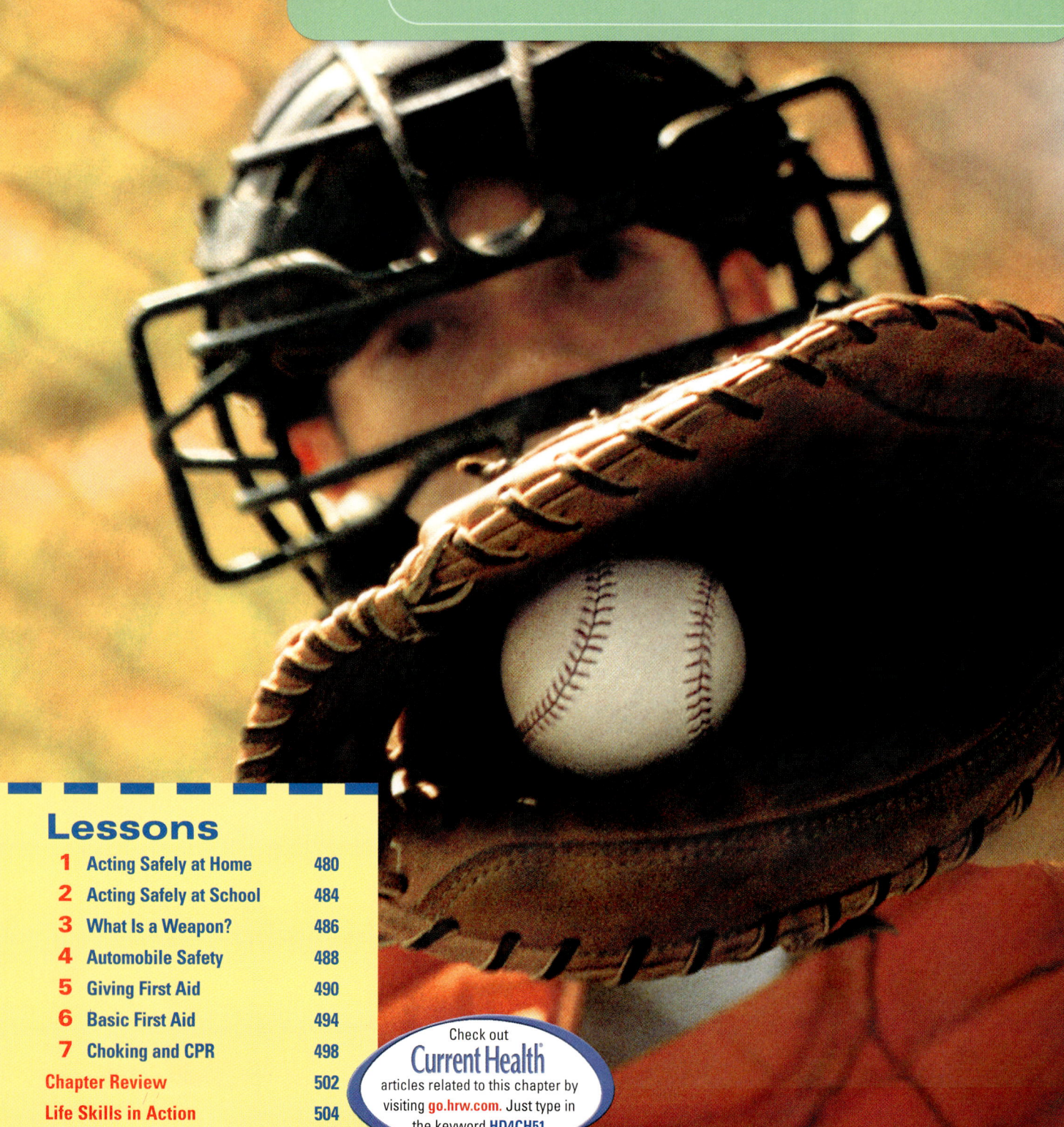

Lessons
1. Acting Safely at Home — 480
2. Acting Safely at School — 484
3. What Is a Weapon? — 486
4. Automobile Safety — 488
5. Giving First Aid — 490
6. Basic First Aid — 494
7. Choking and CPR — 498

Chapter Review — 502
Life Skills in Action — 504

Check out **Current Health** articles related to this chapter by visiting **go.hrw.com.** Just type in the keyword **HD4CH51.**

" I've been **playing baseball** for a couple of **years.** This year, I'm catching for my **school team.**

I put on my safety equipment for every practice and game. You never know when the ball will go wild! "

PRE-READING
Answer the following multiple-choice questions to find out what you already know about health and safety. When you've finished this chapter, you'll have the opportunity to change your answers based on what you've learned.

1. A(n) __ inflates and keeps you from hitting the dashboard of a car during an accident.
   a. seat belt
   b. child safety seat
   c. air bag
   d. None of the above ⭐ 5.A

2. You can protect yourself when you give first aid by
   a. using a breathing mask.
   b. using sterile gloves.
   c. making sure you're safe.
   d. All of the above ⭐ 5.A

3. The first thing you should do during an emergency is
   a. help the victim.
   b. call for help.
   c. make sure you're safe.
   d. None of the above ⭐ 5.A

4. You should not move someone who
   a. has a head injury.
   b. is in shock.
   c. has a cut.
   d. has a burn. ⭐ 5.A

5. An injury in which a bone has been forced out of its normal position in a joint is called a
   a. fracture.
   b. dislocation.
   c. splint.
   d. None of the above ⭐ 5.A

6. If you find someone who has been poisoned, you should
   a. induce vomiting.
   b. call your local poison control center.
   c. make the victim drink milk or water.
   d. None of the above ⭐ 5.A

ANSWERS: 1. c; 2. d; 3. c; 4. a; 5. b; 6. b

Lesson 1

Acting Safely at Home

What You'll Do

- **List** four examples of accidents. ★ 5.A
- **Explain** why you should have a family evacuation plan. ★ 5.A
- **List** eight recreational safety tips. ★ 5.A
- **List** seven ways to stay safe. ★ 5.A

Terms to Learn

- accident

Write

How can you prevent accidents?

Jerry always puts away his in-line skates when he gets home. He used to leave his skates on the stairs. Then, he tripped on them and almost fell. That made him realize it is dangerous to leave his skates on the stairs.

Jerry started putting away his skates because his safety was at risk. Safety is being free of danger and injury.

Accidents at Home

Have you ever heard the phrase "accidents happen"? An **accident** is an unexpected event that may cause injury. The following types of accidents are common:

- **Falls** Some causes of falls are tripping over objects or slipping on spills. Some people fall when they use something other than a ladder to reach a high shelf or cabinet.
- **Fires** Open flames, unattended stoves, and some chemicals can cause fires.
- **Electrical shock** Faulty wiring and overloaded outlets can cause electrical shock.
- **Poisoning** Some people are poisoned by mistaking a poison for something that is safe to drink or eat. Some people are poisoned if they take too much medicine, such as aspirin.

Accidents don't have to happen. Most accidents are easily avoided if everyone watches out for danger. ★ 5.A

Figure 1 Can you see the accidents waiting to happen in this room? Someone could trip and fall!

Figure 2 Smoke detectors and evacuation plans can help families escape fires like this.

Fire Safety

More than one million fires happen in the United States each year. Thousands of people die in fires. There are three things you can do to keep your family safe in a fire: Have working smoke detectors. Keep fire extinguishers in areas where fires are likely to start. Make a family evacuation plan. These three things will help your family get out of the house quickly and safely.

Ask your parents to put smoke detectors in every room. A smoke detector goes off if smoke is in the air. You should check the batteries once a month. You can also keep fire extinguishers in your home. A fire extinguisher releases chemicals that put out small fires. Put fire extinguishers in places where fires may start, such as the kitchen or the garage. Read the directions on the fire extinguishers. Then, you will know how to use the fire extinguisher correctly. When in doubt, don't try to put a fire out. Get out of the building. Call the fire department from your neighbor's home.

Your family will get out of your home more quickly if you have a plan. Sit down with your family, and draw a *family evacuation plan*. Draw a map of your home, and mark all exits and escape routes. Make sure everyone knows at least two ways to get out of each room. Mark a meeting spot outside, away from the building. Most importantly, your family should practice your evacuation plan. Practicing your plan can help you get out more quickly during a fire. Once outside, do not go back in for any reason, even for a pet. It's important to protect yourself first. ★ 5.A

> ## LIFE SKILLS ACTIVITY
>
> **PRACTICING WELLNESS**
>
> Create an evacuation plan for your classroom. Draw a picture of your school. Add the escape routes from your classroom. Don't forget to include a meeting spot outside the building!

Lesson 1 Acting Safely at Home

Figure 3 Outdoor activities, such as this one, are more fun when done safely.

Many states have bicycle helmet laws requiring teens and children to wear bicycle helmets. Some states require people of all ages to wear a bicycle helmet.

Recreational Safety

Many teens get hurt while they're outside having fun. They get hurt while walking down the street, riding a bike, or skating. When you're walking, be sure to wear clothing that is easy to see. Use crosswalks, and look in both directions before crossing the street. If you're biking or skating, be sure to wear a helmet. Skaters should also use elbow pads, knee pads, and wrist guards. You should skate on sidewalks or in other areas that have been designated for skating. Follow the rules of the road when you're cycling. And watch out for traffic.

To stay safe while you're having fun outside, you can also do the following:

- Stay with a group of friends.
- Make sure an adult knows where you are and what you're doing.
- Leave a phone number or another way that you can be reached.
- Make sure you're familiar with the area to which you're going.
- Be aware of your surroundings. Look out for dangerous situations.
- Dress in the right clothes for the activity and for the weather.
- Use your safety equipment.
- Wear sunscreen to prevent sunburn. ★ 5.A

Seven Ways to Stay Safe

Accidents happen all the time. But you can help prevent some of them. First, think before you act. Think about what could result from your actions. Second, pay attention. Be aware of your surroundings and of potential accidents. Third, know your limits. Sometimes, it's hard to admit we have limits. But to stay safe, stay within your limits. Fourth, practice your refusal skills. Don't be afraid to refuse something that may cause injury. Fifth, use your safety equipment. Safety equipment can save your life. Sixth, change risky behavior. If you have a habit that puts you or someone else at risk, try to change it. Changing your habits can be hard. But staying safe is worth the effort. Seventh, change risky situations. Sometimes, someone else's habit might put you at risk. If you see something that might cause an accident, fix it. Or tell someone who can take care of the situation if you can't take care of it. ★ 5.A

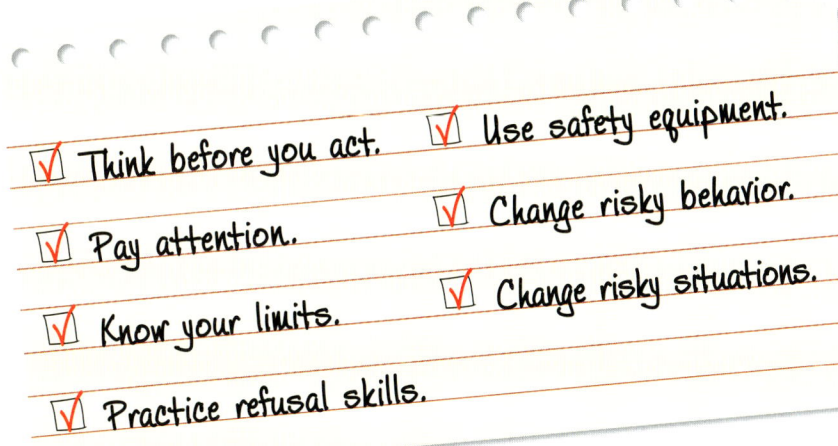

Figure 4 Practicing these seven behaviors can keep you safe.

Lesson Review

Using Vocabulary
1. What is an accident? ★ 5.A

Understanding Concepts
2. List four kinds of accidents.
3. Why should your family have an evacuation plan for fires? ★ 5.A
4. List eight ways to stay safe while having fun outdoors. ★ 5.A
5. What are seven things you can do to prevent accidents? ★ 5.A

Critical Thinking
6. **Using Refusal Skills** Margie's friend wants Margie to try a new skating trick. Margie has just started learning how to skate, and she knows she is not ready for the trick. How can Margie use her refusal skills to let her friend know that she is not ready for the trick?
★ 5.A; 11.D

Lesson 2

Acting Safely at School

What You'll Do

- **Describe** three ways to avoid violence. ★ 5.A; 5.K
- **List** two reasons people join gangs. ★ 5.K; 10.E

Terms to Learn

- violence
- gang

Start Off Write

What do you think causes violence?

Kelvin was walking to class when a couple of other students started fighting. No one got hurt, but the two students were suspended. Kelvin couldn't understand why the students didn't talk out their differences.

We often see images of violence (VIE uh luhns) on television, Web sites, and in video games. **Violence** is using physical force to injure someone or cause damage.

Violence

Unfortunately, violence can happen anywhere, even at school. Many things can lead to violence. For example, anger, stress, drugs, peer pressure, and prejudice can lead to violence. It's important for you to know ways to keep yourself safe. You have a lot of options. The best choice is to avoid violent situations altogether. Avoid people and places that tend to be violent. If things get out of control, walk away.

Using your refusal and conflict management skills can also help you avoid violence. These skills may help you keep people's emotions from erupting into violence. You can also tell an adult. Your parents or school counselor can help you protect yourself. Also, when you tell an adult, you're helping to keep other people from getting hurt. ★ 5.A; 5.K

Figure 5 Anger can lead to violence. Use your conflict management skills to prevent it.

Figure 6 These teens are painting a mural for a community service project. They've found a positive way to avoid gangs.

Gangs

What do you think of when you hear the word *gang*? A **gang** is a group of people who often use violence. Sometimes, it can be tempting to be part of a gang. Gangs make some people feel secure. Some gang members feel as if the gang is a family. But gangs are dangerous. To be part of a gang, you may have to do something violent. Or the gang may use violence against you. It's not worth hurting other people or being hurt to be a part of a group.

Fortunately, you can avoid gangs and gang violence. Use your refusal skills to avoid gangs. If you're having trouble avoiding gang violence, let an adult know you need help. Look for positive alternatives. Join a school club or a sports team. Volunteer at your local community center or a nursing home. Finding positive ways to spend your time can help you stay away from gangs.
★ 5.A; 5.K; 10.E

Health Journal
Describe a violent situation. Write about what you can do to avoid violence.

Lesson Review

Using Vocabulary
1. How are violence and gangs related? ★ 5.K

Understanding Concepts
2. Describe three ways to avoid violence. ★ 5.A; 5.K
3. What are two reasons people join gangs? ★ 10.E

Critical Thinking
4. **Applying Concepts** In what ways are gangs and school clubs different? Are there any similarities between gangs and school clubs? Explain your answer.
★ 5.A; 5.K; 10.A

Lesson 3

What Is a Weapon?

What You'll Do

- **List** two examples of weapons. 5.B
- **List** four ways to be safer from gun violence. 5.A; 5.B; 5.K

Terms to Learn

- weapon

Start Off Write

How can your refusal skills help you stay safe from weapons?

Lonnie accidentally brought a pocketknife to school. He had forgotten he had the knife in his backpack. When he was caught with the knife, he was suspended even though he didn't plan on hurting anyone.

Unfortunately, some students carry weapons to school. A **weapon** is an object or device that can be used to hurt someone. Knives and guns are two examples of weapons. Some students, such as Lonnie, don't plan on hurting anyone. Some students carry weapons to feel safe.

The Danger of Weapons

Some teens have a pocket knife or know how to use a gun. Some teens hunt with their families. Guns and other weapons are found in many homes. But weapons are dangerous, especially if they aren't used or stored properly. Guns are some of the most dangerous weapons. When used and stored responsibly, they are less dangerous. But each year, thousands of people in the United States suffer from gunshot wounds.

There is never a good reason to bring a weapon to school. Many schools have very strict rules against weapons. Students are often punished if they are caught with a weapon, even when they don't want to hurt anyone. Students caught carrying weapons in school are often suspended. Some students are expelled. 5.B; 5.K; 5.L

Figure 7 Many schools have metal detectors to keep students from carrying weapons.

Gun Safety

The second amendment to the U.S. Constitution gives people the right to bear arms. That right doesn't mean guns are safe. If guns aren't handled and stored safely, they become dangerous. The best way to stay safe is to stay away from guns altogether. However, when there are guns around, it is important to make sure guns are stored responsibly. Guns should never be stored loaded. They should always be locked up, especially if there are small children in the house. If you find an unlocked gun, you should walk away. Tell your parents or an adult about the gun right away.

Another way you can stay safer around guns is to learn how to use them properly. If your family hunts, always go with an experienced adult. You can also take classes in gun safety. A shooting range or a local organization may have instructors who can teach you how to use a gun properly. So, you can reduce your risk of injury around guns.

You may have seen or read articles about shootings in schools. Shootings don't happen often. But they are still frightening. You can help keep gun violence from happening. If you know about a student who is carrying a gun or planning to hurt others, you should let an adult know. You're not just protecting yourself when you tell an adult. You're also protecting other people. The student may not want to hurt anyone, but guns have no place in school. ★ 5.A; 5.B; 5.K

Figure 8 Guns and other weapons should be locked up when stored.

Brain Food

In 1999, more than 28,000 people died from gunshot wounds.

Lesson Review

Using Vocabulary

1. What are two examples of weapons?

Understanding Concepts

2. What are four ways to be safer from gun violence?

3. What happens to students caught carrying weapons to school?

Critical Thinking

4. **Making Good Decisions** A friend of yours hunts with his family and knows how to use guns. Your friend wants you to practice shooting targets with him. You know his parents won't be there. What should you do?

internet connect
www.scilinks.org/health
Topic: Gun Safety
HealthLinks code: HD4049

HEALTH LINKS Maintained by the National Science Teachers Association

Lesson 3 What Is a Weapon?

Lesson 4 — Automobile Safety

In 2000, more than 35,000 people died in automobile accidents. Nearly two-thirds of these people were not wearing seat belts.

What You'll Do

- **Describe** how seat belts and air bags protect you during an accident. ★ 5.A
- **List** two ways to be a safe passenger. ★ 5.A

Start Off Write

How does wearing a seat belt help you stay safe in a car?

Automobile accidents are the leading cause of death for teens. One way you can protect yourself is by wearing your seat belt.

Seat Belts and Air Bags

Do you wear your seat belt every time you ride in a car? Does your parents' car have air bags? Seat belts and air bags can keep you from getting hurt during an accident. Seat belts keep you from being thrown around in the car. They also keep you from going through a window. Air bags act as a cushion during a crash. They inflate and keep you from hitting the dashboard. Seat belts and air bags save thousands of lives each year. In fact, if everyone used his or her seat belt, almost 10,000 more lives could be saved each year!

Using you seat belt correctly is important. Small children should use child safety seats. You may also want to sit in the backseat. It's the safest area of a car. The figure below lists some of the things you should know about being a safe passenger.
★ 5.A

Figure 9 Being a Safe Passenger

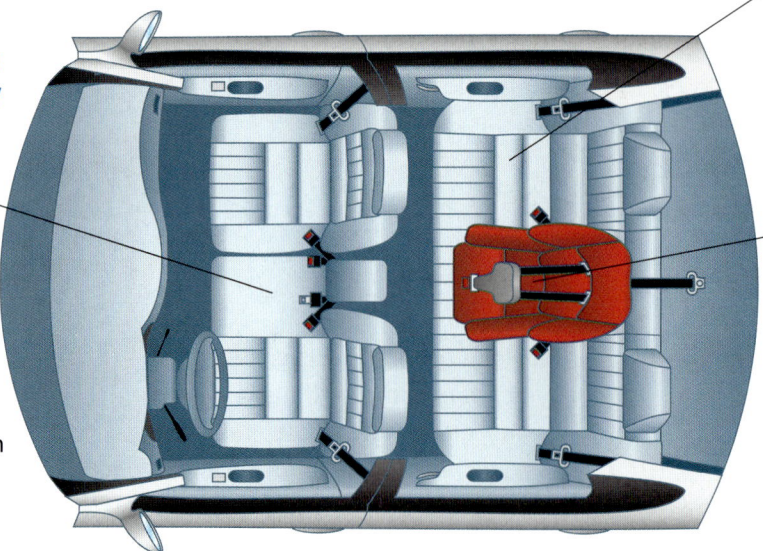

Seat belts should be worn correctly at all times.

Front seat
- Front seats should be moved back from air bags as far as possible.
- Child safety seats should never be used in a front seat that has an air bag.

Back seat
- Children ages 12 and under should sit in the back seat.
- Until children can wear a seat belt correctly, they should use child safety seats or booster seats.

Child safety seat
- Infants who weigh less than 20 to 22 pounds should ride in a rear-facing child safety seat.
- Children who weigh more than 20 pounds should ride in a forward-facing child safety seat.
- Children who weigh 40 to 80 pounds should ride in a booster seat.

Figure 10 Seat belt and air bag designs are tested to make sure they give passengers the best protection.

Being a Safe Passenger

Wearing your seat belt isn't the only way to be a safe passenger. If a driver gets distracted, an accident may happen. You can help by not distracting the driver.

You may ride a bus to school. Are there a lot of students on the bus? With so many students, a bus driver could become distracted easily. You should avoid distracting the bus driver. Obey posted instructions and stay in your seat when the bus is moving. Doing so keeps the driver from getting distracted. It also keeps you safe.

Paying attention to car or bus drivers is very important. It could keep you from getting hurt. If you're ever in an accident, listening to the driver may help you escape injury. ✦ 5.A

Lesson Review

Understanding Concepts

1. How can a seat belt save your life?
2. How does an air bag protect people?
3. What are two things you can do to stay safe in a car or bus?

Critical Thinking

4. **Making Inferences** The back seat is the safest part of a car during an accident. Why do you think this is true?
5. **Applying Concepts** Identify and discuss at least three specific things that you could do to keep a driver from being distracted.

internet connect
www.scilinks.org/health
Topic: Air Bags
HealthLinks code: HD4006

HEALTH LINKS Maintained by the National Science Teachers Association

Lesson 4 Automobile Safety

Lesson 5 Giving First Aid

What You'll Do

- **Describe** the three Cs of an emergency. ⭐ 5.A; 5.G
- **Describe** two ways to protect yourself when you give first aid. ⭐ 5.A; 5.G
- **List** eight phone numbers that should be on an emergency phone number list. ⭐ 5.A; 5.G
- **Explain** why you should be first-aid certified before giving first aid. ⭐ 5.A; 5.G

Terms to Learn

- first aid

Start Off Write

What should you do first during any emergency situation?

Blake has diabetes. His mother gave him a medical alert bracelet to wear. If Blake has an accident and can't talk, the bracelet lets other people know that he is diabetic.

Blake wears his bracelet in case something goes wrong. Knowing that Blake has diabetes will help emergency personnel give him the right care. Medical alert bracelets are just one thing you should look for when you find someone who needs help.

Identifying What's Wrong

Imagine you found someone hurt or unconscious on the floor. Do you know what to do? Remember the three Cs of emergencies:

- **Check out the situation.** First, make sure you're safe. Whatever hurt the victim might hurt you. If you are in danger, leave the area. If you're safe, check the victim for injuries. Try to find out how the victim got hurt. Check for medical alert jewelry, which lets you know about the victim's health.
- **Call for help.** Call 911 or other emergency services.
- **Care for the victim.** How quickly a victim gets help may determine his or her fate. If you have training, you should give the victim first aid right away. **First aid** is emergency medical care for someone who has been hurt or who is sick. Knowing first aid and acting quickly can help you save a victim's life.

Figure 11 Medical Alert Jewelry

Medical alert jewelry may list the following information:

▶ Drug allergies

▶ Illnesses such as diabetes or asthma

▶ Who to call in case of emergency

▶ Doctor's contact information

▶ Current medications

▶ Name, address, and phone number

490 | Chapter 19 Safety

Figure 12 Breathing masks and sterile gloves can keep you from getting sick from giving first aid.

Protecting Yourself

Giving first aid can be risky. You may be exposed to blood, saliva, and other body fluids. These fluids might contain bacteria and viruses that can make you sick. You can protect yourself by using protective equipment, such as breathing masks and sterile gloves. A breathing mask prevents exposure to the victim's saliva when you give rescue breathing. Sterile gloves protect you from blood and other bodily fluids. Breathing masks and sterile gloves are common in first-aid kits.

Sometimes, you may not have a breathing mask or sterile gloves. If you don't, wash all exposed areas with soap and water right after helping a victim. Whether you have protective equipment or not, visit your doctor after you give first aid. Your doctor can make sure you didn't get infected while giving first aid. ★ 5.A; 5.G

LIFE SKILLS ACTIVITY

PRACTICING WELLNESS

One way to be ready for emergencies is to carry a first-aid kit. First-aid kits often have breathing masks and sterile gloves. They also have bandages, antibiotic ointments, and other materials you need to care for a victim.

Create a public service announcement that tells people about the benefits of carrying a first-aid kit. You can create a radio announcement, poster, or brochure to get the word out.

Lesson 5 Giving First Aid

Calling for Help

Responding to an emergency often means making a phone call for help. Keep a list of emergency phone numbers next to every phone in your home. Your emergency phone number list should include numbers for the following:

- 911 or local emergency services
- police department
- fire department
- poison control
- family doctor
- your parents at work
- your neighbors
- your relatives

It's important to stay calm when you call an emergency number. If you panic, the emergency operator may not be able to understand you. You will need to give the operator a lot of information. The figure below lists some of the information you need to give the operator during an emergency call. The emergency operator uses this information to make sure you get the help you need. The operator also uses it to tell you what you can do for the victim.

Your safety must come first. If you are in danger at the location of the accident, leave right away. If you get hurt, you may not be able to help yourself or anyone else. Make the emergency phone call from your neighbor's house or another location. ★ 5.A; 5.G

Social Studies Activity

Research the history of 911. On a piece of posterboard, draw a timeline for the history of 911.

Figure 13 Making an Emergency Phone Call

What you need to do

▶ Stay calm.

▶ Make sure you're safe.

▶ Answer all the operator's questions as best you can.

▶ Follow the operator's instructions.

▶ Stay on the line until the operator tells you to hang up.

What you need to say

▶ Your name

▶ Where you are

▶ The type of emergency

▶ The condition of the victim if someone is hurt

▶ The medical history of the victim if known

▶ What you've done to help the victim

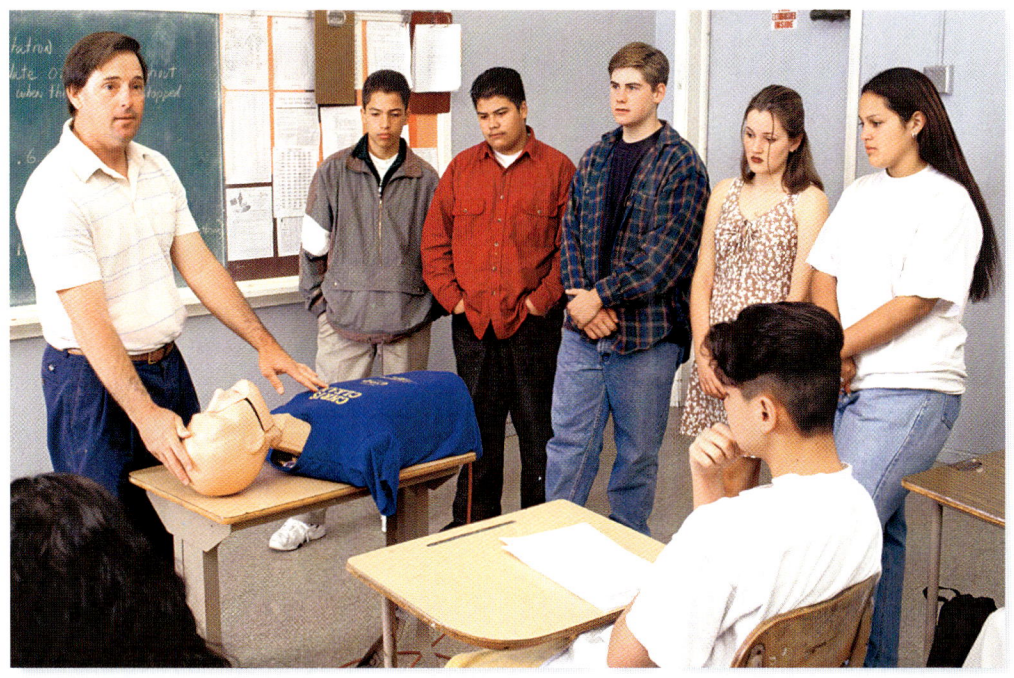

Figure 14 Taking a first-aid class can help you learn how to take care of someone who is hurt.

Why Be Certified?

Have you ever taken a first-aid class? If you haven't, you may want to think twice before you give first aid. Sometimes, helping someone without knowing the right way to do it can cause more injury. You should take a first-aid certification class. People who take first-aid classes are given a special license to give first aid.

First-aid certification classes are available in many places. The American Red Cross and the YMCA are two organizations that teach first aid. Also, talk to your teacher. You may be able to get certified in first aid at your school. ★ 5.G

Lesson Review

Using Vocabulary

1. What is first aid? ★ 5.G

Understanding Concepts

2. What are the three Cs of handling emergencies? ★ 5.G
3. List two things you can use to stay safe when you give first aid. ★ 5.A; 5.G
4. Why should you be first-aid certified before giving first-aid? ★ 5.G
5. What numbers should you have on your emergency phone number list? ★ 5.A; 5.G

Critical Thinking

6. **Making Inferences** There are many dangerous diseases carried in blood. What kind of effect do you think this fact might have on a person's willingness to help someone who is hurt? ★ 5.A; 5.G

internet connect
www.scilinks.org/health
Topic: First Aid
HealthLinks code: HD4042

HEALTH LINKS Maintained by the National Science Teachers Association

Lesson 6 — Basic First Aid

What You'll Do
- **Describe** the treatment for six kinds of injury.  5.A; 5.G
- **Explain** how to treat shock. 5.G

Terms to Learn
- fracture
- dislocation
- shock

Start Off Write
Why shouldn't you move someone with a head injury?

Carlos cut his hand while helping his mom with dinner. The cut bled a lot. His mom took him to the emergency room. He had to get stitches because the cut was so deep.

You've probably cut your hand or scraped your knee. Many cuts and scrapes aren't serious injuries. Carlos's cut needed stitches. Some cuts can bleed so much that a victim may die.

Bleeding

A scraped knee may not seem like a major injury. But it still needs first aid. For small cuts and scrapes, wash the area with mild soap and water. Use antibacterial cream and a bandage to cover the cut or scrape. Doing so can keep the cut or scrape from getting infected.

Some wounds will bleed a lot. Head wounds or cuts on your hands tend to bleed quite a bit even when they are minor. Applying pressure to the injury can stop the bleeding. Cover the injury with sterile gauze, and use your hand to put pressure on the injury. If the bleeding is severe, call for help. Don't take the gauze off the wound. Just add more gauze and maintain pressure if the bleeding continues. If it won't cause more injury, elevate the injured area above the heart to slow the flow of blood.

When in doubt, call for help or go to the emergency room. If you have sterile gloves, use them while helping someone with a cut. Sterile gloves will protect you from diseases carried in blood. They also protect the victim from any diseases you might have. If you get blood on you, wash it off with soap and water as soon as you can. 5.A; 5.G

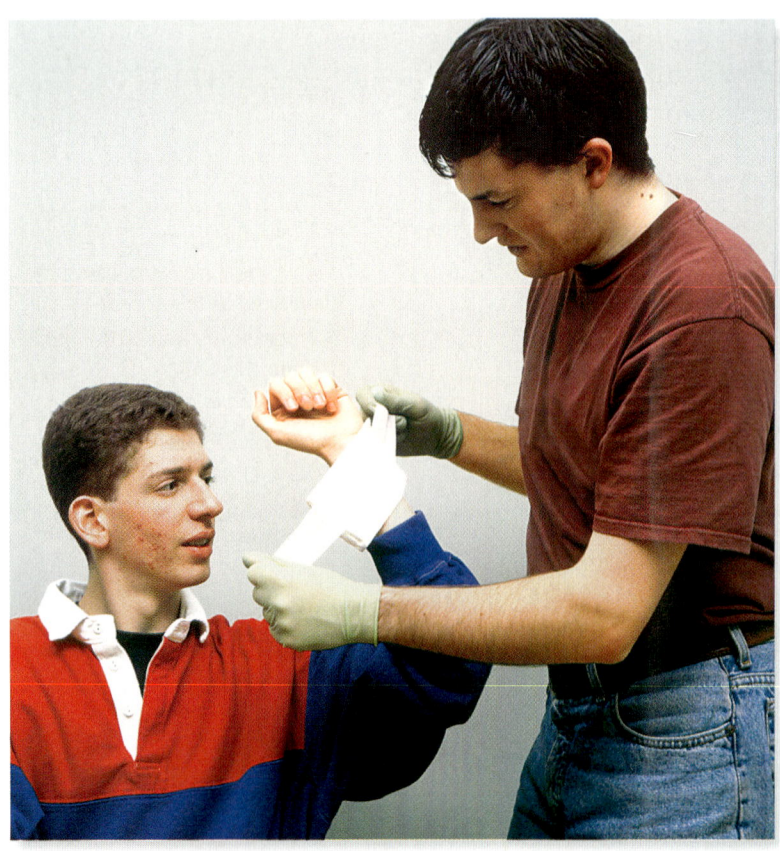

Figure 15 Knowing how to take care of a cut can help you save someone's life.

Poisoning

Many household products can cause poisoning. Cleaning products, automobile fluids, and some medicines are common causes of poisoning. Poisons can enter your body through your stomach, lungs, and skin.

Figure 16 Many common household products can cause poisonings.

Different poisons have different effects. So, how you take care of a poisoning victim depends on the poison. If you find someone who has been poisoned, try to find out what the poison is. If the victim is awake, ask him or her. Or look for nearby boxes and bottles of poisonous substances. Also, aromas and the victim's appearance may help identify the poison. Call your local poison control center right away. The operator can tell you how to take care of a poisoning victim until help arrives. ★ 5.A; 5.G

Burns

Have you ever had a sunburn? A sunburn is an example of a burn. The sun, hot objects, flames, and some chemicals can cause burns. The three types of burns are described below.

- First-degree burns, such as mild sunburn, affect the top layer of skin. The burned area is red, and there is some pain. Run cool water over first-degree burns. Don't put ice or ice water on the burn. Use antibiotic cream while the burns heal. If the burn is large, call a doctor.

- Second-degree burns affect two layers of skin and cause blisters. They are painful. Pour cool water over the area, or use a wet cold compress. Cover the burn with a sterile bandage. If the burn is larger than 2 inches, go to the emergency room or call for help. Do not remove clothing that is stuck to the burn.

- Third-degree burns affect all layers of skin. Some muscle and even bone may be burned. Skin looks dark or dry white. Third-degree burns may not hurt much. This is because pain sensors in the skin may have been damaged or destroyed. Call for help right away. Cover the burn with a clean, wet cloth. Do not remove clothing that is stuck to the burn. ★ 5.A; 5.G

Brain Food

Poisoning results in about 900,000 emergency room visits each year. About 90 percent of these poisonings are caused by items in the home.

Lesson 6 Basic First Aid

Figure 17 Dangerous electrical hazards are not always as obvious as the one in this photo.

Electrical Shock

Never touch someone who is being shocked. Always make sure that someone who has been shocked is no longer touching the electrical source before helping the person. Doing this will help you avoid being electrically shocked.

Electrical Shock

Have you ever wondered why there are warnings on electrical appliances and electrical lines? Did you know that the human body conducts electricity? Electrical shock happens when electricity is passed through the body. Electrical shock can make a victim's heart stop. It also causes burns and internal injuries. Before you touch a victim, make sure he or she is not touching the electrical source. Try to switch off the electrical supply. Use a dry broom handle, dry rope, or dry piece of clothing to move the victim away from the electrical source. If you aren't sure you're safe, don't touch the victim. Call for help. If you can touch the victim safely, give first aid until help arrives. ★ 5.A; 5.G

Fractures and Dislocations

A **fracture** is a broken or cracked bone. If you're helping someone who has a fracture, try not to move the injured area. Moving a broken bone may make the injury worse. Call for help, or go to the emergency room. For some fractures, you can use a splint until help arrives. A splint is a stiff object, such as a stick or board, which you can use to keep the injured area from moving. Put the splint on the area, and wrap it with bandages or cloth. Try to splint the joints closest to the injury as well. This reduces movement even more. Don't try to straighten or set a fracture. If it won't hurt the victim more, elevate the injured area and use ice wrapped in a towel to keep swelling down.

A **dislocation** is an injury in which a bone has been forced out of its normal position in a joint. Do not try to put a dislocated bone back into place. Do your best to keep the joint from moving, and seek medical help. ★ 5.A; 5.G

Head and Back Injuries

If you've bumped your head, you know even minor head injuries can hurt. But some head injuries are very serious. Some people who have head and back injuries never walk again. Do not move someone who has a head or back injury. If the victim is awake, tell him or her not to move. Call 911 or another emergency service right away. Moving someone who has a head or neck injury can make the injury worse. Your main job is to keep the victim still and calm. If the victim is awake, try to keep him or her awake until help arrives. ★ 5.A; 5.G

Shock

Many injuries may cause reduced blood flow. Blood may have been lost, blood flow may be blocked, or the heart may not be working normally. Shock is the body's response to reduced blood flow. A victim in shock has certain symptoms. The victim's skin is pale, cool, and clammy. His or her heart rate is fast but weak. The person feels lightheaded. Breathing is slow and shallow. The victim may seem confused. Call for medical help. Keep the victim warm and awake if possible. Loosen any clothing that might restrict blood flow and elevate the victim's feet. Check for any other injuries, and provide first aid if the victim has visible injuries.
★ 5.A; 5.G

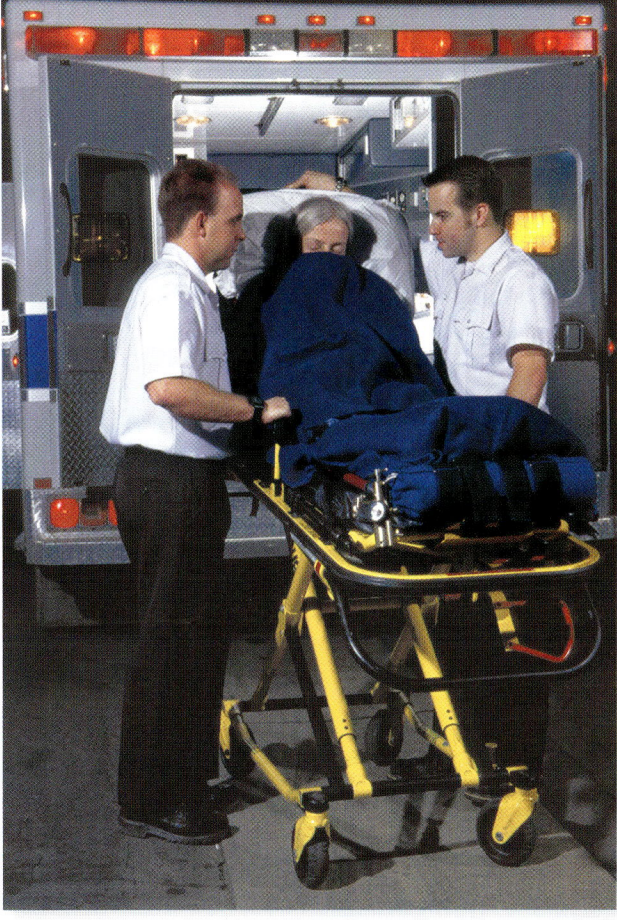

Figure 18 Victims in shock should be kept warm to counter a drop in body temperature.

Lesson Review

Using Vocabulary

1. What is the difference between a fracture and a dislocation? ★ 5.A; 5.G

Understanding Concepts

2. When shouldn't you touch an electrical shock victim? ★ 5.G
3. What are the three types of burns? ★ 5.G
4. Describe how to take care of someone in shock. ★ 5.A; 5.G

Critical Thinking

5. **Applying Concepts** Jerald found someone who was hurt. The victim didn't have any visible cuts. However, the victim's leg was twisted at a weird angle. The victim seemed confused, and her skin was clammy. What should Jerald do? ★ 5.A; 5.G

Lesson 7

Choking and CPR

Serena took a first-aid certification class. She learned how to take care of injuries. She also learned how to help someone who has stopped breathing.

What You'll Do

- **Explain** how to give abdominal thrust to adults, infants, and yourself. ★ 5.G
- **Describe** CPR for adults, small children, and infants. ★ 5.G

Terms to Learn

- abdominal thrusts
- cardiopulmonary resuscitation (CPR)
- rescue breathing

Start Off Write

What should you do if someone isn't breathing?

First-aid courses teach you about taking care of many injuries. But what do you do if someone has stopped breathing? Learning how to save someone who is choking or who isn't breathing is very important.

Abdominal Thrust

Have you ever seen someone grab his or her throat because he or she couldn't breathe? Was this person choking? When you see someone choking, you need to act fast. You will need to give abdominal thrusts. **Abdominal thrusts** (ab DAHM uh nuhl THRUHSTS) are actions that apply pressure to a choking person's stomach to force an object out of the throat.

First, you need to find out if the victim is actually choking. If the victim can cough or speak, he or she can still breathe. Don't try to help the victim. Let the victim try to clear his or her throat. If the victim cannot cough or speak, give abdominal thrusts. Abdominal thrusts compress the victim's abdomen. This increases pressure in the victim's lungs and airway. The pressure forces the air in the victim's lungs to push the object out of the victim's airway.

The figures on the next page show you how to save an adult, child, or infant from choking. You can also use abdominal thrust on yourself. Form a fist. Place the thumb-side of your fist on your stomach between your belly button and breastbone. Cover your hand with your other hand, and quickly push in and upward. You can also use a chair back, counter, or other solid object. Lean forward, and press your stomach against the object. The figure to the left shows this process. ★ 5.G

Figure 19 If you're ever alone and choking, you can use a chair back to give yourself abdominal thrusts.

498

Figure 20 Rescuing Choking Adults and Children — First Aid: Certification required

1. Stand or kneel behind the victim. The victim may be standing or sitting. Wrap your arms around the victim.

2. Form a fist. Place the thumb side of your fist on the victim's stomach, above the belly button and below the breastbone.

3. Cover your fist with your other hand. Give five quick upward thrusts into the victim's stomach.

4. Repeat abdominal thrusts until the object comes loose.

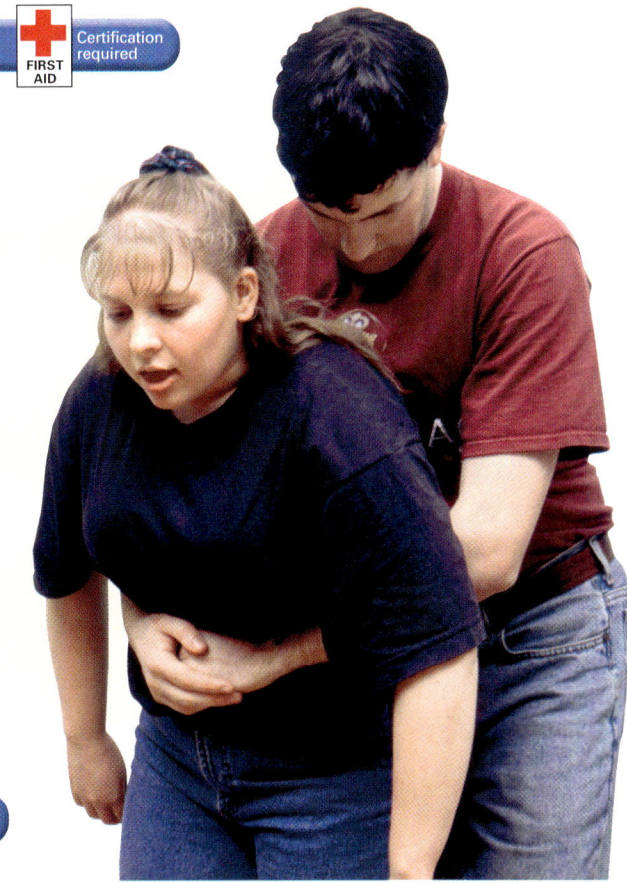

Figure 21 Rescuing Choking Infants — First Aid: Certification required

1. Put the infant face up on your forearm. Place your other arm on top of the infant, and hold the infant's jaw. Make sure the infant's nose and mouth aren't covered. Turn the infant over.

2. Support your arm on your thigh so that the infant's head is lower than his or her chest. Give five firm back blows with the heel of your hand.

3. If the object doesn't come loose, turn the infant back over. Continue to support his or her head and neck. Support your arm on your thigh.

4. Place two fingers on the infant's breastbone, between and just below the infant's nipples. Push the breastbone in five times.

5. Repeat back blows and thrusts until the object comes loose.

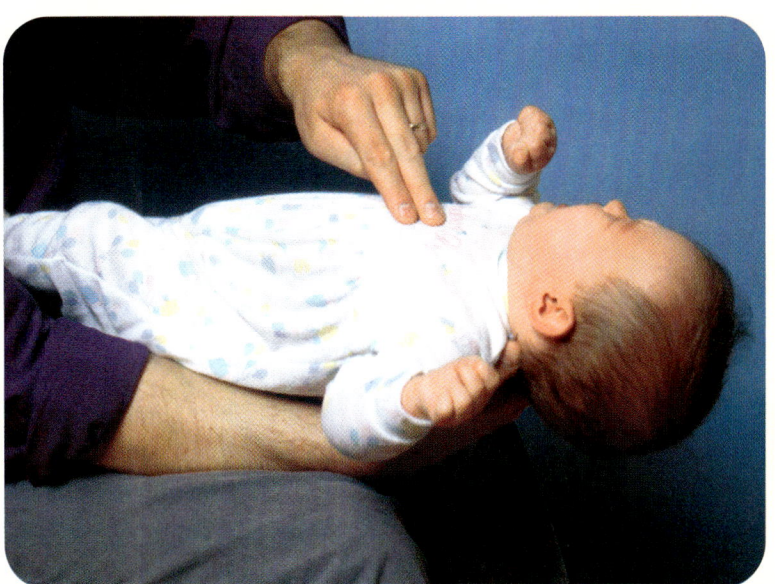

Lesson 7 Choking and CPR

CPR for Adults and Children

Imagine you have found someone unconscious on the floor. Is the victim breathing? Does he or she have a heartbeat? Do you know CPR? CPR stands for cardiopulmonary resuscitation (KAHR dee oh PUL muh NER ee ri SUHS uh TAY shuhn). **Cardiopulmonary resuscitation** is a technique used to save a victim who isn't breathing and who doesn't have a heartbeat.

CPR starts with rescue breathing. **Rescue breathing** is an emergency technique in which a rescuer gives air to someone who is not breathing. CPR also includes chest compressions (kuhm PRESH uhns). Chest compressions stimulate the heart to start beating again. The figures below and on the next page show CPR for adults, small children, and infants. But to give CPR, you'll have to know your ABCs first.

- **Airway** Make sure the victim's airway is clear and open. If it isn't, you won't be able to get air into the victim's lungs.

- **Breathing** Is the victim breathing? Look for movement in the victim's chest. Put your cheek over the victim's mouth, and see if you feel any breath. If the victim isn't breathing, start rescue breathing.

- **Check Pulse** Is the victim's heart beating? You can check at the victim's wrist or neck. If you don't feel a heartbeat, start chest compressions. ★ 5.G

CPR Certification

You should not give CPR unless you have been trained. If you do not know how to give chest compressions properly, you may cause injury. Also, giving chest compressions to someone who still has a heartbeat can interfere with the heart's normal function.

Figure 22 CPR for Adults — Certification required

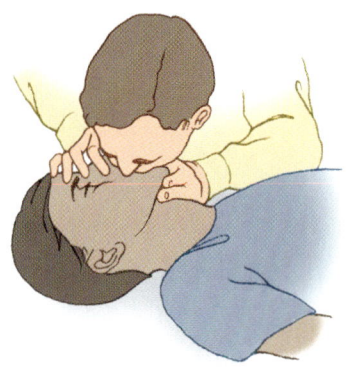

1 If the victim is not breathing, tilt the victim's head back. Pinch the victim's nose shut. Tightly seal your mouth over the victim's mouth. Slowly blow air into the victim's mouth until the victim's chest rises. Remove your mouth, and let the victim exhale. Repeat.

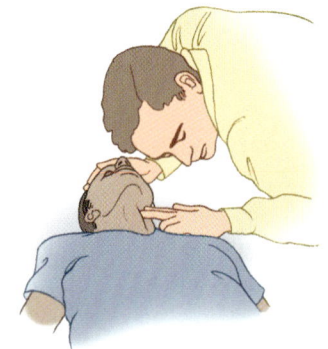

2 Check for the victim's pulse. Place the tips of your index and middle fingers on the side of the victim's neck, just below the victim's jaw. Check for a heartbeat by holding your fingers in place for about 10 seconds.

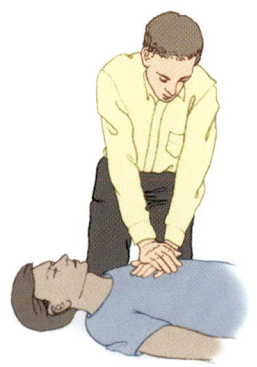

3 If there is no pulse, place the heel of one hand over the victim's breastbone at a point about two fingers' width above where the breastbone and ribs meet. Place your other hand on top of the first. Push straight down on the victim's breastbone. Lift your weight without lifting your hands from the victim's chest. Repeat.

Figure 23 CPR for Small Children and Infants

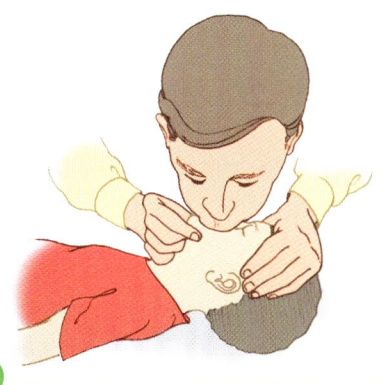

1 Pinch the victim's nose shut. Tightly seal your mouth over the child's mouth. If the victim is an infant, seal the nose and mouth with your mouth. Slowly blow air into the victim's lungs until the chest rises. Let the victim exhale, and repeat.

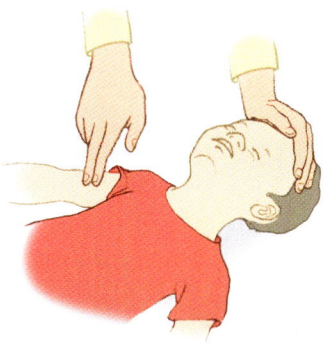

2 Place the tips of your index and middle fingers on the bone on the inside of the victim's arm, between the elbow and shoulder. Check for a pulse for 10 seconds. A pulse may also be found by using the same technique as for adults.

Depending on age of child

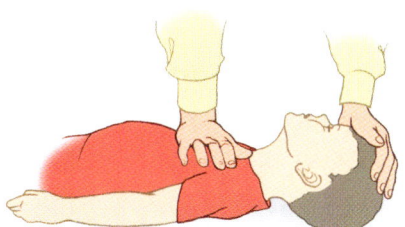

3 Small Children
Place the heel of one hand over the child's breastbone at a point about two fingers' width above where the breastbone and ribs meet. Keep your fingers off the victim's chest to avoid injuring ribs. Push straight down on the victim's breastbone. Lift your weight without lifting your hand from the victim's chest. Repeat.

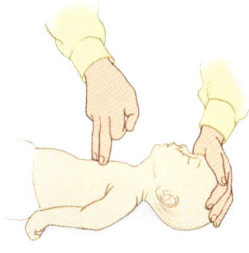

3 Infants
Place your middle and ring fingers on the breastbone at a point about one finger's width below the nipple line. Push the breastbone down no more than 1 inch. Do not lift your fingers from the baby's chest between compressions. Repeat.

Lesson Review

Using Vocabulary
1. What is an abdominal thrust? ★ 5.G
2. What is the difference between rescue breathing and CPR? ★ 5.G

Understanding Concepts
3. Describe how to give abdominal thrusts to adults and infants. ★ 5.G
4. Describe CPR for adults. ★ 5.G

Critical Thinking
5. **Making Inferences** It is very important to take a CPR training course. Someone who tries to give CPR without training may injure a victim. What types of injuries might happen if someone gives CPR without the proper training? ★ 5.A

internet connect
www.scilinks.org/health
Topic: **CPR**
HealthLinks code: **HD4024**

HEALTH LINKS Maintained by the National Science Teachers Association

19 CHAPTER REVIEW

Chapter Summary

- An accident is an unexpected event that may cause injury. - Four common accidents are falls, fires, electrocution, and poisoning. - You can avoid violence by avoiding people and places that tend to get violent, by using your refusal and conflict management skills, and by telling an adult. - Weapons are dangerous, especially if they aren't used or stored properly. - Seat belts and air bags can help prevent injury during a car accident. - The first thing to do during an emergency is to make sure you are safe. - You should be certified before giving first aid. - Abdominal thrusts are a technique used to save a choking victim. - CPR is used to save someone who is not breathing and who does not have a heartbeat.

Using Vocabulary

For each sentence, fill in the blank with the proper word from the word bank provided below.

fracture gangs
accident dislocation
first aid shock
violence weapon
abdominal thrusts

1. ___ is caused by reduced blood flow.
2. ___ are groups of people who often use violence.
3. A(n) ___ is an unexpected event that may cause injury.
4. An object that can be used to hurt other people is called a(n) ___.
5. Using physical force to hurt someone is called ___.
6. ___ are actions that apply pressure to a choking person's stomach.
7. An injury in which a bone has been forced out of its normal position in a joint is called a(n) ___.
8. Emergency medical care for someone who has been hurt is called ___.

Understanding Concepts

9. Describe four kinds of accidents. ★ 5.A
10. Why should you have a family evacuation plan? ★ 5.A
11. List seven ways to stay safe from accidents. ★ 5.A
12. List five reasons violence happens in school. ★ 5.A; 5.K; 10.E
13. What should you do for a victim of electrical shock? ★ 5.A; 5.G
14. Describe how to give abdominal thrusts to yourself. ★ 5.G
15. How does staying seated on the bus keep you safe? ★ 5.A
16. What are the three types of burns, and how do you care for each type? ★ 5.A; 5.G
17. How does a breathing mask prevent the spread of disease? ★ 5.A
18. Describe first aid for poisoning. ★ 5.G
19. What should you do for someone who has a head injury? ★ 5.G
20. Describe CPR for small children and infants. ★ 5.G
21. Where should you keep an emergency phone number list? ★ 5.A

502 | Chapter 19 Review

Critical Thinking

Applying Concepts

22. Roma is going to the park with her friends. They're going skating. What should Roma do while she's skating to make sure she's safe? ★ 5.A

23. Most injuries caused by auto accidents happen when passengers are not wearing their seat belts. Why do these injuries happen? ★ 5.A

24. Before you help someone who is hurt, you should make sure that you're safe. Why is it so important that you're safe when helping others? ★ 5.A; 5.G

25. One way to stay safe when you're doing outdoor recreational activities is to go with a group of your friends. How does going with a group of people keep you safe? ★ 5.A; 10.E

Making Good Decisions

26. Duval knows some people who joined a gang. Now they want him to join the gang. What should Duval do? Explain your answer. ★ 5.A; 5.K

27. Johnny likes to hang out at his friend Kaleb's house. They usually play video games or shoot baskets in the driveway. One day, Kaleb wants to show Johnny his father's gun. Johnny knows that Kaleb and his father hunt together sometimes. But Kaleb's father isn't home. What should Johnny do? ★ 5.A; 5.B

28. Glenn took a first-aid certification class. He and his friend May went mountain biking, and she fell. May has some serious cuts. Glenn usually carries a first-aid kit with him, but he forgot it this time. So, Glenn doesn't have any sterile gloves with him. What should Glenn do? ★ 5.A; 5.G

Interpreting Graphics

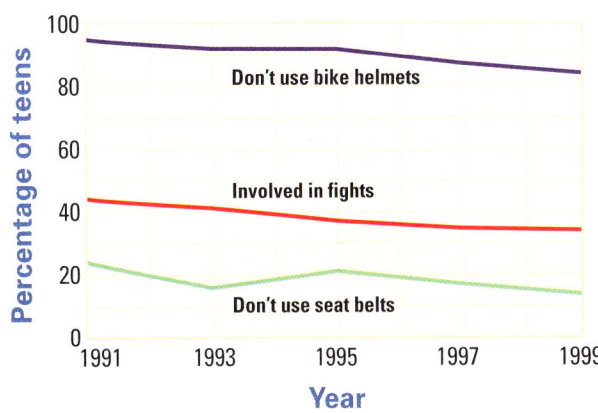

Trends in Teen Risk Behavior

Use the figure above to answer questions 29–32. ★ M8.5.A

29. What percentage of teens didn't wear their seat belts in 1991? in 1999?

30. In 1999, what percentage of teens didn't wear bicycle helmets?

31. What percentage of teens were involved in fights in 1993? in 1997?

32. Are these three risk behaviors decreasing over time, staying the same, or increasing?

Reading Checkup

Take a minute to review your answers to the Health IQ questions at the beginning of this chapter. How has reading this chapter improved your Health IQ?

Life Skills IN ACTION

Making Good Decisions

You make decisions every day. But how do you know if you are making good decisions? Making good decisions is making choices that are healthy and responsible. Following the six steps of making good decisions will help you make the best possible choice whenever you make a decision. Complete the following activity to practice the six steps of making good decisions.

Minhee's Dilemma

Setting the Scene

For several weeks, Minhee and her friends have been planning a long bike ride at a nearby state park. The morning of the outing, Minhee cannot find her bicycle helmet. Her friends are telling her to hurry up. Minhee's brother, Jun-Ho, offers to let her borrow his helmet. But when Minhee tries the helmet on, she discovers that it is too big for her.

The 6 Steps of Making Good Decisions

1. Identify the problem.
2. Consider your values.
3. List the options.
4. Weigh the consequences.
5. Decide, and act.
6. Evaluate your choice.

Guided Practice

Practice with a Friend

Form a group of three. Have one person play the role of Minhee and another person play the role of Jun-Ho. Have the third person be an observer. Walking through each of the six steps of making good decisions, role-play a conversation between Minhee and Jun-Ho. Have Minhee talk to Jun-Ho as she decides what to do next. The observer will take notes, which will include observations about what the person playing Minhee did well and suggestions of ways to improve. Stop after each step to evaluate the process. ★ 5.A; 12.B; 12.C

Independent Practice

Check Yourself

After you have completed the guided practice, go through Act 1 again without stopping at each step. Answer the questions below to review what you did.

1. What options does Minhee have in this situation?
2. What are the possible consequences of each of Minhee's options?
3. Why might it be difficult for Minhee to decide against going on the outing?
4. List some of your own values that help you make good decisions about safety. ★ 5.A; 12.B; 12.C

On Your Own

The next weekend, Minhee and her friend Courtney are riding their bicycles in the same state park. Courtney is very athletic and wants to try riding on one of the harder trails in the park. Minhee doesn't know if she can handle the trail. Courtney promises to go slowly and to help Minhee if she needs it. Write a skit about a conversation between Minhee and Courtney. Have Minhee use the six steps of making good decisions to decide whether to ride on the trail with Courtney. ★ 5.A; 12.B; 12.C

CHAPTER 20
Healthcare Consumer

Lessons

1. **Being a Wise Consumer** — 508
2. **Healthcare Information** — 512
3. **Influencing Healthcare** — 516
4. **Healthcare Services** — 518
5. **Accessing Services** — 522

Chapter Review — 524
Life Skills in Action — 526

Check out **Current Health** articles related to this chapter by visiting **go.hrw.com**. Just type in the keyword **HD4CH52**.

> "I was feeling **pains in my legs** after I ran, so I called my doctor. She said that I need to **stretch** when I run and that I should buy some **shoes** that have better cushioning. Her advice really helped."

PRE-READING

Answer the following multiple-choice questions to find out what you already know about being a healthcare consumer. When you've finished this chapter, you'll have the opportunity to change your answers based on what you've learned.

1. You can find the best value by
   a. always buying the least expensive item.
   b. always buying the most expensive item.
   c. comparison shopping.
   d. None of the above ★ 12.B

2. Advertisements are made primarily to
   a. entertain you.
   b. inform you.
   c. sell products.
   d. All of the above ★ 8.A

3. Healthcare services are provided by
   a. primary care providers.
   b. community organizations.
   c. government agencies.
   d. All of the above

4. Valid healthcare claims are usually
   a. based in facts.
   b. logical.
   c. beneficial.
   d. All of the above ★ 4.A

5. A source that has bias
   a. has good support for what it says.
   b. is a widely recognized authority.
   c. presents information with a slant that prevents the information from being objective.
   d. is wrong. ★ 4.A; 4.B

6. Dermatologists are doctors who can help you with your
   a. mind.
   b. skin.
   c. eyes.
   d. bones.

ANSWERS: 1. c; 2. c; 3. d; 4. d; 5. c; 6. b

Lesson 1

Being a Wise Consumer

What You'll Do

- **List** five influences on your decision to buy healthcare products. ★ 4.A; 7.A; 8.A; 12.E
- **Explain** how a goal can help you spend your money wisely. ★ 12.B; 12.F
- **List** five resources for learning about healthcare products. ★ 4.A; 7.A
- **Describe** how comparison shopping can help you find the best value. ★ 4.A; 12.B

Terms to Learn

- healthcare consumer
- comparison shopping

Start Off Write

How does comparison shopping help you save money?

Marcie's face was starting to break out. Marcie's mom offered to take her to the doctor. But Marcie's best friend used an over-the-counter medicine that seemed to work. Then, Marcie saw an ad in the back of a magazine that promised to make acne "disappear on contact!" Marcie wasn't sure what to do.

When you have acne or any other health concern, you want help. Sometimes, you can fix a problem by changing the way you care for yourself. For example, stretching can help prevent muscle pain later. But for some problems, you may need to see a doctor or to use a healthcare product. If Marcie pays for a visit to the doctor or buys an acne medicine, she is acting as a healthcare consumer (kuhn SOO muhr). A **healthcare consumer** is anyone who pays for a healthcare product or service.

Choosing Products and Services

If you have purchased running shoes, sunglasses, deodorant, or even lip balm, you are a healthcare consumer. Think about the last time you bought a healthcare product. How did you decide what to buy? Maybe you carefully researched which running shoes were the best for you. Maybe the lip balm was just sitting on the checkout counter, and you bought it without really thinking about the choice. Whether or not you realize it, the choice you made was affected by influences. Part of being a wise healthcare consumer is being aware of these influences. ★ 4.A; 4.B; 12.B

Figure 1 When you buy healthcare products, such as the ones shown here, you are a healthcare consumer.

What Influences You?

Many things influence what you buy. A few possible influences are listed below.

- **Tradition** You may choose to buy something because it is what you or your family usually use. For example, your family probably influences your food choices. And if you have grown up using a certain kind of toothpaste, you may not like any other kind.

- **Peers** You may decide to buy something because your friends and classmates like it.

- **Packaging and Placement** You may choose to buy something because it catches your eye or because it was placed in the store where it was easy to grab.

- **Salespeople** Sales clerks can influence what you buy. They may recommend or demonstrate products. They may even offer free samples.

- **Media Advertising** Advertising has a big impact on decisions to buy products. You have probably seen ads your whole life. Companies that make products want to sell the products. These companies spend billions of dollars every year making ads to persuade people to buy their products. ★ 4.A; 7.A; 8.A; 12.E

Figure 2 Sometimes, friends influence what you buy.

Sticking to Your Goal

All of these factors can influence your decision, but the decision to buy something is still up to you. It's your money. Spend it in a way that is right for you and your goals. Many of the things that influence you can help you spend your money wisely. However, sometimes the information you get is not helpful. Sometimes, the information is wrong. Be careful. When you are shopping for something, it's easy to get distracted. For example, you may decide you want to buy toothpaste to fight cavities and plaque. Then, you see a TV ad for a new toothpaste. The ad has a catchy jingle that promises whiter teeth and fresh breath. You may decide to try that brand. But does it help you keep your teeth and gums healthy? Is it recommended by dentists or dental organizations? Remember your original goal, and be sure that the product you buy helps you reach that goal. ★ 12.B; 12.F

Lesson 1 Being a Wise Consumer

Figure 3 You can make better buying decisions by first doing research. Consumer magazines and the Internet are sometimes good sources of product information.

Internet Sources

Be sure that any Web site you use is approved by experts (for example, medical and dental organizations). Always check information found on the Internet with other authoritative sources.

Get the Facts

You can do more than evaluate your influences on your own. Ask your parents or other adults in your family for advice. You can also educate yourself. The following resources can help you make healthcare purchasing decisions:

- medical professionals, such as doctors and nurses
- school staff, such as teachers, counselors, and coaches
- community professionals, such as librarians and health agency workers
- reference material, such as books, consumer magazines, and the Internet

You can make sure the information you find from one source is accurate by checking with other sources. For example, if you find an article that recommends a healthcare product, check with a parent and experts to make sure the claims are true.

★ 4.A; 4.B; 12.B

Choosing for Health

Being a wise consumer can help you be healthier. Wise consumers pay for products and services that are right for them. Spending your money carefully can help you avoid spending money on products and services that are dangerous for you. Careful shopping can keep you from buying things that don't work and things that you don't need. Not buying such things helps you save money for the things that do work and that are good for you. ★ 4.C; 12.B; 12.F

Comparison Shopping

After you research what you need, you can begin comparison shopping. **Comparison shopping** is the process of looking at several similar products and figuring out which one offers the best value. The best value may not be the product that has the lowest price. The best value may be a more expensive, higher quality product. For example, one bottle of shampoo may cost half as much as another bottle. But if the more expensive shampoo lasts three times as long as the cheap one, the more expensive bottle is a better value. Another way comparison shopping can help is by showing you which store offers the best price on identical items. The table below shows how you could comparison shop for toothpaste in a single store. ★ 4.B; 12.B

TABLE 1 Toothpaste Comparison

Toothpaste	Features	Quantity	Cost
Generic	ADA-approved, fluoride	6.4 oz (181g)	$1.49, which is $0.23/oz (or less than 1 cent/g)
Brand-name 1	ADA-approved, fluoride, tartar control	6.4 oz (181g)	$2.89, which is $0.45/oz (or 1.6 cents/g)
Brand-name 2	ADA approved, fluoride, tartar control, whitening agent	4.5 oz (128g)	$6.99, which is $1.55/oz (or 5.5 cents/g)

Hands-on ACTIVITY

THE SMARTEST PURCHASE

1. Research the qualities of safety-approved bike helmets.
2. Create a table using these categories: brand, features, and the lowest price for each model.
3. Fill in the table, and rate the helmets.

Analysis
1. Which helmet is the best value? Explain your answer.

Lesson Review

Using Vocabulary
1. What is a healthcare consumer? ★ 4.B; 12.B
2. Define *comparison shopping*.

Understanding Concepts
3. List five influences on healthcare-purchasing decisions. ★ 4.A; 7.A; 8.A; 12.E
4. Explain how goals can help you spend your money wisely. ★ 12.B; 12.F
5. List five resources for learning about healthcare products. ★ 4.A; 4.B; 12.B

Critical Thinking
6. **Making Good Decisions** Imagine that you have decided to purchase a weight bench and free weights as part of an exercise program. Outline the steps you would take and the questions you would ask before making a purchase. ★ 4.B; 12.B
7. **Analyzing Viewpoints** Your neighbor has had a bad back for years. Is she a good resource for information about treating bad backs, or is she a bad resource? Explain your answer. ★ 4.B; 4.C; 12.B

internet connect
www.scilinks.org/health
Topic: Truth in Advertising
HealthLinks code: HD4103
HEALTH LINKS Maintained by the National Science Teachers Association

Lesson 1 Being a Wise Consumer

Lesson 2

Healthcare Information

What You'll Do

- **Explain** why keeping up with healthcare news is important. ★ 4.A; 4.C
- **Explain** why you should check with an authority about a healthcare claim. ★ 4.A; 4.B
- **Describe** a way to evaluate a healthcare claim. ★ 4.B
- **Explain** how a well-informed consumer can become a resource for others. ★ 4.C; 12.E

Terms to Learn

- bias

Write

Why is it important to check a healthcare claim with more than one source?

Mike wanted to get bigger and stronger. His friend Tyler told him that new dietary supplements would help. Mike asked his health teacher about them and found out that the things Tyler recommended were legal. But the supplements have side effects and could even be harmful. Mike was glad he asked.

Mike was smart. A good healthcare decision begins with good information. He knew that his friend's information needed checking. One reason that health informaton needs checking is that it changes.

Keeping Up with Healthcare News

Developments in many fields can affect health decisions. Nutrition experts develop food pyramids so that people understand how to eat better. Other scientists develop new ways of helping asthma patients. Sometimes, these new developments apply to you or to someone you know. Learning this new information can help make you a smarter consumer. For example, you may read a study that shows that drinking water is just as good for you as drinking sports drinks. That information could help you save money by helping you decide to drink water when you exercise. ★ 4.A; 4.C

Figure 4 Healthcare advances almost always begin in the lab.

Figure 5 Labels offer some helpful information, but they are also designed to help sell the product. You should never use labels as your only source of information.

Consider Your Source

But new information is not always correct. You've probably heard the saying "Don't believe everything you hear." That's especially true about healthcare information. Many people make claims that seem to be true but are not. And sometimes it's hard to tell what is true.

Objective information will be the same no matter who gives it to you. For example, pretend you are going to buy a heating pad and are trying to find out information about one model. The size of the pad will be the same no matter who measures it. But some information about the pad will have a bias (BIE uhs). A **bias** is a slant that changes how information is presented. For example, you may read the label to find out if the pad works well. But the information that you find on the label is probably slanted to persuade you to buy the pad. A rival company may say that its heating pad works much better than the one you are looking at. But that company has a bias, too. Many sources have a bias. However, each source may also make good points. Using several sources can help you see both the bias and the accurate information in each source.

You should always check with an authority about important information. An *authority* is a person or institution that is accepted as an expert in a field. Experts should be widely recognized and concerned with your well-being. Be sure that the information they provide is clear and up-to-date. Your healthcare provider or librarian should be able to help you find good sources. There are also books and reliable Web sites that can help you. Use more than one source to check out a healthcare claim.  4.A; 4.B

SOCIAL STUDIES ACTIVITY

At the top of a piece of paper, write down a healthcare issue you have heard about in the news. Under the issue, write down three questions you have about that issue. Next to each question, write down where you could look for the answer. Research your answers, and write a short report about the issue.

Figure 6 Evaluating a healthcare claim involves asking some important questions.

- Is this claim logical?
- Is this claim based in facts?
- Has this product or service been tested?
- Is this product or service beneficial?

Evaluating Healthcare Claims

Identifying the bias in a source is the first step in evaluating a healthcare claim. The second step is checking with an expert about any information you gather. But sometimes you cannot find an expert. And sometimes the experts that you do find disagree. In the end, you have to decide if a claim is true based on all that you have learned. Asking the questions in the figure above can help. Valid claims are

- based in facts
- tested
- beneficial
- logical

If a claim is not based in facts, has not been tested, isn't beneficial, or isn't logical, then the claim is probably false. Companies that make false claims to sell products or services are guilty of *quackery* (KWAK urh ee). For example, suppose a heating-pad advertisement makes the claim "Our pad not only makes your tired muscles feel younger, it actually makes you younger!" That statement is quackery. Remember that if something sounds too good to be true, it probably is. ★ 4.B

BEING A WISE CONSUMER

Compare the ads or promotional material for two or more similar products. Develop a table illustrating the pros and cons for each product you analyzed. Based on your analysis, choose one product over the other and defend your choice in an oral report. ★ 4.B

Reaching Out

Information is powerful. Learning how to be a careful healthcare consumer teaches you a lot. You learn more than how to be careful with your money. You learn how to think about what you read and hear. Making better choices can help you live a healthier life.

You can use what you've learned to help your family, friends, and community live better, too. For example, you could use a classroom bulletin board to show how recycling motor oil helps protect drinking water. Or you can tell your friends about any research you have done before buying a healthcare product. While keeping up with the news, you may learn about a shortage of volunteers at a hospital or at a foodbank and become inspired to help. The goal of all good healthcare information is to help people live healthier lives. Helping other people live healthier lives shows that you have learned to use healthcare information wisely. ★ 4.C; 12.E

Figure 7 Understanding healthcare information can inspire you to help others.

Lesson Review

Using Vocabulary

1. What is bias? ★ 4.B

Understanding Concepts

2. Explain why keeping up with healthcare news is important. ★ 4.A; 4.C
3. Explain why you should check with an authority about a healthcare claim. ★ 4.A; 4.B; 4.C
4. Explain a way to evaluate a healthcare claim. ★ 4.B
5. Explain how a well-informed consumer can become a resource for others. ★ 4.C; 12.E

Critical Thinking

6. **Applying Concepts** A friend says, "I've lost 15 pounds this week on a new diet! You should try it." Describe how you would evaluate your friend's healthcare claim. ★ 4.A; 4.B

Lesson 3 Influencing Healthcare

Ari bought a bottle of cough syrup at the drugstore. The box looked fine from the outside. When he got home, he noticed that the safety seal around the cap of the bottle was broken. Ari showed the bottle to his mom. She called the store and returned the bottle the next day.

What You'll Do

- **Explain** four ways that consumers can influence healthcare. ★ 4.C; 6.B
- **Explain** how to return a defective product. ★ 4.C; 11.D
- **Describe** three federal agencies that provide consumer protection. ★ 6.B

Start Off Write
What is the proper way to return a defective product?

Ari and his mother did not have to keep the cough syrup, even though they had already paid for it. In fact, consumers have the responsibility to return all damaged products. Returning defective products is one way that consumers affect healthcare.

Money Talks

You may think that healthcare is something so big that you could never have any affect on it. But you can influence healthcare. For example, companies offer products that people buy. If products do not sell, companies have no reason to make them. When you buy products that work and refuse products that do not work, you help influence the kinds of products that are available to everyone.

If you learn about a high-quality healthcare product that you would like to buy, ask a local store to begin stocking it. Take any research you have done to support your request. If the store begins selling the product, buy it. Tell people that this product works for you and helps you stay healthy. Stores stock only products that people buy. You have the power to influence the kinds of products that are available by buying high-quality products. ★ 4.C; 6.B

Figure 8 Stores carry only items that people buy. Choosing high-quality items encourages stores to carry them.

Returning Products

Before buying anything, examine it carefully for signs of tampering. If a seal or shrink-wrap is damaged in any way, take the item to a store representative and choose a different package. If you buy a product and later notice signs of tampering, save the package and your receipts. Take it back to the store, and explain what you found. Do not use any product if the packaging has been damaged. Protect yourself by looking for safety problems before and after you buy healthcare products. If you buy a defective or unsafe product, let the company that made it know. That information helps the company correct the problem. ★ 4.C; 11.D

Consumer Protection

Federal government agencies give consumers protection against dishonest, dangerous, and ineffective products. The Consumer Product Safety Commission (CPSC) alerts the public to recalls of unsafe or even deadly items. The Federal Trade Commission (FTC) assures that companies compete fairly with each other and offer the best quality and value to consumers. The Food and Drug Administration (FDA) oversees the testing and approval of drugs, medical devices, some food products, vaccines, blood products, and cosmetics. All of these agencies have telephone hotlines and Web sites. Use them to report problems or ask questions about defective or dangerous products. ★ 6.B

Figure 9 A respectful letter is helpful when you return a defective product through the mail.

Lesson Review

Understanding Concepts

1. Explain four ways that consumers can influence healthcare.
2. Explain how to return a defective product.
3. Describe three federal agencies that provide consumer protection.

Critical Thinking

4. **Making Good Decisions** After purchasing eye drops, you discover at home that the seal on the box is broken and that there is no seal covering the top of the bottle. What do you do?

internet connect
www.scilinks.org/health
Topic: Consumer Protection and Education
HealthLinks code: HD4023

Lesson 4: Healthcare Services

You can help yourself stay healthy by exercising and by choosing healthy snacks. Your parents help by making sure you have food and clothing. Healthcare professionals help you stay well, too.

What You'll Do

- **Explain** the difference between a primary care provider and a specialist. ★ 4.A; 4.C
- **Contrast** inpatient and outpatient care. ★ 4.C
- **Identify** healthcare needs that may be met by community organizations. ★ 3.A; 4.C; 6.A
- **Identify** the healthcare needs met by government agencies. ★ 4.C

Terms to Learn

- primary care provider
- specialist

Start Off Write

What does a primary care provider do?

You may have a family doctor you see for checkups and when you are sick. But a family doctor is just one of the many kinds of healthcare providers who can help you. Today, many professionals work together as a team to provide healthcare services to individuals and communities.

Types of Healthcare Professionals

A healthcare professional who handles general care is a **primary care provider.** These professionals perform physical examinations, order tests, and diagnose health problems. They may refer patients to specialists. A **specialist** is a healthcare professional who has received training in a specific medical field. Some kinds of medical specialists are listed below. Some medical specialists are doctors, others are not. They all work together to provide healthcare.

★ 4.A; 4.C

TABLE 2 Medical Specialists

Optometrists	doctors who care for the eyes and give eye exams, corrective lens prescriptions, and vision therapy
Dermatologists	doctors who care for the skin, including treatment for acne and rashes
Orthopedic surgeons	doctors who care for bone and skeletal injuries, such as setting broken bones
Radiologists	doctors who locate injuries and signs of disease by reading X rays of and scans of the body
Psychiatrists	doctors who care for the mind through counseling and medicine
Physical therapists	licensed specialists who help restore function after injury, improve movement, relieve pain, and prevent or limit physical disabilities
Pharmacists	licensed specialists who dispense drugs prescribed by another healthcare professional, advise providers on how drugs act in the body, and counsel patients about their medications

Hospitals and Clinics

Hospitals and clinics are *healthcare facilities*, places where you can go to receive healthcare. Generally, hospital care is divided into two types.

- **Inpatient Care** This type of care is given when the hospital can care for a patient best if the person stays at the hospital. Many serious conditions and complicated treatments need inpatient care. For example, major surgery is usually an inpatient procedure.

- **Outpatient Care** This type of care is given when the patient can go home the same day that the treatment is given. Many less-serious conditions and simple procedures can be done through outpatient care. For example, physical therapy is often an outpatient treatment.

But those are just general terms. The typical hospital is a busy place. Emergency departments handle accidents, heart attacks, and other urgent situations. Many hospitals offer wellness programs, such as health screenings, counseling, exercise programs, and education. Outreach programs take specialists to schools, community centers, and neighborhood clinics.

Figure 10 Many hospitals provide physical therapy to people trying to improve movement after an injury or illness.

Some hospitals are general hospitals that treat many kinds of health problems. Other hospitals are specialty hospitals that address specific health concerns. For example, specialty hospitals can focus on helping people who have cancer, heart problems, or burns. General hospitals and specialty hospitals can be teaching hospitals that train healthcare professionals to do their jobs.

Hospitals can help you maintain good health by providing emergency care, education, counseling, and volunteer opportunities. If you are thinking about a career in healthcare, volunteering can help you to learn more about medical care and to help your community at the same time. ★ 4.A; 4.B; 4.C; 6.B

Health Journal

Have you ever spent time in a hospital as a patient or a visitor? If you have, write in your Health Journal your impression of being there.

Myth & Fact

Myth: All healthcare agencies are run by the government.

Fact: Many healthcare facilities are independent community organizations and private businesses.

Community Healthcare Organizations

Not all healthcare services are provided by hospitals. Community healthcare organizations also help communities stay healthy. Many national organizations work to increase awareness and promote research for particular health problems. For example, the American Heart Association raises money to help fund research on heart problems and teach people about cardiovascular health. Some organizations, such as the Red Cross, offer services around the world. Other organizations, such as those who run local hotlines for victims of abuse, give help to a small area.

Whether small or large, community healthcare organizations help meet many needs. For example, these organizations help people who are trying to lose weight, people who have drug problems, and people who have mental health problems. Some community healthcare organizations run safe houses that help people get out of abusive relationships. Some serve the elderly, others help teens who are in trouble. Still others help people who are blind or deaf.

Community organizations serve every healthcare need imaginable. You can find out about the healthcare organizations in your community by doing a little research. An Internet search will help you find the telephone numbers, the addresses, and sometimes the e-mail addresses of many of them. Print directories are available in many libraries. School nurses, counselors, and religious professionals can also link teens and adults to local and national resources. ★ 3.A; 4.C; 6.A; 6.B

Figure 11 Some community organizations specialize in helping the elderly.

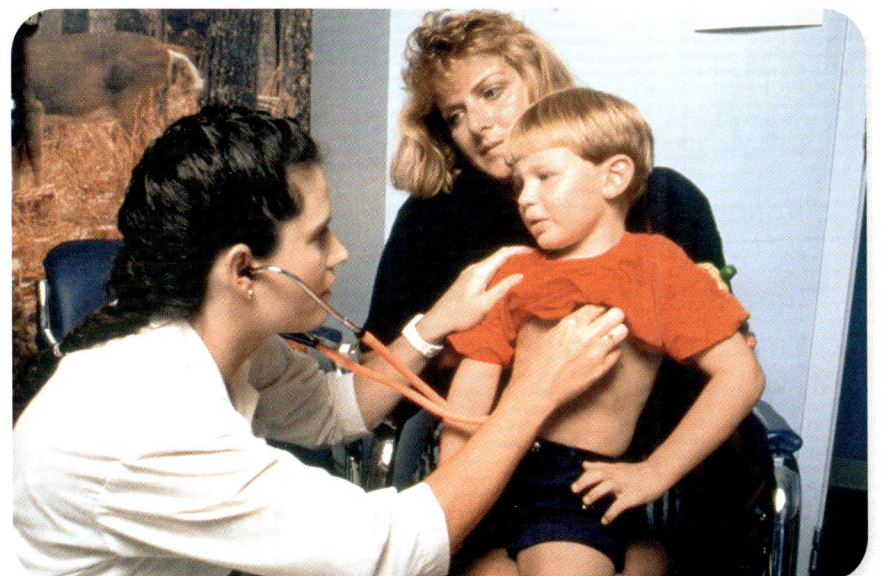

Figure 12 Some agencies provide low-cost checkups.

Government Agencies

Government agencies play a very important role in healthcare. Local agencies are usually run by cities, counties, and states. Some local agencies, such as public health departments, provide free information resources. Some give free or very low-cost vaccines and checkups. Some have nurses who go on home visits to families who have a new baby or to senior citizens whose health is poor. Local agencies test drinking water to make sure it is safe. Rescue crews save countless lives as they move patients safely from the scene of an accident or sudden illness to a hospital.

Federal agencies help the whole country. For example, the Federal Emergency Management Association (FEMA) helps victims of disasters. The National Institutes of Health (NIH) provide money for research for the prevention and treatment of disease. Other agencies help some people pay for medical care. ★ 6.B

LIFE SKILLS ACTIVITY

COMMUNICATING EFFECTIVELY

Choose a federal health agency to study. Conduct library research to learn about it. Prepare a list of questions you have about the services it provides. Contact the agency, and ask your questions. Create a flyer describing the agency and hand out the flyer to your class.

Lesson Review

Using Vocabulary

1. What is a primary care provider? ★ 4.C
2. How are primary care providers different from specialists? ★ 4.A; 4.C

Understanding Concepts

3. Explain the difference between inpatient and outpatient care. ★ 4.A; 4.C
4. Identify healthcare needs that may be met by community organizations. ★ 3.A; 4.C; 6.A
5. Identify healthcare needs met by government agencies. ★ 6.B

Critical Thinking

6. **Analyzing Ideas** Imagine that a major natural disaster has struck your community. Describe how local and national agencies might work with community organizations to provide help. ★ 6.A; 6.B

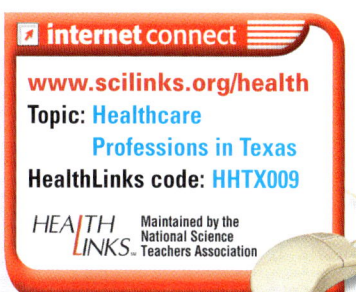

internet connect
www.scilinks.org/health
Topic: Healthcare Professions in Texas
HealthLinks code: HHTX009

HEALTH LINKS. Maintained by the National Science Teachers Association

Lesson 4 Healthcare Services

Lesson 5 — Accessing Services

What You'll Do

- **Explain** why speaking clearly and honestly with healthcare providers is important. ★ 11.B; 11.D
- **Describe** three ways of paying for medical care. ★ 12.A
- **Describe** three responsibilities patients have. ★ 1.A; 4.C; 12.B

Terms to Learn

- health insurance

Start Off Write

Why is it important to speak clearly and honestly with your healthcare provider?

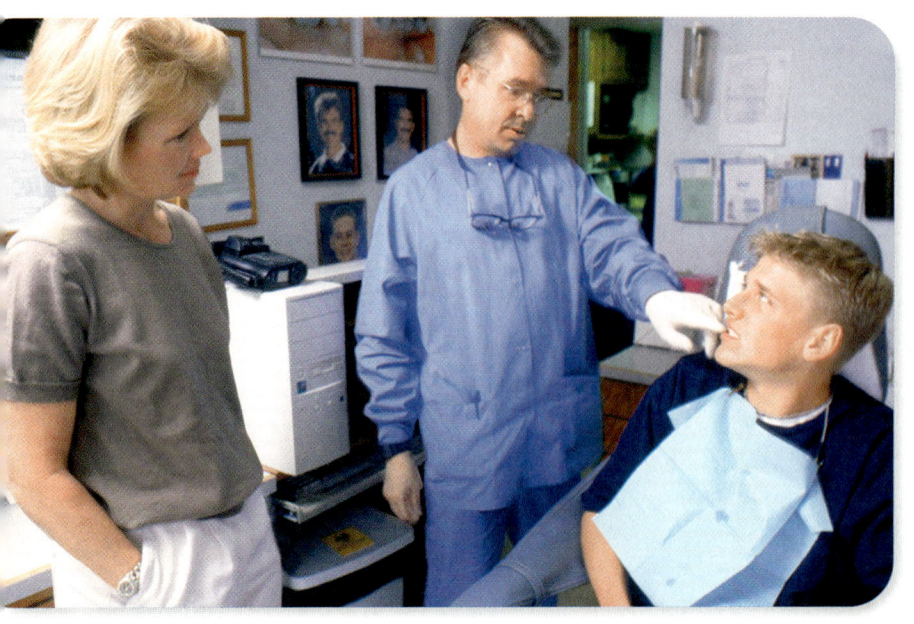

Figure 13 Be clear and honest when speaking with healthcare professionals.

Hannah took her prescription medicine like her doctor told her to, but now she has an upset stomach and feels worse than she did before. She wants to get better, and taking the medicine was supposed to help. She needs to talk to her doctor.

Hannah's doctor prescribed her medicine because it should help her feel better. However, she seems to feel worse. The medicine may actually be making her sicker. It's also possible that the medicine isn't working and that her illness is getting worse. Either way, she needs to call her doctor right away. Anytime your symptoms get worse after you've seen a healthcare provider, be sure to let the provider know.

Using Healthcare Services

Many things can influence how you use medical services. Personal medical history, family tradition, and cultural beliefs may all discourage or encourage you to use healthcare services. But you should never let a fear of talking to healthcare providers keep you from seeking medical help. They are used to talking about personal problems. Talk honestly with them. They cannot help you if you are not clear about your symptoms, feelings, and concerns. If you are confused by words you don't understand, ask questions.

You can also help communication by writing down questions before your visit and by answering all the healthcare provider's questions as well as you can. Be sure to know the names of all medications that you are taking, including herbal medicines and vitamins. You may want to take notes on what the healthcare provider tells you. Before you leave, be sure you understand what is wrong, how you will be treated, and how soon you can expect to see improvement. ★ 11.B; 11.D

522 | Chapter 20 Healthcare Consumer

Paying for Healthcare

Healthcare services can be paid for in several different ways. Some people pay for services with their own money. Others take part in government programs that pay some of their expenses. Some people have private health insurance (in SHUR uhns). **Health insurance** is a policy you buy that covers certain costs in the case of illness or injury. Policies don't usually cover everything. So, knowing what your policy does cover is important.
★ 12.A

Rights and Responsibilities

Everyone has the right to emergency medical care. Patients admitted to a hospital have other rights, too. A list of basic patient rights is listed in the figure at the right.

Patients also have responsibilities. You have the responsibility to live a healthy lifestyle. Eating a healthy diet, exercising regularly, getting plenty of rest, and having regular checkups all greatly reduce the risk of illness. If you do get sick or injured and want care, you have the responsibility to seek medical help as soon as you can. Getting medical care as soon as you need it helps keep one problem from making other problems. Even such common problems as sore throats or sprains can lead to other problems.

You also have the responsibility to take medicine as directed and to do what your healthcare provider tells you to do. For example, you may take medicine to treat an infection. Do not stop taking the medicine just because you begin feeling better. Take the medicine for as long as you were told to take it, or you may get sick again.
★ 1.A; 4.C; 12.B

Figure 14 A Patient's Rights

As a patient, you have the right to

- emergency help for severe pain, injury, or sudden illness
- respectful care
- privacy concerning medical information
- the truth about your medical problem and treatment options
- a role in making medical decisions
- refuse treatment
- an explanation of your bill

Lesson Review

Using Vocabulary
1. What is health insurance? ★ 12.A

Understanding Concepts
2. Explain why talking honestly to healthcare providers is important. List three things you can do to be a good communicator. ★ 11.B; 11.D
3. Describe three ways of paying for healthcare. ★ 12.A
4. Describe three responsibilities patients have. ★ 1.A; 4.C; 12.B

Critical Thinking
5. **Applying Concepts** Your best friend has an earache. Why should she get it taken care of as soon as possible? What would you tell her if she said that she was afraid of getting bad news? ★ 4.C

20 CHAPTER REVIEW

Chapter Summary

- Good information helps consumers make good healthcare decisions. ■ Advertisements are designed to sell products, not provide information. ■ Healthcare consumers should compare prices to get the best value. ■ Health information should come from more than one source. ■ Good healthcare consumers demand good products and services and report problems. ■ Healthcare today is provided by teams of people working together for the benefit of patients. ■ Both government and community organizations play important roles in healthcare. ■ Good healthcare requires good communication. ■ You have rights and responsibilities regarding your healthcare.

Using Vocabulary

For each sentence, fill in the blank with the proper word from the word bank provided below.

health insurance	specialist
comparison shopping	bias
healthcare consumer	primary care provider

1. ___ is one way of paying for healthcare.
2. Using one kind of ___, you check prices on the same item from store to store.
3. Anyone who buys healthcare products and services is a ___.
4. A ___ provides you with basic medical care.
5. A psychiatrist is a medical ___.
6. Information in advertising is likely to have a ___.

Understanding Concepts

7. Provide an example of each of the following: a local community health organization, a national community health organization, and an organization that provides help around the world. ★ 4.C; 6.B

8. Describe why a more expensive product might be a better value. ★ 4.A; 4.B; 4.C; 12.B
9. What is the relationship between a primary care provider and a specialist? ★ 4.C
10. Give one example of an inpatient procedure. ★ 4.C
11. What can make communicating with doctors difficult? ★ 11.D
12. How can you tell which healthcare claims are valid? ★ 4.A; 4.B
13. Describe how tradition, peers, and advertising influence your health decisions. ★ 4.A; 7.A; 8.A; 12.E
14. Describe how to find community organizations that provide healthcare. ★ 6.A; 6.B
15. Explain how healthcare decisions can be influenced by new information. ★ 4.A; 4.B; 4.C
16. Beth wants to reduce the number of cavities she gets. How can that goal help her make good healthcare decisions? ★ 4.C; 12.B
17. Describe two ways that learning healthcare information can make you a good resource for others. ★ 4.C; 12.E
18. Describe three ways you can influence healthcare options. ★ 4.C; 6.B; 12.E

Critical Thinking

Applying Concepts

19. What can you do to be sure you have all the information you need before taking a new prescription medication? ★ 4.A; 12.B

20. Your friend has recently been diagnosed with asthma and is learning how to live with the disease. Where would you suggest he go to find quality information? ★ 4.C

21. During a routine visit, the doctor listens to Matt's heartbeat. She mentions in passing that he has a heart murmur. Matt doesn't know what that means, but he doesn't ask. He is worried that it is serious, and he's embarrassed that he has something wrong. Matt tells you at school the next day about his concern. What would you tell Matt? ★ 4.C; 11.D

Making Good Decisions

22. Marnie read an ad promoting the safety of tanning beds. Then, she read an article that claimed that tanning beds cause skin damage that could lead to cancer. How can Marnie evaluate these claims? What questions should she ask? Which authorities could help her? ★ 4.A; 4.B

23. You hear on the news that a popular kind of bike helmet has been recalled. You don't have that kind, but you know that many kids in your school do. What should you do? Describe two strategies to help with this problem. ★ 4.C; 12.E

24. Imagine that you recently purchased a new pair of running shoes. After only 1 month, the sole and the upper part of the shoe started separating. Write a respectful letter to the manufacturer to notify the company of your experience. What else can you do? ★ 11.C; 11.D

Interpreting Graphics

Sunglasses Comparison

Sunglasses	Features	Materials	Price
A	oval shaped, UV protection	plastic frames only	$8.00
B	oval shaped, scratch-resistant lenses, UV protection	plastic and metal frames	$20.00
C	variety of shapes, UV protection, scratch-resistant lenses, distortion-free vision, designer label	plastic and metal frames	$130.00

Use the table above to answer questions 25–27.

25. Which glasses could you buy if you needed UV protection and had $10?

26. What are the benefits of purchasing the most expensive pair of sunglasses?

27. Which sunglasses would you buy if you wanted glasses that provided UV protection and were scratch resistant but you were not concerned about a designer label?

Reading Checkup

Take a minute to review your answers to the Health IQ questions at the beginning of this chapter. How has reading this chapter improved your Health IQ?

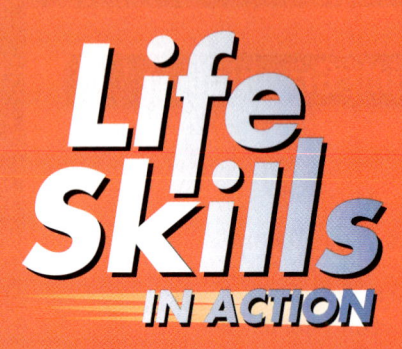

Life Skills IN ACTION

Being a Wise Consumer

Going shopping for products and services can be fun, but it can be confusing, too. Sometimes, there are so many options to choose from that finding the right one for you can be difficult. Being a wise consumer means evaluating different products and services for value and quality. Complete the following activity to learn how to be a wise consumer.

Rafiq's Search

ACT 1 — Setting the Scene

Rafiq has acne. He is embarrassed about it and is trying to figure out how to clear it up. Rafiq has heard that over-the-counter acne medicine will help, but he has also heard that a dermatologist is the only way to go. Rafiq decides to call some dermatologists to see if any of them can help him. ★ 4.A; 4.C

The 5 Steps of Being a Wise Consumer

1. List what you need and want from a product or a service.
2. Find several products or services that may fit your needs.
3. Research and compare information about the products or services.
4. Use the product or the service of your choice.
5. Evaluate your choice.

Guided Practice

Practice with a Friend

Form a group of three. Have one person play the role of Rafiq and another person play the role of a dermatologist. Have the third person be an observer. Walking through each of the five steps of being a wise consumer, role-play Rafiq's selection of a dermatologist to visit. After Rafiq makes his selection, he should talk to the dermatologist of his choice to discuss ways to treat his acne. The observer will take notes, which will include observations about what the person playing Rafiq did well and suggestions of ways to improve. Stop after each step to evaluate the process. ★ 4.A; 4.B; 12.B

Independent Practice

Check Yourself

After you have completed the guided practice, go through Act 1 again without stopping at each step. Answer the questions below to review what you did.

1. Why is it important to research and compare several doctors before selecting one to visit? ★ 4.A; 4.B; 4.C

2. What are some questions Rafiq may ask a dermatologist? ★ 4.C; 12.B

3. How can Rafiq evaluate the dermatologist he visited? ★ 4.B; 12.B

ACT 2 On Your Own

During Rafiq's appointment, the dermatologist gives Rafiq a list of over-the-counter medicines that are effective against acne. Rafiq goes to the store to find facial cleansers and creams that contain the medicines. Make a poster illustrating how Rafiq can use the five steps of being a wise consumer when he goes shopping for skin care products. ★ 4.A; 4.B; 4.C; 12.B

CHAPTER 21
Health and the Environment

Lessons

1. Healthy Environments — 530
2. Meeting Our Basic Needs — 532
3. Environmental Pollution — 536
4. Maintaining Healthy Environments — 540
5. Promoting Public Health — 542
6. A Global Community — 546

Chapter Review — 550
Life Skills in Action — 552

Check out **Current Health®** articles related to this chapter by visiting **go.hrw.com**. Just type in the keyword **HD4CH53**.

" I never realized that **pollution** could affect my **health** until my family moved from a **big** city to a **small** town.

A few weeks after moving, I noticed that my asthma wasn't bothering me. The doctor said the change in my health could be because my new town had less air pollution than the city did. "

Health IQ

PRE-READING

Answer the following multiple-choice questions to find out what you already know about health and the environment. When you've finished this chapter, you'll have the opportunity to change your answers based on what you've learned.

1. People breathe in
   a. only oxygen.
   b. all the gases that make up air.
   c. all the gases that make up air and any pollutants in the air.
   d. only carbon dioxide.

2. Permanent hearing loss can result from
   a. listening to loud music often.
   b. allergies to dust.
   c. poor diet.
   d. contaminated groundwater.
   ★ 6.A

3. A diet that includes a variety of fruits and vegetables
   a. is less important for young children.
   b. is important only for children.
   c. can help keep people from getting sick.
   d. is not a factor in preventing disease.

4. Which of the following is an example of conservation?
   a. recycling the newspaper
   b. driving to the store instead of walking there
   c. not drinking enough water
   d. toxins building up in animals that eat polluted food ★ 6.B

5. Mold inside houses can cause health problems because
   a. some people are allergic to mold particles.
   b. mold can cause lead poisoning.
   c. it is impossible to eliminate mold from a house.
   d. mold can cause skin cancer.
   ★ 6.A

ANSWERS: 1. c; 2. a; 3. c; 4. a; 5. a

Lesson 1 — Healthy Environments

What You'll Do

- **Explain** why living things depend on their environments to survive. ✦ 6.A
- **Describe** how pollution can affect people. ✦ 6.A

Terms to Learn

- environment
- ecosystem
- pollution

What is pollution?

> Don is worried about his fish tank. Since he started feeding the fish more often, the water in the tank has been cloudy. Now, some fish are dying.

Sometimes our actions have unexpected harmful effects on the world around us. This can happen even when we think we are doing something helpful. In Don's case, adding more food to the fish tank caused algae (AL JEE) and bacteria to grow. As a result, the amount of oxygen in the water decreased. This change made it hard for the fish to get enough oxygen.

Depending on the Environment

Living things need food, water, and other resources to survive. They get these materials from their environments. An **environment** is a living thing's surroundings. The Earth is made up of many kinds of environments, such as oceans, forests, and deserts. Different plants and animals depend on each kind of environment.

Organisms that live in an environment interact with, or affect, each other. The living things also interact with the nonliving parts of the environment. A community of living things and the nonliving parts of its environment are called an **ecosystem**. Ecosystems constantly change as new living things are born and others die. Nonliving parts of an ecosystem, such as soil and water, also change over time. Changes in an ecosystem can force living things to find new ways to meet their needs. ✦ 6.A

Figure 1 People depend on the environment. They also affect the environment.

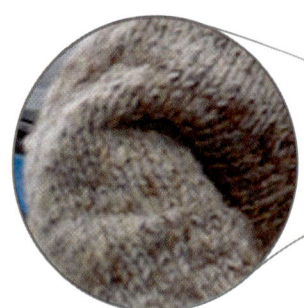

Wool is sheared from sheep.

Metal is mined from the Earth.

530 Chapter 21 Health and the Environment

Figure 2 Water pollution could harm the living things in this beach ecosystem.

Healthy Ecosystems

As healthy ecosystems change, they reuse materials. For ecosystems to work properly, they need energy and clean water, air, and soil.

If an ecosystem is damaged, many living things are affected. Disease, natural disasters, and pollution all can damage parts of an ecosystem. **Pollution** is a change in the air, water, or soil that can harm living things. Often, pollution results from adding poisonous compounds to the environment.

Because humans depend on the environment, pollution can affect their health. Poisonous compounds in air, water, or food can make people ill. A person's reaction to a pollutant depends on how much of it is present and how long the person is exposed to the pollutant. Diseases caused by pollution may take years to develop. ★ 6.A

Myth & Fact

Myth: Technology can solve all our environmental problems.

Fact: Technology can solve some problems, but damage to air, water, and food cannot always be repaired by technology.

Lesson Review

Using Vocabulary
1. Define *pollution* in your own words.

Understanding Concepts
2. Identify three ways living things depend on the environment.
3. Describe how pollution can hurt people.

Critical Thinking
4. **Making Inferences** People used asbestos through the mid-1900s. In 1971, asbestos was identified as an air pollutant that causes lung disease. Why do you think it took so long for people to realize that asbestos is dangerous?

internet connect
www.scilinks.org/health
Topic: Environmental Toxins
HealthLinks code: HD4036

HEALTH LINKS Maintained by the National Science Teachers Association

Lesson 1 Healthy Environments

Lesson 2: Meeting Our Basic Needs

Kris finished her race and felt tired. She was breathing fast, and she was thirsty and hungry. As she rested, she sat under a shady tree to escape the sun. Kris drank a glass of water, ate a banana, and took in a deep breath of air. She felt better.

What You'll Do

- **List** four basic survival needs shared by all people.  1.A; 6.A
- **Explain** why people need air, water, food, and shelter. 1.A; 6.A

Terms to Learn

- dehydration
- nutrient

Start Off Write

What do people need in order to survive?

What would happen if Kris could not find water, food, or shade? At the very least, she would be uncomfortable. Eventually, she might even get sick from thirst, hunger, or heat. All living things have a set of basic needs that must be met for them to live. People need air, water, food, and shelter. They get these things from their environments.

Air to Breathe

You may notice the air only when it is very cold or hot. But you are constantly using the air around you. Air is a mixture of nitrogen, oxygen, carbon dioxide, and other gases. People, like most living things, need oxygen to live. People breathe air in through the nose and the mouth. From there, air passes into the lungs, where oxygen can enter the bloodstream. When people exhale air from the lungs, carbon dioxide gas is released as waste.

The process of breathing brings all of the gases from air—not just oxygen—into a person's lungs. Air pollution can also enter the lungs when a person breathes. Nitrogen and other gases that make up air do not harm people. But air pollution can be harmful to people when they breathe it. 1.A; 6.A

Figure 3 People need a constant supply of air in order to survive. People must bring air with them when they visit places with no air.

Water to Drink

Most animals—including people—are about 70 percent water by weight. Why do people's bodies contain so much water? Water dissolves many substances easily. This trait allows water to carry nutrients and wastes through the body. Without water, the body would not be able to transport these materials. People, like all living things, need water to survive.

Living things must take in enough water each day to replace any water that they lose. People lose water when they sweat or urinate. Water is also lost through breathing. If this lost water is not replaced each day, the body may become dangerously low on water. **Dehydration** (DEE hie DRAY shuhn) is a condition in which the body does not contain enough water to work properly. Dehydration causes discomfort. In extreme cases, it can lead to serious health problems and death. People get some water from the foods they eat. However, people usually need at least eight glasses of water a day to stay healthy.

People use clean water for more than just drinking. For example, people use water for cooking, bathing, brushing their teeth, and cleaning. If water is polluted, bacteria and poisonous compounds in the water can make people sick. If water is unavailable, people may have difficulty keeping their environments clean. Unclean conditions can lead to disease. ★ 1.A; 6.A

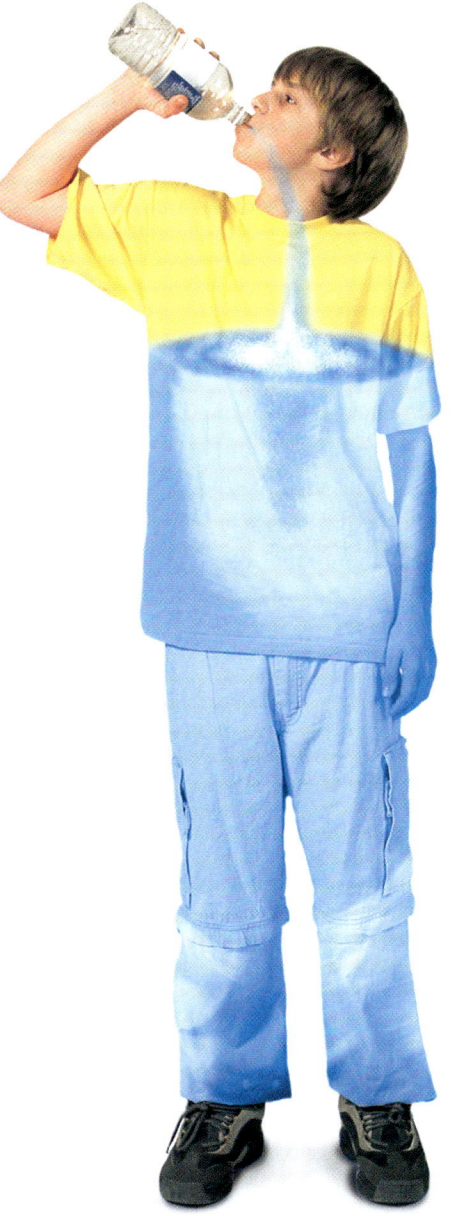

Figure 4 A human body is about 70 percent water! Most people need at least eight glasses of water a day to stay healthy.

Hands-on ACTIVITY

WHAT DISSOLVES IN WATER?

1. Make a prediction about which of the following substances will dissolve in water: salt, sugar, cooking oil, and garden soil. Record your predictions.
2. Mix 1 tablespoon of each substance in a separate cup of water.
3. Record your observations.

Analysis

1. Which substances dissolved in the water? Which substances did not dissolve?
2. Which substances could water carry through the body?
3. Do you think water could carry poisonous compounds through the body?

Lesson 2 Meeting Our Basic Needs

Math Activity

Energy in food can be measured in Calories. The average middle school student needs about 2,200 Calories each day. Young children need only about 1,600 Calories each day. What is the difference between the number of Calories a 4-year-old would eat in a week and the number of Calories a 13-year-old would eat in a week? Why do you think teens need more Calories than young children do?
★ M8.2B

Food to Eat

You probably get most of your food from a grocery store. But where does the food come from? All food can be traced back to the sun's energy. Plants, including those that produce fruits and vegetables, use the sun's energy to make their food. All other living things eat plants, animals, or both. When you eat plants, you depend on the energy that plants use to make their food. If you eat animal products, you depend on the plants that those animals ate.

Food provides you with the energy you need in order to move, think, and grow. Food also supplies you with nutrients, such as proteins, vitamins, and minerals. A **nutrient** is a substance in food that the body needs to function properly. A healthy diet provides all the nutrients your body needs. A healthy diet includes a variety of foods, especially fruits and vegetables. It limits foods with a lot of fat and sugar. These foods don't provide many nutrients.

People who do not eat healthy diets get sick more often. Without proper nutrients, the body is less able to fight disease. A healthy diet is important for everyone. But it is especially important for children. Young people need energy and nutrients for their bodies to grow properly. ★ 1.A; 6.A

Figure 5 Any food you eat can be traced back to a plant and the sun's energy.

Figure 6 People need shelter for protection and comfort.

A Place to Live

You are probably sitting indoors as you read this. People use materials from the environment to make shelters. These places provide shelter from the weather and protection from danger. Buildings keep people dry when it rains outside and warm when it is cold outside.

Shelter helps people maintain their health. Staying at a comfortable temperature helps the body fight off sickness. Having a place to safely store and preserve food makes eating healthy foods easier. Without clean sheltered environments, people may get sick more easily. ★ 1.A; 6.A

STUDY TIP for better reading

Organizing Information
Make a table that has three columns. In the first column, list the four basic human needs. In the next column, list how these needs could be threatened by pollution. In the third column, list what you think people could do to help prevent each kind of pollution.

Lesson Review

Using Vocabulary

1. Define *dehydration* in your own words. ★ 1.A

Understanding Concepts

2. How do people meet their four basic needs? ★ 1.A; 6.A

3. Why do people need food? ★ 1.A; 6.A

4. How much water do people need to drink each day? What could happen to a person who does not drink enough water? ★ 1.A

Critical Thinking

5. **Analyzing Ideas** Imagine that you have a pet dog. How would you make sure that your dog gets air, water, food, and shelter?

Lesson 3 — Environmental Pollution

What You'll Do

- **Describe** three ways that air pollution threatens health. ★ 6.A
- **Describe** five ways that water can be polluted. ★ 6.A
- **Explain** how an indoor environment can be polluted. ★ 6.A

Terms to Learn

- pesticide
- bioaccumulation
- indoor air pollution

Start Off Write

How can water pollution affect human health?

Bert recently started jogging after school instead of in the morning. Since he made this change, his asthma has been much worse. Why is running in the afternoon so much harder?

Bert's asthma symptoms may be irritated by air pollution. Air is often more polluted later in the day. As the day goes on, more fumes from cars and trucks fill the air. Sunlight reacts with these fumes, forming even more pollutants.

Air Pollution

Most air pollution comes from burning fuels. Cars, lawnmowers, and campfires all release wastes into the air. Wastes from factories, businesses, and homes also contribute to air pollution. People cannot avoid breathing in the wastes that pollute the air near Earth's surface. These materials can irritate the eyes and throat. Air pollution can also lead to asthma and other respiratory illnesses.

Air pollution can damage the ozone layer in the upper atmosphere. This layer protects the Earth from ultraviolet (UHL truh VIE uh lit) light, or UV light. UV light is harmful sunlight that can cause sunburns and skin cancer. Damage to the ozone layer allows more UV light to reach the Earth. And greater amounts of UV light increase the risk of getting skin cancer.

★ 6.A

TABLE 1 Primary Waste Products of Gasoline Burning in a Car	
Hydrocarbons (HIE droh KAHR buhnz)	can form smog, irritate the eyes, and cause respiratory problems
Nitrogen oxides (NIE truh juhn AHKS IEDZ)	can lead to ozone formation and contribute to acid rain
Carbon monoxide (KAHR buhn muh NAHKS IED)	can reduce the amount of oxygen in your blood and trap heat in Earth's atmosphere
Carbon dioxide	can trap heat in Earth's atmosphere

Source: EPA.

Water Pollution

Many substances dissolve easily in water. Because of this, many materials that people put in water—on purpose or by accident—can dissolve and pollute the water. For example, pesticides (PES tuh SIEDZ) and other chemicals used in farming can pollute water. A **pesticide** is a chemical used to kill pests, such as insects. Rain can wash these chemicals from the soil into rivers and lakes. The chemicals can also soak into the ground, where they may contaminate underground water supplies. Water that is polluted by these chemicals can harm people and other living things.

Pesticides are only one source of water pollution. Household chemicals can leak from drainage systems into water supplies. Rain can wash chemicals from landfills into soil and nearby water sources. Factory wastes are sometimes released into water sources without being treated properly. Even air pollution can pollute water when rain washes pollutants into lakes or rivers.

Water pollution can cause several health problems. Exposure to pesticides and other chemicals increases the risk of serious diseases such as cancer. Bacteria in untreated water can cause intestinal problems such as diarrhea. Lead from old pipes can get into water and cause fatal lead poisoning. ★ 6.A

Figure 7 Pollution from many sources (shown as red arrows) can build up and spread between air, water, soil, and food.

MAKING GOOD DECISIONS

As a class, write and perform a skit about a summer camp. Imagine that a group of teens is on a hike. They are hot and thirsty. The counselor won't let them drink from the lake because it is untreated water. The group argues that dehydration is also dangerous. Come up with a solution to their problem.

Lesson 3 Environmental Pollution | 537

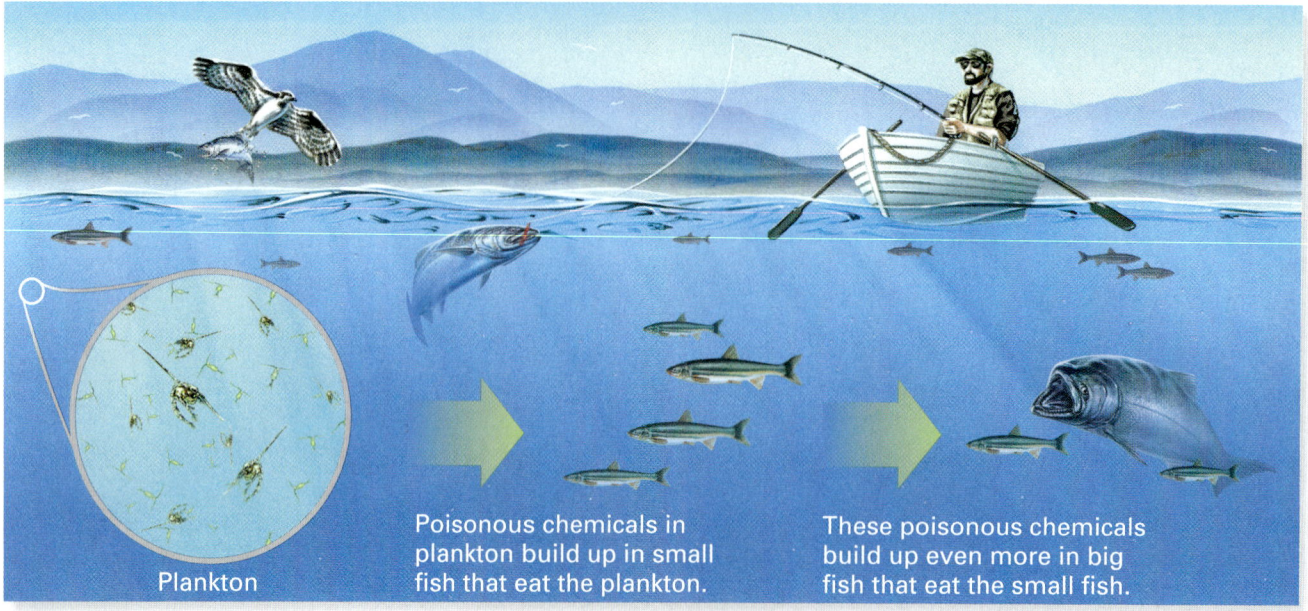

Plankton

Poisonous chemicals in plankton build up in small fish that eat the plankton.

These poisonous chemicals build up even more in big fish that eat the small fish.

Figure 8 In bioaccumulation, poisonous compounds build up in animals that eat polluted food.

Food Safety

Neglecting food safety can make you very sick. Tiny organisms that live in, on, and around some foods can cause serious disease. Be sure to keep yourself, your food, your dishes, and your cooking area clean.

Pollution and Food

People need safe food that is available when they are hungry. If food is polluted, people who eat it can become very sick. If food is not available, people cannot get the nutrients they need. Without proper nutrients, people don't get enough energy and get tired easily. They could also develop a nutritional disease. In severe cases, lack of food can lead to death.

Environmental pollution can decrease the amount of food that is available. For example, damaged soil cannot produce healthy crops. When less food is available, food costs more, making it harder to buy food.

Even when enough food is available, it can be unsafe to eat. Poisonous compounds in the soil and air can pollute food. When an animal eats, it may absorb pollutants from its food. The amount of pollutants an animal absorbs increases with the amount of pollutants in its food. If people eat these animals, pollutants can be passed on to people. **Bioaccumulation** (BIE oh uh KYOOM yoo LAY shuhn) is the process in which chemicals build up in animals that eat polluted food. This process is shown in Figure 8.

Handling food safely at home can prevent some food-related illnesses. Rinsing fruits and vegetables removes chemicals and bacteria from their skin. Thoroughly cooking meat, poultry, and fish kills any bacteria they might carry. Knives and cutting boards can transfer bacteria from raw meat to other foods. Washing these tools can stop bacteria from spreading. Washing your hands with warm, soapy water is also healthy. You should wash your hands after using the bathroom and before cooking or eating. This practice helps keep bacteria from spreading from your hands to food.

★ 6.A; 6.B

Polluted Indoor Environments

Have you ever noticed how the smell of cooking can get trapped inside a house? Most buildings are designed to keep air from leaking in or out. This design helps save energy used in heating or cooling. But it also means that harmful substances can get trapped inside. **Indoor air pollution** is air pollution inside a building. Mold, cigarette smoke, household cleaners, dust, and waste from pests can pollute the air. These materials can cause allergies and respiratory problems.

Noise pollution can also threaten indoor environments. *Noise pollution* consists of loud noises that can damage a person's ears. Loud sounds such as power saws, stereos, and machinery damage hearing over time. To prevent hearing loss, people can try to avoid loud noises or wear earplugs. ★ 6.A; 6.B

Figure 9 Dirty kitchens can attract cockroaches and other pests whose wastes can cause allergies.

Lesson Review

Using Vocabulary
1. Define *bioaccumulation*.

Understanding Concepts
2. What are three ways that air pollution can threaten human health? ★ 6.A
3. Describe five ways that water can be polluted. ★ 6.A
4. How can a building be polluted? ★ 6.A

Critical Thinking
5. **Analyzing Viewpoints** You know that pesticides kill pests on crops. You also know that pesticides can cause health problems by polluting water or food. Why do you think people use pesticides even though pesticides cause health problems? What can you do to protect yourself from pesticides?

internet connect
www.scilinks.org/health
Topic: Environmental Problems in Texas
HealthLinks code: HHTX006

Topic: Skin Cancer
HealthLinks code: HD4089

Topic: Texas Allergies
HealthLinks code: HHTX016

HEALTH LINKS Maintained by the National Science Teachers Association

Lesson 4 Maintaining Healthy Environments

What You'll Do

- **Describe** three ways to use resources wisely. ★ 6.B
- **Explain** how conservation helps other people. ★ 4.C; 6.B

Terms to Learn

- resource
- conservation

Start Off Write

How does recycling help the environment?

Joelle was surprised to learn that oil dumped in a street drain could pollute public water supplies. Luckily, her parents recycle the oil from their car whenever the oil is changed.

Joelle's parents take the oil from their car to a recycling center. After the oil is processed at the center, it can be used again. Recycling is one way to help keep your environment healthy.

Conservation

The paper in this book was made from a tree. Furniture, buildings, some fuels, and many foods also come from trees. Trees are a valuable resource. A **resource** is a material that can be used to meet a need. Some other examples of resources are air, water, oil, plants, and metals.

If resources are not used wisely, environmental problems can occur. Pollution may increase, and some resources could be used up completely. One way to solve these problems is conservation. **Conservation** is protecting and using resources wisely. When people conserve, resources will continue to be available for use in the future.

Many people conserve resources by reducing, reusing, and recycling. By walking instead of driving, you reduce the amount of fuel used. By reusing paper, fewer trees are cut down. By recycling cans, less metal is mined. By using fewer resources, the supplies of these materials will continue to be available for others. ★ 6.B

Health Journal

In your Health Journal, write a paragraph about what you can do to reduce, reuse, and recycle. Include ideas you can use at home, at school, and around your community.

Figure 10 Electric cars help reduce fuel use and air pollution.

540 | Chapter 21 Health and the Environment

Figure 11 Decisions about using pesticides to grow food can affect people in other countries where that food is sold.

Thinking About Others

Conservation encourages people to think about how their actions affect other people. A major reason people conserve resources is to be sure the resources will be available for people in the future. But conservation also affects people in the present. Decisions about resource use can affect people who have no influence over the decision. For example, air pollution that forms in cities affects people in rural areas, too. Reducing fuel use in cities can decrease air pollution everywhere.

Knowing about environmental problems in other places allows people to learn from others' experiences. Newspapers, radio, and TV can provide environmental news from around the world. These news stories describe other people's efforts to combat pollution or control diseases. Knowing which efforts were successful in other places allows people to solve their own environmental problems more effectively. ★ 4.C; 6.B

BEING A WISE CONSUMER

In groups of three or four students, act out a scene in which you go to the grocery store to buy supplies for a party. On your shopping trip, consider the packaging of the products you want to buy. What kinds of packaging can you buy that will allow you to reduce, reuse, or recycle?

Lesson Review

Using Vocabulary

1. How are the terms *resource* and *conservation* related? ★ 6.B

Understanding Concepts

2. Describe three ways to use resources wisely. ★ 6.B

3. How can conservation help other people? ★ 4.C; 6.B

Critical Thinking

4. **Making Inferences** Imagine that you read an article about health problems caused by pesticides used in Costa Rica. Now imagine that you want to plant your own garden. How could the news article be helpful to you when you plan your garden? ★ 4.C; 6.B

Lesson 4 Maintaining Healthy Environments   **541**

Lesson 5

Promoting Public Health

Maria was amazed by the news story she read. The story said that hundreds of people got sick from bacteria in the drinking water of a neighboring town. Bacteria was in the water that came from their faucets.

What You'll Do

- **Describe** how an individual's actions can affect public health. ⭐ 4.C; 6.B
- **Explain** how communities can promote public health. ⭐ 6.B
- **Name** four government agencies that protect public health. ⭐ 6.B
- **Discuss** how scientific discovery has improved community health. ⭐ 6.B

Terms to Learn

- public health

Start Off Write

How can scientific discoveries improve the health of a community?

Access to clean water is one of several basic services that healthy communities need. Individuals, community groups, and governments all contribute to community health. The practice of protecting and improving the health of people in a community is called **public health.**

Your Role in Public Health

To maintain healthy communities, as many people as possible must help. Individuals affect public health through the choices they make. Just one person dumping trash into a water source is unhealthy. One bag of trash may not cause a huge problem. But the actions of many individuals can add up to cause major pollution. Individual homes and businesses are the largest sources of water pollution in the United States.

However, the effects of many individuals can also add up in positive ways. Water pollution can be greatly reduced by individuals deciding to protect water resources. Each person makes a small difference. But together, a group of individuals can make a big difference in community health.

Knowing about local health issues is the first step toward contributing to public health. Understanding the issues allows people to make informed decisions about how to respond. ⭐ 4.C; 6.B

Figure 12 Many products have labels that explain how to safely dispose of the product.

Figure 13 Pollution at Love Canal in New York caused serious health problems until the community worked together to get government support for a major clean-up.

Community Efforts

Community groups join many individuals in efforts to maintain healthy communities. Groups can educate people about local health issues more easily than individuals can. This education encourages people to aim for the same goal. Sometimes these efforts are organized as community programs, such as city recycling projects.

Combining the efforts of several groups can make public health projects even more effective. For example, some cities have separate recycling programs in schools, businesses, and residential areas. Local recycling programs can make big differences in resource use. Each ton of recycled paper saves about 17 trees. It also saves about 380 gallons of oil, 4,100 kilowatt-hours of electricity, 3.3 cubic yards of landfill space, and 7,000 gallons of water. Unfortunately, recycling costs a lot. But if several small recycling programs join efforts, they can share machinery and other resources. Sharing materials can decrease the costs of recycling.

People interested in forming community health groups often get support from government organizations. City health departments and departments of public works can provide helpful information to the public. State and national government agencies can also work with communities to organize environmental health action. Several government organizations publish environmental health information and make it available to the public. For example, the Environmental Protection Agency (EPA) publishes information about environmental health issues occurring throughout the United States. ★ 6.B

PRACTICING WELLNESS

Working in small groups, design a community project that could help your local environment and the health of community members. Does your school have a recycling program? Does your city offer programs to educate people about food safety? Use your imagination to come up with a great project!

Lesson 5 Promoting Public Health | **543**

Figure 14 The government helps make sure that food is safe.

Bread and Vegetables
The bread and vegetables are inspected by the Food and Drug Administration or by state and local government officials, depending on where the food was produced.

Meat
The meat is inspected by the Food Safety and Inspection Service of the US Department of Agriculture. They make sure that the meat is wholesome enough to pass regulated standards.

Cleanliness
Local, state, and federal health departments enforce safety standards by inspecting restaurants, grocery stores, and food production businesses for cleanliness.

Brain Food

The ozone layer in the upper atmosphere is expected to restore itself. International laws against using chemicals that destroy ozone are making a difference!

Government Action

Governments promote public health by educating citizens, passing and enforcing laws, and funding and conducting scientific research. These actions occur in local, state, and national governments. Most states base their environmental laws on national regulations. However, each state has its own environmental and health agencies. Some states make environmental health laws that are even stricter than the national laws.

Two national environmental health laws are the Clean Air Act and the Safe Drinking Water Act. The Clean Air Act gave the federal government power to control air pollution. The Safe Drinking Water Act limits how much pollution is allowed in drinking water. The EPA enforces these and most other federal environmental laws. However, many agencies contribute to public health.

- The Occupational Safety and Health Administration (OSHA) oversees safety and health in workplaces.
- The National Institutes of Health (NIH) funds and conducts medical research. This research can lead to treatments for environmental health problems.
- The Centers for Disease Control and Prevention (CDC) collects and provides public health information. The CDC also investigates disease outbreaks and sets up programs to prevent disease. ★ 6.B

Scientific Discoveries

In 1854, cholera (KAHL uhr uh) was spreading across London. Cholera is a disease caused by bacteria. In 10 days, more than 500 people in one area of London died of cholera. John Snow, a British physician, figured out that the disease was being spread by water from a well. He convinced the local government to keep people from using the well's water. Dr. Snow is credited as the father of modern public health.

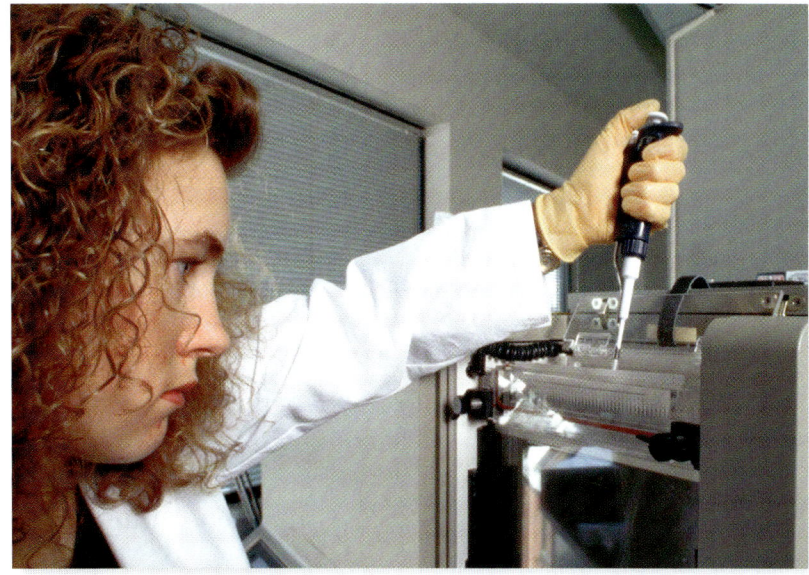

Figure 15 Some scientists conduct research on how the environment affects human health.

Since then, our understanding of public health has grown. Scientists have discovered the causes of many illnesses and the way illnesses spread. Learning that diseases can be spread by water has led to modern water-treatment methods. Cleaner ways to process food have stopped the spread of other diseases. And medical research has led to medicines, antibiotics, and vaccines. These medical discoveries help treat and prevent many illnesses.

Scientific discoveries about the environment also help community health. Understanding environmental processes allows people to predict how human actions will affect the environment. Being able to predict the effects of human actions can help people avoid damaging the environment. A healthy environment allows people to maintain community health. ★ 6.B

STUDY TIP *for better reading*

Compare and Contrast Make a table comparing actions that individuals, communities, and governments can take to protect and maintain public health.

Lesson Review

Using Vocabulary

1. Define *public health* in your own words.

Understanding Concepts

2. How can individuals, communities, and governments improve public health? ★ 4.C; 6.B

3. Name four government agencies that promote public health. ★ 6.B

4. How have scientific discoveries improved public health? ★ 6.B

Critical Thinking

5. **Making Good Decisions** Radon is a dangerous gas that can build up in some homes. Where could you find out more about whether radon is a problem in your area? ★ 4.A; 6.B

Lesson 5 Promoting Public Health

Lesson 6   A Global Community

Cutting down a forest can provide fuel, lumber, and paper. These materials meet important needs. However, cutting down a forest can also damage soil and lead to water and air pollution.

What You'll Do

- **Describe** problems that are caused by population growth.  6.A
- **Explain** how increased energy use is a pollution problem. 6.A
- **Discuss** three factors that speed the spread of disease. 6.A

Terms to Learn

- population

Start Off Write

Could pollution in the United States affect other countries? Explain.

Balancing human needs with conservation is not easy. As the number of people on Earth grows, more people will need resources. And people will need to find new ways to conserve resources for future use.

Population

The total number of people on Earth is the world's human population. A **population** is a group of organisms living in an area at one time. The world's human population tripled from 2 billion in 1927 to 6 billion in 1999. By the year 2150, the world's population could reach 11 billion. The rate of growth is not the same in all countries. Birthrates are declining in some countries, such as the United States. But the populations of many countries continue to grow.

Meeting the needs of a growing population is difficult. In some countries, rural areas do not have enough jobs or food. People move to cities hoping to find work and a better life. Unfortunately, fast city growth leads to shortages of clean food and water. And when more people use resources, more wastes are created. Crowded cities may have difficulty dealing with these extra wastes. As a result, these cities may have more disease. The United Nations estimates that at least 1 billion people live in poor city conditions. 6.A

Figure 16 Population growth forces people to stretch limited resources, such as water.

Figure 17 When completed, China's Three Gorges Dam will provide a large amount of energy. However, this project is polluting and displacing many communities.

Pollution and Energy Use

Growing populations around the world contribute to major pollution problems that affect everyone. For example, increased use of energy resources can cause environmental problems. Fossil fuels, such as coal and oil, are a major source of energy for people. Burning these fuels can cause air pollution. And using large amounts of these fuels decreases the available supply of fossil fuels. Once supplies of fossil fuels are gone, people will have to use different sources of energy. Other resources, such as water, wind, and sunlight, can provide energy. But people are still learning how to use these resources efficiently.

To solve global pollution problems, everyone needs to help. People around the world use resources and create pollution. To decrease pollution and its health effects, people everywhere must decide to conserve resources. ★ 6.A

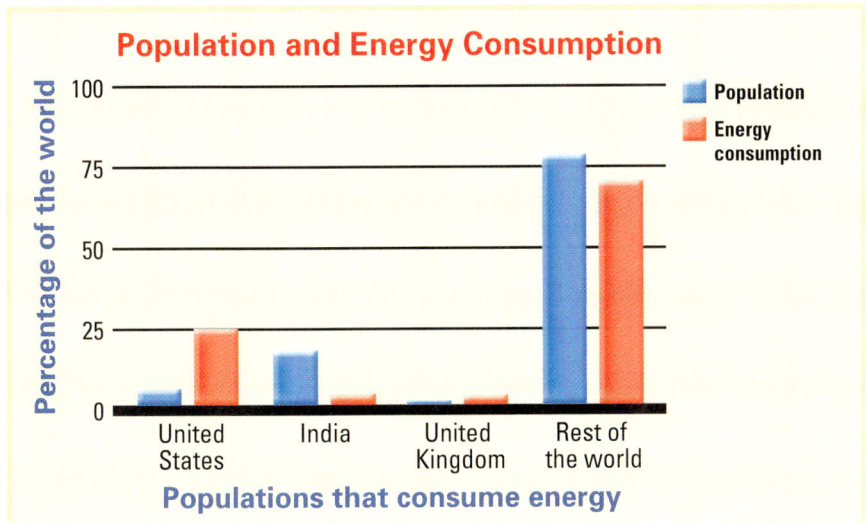

Figure 18 The amount of energy consumed by a country does not always relate to its percentage of the world's population.

Disease

Disease caused by environmental pollution is a health risk for people everywhere. Polluted buildings, food, and water speed the spread of disease. Unclean homes encourage the presence of disease-carrying pests, such as rats. Unclean food and water can spread disease-causing chemicals and bacteria. These problems are worse in places with growing populations. Many diseases can pass more easily from one person to another in crowded places. Diseases that are not controlled can even spread between countries when people travel.

Some international groups help countries that have trouble controlling disease. Two such groups are the United Nations and the World Health Organization. These groups educate people about clean food and water. They also provide medicines and vaccines to treat and prevent disease. These organizations work with governments to improve living conditions and control diseases. ★ 6.A; 6.B

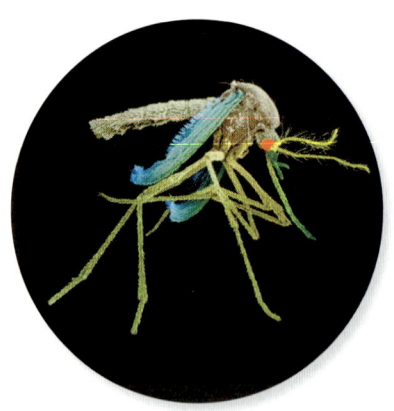

Figure 19 Mosquitoes can spread serious diseases such as dengue fever and malaria.

Figure 20 Educating people about water safety leads to better public health.

Hands-on ACTIVITY

GLITTER HANDSHAKE

1. Your teacher will coat one student's hand with glitter at the beginning of class.

2. A time keeper will tell the class to look where the glitter has spread after every 5 minutes.

3. Every 5 minutes, write down how far the glitter has spread.

Analysis

1. How far did the glitter spread by the end of class?

2. How does this activity relate to the spreading of disease-causing organisms?

3. How do the results of this lab highlight the importance of washing your hands frequently?

Success

In 1969, the Cuyahoga River in Cleveland, Ohio, was so polluted that it burst into flames. The story sparked widespread concern about the quality of national rivers and lakes. The story also helped the Clean Water Act to pass. Today, the river is much cleaner and it is once again home to wildlife. It is even used for swimming and boating. This river's story shows that efforts to solve environmental problems can succeed.

The history of the American bald eagle shows the power of government action. In the 1960s, a pesticide called *DDT* was causing health problems in many living things—including people. DDT weakened bald eagles' eggshells. The weak shells broke before the eagles were ready to hatch. Many baby eagles died, and eagle populations decreased. In the 1970s, the United States banned the use of DDT. And in 1973, the United States passed a law called the Endangered Species Act. This law protects animals and plants that are in danger of becoming extinct. Now eagle populations are healthy.

People can find solutions for many environmental problems. Some problems, such as the water-borne disease cholera, require community public health efforts. Other problems require the cooperation of several countries. For example, more than 160 countries have agreed to stop producing chemicals that may destroy ozone. This action might allow the ozone layer to recover. ★ 6.B

Myth: There's nothing you can do to prevent pollution.

Fact: By making informed choices about resources, you can help maintain a healthy environment.

Figure 21 In the mid-1800s, the deadly disease cholera forced thousands of people into quarantine camps. Today, cholera is much less common.

Lesson Review

Using Vocabulary

1. Use the word *population* in a sentence about problems caused by population growth. ★ 6.A

Understanding Concepts

2. How is increased energy use a global pollution problem? ★ 6.A

3. What are three factors that speed the spread of disease? ★ 6.A

4. Give an example of a successful effort to protect the environment. ★ 6.B

Critical Thinking

5. **Analyzing Viewpoints** You learned that some international organizations help countries that have trouble controlling disease. How do you think disease in these countries could affect people in other parts of the world? ★ 6.A

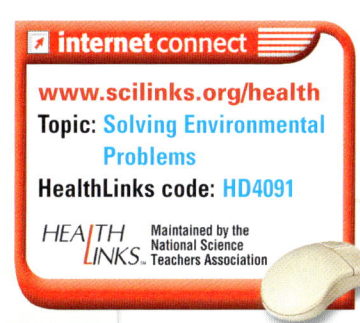

internet connect

www.scilinks.org/health
Topic: Solving Environmental Problems
HealthLinks code: HD4091

HEALTH LINKS. Maintained by the National Science Teachers Association

Lesson 6 A Global Community

21 CHAPTER REVIEW

Chapter Summary

■ Living things get resources from their environments. ■ Basic human needs include air, water, food, and a place to live. ■ Pollution refers to environmental changes that harm the health of living things. ■ Exposure to pollution can cause illness, depending on length of exposure and amount of pollutants present. ■ Outdoor air pollution can cause respiratory illness. ■ Water pollution can cause intestinal problems or serious disease. ■ Cigarette smoke, mold, household chemicals, and loud noises all contribute to pollution inside our homes. ■ Food can be unsafe when it contains harmful chemicals or bacteria. ■ We can conserve resources by choosing to reduce, reuse, and recycle. ■ Communities and governments work together to promote public health.

Using Vocabulary

1. In your own words, write a definition for each of the following terms: *resource*, *dehydration*, and *conservation*.

For each sentence, fill in the blank with the proper word from the word bank provided below.

environments	bioaccumulation
ecosystems	public health
population	pollution
pesticides	nutrients

2. Forests, deserts, and oceans are different kinds of ___.

3. The world's ___ is growing quickly.

4. ___ are chemicals used to kill pests that eat farming crops.

5. A change in the air, soil, or water that harms living things is ___.

6. ___ is the process in which toxins build up in animals that eat polluted food.

Understanding Concepts

7. What are four resources that people need from the environment in order to survive? ★ 1.A; 6.A

8. How can pollution make an ecosystem unhealthy? ★ 6.A

9. How does burning fuel such as coal, oil, or gas pollute the air? ★ 6.A

10. How can pesticides used on farmland pollute a water source? ★ 6.A

11. Name four factors that contribute to indoor air pollution. ★ 6.A

12. How is recycling a way to conserve resources? ★ 6.B

13. Where can you learn about health news from around the world? ★ 4.A; 6.B

14. How has research on antibiotics and vaccines contributed to public health? ★ 6.B

15. How can population growth affect cities? ★ 6.A

16. Why can a poor diet make a person feel tired? ★ 1.A

Critical Thinking

Applying Concepts

17. Think of an environmental health problem that would require action by both individuals and groups in order to be resolved. Give examples of what can be accomplished by individuals alone and what is best accomplished by groups. ★ 4.C; 6.B

18. What steps can your family take to improve the quality of air inside your home? What steps can your class take to improve the quality of air in your school? ★ 6.B

19. Rain-forest destruction can cause soil runoff, large amounts of smoke from burning, and a major increase of carbon dioxide in the atmosphere. How do you think these effects contribute to water pollution and air pollution? ★ 6.A

Making Good Decisions

20. Imagine that you were able to visit a tropical country. You know that many pests, such as mosquitoes, live in this country. You also know that many pests carry diseases. Your doctor tells you that you could use an insect spray to kill insects in the room where you will sleep, use a repellant that you spray on your body, or take medication to prevent catching a disease. What are the pros and cons of each option? What health concerns and environmental impacts should you consider when deciding what precautions to take? ★ 6.A; 6.B; 12.B

Interpreting Graphics

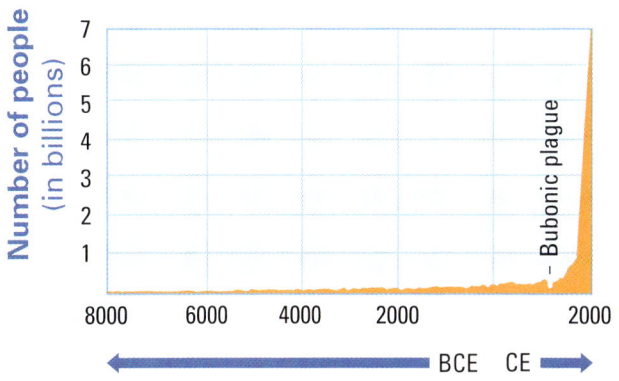

Human Population

Source: U.S. Bureau of the Census 1998.

Use the figure above to answer questions 21–25.

21. What year did the bubonic plague happen?
22. How did the bubonic plague affect population growth?
23. How much did the population grow between 8000 BCE and 1000 CE?
24. How much did the population grow between 1000 CE and 2000 CE?
25. Based on trends in the graph, what do you think will happen to the world's population between 2000 CE and 2500 CE?

Reading Checkup

Take a minute to review your answers to the Health IQ questions at the beginning of this chapter. How has reading this chapter improved your Health IQ?

Chapter 21 Review | 551

Life Skills IN ACTION

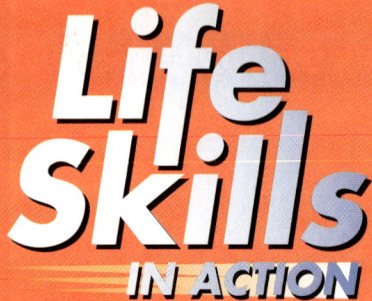

ACT 1

The 5 Steps of Evaluating Media Messages

1. Examine the appeal of the message.
2. Identify the values projected by the message.
3. Consider what the source has to gain by getting you to believe the message.
4. Try to determine the reliability of the source.
5. Based on the information you gather, evaluate the message.

Evaluating Media Messages

You receive media messages every day. These messages are on TV, the Internet, the radio, and in newspapers and magazines. With so many messages, it is important to know how to evaluate them. Evaluating media messages means being able to judge the accuracy of a message. Complete the following activity to improve your skills in evaluating media messages.

Parking Lot or Meadow

Setting the Scene

Tanji can't wait to go to high school next year. Her brother is already in high school. Every month, he brings home the school newspaper so that Tanji can read about her future high school. One day, she reads that the school wants to build a new student parking lot in a meadow next to the school's property. The city's registered voters will decide whether the parking lot will be built. The article, which was written by a high school student, explains why the parking lot is important and urges the students in the school to pressure their parents to vote in favor of it.

Guided Practice

Practice with a Friend

Form a group of two. Have one person play the role of Tanji, and have the second person be an observer. Walking through each of the five steps of evaluating media messages, role-play Tanji analyzing the article in the high school newspaper. Have Tanji use the steps to decide whether to ask her parents to vote for the parking lot. The observer will take notes, which will include observations about what the person playing Tanji did well and suggestions of ways to improve. Stop after each step to evaluate the process. ★ 6.A; 6.B; 12.B

Independent Practice

Check Yourself

After you have completed the guided practice, go through Act 1 again without stopping at each step. Answer the questions below to review what you did.

1. What does the high school student have to gain by having others believe his article?
2. What other sources could Tanji use to compare messages? 📢 4.A; 8.A
3. Did Tanji decide to believe the article? Explain why or why not.
4. Describe a media message that you thought was one sided.

On Your Own

When Tanji goes to talk to her parents about the parking lot, her parents give her a copy of the local newspaper. In the newspaper, an article written by a professor of environmental science explains why people should vote against the parking lot. Make a two-column chart that shows how Tanji could use the five steps of evaluating media messages to compare the article from the school newspaper with the article from the local newspaper.

Appendix

The Food Guide Pyramid

Do you know which foods you need to eat to stay healthy? How much of each food do you need to eat? The Food Guide Pyramid is a tool you can use to make sure you're eating healthfully. Each of the major food groups has its own block on the pyramid. The larger the block, the more you need to eat from that food group. The smaller the block, the less you need to eat from that food group. Use the Food Guide Pyramid as a guide for choosing a healthy diet!

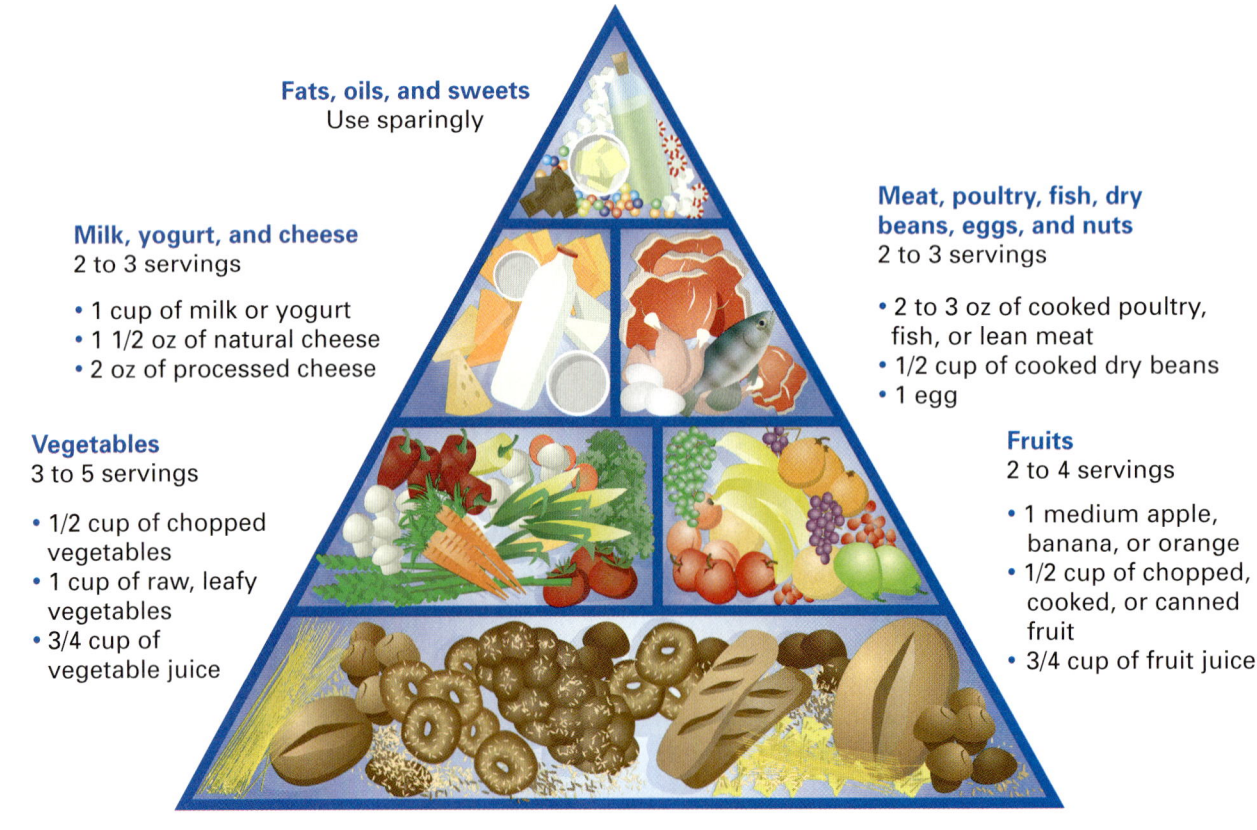

Fats, oils, and sweets
Use sparingly

Milk, yogurt, and cheese
2 to 3 servings
- 1 cup of milk or yogurt
- 1 1/2 oz of natural cheese
- 2 oz of processed cheese

Meat, poultry, fish, dry beans, eggs, and nuts
2 to 3 servings
- 2 to 3 oz of cooked poultry, fish, or lean meat
- 1/2 cup of cooked dry beans
- 1 egg

Vegetables
3 to 5 servings
- 1/2 cup of chopped vegetables
- 1 cup of raw, leafy vegetables
- 3/4 cup of vegetable juice

Fruits
2 to 4 servings
- 1 medium apple, banana, or orange
- 1/2 cup of chopped, cooked, or canned fruit
- 3/4 cup of fruit juice

Bread, cereal, rice, and pasta
6 to 11 servings
- 1 slice of bread
- 1 oz of ready-to-eat cereal
- 1/2 cup of rice or pasta
- 1/2 cup of cooked cereal

Alternative Food Guide Pyramids

The Vegetarian Food Guide Pyramid

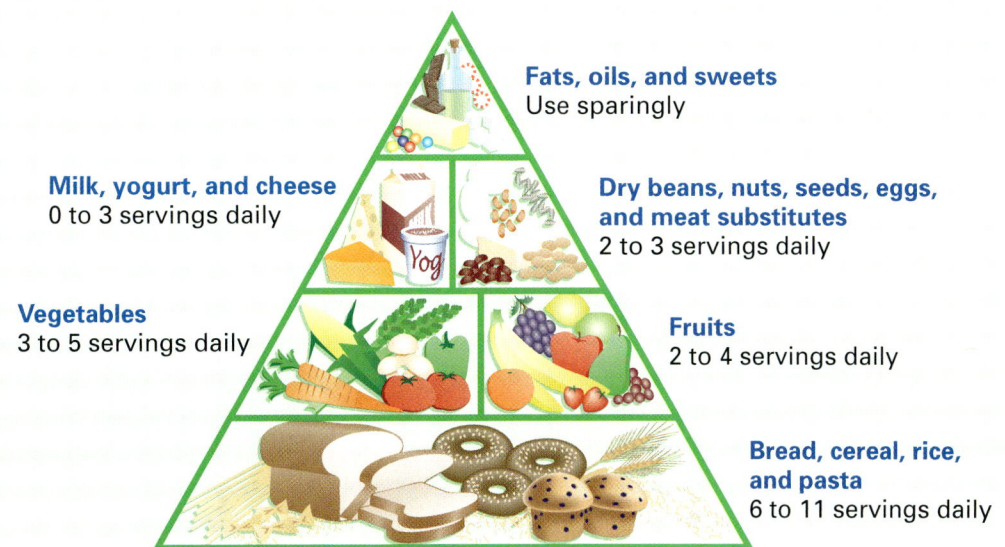

- **Fats, oils, and sweets** Use sparingly
- **Milk, yogurt, and cheese** 0 to 3 servings daily
- **Dry beans, nuts, seeds, eggs, and meat substitutes** 2 to 3 servings daily
- **Vegetables** 3 to 5 servings daily
- **Fruits** 2 to 4 servings daily
- **Bread, cereal, rice, and pasta** 6 to 11 servings daily

The Mediterranean Food Guide Pyramid

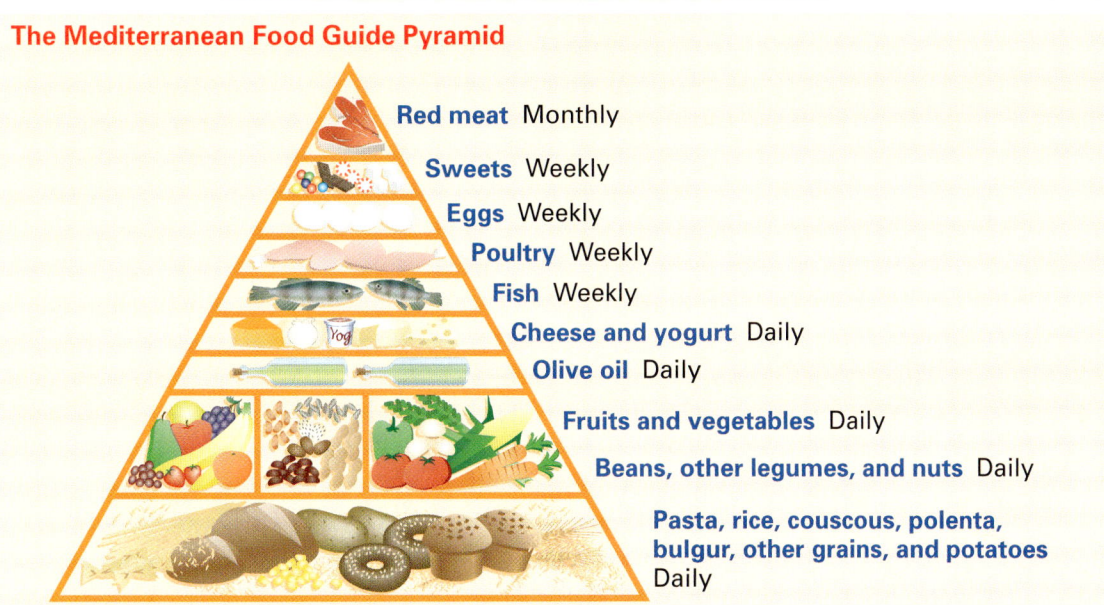

- **Red meat** Monthly
- **Sweets** Weekly
- **Eggs** Weekly
- **Poultry** Weekly
- **Fish** Weekly
- **Cheese and yogurt** Daily
- **Olive oil** Daily
- **Fruits and vegetables** Daily
- **Beans, other legumes, and nuts** Daily
- **Pasta, rice, couscous, polenta, bulgur, other grains, and potatoes** Daily

The Asian Food Guide Pyramid

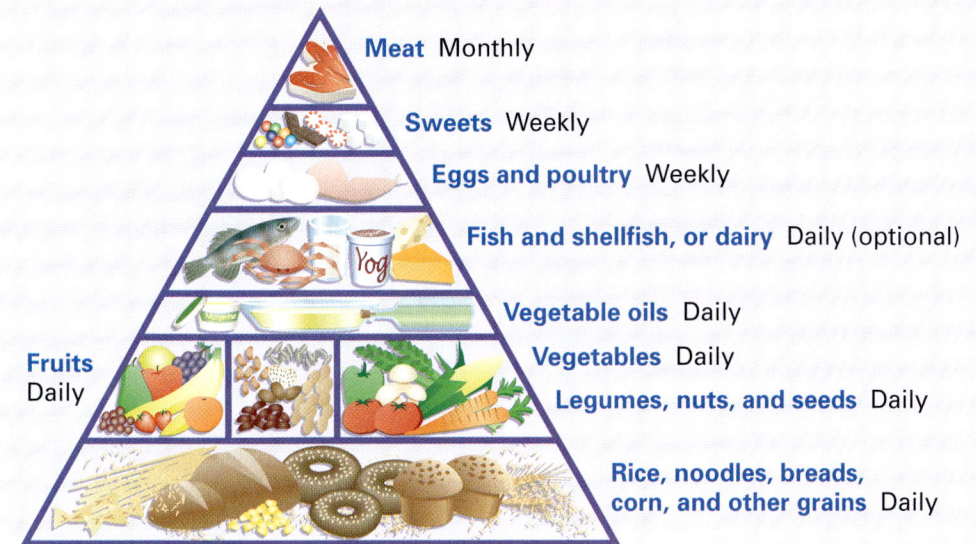

- **Meat** Monthly
- **Sweets** Weekly
- **Eggs and poultry** Weekly
- **Fish and shellfish, or dairy** Daily (optional)
- **Vegetable oils** Daily
- **Vegetables** Daily
- **Fruits** Daily
- **Legumes, nuts, and seeds** Daily
- **Rice, noodles, breads, corn, and other grains** Daily

TABLE 1 Calorie and Nutrient Content of Common Foods

Food group	Food	Serving size	Calories (kcal)	Total fat (g)	Saturated fat (g)	Total carbo-hydrate (g)	Protein (g)
Bread, cereal, rice and pasta	bagel, plain	1 bagel	314	1.8	0.3	51	10.0
	biscuit	1 biscuit	101	5.0	1.2	13	2.0
	bread, white	1 slice	76	1.0	0.4	14	2.0
	bread, whole wheat	1 slice	86	1.0	0.3	16	3.0
	matzo	1 matzo	111	0.2	0.0	22	3.5
	pita bread, wheat	1 pita	165	1.0	0.1	33	5.0
	rice, brown	1/2 cup	110	1.0	0.2	23	2.0
	rice, white and enriched	1/2 cup	133	0.0	0.1	29	2.0
	tortilla, corn and plain	1 tortilla, 6 in.	58	0.7	0.1	12	2.0
	tortilla, flour	1 tortilla, 8 in.	104	2.3	0.6	18	3.0
Vegetables	broccoli, cooked	1 cup	27	0.0	0.0	5	3.0
	carrots, raw	1 baby carrot	4	0.0	0.0	1	0.0
	celery, raw	4 small stalks	10	0.1	0.0	2	0.5
	corn, cooked	1 ear	83	1.0	0.0	19	2.6
	cucumber, raw with peel	1/8 cup	25	0.1	0.0	6	0.6
	green beans, cooked	1 cup	44	0.4	0.0	10	2.4
	onions, raw, sliced	1/4 cup	11	0.0	0.0	3	0.3
	potatoes, baked with skin	1/2 cup	66	0.1	0.0	15	1.4
	salad, mixed green, no dressing	1 cup	10	1.0	0.0	2	0.0
	spinach, fresh	1 cup	7	0.1	0.0	1	0.9
Fruits	apple, raw, with skin	1 medium apple	81	0.1	0.1	21	0.2
	banana, fresh	1 medium banana	114	1.0	0.2	27	1.0
	cherries, sweet, fresh	1 cup, with pits	84	0.3	0.0	19	1.4
	grapes	1/2 cup	62	0.1	0.0	16	0.6
	orange, fresh	1 large orange	85	0.0	0.0	21	1.7
	peach, fresh	1 medium peach	37	0.0	0.0	9	1.0
	pear, fresh	1 medium pear	123	1.0	0.0	32	0.8
	raisins, seedless, dry	1 cup	495	0.2	0.0	131	5.3
	strawberries, fresh	1 cup	46	0.0	0.0	11	0.9
	tomatoes, raw	1 cup	31	0.5	0.0	7	1.3
	watermelon	1/2 cup	26	0.0	0.0	6	0.0
Meat, poultry, fish, dry beans, eggs, and nuts	bacon	3 pieces	109	9.0	3.3	0	6.0
	beans, black, cooked	1/2 cup	114	0.0	0.1	20	7.6
	beans, refried, canned	1/2 cup	127	1.0	0.1	23	8.0
	chicken breast, fried meat and skin	1 split breast	364	18.5	4.9	13	34.8
	chicken breast, skinless, grilled	1 split breast	142	3.0	0.9	73	27.0
	chorizo	1 link	273	23.0	8.6	1	14.5
	egg, boiled	1 large egg	78	5.3	1.0	0	6.0
	humus	1/4 cup	106	5.2	0.0	13	3.0

TABLE 1 Calorie and Nutrient Content of Common Foods (continued)

Food group	Food	Serving size	Calories (kcal)	Total fat (g)	Saturated fat (g)	Total carbo-hydrate (g)	Protein (g)
Meat, poultry, fish, dry beans, eggs, and nuts (continued)	peanut butter	2 Tbsp	190	16.0	3.0	7	8.0
	pork chop	3 oz	300	24.0	9.7	0	19.7
	roast beef	3 oz	179	6.5	2.3	0	28.1
	shrimp, breaded and fried	4 large shrimp	73	3.5	0.6	3	6.4
	steak, beef, broiled	6 oz	344	14.0	5.2	0	52.0
	sunflower seeds	1/4 cup	208	19.0	2.0	5	7.0
	tofu	1/2 cup	97	5.6	0.8	4	10.1
	tuna, canned in water	3 oz	109	2.5	0.7	0	20.1
	turkey, roasted	3 oz	145	4.2	1.4	0	24.9
Milk, yogurt, and cheese	cheese, American, prepackaged	1 slice	70	5.0	2.0	2	4.0
	cheese, cheddar	1 oz	114	9.0	6.0	0	7.1
	cheese, cottage, lowfat	1/2 cup	102	1.4	0.9	4	7.0
	cheese, cream	1 Tbsp	51	5.0	3.2	0	1.1
	milk, chocolate, reduced fat (2%)	1 cup	179	5.0	3.1	26	8.0
	milk, lowfat (1%)	1 cup	102	3.0	1.6	12	8.0
	milk, reduced fat (2%)	1 cup	122	5.0	2.9	12	8.1
	milk, skim, fat free	1 cup	91	0.0	0.0	12	8.0
	milk, whole	1 cup	149	8.0	5.1	11	8.0
	yogurt, lowfat, fruit flavored	1 cup	231	3.0	2.0	47	12.0
Fats, oils, and sweets	brownie	1 square	227	10.0	2.0	30	1.5
	butter	1 tsp	36	3.7	2.4	0	0.0
	candy, chocolate bar	1.3 oz	226	14.0	8.1	26	3.0
	soda, no ice	12 oz	184	0.0	0.0	38	0.0
	cheesecake	1 piece	660	46.0	28.0	52	11.0
	cookies, chocolate chip	1 cookie	59	2.5	0.8	8	0.6
	cookies, oatmeal	1 cookie	113	3.0	0.8	20	1.0
	gelatin dessert, flavored	1/2 cup	80	0.0	0.0	19	2.0
	ice-cream cone, one scoop regular ice cream	1 cone	178	8.0	4.9	22	3.0
	margarine, stick	1 tsp	34	3.8	0.7	0	0.0
	mayonnaise, regular	1 Tbsp	57	4.9	0.7	4	0.1
	pie, apple, double crust	1 piece	411	18.0	4.0	58	3.7
	popcorn, microwave, with butter	1/3 bag	170	12.0	2.5	26	2.0
	potato chips	1 oz	150	10.0	3.0	10	1.0
	pretzels	10 twists	229	2.1	0.5	48	5.5
	tortilla chips, plain	1 oz	140	7.3	1.4	18	2.0

Food Safety Tips

Few things taste better than a hot, home-cooked meal. It looks good and it smells good, but how do you know if it is safe to eat? Food doesn't have to look or smell bad to make you ill. To protect yourself from food-related illnesses, follow the food safety tips listed below.

Tips for Preparing Food

- Wash your hands with hot, soapy water before, during, and after you prepare food.
- Do not defrost food at room temperature. Always defrost food in the refrigerator or in the microwave.
- Always use a clean cutting board. If possible, use two cutting boards when preparing food. Use one cutting board for fruits and vegetables and the other cutting board for raw meat, poultry, and seafood.
- Wash cutting boards and other utensils with soap and hot water, especially those that come in contact with raw meat, poultry, and seafood.
- Keep raw meat, poultry, seafood, and their juices away from other foods.
- Marinate food in the refrigerator. Do not use leftover marinade sauce on cooked foods unless it has been boiled.

Tips for Cooking Food

- Use a food thermometer when cooking to ensure that food is cooked to a proper temperature.
- Red meats should be cooked to a temperature of 160°F.
- Poultry should be cooked to a temperature of 180°F.
- When cooked completely, fish flakes easily with a fork.
- Eggs should be cooked until the yolk and the white are firm.

Tips for Cleaning the Kitchen

- Wash all dishes, utensils, cutting boards, and pots and pans with hot, soapy water.
- Clean countertops with a disinfectant, such as a household cleaner that contains bleach. Wipe the countertop with paper towels, which can be thrown away. If you use a cloth towel, put it in the wash after using it.
- Refrigerate or freeze leftovers within 2 hours of cooking. Leftovers should be stored in small, shallow containers.

BMI

What Is BMI?

The body mass index (BMI) is a calculation that you can use to determine your healthy weight range. It is a mathematical formula that uses height and weight to evaluate body composition. A high BMI indicates that the person being evaluated may be overweight or obese.

How Do You Calculate BMI?

BMI can be calculated by using the following formula:

$$BMI = \text{weight in pounds} \times 704.3 \div \text{height in inches}^2$$

For example, a 14-year-old girl who is 4 feet 8 inches tall and weighs 98 pounds would calculate her BMI as follows:

$$BMI = 98 \times 704.3 \div 56^2 = 22.0$$

Is BMI Accurate?

While BMI works well for many people, it is not perfect. The following are some of the limitations of BMI:

- BMI does not account for frame size. So, someone who is stocky may be considered overweight based on BMI even when that person has a healthy amount of body fat.
- Despite being very fit, athletic people who have low body fat and a lot of muscle may be considered overweight by the BMI. Muscle weighs more than fat which results in a higher BMI measurement.
- Most BMI tables are inaccurate for children and teens because they are based on adult heights. However, some tables have been adjusted to be more accurate for children and teens.

Table 2 Healthy BMI Ranges for Ages 10 to 17

Age	Boys	Girls
10	15.3–21.0	16.2–23.0
11	15.8–21.0	16.9–24.0
12	16.0–22.0	16.9–24.5
13	16.6–23.0	17.5–24.5
14	17.5–24.5	17.5–25.0
15	18.1–25.0	17.5–25.0
16	18.5–26.5	17.5–25.0
17	18.8–27.0	17.5–26.0

Source: *FITNESSGRAM*.

The Physical Activity Pyramid

How often do you exercise during the week? Do you think you get enough exercise to stay fit? Take a look at the Physical Activity Pyramid to find out if you're exercising enough to stay fit!

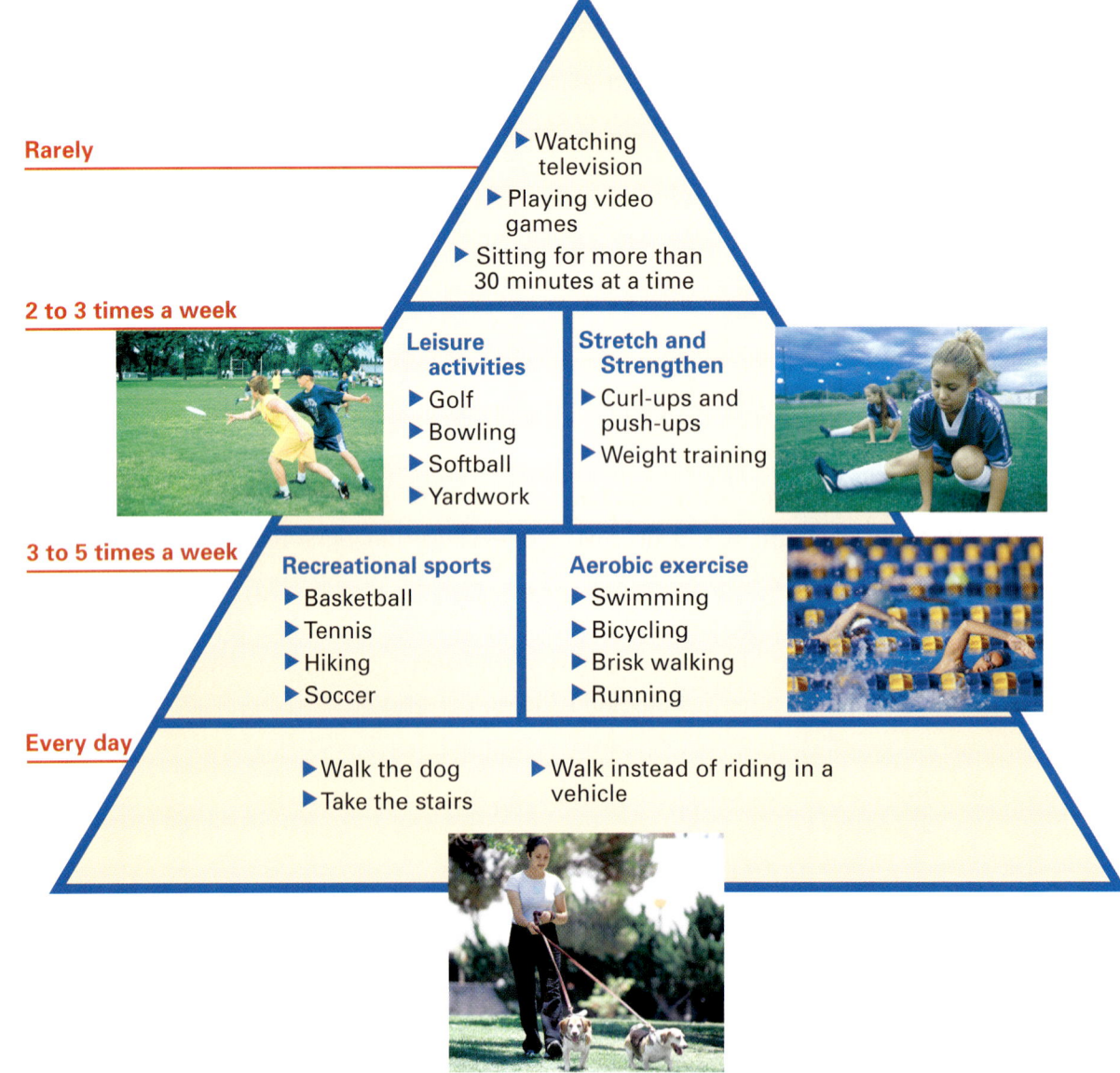

Rarely
- Watching television
- Playing video games
- Sitting for more than 30 minutes at a time

2 to 3 times a week

Leisure activities
- Golf
- Bowling
- Softball
- Yardwork

Stretch and Strengthen
- Curl-ups and push-ups
- Weight training

3 to 5 times a week

Recreational sports
- Basketball
- Tennis
- Hiking
- Soccer

Aerobic exercise
- Swimming
- Bicycling
- Brisk walking
- Running

Every day
- Walk the dog
- Take the stairs
- Walk instead of riding in a vehicle

Emergency Kit

A disaster can happen anytime and anywhere. During a disaster, people lose power, gas, and water. Sometimes, people are not able to get help for a few days. You can prepare for disasters by making an emergency kit. There are six basic things you should keep stocked in your emergency kit.

1. **Water** Store water in plastic containers. You'll need water for drinking, food preparation, and cleaning. Store a gallon of water per person per day. Have at least three days' worth of water in your kit.

2. **Food** Store at least three days' worth of nonperishable food. These foods include canned foods, freeze-dried foods, canned juices, and high-energy foods, such as nutrition bars. You should also keep vitamins in your emergency kit.

3. **First-Aid Kit** Someone may get hurt, so you'll want to have plenty of first-aid supplies. Include the following supplies in your first-aid kit:
   - self-adhesive bandages
   - gauze pads
   - rolled gauze
   - adhesive tape
   - antibacterial ointment and cleansers
   - thermometer
   - scissors, tweezers, and razor blades
   - sterile gloves and breathing mask
   - over-the-counter medicines

4. **Clothing and Bedding** An emergency kit should include at least one complete change of clothing and shoes per person. You should also store blankets or sleeping bags, rain gear, and thermal underwear.

5. **Tools and Supplies** Always keep your emergency kit stocked with a flashlight, battery-operated radio, and extra batteries. Also, include a can opener, cooking supplies, candles, waterproof matches, fire extinguisher, tape, and hardware tools. You should also store emergency signal supplies, such as signal flares, whistles, and signal mirrors.

6. **Special Items** Be sure to remember family members who have special needs. For example, store formula, baby food, and diapers for infants. For adults, you might keep contact lens supplies, special medications, and extra eyeglasses in your emergency kit.

Natural Disasters

The sky is rumbling! The ground is shaking! Knowing what to do during storms and earthquakes can keep you safe. Prepare an emergency kit and put it where you will likely go during a natural disaster. Also, remember the following about natural disasters:

- **Thunderstorms** Lightning is one of the most dangerous parts of a thunderstorm. Lightning is attracted to tall objects. If you are outside, stay away from trees. Lightning may strike the tree you are hiding under and knock it down. If you are in an open field, lie down. Otherwise, you will be the tallest object in the area! You should also stay away from bodies of water. Water conducts electricity. So, if lightning hits water while you are in it, you could be hurt.

- **Tornadoes** If there is a tornado warning for your area, find shelter. The best place to go is a basement or cellar. If you don't have a basement or cellar, go to a windowless room in the center of the building, such as a bathroom or closet. If you are caught outside, try to find shelter indoors. Otherwise, lie down in a large, open field or a deep ditch.

- **Hurricanes** If there is a hurricane, the weather service will give a warning. Some hurricanes can last a few days. Sometimes, people living on the shore are asked to move inland to wait out the storm.

- **Floods** The best thing to do during a flood is to find a high place and wait out the flood. Stay out of floodwaters. Even shallow water can be dangerous if it is fast-moving. Some floodwater moves so quickly that it can pick up cars.

- **Earthquakes** If you are inside when an earthquake happens, the best thing to do is to kneel or lie face down under a heavy table or desk. Stay away from windows, and cover your head. If you are outside, find an open area. Avoid buildings, power lines, and trees. Lie down, and cover your head. If you are in a car, have the driver stop the car in an open area. Stay inside the car until the earthquake is over.

Staying Home Alone

It is not unusual for teens to spend time home alone after school. Their parents may still be at work. Or they may be running errands. If you spend time at home alone, remember the following safety tips:

- Lock the doors and make sure your windows are locked.
- Never let anyone who calls or comes to your door know that you are home alone.
- Don't open the door for anyone you don't know or for anyone that isn't supposed to be at your home. If the visitor is delivering a package, ask him or her to leave it at the door. If the visitor wants to use the phone, send him or her to a phone booth. If the visitor is selling something, you can tell him or her through the door, "We're not interested."
- If a visitor doesn't leave or you see someone hanging around your home, call a trusted neighbor or the police for help.
- If you answer the phone, don't tell the caller anything personal. Offer to take a message without revealing you're alone. If the call becomes uncomfortable or mean, hang up the phone and tell your parents about it when they get home. You can also avoid answering the phone altogether when you're alone. Then, the caller can leave a message on the answering machine.
- Keep an emergency phone number list next to every phone in your home. If there is an emergency, call 911. Don't panic. Follow the operator's instructions. If the emergency is a fire, immediately leave the building and go to a trusted neighbor's home to call for help.
- Find an interesting way to spend your time. Time passes more quickly when you're not bored. Get a head start on your homework, read a book or magazine, clean your room, or work on a hobby. Avoid watching television unless your parents have given you permission to watch a specific program.
- Consider having a friend stay with you. But do so only if your parents have given you permission to have your friend over. That way, you won't be alone and you will have someone to pass the time with you.
- Remember your safety behaviors. By practicing them, you can make sure you stay safe.

☑ Think before you act.
☑ Pay attention.
☑ Know your limits.
☑ Practice refusal skills.
☑ Use safety equipment.
☑ Change risky behavior.
☑ Change risky situations.

Computer Posture

You know that computers can be both fun and helpful. You can play games on a computer, research and write a paper, and e-mail your friends. But sitting in front of a computer for hours at a time can also strain your eyes, neck, wrists, spine, and hands. So, it is important to practice good posture when using a computer. To help prevent injuries related to using a computer, follow the tips listed below.

Tips for Good Computer Posture

- Make sure your entire body faces the computer screen and keyboard.
- Position the computer screen so that you have to look slightly down to see it. The screen should be 18 to 24 inches from your eyes.
- Keep your feet flat on the floor.
- Make sure your thighs are parallel to the floor. You may have to adjust your chair height.
- Keep your shoulders and neck relaxed.
- Keep your back straight, and make sure you have good lower back support.
- Keep your wrists straight while you are typing. Do not flex your wrists up or down.
- Your arms should be bent at a 90° angle.
- Take breaks every 30 minutes to an hour. Stretch, and walk around.

▶ Entire body faces the computer screen and keyboard
▶ Computer screen is slightly below eye level
▶ Feet flat on the floor
▶ Thighs parallel to the floor
▶ Shoulders and neck relaxed
▶ Back straight
▶ Wrists straight
▶ Arms bent at a 90° angle

Internet Safety

The Internet is a wonderful tool. It allows you to communicate with people, access information, and educate yourself. You can also use it to have fun. But when using any tool, there are certain precautions or safety measures you must take. Using the Internet is no different. Listed below are some rules to follow to make sure you stay safe when you are using the Internet.

Rules for Internet Safety

- Set up rules with your parents or another trusted adult about what time of day you can use the Internet, how long you can use the Internet, and what sites you can visit on the Internet. Follow the rules that have been set.
- Do not give out personal information, such as your address, telephone number, or the name and location of your school.
- If you find any information that makes you uncomfortable, tell a parent or another trusted adult immediately.
- Do not respond to any messages that make you uncomfortable. If you receive such a message, tell your parents or another trusted adult immediately.
- Never agree to meet with anyone before talking to your parents or another trusted adult. If your parents give you permission to meet someone, make sure you do so in a public place. Have an adult come with you.
- Do not send a picture of yourself or any other information without first checking with your parents or a trusted adult.

Baby Sitter Safety

Baby-sitting is an important job. You're responsible for taking care of another person's children. You have to make decisions not only for yourself but also for other people. So, you have to make good decisions. Keep the following tips in mind when you baby-sit.

Before you Baby-Sit

- Take a baby-sitting course or a first-aid class.
- Find out what time you should arrive and arrange for your transportation to and from the home.
- Ask the parents how long they plan to be away.
- Find out how many children you will be caring for and what your responsibilities are.
- Settle on how much the parents will pay you for your work.
- Consider visiting the family while the parents are home so you can get to know the children a few days before you baby-sit.

When You Arrive

- Arrive early so the parents can give you information about caring for the children. Ask the parents about the children's eating habits, TV habits, and bedtime routine.
- Find out where the parents are going. Write down the address and phone number for where they will be and put it next to the phone. Find out when they plan to return. If the parents have a cellular phone, be sure to get that number, too.
- Know where the emergency numbers are posted. Also, make sure you have the address for the home so that you can give it to an operator in the event of an emergency.
- If you are watching toddlers or infants, find out where their formula and diaper supplies are stored.
- Learn where the family keeps their first-aid supplies. If the children need any medicine while you care for them, make sure you know how to give it to them. Remember that you shouldn't give children medicine unless you have the parents' permission to do so.
- Ask if the children have any special needs. For example, some children are diabetic or asthmatic. Make sure you know what to do if they have any trouble.

While You Are Baby-Sitting

- Never leave a child alone, even for a short time.
- Don't leave an infant alone on a changing table, sofa, or bed.
- Check on the children often, even when they're sleeping.
- Don't leave children alone in the bathtub or near a pool.
- Keep breakable and dangerous objects out of the reach of children.
- Keep the doors locked. Unless the parents have given you permission, do not open the door for anyone.
- If the phone rings, take a message. Do not let the caller know that you are the baby sitter and that the parents are not home.
- If the child gets hurt or sick, call the parents. Don't try to take care of it yourself. In case of a serious emergency, call 911. Then, call the parents.

FUN THINGS YOU CAN DO WHILE YOU BABY-SIT

Baby-sitting is a huge responsibility. But it is also very rewarding. Children love it when you pay attention to them and when you play with them. Don't be afraid to get down on the floor with them. They like you to play at their level. Consider doing the following fun activities, but remember to always get the parents' permission, first!

- Take children outside or to a local park to play.
- Read stories to each other. Let the children pick their favorite story.
- Go to story time at the local library.
- Draw pictures, or color in coloring books. Take this a step further by pretending there is an art gallery in the house. Hang up the pictures, and pretend to be visiting the gallery.
- Pretend you are at a restaurant during mealtimes. Have the children make up menus and pretend to be waiters.
- Plan a scavenger hunt.
- Bring some simple craft items for the children, and let them get creative.
- Play board games or card games.

Careers in Health

Certified Athletic Trainers

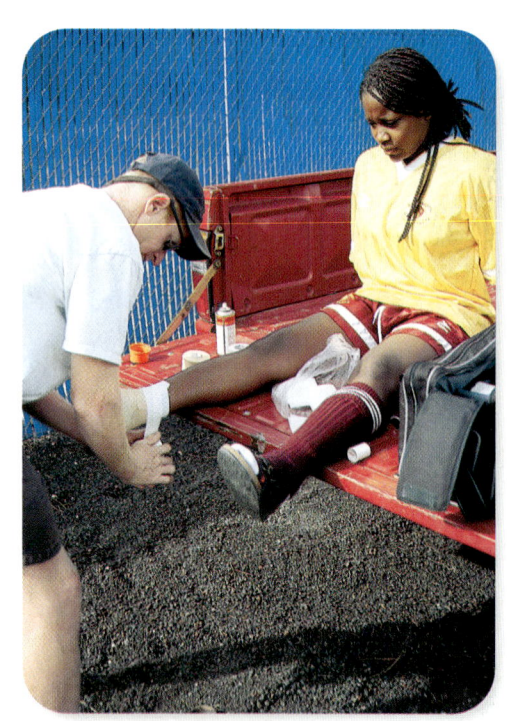

Athletic trainers work with athletes from sports teams and organizations to prevent, recognize, treat and rehabilitate sports-related injuries. They provide first aid and nonemergency medical services at sporting events and practices and help team members get long-term medical care if they need it. Certified athletic trainers usually work for college or professional sports teams. Sometimes, they work for high school sports teams.

How to Become a Certified Athletic Trainer

- four-year bachelor's degree in a National Athletic Trainer's Association (NATA) program or an NATA internship
- training in CPR and first aid
- earn NATA certification

Registered Nurse

Registered nurses (RNs) interpret and respond to a patient's symptoms, reactions, and progress. They teach patients and families about proper healthcare, assist in patient rehabilitation, and provide emotional support to promote recovery. RNs use their knowledge to treat patients and make decisions about patient care. Some RNs are responsible for supervising aides, assistants, and licensed practical nurses. Often nurses choose to work in specialized areas such as obstetrics (childbirth), emergency care, or public health. Registered nurses can work in hospitals, public health departments, nursing homes, and public schools.

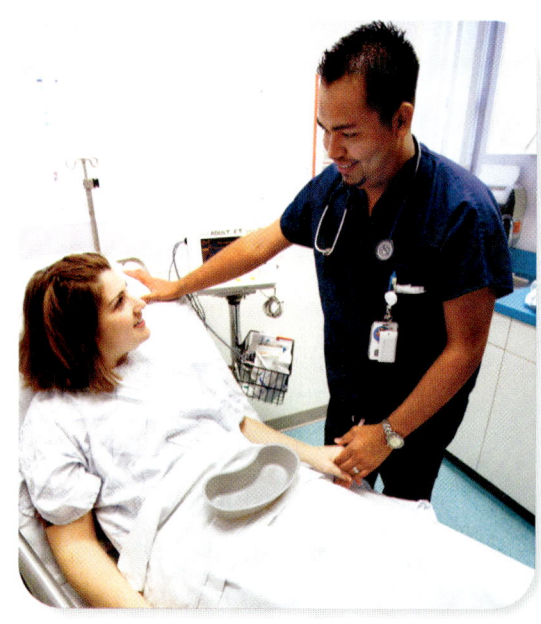

How to Become a Registered Nurse

- two-year associate's degree
- four-year bachelor's degree (optional)
- pass a licensing exam

Emergency Medical Technician (EMT)

Emergency medical technicians (EMTs) respond to healthcare crises. They often drive ambulances, give emergency medical care, and, if necessary, transport patients to hospitals. EMTs respond to emergencies, such as heart attacks, unexpected childbirth, car accidents, and fires. They explain situations and coordinate with local hospital staff. Under the direction of a physician, EMTs are told how to proceed with medical care. They perform cardiopulmonary resuscitation 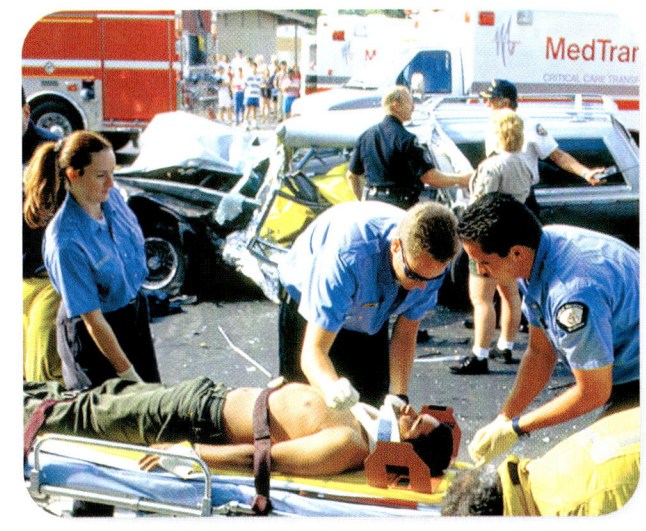 (CPR), control bleeding, place splints on broken bones, and check pulse and respiration. Emergency medical technicians work in hospitals, for fire departments, or with more advanced training, in an ambulance.

How to Become an Emergency Medical Technician

- training depends on duties
- may require basic classes for certification
- may require numerous college courses, depending upon career goal

Medical Social Worker

Medical social workers assist patients and their families with health-related problems and concerns. They lead support group discussions, help patients locate appropriate healthcare, and provide support to patients who have serious or chronic illnesses. They help patients and their families find resources to overcome unhealthy conditions, such as child abuse, homelessness, and drug abuse. They also help patients find legal resources and financial aid to pay for healthcare services. Medical social workers usually work for hospitals, nursing homes, health clinics, or community healthcare agencies.

How to Become a Medical Social Worker

- four-year bachelor's degree
- two-year master's degree (optional)

Glossary

A

abdominal thrusts (ab DAHM uh nuhl THRUHSTS) the act of applying pressure to a choking person's stomach to force an object out of the throat (498)

abstinence the refusal to take part in an activity that puts your health or the health of others at risk; in particular the refusal to engage in sexual activity (440)

abstract thought a thought that extends beyond topics that can be seen or experienced (246)

abuse the harmful or offensive treatment of one person by another person (326)

accident an unexpected event that may lead to injury or death (472, 480)

action plan a map that outlines the steps for reaching your goal (38)

active listening the act of hearing and showing that you understand what a person is communicating (43, 83, 263)

active rest a way to recover from exercise by reducing the amount of activity you do (162)

acute injury an injury that happens suddenly (158)

adolescence the stage of development during which humans grow from childhood to adulthood (233)

adulthood the period of life that follows adolescence and that ends at death (233)

aerobic exercise (er OH bik EK suhr SIEZ) exercise that lasts a long time and uses oxygen to get energy (176)

aggression any action or behavior that is hostile or threatening to another person (308)

AIDS acquired immune deficiency syndrome (uh KWIERD im MYOON dee FISH uhn see SIN DROHM), an illness that is caused by HIV infection and that makes an infected person more likely to get unusual forms of cancer and infection because HIV attacks the body's immune system (442)

alcohol poisoning the result of drinking too much alcohol; a drug overdose that can be fatal (374)

alcoholism a disease caused by addiction to alcohol; a physical and psychological dependence on alcohol (386)

allergy an overreaction of the immune system to something in the environment that is harmless to most people (464)

anaerobic exercise (an er OH bik EK suhr SIEZ) exercise that does not use oxygen to get energy and that lasts a very short time (176)

anorexia nervosa (AN uh REKS ee uh nuhr VOH suh) an eating disorder that involves self-starvation, an unhealthy body image, and extreme weight loss (206)

antibiotic (AN tie bie AHT ik) a drug that kills bacteria or slows the growth of bacteria (434)

anxiety disorder an illness that causes unusually strong nervousness, worry, or panic (91)

artery a blood vessel that carries blood away from the heart (130)

assess to measure one's short-term achievement toward a long-term goal (40)

attitude the way in which you act, think, or feel that causes you to make particular choices (12)

autoimmune disease (AWT oh i MYOON di ZEEZ) a disease in which a person's immune system attacks certain cells, tissues, or organs of the body (464)

B

bacteria (bak TIR ee uh) extremely small, single-celled organisms that do not have a nucleus; single-celled microorganisms that are found everywhere (434)

behavior the way that a person chooses to respond or act (264)

benign (bi NIEN) describes a tumor that is not cancerous and that is usually not life threatening (466)

bias (BIE uhs) a slant that changes how information is presented (513)

binge eating disorder an eating disorder in which a person has difficulty controlling how much food he or she eats (208)

bioaccumulation (BI oh uh KYOOM yoo LAY shuhn) the process in which pollutants build up in animals that eat polluted food (538)

biopsy (BIE op see) a sample of tissue that is removed from the patient and that is sent to a specialist to see if cancer cells are present (468)

birth the passage of a baby from the mother's uterus to outside the mother's body (230)

blood a tissue made up of cells, fluid, and other substances that carries oxygen, carbon dioxide, and nutrients in the body (129)

blood alcohol concentration (BAC) the percentage of alcohol in a person's blood (372)

body composition the proportion of body weight that is made up of fat tissue compared to bones, muscles, and organs (145)

body image the way that you see yourself and imagine your body (200)

body language a way of communicating by using facial expressions, hand gestures, and posture (83, 263, 292)

body mass index (BMI) a measurement that is used to determine one's healthy weight range (210)

body system a group of organs that work together to complete a specific task in the body (106)

bone a living organ of the skeletal system that is made of bone cells, connective tissues, and minerals (116)

brain the major organ of the nervous system; the mass of nervous tissue that is located inside the skull (109)

bulimia nervosa (boo LEE mee uh nuhr VOH suh) an eating disorder in which a person eats a large amount of food and then tries to remove the food from his or her body (207)

bully a person who frequently picks on or beats up smaller or weaker people (299)

C

Calorie a unit used to measure the amount of energy that the body gets from food (192)

cancer a disease in which cells grow uncontrollably and invade and destroy healthy tissues (344, 466)

carbohydrate (KAHR bo HIE drayt) a chemical composed of one or more simple sugars; includes sugars, starches, and fiber (193)

carbon monoxide (KAHR buhn muh NAHKS IED) a gas in cigarette smoke that makes it hard for the body to get oxygen (338)

carcinogen any chemical or agent that causes cancer (467)

cardiopulmonary resuscitation (CPR) (KAHR dee oh PUL muh NER ee ri SUHS uh TAY shuhn) a life-saving technique that combines rescue breathing and chest compressions (500)

cardiorespiratory endurance (KAHR dee oh RES puhr uh TAWR'ee en DOOR uhns) the ability of the heart and lungs to work efficiently during physical activity (143)

cell the simplest and most basic unit of all living things (106)

central nervous system (CNS) the brain and spinal cord (371)

cessation (se SAY shuhn) the act of stopping something entirely and permanently (353)

cheating trying to win by breaking the rules (172)

childhood the stage of development between infancy and adolescence (232)

chronic bronchitis (KRAHN ik brang KIET is) a disease in which the lining of the airways becomes very swollen and irritated (345)

chronic effect a consequence that remains with a person for a long time (340)

chronic injury an injury that develops over a long period of time (158)

circulatory system the body system made up of the heart, of the blood vessels, and of the blood (128)

cirrhosis a deadly disease that replaces healthy liver tissue with useless scar tissue; most often caused by long-term alcohol abuse (376)

clique (KLIK) a group of people who accept only certain types of people and exclude others (251)

collaboration (kuh LAB uh RAY shuhn) a solution to a conflict in which both parties get what they want without having to give up anything important (295)

communication skills methods for expressing one's thoughts and listening to what others say (42)

comparison shopping the process of looking at several similar products to figure out which one offers the best value (511)

competition a contest between two or more individuals or teams (171)

compromise (KAHM pruh MIEZ) a solution to a conflict in which both sides give up things to come to an agreement (295)

conditioning exercise that improves fitness for sports (174)

conflict any situation in which ideas or interests go against one another (288)

consequence a result of one's actions and decisions (32)

conservation the protection and wise use of resources (540)

coping dealing with problems and troubles in an effective way (41)

counselor a professional who helps people work through difficult problems by talking (99)

crosstraining doing different kinds of exercise during conditioning (175)

dating going out socially with someone to whom you are attracted (278)

defense mechanism (di FENS MEK uh NIZ uhm) an automatic, short-term behavior to cope with distress (60, 88)

dehydration (DEE hie DRAY shuhn) a condition in which the body does not contain enough water (533)

depressant any drug that decreases activity in the body (371, 408)

depression a mood disorder in which a person is extremely sad and hopeless for a long period of time (94)

designer drug a drug that is produced by making a small chemical change to a drug that already exists (416)

detoxification (dee TAHK suh fuh KAY shuhn) the process by which the body rids itself of harmful chemicals (422)

diet a pattern of eating that includes what a person eats, how much a person eats, and how often a person eats (190)

Dietary Guidelines for Americans a set of suggestions designed to help people develop healthy eating habits and increase physical activity levels (196)

digestion the process of breaking down food into a form that the body can use (122, 189)

digestive system the group of organs and glands that work together to digest food (122)

disease any harmful change in the state of health of the body or mind (456)

dislocation an injury in which a bone has been forced out of its normal position in a joint (496)

distress any stress response that keeps you from reaching your goals or that makes you sick; the negative physical, mental, or emotional strain in response to a stressor (53)

drug any chemical substance that causes a change in a person's physical or psychological state (396)

drug addiction the condition in which a person can no longer control his or her need or desire for a drug (349, 402)

E

eating disorder a disease in which a person has an unhealthy concern for his or her body weight and shape (205)

ecosystem a community of living things and the nonliving parts of its environment (530)

Ecstasy (EK stuh see) the common name given to the chemical MDMA (416)

elective class a class that you can choose but are not required to take (252)

embryo a developing human, from fertilization until the end of the eighth week of pregnancy (226)

emotion a feeling that is produced in response to a life event (64, 76)

emotional abuse the repeated use of actions and words that imply a person is worthless and powerless (327)

emotional health the way that a person experiences and deals with feelings (76)

emotional spectrum a set of emotions arranged by how pleasant the emotions are (78)

empathy (EM puh thee) sharing and understanding another person's feelings (266)

emphysema (EM fuh SEE muh) a respiratory disease in which oxygen and carbon dioxide have difficulty moving through the alveoli because the alveoli are thin and stretched out or have been destroyed (345)

endocrine system a network of tissues and organs that release chemicals that control certain body functions (112)

environment all of the living and nonliving things around you (9, 530)

environmental tobacco smoke (ETS) the mixture of exhaled smoke and smoke from the ends of burning cigarettes (341)

epinephrine (EP uh NEPH rin) a stress hormone that increases the level of sugar in your blood and directs the "fight-or-flight" response (56)

exercise any physical activity that maintains or improves your physical fitness (146)

extracurricular activities activities that you do and that are not part of your schoolwork (252)

F

fad diet a diet that promises quick weight loss with little effort (211)

fatigue physical or mental exhaustion; a feeling of extreme tiredness (58)

fats an energy-storage nutrient that helps the body store some vitamins (193)

fetal alcohol syndrome (FAS) a group of birth defects that affect an unborn baby that has been exposed to alcohol (377)

fetus the developing human in a woman's uterus, from the start of the ninth week of pregnancy until birth (226)

first aid emergency medical care for someone who has been hurt or who is sick (490)

flashback an incident in which a hallucinogen's effects happen again long after the drug was taken (415)

flexibility (FLEK suh BIL uh tee) the ability to bend and twist joints easily (144)

Food and Drug Administration a government agency that controls the safety of food and drugs in the United States (401)

Food Guide Pyramid a tool for choosing what kinds of foods to eat and how much of each food to eat every day (197)

fracture a crack or break in a bone (496)

gang a group of people who often use violence (485)

GHB a drug that is made from the anesthetic GBL, a common ingredient in pesticides (417)

gland a tissue or group of tissues that makes and releases chemicals such as hormones (113)

goal something that someone works toward and hopes to achieve (34)

good decision a decision in which a person carefully considers the outcome of each choice (24)

grief a feeling of deep sadness about a loss (235)

hallucinogen (huh LOO si nuh juhn) any drug that causes a person to hallucinate (414)

hangover uncomfortable physical effects that are caused by alcohol use, including headache, dizziness, stomach upset, nausea, and vomiting (374)

harassment (huh RAS muhnt) any kind of repeated attention that is not wanted; harassment often affects one's ability to do schoolwork or to live one's life (330)

health a condition of physical, emotional, mental, and social well-being (4)

health insurance (in SHUHR uhns) a policy that you buy and that covers certain costs in the case of illness or injury (523)

healthcare consumer (kuhn SOO muhr) anyone who pays for healthcare products or services (508)

healthy weight range an estimate of how much one should weigh depending on one's height and body frame (210)

hereditary disease a disease caused by abnormal chromosomes or by defective genes inherited by a child from one or both parents (460)

heredity the passing down of traits from parents to their biological child (8)

HIV human immunodeficiency virus (HYOO muhn IM myoo NOH dee FISH uhn see VIE ruhs), a virus that attacks the human immune system and that causes AIDS (442)

hormone a chemical made in one part of the body that is released into the blood, that is carried through the bloodstream, and that causes a change in another part of the body; controls growth and development and many other body functions (77, 112, 242)

immune system a combination of the physical and chemical defenses that your body has to fight infection; the tissues, organs, and cells that fight pathogens (446)

independence the state of being free of the control of others and relying on one's own judgment and abilities (250)

indoor air pollution air pollution inside a building (539)

infancy the stage of development between birth and 1 year of age (232)

infectious disease (in FEK shuhs di ZEES) any disease that is caused by an agent or pathogen that invades the body (432)

influence a force that makes a person choose one way over another when having a decision to make (28)

inhalant (in HAYL uhnt) any drug that is inhaled and that is absorbed into the bloodstream through the lungs (415)

inhibition a mental or psychological process that restrains actions, emotions, and thoughts (378)

interest something that one enjoys and wants to know more about (36)

intervention (IN tuhr VEN shuhn) a gathering in which people who are close to a drug abuser try to get the abuser to accept help by relating stories of how his or her drug problem has affected them (421)

intimidation the act of frightening others by using threatening words and body language (299)

intoxication the physical and mental changes produced by drinking alcohol (374)

joint a place where two or more bones meet in the body (117)

Ketamine (KEET uh MEEN) a powerful drug that is closely related to the hallucinogen PCP (417)

life skills tools that help you deal with situations that can affect your health (14)

lifestyle a set of behaviors by which you live your life (12)

lungs large, spongelike organs in which oxygen and carbon dioxide pass between the blood and the air (131)

malignant (muh LIG nuhnt) describes tumors that are cancerous and that can be life threatening (466)

marijuana (MAR uh WAH nuh) the dried flowers and leaves of the *Cannabis* plant (410)

maximum heart rate (MHR) the largest number of times one's heart can beat during exercise (151)

media all public forms of communication, such as TV, radio, newspapers, the Internet, and advertisements (272)

mediation a process in which a third party, called a *mediator,* becomes involved in a conflict, listens to both sides of the conflict, and then offers solutions to the conflict (296)

medicine a drug that is used to cure, prevent, or treat pain, disease, or illness (398)

menstruation (MEN STRAY shuhn) the monthly breakdown and shedding of the lining of the uterus during which blood and tissue leave the woman's body through the vagina (223)

mental health the way that people think about and respond to events in their lives (76)

mental illness a disorder that affects a person's thoughts, emotions, and behaviors (90)

metabolism (muh TAB uh LIZ uhm) the process by which the body converts the energy in food into energy that the body can use (192, 462)

mineral an element that is essential for good health (194)

modeling changing one's behavior based on how others act (357)

mood disorder an illness in which people have uncontrollable mood changes (92)

muscle any tissue that is made of cells or fibers that contract and expand to cause movement (119)

muscular endurance (MUHS kyoo luhr en DOOR uhns) the ability to use a group of muscles over and over without getting tired easily (143)

muscular strength (MUHS kyoo luhr STRENGKTH) the amount of force that muscles apply when they are used (142)

muscular system the body system made of the skeletal muscles that move the body (119)

negotiation (ni GOH shee AY shuhn) discussion of a conflict to reach an agreement (294)

nerve a bundle of cells that conducts electrical signals from one part of the body to another (110)

nervous system the body system that gathers and interprets information about the body's internal and external environments and that responds to that information (108)

nicotine a highly addictive drug that is found in all tobacco products (338)

nicotine replacement therapy (NRT) a form of medicine that contains safe amounts of nicotine (354)

noninfectious disease a disease that is not caused by a pathogen (456)

nurturing (NUHR chuhr ing) providing the care and other basic things that people need in order to grow (268)

nutrient a substance in food that the body needs in order to work properly (122, 189, 534)

Nutrition Facts label a label that is found on the outside packages of food and that states the number of servings in the container, the number of Calories in each serving, and the amount of nutrients in each serving (198)

opiate (OH pee it) any drug that is produced from the milk of the opium poppy (412)

organ two or more tissues that work together to perform a special function (106)

over-the-counter (OTC) medicine any medicine that can be bought without a prescription (399)

overcommitment the condition of committing too much time to one or more activities (178)

overtraining a condition caused by too much exercise (180)

overuse injury an injury that happens because of too much exercise, poor form, or the wrong equipment (180)

ovum the female sex cell (222)

paranoia (PAR uh NOY uh) the belief that other people want to harm someone (93)

peer a person who is about the same age as you are and with whom you interact every day (251)

peer mediation mediation in which the mediator is of similar age to the people in the conflict (297)

peer pressure a feeling that you should do something because your friends want you to (29, 356)

persistence the commitment to keep working toward a goal even when things make a person want to quit (39)

pesticide (PES tuh SIED) a chemical used to kill pests (537)

physical dependence a state in which the body chemically needs a drug in order to function normally (349, 386, 403)

physical fitness the ability to perform daily physical activities without becoming short of breath, sore, or overly tired (142)

placenta an organ that grows in a woman's uterus during pregnancy, provides nutrients and oxygen to a fetus, and removes waste from a fetus (227)

plan any detailed program, created ahead of time, for doing something (66)

poison something that causes illness or death on contact or if swallowed or inhaled (470)

pollution a change in the air, water, or soil that harms living things (531)

population a group of organisms living in an area at one time (546)

positive self-talk thinking about the good parts of a bad situation (87)

positive stress stress response that makes a person feel good; the stress response that happens when a person wins, succeeds, and achieves (53)

precaution a step that one takes to avoid negative consequences (32)

pregnancy the time when a woman carries a developing fetus in her uterus (226)

prescription medicine (pree SKRIP shuhn) a medicine that can be bought only with a written order from a doctor (398)

preventive healthcare taking steps to prevent illness and accidents before they happen (13)

primary care provider a doctor who handles general care (518)

prioritize (prie AWR uh TIEZ) to arrange items in order of importance (68)

protein (PROH TEEN) a nutrient that supplies the body with energy for building and repairing tissues and cells (193)

psychiatrist (sie KIE uh trist) a medical doctor who specializes in how illnesses of the brain and body are related to emotions and behavior (99)

psychological dependence (SIE kuh LAHJ i kuhl) the state of emotionally or mentally needing a drug in order to function (350, 387, 403)

psychologist (sie KAHL uh jist) a professional who tries to change a person's thoughts, feelings, and actions by finding reasons behind them or suggesting ways to manage emotions (99)

puberty (PYOO buhr tee) the period of time during adolescence when the reproductive system becomes mature (233, 242)

public health the practice of protecting and improving the health of the people in a community (542)

reaction time the amount of time that passes from the instant when the brain detects an external stimulus until the moment a person responds (380)

reframing looking at a situation from another point of view and changing one's emotional response to the situation (63)

refusal skill a strategy to avoid doing something that you don't want to do (15, 44)

rehabilitation the process of regaining strength, endurance, and flexibility while recovering from an injury (159)

relapse to begin using a drug again after you have stopped it for a while (352)

relationship an emotional or social connection between two or more people (262)

resource something that can be used to meet a need or achieve a goal (540)

respiratory system the body system that brings oxygen into the body and removes carbon dioxide from the body (131)

responsibility the act of accepting the consequences of one's decisions and actions (250)

risk factor a characteristic or behavior that increases a person's chances of injury, disease, or other health problem (457)

self-esteem a measure of how much you value, respect, and feel confident about yourself (34, 86, 201)

setback something that goes wrong (41)

sexual abstinence (SEK shoo uhl AB stuh nuhns) the refusal to take part in sexual activity (280)

sexually transmitted disease (STD) any of a number of infections that are spread from one person to another by sexual contact (440)

shock the body's response to reduced blood flow (497)

sibling rivalry competition between siblings (304)

side effect any effect that is caused by a drug and that is different from the drug's intended effect (400)

skeletal system the body system made of bones, cartilage, and the special structures that connect them (116)

specialist a person who has received training in a specific medical field (518)

sperm the sex cell made by males (218)

spinal cord a bundle of nervous tissue that is about a foot and a half long and that is surrounded by the backbone; carries messages to and from the brain (110)

sportsmanship the ability to treat all players, officials, and fans fairly during competition (172)

stimulant (STIM yoo luhnt) any drug that increases the body's activity (406)

stress the combination of a new or possibly threatening situation and the body's natural response to the situation (52)

stress management the ability to handle stress in healthy ways (62)

stress response a set of physical changes that prepare your body to act in response to a stressor; the body's response to a stressor (56)

stressor anything that triggers a stress response (52)

success the achievement of one's goals (38)

suicidal thinking thinking about wanting to take one's own life (95)

support system a group of people, such as friends and family, who will stand by you and encourage you when times get hard (45)

tar a gooey chemical that can coat the airways and that can cause cancer (338)

target heart rate zone a heart rate range that should be reached during exercise to gain cardiorespiratory health benefits; 60 to 85 percent of one's maximum heart rate (151)

teen hotline a phone number that teens can call to talk privately and anonymously about their problems (98)

testes the male reproductive organs that make sperm and the hormone testosterone (218)

THC tetrahydrocannabinol, the active substance in marijuana (410)

threat any serious warning that a person intends to cause harm (320)

time management the ability to make appropriate choices about how to use one's time (68)

tissue a group of similar cells that work together to perform a single function (106)

tolerance (TAHL uhr uhns) the ability to overlook differences and to accept people for who they are (267, 376); a condition in which a person needs more of a drug to feel the original effects of the drug (349)

toxin a poison produced by a living organism (470)

traumatic injury an injury caused by physical force (472)

treatment center a facility where trained doctors and counselors help drug abusers with their problems (422)

trigger a person, situation, or event that influences emotions (80)

tumor a mass of abnormal cells (466)

unhealthy relationship a relationship with a person who hurts you or who encourages you to do things that go against your values (277)

urinary system a group of organs that remove liquid wastes from the blood (125)

urine the liquid waste that is made of excess water and wastes removed from the blood by the kidneys and that is released from the body through the urethra (126)

uterus a muscular organ that has thick walls and that holds a fetus during pregnancy (222)

vaccine a substance that is used to make a person immune to a certain disease (451)

values beliefs that one considers to be of great importance (25)

vein a blood vessel that carries blood toward the heart (130)

violence physical force that is used to harm people or damage property (308, 484)

virus a tiny, disease-causing particle that consists of genetic material and a protein coat and that invades a healthy cell and instructs that cell to make more viruses (435)

vitamin an organic compound that controls many body functions and that is needed in small amounts to maintain health and allow growth (194)

weapon an object or device that can be used to hurt someone (486)

wellness a state of good health that is achieved by balancing physical, emotional, mental, and social health (7)

withdrawal uncomfortable physical and psychological symptoms produced when a person who is physically dependent on drugs stops using drugs (350)

Spanish Glossary

abdominal thrusts/empuje abdominal acción de aplicar presión al estómago de una persona atragantada para lograr que un objeto salga por la garganta (498)

abstinence/abstinencia decisión de no participar en una actividad que ponga en riesgo la salud propia o la de otros; especialmente la decisión de no participar en actividades sexuales (440)

abstract thought/pensamiento abstracto pensamiento que va más allá de temas que se pueden ver o experimentar (246)

abuse/abuso tratamiento dañino u ofensivo de una persona hacia otra (326)

accident/accidente acontecimiento inesperado que puede provocar lesión o muerte (472, 480)

action plan/plan de acción mapa que describe los pasos para alcanzar una meta (38)

active listening/escuchar activamente acción de escuchar y demostrar que comprendes lo que una persona intenta comunicar (43, 83, 263)

active rest/descanso activo forma de recuperarse del ejercicio reduciendo la cantidad de actividad que realizas (162)

acute injury/lesión aguda lesión que se produce de manera repentina (158)

adolescence/adolescencia etapa del desarrollo en la que los seres humanos pasan de la infancia a la edad adulta (233)

adulthood/edad adulta período de la vida que sigue a la adolescencia y termina con la muerte (233)

aerobic exercise/ejercicio aeróbico ejercicio que se realiza durante un período de tiempo prolongado y utiliza el oxígeno para obtener energía (176)

aggression/agresión toda acción o conducta hostil o amenazante hacia otra persona (308)

AIDS/SIDA síndrome de inmunodeficiencia adquirida, enfermedad producida por la infección del VIH que hace que una persona infectada tenga más posibilidades de contraer formas poco comunes de cáncer e infecciones debido a que el VIH ataca al sistema inmunológico del (442)

alcohol poisoning/intoxicación por consumo de alcohol se produce al beber demasiado alcohol; sobredosis que puede causar la muerte (374)

alcoholism/alcoholismo enfermedad ocasionada por la adicción al alcohol; dependencia física y psicológico al alcohol (386)

allergy/alergia reacción del sistema inmunológico del cuerpo ante una sustancia inofensiva (464)

anaerobic exercise/ejercicio anaeróbico ejercicio que no utiliza el oxígeno para obtener energía y que se realiza durante un período de tiempo corto (176)

anorexia nervosa/anorexia nerviosa trastorno alimenticio en el que la persona deja de comer, tiene una percepción enferma de su cuerpo y sufre una pérdida de peso extrema (206)

antibiotic/antibiótico droga que mata a las bacterias o demora su crecimiento (434)

anxiety disorder/trastorno de ansiedad enfermedad que ocasiona nerviosismo, preocupación o pánico (91)

artery/arteria vaso sanguíneo que transporta la sangre desde el corazón (130)

assess/evaluar medir los logros propios a corto plazo para alcanzar una meta a largo plazo (40)

attitude/actitud forma particular de actuar, pensar o sentir de una persona (12)

autoimmune disease/enfermedad autoinmune enfermedad en la que el sistema inmunológico ataca a las células del cuerpo que normalmente protege (464)

bacteria/bacteria organismos unicelulares extremadamente pequeños que no tienen núcleo; microorganismos de una sola célula que se encuentran en todas partes (434)

behavior/conducta la forma en la que una persona decide reaccionar o actuar (264)

benign/benigno describe a un tumor que no es canceroso y que no suele poner en peligro la vida (466)

bias/parcialidad desviación que cambia la presentación de la información (513)

binge eating disorder/trastorno alimenticio compulsivo trastorno alimenticio en el que una persona tiene dificultad para controlar cuánto come (208)

bioaccumulation/bioacumulación proceso en el que se acumulan agentes contaminantes en animales que comen alimentos contaminados (538)

biopsy/biopsia muestra de tejido que se extrae del paciente y se envía a un especialista para verificar la presencia de células cancerosas (468)

birth/nacimiento paso del bebé de la matriz de la madre hacia el exterior de su cuerpo (230)

blood/sangre tejido formado por células, líquidos, y otras sustancias que transportan oxígeno, dióxido de carbono, y nutrientes en el cuerpo (129)

blood alcohol concentration (BAC)/ concentración de alcohol en la sangre (CAS) porcentaje de alcohol en la sangre de una persona (372)

body composition/composición corporal proporción del peso corporal formada por tejido de grasa en comparación con el tejido magro (145)

body image/imagen corporal forma en que piensas en ti mismo y en tu cuerpo (200)

body language/lenguaje corporal forma de comunicarse utilizando expresiones de la cara, gestos con la mano y la postura del cuerpo (83, 263, 292)

body mass index (BMI)/índice de masa corporal (IMC) medición que se utiliza para determinar el peso aproximado de una persona sana (210)

body system/sistema corporal grupo de órganos que trabajan juntos para cumplir una función específica en el cuerpo (106)

bone/hueso órgano vivo del sistema esquelético formado por células óseas, tejidos conectivos y minerales (116)

brain/cerebro órgano principal del sistema nervioso; masa de tejido nervioso que se encuentra dentro del cráneo (109)

bulimia nervosa/bulimia nerviosa
trastorno alimenticio en el que una persona come una gran cantidad de alimentos y luego intenta eliminar la comida del cuerpo (207)

bully/gandalla persona que con frecuencia molesta o golpea a personas más pequeñas o débiles (299)

Calorie/Caloría unidad que se utiliza para medir la cantidad de energía que el cuerpo obtiene de los alimentos (192)

cancer/cáncer enfermedad caracterizada por el crecimiento anormal de las células (344, 466)

carbohydrate/carbohidratos sustancia química compuesta por uno o más azúcares simples; incluye azúcares, féculas y fibras (193)

carbon monoxide/monóxido de carbono gas presente en el humo del cigarrillo que dificulta la llegada del oxígeno al cuerpo (338)

carcinogen/carcinógeno toda sustancia química o agente que causa cáncer (467)

cardiopulmonary resuscitation (CPR)/resucitación cardiopulmonar (RCP) técnica para salvar la vida que combina la recuperación de la respiración y compresiones en el pecho (500)

cardiorespiratory endurance/resistencia cardiorrespiratoria capacidad del corazón y los pulmones para trabajar de manera eficiente durante la actividad física (143)

cell/célula unidad más simple y básica de todos los elementos vivientes (106)

central nervous system (CNS)/sistema nervioso central (SNC) el cerebro y la médula espinal (371)

cessation/cese acción de detener algo de forma completa y permanente (353)

cheating/trampa intentar ganar rompiendo las reglas (172)

childhood/niñez etapa del desarrollo entre la infancia y la adolescencia (232)

chronic bronchitis/bronquitis crónica enfermedad en la que el interior de las vías respiratorias se hincha y se irrita en gran medida (345)

chronic effect/efecto crónico consecuencia que permanece en una persona durante un largo período de tiempo (340)

chronic injury/lesión crónica lesión que se desarrolla durante un largo período de tiempo (158)

circulatory system/sistema circulatorio sistema del cuerpo formado por el corazón, los vasos sanguíneos y la sangre (128)

cirrhosis/cirrosis enfermedad mortal que reemplaza los tejidos sanos del hígado por tejidos cicatrizados inservibles; en la mayoría de los casos está causada por el abuso de alcohol durante un largo período de tiempo (376)

clique/camarilla grupo de personas que aceptan sólo ciertos tipos de gente y excluyen a otros (251)

collaboration/colaboración solución a un problema en el que ambas partes obtienen lo que desean sin tener que renunciar a nada importante (295)

communication skills/habilidades de comunicación métodos para expresar los pensamientos propios y escuchar lo que otros dicen (42)

comparison shopping/comparación de precios proceso de consultar varios productos similares para determinar qué oferta es más conveniente (511)

competition/competencia enfrentamiento entre dos o más personas o equipos (171)

compromise/convenio solución a un problema en el que ambas partes renuncian a ciertas cosas para lograr un acuerdo (295)

conditioning/preparación ejercicio que mejora el estado físico para realizar deportes (174)

conflict/conflicto toda situación en la que las ideas o los intereses se enfrentan (288)

consequence/consecuencia resultado de las acciones y las decisiones de una persona (32)

conservation/conservación protección y el uso correcto de los recursos (540)

coping/sobrellevar manejar los problemas y los inconvenientes de manera eficaz (41)

counselor/consejero profesional que ayuda a las personas a sobrellevar problemas difíciles hablando de ellos (99)

crosstraining/entrenamiento cruzado haciendo tipos de ejercicios diferentes durante preparación (175)

dating/cita salida social con alguien que te resulta atractivo (278)

defense mechanism/mecanismo de defensa conducta automática que se mantiene durante un período de tiempo corto para sobrellevar dificultades (60, 88)

dehydration/deshidratación estado en el que la cantidad de agua que el cuerpo ha perdido es mayor a la que se ha ingerido (533)

depressant/depresivo droga que disminuye la velocidad del funcionamiento del cuerpo y el cerebro (371, 408)

depression/depresión tristeza y desesperanza que impiden a una persona realizar las actividades diarias (94)

designer drug/droga de diseño droga producida mediante un pequeño cambio químico a una droga que ya existe (416)

detoxification/desintoxicación proceso mediante el cual el organismo elimina sustancias químicas dañinas (422)

diet/dieta plan de alimentos que incluye lo que una persona come, cuánto come y cada cuánto come (190)

Dietary Guidelines for Americans/Guía alimenticia para los Estadounidenses conjunto de sugerencias diseñado para ayudar a las personas a crear hábitos alimenticios sanos y aumentar los niveles de actividad física (196)

digestion/digestión proceso de descomponer los alimentos de manera que el cuerpo pueda utilizarlos (122, 189)

digestive system/aparato digestivo grupo de órganos y glándulas que trabajan juntos para digerir la comida (122)

disease/enfermedad todo cambio dañino en el estado de salud del cuerpo o la mente (456)

dislocation/dislocación lesión en la que un hueso sale de su posición normal en una articulación (496)

distress/alteración toda respuesta nerviosa que hace que una persona no logre alcanzar una meta o se enferme; tensión física, mental o emocional negativa que se manifiesta como respuesta a un factor estresante (53)

drug/droga toda sustancia química que provoca un cambio en el estado físico o psicológico de una persona (396)

drug addiction/drogadicción estado en el que una persona ya no puede controlar el consumo de una droga (349, 402)

eating disorder/trastorno alimenticio enfermedad en la que una persona se preocupa de manera negativa por su silueta y su peso corporal (205)

ecosystem/ecosistema comunidad de seres vivos y los elementos no vivientes de su entorno (530)

Ecstasy/éxtasis nombre que habitualmente se le da al químico MDMA (metilendioximetanfetamina) (416)

elective class/clase optativa clase que puedes tomar pero que no es obligatoria (252)

embryo/embrión ser humano en desarrollo, desde el momento de la fecundación hasta la octava semana del embarazo (226)

emotion/abuso emocional uso repetido de acciones y palabras que implican que una persona no tiene valor ni poder (64, 76)

emotional abuse/salud emocional forma en la que una persona experimenta y maneja los sentimientos (327)

emotional health/intimidad emocional condición de estar emocionalmente relacionado con otra persona (76)

emotional spectrum/emoción sentimiento que surge en respuesta a experiencias de la vida (78)

empathy/empatía compartir y entender los sentimientos de otra persona (266)

emphysema/enfisema enfermedad respiratoria en la que el oxígeno y el dióxido de carbono no se pueden desplazar fácilmente a través de los alvéolos dado que éstos se afinaron, se distendieron o se han destruido (345)

endocrine system/sistema endocrino red de tejidos y órganos que liberan sustancias químicas que controlan ciertas funciones corporales (112)

environment/medio ambiente todos los seres vivos y elementos sin vida que rodean a una persona (9, 530)

environmental tobacco smoke (ETS)/ humo de tabaco ambiental(HTA) mezcla del humo exhalado por los fumadores y el humo de los cigarrillos al consumirse (341)

epinephrine/epinefrina hormona de estrés que aumenta el nivel de azúcar en la sangre y dirige la respuesta "luchar o huir" (56)

exercise/ejercicio toda actividad física que mantiene o mejora el estado físico (146)

extracurricular activities/actividades extracurriculares actividades que realizas y que no son parte de las tareas escolares (252)

fad diet/dieta de moda dieta que permite bajar de peso rápidamente con poco esfuerzo (211)

fatigue/fatiga agotamiento físico o mental; sensación de mucho cansancio (58)

fats/grasas nutriente que almacena energía y permite al cuerpo almacenar algunas vitaminas (193)

fetal alcohol syndrome (FAS)/síndrome de alcohol fetal (SAF) grupo de defectos de nacimiento que afectan a un bebé que estuvo expuesto al alcohol durante la gestación (377)

fetus/feto ser humano en desarrollo en el útero de la madre, desde el inicio de la novena semana de embarazo hasta el nacimiento (226)

first aid/primeros auxilios atención médica de emergencia para una persona que se lastimó o está enferma (490)

flashback/retroceso incidente en el que los efectos de un alucinógeno se repiten mucho tiempo después de haber tomado la droga (415)

flexibility/flexibilidad capacidad de doblar y girar las articulaciones con facilidad (144)

Food and Drug Administration/ Administración de alimentos y medicamentos organismo gubernamental que controla la seguridad de los alimentos y las drogas en Estados Unidos (401)

Food Guide Pyramid/Pirámide alimenticia herramienta para escoger qué tipos de alimentos se deben comer y qué cantidad de cada alimento se debe comer cada día (197)

fracture/fractura fisura o rotura de un hueso (496)

gang/pandilla grupo de personas que suelen utilizar la violencia (485)

GHB/GHB droga elaborada a partir de la GBL anestésica, ingrediente común en pesticidas (417)

gland/glándula tejido o grupo de tejidos que elaboran y liberan sustancias químicas; por ejemplo, las hormonas (113)

goal/meta algo por lo que una persona se esfuerza y que espera alcanzar (34)

good decision/buena decisión decisión que toma una persona luego de analizar sus consecuencias detenidamente (24)

grief/duelo sentimiento de profunda tristeza por una pérdida (235)

hallucinogen/alucinógeno toda droga que produce alucinaciones en una persona (414)

hangover/resaca efectos físicos molestos provocados por el consumo de alcohol, incluyendo dolor de cabeza, mareos, malestar estomacal, náuseas y vómitos (374)

harassment/acoso broma, comentario, contacto o comportamiento repetido e indeseado; el acoso suele afectar la capacidad de una persona para realizar las tareas escolares o vivir su propia vida (330)

health/salud condición de bienestar físico, emocional, mental y social (4)

health insurance/seguro de salud póliza que se compra y que cubre ciertos costos en caso de enfermedad o lesión (523)

healthcare consumer/consumidor de servicios de salud toda persona que paga para recibir productos y servicios del cuidado de la salud (508)

healthy weight range/rango de peso saludable cálculo del peso que debería tener una persona según su altura y su estructura corporal (210)

hereditary disease/enfermedad hereditaria enfermedad causada por cromosomas anormales o por genes defectuosos que un niño hereda de uno o ambos padres (460)

heredity/herencia transmisión de rasgos de padres a hijos (8)

HIV/VIH virus de inmunodeficiencia humana, un virus que ataca al sistema inmunológico del ser humano y causa el SIDA (442)

hormone/hormona sustancia química elaborada en una parte del cuerpo que se libera dentro de la sangre, se transporta a través del torrente sanguíneo y produce un cambio en otra parte del cuerpo; controla el crecimiento y el desarrollo y muchas otras funciones del cuerpo (77, 112, 242)

immune system/sistema inmunológico combinación de las defensas físicas y químicas que el cuerpo posee para combatir infecciones; los tejidos, los órganos y las células que combaten a los agentes patógenos (446)

independence/independencia estado de no estar sometido al control de otros y confiar en el criterio y la habilidades propias (250)

indoor air pollution/contaminación del aire interior contaminación del aire dentro de un edificio (539)

infancy/infancia etapa del desarrollo entre el nacimiento y el primer año de edad (232)

infectious disease/enfermedad infecciosa toda enfermedad causada por un agente o un patógeno que invade el cuerpo (432)

influence/influencia fuerza que hace que una persona tome una decisión en lugar de otra al tener que realizar una elección (28)

inhalant/inhalantes drogas que se inhalan en forma de vapor y se absorben en el torrente sanguíneo a través de los pulmones (415)

inhibition/inhibición proceso mental y psicológico que restringe acciones, emociones y pensamientos (378)

interest/interés algo que uno disfruta y desea conocer mejor (36)

intervention/intervención reunión en la que las personas cercanas a un consumidor de drogas tratan de convencer al enfermo de que acepte ayuda mediante el relato de historias sobre cómo el problema de la droga afectó sus vidas (421)

intimidation/intimidación acción de asustar a otros con palabras y lenguaje corporal amenazantes (299)

intoxication/intoxicación cambios físicos y mentales producidos por beber alcohol (374)

joint/articulación parte del cuerpo en la que dos o más huesos se encuentran (117)

Ketamine/quetamina droga potente que está estrechamente asociada al alucinógeno PCP (fenciclidina) (417)

life skills/destrezas para la vida herramientas que te ayudan a manejarse en situaciones que pueden afectar tu salud (14)

lifestyle/estilo de vida conjunto de conductas que marcan tu forma de vivir (12)

lungs/pulmones órganos grandes con aspecto de esponja en los que se produce el intercambio de oxígeno y dióxido de carbono entre el aire y la sangre (131)

malignant/maligno describe tumores que son cancerosos y que pueden poner en riesgo la vida (466)

marijuana/marihuana flores y hojas secas de la planta *Cannabis* (410)

maximum heart rate (MHR)/índice cardíaco máximo (ICM) el mayor número de veces que el corazón de una persona puede latir durante la actividad física (151)

media/medios de comunicación todas las formas públicas de comunicación; por ejemplo, televisión, radio, periódicos, Internet y avisos publicitarios (272)

mediation/mediación proceso en el que un tercero, llamado mediador, participa en un conflicto, escucha a ambas partes y, luego, ofrece soluciones al conflicto (296)

medicine/medicamento toda droga utilizada para curar, prevenir o tratar enfermedades o molestias (398)

menstruation/menstruación proceso mensual de desprendimiento del recubrimiento interior de la matriz durante el que la sangre y los tejidos salen del cuerpo de la mujer a través de la vagina (223)

mental health/salud mental forma en la que una persona piensa y responde a hechos de su vida (76)

mental illness/enfermedad mental trastorno que afecta los pensamientos, las emociones y la conducta de una persona (90)

metabolism/metabolismo proceso de convertir la energía de los alimentos en energía que el cuerpo puede utilizar (192, 462)

mineral/mineral elemento esencial para una buena salud (194)

modeling/modelar cambiar la forma de comportarse según la conducta de los demás (357)

mood disorder/trastorno anímico enfermedad en la que las personas cambian incontrolablemente de estado de ánimo (92)

muscle/músculo todo tejido formado por células o fibras que se contrae y se estira para permitir el movimiento (119)

muscular endurance/resistencia muscular capacidad de utilizar un grupo de músculos durante un tiempo prolongado sin cansarse fácilmente (143)

muscular strength/fuerza muscular cantidad de fuerza empleada por los músculos al utilizarlos (142)

muscular system/sistema muscular sistema del cuerpo formado por los músculos esqueléticos que mueven el cuerpo (119)

negotiation/negociación debate sobre un conflicto para llegar a un acuerdo (294)

nerve/nervio conjunto de células nerviosas (neuronas) que transmiten señales eléctricas desde una parte del cuerpo a otra (110)

nervous system/sistema nervioso sistema del cuerpo que reúne e interpreta la información acerca de los entornos internos y externos del cuerpo y responde a esa información (108)

nicotine/nicotina droga altamente adictiva que se encuentra en todos los productos con tabaco (338)

nicotine replacement therapy (NRT)/ terapia de reemplazo de nicotina (TRN) tratamiento con medicamentos que contienen cantidades seguras de nicotina (354)

noninfectious disease/enfermedad no infecciosa enfermedad que no es causada por un agente patógeno (456)

nurturing/nutrir proporcionar los cuidados y otros elementos básicos que las personas necesitan para crecer (268)

nutrient/nutriente sustancia en los alimentos que el cuerpo necesita para funcionar correctamente (122, 189, 534)

Nutrition Facts label/etiqueta de Valores nutricionales etiqueta que se encuentra en el exterior de los envases de alimentos y en la que se informa el número de porciones que incluye el envase, el número de calorías que contiene cada porción y la cantidad de nutrientes que aporta cada porción (198)

opiate/opiáceo toda droga que se produce a partir de la leche de la adormidera de amapola (412)

organ/órgano dos o más tejidos que trabajan juntos para llevar a cabo una función especial (106)

over-the-counter (OTC) medicine/ medicamentos de venta sin receta (VSR) todo medicamento que se puede comprar sin receta médica (399)

overcommitment/compromiso excesivo condición en la que una persona compromete demasiado tiempo para hacer una o más actividades (178)

overtraining/sobreentrenamiento condición causada por el exceso de ejercicio (180)

overuse injury/lesión por uso excesivo lesión que se produce por exceso de ejercicio, falta de condición física o por el uso incorrecto del equipo (180)

ovum/óvulo célula sexual femenina (222)

paranoia/paranoia la creencia de que otras personas quieren dañar a alguien (93)

peer/par persona de aproximadamente la misma edad que tú y con quien te relacionas todo los días (251)

peer mediation/mediación de pares mediación en la que el mediador tiene una edad similar a la de las personas involucradas en el conflicto (297)

peer pressure/presión de pares sensación de que debes hacer algo que tus amigos quieren que hagas (29, 356)

persistence/persistencia compromiso a seguir trabajando para alcanzar una meta aun cuando las situaciones hacen que se quiera renunciar (39)

pesticide/pesticida sustancia química que se utiliza para matar plagas (537)

physical dependence/dependencia física condición en la que el cuerpo depende de una droga determinada para funcionar (349, 386, 403)

physical fitness/buen estado físico capacidad de realizar actividades físicas todos los días sin sentir falta de aire, dolor o cansancio extremos (142)

placenta/placenta órgano que crece en la matriz de una mujer durante el embarazo, proporciona nutrientes y oxígeno al feto y elimina sus desechos (227)

plan/plan todo programa detallado, diseñado previamente, para hacer algo (66)

poison/veneno algo que causa enfermedad o muerte al tocarlo, tragarlo o inhalarlo (470)

pollution/contaminación cambio en el aire, el agua o la tierra que daña a los seres vivos (531)

population/población grupo de organismos que viven en una misma zona y una misma época (546)

positive self-talk/lenguaje interno positivo pensar sobre los aspectos buenos de una situación mala (87)

positive stress/estrés positivo respuesta de estrés que hace que una persona se sienta bien; respuesta de estrés que se produce cuando una persona experimenta triunfos y logros (53)

precaution/precaución medida que se toma para evitar consecuencias negativas (32)

pregnancy/embarazo período durante el cual una mujer lleva a un feto en desarrollo dentro de la matriz (226)

prescription medicine/medicamento recetado medicamento que se puede comprar sólo con una orden escrita del médico (398)

preventive healthcare/cuidado preventivo de la salud medidas para prevenir enfermedades y accidentes antes de que ocurran (13)

primary care provider/proveedor de cabecera médico que se encarga de los cuidados generales (518)

prioritize/dar prioridad disponer elementos por orden de importancia (68)

protein/proteína nutriente que suministra energía al cuerpo para construir y reparar tejidos y células (193)

psychiatrist/psiquiatra médico que se especializa en estudiar cómo s e relacionan las enfermedades del cerebro y el cuerpo con las emociones y la conducta (99)

psychological dependence/dependencia psicológica estado de necesidad mental o emocional de una droga para poder funcionar (350, 387, 403)

psychologist/psicólogo profesional que intenta cambiar los pensamientos, los sentimientos y las acciones de una persona mediante el descubrimiento de los motivos que los generan o la sugerencia de formas para controlar las emociones (99)

puberty/pubertad período de tiempo durante la adolescencia en el que se produce la maduración del aparato reproductor (233, 242)

public health/salud pública práctica de proteger y mejorar la salud de las personas en una comunidad (542)

R

reaction time/tiempo de reacción cantidad de tiempo que transcurre desde el instante en el que el cerebro detecta un estímulo externo hasta el momento de respuesta de la persona (380)

reframing/reenfocar analizar una situación desde otro punto de vista y cambiar la respuesta emocional a esa situación (63)

refusal skill/habilidad de negación estrategia para evitar hacer algo que no quieres hacer (15, 44)

rehabilitation/rehabilitación proceso de recuperación de fuerza, resistencia y flexibilidad mientras se repone de una lesión (159)

relapse/recaída comenzar a usar una droga nuevamente después de haberlo interrumpido durante un tiempo (352)

relationship/relación conexión emocional o social entre dos o más personas (262)

resource/recurso algo que se puede utilizar para satisfacer una necesidad o alcanzar una meta (540)

respiratory system/aparato respiratorio aparato del cuerpo que absorbe oxígeno y elimina dióxido de carbono (131)

responsibility/responsabilidad acción de aceptar las consecuencias de las decisiones y las acciones propias (250)

risk factor/factor de riesgo característica o conducta que aumenta la posibilidades de lesión, enfermedad u otro problema de salud de una persona (457)

S

self-esteem/autoestima medición de cuánto se valora, respeta y cuánta confianza en sí misma tiene una persona (34, 86, 201)

setback/contratiempo algo que sale mal (41)

sexual abstinence/abstinencia sexual negación de participar en actividades sexuales (280)

sexually transmitted disease (STD)/ enfermedad de transmisión sexual (ETS) cualquiera de un número de infecciones que se transmiten de una persona a otra a través del contacto sexual (440)

shock/choque condición en la que algunos órganos del cuerpo no obtienen suficiente sangre oxigenada (497)

sibling rivalry/ rivalidad entre hermanos competencia entre hermanos (304)

side effect/efecto secundario todo efecto producido por una droga que es diferente al efecto intencional de la droga (400)

skeletal system/sistema óseo sistema del cuerpo formado por huesos, cartílagos y estructuras especiales que los conectan (116)

specialist/especialista persona que recibió capacitación en un campo específico de la medicina (518)

sperm/espermatozoide célula sexual elaborada por los hombres (218)

spinal cord/médula espinal acumulación de tejido nervioso que mide aproximadamente un pie y medio de largo y está rodeado por la columna vertebral; transmite mensajes hacia y desde el cerebro (110)

sportsmanship/actitud deportiva capacidad de tratar a todos los jugadores, funcionarios y espectadores de manera justa durante una competencia (172)

stimulant/estimulante toda droga que aumente la actividad del cuerpo (406)

stress/estrés combinación de una situación nueva o posiblemente amenazante y la respuesta natural del cuerpo a esa situación (52)

stress management/control del estrés capacidad de manejar el estrés de forma sana (62)

stress response/respuesta de estrés conjunto de cambios físicos que preparan el cuerpo para actuar en respuesta a un factor estresante; respuesta del cuerpo a un factor estresante (56)

stressor factor/estresante cualquier factor que origine una respuesta de estrés (52)

success/éxito logro de las metas propuestas (38)

suicidal thinking/pensamiento suicida pensamiento sobre el deseo de quitarse la vida (95)

support system/sistema de apoyo grupo de personas; por ejemplo, amigos y familiares, que estarán a tu lado y te apoyarán en momentos difíciles (45)

tar/alquitrán sustancia química pegajosa que puede cubrir las vías respiratorias y causar cáncer (338)

target heart rate zone/zona de índice cardíaco objetivo rango de índice cardíaco que se debe alcanzar durante el ejercicio para obtener los beneficios de salud cardiorrespiratoria; 60 a 85 por ciento del índice cardíaco máximo (151)

teen hotline/línea de ayuda para adolescentes número de teléfono al que los adolescentes pueden comunicarse para hablar en privado y de forma anónima sobre sus problemas (98)

testes/testículos órganos reproductores masculinos que producen espermatozoides y la hormona testosterona (218)

THC/THC tetrahidrocanabinol, sustancia activa en la marihuana (410)

threat/amenaza toda advertencia grave que una persona hace para ocasionar un daño (320)

time management/administración del tiempo capacidad de tomar decisiones adecuadas sobre cómo utilizar el tiempo (68)

tissue/tejido grupo de células similares que trabajan juntas para cumplir una única función (106)

tolerance/tolerancia capacidad de aceptar a las personas por lo que son a pesar de las diferencias (267, 376); condición en la que una persona necesita más cantidad de una droga para sentir sus efectos originales (349)

toxin/toxina veneno producido por un organismo vivo (470)

traumatic injury/lesión traumática lesión ocasionada por la fuerza física (472)

treatment center/centro de tratamiento institución en la que médicos capacitados y consejeros ayudan a personas con problemas de abuso de drogas (422)

trigger/disparador persona, situación o acontecimiento que afecta a las emociones (80)

tumor/tumor masa de células anormales (466)

unhealthy relationship/relación perjudicial relación con una persona que fomenta acciones que van en contra de sus valores (277)

urinary system/sistema urinario grupo de órganos que elimina desechos líquidos de la sangre (125)

urine/orina desecho líquido formado por el exceso de agua y desechos que los riñones eliminan de la sangre, que sale del cuerpo a través de la uretra (126)

uterus/matriz órgano muscular de paredes gruesas que contiene al feto durante el embarazo (222)

vaccine/vacuna sustancia que generalmente se prepara a partir de patógenos débiles o sin vida o material genético y se introduce en un cuerpo para proporcionar inmunidad (451)

values/valores creencias que uno considera de mucha importancia (25)

vein/vena vaso sanguíneo que transporta la sangre hacia el corazón (130)

violence/violencia fuerza física que se utiliza para dañar a una persona o una propiedad (308, 484)

virus/virus partícula pequeña, capaz de causar enfermedades, formada por material genético y un revestimiento de proteína que invade a una célula sana y le indica que produzca más virus (435)

vitamin/vitamina compuesto orgánico que controla muchas funciones del cuerpo y que es necesario en pequeñas cantidades para mantener la salud y permitir el crecimiento (194)

weapon/arma objeto o elemento que se puede utilizar para lastimar a alguien (486)

wellness/bienestar estado de buena salud que se logra mediante el equilibrio de la salud física, emocional, mental y social (7)

withdrawal/supresión síntomas psicológicos y físicos molestos que se producen cuando una persona que tiene dependencia a una droga deja de consumirla (350)

Index

Note: Page references followed by *f* refer to figures. Page references followed by *t* refer to tables. Boldface page references refer to the main discussion of the term.

911 calls, 492

ABCs for health, 196, 196*t*
abdominal thrust, for choking victims, 498–499, 498*f*, 499*f*
abstinence, sexual, 280–281, 281*t*, 442
abstract thought, 246
abuse, 326–329
   alcohol abuse, 376, 387*t*
   alcohol and physical abuse, 379
   definitions and examples, 327*t*
   drug, 402
   effects of, 327
   getting help for, 328, 328*f*
   reporting, 329
acceptance, by peers, 249
accidents, 472–473
   deaths from, 473
   diseases caused by, 472
   helmets and, 163, 456, 458, 473
   at home, 480
Achilles' tendon, 144
acid, 414*t*.
acne, 114*t*, 244, 245
acquired immune deficiency syndrome (AIDS), 444–447, 446*f*, 447*f*, 448. *See also* **HIV; STDs**
action plans, 38, 38*t*
active listening, 43, 83, 263, 293

active rest, 162
acute injury, 158–159, 159*t*
Adam (MDMA), 416, 416*f*. *See also* **Ecstasy**
addiction
   alcohol, 386–389
   dependence, 349, 386, 402
   drug, 402–405, 407, 412–413
   tobacco, 349–350, 352
   treatment for drug, 420–423
adolescence, 233
adolescent growth and development, 241–257
   attraction to others, 249
   behavior development, 247, 247*f*
   belonging and acceptance, 249
   hormones in, 242, 242*f*
   independence, 250
   individual differences, 243, 243*f*
   interests, 252
   mental ability development, 246
   mood swings, 92*f*, 248
   peer groups and cliques, 251
   physical changes in boys, 244, 244*f*
   physical changes in girls, 245, 245*f*
   planning for your future, 255
   responsibility, 250, 303
adoptive families, 268, 268*f*. *See also* **families**
adrenal glands, 113–114, 113*f*, 114*t*, 242*f*
adrenaline, 56–57
adrenaline rush, 112
adulthood, 233
advertising
   alcohol, 383, 383*f*
   evaluating, 15
   healthcare products, 11, 509

   influences on decisions, 30–31, 272
   tobacco, 357–358
aerobic activity, 143, 176
affectionate behavior, 279
afterbirth, 230. *See also* **labor; placenta**
aggression, 308–311. *See also* **violence**
   avoiding and preventing violence, 311
   body language, 264
   bullying, 299, 308
   controlling anger, 310
   definition, 308
   violence from, 309
agility, 176
aging, 234
AIDS (acquired immune deficiency syndrome), 444–447, 446*f*, 447*f*, 448. *See also* **HIV; STDs**
air, 532
air bags, 488–489, 488*f*, 489*f*
air pollution, 470–471, 532, **536,** 539, 547
alcohol, 370–389
   alcohol abuse, 376, 387*t*
   blood alcohol concentration, 372, 372*t*
   in the body, 371, 371*f*, 373
   driving, injury, and harm, 375, 380–381
   factors in alcoholism, 388
   immediate effects of, 372*t*, 374–375
   individual reactions to, 373
   long-term damage from, 376, 376*f*
   misconceptions, 372, 387
   physical dependence on, 386
   during pregnancy, 227, 227*f*, 377, 377*f*
   pressures to drink, 382–383
   psychological dependence on, 387

recovery from alcoholism, 389
risk behaviors, 377
social decisions and, 378
tolerance of, 376, 386
types of alcoholic beverages, 370
violence and, 379
warning signs, 387t
alcoholism, 386–389, 387t
allergens, 464
allergies, 464–465
asthma from, 133t
description of, 457t, 464, 464f
to drugs, 400, 400f
immune response, 464
treatment, 465
alveoli, 132–133
Alzheimer's disease, 234, 457t
anaerobic exercise, 176
anemia, 131t, 134
angel dust, 414t. See also **PCP**
anger, 81t, 309–310
anorexia nervosa, 206, 206f. See also **eating disorders**
antibodies, 436, 436f
anxiety disorders, 91, 101
appendicitis, 124t
art, expressing emotions through, 84, 262
arteries, 130f
artery disease, 58f
arthritis, 118t, 234
Asian Food Guide Pyramid, 555, 555f
aspirin, 399f
assertion, as defense mechanism, 88t, 331
assertive behavior, 264
asthma, 9, 133t, 457, 457t, 471
athletic trainers, 568
attitudes, healthy, 12
attraction to others, 249
authorities, 513
autoimmune disease, 464–465

automobile safety, 488–489, 488f, 489f

babies
baby-sitting safety, 566–567
birth, 230, 231t
CPR for, 501f
first aid for choking, 499f
hereditary disease tests, 461
infancy, 232
prenatal development, 228–229, 228–229f
baby-sitting safety, 566–567
BAC (blood alcohol concentration), 372, 372t
back injuries, 497
backpacks, organized, 253, 253f
bacteria, 430t, 432
balance, 176
barbiturates, 408
basal cell carcinoma (BCC), 467
B cells, 436, 436f
bee stings, 470t
Beethoven, Ludwig von, 92
behavior
affectionate, 279
definition, 264
development in adolescence, 247, 247f
eating, 204, 204t
risk, 247, 247f, 377, 483
types of, 264
belonging, 249, 485
benign tumors, 466
bias, in information, 513
biceps, 120, 120f
bidis, 339. See also **tobacco**
binge eating disorder, 208. See also **eating disorders**
bingeing, 207
bioaccumulation, 538

bipolar mood disorder (BMD), 92, 92f, 93
birth, 230, 231t
blackout, drug-induced, 409
bladder, 125f
bladder cancer, 344
bleeding, first aid for, 494
blended families, 268, 268f. See also **families**
blood, 107t, **128–131,** 129f, 131t, 346
blood alcohol concentration (BAC), 372, 372t
blood transfusions, HIV in, 445
blood vessel constriction, 346
blotter, 414t
BMD (bipolar mood disorder), 92, 92f
BMI (body mass index), 153, 153t, 210, **559,** 559t
body care, 221, 225
body composition, 145, 153
body fat, 145, 208
body image, 200–203
building a healthy, 203, 203t
definition, 200
influences on, 202
self-esteem and, 201, 201f
body language
aggressive, 309
communicating clearly, 42
during conflict, 292–293
emotions, 79, 83
saying no, 44
understanding, 263
body mass index (BMI), 153, 153t, 210, **559,** 559t
body organization, 105–135
body systems, 106–107, 106f, 107f, 134
brain, 109, 109f
cells, 106, 106f
circulatory system, 107t, 128–130, 131t

digestive system, 107t, 122–124, 124t
endocrine system, 107t, 112–115, 113f, 115t
muscular system, 107t, 119–121, 119f, 121t
nervous system, 107t, 108–111
organs, 106, 106f
respiratory system, 107t, 131–133, 133t
skeletal systems, 107t, 116–118, 116f, 118t
systems, 106–107, 107t
tissues, 106, 106f
body systems, 106–107, 106f, 107t, 134. See also **body organization**
body temperature, 137
bones, 116–118, 116f, 118t
botulism, 558t
boys' bodies, 218–221
physical changes during puberty, 233
reproductive systems, 218–221, 218f, 219f, 220t
brain, 109, 109f
activity during emotions, 76f
effects of alcohol on, 376
problems and diseases, 111t
stress effects, 58t
brain damage
from drugs, 407, 407f, 415, 416f
from not wearing helmets, 456
from traumatic injuries, 472
brainstem, 109f
breast cancer, 460, 467f
breasts, 244, 245
breathing, 107t, 131–133, 131f
breathing, rescue, 500–501, 500f, 501f
breathing masks, 491

breech birth, 231t
broken bones, 118t, 159, 159t, 496
bronchi, 131f
bronchitis, 133t
chronic, 345
bubonic plague, 431
bulimia nervosa, 207, 207f
bullying, 299, 308
burns, 495
buttons, 414t

cactus, 414t
Caesarean section, 230
caffeine, 406, 406f, 407
calcium, 194, 194t
Calories, 192, 193f, 198f, 534, 556–557t
cancer, 466–469
bladder, 344
breast, 460, 467f
cervical, 224t, 443t, 467f
common types of, 467, 467f
description of, 234, 457t, 466, 466f
diagnosis and treatment, 459, 468
kidney, 344
lung, 344, 344f, 467, 467f (see also **lung cancer**)
mouth, 344
of pancreas, 344
prevention, 469
skin, 467, 467f, 469, 536
stomach, 124t
testicular, 220t, 467f
throat, 344
from tobacco, 341, 344
warning signs, 468
Cannabis, 410–411, 410f
capillaries, 130f
carbohydrates, 193
carbon dioxide, 532, 536t
carbon monoxide, 338, 340, 340f, 536t

cardiac muscle, 119f
cardiopulmonary resuscitation (CPR), 500–501, 500f, 501f
cardiorespiratory endurance, 143, 152
cardiovascular disease, 346, 346f
cardiovascular endurance, 152
careers in health, 568–569
carpeting out, 417
carriers, 442
cartilage, 116f
cause and effect, 458
cells, 106
Centers for Disease Control and Prevention (CDC), 544
central nervous system (CNS), 110, 110f, 371
cerebellum, 109f
cerebral palsy, 111t, 134
cerebrum, 109f
certified athletic trainers, 568
cervical cancer, 224t, 443t, 467f
cessation, 353
CF (cystic fibrosis), 8, 461
character, 25, 265, 275
cheating, 26, 172
chemotherapy, 468
chest compressions, 500–501, 500f, 501f
chewing tobacco, 339, 341, 341f. See also **tobacco**
childbirth, 230, 231t
childhood development, 232
child safety seats, 488–489, 488f, 489f
chlamydia, 442, 443t
choking, 498–499, 498f, 499f
cholera, 431, 545
chromosomes, 460f
chronic bronchitis, 345
chronic effects, 340
chronic illnesses, 388
chronic injury, 158–159, 159t

Churchill, Winston, 92
cigarettes. *See also* **tobacco**
    advertising, 357–358
    cardiovascular disease, 346, 346*f*
    chemicals in smoke, 338
    contact lenses and, 342
    deaths caused by, 345*f*, 346, 347*f*
    early effects of, 340, 340*f*
    internal pressures to start smoking, 359
    lung cancer from, 344, 344*f*, 345*f*, 457, 467*f*
    marijuana and, 411
    nicotine, 338, 341, 348, 348*f*, 354
    psychological dependence, 350
    quitting, 349*f*, 350, 352–355
    reasons people start smoking, 356, 356*f*
    refusal skills, 45, 265
    social and emotional health effects of, 343, 363
    tolerance and dependence, 349
circulatory system, 58*t*, 107*t*, 128–131, 131*t*
circulatory system diseases, 457*t*
cirrhosis of the liver, 376, 376*f*
Clean Water Act, 549
Clear Air Act, 544
cliques, 251
clothing, for exercise, 162
CNS (central nervous system), 110, 110*f*, 371
cocaine, 406–407, 407*f*
cola drinks, caffeine in, 406, 406*f*
colds, 347, 440
collaboration, 295
colon cancer, 124*t*, 460, 467*f*
combination therapy, 446
commitment, 280

communication, 42–43. *See also* **listening**
    anger control through, 310
    body language, 42, 44, 83, 263, 292–293
    during conflict, 290–293, 309
    recognizing emotions, 79
    refusal skills, 44–45, 247, 265, 360, 419
    telling people about violence, 324
    through behavior, 264
community health, 542–545
community healthcare organizations, 520
comparison shopping, 511
competitions, 171, 175
compromise, 295
compulsions, 91
computer posture, 564
concussions, 111*t*
conditioning, 174–177
    for competition, 175
    definition, 174
    listening to your body, 177
    overtraining, 180
    sports skills, 176
conflicts, 288–311
    aggression and, 308
    avoiding, 289, 311
    body language, 292–293
    bullying, 299, 308
    communication during, 290–293, 309
    compromise and collaboration, 295
    conflict cycle, 290, 290*f*, 307
    controlling anger, 310
    cultural, 300
    definition, 288
    at home, 302–305
    listening, 293
    major sources, 288
    mediation, 296–297
    negotiation, 294
    with neighbors, 306

    peer mediation, 297, 335
    scaling down, 320, 320*t*
    at school, 298–301
    signs of, 289
    teasing, 298, 330–331
    violence and, 308–311 (*see also* **violence**)
consequences, 32
conservation, 540–541
constipation, 124*t*
Consumer Product Safety Commission (CPSC), 517
consumer protection, 517
contagious diseases, 430, 438–439, 448–449. *See also* **infectious diseases**
Contract for Life, 393
coordination, 176
coping
    changing goals, 41
    definition, 15
    with family problems, 271
    with harassment, 330–331
    with loss, 235
    with threats of violence, 319, 320
    with violence, 322–325
counselors, 99, 325, 421
Cowper's glands, 219
cowpox, 449*f*
CPR (cardiopulmonary resuscitation), 500–501, 500*f*, 501*f*
CPSC (Consumer Product Safety Commission), 517
crack cocaine, 406–407
creative expression, 84, 262
crosstraining, 175
crushes, 249, 278
crystal meth, 407
C-section, 230
cultural conflicts, 300, 307
cuts, first aid for bleeding from, 494
Cuyahoga River (Ohio) fire, 549
cystic fibrosis (CF), 8, 461

D

Daily Values, 198f
date-rape drugs, 417
dating, 278–281
DDT, 549
death and grieving, 234–235, 235t
deaths
  caused by tobacco, 345f, 346, 347f
  leading causes in children, 472f
decisions, 24–45
  choosing healthcare products and services, 509–511
  definition, 24
  effect of alcohol on making, 371, 378–379
  evaluating influences, 31
  family influences, 28
  goal-setting, 34
  good, 14, 24–25
  healthy dietary choices, 196–199
  media messages, 30
  not to drink, 384–385
  not to smoke, 45, 265, 360, 360f
  not to use drugs, 418–419
  peer pressure, 29
  refusal skills and, 44–45, 247, 265, 360, 419
  sexual abstinence and, 281, 281t
  six steps of decision making, 26–27, 26–27f
  weighing consequences of, 32
defective products, returning, 516–517, 517f
defense mechanisms, 60–61, 60f, 88, 88t
dehydration, 195, 533
delusions, 92
dengue fever, 548f
denial, as defense mechanism, 60, 60f, 88

dependence, drug, 349, 386, 402. *See also* **physical dependence; psychological dependence**
depressants, 371, 408–409, 408t
depression, 59, 92, **94–95,** 94f
dermatologists, 518t
detoxification, 422
devaluation, 88t
diabetes, 115t, 231t, 459
diaphragm, 132, 132f
diarrhea, 124t
diazepam (Valium), 408t
diet. *See also* **food; nutrition**
  alternate Food Guide Pyramids, 555, 555f
  Calories, 192, 193f, 198f, 534
  definition, 190
  eating disorders, 204–209
  fad diets, 211
  feelings and, 191
  Food Guide Pyramid, 197, 197f, 554, 554f
  influences on food choices, 190, 190f
  serving sizes, 197, 198, 198f, 199, 199f
  unhealthy eating behaviors, 204, 204t
  vegetarian, 555, 555f
Dietary Guidelines for Americans, 196, 196t
digestion, 123–124, 123f, 124t, 189
digestive system, 58t, 107, 122–124, 124t, 446f
disaster kits, 561
disasters, 562–563
diseases
  caused by injuries, 472
  from contaminated food, 558t
  definition, 456
  hereditary, 460–461
  infectious, 429–451 (*see also* **infectious diseases**)
  infectious vs. contagious, 430
  metabolic, 462–463
  noninfectious, 455–475 (*see also* **noninfectious diseases**)
  pollution and, 431, 545, 548
  signs and symptoms, 456
  smoking-related, 347
  types of infection, 430t
dislocations, 118t, 496
displacement, 60
dissociation, drug-induced, 417
distress, 53
DNA, 466
doctors, 518, 518t, 522–523
Down syndrome, 460–461
drinking water, 533, 533f
drugs, 396–423. *See also* **medicine**
  abuse, 402
  addiction, 402–405
  allergies to, 400, 400f
  combination therapy, 446
  costs of drug abuse, 405, 405f
  date-rape, 417
  definition, 396
  depressants, 408–409, 408t
  Ecstasy, 416, 416f
  FDA approval process, 401, 401f
  flashback, 415
  GHB, 417, 417f
  hallucinogens, 414–415, 414t
  how they enter the body, 396–397, 397f
  inhalants, 415
  interactions, 399
  intervention, 421
  Ketamine, 417
  marijuana, 410–411, 410f
  opiates, 412–413, 412f
  prescription medicine, 398, 398f, 522

recovery, 423, 423f
side effects, 400, 400f
staying drug free, 418–419
stimulants, 406–407
tolerance, 400
treatment for addiction, 420–423
withdrawal symptoms, 403
drug treatment programs, 420–423
drunk driving, 380–381, 393
dust, 414t. See also **PCP**

eagles, banning of DDT and, 549
earthquakes, 562
eating disorders, 204–209
anorexia nervosa, 206, 206f
binge eating disorder, 208
bulimia nervosa, 207, 207f
definition, 205
getting help, 209, 209t
giving help, 208, 209t
overexercising and, 205
signs, 208
unhealthy eating behaviors, 204, 204t
EBV (Epstein-Barr virus), 441
ecosystems, 530–531
Ecstasy (MDMA), 416, 416f
ectopic pregnancy, 231t
eczema, 464f, 465
eggs, 222, 223, 223f, 226f
elective classes, 252
electrical shock, 480, 496
embryo, 226, 228, 228f
emergency calls, 492
emergency kits, 561
emergency medical technicians (EMTs), 569
emotional abuse, 327t
emotional health, 76
emotions, 75–99
alcohol and, 371, 372t, 374
brain activity during, 76, 76f
communicating, 83, 87
as conflict sources, 288–289
creative expression and, 84
defense mechanisms and, 60–61, 88
definition, 64, 76
emotional spectrum, 78, 78f
food and, 191
friendship and, 249
getting help, 96, 97f
grief, 235, 235t
healthy expression of, 82
importance of sharing, 64
knowing your triggers, 80
mood swings, 92f, 248
physical responses to, 81, 81t
positive self-talk, 87
recognizing, 79
self-esteem and, 86
smoking and, 343
teasing and, 298, 330
teens and, 77
unhealthy expression of, 85
empathy, 266
emphysema, 133t, 344, 345, 411, 471
EMTs (emergency medical technicians), 569
Endangered Species Act, 549
endocrine system, 107t, 112–115, 115t, 242, 242f
endometriosis, 224t
endometrium, 223
endorphins, 149
endurance, 143, 152
energy use, 547, 547f
environment, 530–549
air, 532
air pollution, 470–471, 532, 536, 539
conservation, 540–541
dependence on, 530
disease and, 548, 548f
drinking water, 533, 533f
food, 534, 534f
food and pollution, 538
food inspection, 544
healthy ecosystems, 531
homes, 535
indoor air pollution, 539
noise pollution, 539
recycling, 540, 543
scientific discoveries, 545
success stories, 549
water pollution, 533, 537, 545
environmental tobacco smoke (ETS), 341, 344, 346, 361
EPA (Environmental Protection Agency), 543
epidemics, 431. See also **infectious diseases**
epididymis, 218, 219, 219f
epilepsy, 111t
epinephrine, 114t
Epstein-Barr virus (EBV), 441
Escherichia coli (*E. coli*), 558t
estrogen, 114t, 222, 242f
ethanol, 370
ETS (environmental tobacco smoke), 341, 344, 346, 361
euphoria, 407
eustress, 53
excretion, 125–127, 125f, 127t
exercise, 141–163. See also **physical fitness**
active rest, 162
aerobic and anaerobic, 143, 176
anger control through, 310
Calories burned during, 165
clothing for, 162
conditioning skills, 174–177
cool down, 160
eating well and, 147
fitness level, 146, 146f
health and, 135

listening to your body and, 177
mental and emotional benefits of, 86, 89, 149
overexercising, 205
overload, 146, 175
overuse injuries, 180–181
pace, 161
Physical Activity Pyramid, 560, 560f
physical benefits of, 148
safety equipment, 163
social benefits of, 149, 163
specificity of, 156, 175
stretching, 160
taking breaks from, 162
using good form, 161
warm up, 160
warning signs of injury, 158

extended families, 268, 268f. See also **families**
extending muscles, 120
extracurricular activities, 252
eye color, 460
eye diseases, 347

fallopian tubes, 222–223, 222f, 223f, 231t
families
of alcoholics, 389
changes in, 270
conflicts between parents, 305
conflicts within, 302–305
coping with problems in, 271
drug addiction and, 404
as influences on decisions, 28
as influences on relationships, 273
roles within, 269
smokers in, 341, 357
structures of, 268, 268f
teaching about health in, 10

family evacuation plans, 481
Fantasy, 417, 417f
fat
body, 145, 244, 245
dietary, 193, 193f
fatigue, from stress, 58
FDA (Food and Drug Administration), 401, 401f, 544f
fear, 64, 81t
Federal Emergency Management Association (FEMA), 521
Federal Trade Commission (FTC), 517
female bodies, 222–225
body care, 225
changes during pregnancy, 227
menstruation, 223, 223f
ovulation, 223, 223f
physical changes during puberty, 233, 245, 245f
reproductive system, 222–225, 222f, 223f, 224t
reproductive system problems, 224, 224t
fermentation, 370
fertilization, 226, 226f
fetal alcohol syndrome, 227, 227f, 377, 377f
fetus, 226, 228–229, 228–229f
"fight-or-flight" response, 56–57, 59, 112
fire extinguishers, 481
fire safety, 480–481
first aid, 494–497
bleeding, 494
burns, 495
calling for help, 492
certification in, 493
choking, 498–499, 498f, 499f
CPR, 500–501, 500f, 501f
electrocution, 496
fractures and dislocations, 496

head and back injuries, 497
identifying what's wrong, 490
kits, 491, 561
medical alert jewelry, 490f
poisoning, 495
protecting yourself, 491
RICE, 159
shock, 497
first-aid kits, 491, 561
FIT, 156, 161
fitness
cardiorespiratory endurance, 143, 152
exercise and, 146, 146f
FIT, 156
fitness logs, 157
goals for, 154–155
healthy fitness zones, 152t
heart rate monitoring, 151
muscular endurance, 143
muscular strength, 142
Physical Activity Pyramid, 560, 560f
sports and, 183
fitness logs, 157
flashbacks, 415
Fleming, Alexander, 432, 432f
flexibility, 144, 152
flexing muscles, 120
floods, 562
flu, 347, 441
follicle-stimulating hormone (FSH), 223, 242f
food. See also **diet; nutrition**
Calorie and Nutrient Content tables, 556–557t
Calorie needs from, 534
digestion of, 123–124, 123f, 124t, 189
in the environment, 534
feelings and, 191
inspections, 544
Nutrition Facts labels, 198, 198f
pollution and, 538
safety, 544, 544f, 558, 558t

serving size vs. portion, 199
as sources of vitamins and minerals, 194t
Food and Drug Administration (FDA), 401, 401f, 517, 544f
Food Guide Pyramids, 197, 197f, 554, 554f, 555f
food inspection, 544
fossil fuels, 547
fractures, 118t, 159t, 496
Freon, 415
friends. *See also* **relationships**
belonging and acceptance, 249, 485
communicating with, 262–264
drug addiction and, 404
health and, 6, 276
making new, 275
peer groups and cliques, 251
peer pressure, 29, 249, 251, 273, 343
self-esteem and, 274
social skills, 262–265
sports and exercise, 149, 173
unhealthy relationships and, 277
who are victims of violence, 325
FSH (follicle-stimulating hormone), 223, 242f
FTC (Federal Trade Commission), 517
fungus, 430t

G

Gamma-oh (GHB), 417, 417f
gangs, 485
gasoline, pollution from, 536
genes, 219, 460, 460f
genital herpes, 443t
Georgia Home Boy (GHB), 417, 417f
gestational diabetes, 231t

gestures, in different cultures, 292
GHB, 417, 417f
gigantism, 115t
girls' bodies, 222–225
body care, 225
changes during pregnancy, 227
menstruation, 223, 223f
ovulation, 223, 223f
physical changes during puberty, 233, 245, 245f
reproductive system, 222–225, 222f, 223f, 224t
reproductive system problems, 224, 224t
glands, 77, 113, 113f
glaucoma, 194
goals, 34–37
action plans, 38, 38t
assessing progress in, 40
changes in, 41
definition, 34
help from others, 37
interests, 36
long-term, 35
setbacks, 39
short-term, 35
success in achieving, 38
values, 36
gonorrhea, 443t
good decisions, 24–25, 26
government healthcare agencies, 521
grief, 235, 235t
group dating, 278
group pressure, violence and, 309, 318
growth. *See also* **adolescent growth and development**
hair growth, 244, 245
hormones, 114t, 242, 242f
individual differences in, 243, 243f
patterns of, 243
physical changes in boys, 244, 244f

physical changes in girls, 245, 245f
puberty, 233, 244–245, 244f, 245f
guns, 486–487
gunshot wounds, 487

H

hair growth during puberty, 244, 245
hairs, germ defense and, 435
hallucinations, 92, 99
hallucinogens, 91, 99, 414–415, 414t
hangovers, 374
happiness, physical responses to, 81t
harassment, 330–331
head injuries, 456, 472, 497
health
assessment of, 7, 7f, 14
emotional part of, 5
environmental influences on, 9
friendship and, 6, 276
government action and, 544
heredity and, 8
improving, 17
influence of relationships on, 10
life skills and, 14–15
media influences on, 11
mental part of, 5
nutrition and, 188
physical part of, 4
public, 542–545
scientific discoveries in, 545
social part of, 6
staying healthy, 134–135
taking control of your, 12–13
healthcare consumers, 507–525
accessing services, 522–523

choosing healthcare products and services, 508–511, 511t
community healthcare organizations, 520
consumer protection, 517
defective products, 516–517, 517f
evaluating healthcare claims, 514
government agencies, 521
having an influence on healthcare, 516
healthcare news and information, 512–515
hospitals and clinics, 519
medical specialists, 518, 518t
patient's rights and responsibilities, 13, 523
paying for healthcare, 523
preventive healthcare, 13
volunteering, 515
healthcare professionals, 518, 518t, 522–523
health insurance, 523
healthy fitness zones, 152t
healthy weight ranges, 210
heart, 128, 128f, 130
heart attacks, 131t. *See also* **heart disease**
heartburn, 124t
heart disease, 58f, 234, 345, 345f, 346. *See also* **heart attacks**
heart rate, 143, 151
Heimlich maneuvers, 498–499, 498f, 499f
helmet laws, 482
helmets, 163, 456, 458, 473
hemoglobin, 129, 129f
hemophilia, 131t
hemorrhoids, 124t
hemp, 411
herbal supplements, 401
hereditary diseases, 460–461
heredity, 8
hernia, 121t
heroin, 413

herpes, 443t
high blood pressure, 131t, 346
HIV (human immunodeficiency virus), **444–447**
AIDS epidemic, 447, 447f
combination therapy, 446
effects of AIDS on the body, 446, 446f
medications for, 433, 446
origin of, 445, 445f
spread of, 413, 445, 448
virus characteristics, 444, 444f
homework, 254
honesty, 275
hormones
adrenaline, 56, 112
definition, 112, 242
emotions and, 77
estrogen, 114, 114t, 222, 242f
FSH, 223, 242f
functions of, 114t
human growth hormone, 114t, 242f
number in body, 243
during pregnancy, 227
progesterone, 114t, 242f
testosterone, 114t, 118t, 218, 242, 242f
thyroxine, 114t, 242f
hospitals, 519
hotlines, 98
HPV (human papillomavirus), 224t, 443t
human growth hormone, 114t, 242f
human immunodeficiency virus (HIV), **444–447**
AIDS epidemic, 447, 447f
combination therapy, 446
effects of AIDS on the body, 446, 446f
medications for, 433, 448
origin of, 445, 445f
spread of, 413, 445, 448
virus characteristics, 444, 444f

human life cycle, 217–237
adolescence, 233
adulthood, 233
aging, 234
birth, 230, 231t
childhood development, 232
death and grieving, 234–235, 235t
female reproductive system, 222–225, 222f, 223f, 224t
fertilization, 226, 226f
male reproductive system, 218, 218f
pregnancy, 226–231
human papillomavirus (HPV), 224t, 443t
humerus, 144f
humor, as defense mechanism, 88t
hurricanes, 562
hydrocarbons, 536t
hygiene, 4
hypertension, 131t
hyperthyroidism, 115t
hypnotics, 408, 408t, 409
hypothyroidism, 115t

immune system, 434–437
allergies, 464
front-line defenses, 435, 435f
internal defenses, 436, 436f
keeping it strong, 437
stress and, 58t
immunity, 436
implantation, 226
incubation period, 444, 446
independence, 250
indigestion, 124t
indoor pollution, 539
infancy, 232. *See also* **babies**
infatuation, 249

Index | 603

INDEX

infectious diseases, 430–449
  antibiotics, 432, 432f
  bacterial infections, 430t, 432, 438–439
  body's defense system, 434–437, 435f, 436f
  definition, 430
  HIV and AIDS, 444–447, 444f, 445f, 446f, 447f
  how infections spread, 431, 431f
  immune response, 436
  opportunistic infections, 446
  protecting others, 449
  protecting yourself against, 448–449, 448t
  sexually transmitted diseases, 220t, 224t, 442–443, 442f, 443t
  sinus infections, 439
  types of infection, 430–433, 430t
  vaccinations, 441, 449
  viruses, 430t, 433, 433f, 440–441
influenza A/B, 347, 441
inguinal hernia, 121t, 220t
inhalants, 415
inherited diseases, 461
inhibition, 378
injuries
  computer posture, 564
  crosstraining and, 175
  diseases caused by, 472
  head and back, 497
  overuse, 180–181
  preventing, 160–163, 177, 458, 473
  RICE, 159
  warning signs of, 158
inpatient care, 519
insect stings, 470t
insulin, 114t
insurance, 523
interests, 36
Internet safety, 565
intervention, 421
intestines, 122–123, 123f

intimidation, 299
intoxication, 372t, 374
iron, dietary, 194, 194t
"I" statements, 203, 203t, 291

Jenner, Edward, 449f
jock itch, 220t
jogging, 143, 165
joints, 117, 117f, 120, 144

Ketamine, 417
kidney failure, 134
kidneys, 125f
Kit Kat, 417

labor, 230
laughing gas, 415
laughter, 63, 67, 88
lead, 471
leadership, 170
leukemia, 131t, 467f, 468
life expectancy, 234
life skills, 14–16. See also specific life skills
lifestyle, 12
ligaments, 117, 144
Liquid X (GHB), 417, 417f
listening. See also communication
  active, 43, 83, 263
  during conflict, 293, 293t
  to your body, 177
Lister, Joseph, 435
liver, cirrhosis of the, 376, 376f
lockers, organization of, 253, 253f
long-term goals, 35
love, 81t, 249
loyalty, 275
LSD, 414t

lung cancer
  cancerous lung, 344f
  description, 133t
  rate of spread of, 467
  risk factors for, 457, 467f
  from smoking, 344, 344f, 345f, 457, 467f
lungs, 131–133, 340f, 344f, 446f
lymphoma, 467f

macrophages, 436, 436f
MADD (Mothers Against Drunk Driving), 381
magnesium, 194
major depressive disorder (MDD), 94
male body, 218–221
  physical changes during puberty, 233, 244, 244f
  reproductive system, 218–221, 218f, 219f, 220t
malignant tumors, 466
malnutrition, 463
mania, 92
manic depression, 92
marijuana, 410–411, 410f
marrow, 116f
maximum heart rate (MHR), 151
MDD (major depressive disorder), 94
MDMA (Ecstasy), 416, 416f
meat inspection, 544f
media messages
  alcohol use, 383, 383f
  evaluating, 15
  healthcare products, 11, 509
  influences on decisions, 30–31, 272
  smoking, 357–358
mediation, 296–297, 335
medical alert jewelry, 490
medical social workers, 568
medical specialists, 518, 518t

medicine, 396–401. *See also* **drugs**
  antibiotics, 432, 432f
  combination therapy, 446
  definition, 398
  depressants, 408, 408t
  drug interactions, 399
  FDA approval process, 401, 401f
  labels, 398, 398f
  opiates, 413
  over-the-counter, 399, 399f
  prescription, 398, 398f, 522
  safety, 401
  side effects and allergies to, 400, 400f
  stimulants, 406–407
Mediterranean Food Guide Pyramid, 555, 555f
melanoma, 467
meningitis, 111t
menstrual cycle, 223, 223f
menstruation, 223, 223f, 245
mental health, definition, 76. *See also* **emotions**
mental illness. *See also* **depression**
  anxiety disorders, 91, 101
  bipolar mood disorder, 92, 92f, 93
  definition, 90
  finding help for others, 97, 97f
  hallucinogens and, 91
  preventing further problems, 97
  professional help, 99
  schizophrenia, 93
  when to get help, 96
mescaline, 414t
metabolic diseases, 462–463
metabolism, 192, 373, 462
methamphetamine, 406–407, 416
methanol, 370
MHR (maximum heart rate), 151
microorganisms, 430, 430t
minerals, 194, 194t

miscarriage, 231t
modeling, 357
mononucleosis, 441
mood disorders, 92
mood swings, 92f, 248
morning sickness, 227
morphine, 413
Mothers Against Drunk Driving (MADD), 381
mouth cancer, 344
mucus, germ defense and, 435
muscles, 119–120. *See also* **muscular system**
  cardiac, 119
  cramps, 121t
  endurance, 143, 152
  fast-twitch and slow-twitch, 176
  soreness, 158, 177
  strength, 142, 152
muscular dystrophy, 121t, 457t
muscular endurance, 143, 152
muscular strength, 142, 152
muscular system, 107t, 119–121, 119f, 121t
mushrooms, magic, 414t
mycobacteria, 439

National Institutes of Health (NIH), 521, 544
negative peer pressure, 29, 249, 251, 273
negative thinking, 87
neglect, 327t, 328
negotiation, 294
neighbors, conflict with, 306
nervous system, 111
  brain, 108
  central nervous system, 110, 110f, 371
  effects of AIDS on, 446f
  function of, 107t
  nerve impulses, 108, 109, 110
  nerves, 110

  peripheral nervous system, 110
  problems of, 111t
neurogenic bladder, 127t
nicotine, 338, 341, **348,** 348f
nicotine replacement therapy (NRT), 354
night blindness, 194
NIH (National Institutes of Health), 521, 544
nitrogen oxides, 536t
nitrous oxide, 415
"no," learning to say, 44–45, 360, 419. *See also* **refusal skills**
noise pollution, 539
noninfectious diseases, 456–473
  allergies, 464–465, 464f
  autoimmune, 464–465
  cancer, 466–469 (*see also* **cancer**)
  chemicals and poisons, 470–471, 470t
  definition, 456
  examples of, 457t
  hereditary, 460–461
  metabolic, 462–463
  preventing, 458
  risk factors, 457
  treatment of, 459
nonverbal communication, 42, 44. *See also* **communication**
norepinephrine, 114t
NRT (nicotine replacement therapy), 354. *See also* **nicotine**
nuclear families, 268, 268f. *See also* **families**
nurses, 568
nurturing, 268–269
nutrients, 192–195
  absorption of, 122, 124
  carbohydrates, 193
  content in common foods, 556–557t
  definition, 189, 534
  fats, 193

INDEX

how the body uses, 192
minerals, 194, 194t
proteins, 193
six classes of essential, 192
vitamins, 194, 194t
water, 195
nutrition, 188–211. *See also* **diet; food**
ABCs for health, 196
Calorie and Nutrient Content tables, 556–557t
Calorie needs, 534
Dietary Guidelines for Americans, 196, 196t
exercise and, 147
feelings and, 191
Food Guide Pyramid, 197, 197f, 554, 554f, 555f
health and, 188
importance of, 135
nutritional diseases, 462–463
Nutrition Facts label, 198, 198f
during pregnancy, 227
Nutrition Facts label, 198, 198f

obesity, 208, 458, 463. *See also* **weight**
obsessive-compulsive disorder (OCD), 91
Occupational Safety and Health Administration (OSHA), 544
opiates, 412–413, 412f
opium, 412, 412f
opportunistic infections, 446. *See also* **infectious diseases**
optometrists, 518t
organization, 253
organs, definition, 106
orthopedic surgeons, 518t
OSHA (Occupational Safety and Health Administration), 544
osteoarthritis, 118t

osteomyelitis, 118t
osteoporosis, 118t
outpatient care, 519
ova (singular, *ovum*), 222–223, 223f, 226f
ovarian cancer, 224t
ovaries, 113–114, 113f, 222–223, 222f, 242f
overactive bladder, 127t
overcommitment, 178–179
overdose, 400
overload, exercise, 146, 175
over-the-counter medicine, 399, 399f
overtraining, 180
overuse injuries, 180–181
ovulation, 223, 223f
ovum (plural, *ova*), 222, 223, 223f, 226f
oxygen deprivation, 231t
ozone, 414t. *See also* **PCP**
ozone layer, 536, 544, 549

pancreas, 113–114, 113f, 114t
cancer of, 344
panic attacks, 91
paralysis, 111t
paranoia, 93
parasites, 430t
parathyroid glands, 113, 113f
parents. *See also* **families**
conflicts between, 305
conflicts with, 303
smoking by, 341, 357
teen parents, 280
passive behavior, 264
PCP, 414t, 417
peer groups and cliques, 251
peer mediation, 297, 335
peer pressure
alcohol use, 383
health and, 10
positive and negative, 29, 249, 251, 273
sexual abstinence and, 281, 281t
starting smoking and, 356, 356f, 360, 360f, 362

for violence, 309
penicillin, 432, 432f
penis, 218f
period, menstrual, 223, 223f, 245
peripheral nervous system (PNS), 110, 110f. *See also* **body systems**
persistence, 39
personal responsibility, 24, 250, 265, 303
pesticides, pollution from, 537
peyote, 414t
pharmacists, 518t
pharynx, 131f
phenylketonuria (PKU), 461, 462–463
phobias, 91
phosphorus, 194
Physical Activity Pyramid, 560, 560f
physical dependence, 349, 402–403
physical fitness, 142–163. *See also* **exercise**
body composition, 145, 153
cardiorespiratory endurance, 143, 152
definition, 142
exercise and, 146, 146f
FIT, 156
fitness logs, 157
flexibility, 144, 152
goals for, 154–155
healthy fitness zones, 152t
heart rate monitoring, 151
muscular endurance, 143
muscular strength, 142
overtraining, 180
rest, importance of, 178, 180
sports and, 183
sports physicals, 150
physical therapists, 518t
pinch test, 153
pituitary gland, 113, 113f, 114t, 242f
PKU (phenylketonuria), 461, 462–463
placenta, 227, 230

606 | Index

planning, 66–69
    quitting smoking, 353
    schoolwork organization, 254
    stress prevention from, 66–69
    time management, 68, 179, 254
    violence prevention through, 319, 319*f*
    for your future, 255
plasma, 129*f*
platelets, 129*f*
pneumonia, 133*t*
PNS (peripheral nervous system), 110, 110*f*. See also **body systems**
poison ivy, 470*t*
poisons and poisoning, 470, 470*t*, 480, **495**
pollution, 536–539
    air, 470–471, 536, 539, 547
    definition, 531
    disease and, 548
    energy use and, 547, 547*f*
    food and, 538
    indoor environments, 539
    at Love Canal, 543*f*
    noise, 539
    population growth and, 546–547, 547*f*
    water, 533, 537, 545, 549
population growth, 546–547, 547*f*
positive peer pressure, 29, 249, 251, 273. See also **peer pressure**
positive self-talk, 87, 203*t*
positive stress, 53. See also **stress**
posture, computer, 564
potassium, 194
power, in sports, 176
PPD test, 439
precautions, 32
pregnancy, 226–231, 228–229*f*
    alcohol use during, 227, 227*f*, 377, 377*f*
    birth, 230, 231*t*
    changes in the mother's body, 227
    complications, 231*t*
    ectopic, 231*t*
    fertilization, 226, 226*f*
    first trimester, 228, 228*f*
    HIV infection during, 445
    nourishing the fetus, 227
    second trimester, 228–229*f*, 229
    third trimester, 229, 229*f*
    ultrasound images, 239, 239*f*
premature birth, 231*t*
prescription medicine, 398, 398*f*, 522
preventive healthcare, 13
prioritizing, 68
proactive approach, 13
progesterone, 114*t*, 242*f*
progression, in exercise, 175
projection, 60, 60*f*, 88, 88*t*
promotion, of tobacco products, 358
prostate enlargement, 220*t*
prostate gland, 218, 219, 220*t*
proteins, 193
protozoa, 430*t*
psychiatrists, 99, 518*t*
psychological dependence, 350, 387, 403
psychologists, 99
puberty. See also **adolescent growth and development**
    hormones, 242
    physical changes in boys, 244, 244*f*
    physical changes in girls, 245, 245*f*
    timing of, 233, 245
pubic hair, 244, 245
public health, 542–545
purging, 207

Q

quackery, 514

R

rabies, 111*t*
radiation therapy, 468
radiologists, 518*t*
radius, 144*f*
rape, 377, 409, 417
rashes, from drug allergies, 400, 400*f*
rationalization, 60, 60*f*
RBCs (red blood cells), 129*f*
reaction time, 176, 380
recovery, 389, 423, 423*f*
recovery time, heart rate, 143, 151
rectal cancer, 467*f*
recycling, 540, 543
red blood cells (RBCs), 129*f*
Red Cross, 520
reframing, 63
refusal skills, 44–45
    body language, 44
    copying homework, 10
    definition, 15
    importance of, 247, 265
    not drinking alcohol, 247, 384–385
    not smoking, 360, 360*f*, 362
    not using drugs, 419
    to stop harassment, 331
registered nurses (RNs), 568
rehabilitation, from injury, 159
relapse, 352, 361
relationships, 262–281. See also **friends**
    being clear, 279
    belonging and acceptance, 249
    body language, 263, 292–293
    character, 265, 275
    communicating through behavior, 264

INDEX

definition, 262
drug addiction and, 404
empathy in, 266
expressing yourself, 262
in families, 268–271
group dating, 278
health and, 10, 276
influences on, 272–273
making new friends, 275
personal responsibility, 265
refusal skills, 44–45, 247, 265
romantic attraction, 249
self-esteem and, 274
sexual abstinence, 280–281, 281t
showing affection, 279
smoking and, 343, 363
teen parents, 280
tolerance in, 267
understanding others, 263
unhealthy, 277
repression, 60
reproductive systems, 218–221, 222–225. *See also* **body systems**
female, 222–225, 222f, 223f, 224t
male, 218–221, 218f, 219f, 220t
pregnancy and birth, 226–231
problems in, 220, 220t, 224, 224t
rescue breathing, 500–501, 500f, 501f
resources, conservation of, 540–541
respect, 321
respiratory system, 107t, 131–133, 131f
responsibility, 13, 24, 250, 265, 303
resting heart rate (RHR), 143, 151
Rh incompatibility, 231t
RICE, 159. *See also* **first aid**
rickets, 118t, 462f

risk behaviors
in adolescents, 247, 247f
alcohol use and, 377
seven ways to stay safe, 483
smoking, 457, 467f
risk factors, for disease, 457
RNs (registered nurses), 568
roach, 408t, 409
Rohypnol, 408t, 409, 417
roofies (Rohypnol), 408t, 409
rope (Rohypnol), 408t, 409

SADD, 381, 393
sadness, physical responses to, 81t
Safe Drinking Water Act, 544
safety, 480–501
accidents at home, 480
automobile, 488–489, 488f, 489f
baby-sitting, 566–567
checklist, 563f
disasters, 562–563
emergency kits, 561
fire safety, 480–481
first aid, 490–493
food, 544, 544f, 558, 558t
helmets, 163, 456, 458, 473
Internet, 565
recreational, 482
at school, 484–485
seven ways to stay safe, 483
staying home alone, 563
weapons, 486–487
saliva, 123, 435
SARS (severe acute respiratory syndrome), 440
schizophrenia, 93. *See also* **mental illness**
school
acting safely at, 484–485
conflicts during, 298–301
gangs, 485
guns at, 487
marijuana use and, 411

school bus safety, 489
scoliosis, 118t
scooping out, 417
scrotum, 218, 218f
scurvy, 194
seat belts, 488–489, 488f, 489f
Seconal, 408t
secondhand smoke, 341, 344, 346, 361
sedatives, 408, 408t
seizures, 416
self-esteem
acceptance and, 249, 249f
body image and, 201, 201f
emotions and, 86
exercise and, 149
friendships and, 274
goals and, 34, 37
self-examinations, 220, 224
self-talk, 87, 203t
semen, 219
seminal vesicles, 219
seminiferous tubules, 219, 219f
sensitivity skills, 266–267
serving sizes, 197–199, 198f, 199f
setbacks, 39
severe acute respiratory syndrome (SARS), 440
sex hormones. *See also* **hormones**
estrogen, 114t, 222, 242f
progesterone, 114t, 242f
testosterone, 114t, 118t, 218, 242, 242f
sexual abstinence, 280–281, 281t, 442
sexual abuse, 327t
sexual assault, 377, 409, 417
sexual harassment, 330
sexually transmitted diseases (STDs)
causes and symptoms, 442
in females, 224t
HIV and AIDS, 444–447
in males, 220t
types of, 443t

sherm, 414t. See also **PCP**
shin splints, 121t
shock, electrical, 480, 496
shock, first aid for, 497
short-term goals, 35
sibling rivalry, 304
sickle cell anemia, 131t
sickle cell disease, 460
side effects, drug, 400
Simian immunodeficiency virus (SIV), 445
sinus infections, 439
sinusitis, 439
six steps of decision making, 26
skeletal system, 107t, 116–117, 116f, 118t
skin
    acne, 114t, 244, 245
    cancer, 467, 467f, 469, 536
    effects of AIDS on, 446f
    germ defense and, 435
    stress and, 58t
skinfold calipers, 153
sleep needs, 4f
slow-twitch muscles, 176
smallpox vaccine, 449f
smoke detectors, 481
smokeless tobacco, 339, 341, 341f, 361
smoking. See also **tobacco**
    advertising about, 357–358
    cardiovascular disease and, 346, 346f
    deaths caused by, 345f, 346, 347f
    early effects of, 340, 340f
    lung cancer from, 344, 344f, 345f, 457, 467f
    marijuana, 411
    nicotine, 338, 341, 348, 348f
    physical dependence and, 349
    psychological dependence and, 350
    quitting, 349f, 352–355
    reasons people start, 356, 356f, 359
    reducing effects of, 342
    refusal skills, 45, 265, 360, 360f
    smoker's face, 341
    social and emotional health effects of, 343, 363
    tolerance and, 349
    withdrawal symptoms of, 349f, 350
smooth muscle, 119
snot, germ defense and, 435
Snow, John, 545
snuff, 339, 341, 341f. See also **tobacco**
social health, 6
social skills, 262–265
social workers, 99
sodium, 194
specialists, 518, 518t
Special K (Ketamine), 417
specificity of exercise, 156, 175
speed, 176
sperm, 218, 219, 219f, 226f
spinal cord, 110
spleen, during mononucleosis, 441
splints, 496
sports, 170–181
    basic sports skills, 176
    competitions, 171
    conditioning skills, 174–177
    friends and, 173
    listening to your body and, 177
    overcommitment to, 178–179
    overtraining, 180
    physical fitness and, 183
    sportsmanship, 172
    team and individual, 170
    walking away, 181
sportsmanship, 172
sports physicals, 150
sprains, 118t, 159t
starches, 193
STDs (sexually transmitted diseases)
    causes and symptoms, 442
    in females, 224t
    HIV and AIDS, 444–447
    in males, 220t
    types of, 443t
stillbirth, 231t
stimulants, 406–407
stomach acid, germ defense and, 435
stomach cancer, 124t
stones, 127t
strains, muscle, 121t, 159t
strength, 142, 152
strep throat, 432, 438, 438f
Streptococcus, 438
stress, 52–69. See also **stress management**
    bad and good, 53
    body's response to, 56
    common signs of, 62, 62t
    defense mechanisms and, 60–61, 88
    definition, 52
    eczema and, 465
    long-term effects of, 58, 58f, 58t
    major life changes and, 55, 55t
    relationships and, 59, 276
    short-term responses to, 57
    stressors in your life, 53t, 54
stress fractures, 159t, 180
stress management, 52–69
    common signs of stress, 62
    good health and, 67
    preventing distress, 66–67
    sharing emotions, 64
    strategies for dealing with, 63
    taking time for yourself and, 65
    time management and, 68–69
stressors, 52–54, 53t
stress response, 56

stretching exercises, 144, 160
strokes, 111*t*, 345, 345*f*, 346
Students Against Destructive Decisions (SADD), 381, 393
Students Against Drunk Driving (SADD), 381, 393
study skills, 254
sublimation, 88*t*
success, 38
sugars, 193
suicidal thinking, 95
suicide, 59, 95
sunblock, 469
sunburns, 495
superweed, 414*t*
support groups, for drug treatment, 422
support systems, 45
symptoms, 456
syphilis, 443*t*

tar, 338, 340
target heart rate zone, 151
T cells, 436, 436*f*
teachers, conflict with, 300
teamwork, 170
tears, germ defense and, 435
teasing, 298, 330–331
teen hotlines, 98
teen parents, 280
tendinitis, 121*t*, 159*t*
tendons, 119, 144
testes, 218
  hormones from, 114*t*, 242*f*
  location of, 113*f*, 218, 218*f*, 219*f*
  sperm made in, 219
  testicular cancer, 220*t*, 467*f*
testicles, 218, 218*f*
testicular cancer, 220*t*, 467*f*
testicular torsion, 220*t*
testosterone, 114*t*, 118*t*, 218, 242, 242*f*. See also hormones

THC (tetrahydrocannabinol), 410. See also marijuana
threats of violence, 311, 320
three-dimensional ultrasound, 239, 239*f*
Three Gorges Dam (China), 547*f*
throat cancer, 344
throat culture, 438, 438*f*
thunderstorms, 562
thyroid gland, 113, 113*f*, 114*t*, 242*f*
thyroxine, 114*t*, 242*f*
time management, 68, 179, 254
tissue, 106
tobacco, 338–363
  addiction, 349
  advertising, 357–358
  bidis, 339
  cancer from, 341, 344, 344*f*, 345*f*, 467*f*
  cardiovascular disease and, 346, 346*f*
  cigarettes, 338
  deaths caused by, 345*f*, 346, 347*f*
  different responses to, 351
  early effects of smoking, 340, 340*f*
  environmental tobacco smoke (ETS), 341
  nicotine in, 338, 341, 348, 348*f*
  other health problems from, 347
  physical dependence, 349
  psychological dependence, 350
  quitting, 349*f*, 352–355
  reasons people start using, 356, 356*f*, 359
  reducing effects of, 342
  refusal skills, 360–361, 360*f*
  respiratory disease and, 345, 345*f*
  smokeless, 339, 341, 341*f*, 361
  social and emotional health effects of, 343, 363
  tolerance, 349
tolerance
  to alcohol, 376, 386
  to drugs, 400
  to medicines, 400
  to tobacco, 349
  toward others, 267
tornadoes, 562
toxemia, 231*t*
toxic shock syndrome, 224*t*
toxins, 470
traits, 8
tranquilizers, 408, 408*t*
transdermal patches, 397*f*
traumatic injuries, 472
treatment centers, 422
triceps, 120, 120*f*
trichomoniasis, 443*t*
triggers, emotional, 80
trimesters, 228–229, 228–229*f*. See also pregnancy
tuberculosis, 133*t*, 432, 438, 439, 439*f*
tumors, 344, 466. See also cancer
type 2 diabetes, 115*t*, 459. See also diabetes

ulcers, 124*t*
ulna, 144*f*
ultrasound images, 239, 239*f*
ultraviolet light (UV light), 536
undescended testicle, 220*t*
unhealthy relationships, 277
ureters, 125*f*
urethra, 219
urinary incontinence, 127*t*
urinary system, 107*t*, 125–127, 125*f*, 127*t*
urinary tract infection (UTI), 127*t*, 220*t*, 224*t*

uterine cancer, 224t
uterus, 222, 222f, 223, 223f
UTI (urinary tract infection), 127t
UV light (ultraviolet light), 536

V

vaccinations, 441, 449
vagina, 222, 222f
vaginitis, 224t
Valium, 408t
values, 25, 36, 384
vas deferens, 218f, 219, 219f
Vegetarian Food Guide Pyramid, 555, 555f
veins, 130f
verbal abuse, 327t
vinyl chloride, 471
violence, 318–331
  abuse, 326–329
  aggression and, 308
  alcohol use by victims of, 377
  by alcohol users, 379
  avoiding and preventing, 311, 319, 319f, 323
  bullying, 299, 308
  conflicts leading to, 309
  gangs, 485
  group pressure for, 309, 318
  harassment, 330–331
  helping your friends recover, 325
  recognizing, 322
  recovering from, 325
  reporting, 324, 329
  respect and, 321
  at school, 484
  seeking safety from, 323
  sexual assault, 377, 409, 417
  spotting dangerous situations, 318
  threats of, 311, 320
  weapons, 486–487
viruses, 430t, 433, 433f, 440–441, 444–447
vision, 8, 194, 347
vitamin A, 194t, 463
vitamin B-12, 194t
vitamin C, 194t
vitamin D, 118t, 462f
Vitamin K (Ketamine), 417
vitamins, 118t, 194, 194t, 462f
volunteering, 255, 515

W

walking, 143, 165
warts, genital, 443t
water, importance of drinking enough, 135, 195, 533, 533f
water pollution, 533, 537, 545, 549
weapons, 486–487
weight, 210–211
  body mass index, 153, 153t, 210, 559, 559t
  eating disorders and, 204–209
  finding your healthy weight range, 210
  healthy energy balance and, 211
  obesity, 208, 458, 463
  stress and, 58t
  weight loss diets, 206, 211
wellness, 4–7, 15, 17. *See also* health
whip-its, 415. *See also* inhalants
white blood cells, 129f
withdrawal symptoms, 349f, 350, 403, 412, 422

X

XTC (Ecstasy), 416, 416f

Y

yeast infections, 222, 222f

Z

zinc, 194

Acknowledgments continued from page iv.

Academic Reviewers

Leslie Mayrand, Ph.D., R.N., C.N.S.
Professor of Nursing
Pediatrics and Adolescent Medicine
Angelo State University
San Angelo, Texas

Karen E. McConnell, Ph.D.
Assistant Professor
School of Physical Education
Pacific Lutheran University
Tacoma, Washington

Clyde B. McCoy, Ph.D.
Professor and Chair
Department of Epidemiology and Public Health
University of Miami School of Medicine
Miami, Florida

Hal Pickett, Psy.D.
Assistant Professor of Psychiatry
Department of Psychiatry
University of Minnesota Medical School
Minneapolis, Minnesota

Philip Posner, Ph.D.
Professor and Scholar in Physiology
College of Medicine
Florida State University
Tallahassee, Florida

John Rohwer, Ph.D.
Professor
Department of Health Sciences
Bethel College
St. Paul, Minnesota

Susan R. Schmidt, Ph.D.
Postdoctoral Psychology Fellow
Center on Child Abuse and Neglect
The University of Oklahoma Health Sciences Center
Oklahoma City, Oklahoma

Stephen B. Springer, Ed.D., L.P.C., C.P.M.
Director of Occupational Education
Southwest Texas State University
San Marcos, Texas

Richard Storey, Ph.D.
Professor of Biology
Colorado College
Colorado Springs, Colorado

Marianne Suarez, Ph.D.
Postdoctoral Psychology Fellow
Center on Child Abuse and Neglect
The University of Oklahoma Health Sciences Center
Oklahoma City, Oklahoma

Nathan R. Sullivan, M.S.W.
Associate Professor
College of Social Work
The University of Kentucky
Lexington, Kentucky

Josey Templeton, Ed.D.
Associate Professor
Department of Health, Exercise, and Sports Medicine
The Citadel, The Military College of South Carolina
Charleston, South Carolina

Marianne Turow, R.D., L.D.
Associate Professor
The Culinary Institute of America
Hyde Park, New York

Martin Van Dyke, Ph.D.
Professor of Chemistry Emeritus
Front Range Community College
Westminster, Colorado

Graham Watts, Ph.D.
Assistant Professor of Health and Safety
The University of Indiana
Bloomington, Indiana

Teacher Reviewers

Dan Aude
Magnet Programs Coordinator
Montgomery Public Schools
Montgomery, Alabama

Judy Blanchard
District Health Coordinator
Newtown Public Schools
Newtown, Connecticut

David Blinn
Secondary Sciences Teacher
Wrenshall School District
Wrenshall, Minnesota

Johanna Chase, C.H.E.S.
Health Educator
California State University
Dominguez Hills, California

JeNean Erickson
Sports Coach, Physical Education and Health Teacher
New Prague Middle School
New Prague, Minnesota

Stacy Feinberg, L.M.H.C.
Family Counselor for Autism
Broward County School System
Coral Gables, Florida

Arthur Goldsmith
Secondary Sciences Teacher
Hallendale High School
Hallendale, Florida

Jacqueline Horowitz-Olstfeld
Exceptional Student Educator
Broward County School District
Fort Lauderdale, Florida

Kathy LaRoe
Teacher
St. Paul School District
St. Paul, Nebraska

Regina Logan
Sports Coach, Physical Education and Health Teacher
Dade County Middle School
Trenton, Georgia

Alyson Mike
Sports Coach, Science and Health Teacher
East Valley Middle School
East Helena, Montana

Elizabeth Rustad
Sports Coach, Life Science and Health Teacher
Centennial Middle School
Yuma, Arizona

Rodney Sandefur
Principal
Nucla Middle School
Nucla, Colorado

Helen Schiller
Science and Health Teacher
Northwood Middle School
Taylor, South Carolina

Gayle Seymour
Health Teacher
Newtown Middle School
Newtown, Connecticut

Bert Sherwood
Science and Health Specialist
Socorro Independent School District
El Paso, Texas

Beth Truax, R.N.
Science Teacher
Lewiston-Porter Central School
Lewiston, New York

Dan Utley
Sports Coach and Health Teacher
Hilton Head School District
Hilton Head Island, South Carolina

Jenny Wallace
Science Teacher
Whitehouse Middle School
Whitehouse, Texas

Kim Walls
Alternative Education Teacher
Lockhart Independent School District
Lockhart, Texas

Alexis Wright
Principal, Middle School
Rye Country Day School
Rye, New York

Joe Zelmanski
Curriculum Coordinator
Rochester Adams High School
Rochester Hills, Michigan

Teen Advisory Board

Teachers

Melissa Landrum
Physical Education Teacher
Hopewell Middle School
Round Rock, Texas

Stephanie Scott
Physical Education Teacher
Hopewell Middle School
Round Rock, Texas

Krista Robinson
Physical Education Teacher
Hopewell Middle School
Round Rock, Texas

Hopewell Middle School Students

Efrain Nicolas Avila
Darius T. Bell
Micki Bevka
Kalthoom A. Bouderdaben
La Joya M. Brown
Jennafer Chew
Seth Cowan
Mariana Diaz
Marcus Duran
Timothy Galvan
Megan Ann Giessregen
Shane Harkins
Ryan Landrum
Maria Elizabeth Ortiz Lopez
Travis Wilmer

Staff Credits

Editorial
Robert Todd, *Associate Director, Secondary Science*
Debbie Starr, *Managing Editor*

Senior Editors
Leigh Ann García
Kelly Rizk
Laura Zapanta

Editorial Development Team
Karin Akre
Shari Husain
Kristen McCardel
Laura Prescott
Betsy Roll
Kenneth Shepardson
Ann Welch
David Westerberg

Copyeditors
Dawn Marie Spinozza, *Copyediting Manager*
Anne-Marie De Witt
Jane A. Kirschman
Kira J. Watkins

Editorial Support Staff
Jeanne Graham
Mary Helbling
Shannon Oehler
Stephanie S. Sanchez
Tanu'e White

Editorial Interns
Kristina Bigelow
Erica Garza
Sarah Ray
Kenneth G. Raymond
Kyle Stock
Audra Teinert

Online Products
Bob Tucek, *Executive Editor*
Wesley M. Bain
Catherine Gallagher
Douglas P. Rutley

Production
Eddie Dawson, *Production Manager*
Sherry Sprague, *Senior Production Coordinator*
Mary T. King, *Administrative Assistant*

Design

Book Design
Bruce Bond, *Design Director*
Mary Wages, *Senior Designer*
Cristina Bowerman, *Design Associate*
Ruth Limon, *Design Associate*
Alicia Sullivan, *Designer, Teacher Edition*
Sally Bess, *Designer, Teacher Edition*
Charlie Taliaferro, *Design Associate, Teacher Edition*

Image Acquisitions
Curtis Riker, *Director*
Jeannie Taylor, *Photo Research Supervisor*
Stephanie Morris, *Photo Researcher*
Sarah Hudgens, *Photo Researcher*
Elaine Tate, *Art Buyer Supervisor*
Angela Parisi, *Art Buyer*

Design New Media
Ed Blake, *Design Director*
Kimberly Cammerata, *Design Manager*

Media Design
Richard Metzger, *Director*
Chris Smith, *Senior Designer*

Graphic Services
Kristen Darby, *Director*
Jeff Robinson, *Senior Ancillary Designer*

Cover Design
Bruce Bond, *Design Director*

Design Implementation and Page Production
Preface, Inc.,
Schaumburg, Illinois

Electronic Publishing

EP Manager
Robert Franklin

EP Team Leaders
Juan Baquera
Sally Dewhirst
Christopher Lucas
Nanda Patel
JoAnn Stringer

Senior Production Artists
Katrina Gnader
Lana Kaupp
Kim Orne

Production Artists
Sara Buller
Ellen Kennedy
Patty Zepeda

Quality Control
Barry Bishop
Becky Golden-Harrell
Angela Priddy
Ellen Rees

New Media
Armin Gutzmer, *Director of Development*
Melanie Baccus, *New Media Coordinator*
Lydia Doty, *Senior Project Manager*
Cathy Kuhles, *Technical Assistant*
Marsh Flournoy, *Quality Assurance Project Manager*
Tara F. Ross, *Senior Project Manager*

Ancillary Development and Production
General Learning Communications, Northbrook, Illinois

Illustration and Photography Credits

Abbreviations used: (t) top, (c) center, (b) bottom, (l) left, (r) right, (bkgd) background

Illustrations

All work, unless otherwise noted, contributed by Holt, Rinehart & Winston.

Table of Contents: xxii (t), Argosy.

Chapter One: L1: Page 7 (t), (tl), Leslie Kell; L2: 8 (bl), Mark Heine; REV: 19 (tr), Leslie Kell.

Chapter Two: L1: Page 26–27 (t), Marty Roper/Planet Rep; L2: 30 (t), Rick Herman; L3: 32 (br), Argosy; L5: 38 (br), Rita Lascaro; L6: 40 (br), Leslie Kell; REV: 47 (tr), Leslie Kell.

Chapter Three: L1: Page 54 (b), Marty Roper/Planet Rep; L3: 60 (b), Rita Lascaro; L5: 68 (br), Argosy; 69 (tc), Argosy.

Chapter Four: L2: Page 78 (b), Rick Herman; L5: 92 (br), Leslie Kell; L6: 94 (b), Stephen Durke/Washington Artists; L7: 97 (t), Leslie Kell; FEA: 103, Laura Bailie.

Chapter Five: L1: Page 106 (b), Christy Krames; L2: 109 (t), Christy Krames, 110 (bl), Christy Krames; L3: 113 (b), Christy Krames; L4: 116 (b), Christy Krames, 117 (c), Christy Krames, 119 (b), Christy Krames, 120 (b), Christy Krames; L5: 123 (cr), Christy Krames, 124 (tl), Christy Krames, 125 (cr), Christy Krames, 126 (c), Christy Krames; L6: 128 (bc), Christy Krames, 130 (t), Christy Krames, 131 (br), Christy Krames, 132 (c), Christy Krames; REV: 137 (tr), Leslie Kell.

Chapter Six: L1: Page 144 (b), Christy Krames; L2: 146 (bc), Leslie Kell; L5: 157 (t), Argosy; L6: 162 (bl), Argosy, 162 (bl), (bc), (br), Argosy; REV: 165 (tr), Leslie Kell.

Chapter Seven: REV: Page 183 (tr), Leslie Kell.

Chapter Eight: L2: Page 193 (br), (bl), Mark Heine; L4: 201 (t), Mark Heine; L5: 206 (b), Mark Heine; 208 (br), Argosy; REV: 213 (tr), Leslie Kell.

Chapter Nine: L1: Page 218 (bl), (br), Christy Krames, 219 (tc), Christy Krames; L2: 222 (bl), (br), Christy Krames; 223 (r), Christy Krames; REV: 237 (tr), Christy Krames.

Chapter Ten: L1: Page 242 (b), Christy Krames, 243 (cl), Leslie Kell; 244 (tc), Marcia Hartsock/The Medical Art Company; 245 (tc), Marcia Hartsock/The Medical Art Company; L2: 247 (tl), Leslie Kell; REV: 257 (tr), Leslie Kell; FEA: 259 (c), Laura Bailie.

Chapter Eleven: L3: Page 268 (b), Leslie Kell; L4: 272 (b), Rick Herman.

Chapter Twelve: L2: Page 290 (br), Leslie Kell; 293 (cr), Rita Lascaro; L4: 298 (br), Marty Roper/Planet Rep; L7: 308 (br), Leslie Kell; REV: 313 (tr), Leslie Kell.

Chapter Thirteen: L1: Page 319 (cl), Leslie Kell; L3: 328 (b), Rick Herman; 329 (tr), Argosy; L4: 331 (tl), Marty Roper/Planet Rep.

Chapter Fourteen: L2: Page 340 (bl), Christy Krames; L3: 345 (br), Leslie Kell; 347 (cl), Leslie Kell; L4: 348 (br), Christy Krames, 350 (br), Leslie Kell; L5: 352 (bl), Leslie Kell; L6: 356 (b), Leslie Kell; L7: 360 (bl), Leslie Kell; REV: 365 (cr), Rick Herman.

Chapter Fifteen: L1: Page 371 (cr), Christy Krames, 372 (t), Stephen Durke/Washington Artists; L6: 383 (tr), Marty Roper/Planet Rep.

Chapter Sixteen: L1: Page 397 (t), Christy Krames; L2: 398 (bc), Leslie Kell, 399 (tc), Leslie Kell, 401 (c), Argosy; L3: 403 (tc), Leslie Kell, 405 (cl), Leslie Kell; L10: 423 (c), Leslie Kell; REV: 425 (tr), Leslie Kell.

Chapter Seventeen: L1: Page 430 (b), Stephen Durke/Washington Artists; 431 (tl), Argosy; 433 (c), Stephen Durke/Washington Artists; L2: 435 (tc), Christy Krames, 436 (t), Stephen Durke/Washington Artists; L6: 444 (bc), Stephen Durke/Washington Artists; 445 (t), Mark Heine; 445 (t), Ortelius Design; 446 (t), Christy Krames; 447 (cl), Leslie Kell.

Chapter Eighteen: L6: Page 470 (br), Argosy; L7: 472 (br), Leslie Kell.

Chapter Nineteen: L1: Page 483 (c), Argosy; L4: 488 (b), Rick Herman; L7: 500 (b), Marcia Hartsock/The Medical Art Company; 501 (t), Marcia Hartsock/The Medical Art Company; REV: 503 (tr), Leslie Kell.

Chapter Twenty: L3: Page 517 (tr), Argosy; L5: 523 (cr), Rick Herman.

Chapter Twenty-One: L1: Page 531 (t), Mark Heine; L3: 536 (br), Argosy; 537 (t), Stephen Durke/Washington Artists; 538 (t), Mark Heine; L6: 547 (bl), Leslie Kell; REV: 551 (tr), Leslie Kell; FEA: 552 (b), Laura Bailie.

Appendix: Page 554 (c), Argosy; 555 (tl), (bl), (cr), Rick Herman; 560 (c), Rick Herman; 563 (br), Argosy.

Photography

Cover: Gary Russ/HRW.

Table of Contents: v, Corbis Images; vi, (tr), Cory Sorensen/Corbis; (tl), Sam Dudgeon/HRW; (b), John Langford/HRW; vii, (t), Nathan Bilow/Getty Images/Allsport Concepts; (bl), Skjold Photographs; (br), Tony Freeman/PhotoEdit; viii (t), Peter Van Steen/HRW Photo; (b), Peter Cade/Getty Images/Stone; ix (t), David Young-Wolff/PhotoEdit; (b), Sam Dudgeon/HRW; x (t), Mike Powell/Getty Images/Allsport Concepts; (b), Joe Patronite/Getty Images/The Image Bank; xi (t), Index Stock/Roberto Santos; (c), Victoria Smith/HRW; (b), Corbis; xii (tl), Sam Dudgeon/HRW; (b), Myrleen Ferguson Cate/PhotoEdit; xiii (t), Myrleen Ferguson Cate/PhotoEdit; (b), David Young-Wolff/PhotoEdit; xiv, Michael Newman/PhotoEdit; xv (t), PhotoDisc, Inc.; (cr), Tony Freeman/PhotoEdit; (b), Peter Van Steen/HRW; xvi (t), PhotoDisc, Inc.; (b), Peter Van Steen/HRW; xvii (tl), PhotoDisc, Inc.; (tr), Gallo Images/Corbis; (c), PhotoDisc, Inc.; (b), Bobbie Deherrera/Getty Images News Service; xviii (tl), Wood River Gallery/PictureQuest; (tr), Brian Brown/Getty Images/FPG International; (b), Victoria Smith/HRW; xix (tl), Ken Sherman/Phototake; (tr), Peter Van Steen/HRW; (b), Superstock; xx (t), E. Dygas/Getty Images/Taxi; (c), Victoria Smith/HRW; (b), Alvis Upitis, Brand X Pictures; xxi (t), Sam Dudgeon/HRW; (b), Spencer Jones/Getty Images/FPG International; xxii, Corbis Images; xxiii, Gail Mooney/Masterfile.

Chapter One: Page 2–3, © Arthur Tilley/Getty Images/FPG International; L1: 4, John Langford/HRW Photo; 5, Layne Kennedy/CORBIS; 6, Yellow Dog Productions/Getty Images/The Image Bank; L2: 9, Victoria Smith/HRW; 10, Jeff Greenberg/PhotoEdit; 11, Cory Sorensen/CORBIS; 11 (bl), Sam Dudgeon/HRW; L3: 12, Image Copyright © 2004 PhotoDisc, Inc.; 13, David Hanover/Getty Images/Stone; L4: 14, Tony Freeman/PhotoEdit; 15, Rachel Epstein/PhotoEdit; 16, Lori Adamski Peek/Getty Images/Stone; 17, Image Copyright © 2004 PhotoDisc, Inc.; FEA: 20, CC Studio/Science Photo Library; 21, Sam Dudgeon/HRW.

Chapter Two: Page 22–23, © Syracuse Newspapers/The Image Works; L1: 24, David Young-Wolff/PhotoEdit; 25, Skjold Photographs; L2: 28, Leo Meyer/Painet Inc.; 29, Skjold Photographs; 31, Bob Daemmrich/The Image Works; L3: 33, Dana White/PhotoEdit; L4: 34, David Young-Wolff/PhotoEdit; 35 (l), Skjold Photographs; (r), Tony Freeman/PhotoEdit; 36, Richard T. Nowitz/CORBIS; 37, Nathan Bilow/Getty Images/Allsport Concepts; L5: 39 (l,r), Michael Newman/PhotoEdit; L6: 41, Skjold Photographs; L7: 42, Gary Russ/HRW; 43, Index Stock/Kindra Clineff; L8: 44, Peter Van Steen/HRW; 45, David Young-Wolff/PhotoEdit; FEA: 48, Reza/Webistan/CORBIS; 49, PhotoDisc, Inc.

Chapter Three: Page 50–51, Digital Image Copyright © 2004 PhotoDisc, Inc.; L1: 52, Peter Van Steen/HRW; L2: 56, © Galen Rowell/CORBIS; 57 (all), Peter Van Steen/HRW; 58 (all), Custom Medical Stock Photo; 59 (all), Peter Van Steen/HRW; L3: 61 (all), Don Couch/HRW; L4: 63 (all), David Young-Wolff/PhotoEdit; 64, Michelle D. Bridwell/PhotoEdit; 65, Index Stock/Myrleen Cate; L5: 66, Don Couch/HRW; 67 (c), Spencer Grant/PhotoEdit; (l), David Young-Wolff/PhotoEdit; (r), Peter Cade/Getty Images/Stone; 69 (all), Don Couch/HRW; FEA: 72, Markus Boesch/Getty Images/Allsport Concepts; 73, Bill Aron/PhotoEdit.

Chapter Four: Page 74–75, © Lawrence Manning/CORBIS; L1: 76, WELLCOME DEPT. OF COGNITIVE NEUROLOGY/SPL/Photo Researchers, Inc.; 77, CORBIS; L2: 79 (all), Sam Dudgeon/HRW; 80, Richard Hutchings/CORBIS; L3: 82, Cleve Bryant/PhotoEdit; 83, David Young-Wolff/PhotoEdit; 84, Stewart Cohen/The Image Works; 85, Paul Thompson; Eye Ubiquitous/CORBIS; L4: 86, Tony Freeman/PhotoEdit; 87, Dale C. Spartas/CORBIS; 89, David Young-Wolff/PhotoEdit; L5: 90, Mug Shots/Corbis Stock Market; 91, Romilly Lockyer/Brand X Pictures/PictureQuest; 93, International Stock/Image State; L6: 95, SW Production/INDEX STOCK; L7: 96, Michelle Bridwell/PhotoEdit; L8: 98, Mary Kate Denny/PhotoEdit; 99, Sunbathing/INDEX STOCK; FEA: 102, Image Copyright © 2004 PhotoDisc, Inc.

Chapter Five: Page 104–05, © Richard Cooke/Getty Images/FPG International; L1: 106, Sam Dudgeon/HRW; L2: 108, Sam Dudgeon/HRW; L3: 112, 113, Sam Dudgeon/HRW; 114, Index Stock/Grantpix; L4: 117, Sam Dudgeon/HRW; 118, Index Stock/IT STOCK INT'L; 120 (all), Sam Dudgeon/HRW; L5: 122, 123, 125, Sam Dudgeon/HRW; L6: 129 (b), D. Phillips/Photo Researchers, Inc.; (bc), Becker/Custom Medical Stock Photo; (l), YOAV LEVY/Phototake; (t), C Abraham, M.D./Custom Medical Stock Photo; (tc), MICROWORKS/Phototake; 131, Sam Dudgeon/HRW; L7: 134, DAVID M. GROSSMAN/Phototake; 135 (all), Victoria Smith/HRW; FEA: 138, Gary Conner/Index Stock; 139, Myrleen Ferguson Cate/PhotoEdit.

Chapter Six: Page 140–41, Digital Image Copyright © 2004 PhotoDisc, Inc.; L1: 142, David Young-Wolff/PhotoEdit; 143, JOHN TERENCE TURNER/Getty Images/FPG International; 145, Mark E. Gibson/Stock Photography; L2: 147, David Young-Wolff/PhotoEdit; L3: 148, Tom & Dee Ann McCarthy/CORBIS; 149, Lori Adamski Peek/Getty Images/Stone; L4: 150, Michael Newman/PhotoEdit; 151, Sam Dudgeon/HRW; 153, M. Carr/Custom Medical Stock Photo; L5: 154, Jonathan Nourok/PhotoEdit; 155, TONY ANDERSON/Getty Images/FPG International; 156, Mark Richards/PhotoEdit; L6: 158, Skjold Photographs; L7: 160, Index Stock/Omni Photo Communications Inc.; 161, Mark Burnett/Stock Boston Inc./Picture Quest; 163, Mike Powell/Getty Images/Allsport Concepts; FEA: 166, Novastock/Indexstock; 167, Tom Stewart/CORBIS.

Chapter Seven: Page 168–69, © Tracy Frankel/Getty Images/The Image Bank; L1: 170, Tony Freeman/PhotoEdit; 171, Clive Brunskill/Getty Images/Allsport Concepts; 172, Rudi Von Briel/PhotoEdit; 173, Spencer Grant/PhotoEdit; L2: 174, Mike Powell/Getty Images/Allsport Concepts; 175, Bob Daemmrich/The Image Works; 176, Index Stock/Dean Berry; 177, Joe Patronite/Getty Images/The Image Bank; L3: 178, Gary Russ/HRW; 179, Peter Van Steen/HRW; 180, Bob Mitchell/CORBIS; 181, John Langford/HRW; FEA: 184, Sam Dudgeon/HRW; 185, David Young-Wolff/PhotoEdit.

Acknowledgments | 615

Photography (continued)

Chapter Eight: Page 186–87, © 2002/StockImage/ImageState; L1: 188 (all), 189 (all), Don Couch/HRW, 190, Peter Van Steen/HRW; 191, Index Stock/Roberto Santos; L2: 192, Peter Van Steen/HRW; 194 (b,tl), CORBIS Images/HRW; (bc), Don Couch/HRW; (bc,tc,tl), Image Copyright © 2004 PhotoDisc, Inc./HRW; 195, Barbara Stitzer/PhotoEdit; L3: 197, © John Kelly/Getty Images/Stone; 199, Victoria Smith/HRW; L4: 200, Sam Dudgeon/HRW; 202, Michael Newman/PhotoEdit; L5: 205, Michael Newman/PhotoEdit; 207, Peter Van Steen/HRW; L6: 210, Rudi Von Briel/PhotoEdit; 211, Peter Van Steen/HRW; FEA: 215, Vincent Hobbs/SuperStock.

Chapter Nine: Page 216–17, David Young-Wolff/PhotoEdit; L1: 221, Victoria Smith/HRW; L2: 225, Peter Van Steen/HRW; L3: 226, DENNIS KUNKEL/Phototake; 227, © George Steinmetz; 228 (c), Lennart Nilsson; (l), David M. Phillips/Photo Researchers; (r), Claude Edelmann/Photo Researchers; 229 (l), Lennart Nilsson Albert Bonniers Forlag AB, *A CHILD IS BORN*; (r), David M. Phillips/Photo Researchers; 230, 2001 ImageState; L4: 232, Rachel Epstein/PhotoEdit; 233, Gail Mooney/Masterfile; 234, Tom & DeeAnn McCarthy/CORBIS STOCK MARKET; 235, CORBIS Images; FEA: 238, 239, David Young-Wolff/PhotoEdit.

Chapter Ten: Page 240–41, © VCL/Getty Images/FPG International; L1: 242, (bkgd), Sam Dudgeon/HRW; 243, Spencer Grant/PhotoEdit; L2: 243, Tony Freeman/PhotoEdit; L3: 248 (br), Steve Skjold/PhotoEdit; (bl), Image Stock/Randi Sidman; (bc), Index Stock/SW Production; 249, ROB GAGE/Getty Images/FPG International; 250, David Young-Wolff/PhotoEdit; 251, Gary Conner/PhotoEdit; L4: 252, Robert Brenner/PhotoEdit; 253 (all), Peter Van Steen/HRW; 254, David Young-Wolff/PhotoEdit; 255, Myrleen Ferguson Cate/PhotoEdit; FEA: 258 (b), Kevin R. Morris/Corbis; (t), Wartenberg/Picture Press/Corbis; 259, Sam Dudgeon/HRW.

Chapter Eleven: Page 260–61, © Nathan Bilow/Allsport/Getty Images; L1: 262 (bl), David Young-Wolff/PhotoEdit; (br), Lawrence Migdale, 263, Image Copyright © 2004 PhotoDisc, Inc.; 264, Michelle Bridwell/PhotoEdit; 265, Larry Bray/Getty Images/FPG International; L2: 266, Nova Stock/International Stock; 267, Myrleen Ferguson Cate/PhotoEdit; L3: 269, Michael Krasowitz/Getty Images/FPG International; 270, Rob Lewine/Corbis; 271, Lawrence Migdale/Getty Images; L4: 273, Skjold Photographs; L5: 274, Peter Van Steen/HRW; 275, David Young-Wolff/PhotoEdit; 276, Michael Newman/PhotoEdit; L5: 277, Peter Van Steen/HRW; L6: 278, Mary Kate Denny/PhotoEdit; 279 (b), Victoria Smith/HRW; (t), David Young-Wolff/PhotoEdit; 280, Peter Van Steen/HRW; FEA: 284, 285, Tony Freeman/PhotoEdit.

Chapter Twelve: Page 286–87, George Emmons/Index Stock Imagery, Inc.; L1: 288 (c), Richard Hutchings/CORBIS; (l), Tony Freeman/PhotoEdit; (r), copyright 2001 SWP Incorporated; 289, Michael Newman/PhotoEdit; L2: 291, David Simson/Stock Boston; 292 (all), Gary Russ/HRW; L3: 294, EUGENE HOSHIKO/Associated Press, AP; 295, Sam Dudgeon/HRW; 296, David Young-Wolff/PhotoEdit; 297, Jonathan Nourok/PhotoEdit; L4: 299, Eye Ubiquitous/CORBIS; 300, Ariel Skelley/Corbis Stock Market; 301, FLASH ! LIGHT/Stock Boston; L5: 302 (bl), Alan Levens/Stock Boston; (br), Francisco Villaflor/CORBIS; (tl), CORBIS; (tr), Michael Newman/PhotoEdit; 303, Image Copyright © 2004 PhotoDisc, Inc.; 304, John Langford/HRW; 305, David Young-Wolff/PhotoEdit; L6: 306, CLEO PHOTOGRAPHY/PhotoEdit; 307, Jeff Greenberg/PhotoEdit; L7: 309, Jonathan Nourok/PhotoEdit; 310, Cleo Photography/PhotoEdit; 311, Sam Dudgeon/HRW; FEA: 314, Victoria Smith/HRW; 315, PhotoDisc.

Chapter Thirteen: Page 316–17, © Color Day Production/Getty Images/The Image Bank; L1: 318, Image Copyright © 2004 PhotoDisc, Inc.; 320, Tony Freeman/PhotoEdit; 321, David Young-Wolff/PhotoEdit; L2: 322, Peter Van Steen/HRW; 323, William Wittman/Painet Inc.; 324, EyeWire; 325, Barbara Haynor/Index Stock; L3: 326, David Young-Wolff/Getty Images/Stone; L4: 330, Image Copyright ©2004 PhotoDisc, Inc.; FEA: 334, Image Copyright © 2004 PhotoDisc, Inc.; 335, Tony Freeman/PhotoEdit.

Chapter Fourteen: Page 336–37, © Ghislain & Marie David de Lossy/Getty Images/The Image Bank; L1: 338, GERD GEORGE/Getty Images/FPG International; 339, Peter Van Steen/HRW; L2: 341, AP Photo/Eric Paul Erickson; 342, Tony Freeman/PhotoEdit; 343, AP Photo/Jerge JF Levy, Sringer; L3: 344 (l), SIU BioMed/Custom Medical Stock Photo; (r), Siebert/Custom Medical Stock Photo; 345, Peter Van Steen/HRW; 346, A. Pasieka/Photo Researchers; L4: 349, Image Copyright © 2004 PhotoDisc, Inc.; 351, Ken Fisher/Getty Images/Stone; L5: 353, Lori Adamski Peek/Getty Images/Stone; 354, JPL/Anne/Photo Researchers; 355, Alan Bailey/RubberBall/Alamy Images; L6: 357, Photo Reasearchers; 358, Lee Snider/The Image Works; 359, Gary Russ/HRW; L7: 361, David Young-Wolff/PhotoEdit; 362, AP Photo/Steven Wayne Rotsch; 363, David Grossman/The Image Works; FEA: 366, CORBIS; 367, Tony Freeman/PhotoEdit.

Chapter Fifteen: Page 368–69, © Vincent Dewitt/Stock Boston; L1: 370, Peter Van Steen/HRW; 371, Sam Dudgeon/HRW; L2: 374, Dennis MacDonald/PhotoEdit; 375, Mark E. Gibson/PhotoEdit; L3: 376 (l), SIU BioMed/Custom Medical Stock Photo; (r), PHOTOEDIT/PhotoEdit; 377, Claude Edelmann/Photo Researchers; L4: 378, Image Copyright © 2004 PhotoDisc, Inc.; 379, Bruce Ayres/Getty Images/Stone; L5: 380, Index Stock/Mark Reinstein; 381, PHOTOMONDO/Getty Images/FPG International; L6: 382, Mary Kate Denny/PhotoEdit; L7: 384, Mark Gibson; 385, Michael Newman/PhotoEdit; L8: 386, Bruce Ayres/Getty Images/Stone; 388, Carl & Ann Purcell/CORBIS; 389, Mark Peterson/Corbis SABA; FEA: 392, David Young-Wolff/Getty Images/Stone; 393, Nick Dolding/Getty Images/Stone.

Chapter Sixteen: Page 394–95, © Leland Bobbe/Getty Images/Stone; L1: 396, Peter Van Steen/HRW; 397, Victoria Smith/HRW; L2: 398, 399, Peter Van Steen/HRW; 400, Scott Camazine/Photo Researchers, Inc.; L3: 402 (all), Image Copyright © 2004 PhotoDisc, Inc./HRW; 404, Image Copyright © 2004 PhotoDisc, Inc.; L4: 406, Peter Van Steen/HRW; 407, Roseman/Custom Medical Stock Photo; 408 (all), Victoria Smith/HRW; 409, Bobbie DEHERRERA/Getty Images News; L5: 410 (b), Eric Neurath/Stock Boston; (t), EyeWire; 411, Index Stock/Craig Witkowski; L6: 412, BERGSAKER TORE/CORBIS SYGMA; 413, Peter Van Steen/HRW; L7: 415, G & M David de Lossy/Getty Images/The Image Bank; L8: 416, National Institute on Drug Abuse, National Institutes of Health; 417, Bill Varie/CORBIS; L9: 418, John Terence Turner/Getty Images/FPG International; 419, Peter Van Steen/HRW; L10: 420, Bruce Ayres/Getty Images/Tony Stone; 421, John Bradley/Getty Images/Tony Stone; 422, CUSTOM MEDICAL STOCK PHOTOGRAPHY; FEA: 426, Steve Skjold/Painet; 427 (cl), Eye Wire/Getty Images; (cr), Arthur Tilley/Taxi/Getty Images.

Chapter Seventeen: Page 428–29, David Young-Wolff/PhotoEdit; L1: 432, Bettmann/CORBIS; L2: 434, Judy Gelles/Stock Boston Inc./PictureQuest; 435, Victoria Smith/HRW; 437, Jonathan Nourok/PhotoEdit; L3: 438, Will & Deni McIntyre/Photo Researchers, Inc.; 439, Hulton Archive/Getty Images; L4: 440, David Young-Wolff/PhotoEdit; 441, Jeff Greenberg/PhotoEdit; L5: 442, LUIS M. DE LA MAZA, Ph.D. M.D./Phototake; L7: 449 (b), Wood River Gallery/PictureQuest; (t), BRIAN BROWN/Getty Images/FPG International; FEA: 452, Skjold; 453, Michael Newman/PhotoEdit.

Chapter Eighteen: Page 454–55, Donna Day/ImageState; L1: 456, International Stock/ImageState; 458 (l), SPL/PHOTO RESEARCHERS, INC.; (r), COLIN CUTHBERT/SPL/PHOTO RESEARCHERS, INC.; 459, Susan Van Etten/PhotoEdit; L2: 460, Phototake; 461, KEN SHERMAN/Phototake; L3: 462, Superstock; 463, CORBIS; L4: 464, BARTS MEDICAL LIBRARY/Phototake; 465, Peter Van Steen/HRW; L5: 466 (l), SPL/Photo Researchers, Inc.; (r), DR P. MARAZZI/SPL/Photo Researchers, Inc.; 467, Daphne Hougard/See Jane Run; 469, Peter Van Steen/HRW; L6: 471, Mark E. Gibson/HRW; L7: 473, The Image Works; FEA: 476, Rudi Von Briel/PhotoEdit; 477, Sam Dudgeon/HRW.

Chapter Nineteen: Page 478–79, Image Copyright © 2004 PhotoDisc, Inc.; L1: 480, Richard Hutchings/CORBIS; 481, Tom Carter/PhotoEdit; 482, Jock Montgomery/Bruce Coleman Inc.; L2: 484, Bob Daemmrich/The Image Works; 485, Michael Newman/PhotoEdit; L3: 486, Image Copyright © 2004 PhotoDisc, Inc.; 487 (all), Victoria Smith/HRW; L4: 489, SuperStock; L5: 490, Victoria Smith/HRW; 491, Sam Dudgeon/HRW; 492, E. Dygas/Getty Images/Taxi; 493, Michael Newman/PhotoEdit; L6: 494, Photo Researchers; 495, Peter Van Steen/HRW; 496, Gary W. Carter/CORBIS; 497, Spencer Grant/PhotoEdit; L7: 498, Michael Newman/ PhotoEdit; 499 (b), J. Watson/Custom Medical Stock Photo; (t), A. Bartel/Custom Medical Stock Photo; FEA: 504, Sam Dudgeon/HRW; 505, Copyright 2001 ImageState.

Chapter Twenty: Page 506–07, © Eric O'Connell/Getty Images/Taxi; 508, Victoria Smith/HRW; 509, Michael Newman/PhotoEdit; 510, LWA-Dann Tardif/CORBIS STOCK MARKET; L2: 512, BSIP Agency/Index Stock; 513, Mark E. Gibson; 514, Gary Russ/HRW, 515, Alvis Upitis, Brand X Pictures; L3: 516, David Young-Wolff/PhotoEdit; L4: 519, Tom Stewart/CORBIS; 520, Roger Ball/Corbis StockMarket; 521, Rob Crandall/Stock Connection/PictureQuest; L5: 522, Table Mesa Prod./Index Stock; FEA: 526, 527, Sam Dudgeon/HRW.

Chapter Twenty One: Page 528–29, Jason Tanaka Blaney/Index Stock Imagery, Inc.; L1: 530, David Young-Wolff/PhotoEdit; L2: 532, Charle Avice/AgefotoStock; 533, Sam Dudgeon/HRW; 533, Evan Sklar/Getty Images/FoodPix; 534 (bc), Peter Van Steen/HRW; (bl), George D. Lepp/Corbis; (br), Index Stock/photolibrary.com pty. ltd.; 535, David Young-Wolff/Getty Images/Stone; L3: 539, Sam Dudgeon/HRW; L4: 540, MARKOW TATIANA/CORBIS SYGMA; 541, Spencer Grant/PhotoEdit; L5: 542 (all), Peter Van Steen/HRW; 543, Galen Rowell/Corbis; 544, SPENCER JONES/Getty Images/FPG International; 545, Roger Ressmeyer/Corbis; L6: 546, David Samuel Robbins/Corbis; 547, Keren Su/CORBIS; 548 (b), AP Photo/FEMA, Andrea Booher; (t), DENNIS KUNKEL/Phototake; 549, Hulton Archive/Getty Images; FEA: 552, Raymond Gehman/CORBIS; 553, David Young Wolff/PhotoEdit.

Appendix: 558, Sam Dudgeon/HRW; 560 (tr), Nathan Bilow/Getty Images; (cr), David Young-Wolff/PhotoEdit; (br), Davis Barber/Photo Edit; (tl), Mark E. Gibson Stock Photography; 561, Peter Van Steen/HRW; 562, Alan R Moller/Getty Images/Stone; 564, Sam Dudgeon/HRW; 565, Cindy Charles/PhotoEdit; 566, Mary Kate Denny/PhotoEdit; 567, Victoria Smith/HRW; 568, (tl), Mark Gibson Photography; (br), Spencer Grant/PhotoEdit; 569 (b), A. Ramey/PhotoEdit; (t), Tony Freeman/PhotoEdit.

Models are for illustrative purposes only. Models do not directly promote, represent, or condone what is written within the text of the book, and are not ill.